The Handbook of Global Trade Policy

Handbook of Global Policy Series

Series Editor
David Held
Master of University College and Professor of Politics and International Relations at Durham University

The Handbook of Global Policy series presents a comprehensive collection of the most recent scholarship and knowledge about global policy and governance. Each Handbook draws together newly commissioned essays by leading scholars and is presented in a style which is sophisticated but accessible to undergraduate and advanced students, as well as scholars, practitioners, and others interested in global policy. Available in print and online, these volumes expertly assess the issues, concepts, theories, methodologies, and emerging policy proposals in the field.

Published

The Handbook of Global Climate and Environment Policy
Robert Falkner

The Handbook of Global Energy Policy
Andreas Goldthau

The Handbook of Global Companies
John Mikler

The Handbook of Global Security Policy
Mary Kaldor and Iavor Rangelov

The Handbook of Global Health Policy
Garrett Brown, Gavin Yamey, and Sarah Wamala

The Handbook of Global Science, Technology, and Innovation
Daniele Archibugi and Andrea Filippetti

The Handbook of Global Education Policy
Karen Mundy, Andy Green, Bob Lingard, and Antoni Verger

The Handbook of Global Trade Policy
Andreas Klasen

The Handbook of Global Trade Policy

Edited by

Andreas Klasen

WILEY Blackwell

This edition first published 2020
© 2020 John Wiley & Sons Ltd

The right of Andreas Klasen to be identified as the author of the editorial material in this work has been asserted in accordance with law.

Registered Offices
John Wiley & Sons, Inc., 111 River Street, Hoboken, NJ 07030, USA
John Wiley & Sons Ltd, The Atrium, Southern Gate, Chichester, West Sussex, PO19 8SQ, UK

Editorial Office
9600 Garsington Road, Oxford, OX4 2DQ, UK

For details of our global editorial offices, customer services, and more information about Wiley products visit us at www.wiley.com.

Wiley also publishes its books in a variety of electronic formats and by print-on-demand. Some content that appears in standard print versions of this book may not be available in other formats.

Library of Congress Cataloging-in-Publication Data

Name: Klasen, Andreas, editor.
Title: The handbook of global trade policy / edited by Andreas Klasen.
Description: Hoboken, NJ : John Wiley & Sons, 2020. | Series: Handbook of global policy series | Includes bibliographical references and index.
Identifiers: LCCN 2019030967 (print) | LCCN 2019030968 (ebook) | ISBN 9781119167396 (paperback) | ISBN 9781119167433 (adobe pdf) | ISBN 9781119167426 (epub)
Subjects: LCSH: Commercial policy. | International trade. | International economic relations.
Classification: LCC HF1411 .H25767 2020 (print) | LCC HF1411 (ebook) | DDC 382/.3–dc23
LC record available at https://lccn.loc.gov/2019030967
LC ebook record available at https://lccn.loc.gov/2019030968

Cover Design: Wiley
Cover Image: © Fabian Wentzel/Getty Images

Set in 10/12.5pt Sabon by SPi Global, Pondicherry, India

10 9 8 7 6 5 4 3 2 1

Contents

Notes on Contributors

Omar Alam was working at the European Commission's Directorate-General for Trade at the time of writing. He previously worked in the private sector, where he specialised in EU affairs and EU-Asia political and trade relations. His research interests include global trade policy and the inter-linkages between trade, geopolitics and development. He currently works in the UK Civil Service.

Marc Auboin is Economic Counsellor at the World Trade Organization (WTO), responsible for the institution's trade and finance agenda, including trade finance, and for WTO relations with the International Monetary Fund (IMF) and World Bank. Previously he held several positions at the IMF, was Deputy-Secretary General of the Monetary Committee of the European Union and worked for the French Treasury. Mr Auboin holds a PhD in economics and published extensively on trade finance issues in academic books and articles. He runs the WTO Expert Group on Trade Finance.

Fiona Bannert is Financing Partnerships Specialist at the Asian Development Bank. Previously, she was a Manager with PricewaterhouseCoopers advising the German Export Credit Agency in various roles in Hamburg and Berlin from 2010 to 2017. Her current research is focused on climate finance, economic development, trade and public policy. Her publications include among others *The Future of Foreign Trade Support* (co-editor with Andreas Klasen, 2015). Fiona has two Master's degrees from the University of Munich, Germany, and Nottingham University, UK.

Steven Beck is the Head of Trade and Supply Chain Finance at the Asian Development Bank (ADB). He built ADB's multibillion trade finance business. He also created the Trade Finance Register of the International Chamber of Commerce, which compiles the only global statistics on trade finance default and loss rates. He created the ADB study that, for the first time, quantified trade finance market gaps and their impact on economic growth and jobs. His career began with roles as a Special Assistant to the Canadian Minister for International Trade and as a Senior Manager at the Canadian Imperial Bank of Commerce (CIBC). He left CIBC to help start up the Black Sea Trade & Development Bank. Mr Beck is on the Advisory Board of the International Chamber of Commerce (ICC) Banking Commission and the World Trade Board. He has an MA from Fletcher School, Tufts University, and a BA from Queen's University in Canada.

Lucian Cernat is the Chief Trade Economist of the European Commission. Until 2008, he held various positions at the United Nations in Geneva dealing with trade and development issues. He has authored more than 20 publications on the development impact of trade policies, World Trade Organization negotiations, European Union preferential market access, regional trade agreements, competition policy and corporate governance. Prior to his UN experience, he has been a trade diplomat with the Romanian Ministry of Foreign Affairs. Cernat obtained a PhD from the University of Manchester and a Postgraduate Diploma from Oxford University.

Banu Demir is an Assistant Professor of Economics at Bilkent University in Ankara, a Research Affiliate at the Centre for Economic Policy Research in London and a Research Affiliate at the CESifo Institute in Munich. She was a Visiting Assistant Professor at the Department of Economics, Princeton University, for the academic year 2016–2017. She also worked as a Research Analyst at the Poverty Reduction and Economic Management (PREM) unit at the World Bank between 2006 and 2008. She holds a DPhil from the University of Oxford, an MA from Bilkent University and a BSc from Middle East Technical University, all in economics. Her research interests lie in the areas of international trade and development, with a focus on trade financing and transportation costs.

Alisa DiCaprio is the Head of Trade and Supply Chain at R3 in New York City. In addition to strategy, she also covers trade governance and global standards initiatives. She joined from the Asian Development Bank where she was a Senior Economist working on digital trade, trade finance and innovation. She has also worked in both the public and private sectors on export promotion, trade negotiations and labour issues. She co-chairs the Bankers Association for Finance and Trade (BAFT) Innovation Council and is a Vice Chair of the US Department of Commerce's Trade Finance Advisory Council. She has worked in Cambodia, Chile, Finland, Japan, the Philippines, Thailand and the United States. Her PhD is from MIT, and she holds a BA and an MA from Johns Hopkins University.

Gabriel Felbermayr is President of the Kiel Institute for the World Economy. He concurrently holds a chair in economics and economic policy at Kiel University and is a member of the Scientific Advisory Board of the German Federal Ministry of Economics and Energy. Previously, he was an Associate Consultant with McKinsey & Co., Assistant Professor at the University of Tübingen, held a chair in international economics at the University of Hohenheim (Stuttgart) and led the ifo Center for International Economics at the University of Munich, where he also served as a full professor in international economics. His research and advisory activities focus on questions of economic global governance, European economic integration and German economic policy.

Judith Goldstein is the Janet M. Peck Professor of International Communication at Stanford University. She is also the Chair of the Department of Political Science and Senior Fellow at the Stanford Center for Economic Policy and the Freeman Spogli Institution and has held the Kaye University Fellow in Undergraduate Education. Goldstein has a BA in political science and Near Eastern languages from University of California, Berkeley, a Master's in international affairs from Columbia University and an MA and PhD in political science from UCLA. She has written and/or edited five books and numerous articles, many of which centre on issues of globalisation, international law and the World Trade Organization.

Steffen Gröning is a lecturer in economics and freelance consultant. He holds a Bachelor degree in economics and a Master's degree in international economics. He completed his studies at the University of Göttingen, Germany, UC San Diego, California, USA, and the Universidad Torcuato di Tella, Buenos Aires, Argentina. Focusing his research on econometrics, international trade relations and institutional economics, he received his Dr rer. pol. in 2011 at the University of Hamburg, where he was a postdoctoral fellow at the chair of international economics.

Jack Harding is Head of Political Risk at Coriolis Technologies. He has nearly ten years' experience in political risk analysis and forecasting for financial institutions. He is the co-author of *The Weaponization of Trade: The Great Unbalancing of Policy and Economics* (with Rebecca Harding, 2017). Alongside his work for Coriolis, he is studying for a PhD at the University of Glasgow, where he is examining British, French and German responses to terrorism post-2001. He holds a distinction in his MA in intelligence and international security from King's College London, where his work on German intelligence operations earned him the prize for best MA dissertation. He has taught political science at Sciences Po (Reims Campus) and recently co-organised a North Atlantic Treaty Organization (NATO) conference on military exercises held in Brussels.

Rebecca Harding is an independent economist specialising in trade and trade finance and is Chief Executive Officer (CEO) of Coriolis Technologies, providing data as a service to the trade finance and banking sectors. She is also a Fellow at the Institute for Trade and Innovation at Offenburg University. She is the co-author of *The Weaponization of Trade: the Great Unbalancing of Policy and Economics* (with Jack Harding, 2017). Until February 2017, she was the Chief Economist of the British Bankers' Association. Her senior roles also include CEO of Delta Economics, Senior Fellow at London Business School, Head of Corporate Research at Deloitte and Chief Economist at the Work Foundation. Ms Harding was also a Specialist Advisor to the Treasury Select Committee and Chief Economic Advisor to the All Party Parliamentary Group on Entrepreneurship.

Jennifer Henderson is a Senior Consultant for International Financial Consulting Ltd., with extensive experience in the field of trade and development finance. She has lived and worked around the world focusing on strategy, institutional development and impact measurement; advising governments, development banks and export credit agencies. A key theme in her publications and work to date has been examining how public sector institutions might catalyse private sector activities to maximize development or social-economic impact. She studied economics and international relations at the Australian National University and will complete her Master's in public policy from Cambridge University in 2020.

Thomas Hoehn is an experienced economist with a background in applied economic research, business consulting, regulation and public policy advice. He was a Visiting Professor at Imperial College Business School between 2003 and 2009 and Director of the Intellectual Property Research Centre at Imperial College until 2013. He previously held teaching and research positions at the University of Zurich and the London School of Economics. From 2009 to 2017 Tom was a Panel Member of the UK Competition and Markets Authority. Tom has spent his career analysing markets and competition and has held senior management and advisory positions with several major international consulting firms.

Martina Höppner heads the Commercial Department of Kleemeier, Schewe & Co., KSH GmbH, a company co-founded by her father. Previously, she was in charge of the Department Economic Research at the German Export Credit Agency. Furthermore, she is a Visiting Lecturer for country risk analyses at the Institute for Trade and Innovation (IfTI) at Offenburg University. Her educational background includes a Doctoral degree in economic sciences from the University of St Gallen, an Executive Master's in finance from Vlerick Business School, a Master's in development studies from the London School of Economics (LSE) and a Master's in business administration from the University of Gothenburg.

Marion Jansen is Chief Economist and Director of the Division for Market Development at the International Trade Centre (ITC) in Geneva. Previously she held senior positions in the World Trade Organization (WTO) and the International Labour Organization (ILO). Her publications include *Making Globalization Socially Sustainable* (co-editor with Marc Bacchetta, 2011) and *The Use of Economics in International Trade and Investment Disputes* (co-editor with Joost Pauwelyn and Theresa Carpenter, 2017). She has lectured at the University of Geneva, the World Trade Institute, the Universitat Pompeu Fabra and the European University and holds a PhD in economics from the Universitat Pompeu Fabra.

Cindy Jane Justo is a Consultant at the Economic Research and Regional Cooperation Department of the Asian Development Bank. She works on development economics and policy research. Previously, she was a Research and Programme Associate at the Asian Institute of Management and a Programme Assistant for the United Nations Development Programme (UNDP). She holds a BA in social science and is currently studying for a Master's in population studies at the University of the Philippines.

Fahad H. Khan is an Economist in the Regional Cooperation and Integration Division of the Asian Development Bank's Economic Research Department. Mr Khan has worked on a wide range of issues of regional integration and inclusive economic growth. He joined ADB after completing a Doctoral degree in economics from Australian National University, and also holds a Bachelor degree in economics from Yale University.

His primary research fields are international and development economics, applied macroeconomics and empirical political economy.

Andreas Klasen is Professor of International Business and Head of the Institute for Trade and Innovation at Offenburg University, Visiting Professor at Northumbria University and Senior Honorary Fellow at Durham University. Previously, he was a Partner with PricewaterhouseCoopers and Managing Director of the German Export Credit Agency. His current research is focused on trade policy, export finance and economic development. His publications include *The Future of Foreign Trade Support* (co-editor with Fiona Bannert, 2015) and *Beyond Gridlock* (contributing author, 2017). He also advises multilateral development banks, governments, innovation funds and export credit agencies on policy, strategy and programme management. Mr Klasen holds LLM and DBA degrees from Northumbria University, an MLitt from the University of St Andrews and the 1st and 2nd Legal State Exam from the University of Hannover.

Sebastian Klotz is a PhD candidate in international political economy at the World Trade Institute (WTI), University of Bern. His current research focuses on the governance of regulatory standard-setting and international trade. Before joining the WTI, he worked as a Carlo-Schmid Fellow and Trade and Competitiveness Consultant for the Office of the Chief Economist of the International Trade Centre, the joint agency of the United Nations Conference on Trade and Development and the World Trade Organization. He holds degrees in economics from the Barcelona Graduate School of Economics and the University of Strathclyde.

Simone Krummaker is Senior Lecturer in Insurance at Cass Business School, City, University of London, and Fellow in the Institute for Trade and Innovation (IfTI) at Offenburg University. She is also a Senior Research Associate at the Center for Risk and Insurance, Hannover. Previously, she worked as Senior Lecturer in Finance at the University of Westminster, at the University of East Anglia London and as Senior Researcher at the Center for Risk and Insurance and Associate Lecturer at the Institute for Insurance Economics, both at Leibniz University of Hannover. Her research focuses on insurance and risk management, in particular on corporate demand for insurance. She holds a Dr rer. pol. and a high-level German University degree (Diplom Ökonom) from Leibniz University of Hannover.

Elisabeth van Lieshout is a PhD candidate in political science at Stanford University. She previously obtained a BA in philosophy, politics and economics from the University of Oxford, an MSc in global politics from the London School of Economics and an MA in economics from Stanford University. Her research focuses on trade policy and, in particular, the evolving nature of preferential trade agreements. She also studies public preferences about international cooperation on trade and the environment.

Alexander Malaket is President of Canadian consultancy OPUS Advisory Services International, focusing on international business, trade and investment with a specialism in trade finance/supply chain finance and trade-related international development. He is the author of *Financing Trade and International Supply Chains*

(2014) and has authored numerous white papers, policy briefs and articles. He speaks at top-tier events and has delivered training and educational material around the world. He serves on several industry boards and advisory bodies, including as Deputy Head of the Executive Committee, International Chamber of Commerce (ICC) Banking Commission, Chair of the International and Technical Advisory Committee, Global Trade Professionals Alliance, member of the World Economic Forum E-15 Initiative and member of the Advisory Board of Tin Hill Capital among others.

Mina Mashayekhi is Senior Advisor at RockCreek, a leading global investment management firm, and Associate Professor at Shanghai University of International Business and Economics. Previously, she led the Division of International Trade and headed the Trade Negotiations and Commercial Diplomacy at United Nations Conference on Trade and Development (UNCTAD) where she directed the work on making international trade, trade negotiations and globalisation work for sustainable and inclusive development including the Sustainable Development Goals (SDGs). She has also worked and published on services development and trade, the financial sector, global value chains, the digital economy, technology and innovation, trade policy and the future of work. She acted as the Vice Chairman of the Focus Group on Digital Financial Services (DFS) and Co-Chair of the DFS Ecosystem Working Group at International Telecommunication Union (ITU) in partnership with the Bill and Melinda Gates Foundation.

Benedict Okey Oramah is a Professor of International Trade and Finance and President and Chairman of the Board of Directors of the African Export-Import Bank (Afreximbank). Previously, he was the Executive Vice President responsible for business development and corporate banking at Afreximbank. His current research is focused on export credit arrangements in developing countries, trade finance during commodity crisis, structured trade and receivable finance, and intra-African trade. His is the author of *Foundations of Structured Trade Finance* (2016). He has also authored chapters in several books. He serves on the Practitioner Advisory Board in the Institute for Trade and Innovation at Offenburg University. He also serves on other boards and advisory councils.

Cyn-Young Park is Director of the Regional Cooperation and Integration Division in the Economics Research and Regional Cooperation Department of the Asian Development Bank (ADB). During her progressive career within ADB, she has been a main author and contributor to ADB's major publications, including ADB's flagship publication *Asian Development Outlook*. She has also participated in various global and regional forums, including the G20 Development Working Group. Ms Park has written and lectured extensively about the Asian economy and financial markets. Her work has been published in peer reviewed academic journals, including the *Journal of Banking and Finance*, the *Journal of Futures Markets*, the *Review of Income and Wealth* and *The World Economy*. She received her PhD in economics from Columbia University and holds a Bachelor degree in international economics from Seoul National University.

Nikos Passas is Professor of Criminology and Criminal Justice at Northeastern University, where he served for a number of years as Co-Director of the Institute for Security and Public Policy. He is also Distinguished Visiting Professor at Beijing Normal University and Distinguished Practitioner in Financial Integrity and Senior Fellow of the Financial Integrity Institute at Case Western Reserve Law School. He serves on numerous advisory boards. He specialises in the study of corruption, illicit financial/trade flows, sanctions, informal fund transfers, remittances, terrorism, white-collar crime, financial regulation, organized crime and international crimes and has published more than 230 articles, book chapters, reports and books in 14 languages. He is often an expert witness in court cases or public hearings and consults with law firms, financial institutions and various organizations, including the Financial Crimes Enforcement Network (FinCEN), the Organisation for Economic Co-operation and Development (OECD), Organization for Security and Co-operation (OSCE), the International Monetary Fund (IMF), the World Bank, multilateral and bilateral institutions, the United Nations and the European Union.

Karla Simone Prime is a Doctoral Researcher in economic growth and a Lecturer at Newcastle Business School, Northumbria University. Primary research interests are economic growth and development, institutional economics and international business, with special focus on developing economies. Current research concerns the impact of institutional quality on economic growth in former colonies. Ms Prime holds an MBA as well as a Postgraduate diploma in law from Northumbria University and an LLB from the University of London.

Cyrus de la Rubia is Chief Economist at Hamburg Commercial Bank, Lecturer at Frankfurt School of Finance & Management and Consultant at Berlin Economics, an economic policy consulting firm with a focus on emerging economies. He has a Master's degree in economics from the University of Kiel and holds a PhD in economics from the University of Potsdam. He started his career at Dresdner Bank Latin America, heading the Economics Department. His main research fields are monetary policy, international trade and business cycles as well as digitalization in connection with blockchain technology.

Yasuyuki Sawada is Chief Economist of the Asian Development Bank (ADB) and Director General of its Economic Research and Regional Cooperation Department. He is chief spokesperson on economic and development trends, and leads the production of ADB's flagship knowledge products and support for regional cooperation fora. Before joining ADB, Mr Sawada was Professor of Economics at the University of Tokyo, and he has led numerous large-scale development policy evaluation projects for various institutions. His key research areas are development economics, microeconometrics, economics of disasters, and field surveys and experiments. Mr Sawada obtained his PhD in economics from Stanford University.

Diana Smallridge is President and Chief Executive Officer of International Financial Consulting Ltd. She is a global expert in export credit agencies and development banks. Since founding the firm in 2000, she has worked with clients from over 50 countries and has developed a methodology, the Health Diagnostic Tool©, to measure the overall performance of financial institutions with a mandate to promote trade, investment or development. She is a sought-after speaker and facilitator at international workshops and conferences, has been the Conference Chairman for the Annual Global Convention on Insuring Export Credit and Political Risk since 2000 and has authored multiple publications.

Marina Steininger is a Junior Economist at the ifo institute for International Economics and a Doctoral student at the Ludwig-Maximilians-University in Munich. She studied at the universities of WU Vienna, Harvard and Passau. Her research focuses on the quantitative assessment of international trade policies and the effects of trade on environment. Her publications include *Revisiting the Euro's Trade Cost and Welfare Effects* (contributing author, 2019) and *Quantifying the EU-Japan Economic Partnership Agreement* (contributing author, 2019). She has advised governmental organizations such as the European Commission and the German Federal Ministry for Economic Affairs and Energy.

Thomas Straubhaar is Professor of Economics at the University of Hamburg, and chairs the Department of International Economic Relations. He was President of the Hamburg Archive of International Economics (HWWA) and thereafter Head of the Hamburg Institute of International Economics (HWWI) from 1999 to 2014. Straubhaar studied economics at the University of Bern, where he received his Dr rer. pol. degree in 1983 and completed his habilitation in 1987. He was an Assistant Professor at the universities of Bern, Constance, Basel and Freiburg im Breisgau, Professor for Economics at the Helmut-Schmidt-University (HSU) in Hamburg and Visiting Professor at the Instituto Tecnológico Autónomo de México (ITAM) and the Universidad Nacional Autónoma de México (UNAM) in Mexico City.

Jasmeer Virdee is a Trade Economist in the Office of the Chief Economist at the International Trade Centre (ITC), based in Geneva, Switzerland. ITC is a joint agency of the World Trade Organization and the United Nations, and is devoted to promoting trade to foster sustainable development. His current research focuses on investments in small businesses. Other areas of focus include small business competitiveness, standards and regulations, and trade policy. He holds a PhD in astrophysics from the University of Oxford and an undergraduate degree in physics from Imperial College London.

Roseline Wanjiru is Associate Professor and Faculty Director of Student Engagement at Newcastle Business School, Northumbria University. She is a Fellow of the Institute of Trade and Innovation (IfTI) at Offenburg University. Roseline is an advisor to the UK government on export financing, and an expert member of the Export Guarantees Advisory Council which advises the Secretary of State on the operations of UK Export Finance, the UK's export credit agency. Her academic research is focused on economic development, institutions and international trade policy.

Erdal Yalcin is Professor of International Economics at the University of Applied Sciences Constance (HTWG). Previously, he was the Deputy Director of the ifo Center for International Economics, ifo Institute, leaving in 2018. He is member of the CESifo research network and further high-level academic expert groups. His research focuses on economic effects of international trade agreements, on the interaction between international value chains and firm dynamics and on the role of uncertainty for trade policy. He has published numerous articles and policy reports in the field of international economics. He is a regular consultant to various European institutions and ministries.

Introduction

Chapter 1

Quo Vadis, Global Trade?

Andreas Klasen

Introduction

Global trade is a key driver for economic growth, and trade is related to several dimensions: The Fourth Industrial Revolution (4IR), with disruptive technologies, globalisation of markets and innovation leading to new trade opportunities, as well as foreign investments following exports, lead to both challenges and opportunities for companies to be active in cross-border business. Digital technologies are changing the business environment at breathtaking speed; exports are important drivers to increase economies of scale, boost sales volumes and diversify companies' customer base; and foreign direct investment (FDI) can yield substantial competitive advantages for firms. From an economic perspective, growth is powered by innovation, investments and exports, helping both industrialised and developing countries to reduce poverty and prosper.

For thousands of years, benefits and harms of economic interaction across borders have been the subject of political contestation. Ancient philosophers such as Hesiod (c. 750–650 BCE) and Plato (c. 427–347 BCE) mention the benefits of foreign trade and the importance of international exchange of merchandise goods. Democritus (c. 460–370 BCE) and Xenophon (c. 430–354 BCE) describe basic economic concepts such as comparative advantages (Michaelidis *et al.*, 2011; Amemiya, 2007; Skultety, 2006). Today, a global economy producing, trading and consuming goods and services across borders is a reality for billions of people and firms. The expansion of international business activities through a multilateral trading system has provided a major pillar for growth enjoyed by industrialised countries in the past century (Klasen, 2017a). Developing countries also opened their economies to take full advantage of opportunities for growth through trade (Were, 2015). Our extraordinarily global economy would not exist but for a complex series

The Handbook of Global Trade Policy, First Edition. Edited by Andreas Klasen.
© 2020 John Wiley & Sons Ltd. Published 2020 by John Wiley & Sons Ltd.

of institutions and rules, which governments, international organisations and private bodies have created over the previous decades of globalisation.

The external environment for businesses has changed dramatically over the past decade. Following the 2008 Global Financial Crisis, financial systems have recovered to the greatest possible extent. Expected real gross domestic product (GDP) growth in the Euro Area reached 1.9% in 2018, and higher domestic demand including investment led to an expected real GDP growth of 2.9% in the United States (World Bank, 2019). Economic activity continues to flourish in highly industrialised countries and is anticipated to remain robust to reach more than 2% in 2019. A cyclical recovery is also expected for most emerging markets and developing economies, especially if engaged in commodity exports. GDP in China is projected to grow by 6.2% on average in 2019 and 2020. Global trade of goods and non-factor services experienced a substantial recovery with a 5.4% growth in 2017 and expected 3.8% growth in 2018. Drivers for growth relevant for exporters were not only stronger intra-regional trade developments in Asia but also rising imports in the United States, in particular due to additional fiscal stimulus. The rebound of international trade has also boosted exports and business investments in other economies.

However, there is a projected global economic weakening over the coming years in many economies. Moderate trade growth is anticipated over the coming years because of structural developments and broader trends, putting the global trading system into question. In some industries, digitalised processes and new forms of production involving automation or three-dimensional printing are eroding the economic rationale for cross-border production. The rebalancing of the Chinese economy will affect trade, as it moves away from investment including high import components towards higher domestic consumption. Slower growth of global value chains might lead to substantial problems for exporters. The unanticipated rise of inflation rates with central banks increasing interest rates could also lead to negative consequences on trade. In addition, economic performance is increasingly overshadowed by heightened political risks and other policy challenges for businesses: A rising number of armed conflicts on a global scale endangers continuous economic prosperity. Furthermore, trade tensions between major economies have further intensified in recent years leading to increasing problems for companies engaged in exports and FDI.

In particular, the rise of nationalist and populist politicians in key economies such as the United States has put in question the consensus around trade and investment liberalism that sustained economic openness for decades (Hale and Held, 2017; Ruggie, 1982). Despite numerous gains from free trade between countries, multilateral efforts to enhance the global governance of trade seem to have come to a standstill, most notably already with the collapse of the Doha Round of negotiations under the World Trade Organization (WTO) (Destradi and Jakobeit, 2015; Lee, 2012; Narlikar, 2010). As a consequence, the multilateral trading system faces a new set of challenges with harder problems and a fragmented policymaking landscape leading to a breakdown of international cooperation in many areas (Hale *et al.*, 2013). At the same time, there has been a vast proliferation of trade agreements at bilateral and regional levels, including a series of proposed "mega-regional" agreements such as the Regional Comprehensive Economic Partnership in Asia (Klasen, 2017b).

Key questions for trade policy are: Are regional or bilateral investment and trade partnerships a solution to gridlock, or part of the problem? Is the WTO's crisis the new reality, or are multilateral agreements still realistic? Away from the gridlock of global trade negotiations, do less formal or more technocratic processes and organisations offer a way forward? And have the politics of economic openness now shifted against globalisation, putting the future of the existing regime into question?

This Handbook presents several approaches on how to discuss and answer these questions. It deals with a general overview and in-depth discussion of new realities, trends and further challenges for trade in the 21st century in Part I. It also sheds light on global governance and international institutions in Part II, focusing on the future for multilateral trade agreements and the activities of international financial institutions, as well as banking regulation and illicit flows. It shows in Part III how global trade and regional development are linked up, for example by looking at the next wave of regional integration as well as what to expect from a protective US trade policy. And, last but not least, in Part IV it has a look at the question of how to finance international trade.

Foreign Trade in the 21st Century

History and Developments of Foreign Trade Liberalisation

Successful free trade in a truly global setting is a comparatively recent phenomenon. As discussed by Klasen (2017b), trade liberalisation among European states in the latter part of the 19th century contributed to a first wave of globalisation, although it coexisted with colonial trading relationships between Europe and territories around the world. Support for liberalisation in major countries, notably the United States, receded after World War I before succumbing totally to the nationalist turn in the 1930s. After World War II, countries sought to rebuild a managed form of trade integration. The creation of the General Agreement on Tariffs and Trade (GATT), signed in 1947, was one of the key achievements after World War II. The rules of GATT enhanced trade relationships in several ways. In particular, concessions between any two members were passed to other participants according to the principle of the "most-favoured nation." Since the 1950s, many multilateral organisations have adopted a rule-based approach that has given states increasing confidence to liberalise their economies and reduce tariffs, quotas, and other barriers to trade. Some 20 years ago, a strengthening of GATT led to the development of the most important organisation for world trade governance, the WTO.

Growing out of the GATT in 1995, and now the only truly global multilateral organisation dealing with the rules of trade between countries, the WTO aims to help manufacturers, services providers and thus exporters and importers to conduct their business (Matsushita *et al.*, 2015; Hoekman and Mavroidis, 2007). In providing legal rules for international commerce, the overall purpose is to help trade flow between countries and regions by removing obstacles and ensuring transparent and predictable rules of international trade. These rules give individuals, companies and governments confidence that there will be no sudden changes of policy, and that conflicting interests can be resolved in a fair manner. Since 1995, the international trade regime has, for the first time ever, a strong legal basis, a sustainable organisational structure and an effective dispute settlement process (Capling and Higgott, 2009). During the first decade of its existence, the WTO had several positive effects on free trade policy and dispute enforcement. Countries have tended to comply with WTO rules, and, when they have not, the dispute settlement mechanism has been largely effective at compelling compliance. The principle of transparency in negotiations and disputes found its way into the trade regime through the introduction of the WTO's decision-making procedures and the dispute settlement system (Klasen, 2017b; Delimatsis, 2014).

As a result, the expansion of international business activities through a multilateral trading system provided a major pillar for growth enjoyed by industrialised countries in the past century. Although developing economies were latecomers to international trade and FDI, many of them have significantly benefited from open markets and the prevention of protectionist measures (Klasen and Bannert, 2015), especially through concessional trade access. The WTO was able to prevent numerous unilateral tariff increases or quantity restrictions, and even extremely difficult trade disputes such as the multibillion-dollar Airbus–Boeing dispute between the European Union and the United States are now transparently resolved in an international forum.

New Realities, New Vistas

In her chapter about new realities of a global trade environment, Martina Höppner looks at historic and current trends in trade. She disentangles to what extent economic developments are driven by global trade as opposed to innovation, automation and new technologies, while acknowledging that all these factors are intertwined. Chapter 2 also discusses current trends in free trade and contrasts these with rising protectionist tendencies. In addition, she looks into the impact of global trade, its advantages but also its disadvantages, as well as challenges of adjusting to these developments in industrialised, emerging and frontier economies. Finally, determinants for future trends in trade are stipulated. Höppner concludes that benefits from trade must be gained, quantified and made public, whereas the negative side effects should also be quantified, made clear and discussed, but alleviated through adequate policies.

Steffen Gröning, Cyrus de la Rubia and Thomas Straubhaar pick up the aspect of technological changes and digitisation of trade in Chapter 3. They present the substantial increase of international transactions between World War II and the financial market crisis in 2008, and argue that globalisation did not stop, and trade did not peak but simply changed its clothes. Their chapter analyses that trade no longer focuses on trade in goods, but increasingly appears in the form of trade in services and trade in data. In addition, the authors search for new concepts to solve the "trade puzzle", for example how new trade patterns could be reflected in trade statistics. Their analysis is a starting and not an end point of a new discussion on the future of globalisation.

Mina Mashayekhi then looks at challenges and opportunities of services trade, focusing on structural transformation and the Sustainable Development Goals (SDGs). In an in-depth analysis, she shows that services play a crucial role in support of economic and social transformation. Adequate regulation and international trade can generate further transformation opportunities, particularly for developing countries. Chapter 4 discusses that trade in services plays an important role in employment

creation and value addition, enabling countries to diversify and upgrade their economies. However, significant efforts are needed at international level to advance a
services trade agenda in the global trading system that is supportive of the SDGs.
This includes crucial aspects such as preferential treatment, flexibilities, experimentation, adjustment mechanisms and capacity-building for developing countries.

Chapter 5 opens up new vistas of the global trade economy through the unusual
lens of cities. Thomas Hoehn shows that urban perspectives rather than national or
international country perspectives generate valuable insight into patterns of economic
development. Major cities produce unique products and services that are traded on
a global scale and support the international trading system. In the superleague of
global cities, he finds cities that have much more in common with each other than
they do with other cities in their respective home countries. Hoehn surveys different
strands of the economic, sociological, political and historical literature analysing the
relationship between cities and trade from different but always cities-based perspectives. He also shows how cities have been central to the growth and development of
global trade and the world economy.

Strategic trade as a means to global influence is discussed by Rebecca Harding
and Jack Harding in the final chapter of Part I. They describe a *de facto* weaponisation of trade which is clearly damaging, not just for the global economy with its
reliance on multilateralism to support the principle of free trade, but also because it
puts trade in a battlefield, not a boardroom. From the authors' point of view, more
nationalistic policies create an "us versus them" mentality which then becomes
entrenched by more aggressive political rhetoric transforming trade irreparably from
an economic tool into a political one. It is also discussed that "strategic trade" wars
are "indirect" wars and are the result of Western failures in recent conflicts: Countries
use trade as a vehicle for coercion – either through orthodox trade wars with protectionism and sanctions, or through trade in specific sectors with specific countries.

Global Governance and International Institutions

Success and Failure of the WTO

While Part I of this Handbook establishes the history, new realities and new vistas of
foreign trade from a general perspective focusing on goods, services, digitisation, cities and the weaponisation of trade, the emphasis of Part II is on global governance
and institutions.

The expansion of the multilateral trading system shaped by the WTO was and still
is effective in many cases. It gives developed and developing economies greater
leverage than they would have outside the system. However, the Doha Round, also
known as the Doha Development Agenda, the latest round of multilateral trade negotiations, has shown the immense difficulties that face the WTO. Launched in 2001, the
key objective was to make the international trading system fairer for developing economies. The main issues at stake were to improve developing countries' access to global
markets and to revise rules with regard to agricultural subsidies (Klasen, 2017b).

Two major problems made it difficult to bring talks to a successful conclusion:
Although highly industrialised countries committed to promote development in
poorer economies without asking them to reduce import barriers to the same extent,

disagreement grew with regard to protection of industries and market access. This applied, in particular, for the agricultural sector. Second, economic conditions in countries such as China and India substantially changed during the decade of talks over which negotiations took place. Some emerging economies started producing export surpluses but insisted on sticking with the original principles exempting them from opening their markets, refusing requests from European members and the United States to lower import barriers and cut agricultural subsidies.

Faith in the WTO was partially restored after the Bali Ministerial Conference in 2013. Governments formally agreed on the WTO's first truly multilateral pact in nearly 20 years, accepting a new agreement on trade facilitation. There were further substantial successes at the 2015 Ministerial Conference in Nairobi, for example by outlawing agricultural export subsidies. However, major challenges remain to revive multilateral negotiations after the *de facto* failure of the Doha Round. Bali and Nairobi were significant in showing that the WTO is still a living animal, but the agreed results are only small steps forward. The agreements on trade facilitation that emerged have been described as asymmetric deals: although developing economies benefit from Bali, gains from trade facilitation will be primarily realised by developed countries (Wilkinson *et al.*, 2014).

While the WTO sits at the centre of the global trade regime, it is hardly alone. Over the past decades there has been a proliferation of bilateral investment treaties and preferential and free trade agreements (FTAs) on a bilateral or regional basis (Garcia *et al.*, 2015), which now number over 300, making the landscape of global trade liberalisation into a "spaghetti bowl". There have also been a number of "plurilateral" trade deals on specific issues – for example, on trade in services – under which a subgroup of WTO members liberalise trade on a certain set of issues. While most of these agreements have no formal links to the WTO, many rely on the WTO's dispute settlement procedures to guarantee their credibility.

Multipolarity and Institutional Inertia

Looking at global governance and institutions, the global trade environment is increasingly multipolar. For decades, governance of the multilateral trading system has been configured around political and economic interests of highly industrialised states. But from a perspective of relative economic size, the world today is more multipolar than it has ever been since the 1960s. The impasse of the failure of the Doha Round is partly the consequence of two major trends, and it is expected that greater diffusion is set to continue into the future.

The first trend is the significant role of the BRICS countries (Brazil, Russia, India, China and South Africa) in the export of goods and services, showing substantial growth and increasing their share in world exports. These structural changes over past years parallel the BRICS countries' behaviour in international institutions. Economies such as China and India are increasingly assuming an importance in the growth picture relative to the advanced economies, such as the Eurozone and Japan. And while they may not yet have reached an advanced level of development, the trend towards regional integration is progressing rapidly. The BRICS are, and this applies in particular for China, at the forefront of the entire multipolarity phenomenon. Their greater involvement in the future direction of the global economy means that decoupling between the advanced and emerging world may finally come to pass (Klasen, 2017b).

The second trend is a profound eastward shift in economic activities and growing South–South trade. Both developments are becoming increasingly important, further reducing the relevance of traditional industrialised countries in the northern hemisphere. In particular, China's activities are most remarkable as the country is at the forefront of the entire multipolarity phenomenon: China as well as other countries increasingly use their political influence for export promotion or development policy while representing a diverse range of opposed interests. Converting from a long-time aid recipient to a new leading donor, China now has a crucial role as an assertive provider of development and export financing. In addition, the government has signed numerous FTAs in order to expand its markets and secure long-term supply of national resources. The Belt and Road Initiative (BRI) is a vivid example of the strategic move in trade, investment and economic development transforming politics at multiple scales (Flint and Zhu, 2019; Shimomura and Ohashi, 2013; Quah, 2011).

In addition, institutional inertia is a major area of concern. Power structures of international organisations with great importance for international trade, such as the International Monetary Fund (IMF), the World Bank and the WTO, have been regarded as dominated by the United States and larger European countries (San Juan, 2011; Wade, 2011; Harrigan *et al.*, 2006). There is severe criticism that there is still systematic bias towards rich economies and multinational corporations. Institutional inertia is also a pressing topic because important areas such as social and environmental issues seem to be continuously ignored. In particular, traditional multilateral organisations have been criticised for being an "economic cartel" dominated by the United States, and for pursuing free trade and open markets at the expense of the poorest and least developed countries. Emerging economies feel discriminated against regarding power and influence within multilateral institutions, although there is an obvious transformation in the global economic structure described above.

The question of global governance and international institutions, however, is not only related to the IMF, the World Bank and the WTO. Another example that is highly relevant for global trade policy is the Organisation for Economic Co-operation and Development (OECD). Many OECD member countries have cooperated since the 1970s with regard to trade policy and official export credit support in order to create a "level playing field" for businesses involved in international trade. Governments have jointly agreed on improved rules and regulations through the OECD Arrangement or the Common Approaches, ensuring coherence between exports supported by national governments and environmental protection (Drysdale, 2015). As compliance with these standards is limited to OECD participants, and emerging economies such as China and India are very active in supporting and financing exports, many stakeholders see a need to establish additional rules and regulations on a global level.

Exporters in highly industrialised countries need these regulatory frameworks and require transparent rules and regulations. An application of truly international norms ensuring global trade governance is crucial for businesses. There is a continuous criticism regarding the limits of the OECD framework, which captures less and less trade due to the fact that both non-exporting-related export finance operations and non-OECD export credit agency (ECA) activities continue to grow. Mildner and Bartel (2015) as well as Ron and Terzulli (2015) mention that the Arrangement failed to accommodate and adjust to the transformed global landscape. Many businesses in the OECD believe they are at a disadvantage vis-à-vis non-OECD exporters because countries outside the OECD are not bound by similarly stringent export finance rules. Exporters in OECD countries would celebrate a success of the International Working Group on Export Credits (IWG) initiated by former US President Obama and China's President Xi Jinping. However, there is limited progress locking domestic decision-makers into a global framework.

Governance and Regulation that Matter

Due to the obvious importance of the WTO, Judith Goldstein and Elisabeth van Lieshout examine its history and its relevancy today in Chapter 7. Their review looks at the central norms of the system and compares trade liberalisation under the multilateral WTO with the more exclusive regional and preferential trade agreements (PTAs). In times of deep concern about the role of the WTO and the future of the trading order, the authors also explain in detail why the crisis arose, and how it affects the future of the trade regime. While some people suggest that the WTO has outlived its purposes, Goldstein and van Lieshout counter with the observation that on the whole, member nations have complied with the significant commitments made in earlier negotiations, and in general, WTO members have resisted protectionist pressures. They also find that it is wrong to assume that the popular malaise about the virtues of trade is a function of something the WTO did or did not accomplish.

Chapter 8 looks at international financial institutions and their role and relevance regarding global trade. The objective is to detail the development impacts of trade finance as the basis for a discussion of the role multilateral development banks (MDBs) have played. Steven Beck and Alisa DiCaprio analyse ways in which MDBs have reduced friction in global trade finance markets. Furthermore, the chapter describes and analyses, for example, that MDBs can play an important role developing basic infrastructure to infuse blockchain and other technology into trade finance. The authors give evidence that, as technology advances, multilateral development banks have the incentive and mandate to introduce new resources to meet development goals.

Then, Diana Smallridge and Jennifer Henderson elaborate the challenging relationship between trade policy and banking regulation. Their chapter's primary purpose is to examine the impact that banking regulation has on those financial institutions serving small and medium-sized enterprises (SMEs), women-led businesses and emerging economies. The authors argue that the mismatch in mandate between trade ministers and financial regulators, with each singing from a different songbook, creates policy conflict and opens up new market gaps. Chapter 9 also discusses the questions of whether regulators should compromise on their standards, or if trade ministers should ignore the business realities of their local companies. The authors' conclusion is that the road ahead is uncertain and coordinated efforts of different stakeholders are required.

A less considered but important aspect of global governance in trade is the relationship between trade and illicit flows. In a case involving the United States, China and Mexico, Nikos Passas provides information about processes that have been developed by customs authorities for detecting and intercepting criminal activities within trade movements. In particular, Chapter 10 examines the vulnerabilities for trade-based money laundering in cargo flows across the US–Mexican border. The author provides evidence of transaction irregularities suggesting that trade-based money laundering involving China, the United States and Mexico is ongoing, while also identifying additional problem areas that warrant close attention by trade authorities. In his conclusion, Passas also recommends important next steps such as improved data quality and systematic comparison, as well as closer monitoring of border warehouses and businesses re-packaging in-bond shipment.

Global Trade and Regional Development

Regional Trade Policies and Fragmentation

Part III of this Handbook deals with global trade and regional development, and a major aspect of regional development is the above-mentioned economic shift towards the East as well as South–South exports, which have doubled over the past two decades. The substantial growth resulting in a share of 42% of developing countries' total merchandise trade in 2015 is visible in South American and Asian developing economies, coinciding with the economic dynamism in these regions. And although Asia, Europe and North America have accounted for 88% of total merchandise trade of WTO members over the past ten years, South–South trade from least developed countries in Africa also significantly climbed. As a result of this development, countries engaged in South–South trade are now influential players building coalitions in multilateral trade negotiations to increase their power and interests (Rolland, 2007). They are also much more willing and able to challenge industrialised WTO member countries because of their divergent interests, in particular regarding agricultural policies. Activism of developing economies during the Doha Round negotiations has made gridlock the standard rather than the exceptional circumstance (Lee, 2012).

Fragmentation, which is related to increased transaction costs but also excessive flexibility, complements the different trends such as multipolarity and institutional inertia. As noted above, in part due to a persistent deadlock in multilateral talks, regional initiatives to advance trade liberalisation or to protect economies have grown outside the WTO framework. The new regional and bilateral trade agreement landscape is an immense challenge. Trade initiatives are not only sprouting on a regional level, a major trend in trade policy is also bilateral solutions. Policymakers increasingly remove existing multilateral trade strategies, focusing much more on FTAs. Nationalism and regionalism are thus likely to occupy a growing role in trade governance (Reyes *et al.*, 2014). Drivers of these trends include different policy preferences affected by interest configuration, defensive motives with economies experiencing limitations to economic growth, and the growth of lobbying by companies towards their national government to bolster their competitive position via FTAs (Manger, 2005).

India, in particular, has been aggressively pushing bilateral foreign trade agreements, with mixed results. While the country's exports stagnated, imports from bilateral partner countries into India increased. Bilateral agreements have been immensely popular throughout Asia (Aggarwal and Lee, 2011; Park, 2009). China signed FTAs with, for example, Australia, India and Korea in order to expand its markets and secure long-term supply of natural resources. The increasing number of bilateral deals in Asia is described as a "noodle bowl", often doing more harm than good. Bilateral FTAs mostly include complicated rules, and too many and overlapping "noodles" create complex regulatory environments leading to higher costs for exporters.

Sailing Against the Storm of Protectionism

In Chapter 11, Marion Jansen, Sebastian Klotz and Jasmeer Virdee discuss regional integration within the context of three phenomena: the rise of China as a major global player, the appearance of a new "industrial revolution" due to the fast development of the digital economy, and the increased complexity of trade rules as further liberalisation increasingly implies the need to move "behind the border". The authors give an overview of regional integration with a focus on the past century and the interplay between multilateral and regional trade rules. Then, they examine the surge of so-called mega-regionalism in the light of the relationships between Northern America, the European Union and China. The interaction between different "domestic" policy areas and international trade is a further focus, as is the advent of the digital economy and its impact on trade rules. In the conclusion, the authors venture into the future by asking what the next wave of regional integration may look like.

Erdal Yalcin, Gabriel Felbermayr and Marina Steininger then look at the United States, and what to expect from a protective US trade policy. Their analysis shows that the US administration's promise to create more jobs and investment in the United States through the presented trade policies is a fallacy. In all of the simulated scenarios, an isolation of the US market would primarily have a negative impact on the US economy itself in the long term. It is also clear for the authors that a protectionist trade policy would most likely lead to a worldwide policy of retaliation against the United States. Overall, the comprehensive analysis in Chapter 12 discourages the United States from pursuing the protectionist trade policy executed by the Trump administration for its own sake. Seeking new forms of cooperation between the United States and its main trading partners like China and Germany, as well as Canada and Mexico, would be a far more sensible strategy.

The aspect of trade and developing-country exporters is key for Banu Demir. She looks at the significance of bank-intermediated trade finance for developing-country exporters and importers. Chapter 13 relies on currently available survey data on trade finance practices, as well as insights and findings of the recently growing literature on trade finance with a geographical focus on Central and Latin American, and Caribbean countries. In her conclusion, Banu Demir particularly discusses that supply chain finance is an important innovation in the global trade finance market, and it is particularly relevant for developing-country businesses. She discusses that main benefits include transition from paper-based transactions to electronic invoicing and using transaction-level data to assess the creditworthiness of potential borrowers. However, the author also concludes that supply chain finance is still not widely used in Latin America except in Mexico and Brazil.

Lucian Cernat and Omar Alam then look at the role of the European Union (EU) in shaping global trade policy, sailing against the storm of protectionism. The authors discuss that the EU has been playing a leading role in shaping global trade flows and the rules governing them, and trade is arguably the EU's most significant link to the world beyond its borders. Focusing on future challenges for EU trade policy, Chapter 14 discusses improving market access implementation and enforcement, facilitating trade for SMEs, and revamping key performance indicators. Further aspects include enhancing trade policy communication, as well as using trade to benefit all Europeans. One takeaway of the latter is that EU trade policy objectives need to be well embedded in the overall set of policies, aimed at ensuring that the future looks bright to all Europeans. In this respect, the authors emphasise that concerns need to be properly addressed that globalisation and further trade integration will widen social inequality in Europe.

The following chapter discusses trade, global value chains and inclusive growth in Asia and the Pacific. Yasuyuki Sawada, Cyn-Young Park, Fahad H. Khan and Cindy Jane Justo create a colourful picture of developing Asia, the world's fastest growing region. Asia has emerged as a growth pole in the world economy, and policies promoting export-oriented industrialisation while mobilising high savings have bolstered growth, outperforming the industrialised economies and other parts of the developing world. The authors discuss trade and investment as engines of growth and development in Asia and the Pacific, but also look at growth- and trade-related policy implications. Examples include policies to unlock trade potential in achieving SDGs, as well as trade facilitation for inclusive growth. A particular focus of Chapter 15 is on support for trade-related infrastructure equipping developing countries with the preconditions to trade.

At the end of Part III, Roseline Wanjiru and Karla Simone Prime investigate the changing trade and economic performance of African economies, and the influence that institutional capacities in different host economies have on a country's economic performance. Building upon insights from existing empirical studies, Chapter 16 focuses on the role of institutions and their respective influence on trade and investment performance within Africa. The chapter specifically investigates institutions as key factors impacting the current performances on trade and inward FDI flows within African economies. The authors' results demonstrate that institutions have a long-run effect on investment flows. In order to further increase economic benefits from rising trade participation and inward investment in African economies, there is a need to pay attention to the role of effective institutions in regulating business, and implementation of supportive institutions more adapted to entrepreneurs and investors in high-risk environments.

Financing Trade

A Need for A Functioning Trade Finance Environment

Part IV of the Handbook focuses on financing trade. International trade is strongly connected with a functioning financial environment, and commercial banks and private credit insurers play an important role in the financial system. However, exporters are regularly facing challenges in financing and insuring trade because of limited appetite from commercial players in certain markets or sectors.

In general, markets are mechanisms for allocating resources and are, by and large, the most efficient way to coordinate a global economy. As discussed by Stiglitz and

Walsh (2006), if markets are perfectly competitive, market participants have perfect information, and there are no externalities and no public goods, market outcomes will be efficient. However, shortcomings of markets are widely acknowledged in certain situations in which conditions for perfect competition are not met. In such events, markets may lead to inefficient outcomes, which provide a rationale for government intervention (Klasen and Eicher, 2017). There are four main types of situations in which market failure can occur: Monopolies and oligopolistic markets, externalities or third-party effects, imperfect information or public goods (see e.g. Lipsey and Chrystal, 2011). Markets for the provision of export or development finance can fail to achieve efficient outcomes as they suffer, in particular, from imperfect information and externalities.

Imperfect information or information asymmetries between potential transaction partners may prevent mutually beneficial investment from occurring. Stiglitz and Weiss (1981) have shown that this can result in unmet demand for credit. Potential borrowers might not receive investment or export finance loans even if they indicate a willingness to pay more than the market interest rate, or to put up more collateral than demanded. Information asymmetries can also be the underlying reason for market failure in insurance markets that suffer from adverse selection and moral hazard (Williamson, 1973). Externalities are typically a main justification given for government intervention to support export industries (Harrison and Rodríguez, 2009). Wider positive effects on economic development associated with trade represent positive externalities for which providers of export finance will not receive payments. As a result, private market actors will provide less export finance than socially desirable.

In addition to market failure, policy goals can be a key reason for public interventions. As governments play an important role in growth processes, goals can be related to provision of domestic infrastructure such as transportation and communication, education and health in the national economy (Lipsey and Chrystal, 2011). However, emphasis can also be placed on SDGs such as poverty reduction, reduced inequalities, and responsible consumption and production focusing on foreign countries. In recent years, a number of governments started to combine trade and development cooperation policy objectives. Policies then can focus, for example, on reducing poverty and social inequality and promoting sustainable and inclusive growth, as well as enhancing international earning capacity by pursuing a progressive international trade agenda (Klasen, 2017a).

As a consequence, many governments in both developed and developing economies have set up government financial vehicles to finance economic development, exports or innovation not only to alleviate market failure but also to reach national or international policy goals. A principal success factor of government financing vehicles is an integration into a concise national strategic framework to leverage impact (Meyer and Klasen, 2013). Within this strategic framework, different institutions such as bilateral development finance institutions (DFIs), national ECAs, national development banks and innovation funds have different mandates and strategic approaches but follow a coherent set of policy objectives.

The establishment of development banks goes back to the 19th century when the rapid industrialisation could often only be achieved by a government provision of long-term financing for risky transactions (see e.g. Diamond, 1957). A necessity for reconstruction after World War I was another driver for government-sponsored financial institutions for development (Armendáriz de Aghion, 1999). After 1945, state intervention banks such as the Business Development Bank of Canada (BDC) and Kreditanstalt für Wiederaufbau (KfW) in Germany were launched for capital assistance to the local industry (Fergusson, 1948). Applying a narrower approach of development banks, contributions focus only on bilateral DFIs and MDBs with the policy mandate to invest in shortcomings of developing countries. Mostly funded after World War II, this group includes bilateral institutions such as Nederlandse Financierings-Maatschappij voor Ontwikkelingslanden (FMO) in the Netherlands, Deutsche Investitions- und Entwicklungsgesellschaft (DEG) in Germany and France's Société de Promotion et de Participation pour la Coopération Economique (Proparco).

Multilateral institutions include the African Development Bank (AfDB), the Asian Development Bank (ADB) and the World Bank. Most recently, new multilateral development banks such as the Asian Infrastructure Investment Bank (AIIB) or the New Development Bank (NDB) were founded, some of them focusing on infrastructure or energy projects in order to intensify regional and global trade relations (Flint and Zhu, 2019; Gallagher *et al.*, 2018). Initially mostly focusing on official development assistance (ODA), the area of development finance has substantially changed since 2000: On the one hand, financing with more than 25% grant elements particularly from bilateral institutions based in OECD countries substantially went down. On the other hand, financing of private sector development dramatically increased, a consequence of the reorientation in development thinking in the 1980s (Savoy *et al.*, 2016; Gibbon and Schulpen, 2004). Important rationales are now to provide private sector firms with equity or loans, which are difficult to obtain in developing countries, or to invest in businesses, projects and financial institutions to support sustainable growth. DFI and MDB activities and contributions are often associated with SDGs such as decent work and economic growth, a reduction of inequalities and climate action. Financing trade plays an increasing role in this context.

To expand economic growth and foreign trade, many governments around the globe also promote trade through financing and risk mitigation instruments focusing on exports and FDI. Although some instruments have been labelled as export development banks or export-import banks, we define these instruments as ECAs. The first agency, now branded UK Export Finance, was established 100 years ago in the United Kingdom, followed by other industrialised countries such as Germany, Italy and Spain. As private credit insurers and commercial banks today sometimes restrict their offerings, in particular for exports to high-risk markets and transactions with extended credit periods involving capital goods, many other governments also started to provide export credit and trade credit insurance facilities (see e.g. Broocks and Biesebroeck, 2017; Klasen, 2014; Klasen, 2012; Gianturco, 2001). In 2017, more than 60 governments provided noteworthy financing and insurance for trade transactions, with China at the top.

Similar to the field of development finance, the ECA environment has substantially changed in response to new challenges in recent decades. A main driver was the 2008 Global Financial Crisis. Agencies around the globe substantially expanded their product offering, including direct lending, working capital facilities, or even equity and mezzanine financing. Other ECAs increased their risk appetite, supporting key industries or financing projects in developing economies. Some institutions are moving towards an integrated solutions provider approach: They insure risk and enable refinancing in the traditional European model, support companies also in the full financing cycle through direct lending or less export-related financing, and additionally provide knowledge products and technical assistance.

How Trade Finance and Government Interventions Work

Chapter 17 summarises some of the economic and policy knowledge developed by analysts and policymakers in past decades with regard to trade finance. Marc Auboin examines the links between trade and trade finance, and analyses the markets – large, liquid, but prone to temporary or permanent gaps. The author also looks at challenges affecting developing countries, some of which are structural, and some linked to the retrenchment of the global financial industry from countries seen as "challenging" since the Global Financial Crisis. The chapter also discusses recent efforts to evaluate global trade finance gaps, describing policy initiatives to address them.

A more technical perspective of how trade finance works is provided by Alexander Malaket. He discusses the four key elements of trade financing: The facilitation of appropriate, secure and timely payment across borders; the provision of financing to one or more parties in a transaction or supply chain; the effective mitigation or optimisation of a range of risks, as dictated by the characteristics of the transaction or trade flows, and the risk tolerances of trading parties; and the flow of information about the physical movement of the goods or services and the related financial flows. Chapter 18 also analyses policy measures that help develop a healthy and robust trade finance market. The question is how these measures contribute to a dynamic capability to trade, considering the value and impact as well as opportunities that can derive from closing the global trade finance gap.

Benedict Okey Oramah focuses on export credit arrangements in capital-scarce developing economies in the following chapter. His key questions are: What is the rationale behind the use of ECAs in export promotion in capital-scarce economies, which would ordinarily not be in a position to export capital goods or offer export credits? What are the differences, if any, between traditional advanced economy ECAs and developing economy ECAs? Are ECAs that are designated as export-import banks more prevalent in advanced or developing economies and why? And how have ECAs in developing economies evolved as economies have moved up the development ladder? Chapter 19 also looks at important lessons learned for developing economies contemplating setting up ECAs, and provides a case study approach focusing on the Nigerian Export-Import Bank, as well as the African Export-Import Bank.

An analysis of motives and factors for demand for credit insurance is provided by Simone Krummaker. She focuses on aspects of managing risk connected with the provision of trade credit in international trade. Chapter 20 looks at export credit insurance markets and products, but also at export credit market governance. The chapter then analyses firm factors affecting the demand for risk mitigation instruments in financing foreign trade. A further important aspect is the reduced risk appetite of commercial banks leading to a persistent lack of export funding, as well as the funding and insurance gap for SMEs. Other important issues in the analysis are factors affecting trade and export credit insurance as consequences of globalisation and shifts in the geopolitical landscape.

The final chapter looks at climate finance, trade and innovation systems. Fiona Bannert discusses climate finance from a variety of angles. She starts with outlining the current landscape of climate finance, its actors, instruments, final use and location. Her chapter then discusses the challenge of mobilising additional private investment and ways to leverage public funds before making reference to the role of international trade in this setting. Finally, Chapter 21 sketches out a theoretical framework, which can be a helpful tool for placing the current discussions around climate finance in a holistic framework. Fiona Bannert concludes that there is no way around an agreed definition of what constitutes climate finance on an international level. She also highlights that more attention should be spent on an appropriate national investment policy and the establishment of the right climate finance incentive framework on a country level. Finally, the contribution shows that it remains important to foster the dialogue and enhance the integration of climate change considerations into the financial system.

Summary and Conclusion

International trade is a key driver for prosperity and economic growth, and doing business with and in other countries is vital for the success of companies of all sizes and sectors. Many countries have prospered by establishing competitive industries, and GDP growth has helped to generate financial resources needed to improve people's living conditions. Firms and countries that open up to trade enjoy long-run growth through several impacts: There is evidence of a market share's shift towards more efficient exporters, and a direct effect of trade liberalisation on aggregate productivity. In addition, host country governments often adopt policies to encourage inward FDI through bilateral investment treaties and national investment law including most-favoured-nation clauses and tax incentives. The expansion of international business activities through a multilateral trading system has provided a major pillar for growth enjoyed in the past century by industrialised and developing countries.

Trade in the 21st century faces a number of challenges: challenging economic and social developments such as the 4IR with new and rapidly changing technologies are altering the competitiveness of countries and their exporters in many ways. Artificial intelligence, cloud computing or autonomous systems create new industries and revolutionise or even destroy traditional industry sectors and global supply chains. Services trade becomes much more important, and rising global uncertainty leads to a new set of problems. A major challenge is often described as growing multipolarity: a growing number of countries use their political influence for export promotion or development policy while representing a diverse range of opposed interests.

The global trade landscape suffers from extensive gridlock, a condition that has brought its core post-war function, negotiating progressively lower barriers to trade, to a halt. But at the same time, elements of the trade regime have proven remarkably resilient and adaptive, including the WTO dispute settlement mechanism and technical organisations such as the International Chamber of Commerce, the Berne Union, and the OECD. Though the trade regime remains gridlocked, it still functions thanks to these different institutions working at different levels. At the same time, the pluralisation of trade agreements has not necessarily brought coherence. Gridlock trends like rising multipolarity can be so strong as to prevent the minimum level of coherence required to make plurality work. But can the trading regime endure? With political leaders threatening to turn away from free trade across major economies, the question arises of whether "business as usual" will be sufficient, or if deeper transformations are required to move global trade arrangements through or even beyond gridlock. Or, indeed, to prevent them from deteriorating. In this context, innovative and adaptive leadership from the WTO itself may be able to at least partially reinvigorate the regime as a whole. Since 1995, the WTO has been a main pillar of multilateral economic governance in trade. Despite its weaknesses, solutions through and beyond gridlock without a strong involvement of the WTO are hardly imaginable. To reinvigorate the WTO, however, policymakers in developed and developing countries would have to admit and accept that amendments in policy-making and organisational settings are necessary.

A continuous expansion of export depends not only on appropriate trade policies in a challenging political context but also on a supportive financial environment. Credit availability is important for all countries and industries, and there is a causal link between finance and economic growth. However, external financing is particularly required for production and exporting in the machinery industry in many countries, and for transportation infrastructure necessitating large capital expenditures. Other sectors such as energy are also highly dependent on export and development finance. International trade and economic development are thus strongly connected with a well-developed and functioning financial environment including export credit.

With plenty of liquidity from commercial banks in the market, the availability of credit has improved with declining interest rates after the 2008 Global Financial Crisis. However, many commercial banks active in export financing particularly in Europe have consolidated their operations. Banks have reduced the number of clients, focusing on a few large corporates. Commercial bank cross-border lending has been flat over past years, and banks often consider long-term transactions for capital goods to be too costly and risky to finance. The same applies for challenging transactions for large infrastructure projects in difficult markets, or for complex project finance structures. This is due to the fact that commercial banks are less willing to tie up liquidity in long-term transactions with low yields. In addition, SMEs continue to face substantial difficulties in obtaining financing. There is no sufficient offering from commercial banks for "small ticket" transactions below US$5 million due to limited risk appetite and competition.

The trend of commercial banks' balance sheet optimisation in many economies is expected to continue. Compliance and regulatory issues are additional impediments for the provision of export, development and innovation financing. As a consequence, offerings made available by commercial financial institutions often mismatch to exporters' requirements with regard to size and maturity. The search for finance is greater for smaller export projects and longer maturities. Substantial financing gaps for exporters and investors also occur for large export transactions with long tenors, in particular for infrastructure investments.

In recent years, the world of Exim-Banks and ECAs has changed considerably in response to new challenges of the foreign trade environment and financial markets. ECAs around the globe have substantially expanded their product offering including direct lending, working capital facilities or even equity and mezzanine financing.

Other ECAs took steps to substantially increase their risk appetite, supporting key industries or financing projects in developing economies. As described above, several ECAs are now also moving towards an integrated solutions provider approach. With fast-growing export finance activities in emerging economies, countries such as China are cementing the importance of their institutions: The Export-Import Bank of China (CEXIM), for example, is very active in Africa with both export credits and concessional loans. The multilateral Afreximbank intends to substantially increase its business with the implementation of the Afreximbank Guarantee Programme (AFGAP), a new programme for exports and imports.

Bilateral development finance institutions went through a change process in recent years and DFIs today follow diverse objectives. Products and programmes now include microfinance and guarantee mechanisms as well as working capital and bridge financing, credit allocation to climate change mitigation, and women and youth entrepreneurship. Some development finance institutions are still financial gap fillers focusing solely on additionality. Others started to undertake more entrepreneurial roles in order to meet capital needs of SMEs. Many DFIs focus not only on economic growth but also on private sector development, gender and development, as well as regional cooperation. Consistent themes are emerging globally for DFIs, including funding, governance, risk management and changing real economies, as well as a broader approach regarding financial instruments. There is also a trend that some development finance institutions are looking into new areas such as trade and export finance. Due to the fact that participation in global value chains is an important objective for exporters, trade financing becomes a building block of future frameworks for some DFIs as well. There is an increasing number of development finance institutions offering trade-related financing products, or planning to establish respective programmes. This is often driven by a political will to mobilise private sector finance towards SDGs and putting pressure on governments to honour global political commitments.

The *Handbook of Global Trade Policy* provides a comprehensive resource for the study of global policy and governance, as well as economics and financing of international trade. It brings together internationally recognised experts to produce surveys of recent academic research and to assess its policy implications. The contributions provide a state-of-the-art overview of the research landscape in a number of related disciplines, from economics and international business to international relations, law and global politics.

References

Aggarwal, V.K. & Lee, S. (2011) The Domestic Political Economy of Preferential Trade Agreements in the Asia-Pacific. In: Aggarwal, V.K. & Lee, S. (eds.) *Trade Policy in the Asia-Pacific: The Role of Ideas, Interests, and Domestic Institutions*. New York: Springer, pp. 1–28.

Amemiya, T. (2007) *Economy and Economics of Ancient Greece*. New York: Routledge.

Armendáriz de Aghion, B. (1999) Development Banking. *Journal of Development Economics*, 58, 83–100.

Broocks, A. & Biesebroeck, J.V. (2017) The Impact of Export Promotion on Export Market Entry. *Journal of International Economics*, 107, 19–33.

Capling, A. & Higgott, R. (2009) Introduction: The Future of the Multilateral Trade System – What Role for the World Trade Organization?. *Global Governance*, 15, 313–325.

Delimatsis, P. (2014) Transparency in the WTO's Decision-Making. *Leiden Journal of International Law*, 27, 701–726.

Destradi, S. & Jakobeit, C. (2015) Global Governance Debates and Dilemmas: Emerging Powers' Perspectives and Roles in Global Trade and Climate Governance. *Strategic Analysis*, 39(1), 60–72.

Diamond, W. (1957) *Development Banks*. Baltimore: Johns Hopkins Press.

Drysdale, D. (2015) Why the OECD Arrangement Works (Even Though It Is Only Soft Law). In: Klasen, A. & Bannert, F. (eds.) *The Future of Foreign Trade Support*. Durham: Global Policy and Wiley, pp. 5–7.

Fergusson, D. (1948) The Industrial Development Bank of Canada. *Journal of Business of the University of Chicago*, 21, 214–229.

Flint, C. & Zhu, C. (2019) The Geopolitics of Connectivity, Cooperation, and Hegemonic Competition: The Belt and Road Initiative. *Geoforum*, 99, 95–101.

Gallagher, K.P., Kamal, R., Jin, J. *et al.* (2018) Energizing Development Finance? The Benefits and Risks of China's Development Finance in the Global Energy Sector. *Energy Policy*, 122, 313–321.

Garcia, F.J., Ciko, L., Gaurav, A. & Hough, K. (2015) Reforming the International Investment Regime: Lessons from International Trade Law. *Journal of International Economic Law*, 18, 861–892.

Gianturco, D.E. (2001) *Export Credit Agencies*. Westport: Quorum.

Gibbon, P. & Schulpen, L. (2004) Comparative Appraisal of Multilateral and Bilateral Approaches to Financing Private Sector Development. In: Odedokun, M. (ed.) *External Finance for Private Sector Development*. Basingstoke: Palgrave Macmillan, pp. 42–91.

Hale, T. & Held, D. (2017) Pathways beyond Gridlock. In: Hale, T. & Held, D. (eds.) *Beyond Gridlock*. Cambridge: Polity Press, pp. 1–27.

Hale, T., Held, D. & Young, K. (2013) *Gridlock: Why Global Cooperation is Failing When We Need It Most*. Cambridge: Polity Press.

Harrigan, J., Wang, C. & El-Said, H. (2006) The Economic and Political Determinants of IMF and World Bank Lending in the Middle East and North Africa. *World Development*, 34(2), 247–270.

Harrison, A. & Rodríguez-Clare, A. (2009) Trade, Foreign Investment, and Industrial Policy for Developing Countries. *NBER Working Paper* No. 15261.

Hoekman, B.M. & Mavroidis, P.C. (2007) *The World Trade Organization*. London: Routledge.

Klasen, A. (2012) Generating Economic Growth – How Governments Can Help Successfully. *Global Policy*, 3(2), 238–241.

Klasen, A. (2014) Export Credit Guarantees and the Demand for Insurance. *CESifo Forum*, 15(3), 26–33.

Klasen, A. (2017a) Policy Instruments of Innovation, Investment and Global Trade. *Global Policy*, 8(3), 389–391.

Klasen, A. (2017b) Trade: Gridlock and Resilience. In: Hale, T. & Held, D. (eds.) *Beyond Gridlock*. Cambridge: Polity Press, pp. 65–82.

Klasen, A. & Bannert, F. (2015) The Future of Foreign Trade Support. In: Klasen, A. & Bannert, F. (eds.) *The Future of Foreign Trade Support*. Durham: Global Policy and Wiley, pp. 1–4.

Klasen, A. & Eicher, B. (2017) Instrumente staatlicher Innovationsfinanzierung für Infrastruktur [Public Innovation Financing Instruments for Infrastructure]. *Recht der Internationalen Wirtschaft*, 11, 726–734.

Lee, D. (2012) Global Trade Governance and the Challenges of African Activism in the Doha Development Agenda Negotiations. *Global Society*, 26(1), 83–101.

Lipsey, R. & Chrystal, A. (2011) *Economics*. Oxford: Oxford University Press.

Manger, M. (2005) Competition and Bilateralism in Trade Policy: The Case of Japan's Free Trade Agreements. *Review of International Political Economy*, 12(5), 804–828.

Matsushita, M., Schoenbaum T.J. & Mavroidis, P.C. (2015) *The World Trade Organization*. Oxford: Oxford University Press.

Meyer, H. & Klasen, A. (2013) What Governments Can Do to Support their Economies: The Case for a Strategic Econsystem. *Global Policy*, 4(Suppl. 1), 1–9.

Michaelidis, P., Kardasi, O. & Milios, J. (2011) Democritus's Economic Ideas in the Context of Classical Political Economy. *European Journal of the History of Economic Thought*, 18(1), 1–18.

Mildner, S.-A. & Bartel, R. (2015) German Industry Needs a Level Playing Field in Export Finance. In: Klasen, A. & Bannert, F. (eds.) *The Future of Foreign Trade Support*. Durham: Global Policy and Wiley, pp. 105–107.

Narlikar, A. (2010) New Powers in the Club: The Challenges of Global Trade Governance. *International Affairs*, 86(3), 717–728.

Park, I. (2009) Regional Trade Agreements in East Asia: Will They Be Sustainable? *Asian Economic Journal*, 23(2), 169–194.

Quah, D. (2011) The Global Economy's Shifting Centre of Gravity. *Global Policy*, 2(1), 3–9.

Reyes, J., Wooster, R. & Shirrell, S. (2014) Regional Trade Agreements and the Pattern of Trade: A Network Approach. *World Economy*, 37(8), 1128–1151.

Rolland, S.E. (2007) Developing Country Coalitions at the WTO: In Search of Legal Support. *Harvard International Law Journal*, 48, 483–551.

Ron, M. & Terzulli, A. (2015) Regulations, Subsidies and ECAs – Are We Sure the More the Merrier? In: Klasen, A. & Bannert, F. (eds.) *The Future of Foreign Trade Support*. Durham: Global Policy and Wiley, pp. 33–35.

Ruggie, J.G. (1982) International Regimes, Transactions, and Change: Embedded Liberalism in the Postwar Economic Order. *International Organization*, 36(2), 379–415.

San Juan, E. (2011) Contemporary Global Capitalism and the Challenge of the Filipino Diaspora. *Global Society*, 25(1), 7–27.

Savoy, C.M., Carter, P. & Lemma, A. (2016) Development Finance Institutions Come of Age. Washington DC: CSIS.

Shimomura, Y. & Ohashi, H. (2013) Why China's Foreign Aid Matters? In: Shimomura, Y. & Ohashi, H. (eds.) *A Study of China's Foreign Aid*. Basingstoke: Palgrave Macmillan, pp. 3–15.

Skultety, S. (2006) Currency, Trade and Commerce in Plato's Laws. *History of Political Thought*, 27(2), 189–205.

Stiglitz, J.E. & Walsh, C.E. (2006) *Economics*. New York: W.W. Norton.

Stiglitz, J.E. & Weiss, A. (1981) Credit Rationing in Markets with Imperfect Information. *The American Economic Review*, 71(3), 393–410.

Wade, R.H. (2011) Emerging World Order? From Multipolarity to Multilateralism in the G20, the World Bank, and the IMF. *Politics & Society*, 39(3), 347–378.

Were, M. (2015) Differential Effects of Trade on Economic Growth and Investment: A Cross-Country Empirical Investigation. *Journal of African Trade*, 2, 71–85.

Wilkinson, R., Hannah, E. & Scott J. (2014) The WTO in Bali: What MC9 Means for the Doha Development Agenda and Why It Matters. *Third World Quarterly*, 35(6), 1032–1050.

Williamson, O.E. (1973) Markets and Hierarchies: Some Elementary Considerations. *The American Economic Review*, 63(2), 316–325.

World Bank (2019) *Global Economic Prospects January 2019: Darkening Skies*. Washington, DC: World Bank Group.

Part I Foreign Trade in the 21st Century

Chapter 2

The Global Trade Environment – A New Reality

Martina Höppner

Introduction

Global trade has been one of the major pillars of global economic development and growth. Not only today's industrialised countries but also emerging economies have profited. The "export-led growth" strategies of Asian countries have long been promoted as a model of development for emerging and frontier markets. The integration of value chains has linked countries to an unprecedented extent (Constantinescu *et al.*, 2014). However, since the 2008 Global Financial Crisis, global trade has slowed, whereby both cyclical and structural factors are at play. Doubts regarding the benefits of trade are becoming increasingly vocal. Free trade is blamed for everything from lost jobs in Detroit to the danger of chlorine-washed chicken in Germany (Sinn, 2014). Free trade agreements have become contentious (Felbermayr and Kohler, 2015). While it is important to acknowledge that free trade can create some losers, blaming trade for developments that are not induced by it is not only unjustified but even dangerous, as policy responses will be ill-targeted and therefore limited in their effectiveness. Having a clear picture of the global trade environment is therefore highly relevant.

The aim of this chapter is fourfold. First, it will look at historic and current trends in trade. Second, it will search to disentangle the extent to which current economic developments are driven by global trade as opposed to innovation, automation and new technologies, while acknowledging that all of these factors are intertwined. Third, it will discuss current trends in free trade and contrast these with rising protectionist tendencies. Forth, it will look into the impact of global trade, its advantages and disadvantages, as well as the challenges of adjusting to these developments in industrialised, emerging and frontier economies. Finally, based on the issues discussed, determinants for future trends in trade will be stipulated.

The Handbook of Global Trade Policy, First Edition. Edited by Andreas Klasen.
© 2020 John Wiley & Sons Ltd. Published 2020 by John Wiley & Sons Ltd.

Ever since David Ricardo, one of the earliest economists establishing the principle of comparative advantage, the notion that global trade is largely beneficial remains undisputed among economists. Just as undisputed is the notion that not everybody will gain from trade (Krugman and Obstfeld, 2000). While winners of trade are often numerous but diffuse and their gains tend to be relatively small, losers – facing comparatively large losses – tend to be clearly identifiable. Although the gains from trade generally outweigh the losses, thus allowing losers of trade to be compensated, in reality this compensation has often not happened, or at least not successfully. Add to this Olson's theory of lobbies – which states that when there is a large group and a small group with divergent interests, the small group always wins out in the political process as it enjoys a higher per capita gain from lobbying (Sinn, 2014) – and the success of recent tendencies towards populism and protectionism become comprehensible.

Given that this dilemma is anything but new, why have populist tendencies and protectionism recently surged? Four phenomena may be contributing to this development.

First, trade has decelerated considerably since the early 2000s and particularly since the 2008 Global Financial Crisis. Between 1986 and 2000, merchandise trade volume growth was approximately 6% a year on average, roughly twice the rate of world real gross domestic product (GDP) growth. While this period was certainly exceptional – including compared with preceding years – ever since the 2000s, and particularly since the financial crisis, trade growth has been sluggish. From 2008 to 2014, international trade grew at half the rate of 1986–1990 and at the same pace as global output (Constantinescu et al., 2016). While reasons for this development will be discussed later in this chapter, slower growth in trade may very well contribute to smaller gains from trade, leading to increasing dissatisfaction.

Second, trade is often used as a scapegoat for dislocations in communities and lost jobs. According to the World Trade Organization (WTO), innovation, automation and new technologies are responsible for roughly 80% of the manufacturing jobs that have been lost (WTO, 2017a; Rotman, 2013). Trade is thus only responsible for a small part of the disruption, although the factors and developments are certainly intertwined. Nonetheless, it appears that losses from trade are particularly long-lasting, thus contributing to trade aversion (IMF, 2017a).

Third, free trade agreements have become much more contentious. They are blamed for job losses, particularly in advanced economies. In addition, rightly or wrongly, they are associated with deteriorations of standards. Consequently, the distrust towards free trade agreements has increased while their benefits are often less discussed (Felbermayr and Kohler, 2015; Sinn, 2014).

Forth, while it remains true that the gains from trade should be sufficient to compensate the losers from trade, it has become increasingly clear that some trends complicate putting this theoretical assumption into practice. Two trends have been prevailing since the 1990s: whereas poorer economies have been catching up with industrialised ones, regional inequalities in rich economies have been increasing. The first part of this observation fits well with trade theories: when poorer countries with low-wage workers start trading with richer countries, pay for similar skilled workers should converge, i.e. workers in poor countries grow richer at the expense of low-skilled workers in rich countries. The challenge appears to be that those losing out from trade in rich countries tend to live in similar places. Trade is thus hurting entire local and regional economies (although innovation, automation and new technologies have certainly also played their role in this phenomenon). However, the ability of these regions to adjust, or its inhabitants to move to more prosperous environments, has been less pronounced than expected. Consequently, losers from trade become easily visible. Moreover, emerging and frontier economies – despite generally being clear winners of trade – have their challenges cut out. Emerging markets – many of them profiting from export-led growth and the inclusion in global value chains – have to find strategies of moving up the ladder in terms of value added of their products (UNCTAD, 2017). Frontier markets may face a plateauing of global value chains due to the increasing automation of production. They may therefore not be able to rely to the same extent on an export-led growth strategy compared with their role models. They may thus face the challenge of having to create their own catch-up model.

These four phenomena – the slowdown of trade since the 2000s, the lack of distinction between the effects of technological change and trade, the mixed picture of advances in global free trade and the challenges handling current trade and economic developments – have thus all played their role in dampening the enthusiasm for global trade.

However, retreating from global trade would only make matters worse. Gaining a clear understanding of the characteristics of the current global trade environment is thus vital to shape the discussion among both economists and the general public, to make a case for global free trade and mitigate its negative consequences for those at risk of losing out.

Historical and Current Trends in International Trade

In order to understand the new reality of trade, it is important to put the development of global trade into a historic perspective. Such a perspective also helps to understand that, apart from historic developments, it was often technological change leading to lower transport, communication or other transaction costs that helped trade to reach a next level. After World War II, the push to foster free trade helped to reinforce this development.

Trade Throughout History

Trade has been a common feature throughout the history of mankind. Even among the first humans, barter trade intuitively played a vital role. Throughout the centuries, trade has often been a driving force for various historic developments. Greeks and Romans were important traders. Later, the Silk Road, the Hanseatic League and the quest for colonies were all largely driven by the interest in trade. At that time, trade was still more focused on products not available in other regions, e.g. silk from China or certain spices. Hubs of trade grew rich and were leading in the quest for scientific developments and the arts.

From the 16th to the 19th century, trade was boosted by colonialism, and thus again the search for new, rare and valuable goods. Costa *et al.* (2015) show that Portugal and Spain took an early lead in the 16th century, followed and overtaken by England and the Netherlands from around 1600. The Dutch Golden Age of the 17th century is certainly a case in point.

Ortiz-Ospina *et al.* (2018) highlight that over the course of the 19th century, international trade became ever more important for a growing number of nations. Trade within Europe also gained in importance, thus reflecting increasing economic integration. Until 1913, trade grew by more than 3% annually. Technological advances such as the steam engine and improved logistics triggered this "first wave of globalisation". On the eve of World War I, leading politicians thought that the (trade) interdependence of nations – particularly in Europe – was too strong for a war to erupt in the region. They were proven incorrect.

The process of global trade growth stopped with the beginning of World War I and was even reversed in the inter-war period and by World War II, when the decline of liberalism and the rise of nationalism led to a slump in international trade. However, since World War II international trade has been growing again, at times faster than ever before. Ortiz-Ospina *et al.* (2018) underline that today, the sum of exports and imports across nations is higher than 50% of global production. At the turn of the 19th century, this figure was below 10%.

It is impressive the extent to which trade has been growing over the past two centuries: growth roughly followed an exponential path in the period up to the turn of the 21st century. Even more recently, trade growth figures have been impressive. According to the International Monetary Fund (IMF), from 1960 to the eve of the Global Financial Crisis in 2007, global trade in goods and services grew at an average real rate of about 6% a year, while the WTO highlights that since World War II, the volume of merchandise trade has tended to grow about 1.5 times faster than world GDP, emphasising that in the 1990s, trade grew more than twice as fast. Only since the 2008 Global Financial Crisis has the ratio of trade growth to GDP fallen to around 1:1.

Drivers of Trade since World War II

Driving factors for the strong growth in trade since World War II have been again decreasing transport, communication and other transaction costs. However, in addition, stronger trade integration and free trade agreements have contributed to trade growth. In terms of decreasing transport and communications costs, there are three developments: the development of commercial civil aviation, increasing productivity of the merchant marine, and telephone costs. Special attention must be drawn to the invention of containers in 1956 (*The Economist*, 2013). This invention prompted the costs of goods shipped by container to decline to US$0.16 per tonne compared with US$5.83 per tonne for loose cargo. Looking at 22 industrialised countries, containerisation was associated with a 320% increase in bilateral trade over the first five years and 790% over 20 years. A bilateral free trade agreement generally boosts trade by 45% over 20 years, and membership of the General Agreement on Tariffs and Trade (GATT) raised it by 285%. Containers thus have boosted globalisation more than all trade agreements in the past 50 years put together.

The impact of free trade should also not be neglected. Continuous rounds of trade negotiations once GATT came into force in 1948 have contributed to a steady reduction of tariffs, culminating in the foundation of the WTO in 1995. However,

ever since the foundation of the WTO, global free trade agreements have seen a marked slowdown, with the failure of the Doha negotiations being the most prominent example. In 2013, a consensus on the Trade Facilitation Agreement (TFA) or Bali Package, which had its roots in the Doha Round, was finally found, making it the first agreement reached through the WTO approved by all its members (WTO, 2017a). The major goal of the agreement is to streamline customs procedures and speed up the flow of goods across borders. The agreement entered into force in February 2017. According to the WTO, it is estimated that the full implementation of the TFA could lead to an increase of as much as 2.7 percentage points per year to world trade growth by 2030. Nonetheless, criticism of the WTO for not having kept pace with economic change, especially in services and information technology (IT) developments, as well as for not having been able to handle China's state-led economic development, have not abated. In the meantime, bilateral and regional trade agreements have substantially expanded in scope and number. According to the IMF (2017a), the number of agreements notified to the WTO has risen from about 50 in 1990 to around 280 in 2015, while their scope has also expanded. After the failure of the Transatlantic Trade and Investment Partnership (TTIP) – a free trade and investment agreement between the United States and the European Union (EU) – the revival of the Trans-Pacific Partnership (TPP) – a free trade agreement initially among 12 countries in Asia and North and South America – as well as the Comprehensive and Progressive Agreement for Trans-Pacific Partnership (CPTPP), the future outlook for free trade appears to be more varied. While the CPTPP survived the withdrawal of the United States as the remaining 11 countries decided to continue with its implementation, the Trump administration's negative attitude towards trade and its disrespect for the WTO and other trade agreements, as well as its readiness to risk trade wars, certainly pose one of the major risks for the nearer-term future of free trade, which may not always be healed by the action of other countries. Indeed, this issue will be taken up again later.

Another factor strongly influencing trade patterns has been the expansion of global value chains in the late 1990s and early 2000s (Constantinescu *et al.*, 2014), which have been a strong driver of productivity and manufacturing exports. The trend has been made possible by the information and communication revolution, as well as the strong decrease of transportation costs and an improved logistical landscape. The global economy has become increasingly structured around global value chains that account for a rising share of international trade. With different stages of the production process being located across multiple countries, intermediate goods cross borders several times along the chain, often passing through many countries more than once.

On the one hand, this trend has made a huge positive contribution to global trade as it has contributed to the diversification of trade. It has allowed for the increasing integration of emerging markets into global trade, particularly the trade of manufactured goods, as it is no longer necessary to produce a complete product for exports. Instead, primary manufactured goods, or even primarily manufactured value added are sufficient. Particular importance has to be attributed to China. The acceleration of the expansion of global value chains occurred shortly after China joined the WTO in 2001. The financial crisis led to a marked slowdown of this development. Since 2011, global value chains have not been able to return to their pre-crisis growth patterns (Constantinescu *et al.*, 2015). The importance of the phenomenon of global value chains is stressed by Dollar (2017), estimating that global value chain trade accounts for 60–67% of global trade in value-added terms.

On the other hand, this trend obscures the picture when examining global trade patterns based on conventional statistical measures as global trade looks very different when examined in value-added terms rather than in gross flows of exports and imports. Conventional measures of trade still measure the gross value of transactions between partners instead of their true value added as most of today's official statistical information systems, designed to measure economic activity in a world before the development of global value chains, have struggled to keep pace with these changes. Global value chains, however, require intermediate goods to cross borders multiple times through the stages of production, thus leading to double counts in traditional trade statistics each time that a product crosses a border. Simola (2015) cites a United Nations Conference on Trade and Development (UNCTAD) evaluation estimating that 28% of global exports in 2010 were actually due to this kind of double counting. The implication is that gross trade flows from traditional statistics no longer provide a clear picture for understanding trade patterns as they provide inflated figures. Analyses focusing on the value added based on e.g. Organisation for Economic Co-operation and Development (OECD) input–output tables intend to address these shortcomings but remain a relatively new field (Simola, 2015). Adjusting global trade data to the impact of global value chains is thus still work in progress but strongly needed to gain a better understanding of trade patterns.

The Slowdown of Trade since the Global Financial Crisis

The 2008 Global Financial Crisis marked a turning point in trade flows. After a sharp decline during the crisis and a brief rebound in its immediate aftermath, trade growth has again slowed, with trade being comparatively weak when taking into consideration past developments (WTO, 2017b). However, this sharp slowdown in global trade in recent years is both a symptom of and a contributor to low growth. According to the IMF, main culprits are changes in the composition of economic activity away from import intensive investment, a slowing pace of global value chain growth and trade liberalisation, and an uptick in trade protectionism. Recent trade growth has been some 1–2 percentage points a year less than would have been expected based on historical relationships between trade and macroeconomic factors. To understand the current slowdown of trade, which is not only occurring in value terms but also and more importantly in volume terms, both a geographical perspective and a distinction between cyclical and structural factors is helpful.

Most trade still takes place between North America, particularly the United States, Europe and Emerging Asia, particularly China, leaving trade still highly concentrated (WTO, 2017a). The top ten traders represent more than half of world trade in both merchandise trade and trade in commercial services. The five major merchandise traders in 2016 were China, the United States, Germany, Japan and France, accounting for more than 38% of world merchandise trade. Therefore, current developments in China, the United States and Europe (which in total accounts for about one third of global trade, with intra-European trade representing about one-fourth of trade) are highly relevant to understand the current trade slump.

Constantinescu *et al.* (2015) highlight that cyclical factors related to developments in various countries and regions account for approximately half to two thirds of the trade slowdown in 2013 and 2015. They find Emerging Asia, which accounts for more than a quarter of world trade, to be the epicentre of the 2015 downturn and the recent rebound, while developments in other regions also matter. At the heart of this development is China, where several trends have been at work.

A Regional Perspective on the Current Trade Slowdown

As far as China's contribution to the trade slowdown since the financial crisis is concerned, a number of factors have been at play. First of all, there has been a general slowdown of growth rates in China. Since reaching its peak in 2007 of just over 14%, growth rates have come down to 6.9% in 2017 (IMF, 2018). This adjustment differs by sector and expenditure components. Data by industry suggests that China's secondary sector has seen a more marked reduction, whereas its tertiary sector has shown a more muted deceleration. On the expenditure side, the contribution of investment activity has slowed more than consumption. This corresponds well with China's overall strategy to move from industry activity to services and from investment to consumption. This slowdown in GDP growth and the changing patterns of industry and expenditure composition all negatively influence trade, especially as both services and consumption are associated with much higher domestic shares of contribution, as opposed to industry production and investment.

In addition, the share of domestic production in both China's investments and its exports has increased. The import content of Chinese investment spending fell from around 30% in 2004 to 18% in 2014 as China sourced more intermediate goods domestically (WTO, 2017a): 65% of the ingredients in goods China sells to the world are made at home, up from 40% in the mid-1990s (*The Economist*, 2015). And again, two mechanisms are at work: on the one hand, China has been climbing up the value chain ladder, thus hosting increasingly more of the complex parts of the value chain. One the other hand, while wages in the coastal regions of the country have been rising fast – thus pushing these regions out of the low end of the value chain – low-skill parts of the value chain have only partly left the country (e.g. to Bangladesh, Cambodia and Myanmar) with other parts moving to the vast Chinese hinterland, which is well connected to the coastal region through an excellent infrastructure. However, this phenomenon – paired with the extreme importance of China for global trade – has played its part in the recent trade slowdown (*The Economist*, 2015).

The huge impact that China has on international trade can probably best be understood when examining market trends especially for the export of hard commodities, on which a large number of emerging and frontier markets depend. China accounts for 13% of world commodity imports and up to 40% for certain materials (Constantinescu *et al.*, 2016). Commodity prices all but collapsed in 2014 and 2015. It is thus unsurprising that emerging markets were in fact stronger hit by the trade slowdown of recent years than developed countries.

However, policy-induced infrastructure spending in China has recently supported demand for industrial commodities, thus benefitting countries exporting raw materials. For the future, the speed and style of China's rebalancing as well as its attempts to limit the country's increasing debt may have a negative impact on international trade. China's Belt and Road Initiative, in contrast, with the enormous investments associated with it, will have a substantial positive impact on global trade.

Looking at the United States, two factors should be highlighted, the first of which is the shale oil sector. While the emergence of the shale oil sector at first led to increased investments, usually associated with higher imports, it consequently reversed the US's position as a substantial oil importer, with the logical reduction of trade. With the slump of the oil price, investments in the shale oil sector substantially declined. However, the recent rise of oil prices has been sufficient to boost new spending on oil rigs, which increased in number from 568 in 2016 to 907 in November 2017, based on renewed investments (*The Economist*, 2017a). Nonetheless, whether investments in the sector and US exports of oil and gas will compensate for the reversal of the US position as oil and gas exporter remains to be seen. The second factor relevant for future US trade patterns is the US trade policy. The impact of the extremely hostile position towards trade under President Trump remains difficult to quantify for the time being, with a plethora of threats being put forward (e.g. ending the North American Free Trade Agreement (NAFTA), tariffs on steel and aluminium, lists of sanctioned goods from China), as well as potential counter-reactions by other regions.

As far as Europe is concerned, the trade slump appears to be mainly attributable to the prolonged cyclical downturn of the region, with the crisis depressing imports across the regions. However, the expansion of supply chains to Eastern and Central Europe still appears to be continuing, thus boding well for future trade.

A Structural Perspective on the Current Trade Slowdown

While some of the aforementioned factors are clearly cyclical, such as the slowdown in trade in Europe, other factors, such as China's rebalancing, are of a more structural and thus persistent nature. Constantinescu *et al.* (2015) intend to disentangle cyclical from structural factors to see whether there is a deeper structural shift in trade. Long-term elasticity of trade with respect to income has changed over time, from an elasticity of 1.3[1] between 1970 and 1985, to 2.2 from 1986 to 2000, and back to 1.3 in the 2000s, underlining that the decline in long-run trade elasticity actually set in before the financial crisis. Subdividing the latter period, during the period before the financial crisis, i.e. 2001–2007, a 1% increase in income was associated with a 1.5 increase in trade, whereas this figure decreased to 0.7 in the period from 2008 to 2013. The clear implication of these findings is that global trade is growing slowly not only due to the sluggish GDP growth of recent years, but also because the trade–GDP relationship has changed. As to the magnitude of the phenomenon, about 48% of the downturn can be explained by structural factors for 2013, whereas 52% can be attributed to cyclical factors.

The question is which factors lie behind this change in the elasticity of trade, looking into four possible explanations (Constantinescu *et al.*, 2015): changes in composition to world trade, changes in the structure of trade associated with the international fragmentation of production, changes in the composition of GDP, and changes in the trade regime, particularly the presumed rise in protectionism. For China and the United States, both accounting for an important share of global trade, the elasticity of imports to their GDP is significantly lower in the 2000s compared with the 1990s. This contrasts with the Euro Area, where an increasing elasticity is found. One possible explanation is that the slower pace of expansion of global supply chains is an important determinant of the trade slowdown, given that the 1990s and early 2000s were characterised by the increasing production fragmentation associated with global supply chains. However, this engine of growth appears to have lost its strength, particularly in China and the United States (whereas the Euro Area appears to be less affected). In addition, the changing composition of GDP, mainly the smaller share of investment, explains the lower trade elasticity in the post-crisis period, but not its historical decline since the early 2000s. The other two possible explanations – i.e. changes in the composition of world trade and a rise in protectionism – are not found to be relevant.

These results fit well with the geographical observations illustrated before. However, it remains doubtful that global value chains have really come to a halt. Instead, the unfortunate combination of the 2008 Global Financial Crisis followed by the Euro crisis and the slowdown in China strongly reduced companies' enthu- siasm to invest in further global value chain expansions. With the picture starting to look brighter from 2017 onwards, it is assumed that there is a recovery of the quest for global value chains (UNCTAD, 2017). It will thus remain interesting to see whether global value chains will increase their vigour in the years to come and whether this phenomenon will be global or limited to certain regions with Europe, which had never been affected by the slowdown of global value chains to the same extent as, above all, Asia.

Regarding recent developments, 2016 proved to be a particularly poor year for trade. According to the IMF (2018), trade grew by 2.3% in volume terms (GDP growth reached 3.2%, so that trade lagged behind growth once more), the slowest pace since 2009, with weak growth in advanced economies, emerging markets and developing economies. The IMF attributes this slow growth to an investment slow- down and inventory adjustment in advanced economics, while China's protected trade slowdown has been driving poor growth in emerging markets and developing economies. In 2017, on the back of a brightening macroeconomic picture, trade expe- rienced a substantial rebound with growth of 4.9%, and thus a return of trade growth above global GDP growth of 3.8% (IMF, 2018). For 2018, estimates are positive, with a forecast trade growth of 5.1% (with GDP growth of 3.9%). Reasons for this positive outlook for trade are a cyclical recovery in global demand with a synchro- nised upsurge in global economic activity in industrialised countries and emerging markets as well as broad-based growth and recovering investments. Nonetheless, the IMF cautioned that protectionist tendencies and potential trade wars could hamper this positive development.

Finally, despite still substantial policy barriers, a slightly different trend can be observed in the trade of services over the past ten years. According to the WTO (2017a), world exports of commercial services increased by 65.5% over the past ten years (from US$2.9 trillion in 2006 to US$4.8 trillion in 2016) whereas world exports of manufactured goods grew by 37.5% over the same period (from US$8 trillion in 2006 to US$11 trillion in 2016) – with trade in services still being much smaller than in merchandise goods. According to the IMF (2017a), even after the financial crisis, global commercial services imports grew at some 5% per year between 2010 and 2015, compared with a 1% growth for merchandise trade. The growth in service trade was mainly driven by travel and other commercial services. This development has been supported by new business models – for example, in financial services and communication technology – as well as an increasing provision of services attached to manufactured goods. For example, service updates and maintenance are increasingly part of goods sold (e.g. smartphones, TVs) and have become much more important. In addition, innovation in digital technology and other services has helped to reshape the trade landscape and fostered the development of global value chains. For the future of service trade, the developments in digital technology and the increasing integration of services in merchandise exports will bode well. In addition, the upward trend in travelling, especially of Chinese travellers, does not seem to have reached its limit yet.

To sum up, while trade currently appears to be profiting from an economic upturn and a reinvigoration of investments, trade is currently not profiting from any major trade boosters or game changers – be it containers, the establishment of global value chains or major trade agreements. For a return to trade figures seen in the 1990s, a strong resurgence of global value chains, a technological breakthrough in the fields of communication or transport or a major trade agreement would be better. As far as the resurgence of value chains is concerned, while practitioners in Europe remain optimistic, literature hitherto does not support this enthusiasm. China's increasingly national value chains also do not bode well. As for trade agreements, the WTO seems to face many challenges in dealing with the current trade environment (e.g. China's state-led growth model, the Trump administration's handling of trade matters). However, some hope may be put on the CPTPP as well as on a counter-reaction to the negative position towards trade put forward by the United States. As far as innovation is concerned, current trends appear to be rather neutral if not harmful for global trade, as will be explored in the flowing section, with potential improvements only in the more distant future. Finally, protectionism poses a substantial threat. Here, much will depend on future trends in politics and the extent to which economists and policymakers are able to convey the overall beneficial impact of trade while dealing with its negative side impacts. One vital component in this venture is to disentangle the extent to which trade is responsible for current developments from the degree to which innovation and automation are responsible, an issue upon which the next section will focus.

What Drives Current Developments, and How Are They Related?

Differentiating between the effects of trade and those of innovation, automation and new technologies remains a major challenge, especially considering that all of these factors are intertwined. Trying to understand what the driving forces behind current disruptive developments are is vital to put well-targeted policies into practice without harming the positive effects of both trade and innovation. This is, however, further complicated by the fact that the distinction between trade and innovation is blurred, and that innovation and technological advances have a strong impact on trade developments, often enabling new trade patterns or facilitating them. It thus remains contested whether a clear distinction is possible.

As discussed above, global value chains are a case in point. Without advances in both communication and transport, global value chains, with their huge advantage for large groups of consumers but also their disturbing impacts for basic manufacturing in advanced economies, would not exist. However, as global value chains have also had a substantial impact on trade, it is often trade that is blamed for the consequences. Indeed, it appears that trade is the consequence and most obvious sign of technological disruption, rather than the cause of disruptive effect. However, since trade with lower-cost countries and technological change have similar effects on labour-intensive production in the rich world, an attempt to disentangle phenomena is not always pursued.

Despite all the challenges that are related to the attempt of differentiating between the impact of trade and that of innovation, most current studies point to the fact that it is actually technological development that is the driving force behind current job losses in most sectors and regions. The WTO (2017b) highlights that innovation, automation and new technologies are responsible for roughly 80% of the manufacturing jobs that have been lost. Job losses in certain sectors or regions in advanced economies have resulted to a large extent from technological change rather than from trade (IMF, 2017a). A study of the Center for Business and Economic Research at the Ball State University finds that 85% of the 5.6 million job losses that occurred in the United States between 2000 and 2010 are actually attributable to technological change – largely automation – rather than trade (Cocco, 2016). Only 13% of overall job losses in manufacturing are attributed to trade. As manufacturing has become more productive and industrial output has been growing, fewer workers are necessary to produce the same quantity of goods. This argument is supported by the fact that car manufacturing's contribution to GDP has fallen by about 10% since 1994 in the United States, whereas there are 30% fewer car manufacturing jobs (*The Economist*, 2016a).

Just as is the case with trade, the benefits of the rise and spread of technological innovations on the whole outweigh the costs. Yet again, the costs of innovative disruption tend to be concentrated on a few industries and regions, whereas its benefits are widespread but also diffuse. The rise and spread of new technologies and the associated breakdown of existing ways of life have been a recurring source of disruption since at least the Industrial Revolution, if not earlier.

While the increasing use of robot technology and additive manufacturing including 3-D printing is mainly visible in manufacturing, advances in big data as well as the digital revolution will not be limited to manufacturing but will have a strong impact on clerical work and professional services. Obviously, investment in new capital equipment still depends on the potential savings on labour costs. Consequently, job displacement by robots is economically more interesting in skill-intensive and well-paying (manufacturing) jobs than in relatively labour-intensive low-paying sectors. It is thus no surprise that countries currently most exposed to automation through industrial robots are advanced economies with a large manufacturing sector and relatively well-paying jobs, such as automotive and electronics. Germany, Japan and the United States combined already account for 43% of the world's operational industrial robots (UNCTAD, 2017). And while the use of robots still remains relatively small, their use has increased rapidly since 2010. Interestingly, the increase in robot deployment has recently been the most rapid in developing countries, a trend that is mainly driven by China. According to *The Economist* (2017b), in 2016 86% of industrial robots bought went to Asia, again particularly to China. It thus appears that China is putting a huge effort into moving up the value chain without losing current parts of production and potentially even servicing increasingly more parts of the value chain in its own country.

In terms of sectors, robot deployment has remained very limited in those manufacturing sectors where labour compensation is low (UNCTAD, 2017). Thus, robot deployment in the textiles, apparel and leather sector – for example – have been lowest among all manufacturing sectors. This is mainly attributed to the fact that the pliability of fabrics makes automation relatively complicated as compared with automation in the automotive or electronics sector. Consequently, developed countries and developing countries other than least-developed countries are exposed to robot-based automation, with only least-developed countries in the very initial stage of industrialisation relying on labour-intensive manufacturing and having traditional labour cost advantages that still remain largely unaffected. However, leaving this very early stage of manufacturing will become all the more difficult.

However, these innovation-driven trends will have a substantial impact on trade. To begin with, automation and innovative production technologies used in advanced economies will have a negative impact on trade figures. This is especially true for the United States. Those types of production returning to the United States (for which the cost reduction through automation is sufficiently large to make production viable in the United States and which profit from being close to the customer) will probably be tailored to the US market and will hardly be exported. In Europe, the same effect may occur. However, due to much smaller national markets as compared with the United States and relatively low transport and communication costs within Europe, intra-European trade should remain viable – especially considering that several clusters of markets strongly resemble each other (e.g. German-speaking market, Scandinavian market, Benelux market etc.). It will thus probably still make sense to service several markets from one production hub, thus keeping trade stable.

As far as developing markets are concerned, trends in China (the increasing part of the value chain being serviced from China with the upgrading of coastal regions and the inclusion of the hinterland as well as the automation) will probably also have a negative impact on trade. This remains true even if parts of the value chain that are not fit for automation, in particular the textile and apparel sector, may move not only to China's inner territory but also to other countries such as Vietnam, Cambodia or Bangladesh, as it would only be a relocation of parts of an existing value chain.

Finally, least-developed countries will continue to profit from an inclusion in the very lowest levels of the value chain, i.e. inclusion in the production of textiles, apparels and leather, but will find it difficult to move further up due to increasing automation of the sectors that traditionally followed in a strategy of industrialisation and export-led growth. Again, even the inclusion of least-developed countries will be largely trade-neutral, as it is mainly based on the relocation of production facilities and in lesser part their extension.

To sum up, trade can certainly not be held responsible for the disruptive developments of recent years, as various studies underline. However, trade is strongly influenced by technological developments – making the disentangling of the two phenomena all the more difficult. It has to be acknowledged that the trade surge of the 1990s and early 2000s was mainly driven by the fast rise of global value chains based on declining transport and communication costs. Recent innovations, trends of automation and technological changes, in contrast, may not hold the same promises of a surge in trade. Instead, in the short-term future, trade increase appears to be mainly limited to the increase in global world GDP, with a slightly positive momentum of increasing investments after a long period of under-investment following the financial crisis – especially in Europe. Strong reasons for a boost of trade from innovation and techno-logical change, pushing trade growth significantly above world GDP growth, are currently not clearly discernible. The main possible exception could be an increasing trend in services, made possible by increasing enthusiasm for travelling, technological innovations and the increasing integration of services into manufactured goods. However, the speed of these developments will probably vary from region to region and sector to sector. Whereas advances in robotics have reached a level of steady development, albeit still coming from a low level, additive manufacturing – still in its infancy and thus more difficult to judge– leaves more questions open concerning how quickly its impact on trade will be felt. Nonetheless, both would probably not bode well for trade. By contrast, blockchain technology – which has the potential to strongly facilitate both trade and trade finance and could thus be a game changer that boosts trade – remains in an early stage of development, which makes the size and speed of its impact still difficult to predict.

Trade Liberalisation vs. Protectionism

As discussed above, the future of trade liberalisation appears relatively varied – and certainly difficult to predict. On the one hand, rhetoric in the United States has been strongly adverse towards trade liberalisation. TTIP is no longer on the table, the United States withdrew from the TPP and even NAFTA is being renegotiated. Threats of imposing tariffs on specific sectors such as the steel or aluminium sector or on products from specific countries such as China are currently being pushed forward. Support for free trade can thus not be expected from a United States under the Trump administration, whose protectionist policies might lead to retaliations and escalating trade wars.

On the positive side, the remaining members of the TPP have not given up on the deal. Not only have they decided to continue with the TPP under its new name of the CPTPP, the renaming was also to show the intention of pursuing a particularly advanced trade agreement. In addition, the Regional Comprehensive Economic Partnership (RCEP) – an Asian free trade agreement often viewed as an alternative to TPP and including China – remains on the negotiating table. It would create one of the world's largest free trade zones, with roughly 45% of the world's population and 24% of the world's GDP.

As the remaining trade hub, Europe offers a varied picture. The EU–Canada Comprehensive Economic and Trade Agreement (CETA) faced huge opposition on its way through the European Council and Parliament, although part of this opposition probably has to be attributed to the fact that it was feared to be a blueprint for TTIP. For example, the EU–Japan Free Trade Agreement has hitherto not faced the same opposition. As Cameron (2017) highlights, the strategic partnership agreement (SPA) and the economic partnership agreement (EPA) with Japan may be the largest booster to global trade since China joined the WTO in 2001. However, as negotiations have been conducted behind closed doors, public scrutiny may still pick up. The EU–

Vietnam Free Trade Agreement – one of the most comprehensive and ambitious free trade and investment agreements that the EU has ever negotiated with a developing country – is expected to enter in force in 2018/2019 and has not received the same level of negative attention. In addition, the EU has concluded trade agreements with South Korea and Singapore. Moreover, negotiations are intensifying again with the South American trade bloc Mercosur, a region where free trade is on the rise again. Negotiations with India, Indonesia, the Philippines, Thailand and Malaysia are either ongoing or waiting to be resumed when political conditions change.

Although the picture for trade agreements with US involvement is certainly bleak, it is much more diverse in Europe, Latin America and Asia. Further global agreements – especially at the WTO level – are difficult to expect in this climate. Nonetheless, regional agreements may still be on the table and may even be fostered by the strongly adverse position of the United States and the vacuum that it is leaving. However, it has to be acknowledged that regional agreements always carry the risk of not only fostering trade but also diverting it and thus not being as beneficial as global trade agreements. Finally, the field of non-tariff measures and barriers to trade in services should be accounted for. Smaller-scale measures such as local content requirements do appear to be on the rise. The same applies for protectionist (counter-) measures, particularly aiming at China and often originating in the United States.

Consequently, the future of free trade is far from secured, and protectionism is certainly on the rise. Whereas the negative attitude towards free trade agreements in Europe seems to have calmed down for the moment, the same is not true for the United States. There, anti-trade feelings are stirred up stressing the negative impact of trade on the country. It will therefore remain vital to highlight costs and the overall negative impact of protectionist measures to make sure that policymakers understand the effects such measures have.

The Distribution of Trade Benefits

Already in 1824, Thomas Macaulay noted that "free trade, one of the greatest blessings which a government can confer on a people, is in almost every country unpopular" (IMF, 2017a). So, what are the benefits of trade and why is it nevertheless so unpopular? Once these questions have been answered, a closer look will be taken at different regional developments.

Benefits and Adverse Consequences from Trade

Cross-country evidence links greater trade openness to higher per capita income. It also links positive trade reforms (proxied as reduction in tariffs) to higher rates of productivity, income growth and declining poverty. Moreover, the causality may run mainly from trade reforms and trade to higher incomes – although admittedly, econometric challenges to prove causality remain substantial.

Examining these factors in more depth, there is evidence that a 1 percentage point increase in trade openness raised productivity by 1.23% in the long run (IMF, 2017b). Ahn *et al.* (2016) found that a 1 percentage point reduction in tariffs on inputs used in a sector improves total factor productivity in that sector by 2%. Such sector-level productivity gains were found to hold both for advanced and emerging markets. Reasons for this productivity boost are reallocations of resources, with production shifting towards sectors and firms with comparative advantage and higher efficiency as well as the ability to sell to larger markets, which consequently allows firms to invest more in innovation. Moreover, import competition may very well spur technology upgrading just as knowledge spillovers and diffusion contribute to productivity growth. Indirectly, trade may also enhance productivity by encouraging institutional reform, improving governance and contributing to financial deepening. For example, the ease of doing business is found to be strongly correlated with a country's level of trade integration (IMF, 2017a).

As far as consumers are concerned, trade allows them to profit from lower prices as well as access to a wider variety of goods and services. Trade integration reduces prices directly through lower tariffs on imported goods and related pro-competition effects as well as indirectly through productivity gains. As far as the introduction of a greater variety of goods and the introduction of new goods are concerned, these can have major positive effects on the cost of living. Citing the example of the United States, *The Economist* (2016a) stresses that clothes there now cost the same as they did in 1986, while furnishing a house is as cheap as it was 35 years ago.

By contrast, there is an impact to the imposition of tariffs: for example, in 2009 the United States imposed additional tariffs on Chinese tyre imports, which cost at least US$900,000 for each job saved on an estimated annual basis, about 22 times the average wage of the workers whose jobs were saved (IMF, 2018). Additionally, the policy was associated with three times as many job losses in other sectors.

Finally, there is a strong pro-poor bias in the benefits of lower prices and consumer choice induced by trade. This pro-poor bias arises because poorer consumers spend relatively more on sectors that are more traded and thus experience larger price drops. Studies suggest that on average, people with high incomes would lose 28% of their purchasing power if borders were closed to trade whereas the poorest 10% of consumers would lose 63% of their spending power, because they buy relatively more imported goods. Overall, there can be a bias of trade in favour of poorer people (*The Economist*, 2016a).

Greater trade openness has been associated with lower poverty and inequality in emerging markets and developing economies as long as appropriate supporting policies are put into place (World Bank, 2017). For example, income inequality fell in many emerging markets and developing economies after the extensive trade liberalisation of the 1990s. Trade expansion is thus seen as an important factor in the transition of countries out of low-income status.

Despite the general benefits from trade, the reallocation of resources associated with open trade can also have adverse consequences. Trade is not a main factor behind increased inequality overall, as technology has played the key role. Nevertheless, as reallocation is costly, adverse effects on certain individuals and communities can be large and long-lasting if not addressed properly (IMF, 2017b). Trade, through the reallocation of resources, changes the demand for labour and skills, which affects wages. Mobility frictions and skills mismatches exacerbate these trends as switching occupations, industries or regions is costly. Moreover, policy distortions such as labour market frictions and job security legislations, but also imperfect credit markets, can impede adjustment.

In addition, although trade integration has generally brought greater prosperity, the extent of benefits depends on country characteristics and supporting policies, notably the nature of export specialisation, the degree of product diversification and the quality of institutions.

Trade Impact on Different Regions – the United States, Asia and Sub-Saharan Africa

As far as the United States is concerned, its economy has gradually opened up to imports since the 1980s. The opening up to trade greatly accelerated when NAFTA came into force in 1994. Nonetheless, most important for US imports was China joining the WTO in 2001. Although this did not change any tariffs, a surge in imports from China took place in the following years because WTO membership gave certainty to investors in China's export industries. Chinese imports surged from 1% of GDP in 2000 to 2.7% by 2015. The positive consequences for consumers, in terms of falling prices for goods and a broader choice, have already been mentioned. At the same time, American firms have gained access to new markets. For example, US car exports to Mexico have grown from US$10 billion (at today's prices) to US$70 billion. In addition, US exports to China grew by almost 200% between 2005 and 2014. Workers in export-intensive sectors have thus benefitted from rising exports with an export wage premium of 18% (*The Economist*, 2016a). In addition, outsourcing low-wage parts of the value chain has increased US productivity. Thus, consumers, exporters and workers in exporting industries have been profiting from the opening up of trade.

Regarding those losing out from trade, the problem of disentangling trade from other relevant factors, particularly automation and technological change in general, is again extremely difficult, especially as those who have been hit hardest by the impact of trade are also those highly exposed to the effects of technological change, above all automation. Nonetheless, for some sectors, at least part of the effect has to be attributed to trade. Manufacturers – especially in the Midwestern rustbelt and in the South – have been hit by cheaper imports. Moreover, as trade theory predicts, unskilled workers have been affected most. For example, Acemoglu *et al.* (2014) highlight that the increase in US imports from China was a major force behind the recent reduction in US manufacturing employment, and between 2.0 and 2.4 million jobs were lost between 1999 and 2011 due to the rise in import competition from China.

Trade-induced job losses in the United States – while considered to be relatively small compared with job losses from technological change – appear to be particularly painful. Employment falls at least one-for-one with jobs lost to trade, and displaced workers are unlikely to move to seek new work (*The Economist*, 2016b). In addition, in areas affected by trade with China, new spending on disability benefits increased disproportionally, implying that not all unemployment from trade may be captured in official unemployment statistics. While economic theory would suggest that people in regions strongly affected by cheaper imports would move to more prosperous regions, several impediments appear to dampen this effect. On the one hand, costs of moving and expensive housing in more prosperous regions make moving there less appealing. For example, unskilled workers find it difficult to earn a reasonable income in cities and areas such as New York, San Francisco or Silicon Valley, strongly limiting the appeal of moving there. On the other hand, state and local benefits, as useful and important as they are, often incentivise staying put. However, the total effect is that the losers from trade remain concentrated in depressed areas. Once an area is set for decline, decreasing tax intakes make the decent provision of services, above all health care and education, all the more difficult, thus setting in motion a vicious circle of decline. Such places are even unlikely to participate in an economic upturn, thus perpetuating negative trends. Counteracting these tendencies through adequate policies and incentives is therefore highly relevant.

Turning to Asia as the region representing emerging markets, trade has certainly been one of the major factors fostering Asia's rapid economic growth. Asia's share of global merchandise trade has doubled since 1973 to just over 30%, with its exports growing at three times the rate for the rest of the world over the past decade. China is now the world's largest exporter. However, differences in economic development in the region are enormous with, for example, Japan or Singapore having closed up to the forefront of economic development whereas, for example, Myanmar or Laos remain at very early stages of economic development. Nonetheless, for almost every country in the region, two developments appear to hold particular importance: the state- and export-led development strategies that, for example, Japan, Taiwan and Korea were among the earliest to pursue and that have been copied and adjusted by various countries in the region; and the region's increasing integration into global value chains.

In terms of the state- and export-led growth strategy of various countries in the region, China's rise – especially after its entry into the WTO in 2001 – has certainly had the deepest impact on economic and trade patterns. However, it should not be forgotten that, for example, Japan, Taiwan and South Korea pursued such strategies much earlier than China. Moreover, while China certainly differs from these earlier countries in the pure heft of its economic development, the economic development of, for example, Japan, Taiwan and Korea may still hold important lessons for both China's further development and that of other economies in the region. In essence, the state- and export-led strategy that countries such as Japan, Taiwan and Korea have pursued is to put in place economic policies that strongly support those industries and sectors in which the country has a comparative advantage. At the beginning of economic development that is often cheap labour, but with increasing exports and industrialisation, wages start to increase and economic policies have to be readjusted. Over time, the country moves up the ladder of production, that is, the value added, complexity and sophistication of produced goods increase. The state plays a vital role in choosing the sectors that are to be supported and putting in place relevant economic policies. Although the impact of state- and export-led developmental strategies remains the subject of lively debate, and other factors (e.g. institutional quality, infrastructure, education, historic circumstances) may have been relevant for the successful implementation in, for example, Japan, Taiwan and South Korea (especially as the strategy does not appear to lead to the same success in some other countries), the notion that the state- and export-led growth strategy has been beneficial for a number of Asian countries and their people can hardly be debated.

An additional factor occurring since the mid-1990s has been Asia's increasing integration in global value chains, which has given the export-led strategies a further boost. However, as Choi (2015) highlights, while global value chains have caused a dramatic shift in Asia's trade patterns, with vertical trade in intermediate goods and assembly production being the main driver of global value chains in the region, not all of Asia has hitherto managed to play a leading role with respect to technological innovation in global value chains. However, even if global value chains might not have allowed all Asian countries to move to the forefront of technological innovation (yet), they certainly have contributed to the industrialisation of the countries involved and contributed to increasing industrial employment. Historical evidence shows that attaining a high share of manufacturing employment is critically important for sustained economic development and a relevant predictor of eventual prosperity. Consequently, the expansion of global value chains has been beneficial for the economic development of most Asian countries, albeit at varying degrees. To sum up, even if challenging to prove through econometric models (due to endogeneity, potentially omitted variables and other econometric problems), trade, state- and export-led growth as well as integration into global value chains appear to have helped take millions out of poverty in Asia and improve their economic lot.

Turning to Sub-Saharan Africa with its 49 countries, there are obviously huge differences from country to country. The major focus of this section will be on the low-income developing countries. Low-income developing countries remain underrepresented in global value chains, even though their integration has expanded from US$259 billion in 1995 to about US$1.5 trillion in 2011 (OECD and World Bank Group, 2015). Whereas the commodity-exporting countries of this group saw their exports increase substantially during the commodities super cycle, the sharp realignment of global commodity prices has been a major setback. This development delivers further evidence of the hypothesis that export-led growth strategies tend to be more successful if they are based on manufacturing rather than on raw materials. It also supports the findings mentioned above that it is mainly employment in manufacturing that is a good predictor of eventual prosperity. However, in terms of employment in manufacturing, Africa still lags behind all other regions, with the share of manufacturing in total employment only amounting to 6.9% in 2014 in comparison with a global share of 13.3%, and a share for Asia of 14.7% (UNCTAD, 2017). Moreover, although the share of employment in manufacturing in Africa has been increasing as employment has been shifting from the primary to the manufacturing sector, labour productivity in the manufacturing sector has in fact been decreasing, suggesting very low technological dynamism in African manufacturing. It is therefore unsurprising that Africa's integration into global value chains remains in its infancy. In addition, a number of further trade impediments – both hard and soft – hinder trade in the region. As Brückner and Lederman (2012) highlight, African economies have the highest import tariffs in the world. Non-tariff barriers are also prevalent. Governance – especially corruption and misrule – and institutional challenges as well as infrastructure are further impediments to both trade and economic development. Africa's weak infrastructure, such as inefficient ports, is a major challenge that puts many potential exporters off investing there. The lack of reliable electricity at competitive prices is certainly another problem worth mentioning as is the quality of education. In addition, a lack of trade financing is particularly prevalent. Moreover, Wignaraja *et al.* (2015) argue that low-income countries that export unskilled labour or natural-resource-intensive products are not expected to trade much with each other as they specialise in the same type of homogeneous products. However, the majority of global trade takes place between countries producing heterogeneous products such as automobiles or electronics. It is thus unsurprising that intra-African trade remains low.

The fact that Sub-Saharan Africa is only marginally integrated in global value chains and that its trade still mainly depends on commodities is all the more worrying as the region continues to lag behind other regions in terms of economic development and poverty reduction, as its runs huge trade deficits with the rest of the world thus needing to export more and as the region needs to provide employment for the huge numbers of young people leaving school each year and searching for jobs. With all this in mind, the prospect that the traditional path of industrialisation may be affected and indeed hampered by the increasing use of robots appears all the more worrying. Whether Africa will be able to use technological advances to leapfrog ahead is far from clear. Certainly, drone technology may – for example – compensate for a lack of roads, and mobile money for a lack of access to banks and thus trade finance. Huge investments in hydropower may help solve the electricity issue (although grids would still have to be upgraded to get the electricity to where it is needed).

To summarise, examining Sub-Saharan Africa certainly holds some lessons as far as trade is concerned. First, trade in commodities is possible if prices are sufficiently high, even if the circumstances for trade in a given country are dismal. However, this sort of trade is highly dependent on commodity prices and will only have a beneficial effect for the entire country if the right types of policies for using the windfall profits from commodities are put in place. To date the track record has been mixed at best. Second, there is little doubt that economic growth and trade are interrelated and that often the same impediments that hinder growth also hinder trade, that is, political turmoil or corruption, a lack of infrastructure or electricity, or a lack of education and institutional capacity. It is therefore worthwhile addressing these impediments for the sake of both economic development and trade growth. Third, although these various interconnections complicate the assessment of the impact of trade on a given country, trade should have a positive (or at worst neutral) impact as long as windfall profits are not abused through rent-seeking by one part of the population at the expense of the rest of the population. Finally, in order to foster long-term growth and stable trade relations, the broad-based involvement of the population in the respective economic activities – particularly in manufacturing but potentially increasingly in services – is vital.

Overall, some conclusions from the regional developments described can be drawn. First of all, trade still appears to be a relevant strategy for low-income countries to foster development, thus following the Asian example. However, it may become more difficult as new technologies may reduce the advantage of low employment costs. In combination with other common disadvantages in low-income countries, such as poor governance and high transport costs, this could make following the Asian example more difficult. Nonetheless, trade in services might hold new options, for example by providing worldwide services via internet platforms. Asian countries have certainly been major winners from trade, as have advanced economies. However, especially among the latter, losers from trade are also clearly identifiable. While the fact that some groups may lose out from trade is anything but surprising, the strong impact and long-lasting effect may have been underestimated and should be corrected through adequate policies.

Conclusion and Trends

When looking beyond the immediate future, the trends for global trade are diverse. Some structural changes in major trade centres, such as the increasing intra-China trade and the US self-sufficiency of oil, certainly have a dampening effect on global trade. I addition, the uncertain future development of global value chains and their possible plateauing do not bode well for an increase in global trade. A trade finance gap may very well increase with international banks cutting their correspondent bank relationships due to the transaction costs.

In addition, technological changes, with increasing automation, use of robots and additive manufacturing, do not appear to be positive contributors for international trade in manufactured goods. Instead, they may very well lead to the relocation of production to advanced economies where customers are to be found or to the freezing of current patterns of value chains, with especially China investing hugely in automation to keep production in the country. Countries still intending to climb the value chain might thus find it increasingly difficult as fewer industries remain for which a competitive advantage in cheap labour has an impact and outweighs other trade impediments such as higher transportation costs or institutional difficulties that are common in countries featuring cheap labour.

Protectionism is all but defeated. However, whereas countries such as India have long been cautious and reluctant to open up their markets, the US change of position to "America first" may have a vital impact on global trade patterns and rules. With the United States withdrawing from TPP, the previous intention of spreading US standards in Asia has been undermined. Nonetheless, the continuation of the TPP as the CPTPP may alleviate this consequence. However, China will certainly find it easier to spread its standards now if the country so choses. Furthermore, growing US threats and the increasing use of protectionist measures risk undermining the WTO as a guardian of global trade. Finally, the risk of trade wars has certainly increased.

However, the picture for trade is not entirely bleak. The adverse US position towards trade does not seem to have led to a global renunciation of trade. Meanwhile, remaining countries that had signed up for the TPP are heading for an even more comprehensive agreement. Moreover, Asia does not appear to have lost its interest in free trade, with the CPTPP and RCEP still being negotiated. Latin America is rediscovering its enthusiasm for free trade, leading to a push in EU–Mercosur negotiations. Indeed, even Europe – after the controversy regarding CETA and TTIP – appears to have calmed down as far as the move against free trade is concerned.

As far as technological change is concerned, one area that may profit from increased trade thanks to technological advances is the trade in services. While this type of trade is certainly still hampered by a lack of international standards, the increasing integration of services into exported manufactured goods and the increasing possibility to provide services internationally via international networks or the internet open up new possibilities. Phones and the internet have already enabled providing services from distant places, whether help desks, call centres or service hotlines. International internet platforms on which services can be traded may foster this development. Moreover, blockchain technologies with the ability to facilitate both trade and trade finance could prove to be an innovation that boosts trade once further developed.

What will not disappear is the discussion concerning how to ensure that benefits from trade are fairly distributed, and how losers from trade are compensated for their losses. Without tackling this challenge, not only through adequate policies but also through better information regarding the pros and cons of trade, trade will remain the scapegoat both for its own negative side effects and for the disruptive effects of technological change. Consequently, benefits from trade must be gained, quantified and made public, while the negative side effects should also be quantified, made clear and discussed, as well as alleviated thorough adequate policies.

Note

1   For Constantinescu *et al.*'s calculation of elasticity, see Constantinescu *et al.* (2015), p. 9.

References

Acemoglu, D., Autor, D., Dorn D. *et al.* (2014) Import Competition and the Great U.S. Employment Sag of the 2000s. *NBER Working Paper* No. 20395. Retrieved from: http://www.nber.org/papers/w20395.pdf (accessed 2 July 2019).

Ahn, J., Dabla-Norris, E. Duval, R. *et al.* (2016) Reassessing the Productivity Gains from Trade Liberalisation. *IMF Working Paper* No. 16/77. Retrieved from: https://www.imf.org/external/pubs/ft/wp/2016/wp1677.pdf (accessed 2 July 2019).

Brückner, M. & Lederman, D. (2012) Trade Causes Growth in Sub-Saharan Africa. *World Bank Policy Research Working Paper* No. 6007. Retrieved from: https://openknowledge.worldbank.org/handle/10986/19874 (accessed 2 July 2019).

Cameron, F. (2017) It's Asia, Stupid: Time for the EU to Deepen Relations with Asia. *GIGA Focus Asia*, 6, 1–11.

Choi, N. (2015) Global Value Chains and East Asian Trade in Value-Added. *Asian Economic Papers*, 14(3), 129–144.

Cocco, F. (2016) Most US Manufacturing Jobs Lost to Technology, Not Trade. *Financial Times* (2 December). Retrieved from: https://www.ft.com/content/dec677c0-b7e6-11e6-ba85-95d1533d9a62 (accessed 2 July 2019).

Constantinescu, C., Mattoo, A. & Ruta M. (2014) Slow Trade. *Finance & Development*, 51(4), 39–41.

Constantinescu, C., Mattoo, A. & Ruta M. (2015) The Global Trade Slowdown: Cyclical or Structural? *IMF Working Paper No. 15/6.*

Constantinescu, C., Mattoo, A. & Ruta M. (2016) Trade Developments in 2015. *World Bank Group.* Retrieved from: http://documents.worldbank.org/curated/en/913061468196142457/Global-trade-watch-trade-developments-in-2015 (accessed 2 July 2019).

Costa L.F., Palma N. & Reis, J. (2015) The Great Escape? The Contribution of the Empire to Portugal's Economic Growth, 1500–1800. *European Review of Economic History*, 19(1), 1–22.

Dollar, D. (2017) Executive Summary, Measuring and Analysing the Impact of GVCs on Economic Development. Washington, DC: International Bank for Reconstruction and Development/The World Bank, pp. 1–14. Retrieved from: https://www.wto.org/english/res_e/booksp_e/gvcs_report_2017.pdf (accessed 2 July 2019).

Felbermayr, G. & Kohler W. (2015) Welthandel: Frei und fair? Handelsabkommen in der Kritik [World Trade: Free and Fair? Critisising Free Trade Agreements]. *ifo Schnelldienst*, 68(7), 3–11.

International Monetary Fund (2017a) Making Trade and Engine of Growth for All. Prepared for discussion at the meeting of G20 Sherpas, Frankfurt, Germany, 23–23 March 2017.

Retrieved from: https://www.wto.org/english/news_e/news17_e/wto_imf_report_07042017.pdf (accessed 2 July 2019).

International Monetary Fund (2017b) *World Economic Outlook, October 2017*. Available from: https://www.imf.org/en/Publications/WEO/Issues/2017/09/19/world-economic-outlook-october-2017 (accessed 2 July 2019).

International Monetary Fund (2018) World Economic Outlook, *April 2018*. Available from: https://www.imf.org/external/pubs/ft/weo/2018/01/weodata/index.aspx (accessed 2 July 2019).

Krugman, P.R. & Obstfeld, M. (2000) *International Economics: Theory and Policy* (5th ed.). Reading: Addisson-Wesley.

OECD and World Bank Group (2015) *Inclusive Global Value Chains: Policy Options in Trade and Complementary Areas for GVC Integration*. Retrieved from: https://www.oecd.org/publications/inclusive-global-value-chains-9789264249677-en.htm (accessed 2 July 2019).

Ortiz-Ospina, E., Beltekian, D. & Roser, M. (2018) Trade and Globalization. Retrieved from: https://ourworldindata.org/trade-and-globalization (accessed 2 July 2019).

Rotman, D. (2013) How Technology Is Destroying Jobs. *Technology Review*, 116(4), 25–35.

Simola, H. (2015) Tracing Trade Interdependence between EU and East Asia. *Global Economic Review*, 44(4), 420–430.

Sinn, H.W. (2014) Free Trade and Prosperity. *CESifo Forum*, 15(4), 8–13.

The Economist (2013) Why Have Containers Boosted Trade So Much? Retrieved from: https://www.economist.com/the-economist-explains/2013/05/21/why-have-containers-boosted-trade-so-much (accessed 2 July 2019).

The Economist (2015) A Tightening Grip. Retrieved from: https://www.economist.com/briefing/2015/03/12/a-tightening-grip (accessed 2 July 2019).

The Economist (2016a) Trade, At What Price? Retrieved from: https://www.economist.com/united-states/2016/04/02/trade-at-what-price (accessed 2 July 2019).

The Economist (2016b) Coming and Going. Retrieved from: https://www.economist.com/special-report/2016/09/29/coming-and-going (accessed 2 July 2019).

The Economist (2017a) Blue-Collar Wages Are Surging. Can It Last? Retrieved from: https://www.economist.com/united-states/2017/11/14/blue-collar-wages-are-surging-can-it-last (accessed 9 July 2019).

The Economist (2017b) The Leapfrog Model. Retrieved from: https://www.economist.com/special-report/2017/11/10/what-technology-can-do-for-africa (accessed 2 July 2019).

UNCTAD (2017) *Trade and Development Report 2017*. Geneva: United Nations.

Wignaraja, G., Morgan, P., Plummer, M.G. & Zhai F. (2015) Economic Implications of Deeper South Asian-Southeast Asian Integration: A CGE Approach. *ADBI Working Paper* No. 494. Tokyo: Asian Development Bank Institute.

World Bank (2017) Global Economic Prospects, A Fragile Recovery. A World Bank Flagship Report, Retrieved from: https://openknowledge.worldbank.org/handle/10986/26800 (accessed 2 July 2019).

World Trade Organization (2017a) World Trade Statistical Review 2017. Retrieved from: https://www.wto.org/english/res_e/statis_e/wts2017_e/wts17_toc_e.htm (accessed 2 July 2019).

World Trade Organization (2017b) Trade Recovery Expected in 2017 and 2018, Amid Policy Uncertainty. Press release, 12 April 2017, 17-1964. Retrieved from: https://www.wto.org/english/news_e/pres17_e/pr791_e.htm (accessed 2 July 2019).

Chapter 3

On the Remeasurement of International Trade in the Age of Digital Globalisation

Steffen Gröning, Cyrus de la Rubia, and Thomas Straubhaar

Introduction

Globalisation – nothing else has characterised better the fundamental economic changes of the past that preceded the financial crisis that hit the markets at the beginning of the 21st century. *Digitalisation* – no other trend will influence economic activities more strongly in the future. *Digital globalisation* – the effective and efficient merger of both long-term developments – is the offspring that will reshape production decisions and factor allocation in many ways. How does it affect trade patterns and the (re)measurement of (international) transactions? This is the question that motivates the following chapter. How well are old concepts of trade statistics able to reflect the newly emerging options for (international) exchange of value added in times of a *digital globalisation*? We aim to detect and discuss new approaches and options to answering this question in the course of the following chapter.

The influences of digitalisation are countless. Nevertheless, we try to address important aspects that will lead to a coherent picture with regard to economic trade analysis. Looking at internal challenges that enterprises worldwide share, it becomes clear that new technologies are not only influencing but changing ways in which business is done. Logistics, payment streams, securities, real-time procurement and many other areas are rebuilt. Blockchain technologies allow new closed-circuit and real-time communication and information. This has and will change the way trade deals are done. The speed and availability of information will lead to breaking changes that will change internal processes. And while we certainly include the outcomes in our analysis, due to the nature of blockchain technologies a thorough analysis requires an internal business focus. We will hence focus on a macroeconomic perspective in this chapter and will guide the reader to a global understanding of issues associated with digitalisation.

The Handbook of Global Trade Policy, First Edition. Edited by Andreas Klasen.
© 2020 John Wiley & Sons Ltd. Published 2020 by John Wiley & Sons Ltd.

In the first section, we briefly present the impressive increase in international transactions between World War II and the financial market crisis in 2008. Trade on goods and services have multiplied, and growth rates of trade and service flows have outreached by far growth rates of value added. Consequently, the world economy has become more and more strongly connected while a steadily increasing share of the worldwide gross domestic product (GDP) has been traded internationally. However, the Great Recession following the financial market crisis has changed international transaction patterns dramatically. For the first time in decades, growth of international trade flows remains below growth of value added. Does this mean a pause in or even the end of *globalisation*? At first glance, we might indeed judge the slowdown of pace as a "trade peak". But is this the correct conclusion?

In the second section, we argue that globalisation did not stop and trade did not peak. It has simply changed its clothes. It is no longer focused on trade in goods, but increasingly appears in the form of trade in services and trade in data. However, neither (international) service trade nor (international) data trade is easily measurable with concepts traditionally used for goods. Boundaries blur because of geographic latitudes, the new options of a sharing economy and the increasingly hybrid structure of global value chains. As much as actual processes change, new technologies also change the rules of the game. Blockchain technologies have enabled new approaches toward traditional tasks. This is by no means limited to trade financing, but it is one topic that is closely related to our topic and will hence be discussed as well. Taking these new tendencies into account, we argue that the "trade peak" is rather a measurement consequence than a real phenomenon.

In section three, we search for new concepts to solve the "trade puzzle". How could new trade patterns be reflected in trade statistics? A remeasurement of international transactions in the age of digital globalisation has to include a more careful consideration of the specifics of service trade, data trade and the consequences of blurry boundaries than in the past. Otherwise statistics on international activities might mislead policymakers. They could indicate a "trade peak" and underestimate the still increasing worldwide interdependence.

In a final section we conclude that globalisation is not reaching its end. It does not even pause. It simply changes to new patterns reflecting new options of *digital globalisation*. Consequently, our analysis is a starting point and not an end point of a new discussion on the future of globalisation. Many other researchers and institutions are dealing with the consequences of digitalisation on trade patterns and trade measurement. They also aim to provide more insights on what is attributed to digitalisation and what is attributed to the advancement of technology.[2] With the following we hope to support this research.

From Trade to Digitalism – Globalisation Trends

At the beginning of the 19th century, globalisation was about trading goods and commodities through borders. It was enabled on an unprecedented scale by the steam revolution of 1820. The later phase of globalisation starting in the 1980s underwent a fundamental structural change. International trade was influenced by countries that moved up the development ladder, as services started to play an increasing role (Figure 3.1).

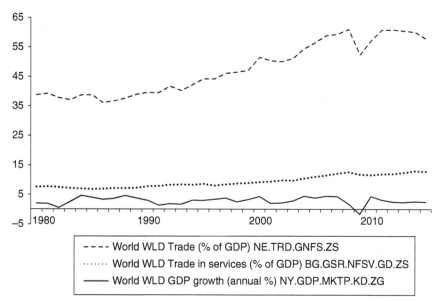

Figure 3.1 Development of trade, trade in services, and GDP growth 1980–2015.
Source: World Bank (2016).

Goods	Services	Data
Tangible	Intangible	Intangible
Can be stored	Not storage possible	Can be stored
Consumption is usually separated from production	Consumption often happens at the same moment as production	Consumption is usually separated from production

Figure 3.2 Categorisation of goods, services and data.
Source: Own depiction following Mandel (2012), p. 5.

Since then, the separation of trade in goods and services has been widely accepted and seemed to capture human activities well. The dichotomy between goods and services has been taken as an almost natural separation. While this may have been true in the past, digital globalisation has navigated the world economy into a more complex world. A fast-growing demand for immaterial goods in areas such as communication, information, knowledge-organisation, finance, insurances and consulting has driven international economic relations in recent decades.

Mandel (2012) expands therefore the traditional divide of goods and services by a third category, data (Figure 3.2). The reason for doing so is that – as Mandel (2014) shows with various examples – data flows are mostly not connected to monetary payment and are therefore underestimated in the concept of GDP (and thus also international trade), which is based on monetary transactions. Considering data as a third category allows him to recalculate the real GDP of the United Kingdom. While the official rate for the first half of 2012 is 1.7%, he sees a growth of 2.3%, an increase of 0.6 percentage points.

While the methodological issue may be grasped by the introduction of another category, the measurement issues are still ahead. How does digitalisation change our view so far? Research from Goldman Sachs gives an idea. It suggests that the mismeasurement of quality change in information technology (IT) output could lead to a 0.7

percentage points underestimation of annual GDP growth in the United States and up to 0.5 percentage points in European countries (Bean, 2016). This problem, as a logical consequence, also arises when measuring international trade flows. In the following chapter we aim to address the drivers of change, show that trade has changed and consider what should be done about it. We will argue that the separation of trade in goods and trade in services still makes sense, but that data flows have a deep impact on the dynamics of goods and services trade in various ways. Before doing so we will analyse how trade in goods and trade in services have evolved in recent decades.

On Trade of Goods

Between 1998 and 2007 global trade of goods increased (in real terms, i.e. corrected for inflationary tendencies) every year by 6% (Figure 3.3). This growth was almost double the growth of productivity. Before the end of the Cold War at the end of the 1980s less than one fifth of world production was traded internationally. In 2008, this share rose to about one third. After the deep recession at the end of the past decade and as a consequence of the financial crisis, trade growth between 2012 and 2014 only reached a maximum of 2.5%. The average was at 2.4%, which equals worldwide productivity growth. One could take this as a pointer towards a barrier for international trade exchange.

The classical trade export leader is China with a world market share of 12%, followed by the United States and Germany, which both reach levels of 8%.

Figures 3.4 and 3.5 show that trade in general, as well as in almost all product categories individually, has slowed down significantly over the past few years, especially

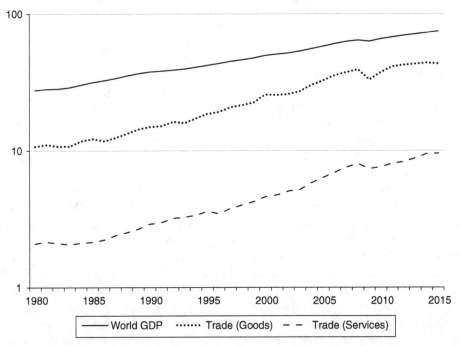

Figure 3.3 Trade development (in logarithms of constant 2010 US$ trillion).
Source: World Bank (2016).

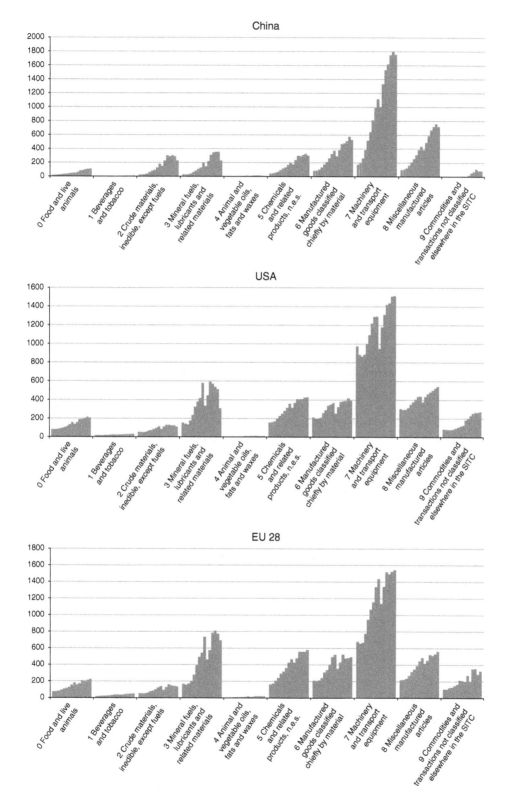

Figure 3.4 Total trade as exports and imports 2000–2015 in US$ billion by 1-digit classification (Standard International Trade Classification, Revision 3).
Source: UN Comtrade Database (2017).

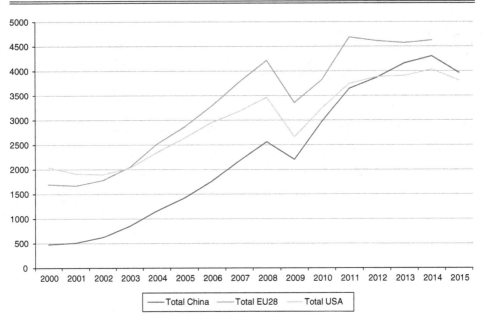

Figure 3.5   Total trade to world of China, EU28, and USA 2000–2015 in current US$ billion.
Source: UN Comtrade Database (2017).

after the financial market crisis of 2008/2009. There are various factors behind this
slowdown in trade growth. For once the end of the integration process of China and
Eastern Europe into the global economic division of labour may be a reason. This is
linked to diminishing wage differentials between China and developing countries. As
wages are rising, the incentive to trade at a comparative cost advantage, according to
the Heckscher–Ohlin theory, is fading (Heckscher, 1913; Ohlin, 1933).

It should also be noted that the structural change of China from an industry- and
investment-driven economy towards a more consumer- and services-oriented
economy is less trade intensive. In addition, the boom of the information technology
(IT) industry at the beginning of the 1990s caused the creation of global value chains
(GVC) which are very trade intensive. However, this process has gradually come to
a standstill. One could argue that the technology shock was absorbed. And lastly the
global decline of investment means that many fewer goods are imported and
exported, because the import content of investment goods is estimated to be twice as
high as the import content of consumer goods (see Figure 3.4).

On Trade of Services

For a long time, supplier and consumer would have needed to get together spatially
to exchange services. A classical text book example would be the service of a hairdresser. If you want to get your hair cut, you have to move to wherever the hairdresser
is (or vice versa). Modern trade of services is rather the exception than the rule.
Figure 3.6 shows the four types (modes) of services that are commonly identified.

The ease of transferability has led international trade of services to grow stronger
than ordinary trade flows – at least in the past couple of years. Between 2012 to
2014, worldwide trade in services grew (on average) 4.5%, almost double the growth

Mode 1: Cross-border

A user in country A receives services from abroad through its telecommunications or postal infrastructure. Such supplies may include consultancy or market research reports, tele-medical advice, distance training or architectural drawings.

Mode 2: Consumption abroad

Nationals of country A have moved abroad as tourists, students or patients to consume the respective services.

Mode 3: Commercial presence

The service is provided within country A by a locally established affiliate, subsidiary, or representative office of a foreign-owned and -controlled company (bank, hotel group, construction company etc.).

Mode 4: Movement of natural persons

A foreign national provides a service within country A as an independent supplier (e.g., consultant, health worker) or employee of a service supplier (e.g. consultancy firm, hospital, construction company).

Figure 3.6 Service modes.
Source: WTO (2016).

of overall production and faster than the trade of goods. With respect to the contribution to services trade of different countries, the picture for services differs from the picture for goods. The United States leads with a global share of 14%, far above all other countries. Runners-up are Great Britain with 7% and Germany with 5.5%. However, among the developing and transition economies, China leads in terms of total exports and imports of services.

On Trade of Data

Digitisation,[3] according to Shapiro and Varian (1998), refers to the process of encoding something "as a stream of bits". This information is created virtually and thus detached from physical products that are traded on markets. Furthermore, through the collecting, compacting, reviewing, dissemination, networking and usage of data and the transformation of information into knowledge and production, a new value is created outside of goods and services. To analyse the special challenges a digitalised economy entails, we need to understand how continued technological innovation made this change possible. Two main factors can be identified: the development of microprocessors and the distribution of an international network that links computers, and hence people, and devices with one another. The main feature with respect to microprocessors is the exponential increase in performance in production.

This exponential growth was observed already in 1965 (Moore, 1965) and held roughly true for the past 40 years (doubling roughly every two years). It allowed for an immense increase in performance and productivity which has been a substantial factor in cutting down the cost of information. Another decisive factor that enables digitalised globalisation is the world-spanning decentralised organised data network, which is generally referred to as the internet. Through the enormous performance increases in the computer industry, internet-capable devices became affordable and the reach of this network grew exponentially: from the early days of the internet in 1968 as a military network (ARPANET: Advanced Research Projects Agency Network) to a network with currently about 3 billion subscribers. But not only did it spread exponentially, at the same time its special properties as a network good increased the new opportunities.

In economic theory, network effects are dependent on the number of participants. A classic example would be the telephone network: the more subscribers can be reached, the higher the value of said network for each individual subscriber. Hence, the total utility for each user depends on the total number of users. The effects are, driven by the huge spread of the internet (almost 50% of the world population has access to the internet), correspondingly large. Another factor is the ubiquitous information delivery. Only two decades ago, at least a phone call was necessary to receive information. Today in many cases a largely automated query suffices. The spread of the internet has to a large extent automated the provision of information. Knowledge is no longer restricted to human interaction (and hence working hours etc.) but can be accessed and used across borders and time zones (Box 3.1).

The more rapid growth of trade in services seems to reflect partly the rapid expansion of trade in data. Indeed, the traditional statistical framework tries to include trade in data in the trade in services. However, given the huge measurement problems, this does not look to be very successful.

Box 3.1   Digitalisation in the media industries.

The music industry was probably first to notice the backlash of technological invention. In 1992 mp3 was introduced as a standard and by combination with increased transmission speeds allowed a full music album to be downloaded in only twice the time it took for playback. When technology had caught up, the film industry experienced a similar process. Both industries involve the production of intangible goods, which are highly scalable and hence suited perfectly for digital distribution channels. They can be copied without any decrease in quality, with low (almost no) variable per unit cost, and depend only on connection quality to reach the consumer. However, as straightforward as the properties of these goods are, it seems equally difficult to establish fair pricing and find a mechanism to protect the content from illegal activities. Part of this problem is that the marginal cost of reproduction is close to zero. Reproduction does not require a sophisticated facility but can be achieved within the shortest time periods and by almost everyone with basic access to IT. To date it is unclear whether the distribution models of the music industry allow for a sustainable market. The increasingly popular subscription models for music that allow nearly unlimited streaming at around 10 euros a month (Apple Music, Google Play, Spotify, Deezer, Tidal, Napster etc.) are based on a system that pays artists by actual playing occurrences. It is estimated that an artist receives around US$0.001128 per play (Dredge, 2015). With remuneration this small the total number of plays is important, and hence the big stars are less affected by such models than are new or special interest bands that may not be able to gather a big fan base. It remains to be seen which path this development will take. What it already shows is the shift of power that the formerly free distribution channels made possible. In addition, it shows how illegal channels gain leverage on legal companies, as jurisdiction and governments are not able to protect them.

A recent study by the McKinsey Global Institute shows that one eighth of world trade in goods is mandated through e-commerce and about half of all internationally traded services is digitised (McKinsey Global Institute, 2016). Thus, it seems clear that trade in data is very much underestimated. It also makes clear that a thorough analysis is needed and relevant in understanding new trade patterns and associated consequences. There are some estimates with respect to the expansion rate of trade in data. For example, Mandel (2014) points out that the "data-carrying capacity of transatlantic submarine cables rose at an average annual rate of 19% between 2008 and 2012". Given that video streaming dominates data flows in general, one may object to the measurement above. However, Netflix and other providers usually have servers all over the world. Hence, most videos are not streamed via the Atlantic. Thus the "video streaming effect" may be less relevant.

In addition to the effects on data streams, which could be seen as an internal digitalisation issue (d2d, digital 2 digital), because it stems from digital businesses and has an effect on digital issues (data streams), there certainly is the somewhat traditional digitalisation effect (d2a, digital to analogue). This means that certain formerly non-digital (aka. analogue) markets are severely modified by digitalisation. Keeping to the example of video streaming, this is an issue, for example, for cinemas, video rental businesses and department stores which experience the transformation of an onsite market to a hybrid market that allows a direct delivery into homes.

How Trade of Goods and Services is Influenced by Data Flows

The extraordinary growth of trade in data has implications for the traditional trade in goods and services. Roughly speaking, there are substitution effects and complementary effects.

Substitution effect

In many cases, trade in goods will be substituted with the transport of data (Box 3.2). This can be seen very vividly with encyclopaedias. Wikipedia, a free-to-use online encyclopaedia created using free content provided by anybody who wishes to contribute, was founded in 2001. In the first year 19,000 articles were published. At the beginning of September 2016, the English version of Wikipedia had 5.2 million articles (see Figure 3.7). Currently, about 8 billion page views accumulate per month across all language versions of Wikipedia. In stark contrast to this development, the value of traded encyclopaedias has shrunk from US$1.77 billion in 2008 to US$564 million in 2015.

Box 3.2 Example of borderless production.

The On Demand Books, LLC sells the Espresso Book Machine to retailers or libraries that wish to add the service of on-demand book printing. Currently there are 67 locations worldwide that offer the on-demand production of books within minutes, and not much fantasy is needed to envision a growing demand. One could argue that books may be replaced by e-books before too long, which shows how quickly traditional boundaries can be overcome by technology.

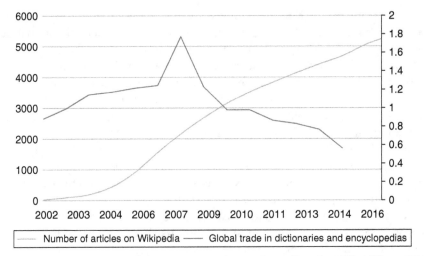

Figure 3.7 Global exports of dictionaries and encyclopaedias (in US$ billion; HS92[26]: 490191) and number of articles on the English Wikipedia (in thousand).
Source: UN Comtrade Database (2017), Wikimedia Foundation (2017).

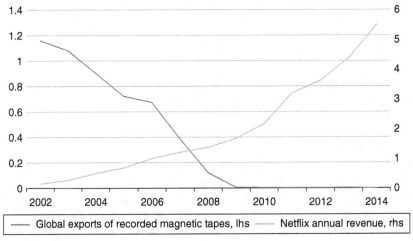

Figure 3.8 Global exports of magnetic tapes (in US$ billion; HS92[27]: 852421, 852422, 852423) and film streaming company Netflix's revenues (in US$ billion).
Source: UN Comtrade Database (2017), Statista (2017a).

Globally this also holds true for the newspaper trade, which has dwindled since 2008 and can be explained by the growing importance of online news. A survey by the Pew Research Center (cited by Caumont, 2013) among US citizens found that in 2001 a mere 13% named the internet as their most important source of news. This figure rose to 50% in 2013 and is most likely to increase further as digital formats are becoming more sophisticated and content that used to be print-only is being offered in other digital formats and can be consumed with specific applications designed for a smartphone or a tablet. Figure 3.8 shows the deterioration of trade of magnetic video tapes from 2002 to 2009. In the same period, revenue of the online video streaming portal Netflix increased. While the decline of magnetic video tapes started with the distribution of DVDs (digital

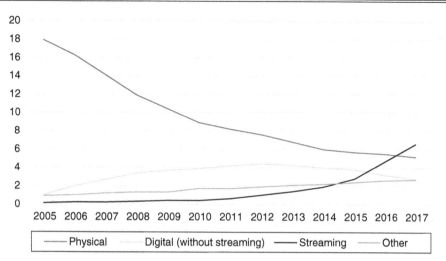

Figure 3.9 Global recorded music industry revenues (includes performance rights and synchronisation revenues) (in US$ billion).
Source: IFPI (2017).

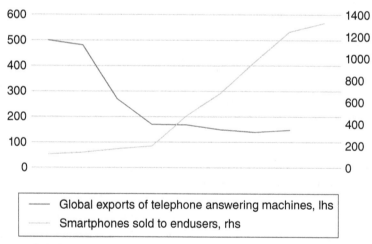

Figure 3.10 Global exports of photographic cameras in US$ million (HS92[28]; 9006) and number of smartphones sold to end users (in million).
Source: UN Comtrade Database (2017), Statista (2017b).

versatile discs) and Blu-rays, the streaming of movies is gaining momentum continuously. The music industry has been witnessing this process for even longer (see Figure 3.9).

Inclusive effect

Digitalisation also has an inclusive effect where it unifies two or more "old" products in one new one. The most memorable example is probably the introduction of the first touch-capable smartphone (the iPhone) by Apple in 2007, which has since integrated even more devices (such as a camera, to name only one of dozens of examples). Sales numbers of smartphones have risen from 122 million units in 2007 to 1.32 billion units in 2015. At the same time, international trade in cameras has gone down (see Figure 3.10).

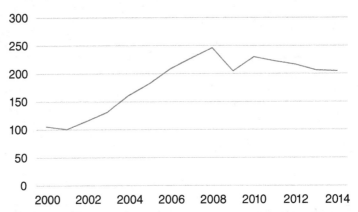

Figure 3.11 Consumer electronic equipment, bilateral trade flows (in US$ billion).
Source: UNCTADstat (2017).

With new devices including more functionality in one device, old devices tend to become superfluous. This is notable in the international trade in consumer electronics, where, despite the increasing spread of electronics in households, stagnation has set in since 2009 (see Figure 3.11).

Efficiency gains
The cost of international trade has dropped dramatically in past decades through gains in efficiency, and this has been a driver for growth in trade. One example of these efficiency gains is container-based trade, where digitalisation is playing an important role. A modern container terminal can unship 20,000 standard containers in less than 24 hours. Fifty years ago, when the first container ships where unloaded, this number of containers would have needed 75 days.[4] Since 1980, freight rates of container ships have decreased by 80% (adjusted for inflation) (see Figure 3.12). While these rates have certainly been affected by digitalisation, the main decrease in transportation cost has its root in rather traditional engineering advances and lower fuel prices. However, digitalisation has the potential to further lower cost for international trade by improving efficiency. This in turn will allow for further development and changes in trade that may be as extreme as we are already witnessing. One example is that of self-driving trucks, which could transport commodities without the necessary breaks for human drivers. Tracking of goods with sensors, which is already widely used today, has lowered product losses along the logistical chain. These cost savings may allow businesses to realise new opportunities to outsource the production of intermediate goods or even expand global value chains.

In addition, without the progress in information and communication technology it would not be feasible to coordinate different stages of production at great distance. Thus, international trade along more efficient value chains built up by international companies in recent decades was only made possible by cross-border data flows (Baldwin, 2016). Furthermore, blockchain technologies could facilitate documentary compliance in cross-border trade and make trade cheaper. According to the World Bank, it takes some 68.2 hours for an average East Asian & Pacific export company to comply with the documentary requirements when a standardised export unit is shipped abroad. Around the same time (65.6 hours) is needed for the import of a standardised import unit.[5]

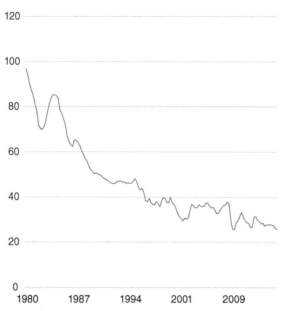

Figure 3.12 Freight rates, inflation adjusted.
Source: HSH Nordbank (2017).

These costs have to do with the fact that many parties are involved in a cross-border transaction, starting with the export company and the import company, the insurance company, border control and at least two banks (one for the exporter and one for the importer), which often both finance the deal and grant that the documents attached to the trade are correct. In each step of this chain, paper is mostly still the dominant form in making sure the handling of international transactions is done properly. Obviously, this is not only time-consuming, but also error-prone and fraud-sensitive. One way to streamline the whole process could be to use the technology of blockchain. Indeed, some market participants are already underway in trying to implement blockchain in handling documentary compliance with respect to trade finance and other applications.[6] To get an idea of how blockchain technology may streamline international trade transactions, a traditional cross-border transaction financed by a letter of credit (L/C) should be compared with a modern blockchain-based transaction, as shown in Figure 3.13.

In a traditional and simply structured L/C transaction, five parties are involved: the seller, the buyer, the seller's bank, the buyer's bank and the carrier. When the goods are laded (for example on a vessel), the seller receives a bill of lading (BoL) from the shipper, who confirms that the lading of the goods has taken place.[7] This BoL is sent in paper form to the seller's bank which (after having checked the BoL for validity) sends it to the buyer's bank, which is the one that has issued the L/C with the seller as the beneficiary. The buyer's bank checks the documents and transfers the money to the seller's bank. The documents are transferred to the buyer, who presents the BoL to the shipper on arriving at the port of destination. These documents entitle the buyer to take possession of the transported goods. Obviously, this process takes some time as the BoL is transported in a physical way. It often happens that the traded goods arrive earlier than the transaction documents.[8] A blockchain-based cross-border trade has the potential to speed up the whole process and to make it more secure and less prone to fraud.

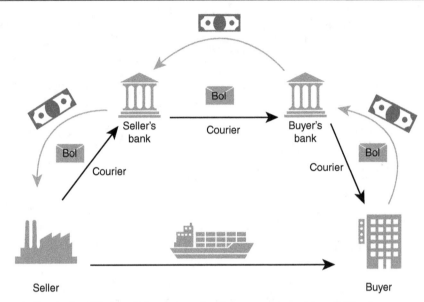

Figure 3.13   A simplified traditional cross-border transaction with an L/C.
Note: The L/C is issued by the buyer's bank for the beneficiary of the seller's bank. The payment is triggered by the bill of lading (BoL) if and when it is fulfilling the condition agreed upon.

What would such a transaction look like? The basic idea is that there is no central entity controlling the transaction but instead a decentralised system where all parties involved in the transaction are required to validate the transaction (Figure 3.14). There is no international standard established yet as blockchain-based transactions are in the stage of being tested.[9] However, there are certain ideas about what an ideal blockchain-based transaction in international trade could look like:[10]

- In contrast to Bitcoin, the model blockchain for international trade finance should be a private blockchain. Thus, only the buyer and seller of the goods, the carrier and the financial institutions that finance the trade should be involved.
- There should be no anonymity. Each member would therefore be able to identify any other by their digital signature.
- The core of the blockchain idea is that each transaction has to be validated by the members, while a single member alone could not validate a transaction. Fraud and double spending would be very difficult.
- When the members have validated the transaction, it could be added to the blockchain. Data would be encrypted, which would make it nearly impossible to modify them.
- Adding smart contracts to the blockchain would enable the automatic triggering of payments when certain conditions are fulfilled.

Summing up, blockchain technology is still in its infancy. As cross-border transactions involve many parties, it is a challenge to convince all of them to participate in this new technology, since the chain is only as strong as its weakest link. However, given the huge potential efficiency gains from using blockchain technologies, it

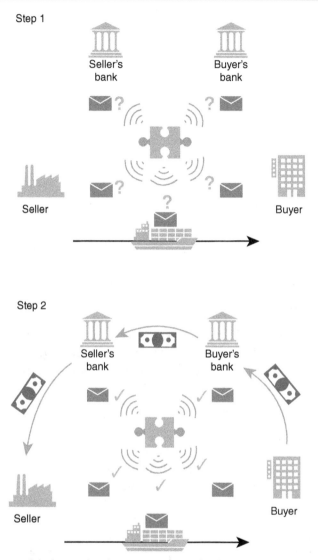

Figure 3.14   A simplified cross-border transaction with Blockchain.

should only be a matter of time before international trade documents are being processed digitally instead of paper forms being shipping around.

Online trading

In recent decades, digitalisation has led to global online trading platforms that have made international trade for small and medium-sized enterprises (SMEs) and individuals much easier. It is perfectly normal to order goods from abroad directly via platforms such as Amazon, eBay and Etsy. An indication of the dynamics in e-commerce, which now accounts for 12% of international trade (McKinsey Global Institute, 2016), is the increase in turnover achieved by parcel services over the past few years (Figure 3.15). Some of this growth is likely at the expense of traditional distribution channels, such as wholesalers. However, an important part of the

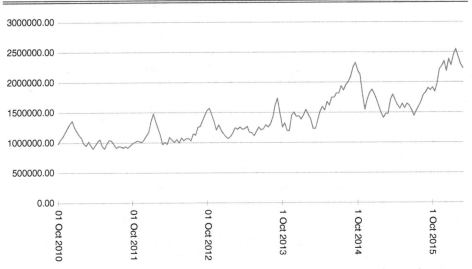

Figure 3.15 Daily parcel tonnage transported through the international postal systems.
Source: Universal Postal Union, cited by UNCTAD (2016).

increase is probably due to lower market entry barriers that allow SMEs to offer their goods abroad. And this trend doesn't stop with SMEs, but also allows private individuals to produce goods and sell them on online platforms. Etsy (www.etsy.com), for example, has specialised in offering people a marketplace where they can offer their own products.

In terms of selling opportunities, the gap between a hobbyist and a professional tailor or between an occasional dressmaker and the head of a small craft business is narrowing. Rifkin (2014) speaks in this context of so-called prosumers (*producers and consumers*). The classic separation between consumers and producers may no longer be valid. The increased distribution of 3-D printers in private households can additionally lead to growing business opportunities for small-sized households. Hence it is unclear whether, with the invention of the 3-D printer, trade in goods will be replaced with trade in blueprints or whether the finished products will not be traded.[11] Closely related is the development of online payment systems, such as PayPal, which have helped to facilitate online trading for the consumer. This easy and seemingly boundary-free transfer of monetary resources again raises the question of accountability in the context of GDP measurement.

Data enabling the tradability of certain services

The increased tradability of correspondence services has led to a dynamic element of internationalisation. It strengthens the vertical dimension of international trade of services and pushes added value chains across national boundaries, making them global value chains. Similar to the production process of commodities in international production compounds, services are split into several segments and divided into countries according to locational advantages. The integration of these segments is achieved by trading with location-unbound services (at-arm's-length services). This separation is usually home to multinational enterprises (MNEs) that specialise in services.

A simple integration is achieved when foreign subsidiaries provide a service or a service component for their parent company. A typical example might be back-office functions, such as financial services, controlling and accounting for a foreign regional headquarters of an MNE or the coordination of multinational activities in a certain region through a wholly owned foreign subsidiary. One way to realise a complex integration of more than one subsidiary would be for the parent to take part in the international labour division. Another way could be for a single foreign subsidiary to deliver services for all other members (or geographically limited subsidiaries, e.g. North America) of an MNE. In addition, a number of subsidiaries could jointly provide a service, such as research and development, on an integrated data basis with rotating tasks.

Beyond assembling value chains between countries, international services can act as grease for certain – and frequently – far-reaching production compounds in the commodity sector. This is especially true for company-based (in contrast to household- or person-based) services. They can be directly related to the trade of commodities and foreign direct investment (FDI) (such as transport, distribution, service, telecommunication), or substitute both (as it is the case with leasing or licensing contracts). In the same regard, company-based services can disconnect completely from commodity trade and direct investments, in the form of general banking and insurance services. For the trans-border fragmentation of production in the commodities sector, the corresponding production sites specialise in those steps of production in which they (the country) have a comparative advantage. Production components can be transferred within the same MNE (this creates intra-firm trade) or parts of the production can be outsourced to companies that are independent of one another (these companies would then need to trade via the market internationally with one another).

In both cases, services play a central role: they enable the existence as well as the execution of the relevant trade flows. For the first scenario, they also have an important coordination function between the countries. As a consequence, outsourcing and offshoring are used more and more by international services. All this would not have been realised without the internet and the corresponding ease of transfer of data from one point in the world to another. For example, the United States (see Figure 3.16) shows an impressive shift of shares in value added of GDP towards services, which may well have to do with the above described trend of increasing growth in international trade of data. One may argue that this shift is simply a reflection of a normal structural change of an economy becoming wealthier as well as the relocation of industrial production to emerging economies, which certainly is true for the decades between 1950 and 1990. However, as argued above, later on this relocation of production was very much enabled by the flow of data allowing the control and monitoring of value-added chains across the world. An example is the technology firm Apple: while this company started producing its devices in the United States during the 1980s and 1990s, it closed down the last US production facility in 2004. However, the whole process of innovation and product development does take place in Cupertino, California.[12]

The future of globalisation will no longer be dominated by commodity trade, but by the transfer of services and, to be more precise, by the exchange of data. Digitalisation will accelerate and change the international trade in services.

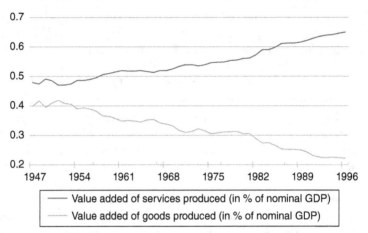

Figure 3.16 Value added for goods and service producing sectors in the United States, 1947–1997, in % of total GDP.
Source: US DOC/BEA, cited by Berg-Andreassen (2015).

Blurry Boundaries

While the above concepts sound straightforward, the implication may not always be. Some concepts and developments fail to surrender to one category. Hence a further look into the shifting and transitioning borders is necessary.

Geographic Latitude

One key factor of the ongoing change is the geographic latitude of digitalisation (Box 3.3). The traditional idea of national borders is no longer as clear cut as it used to be. We have shown that a book today can be created, produced and consumed in different locations without the need of ever being shipped.

Sharing Economy

Modern applications may also work towards a sharing economy, which allows a far more efficient use of existing goods, cars or apartments.[13] Figure 3.17 shows the huge growth in business models which are based on the idea of a sharing economy.

Box 3.3 Geographic examples (firms).

This was very much to the liking of Luxembourg, which initially was very pleased with the settling of Amazon, when all revenue made in the EU had to be taxed with them. It is only since May 2015 that Amazon has had to file taxes in Germany for revenue made in Germany. This shows the problems a digital distributor can have with the foundations of traditional national accounting. Two other major IT-related companies use similar models. Apple and Google both bundle their revenues in Ireland to make use of its tax laws. This challenges the community of states, but also the countries themselves. This is especially true for economic policy: what should an adequate policy framework look like if it is unclear whether (i) it is useful (financial streams) and (ii) somebody else might get to pick the cherries (national borders)?

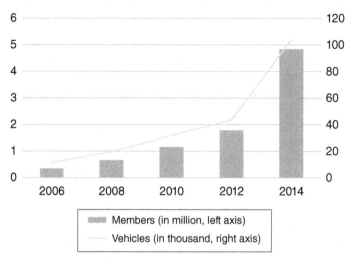

Figure 3.17 Global trends in car sharing.
Source: Shaheen and Cohen (2016).

The mobility service Uber, which is directly targeted at customers using traditional taxis, is one example. As an online middleman, it arranges a car and a driver for a customer to go from A to B on an app or online basis. As a new participant in the market, Uber has greatly increased the supply of available taxis. This is especially true for those rides offered by private drivers. This tendency, in the long run, can lead to fewer private cars being needed in this area, which is one of the aims of Uber boss Travis Kalanick. He wants to make Uber so cheap and reliable that there is little to no incentive to own your own car. Other car sharing projects, such as the self-driving mobility service project nutonomy.com – starting in Singapore in August 2016 – reinforce this trend. Should this vision become reality, the international trade in cars could be reduced significantly. Another example of the sharing economy is the accommodation service Airbnb, which has gained a considerable market share of overnight stays. This may develop to become serious competition for hotels and may even aggravate apartment shortages in cities (FAZ, 2016). In this case, the international trade in goods needed for the hotel business (e.g. building materials, elevators, room decor) would be reduced. Zervas *et al.* (2017) show for Texas that Airbnb significantly alters the price-setting power of hotels and hence impairs revenues.

Hence, we conclude that an expanded sharing economy may lead to fewer goods being traded. Two other issues also arise as a consequence. While not specifically aimed at the sharing economy, Grömling (2016) describes the general statistical problems that arise when consumer goods are being supplied without cost through the internet and hence substitute traditional products. Examples could be user-generated contents, such as games, music and Wikipedia, the use of which is not captured by GDP, or shared economy as discussed above. Another issue stems from the measurement of utility. Hitherto, it could be argued that buying constituted utility. This, however, has changed to usage instead of buying. Hence a shift from trade to services is evident. No longer is owning and driving a car a standard but the service of being driven enters the markets as a more efficient and hence economic alternative. This change from physical to tangible (see Figure 3.2) bears important challenges that stem from the digitalisation of the economy.

Hybrid Goods

In digitalised globalisation, the internet can replace transportation of goods and data transfer the trade in goods. Instead of producing standard goods centrally and in bulk, which would then need to be transported thousands of miles to the consumer, 3-D printers can produce these goods decentrally and tailored to the specific needs of the consumer. It is difficult, if not impossible, to project the influence the technology of 3-D printing will have on industrial production processes. Between 2009 and 2013, the market grew dynamically by an average of 30.2% per year (Consultancy.uk, 2016), while the global market volume of US$3.1 billion is estimated to have more than quadrupled to U12.57 billion. While at present the technology is still very capital intensive and needs intensive research, first examples (see below) show that mass production with 3-D printers could be possible in the future.

If technical progress leads to further acceleration of the printing process and 3-D printing is widely used in industry, massive negative repercussions are likely for the international trade of goods; around 50% of international trade is in intermediary goods. 3-D printers can shorten the length of the value chain in which the intermediate goods are traded. For various reasons, companies could have an incentive to carry out the production of intermediate goods by means of 3-D printers (Box 3.4). Value chains across countries and jurisdictions are always at risk of disruption. The shortening of value chains reduces this risk. Just-in-time delivery could transform into print-on-demand production. It is also possible that companies will install 3-D printers even if they receive their intermediate goods from suppliers. This allows them the ability to switch to their own production in urgent cases and also allows them to reduce dependency on suppliers or to react to a more protectionist trade policy at home.

The production of consumer goods can take place closer to the end user by using 3-D printing. This advantage is particularly relevant with people increasingly demanding individualised products, which could challenge traditional centralised mass production systems.

While nowadays investment goods, industrial machinery, tools and vehicles are being shipped into the most diverse geographical regions, this may decline in the near future and we may only need to ship the blueprints or technical sketches. The final product will be produced and assembled right where the customer needs it. Hence data transfer can make traditional trade of products redundant. This leads

---

Box 3.4   Cost savings of 3-D printing.

The cost savings of using 3-D production technology depend on how efficiently 3-D printers can produce in the future. Basically, the transport costs for the intermediate material are not included in the 3-D printer, but one has to calculate the transport of the "ink". Efficiency gains can in any case result from there being virtually no waste in this production technology and thus raw material is saved. Storage is also not necessary. Whether the application of 3-D production technology provides better quality results depends on the requirements of the product and the materials used. In the example given in Box 3.5 (GE injection nozzles), the reason for the production change is the improvement in quality with simultaneous cost savings.

to another hypothesis: The trade of traditional goods is increasingly less useful to describe the abilities of an economy. It will certainly not become extinct, but it will change: it will be lower in volume, more specific and of higher quality. It will be replaced by long-range transfers of locally unbound information, electronic data and remote-controlled activities. The world is (becoming) flat: business meetings are already increasingly taking place via telephone conferences and video conferences. Skype, WhatsApp, FaceTime and other services allow users to conduct such conferences at virtually no cost and with minimal technological knowledge and investment. It is conceivable that 3-D video conferencing will develop, for example using 3-D glasses, to make interaction with people more authentic.

While this may be a long shot for a conversational scenario, lectures or presentations could easily be carried out without the physical presence of the lecturer while preserving the interaction with the listeners. If an increasing part of value is created without geographic restrictions in the orbit of the World Wide Web, a "domestic" scale is increasingly losing its function. Automation and artificial intelligence as well as the mutual interconnection between humans and machines allow time and space to merge as much as they help make the physical boundaries of and between value creators, companies and nations disappear. To aggravate this, we also have to deal with free provision by consumers (this includes so-called user-generated content – UGC). Be it consumer to business (C2B) or consumer to consumer (C2C), a shadow economy has been created (Grömling, 2016), which is not reflected in GDP and will be dealt with later in this chapter.

Disruptive Structural Change

In many industries, digitalisation challenges traditional business models. The speed of this change is breathtaking and may lead to a disruptive structural change, i.e. people become unemployed without having time to adapt to the new structures. The result may be a deep and lasting recession that includes even less international trade. In addition to the above examples in the context of the sharing economy, other developments can also lead to a disruptive structural change. For example, the traditional banking sector has to deal with the so-called fintechs,[14] the stationary retail trade needs to cope with online trading platforms and in the logistics sector, millions of truck drivers might lose their jobs in just a few years if the self-propelled truck proves to be a successful idea. Even the educational sector may face profound change, if so-called MOOC (massive open online courses) are implemented and entire lecturer positions become redundant. Another example of this development is the Internet of Things. It not only connects machines to humans, but also machines to machines (M2M) on a worldwide scale. Not only national borders, regulations, provisions and tax law, but also national trade statistics become obsolete when the digitalisation of globalisation takes place. Already today – and with a daily reinforced trend – data packets are sent around the world in nanoseconds. It is only by means of 3-D printers that they become local in their final destination. They then construct "values", e.g. as construction segments, special tools, prostheses of almost all body parts, eyeglass frames or even clothes or shoes.

Box 3.5   Impact of 3-D printing on GVC and international trade of goods.

Two examples illustrate the impact on GVC and international trade of goods. In 2014, General Electric (GE) changed the production of engine injection nozzles from conventional production to 3-D printing. While the original product consisted of 20 different parts that had to be produced separately and then assembled, the 3-D printer is able to "print" the injection nozzle in one piece in up to 120 hours. This dramatically shortens the value chain. A procedure like this can well be applied in automotive production. Another example refers to a company from the United States, Local Motors (LM). Since its incorporation in 2007, LM has produced a specific type of car for which 75% of the parts originate from a 3-D printer. Although the company has produced only a few hundred cars, they have different production locations so that neither the 3-D parts nor the car produced has to be traded internationally. Since the development costs are shared in a collaborative manner based on an open source licence, it is conceivable that new production forms could become even more favourable than traditional production lines.

Outlook

In the digital age, many values are no longer *in rem* prepared. They are no longer measured by themselves or as local attributable numbers, vehicles or material units, but in "data". But there is neither a clearly defined value nor an export value in the classical sense – neither for the product itself, nor for the logistical services of data transport. An increasing amount of the human workforce is being replaced by machines and the degree of automating rises. Intelligent communication systems, smart grids, robots, self-driving cars, trains and many other innovations help to lower the physical and mental workload of workers or even take over completely. Labour productivity will be increased by self-driving, self-flying, self-steering, always-on systems with a low margin of error that are highly connected and equipped with artificial intelligence. In the future, few(er) people will create more value added with more capital. A "functional mobility with personal immobility" enables a growing disentanglement of living and working, production and consumption, saving and investment. Modern means of transportation, a powerful telecommunication network, satellite technology, internet and a hybrid place of networked communication allow (at least within Europe) us to choose a place of living, a place of business, a place for taxation, a place for a bank account almost *ad libito*. Traditional, often sovereignly enforced, social societies are being opened up. Individual decisions are freed of national practical constraints, of historically grown location-specific values, norms and moral concepts and behaviours. All this becomes possible, if not necessary. How far reaching and quickly the ongoing digitalisation and "functional mobility with personal immobility" will displace the traditional trade and service transactions is dependent on many factors. Political, societal, cultural and economic parameters equally determine the transactions of cross-border activities.

How to Remeasure Trade Globalisation

How can the value created in an economy be measured reliably when the geographic origin of a product can only be determined less and less accurately? In which part of GDP statistics should the signals and impulses of drones and other machinery or even cloud-based data solutions be counted? Only looking at the European Union with labour, factor and capital mobility, the idea of calculating a GDP for one country becomes obsolete. While truckloads of products are carried across borders every second, back and forth without any government taking note, another issue comes into play. Even if transfers were noted, transfer pricing of MNE has to be taken into account, and most likely other factors (such as tax avoidance) may play a larger role for transfer pricing than a value-added determination.[15] Can GDP adequately capture these new forms of economic action?[16] It has been used (quite successfully) as a proxy to indicate the state of development of nations and has its very own advantages (availability being the most prominent). However, once countries have reached a certain income level, this also changes what the GDP calculation is founded on and will or should be seen as a performance indicator rather than a measure of economic well-being and development. Very often though, GDP is seen as the "core measure of economic prosperity" (Thewissen *et al.*, 2016). And still, when we are talking about growth and productivity, we look towards this seemingly most important figure: GDP. But really it is not just a figure but an abstract idea, a very complex tool (Coyle, 2014, even describes it as artificial), and it may even be highly political[17] as it is often seen as the one singular figure that represents an economy's well-being and economic power.

This, however, is flawed. GDP is explicitly not a measurement for well-being, but for total market production and associated income (Grömling, 2016). As the share of services has increased in high-income economies, GDP has been put further to the test.[18] Adam Smith even advocated that services should be seen as something negative: "A man grows rich by employing a multitude of manufacturers: he grows poor by maintaining a multitude of menial servants" (Smith, 1776).[19] This view did not succeed, and services today are an important part of GDP.[20]

In a quite thorough attempt "to identify the limits of GDP as an indicator of economic performance and social progress" Stiglitz *et al.* (2015) found a plethora of shortcomings. They found that "it is difficult even to define [these] services, let alone to measure them" and they also acknowledged the existence of the internet today as "an era when an increasing fraction of sales take place over the internet", but they did not go into any detail on the challenges and operations that arise from new technology and data transfers.[21] In this section we aim to fill exactly this gap.

To measure economic power, GDP relies on financial streams that are associated with economic transactions. But these very streams are changing more and more and they may not (or only partly) show up in GDP at all, because the calculation runs via market transactions or – when there is no market transaction – via cost.[22] Mandel (2014) points to this fact with respect to data flows via the internet: "The global and national statistics on trade in services are based on tracking monetary exchanges between residents of different countries. In theory, this principle can be applied to trade in data as well. If a person in the United States downloads a file from a website in a different country, it's theoretically possible that he or she could be charged for both the cross-border telecommunications link and for the content in the file. However, in practice the architecture of the Internet has developed in such a way that many or perhaps most cross-border data flows do not result in an exchange of money between residents of different countries." Instead, almost all networks connections (99.5%) are based on peering agreements, which means that they exchange traffic without exchanging money.

The distribution and usage of a digital good, however, does not necessarily imply a financial stream. In fact, the opposite is true when we look at the original provision of information in the internet, which was entirely without paywalls. It was only once the distribution of personal computers in households and the provision of goods increased substantially that things changed. One example is the change that was brought about in the music industry by the decentralised, peer-to-peer exchange of music by private individuals (often conducted illegally through software such as Napster): it massively withdrew earnings from record companies and only then did new means of central provision by enterprises allow sales to be conducted online.

Thus, it is not surprising if the effects of the digitalisation are not found in common GDP measuring practices. Looking at the "productivity puzzle" from the beginning of the computer age, a notion that Nobel Prize winner Robert Solow put so well as: "You can see the computer age everywhere but in the productivity statistics" (Solow, 1987), one could assume that history may repeat itself.[23] There are many reasons for the "productivity puzzle" of digitalisation. Certainly important is that GDP can only measure the "old" and familiar, for which there are "classifications", where "goods" can be identified and a clear distinction between "domestic" and "foreign" can be made. The "new" and, to the naked eye, invisible data-driven digitalisation, i.e. networking, the merging of man and machine, and the displacement of physical products into virtual spaces, however, remains more or less ignored in GDP (Triplett, 1999).

Furthermore, the inclusion (and dominance) of services aggravates measurement errors that have always been present. Services can be particularly problematic as they sometimes do not provide adequate statistical information on production and market value (Brümmerhoff and Grömling, 2015). If costly print magazines are substituted by freely accessible e-papers, GDP may fall as a result, even if the e-paper has benefits and prosperity rises, because more people can find cheaper, faster and easier access to information. Likewise, investment in GDP will only be accounted for if it comes in physical (fixed or tangible) goods, but not if it is expenditure on education, which in turn will enable people to accumulate more knowledge. This is a serious deficiency when, in the age of knowledge, human capital is increasingly becoming the micro- and macroeconomic key to success.

Some scholars such as Gordon (2014) bring up that GDP has never accurately measured huge amounts of consumer surplus. He also points out that even while Moore's Law[24] (as depicted above) may hold true, the increased distribution of smartphones and tablets has not had any stimulus on the economy. He goes on to argue that this should not come as a surprise since economics tell us that marginal cost equals marginal benefit, hence when the cost is low (which it is) so is the benefit. Another reason why the influence of new technology may be underestimated is the argument that a critical mass must be reached before any positive effect will significantly enter the data. This would be especially true for goods with network properties. However, it is hard to argue that the significant amount of internet penetration in high-income countries has yet to be reached. Brynjolfsson and McAfee (2014) note that to achieve certain benefits of technology, complementary factors first need to be introduced. So it may take a while for technology to penetrate the economy. Hence it seems necessary to evaluate new means of remeasuring trade and services in a digitalised world.

Brynjolfsson and Oh (2012) try to put a number to the digital shadow economy by estimating the gains from TV and the internet (see Figure 3.18) using an opportunity cost approach. These numbers may seem somewhat high, and Nakamura *et al.* (2016) find that advertising-supported media (such as the internet) are "too small to impact aggregate economic statistics much". While the truth may be somewhere between these two, it certainly shows a tendency towards underestimation.

Gordon (2014) also does not share a "techno-optimist" view. He notes four major factors that are and will be responsible for driving down growth rates: demography, education, growing inequality and government spending (increasing tax rates). Grömling (2016) identifies further factors that have been hindering productivity growth in the recent years. While Gordon (2014) does not dispute the effect of IT in general, he does note how short-lived the productivity increase due to the introduction of email, the internet, the web and e-commerce was. He writes that it was mainly driven by a never before experienced decline in the price for computer speed and memory. But despite his diagnosis that many of the available techniques took a very long time to be introduced into everyday life and hence unleash their full potential, he sees the contributions of early IT as masking an otherwise even "more severe slowdown in productivity growth".

With regard to future developments, he is very critical and notes that even though some inventions are within reach, they will never reach any level of innovation compared to those we have seen in what he calls the second industrial revolution, namely electricity, the internal combustion engine and wireless transmission. As a consequence, no substantial impact can be expected from these technologies. Without doubt this is a bad outlook and the arguments weigh heavily. However, we may need to take a

Comparison of consumer surplus from
television, internet, and free sites (in bn USD)

Year	Television	Annual gain from television	Internet	Annual gain from Internet	Free sites	Annual gain from free sites
2007	$1,715		$562		$375	
2008	$1,410	$305	$718	$156	$478	$104
2009	$1,080	$330	$676	$42	$451	$28
2010	$1,706	$615	$1,040	$364	$693	$243
2011	$1,399	$306	$1,196	$156	$797	$104
Average (2007–2011)	$1,462	$72	$838	$159	$559	$106
Average (2007–2011) in % of GDP	10.17%	0.50%	5.83%	1.10%	3.89%	0.74%

Figure 3.18 Consumer surplus.
Source: Own depiction following Brynjolfsson and Oh (2012).

closer look at the calculation of GDP. As noted earlier (and seen in Brynjolfsson and Oh, 2012), an underestimation of actual effects may be taking place (Box 3.6).

Conclusion

Gordon (2014) sees innovation as a free good: once it has been created (by whomever), it can be consumed by everyone else. As he puts it: "other countries can have the free lunch of enjoying American innovation including thousands of smart-phone apps without being saddled with American socio-economic decay, poor educational test scores, massive student debt, high school drop-outs, rising poverty together with explosive growth of incomes at the very top, and the need to reform entitlement programs that are in trouble in part because the USA have refused to make medical care a right of citizenship."

As a consequence, a catch-up process may take place that could even result in a takeover process and remove the United States from its position of leadership. In a very pessimistic outlook (after all, all other innovation can also be consumed by the United States), he warns of a series of countries "taking over" and the United States hence falling back. Brynjolfsson and McAfee (2014) see a similar trend. However, their conclusion is different. While Gordon takes the United States as his focal point, Brynjolfsson and McAfee take on a global focus. No resource could better help to advance the world than humans themselves, and with currently 7.1 billion people there have never been more potential ideas or a greater workforce to realise them.

In Europe, as much as in the United States, more or less populist movements are gaining attention. Their main pillars are nationalism rather than globalisation and encapsulation rather than opening up towards foreigners and foreign produce. These national(istic) tendencies will hinder the "old" globalisation, and maybe even stop it.[25] Against the "new" globalisation, however, these national(istic) tendencies will not be as successful. That is one reason why the structure of globalisation is likely to keep changing: away from traditional trade of goods towards the modern exchange of data. Even before the financial market crisis a slowdown in world trade could be observed and continued into the recent past. It coincides with a growing role of digitalisation on the consumer and producer side.

The impact of digitalisation on international trade is extremely evident in some sectors: CDs and DVDs are scarcely shipped, as streaming services have prevailed (substitution effect), the demand for cameras has reduced significantly, since smartphones can act as cameras (multi-functionality), and the 3-D printer is succeeding in the creation of value chains in the aircraft industry. All these make international transactions on the goods market superfluous. Furthermore, Uber (among others) may be part of the reason to buy fewer cars (sharing economy), while other technological solutions ensure that the world really is flat. Many of today's business trips may no longer be necessary. This will have corresponding negative repercussions on demand and world trade. The latter could also be the result of a disruptive structural change associated with digitalisation, which could be accompanied by a long-lasting recession.

The negative effects of digitalisation mentioned here are countered by a number of attenuating factors, which can also be attributed to digitalisation. New technology requires highly sophisticated hardware, which is still transported across country

> **Box 3.6   When a lot doesn't mean much – on the difficulties of measuring data.**
>
> Data will be a vehicle for values and the exchange of data will substitute commodity trade to a certain extent. Some of this change is already reflected in external trade statistics, where the traditional commodity trade loses its dynamic pattern while the global trade in services and most of all the international data traffic increases. However, the increase in global data usage has to be taken with a grain of salt, as it frequently reflects a rather consumptive and less productive usage. To give one example, Netflix, an on-demand supplier of TV series, movies and other videos, accounted for more than a third of all internet traffic (i.e. data transfers) on North American fixed networks. The total of all streamed audio and video broadcasts even accounted for 71% of evening traffic in North American fixed access networks and it is expected that this figure will reach 80% by 2020. This certainly does reflect a change in consumption of consumers, away from the traditional TV reception mechanism towards an on-demand system. However, it also reflects a qualitative aspect. The data transfer of a book (take for example Goethe's *Faust*) will be around 200 kilobytes. However, one hour of a typical series broadcasted in 4K quality will take up to 20 gigabytes, even with current and very sophisticated data compression standards applied. This is a factor of 100,000 for a standard TV programme that is consumed a lot more than any book may ever be in a comparable time span. And even the step of the now almost established Full HD standard will expand fourfold once 4K is made available. All other industrial use almost vanishes in this pile of data.

boundaries. At the same time, enormous efficiency gains in logistics have been realised and will continue by means of digitalisation. This could make international trade even more attractive to many companies. Many of the cumbersome practices that are still necessary today may be obsolete in the future. By using blockchain technologies, a decentralised approach may help to overcome and substitute intermediaries that have seemed irreplaceable up to now. This also works for the *prosumers*: new digital trading platforms give international trade a positive boost and are likely to expand in the near future. The bottom line, however, is that the negative effects of digitalisation are predominant in international trade of goods.

These fundamental changes, as well as the inability of traditional GDP to depict the digitalisation change, leave two main options. One is redesigning the GDP measure to reflect current events. For example, the opportunity cost of individuals, i.e. the valuation of time spent on the internet when taking into account wages, could be used to calculate a valuation. Grömling writes that this would lead to an increase in GDP growth of around 0.3 percentage points; however, he fails to disclose his calculations.

In general, a solution could be to estimate the value added by digitalisation, i.e. the benefit or sales that arise from digital goods and services, at the desk of statisticians in the calculation of GDP. However, doing so will shift the accounting process even further away from reality into the artificial world of statisticians, who may or may not have their very own agenda. This will increase the risk of losing traction on reality by using artificially created figures.

Notes

1 Financial support from the NORDAKADEMIE Stiftung Elmshorn/Hamburg is acknowledged.

2 The WTO (2017) investigated the use of data by firms as an input into production and operations across a broad array of sectors – whether in goods, services, agriculture or public institutions – specifically looking at the impact of business-to-business (b2b) exchange of goods, services and data on the productivity development of firms. The Organisation for Economic Co-operation and Development, the European Commission and the IMF are also looking for new measurements of the digital economy (see Deutsche Bank Research, 2018).

3 Digitisation should not be confused with digitalisation. The former refers to the handy process of converting analogue information into digitally accessible information, while the latter can be seen as a broader term to describe a whole development, which may or may not involve elements of digitalisation.

4 The first container ship that came to Germany, about 50 years ago, unloaded 110 containers (Weser Kurier, 2016).

5 See World Bank (2017a, b) where it is shown how the shipments are standardized.

6 See for example Wild *et al.* (2015).

7 For a simple bill of lading see Freightquote (2017).

8 See for example Gil-Pulgar (2015).

9 See for example Michel (2016).

10 See McDermott et al. (2017).

11 One reason for this development could be that developers of such blueprints might fear their work is being illegitimately copied after it has been sold.

12 The topic of financial havens abroad or offshore has gained increased attention. This is especially true for some US companies that have dominating positions. While this certainly is a very important topic, it is not created by digitalisation. However, it may, as other examples have shown in this chapter, have further aggravated the existing issue. Hence, it is a relevant topic which deserves a proper examination, but unfortunately is beyond the scope of this chapter.

13 Grömling (2016, p. 137) describes the statistical problems that arise when consumer goods are being supplied without cost through the internet and hence substitute traditional products. Examples include user-generated content, such as games, music or Wikipedia, the use of which is not captured by GDP.

14 Fintech is collective term that is used to describe companies (here) or technologies that use modern technologies in the realm of financial services.

15 See e.g. Bartelsman and Beetsma (2003) and Clausing (2003).

16 In addition to these errors, calculative revisions of GDP need to be taken into account. These revisions can "correct" data even years after it has been published, but as Mauldin (2015) writes wittily: "When's the last time the mainstream media reported a five-year-old revision?" To the question of how much influence these revisions can have in historic data, a look at 2005 in Germany is in order, when a revision ex-post increased the yearly growth rate by 0.5 percentage points (Nierhaus 2007, p. 25).

17 See Mauldin (2015).

18 Further challenges for GDP may be the need to distinguish between the demand (consumption) and supply (production) sides. While there are typically three approaches to calculating GDP (expenditure, production and income), the latter approach is, due to lack of data, usually not feasible (Statistisches Bundesamt, 2016). Both sides have their very own needs, and adequate instruments for measurement need to be found. In addition, the difference between a country and world perspective should not be underestimated. While the former may be seen as rather dark (as Gordon, 2014, puts it) for high-income countries, the latter surely is bright for countries that are catching up.

19 Mauldin (2015) notes that Karl Marx had a similar view and that the Soviet Union's statistics department ignored services until communism collapsed in 1989.

20 A thorough overview of the historic development and the associated shortcomings of GDP can be found in Coyle (2014).

21 The report is nearly 300 pages.

22 See Grömling (2016, pp. 135–139). He shows that especially during transition phases of technology a dampening of production is to be expected, because the substitution effects will be acknowledged immediately in the national accounting, while the new goods will not.

23 Though Mark Twain and Charles Dudley Warner (1873) claim: "History never repeats itself, but the kaleidoscopic combinations of the pictured present often seem to be constructed out of the broken fragments of antique legends", which seems like a good description for what we are seeing.

24 While Gordon's general understanding of the results of Moore's Law is correct, he draws a rather shaky conclusion when he connects Moore's Law to price development (Gordon, 2014, p. 29). Moore's Law is a technological deduction that describes the space needed to place a transistor. The "law" does not make any assumptions on price or productivity and hence an interpretation towards an economic reality is unwarranted.

25 Compare the ongoing sideways movement of the globalization index of the ETH Zürich (2016).

26 HS stands for Harmonized Commodity Description and Coding System of 1992. More information can be found here: https://unstats.un.org/unsd/trade/classifications/correspondence-tables.asp and here: https://unstats.un.org/unsd/tradekb/Knowledgebase/50018/Harmonized-Commodity-Description-and-Coding-Systems-HS.

27 See endnote 4.

28 See endnote 4.

References

Airbnb (2015) Airbnb Summer Travel Report 2015. Retrieved from: https://blog.atairbnb.com/wp-content/uploads/2015/09/Airbnb-Summer-Travel-Report-1.pdf (accessed 2 July 2019).

Baldwin, R. (2016) *The Great Convergence, Information Technology and the New Globalization*. Cambridge, MA: Harvard University Press.

Bartelsman, E.J. & Beetsma, R.M.W.J. (2003) Why Pay More? Corporate Tax Avoidance through Transfer Pricing in OECD Countries. *Journal of Public Economics*, 87(9–10), 2225–2252.

Bean, C. (2016) *Independent Review of UK Economic Statistics*. Retrieved from: https://www.gov.uk/government/uploads/system/uploads/attachment_data/file/507081/2904936_Bean_Review_Web_Accessible.pdf (accessed 2 July 2019).

Berg-Andreassen, J. (2015) The Rise of US Income Inequality and the Demise of the Manufacturing Industries. *Industry Week*. Retrieved from: http://www.industryweek.com/competitiveness/rise-us-income-inequality-and-demise-manufacturing-industries (accessed 2 July 2019).

Brümmerhoff, D. & Grömling, M. (2015) *Volkswirtschaftliche Gesamtrechnungen* [National Accounts] (10th ed.). Munich: De Gruyter Oldenbourg.

Brynjolfsson, E. and McAfee, A. (2014) *Second Machine Age: Work, Progress, and Prosperity in a Time of Brilliant Technologies*. New York: W.W. Norton.

Brynjolfsson, E. and Oh, J.H. (2012) The Attention Economy: Measuring the Value of Free Digital Services on the Internet. In: *Thirty Third International Conference on Information Systems*, Orlando 2012. Retrieved from: https://pdfs.semanticscholar.org/9ff9/bec84357dacc286b570937a955f358a9a8b5.pdf (accessed 2 July 2019).

Caumont, A. (2013) 12 Trends Shaping Digital News. Retrieved from: http://www.pewresearch.org/fact-tank/2013/10/16/12-trends-shaping-digital-news (accessed 2 July 2019).

Clausing, K.A. (2003) Tax-Motivated Transfer Pricing and US Intrafirm Trade Prices. *Journal of Public Economics*, 87, (9–10), 2207–2223.

Consultancy.uk (2016) 3D Printing Market to Grow to 12.5 Billion by 2018. Retrieved from: https://www.consultancy.uk/news/11904/3d-printing-market-to-grow-to-125-billion-by-2018 (accessed 2 July 2019).

Coyle, D. (2014) *GDP – A Brief But Affectionate History*. Princeton: Princeton University Press.

Deutsche Bank Research (2018) Digital Economics: How AI and Robotics Are Changing Our Work and Our Lives. 14 May 2018. Retrieved from: www.dbresearch.com (accessed 2 July 2019).

Dredge, S. (2015) How Much Do Musicians Really Make from Spotify, iTunes and YouTube? Retrieved from: https://www.theguardian.com/technology/2015/apr/03/how-much-musicians-make-spotify-itunes-youtube (accessed 2 July 2019).

ETH Zürich (2016) KOF Globalisation Index. Retrieved from: https://kof.ethz.ch/en/forecasts-and-indicators/indicators/kof-globalisation-index.html (accessed 2 July 2019).

FAZ (2016) Airbnb begrenzt Londoner Vermietungen [Airbnb Restricts Rentals in London]. Retrieved from: http://www.faz.net/aktuell/finanzen/wohnungsnot-airbnb-begrenzt-londoner-vermietungen-14555772.html (accessed 2 July 2019).

Freightquote (2017) What Is Bill of Lading? Retrieved from: https://www.freightquote.com/how-to-ship-freight/bill-of-lading (accessed 2 July 2019).

Gil-Pulgar, J. (2015) Bitcoin and Its Blockchain Will Shape the Future of International Trade. Retrieved from: https://news.bitcoin.com/bitcoin-blockchain-will-shape-future-international-trade/ (accessed 2 July 2019).

Gordon, R. (2014) The Demise of US Economic Growth: Restatement, Rebuttal, and Reflections. *National Bureau of Economic Research Working Papers* No. 19895. Retrieved from: http://www.nber.org/papers/w19895 (accessed 2 July 2019).

Grömling, M. (2016) Digitale Revolution – eine neue Herausforderung für die Volkswirtschaftlichen Gesamtrechnungen? [Digital Revolution – A New Challenge for the Calculation of National Accounts?] *Wirtschaftsdienst*, 96(2), 135–139.

Heckscher, E. (1919) The Effect of Foreign Trade on the Distribution of Income. *Ekonomisk Tidskriff*, 497–512. Translated as Chapter 13 in American Economic Association (1949) *Readings in the Theory of International Trade*. Philadelphia: Blakiston, 272–300.

HSH Nordbank (2017) HSH Nordbank Economics & Research Calculations Based on CI Containerisation International; Container Trade Statistics; CCFI China Container Freight Index; US Bureau of Labor statistics.

IFPI (2017) Global Music Report 2017. Retrieved from: http://www.ifpi.org/downloads/GMR2017.pdf (accessed 2 July 2019).

Kommerskollegium (2016) *Trade Regulation in a 3D Printed World – A Primer*. Retrieved from: http://unctad.org/meetings/en/Contribution/dtl_eweek2016_Kommerskollegium_en.pdf (accessed 2 July 2019).

Mandel, M. (2012) Beyond Goods and Services: The Unmeasured Rise of the Data Driven Economy. *Policy Memo*. Retrieved from: http://www.progressivepolicy.org/wp-content/uploads/2012/10/10.2012-Mandel_Beyond-Goods-and-Services_The-Unmeasured-Rise-of-the-Data-Driven-Economy.pdf (accessed 2 July 2019).

Mandel, M. (2014) Data, Trade and Growth. *Policy Memo*. Retrieved from: http://www.progressivepolicy.org/wp-content/uploads/2014/04/2014.04-Mandel_Data-Trade-and-Growth.pdf (accessed 2 July 2019).

Mauldin, J. (2015) Weapons of Economic Misdirection. Retrieved from: https://www.mauldineconomics.com/frontlinethoughts/weapons-of-economic-misdirection (accessed 16 July 2019).

McDermott, C., Nagle, J., Horowitz, M. & Johnson, S. (2017) From Bills Of Lading To Blockchain Structures: Part 1. Retrieved from: https://www.law360.com/articles/952871/from-bills-of-lading-to-blockchain-structures-part-1 (accessed 2 July 2019).

McKinsey Global Institute (2016) Digital Globalization: The New Era of Global Flows. Retrieved from: http://www.mckinsey.com/business-functions/digital-mckinsey/our-insights/digital-globalization-the-new-era-of-global-flows (accessed 2 July 2019).

Michel, M. (2016) First Live Blockchain Trade Transaction Conducted. Retrieved from: https://www.gtreview.com/news/global/first-live-blockchain-trade-transaction-conducted/ (accessed 2 July 2019).

Moore, G.E. (1965) Cramming More Components onto Integrated Circuits. *Electronics*, 38(8), 114–117.

Nakamura, L.I., Samuels, J.D. & Soloveichik, R.H. (2016) Valuing "Free" Media in GDP: An Experimental Approach. *FRB of Philadelphia Working Paper* No. 16-24. Retrieved from: http://ssrn.com/abstract=2833772 (accessed 2 July 2019).

Nierhaus, W. (2007) Wirtschaftskonjunktur 2006: Prognose und Wirklichkeit [Economic Activity 2006: Forecasting and Reality]. *ifo Schnelldienst*, 60(2), 23–28.

Ohlin, B. (1933) *Interregional and International Trade*. Cambridge, MA: Harvard University Press.

Rifkin, J. (2014) *The Zero Marginal Cost Society: The Internet of Things, the Collaborative Commons, and the Eclipse of Capitalism*. Basingstoke: Palgrave Macmillan.

Shaheen, S. & Cohen, A. (2016) Innovative Mobility Carsharing Outlook: Carsharing Market Overview, Analysis, and Trends. Retrieved from: http://innovativemobility.org/wp-content/uploads/2016/02/Innovative-Mobility-Industry-Outlook_World-2016-Final.pdf (accessed 2 July 2019).

Shapiro, C. & Varian, H.R. (1998) *Information Rules: A Strategic Guide to the Network Economy*. Brighton: Harvard Business School Press.

Smith, A. (1776) *Wealth of Nations*. Book II. London: Methuen & Co.

Solow, R. (1987) We'd Better Watch Out. *New York Times Book Review*, 12 July.

Statista (2017a) Statista/Netflix Annual Reports. Retrieved from: http://www.statista.com (accessed 2 July 2019).

Statista (2017b) Statista/Gartner. Retrieved from: http://www.statista.com (accessed 2 July 2019).

Statistisches Bundesamt (2016) Bruttoinlandsprodukt (BIP) [Gross Domestic Product]. Retrieved from: https://www.destatis.de/DE/ZahlenFakten/GesamtwirtschaftUmwelt/VGR/Methoden/BIP.html (accessed 2 July 2019).

Stiglitz, J.E., Sen, A. & Fitoussi, J.-P. (2015) Report by the Commission on the Measurement of Economic Performance and Social Progress. Retrieved from: https://ec.europa.eu/eurostat/documents/118025/118123/Fitoussi+Commission+report (accessed 2 July 2019).

Thewissen, S., Roser, M. & Nolan, B. (2016) Household Income Growth Is Lagging Behind GDP Per Capita. This Is Why. Retrieved from: https://www.weforum.org/agenda/2016/08/household-income-growth-is-lagging-behind-gdp-per-capita-this-is-why (accessed 2 July 2019).

Triplett, J.E. (1999) The Solow Productivity Paradox: What Do Computers Do to Productivity? *The Canadian Journal of Economics,* Special Issue, 32(2), 309–334.

Twain, M. & Warner, C.D. (1873) *The Gilded Age: A Tale of Today*. Chicago: American Publishing.

UN Comtrade Database (2017) Comtrade. Retrieved from: https://comtrade.un.org/db/ (accessed 2 July 2019).

UNCTAD (2016) In Search of Cross-border E-commerce Trade Data. *Technical Note* No. 6. Retrieved from: http://unctad.org/en/PublicationsLibrary/tn_unctad_ict4d06_en.pdf (accessed 2 July 2019).

UNCTADstat (2017) UNCTAD Datacenter. Retrieved from: http://unctadstat.unctad.org/wds/ReportFolders/reportFolders.aspx?sCS_ChosenLang=en (accessed 2 July 2019).

Weser Kurier (2016) Der Tag, an dem die Blechkisten kamen [The Day When the Tin Boxes Arrived]. Retrieved from: https://www.weser-kurier.de/bremen/bremen-wirtschaft_artikel,-Der-Tag-an-dem-die-Blechkisten-kamen-_arid,1369473.html (accessed 2 July 2019).

Wikimedia Foundation (2017) Wikipedia Statistics. Retrieved from:_ https://stats.wikimedia.org/EN/TablesWikipediaEN.htm (accessed 2 July 2019).

Wild, J., Arnold, M. & Stafford, P. (2015) Technology: Banks Seek the Key to Blockchain. *Financial Times* (1 November). Retrieved from: https://www.ft.com/content/eb1f8256-7b4b-11e5-a1fe-567b37f80b64 (accessed 2 July 2019).

World Bank (2016) World Development Indicators Database. Retrieved from: https://databank.worldbank.org/reports.aspx?source=world-development-indicators (accessed 2 July 2019).

World Bank (2017a) Doing Business: Trading Across Borders. Retrieved from: http://www.doingbusiness.org/data/exploretopics/trading-across-borders (accessed 2 July 2019).

World Bank (2017b): Doing Business: Trading Across Borders Methodology. Retrieved from: http://www.doingbusiness.org/methodology/trading-across-borders (accessed 2 July 2019).

World Trade Organization (2016): World Trade Organization Database. Retrieved from: https://www.wto.org/english/tratop_e/serv_e/cbt_course_e/c1s3p1_e.htm (accessed 2 July 2019).

World Trade Organization (2017) Conference on the Use of Data in the Digital Economy, Geneva, 2–3 October 2017. Retrieved from: https://www.wto.org/english/res_e/reser_e/datadigitaleco17_e.htm (accessed 2 July 2019).

Zervas, G., Proserpio, D. & Byers, J.W. (2017) The Rise of the Sharing Economy: Estimating the Impact of Airbnb on the Hotel Industry. *Journal of Marketing Research*, 54(5), 687–705.

Chapter 4

Services Trade, Structural Transformation and the SDG 2030 Agenda

Mina Mashayekhi

Introduction

The long-term trends in many countries confirm the increased contribution of services to economies. This is reflected in the major contributions of the services sector to output, employment, trade and foreign direct investment (FDI). Between 1980 and 2015, the proportion of services in GDP increased for all categories of countries – from 61 to 76% in developed economies and from 42 to 55% in developing economies (Figure 4.1). In 2016, services were responsible for a 56% share of GDP in developing countries. Services are predominant in all developing regions, mainly in Latin America and the Caribbean (65% share of GDP).

This preponderance of services is true also for employment. In 2017, the services sector was estimated to account for more than half of global jobs (59%). As in output, the importance of services in employment is more pronounced in developed economies – where services jobs represent over 75% of the total – than in developing economies (54%). Services have been the main job provider since the mid-2000s, even during the 2008–2009 global economic and financial crisis. This role is particularly important as in 2017 the number of unemployed persons globally rose by 3.4 million with an additional 2.7 million expected in 2018. Employment in services is particularly relevant for women, as it is the services sector where women have the highest share of jobs globally and in developed countries. The participation of women in services jobs in developing economies is 51%, second only to the agriculture sector. In developed countries it is 89%. Services employment is also important for migrant workers as some host countries, such as Canada and the United States, rely heavily on migrants in their broad services sector (International Labour Organization [ILO], 2017).

The Handbook of Global Trade Policy, First Edition. Edited by Andreas Klasen.
© 2020 John Wiley & Sons Ltd. Published 2020 by John Wiley & Sons Ltd.

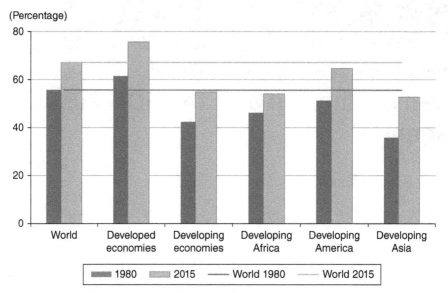

Figure 4.1   Share of services in GDP by income level and region, 1980 and 2015 (%).
Source: UNCTADStat (https://unctadstat.unctad.org/EN/).

Services as a Growing Part of the Economy

Between 2001 and 2017, construction, tourism and other business services were sectors whose importance for the global job market grew more annually, above 3%. The same occurred in developing economies, where these sectors had even higher annual growth of their employment share, above 4%. Although to a lesser extent, transport and financial services also had important annual growth of their employment share in the same period. The same trends were followed in Latin America and the Caribbean, although with lower growth rates than for the average of developing countries. Other business services account for the biggest employment share annual growth rate between 2001 and 2016, of 2.8% (Figure 4.2).

Services are also increasingly important for the creation of jobs related to global value chains (GVCs). Between 2000 and 2013, services accounted for the greatest part of new trade-related jobs in advanced economies and were the second-largest contributor, after manufacturing, to new trade-related jobs in emerging economies. Between 2000 and 2011, some services sectors revealed more potential to create trade-related jobs, namely business services, transport and communication in developed economies, and business services, hotels and restaurants in emerging economies. Data from 2014 revealed that although women account for large shares of employment in several services sectors, they represent a small share of employment in the sectors that create the most jobs linked to GVCs. The indirect effects of services exports were stronger in some sectors, with one job in tourism creating three jobs elsewhere, and in India one job in information technology creating four jobs elsewhere. Infrastructure services in particular are a key factor in creating supply and export capacity and taking advantage of employment benefits from trade (UNCTAD, 2016a).

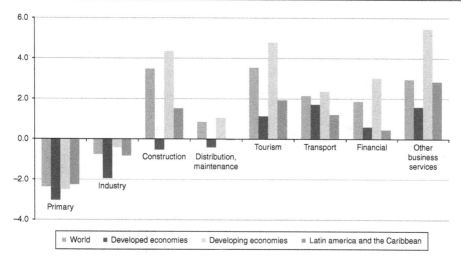

Figure 4.2   Annual change of employment distribution in selected sectors by income level, 2001–2016 (%).
Source: UNCTAD secretariat calculations, based on International Labour Organization (ILO) econometric models; UNCTAD (2017c).
Note: Estimates for 2014 and projections for 2015 and 2016.

Still, the services policy agenda needs to be mindful of employment risks related to services. Technology, infrastructure and knowledge-related services increase productivity and may cause job losses by automation. Notwithstanding, this is to a certain extent a job replacement since indirect effects have to be taken into account as there are job gains in technology-producing sectors and these might be more important (UNCTAD, 2017a). Trade in services contributes to the potential of the services sector in generating employment and inducing skills upgrading, although a set of policies needs to be in place to enable this role (UNCTAD, 2016b). In South America, trade liberalisation has prompted firms, especially exporting firms, to upgrade their technology and to increase the skill intensity of their workforce as exporters increased the share of high-skilled workers in their workforce (ILO and WTO, 2017). Nevertheless, trade creates jobs with a different skill set from jobs being replaced. With labour frictions, workers cannot easily move across sectors, and a net job loss may occur.

Overall services-related policies are relevant for inclusive employment, especially in a current context of persistent high unemployment where global unemployment is expected to rise in 2017 to just over 201 million people and vulnerable employment remains pervasive at 1.4 billion people worldwide (ILO, 2017). It is crucial to put a strong emphasis on skills development, not only because of their role in strengthening productive and export capacity, but also because appropriate skills development policies help workers who lose their jobs to make a smoother and faster transition to new jobs with equal or higher wages (ILO and WTO, 2017).

Services sector employment will be impacted by automation technologies, including AI and robotics, which may displace workers, depending on the pace of their development and adoption, economic growth and growth in demand for work in new occupations. Some occupations will decline and others will change. It is estimated that 60% of occupations have at least 30% of constituent work activities that

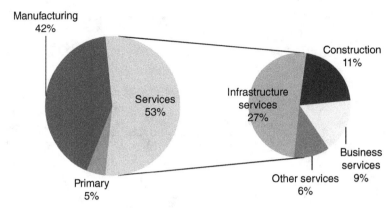

Figure 4.3   Sectoral distribution of announced greenfield foreign direct investment projects, 2015 (%).
Source: UNCTAD secretariat calculations, based on UNCTAD (2016c) annex tables.

could be automated and that by 2030, between 75 million and 375 million workers (3–14% of the global work force) will need to switch occupation. Half of all work activities have the technical potential to be automated by adapting current technologies. Rising incomes and consumption particularly in developing countries, health care for aging populations, infrastructure building, raising energy efficiency and climate adaptation, use of renewable energy, producing goods and services for the expanding consuming and middle classes, investing in technology, research and development, infrastructure and construction and other trends will create demand for work that could help offset the displacement of workers. In developing and emerging countries and China, middle wage occupations, particularly services, will see the most net job growth. These changes and the market needs will require new educational and workforce training and reskilling models and the strengthening of social safety nets and income support for workers impacted by automation (McKinsey Global Institute, 2017)

Services are also prevalent in FDI, with announced greenfield investment in the last ten years mainly concentrated in the services sector. On average about 40–50% of greenfield investment announcements and cross-border mergers and acquisitions are labelled as projects in services. In 2017, services received 50% of investment. FDI in services has grown 6% annually between 2005 and 2015, faster than investments in the primary and manufacturing sectors. Investment in the infrastructure services sector (ISS) has grown even faster in the same period – 7% annually – and accounted in 2015 for more than half of announced greenfield investment in services. Construction and business services also received important shares of FDI in services (Figure 4.3). By 2015, about two thirds of global FDI stock was concentrated in the services sector, in line with its share in the global economy.

Trends in Trade in Services

Services trade has become a vibrant component of world trade, and developing countries have increased their participation in this trade. In 2017 world commercial services exports increased by 7% to US$5.25 trillion following two years of weak to negative

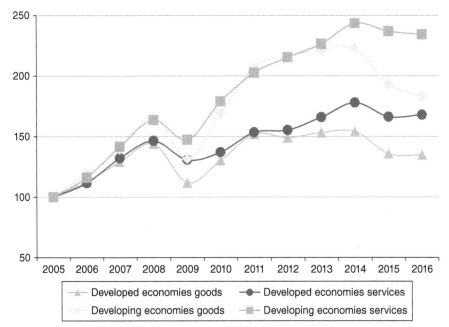

Figure 4.4   Growth of goods and services exports by income level, 2005–2016 (index: 2005=100).
Source: UNCTADstat (https://unctadstat.unctad.org/EN/); UNCTAD (2017c).

growth. Transport services grew faster than the world average, at 8%. Goods-related services had the weakest growth, with a 5% increase. Between 2005 and 2017, the share of services exports in the total exports of goods and services increased from 24 to 28% in developed economies and from 14 to 17% in developing economies (Figure 4.4). In this period, services exports had an annual growth of 5% in developed economies and 8% in developing economies, higher than the annual growth of goods exports for both income levels. In addition, services exports have been more resilient than goods exports. Globally, services exports decreased 11% in 2009, in the global economic and financial crisis, and 6% in 2015, in the trade downturn, much less than goods exports, which have decreased 22% in 2009 and 13% in 2015. Global services exports have resumed growth in 2016, in opposition to goods exports. In developing countries, services exports decreased 3% in 2015 while goods exports decreased 13% (Figure 4.4).

Trade in services has a direct contribution for development, with services exports growing faster in developing economies than in developed economies. Between 2005 and 2017, the fastest growth of services exports in developing countries was associated with the share of developing economies in global services exports growing from 23 to 30%. Developing countries experienced much lower declines in services trade than in goods trade, both in the global economic and financial crisis and in the 2015 trade downturn (Figure 4.5).

In 2017, the world's five largest exporters and importers were mainly developed economies: the United States with 14.5% of global exports of services; the United Kingdom with 6.7%; Germany with 5.6%; France with 4.7%; and China with 4.3%. These countries were also the main importers in the same year. Their share of

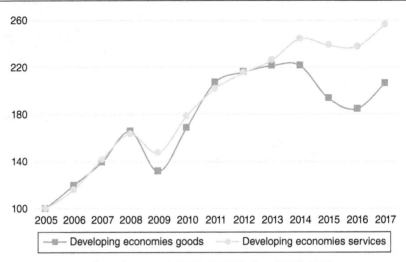

Figure 4.5 Services and goods exports, 2005–2017 (index: 2005=100).
Source: UNCTAD secretariat calculations based on UNCTADstat (https://unctadstat.unctad.org/EN/); UNCTAD (2017c).

Table 4.1 Main exporters and importers of services, 2016 (US$ million and %)

Main services exporters	Value of services exports	Share of global services exports	Main services importers	Value of services imports	Share of global services imports
United States	752 411	15.6	United States	503 053	10.7
United Kingdom	327 176	6.8	China	453 014	9.6
Germany	272 738	5.6	Germany	312 074	6.6
France	236 760	4.9	France	235 679	5.0
China	208 488	4.3	United Kingdom	198 653	4.2
Netherlands	179 776	3.7	Ireland	191 939	4.1
Japan	173 821	3.6	Japan	184 710	3.9
India	161 845	3.3	Netherlands	169 458	3.6
Singapore	149 642	3.1	Singapore	155 581	3.3
Ireland	146 678	3.0	India	133 710	2.8
Total	2 609 334	53.9	Total	2 537 870	53.9

Source: UNCTADstat (https://unctadstat.unctad.org/EN/); UNCTAD (2017c).

global services exports has gone down since 2016. The first ten exporters account for more than 50% of global services exports and the same occurs with the first ten importers, revealing heterogeneity in the participation of developed and developing economies in trade in services (Table 4.1).

The export data disaggregated by services category reveals that between 2005 and 2017 exports in developing countries were growing more strongly in telecommunications, computer and information services (with a 12% annual growth rate), financial services (11%) and other business services (9%) (Figure 4.6). This has contributed

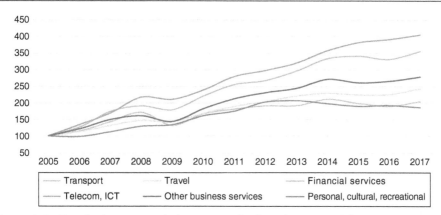

Figure 4.6 Developing economies' exports of selected commercial services categories, 2005–2017 (index: 2005=100).
Source: UNCTAD secretariat calculations based on UNCTADstat (https://unctadstat.unctad.org/EN/); UNCTAD (2017c).

to the reduction of the gap between trade in services' profiles of developed and developing countries and achieving the Sustainable Development Goals (SDGs).

Nevertheless, the sectoral distribution of commercial services exports in 2017 confirms that developed and developing economies still have different trade profiles. Although transport, travel and other business services are the largest categories for all types of economies, the share of transition and developing economies in transport and travel services continues to be higher – 58 and 55% of their total commercial services exports. This is more important in Africa and in least developed countries (LDCs), where transport and travel represent 71 and 76%, respectively, of their total commercial services exports (Table 4.2).

The revealed comparative advantages (RCAs) of developing countries are in transport, travel and construction services (Figure 4.7). In contrast, developed economies continue to be more specialised in higher value-added services categories, such as financial services and charges for the use of intellectual property.

It should be noted that there is also inequality in the services sector among developing countries and regions. Asia registered the fastest growth in services exports between 2005 and 2017, and Africa the slowest growth. In 2017, developing Asia accounted for 24% of global services exports, much above the 3.5% share of Latin America and the Caribbean. Africa has 2% share, and the LDCs, despite a strong growth in the services sector, have started from a low base and still account for less than 1% of global services exports. In Latin America and the Caribbean, between 2008 and 2017, exports were growing more in telecommunications, computer and information services, followed by travel and other business services (Figure 4.8). Still, this region has a lower focus than developing Asia on exports of higher value-added services categories, such as financial services; telecommunications, computer and information services; and other business services (Table 4.2). These developments underscore the importance of the contribution of services for the achievement of target 17.11 of SDGs, which calls for the increase in exports of developing countries and LDCs.

In line with developed and transition economies, the Russian Federation underwent a change in its economic structure between 1992 and 2015. It had a 12%

Table 4.2 Commercial services exports by region, income level and category, 2017 (%)

Services categories	Developed economies	Transition economies	Developing economies	Developing Africa	Developing America	Developing Asia	LDCs
Goods-related	3.5	6.3	3.5	2.2	2.2	3.8	1.7
Transport	16.0	34.4	21.2	27.9	16.0	21.4	22.5
Travel	21.4	23.7	33.9	43.3	48.2	31.0	53.0
Construction	1.3	5.8	3.1	2.1	0.1	3.7	1.8
Financial services	13.4	1.9	6.6	3.8	5.7	6.9	2.4
Intellectual property	9.6	0.9	1.7	0.3	0.7	2.0	0.3
Telecom, computer and information	10.4	10.0	9.2	6.1	4.7	10.1	7.8
Other business services	23.3	16.2	19.9	13.7	20.0	20.5	10.0
Personal, cultural and recreational	1.0	0.8	0.8	0.7	2.3	0.6	0.5
Total	100.0	100.0	100.0	100.0	100.0	100.0	100.0

Source: UNCTAD secretariat calculations based on UNCTADStat (https://unctadstat.unctad.org/EN/); UNCTAD (2017c).

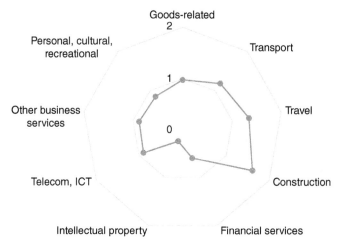

Figure 4.7 Developing economies' RCAs in services, 2017 (index: RCA > 1).
Source: UNCTAD secretariat calculations based on UNCTADstat (https://unctadstat.unctad.
org/EN/); UNCTAD (2017c).

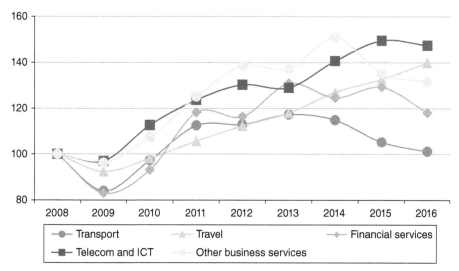

Figure 4.8 Developing America: exports of selected commercial services, 2008–2016
(index: 2008=100).
Source: UNCTADstat (https://unctadstat.unctad.org/EN/); UNCTAD (2017c).
Note: Other business services covers miscellaneous business, professional and technical services.

increase in the contribution of services to national GDP, which reached 64% in
2015. This corresponds largely to a 10% drop in industry's contribution to national
GDP, which fell to 32% in 2015 (see Figure 4.9).

The Russian Federation followed the global trend between 2005 and 2016, which
was also the trend in transition economies, where trade in services has been more resilient
than trade in goods. In 2015, during the trade downturn, trade in services fell 21% in the
Russian Federation against a 31% drop in trade in goods. In 2016, trade in services stabilised with a slight decrease of 2% against a new plunge of 17% of trade in goods. Most

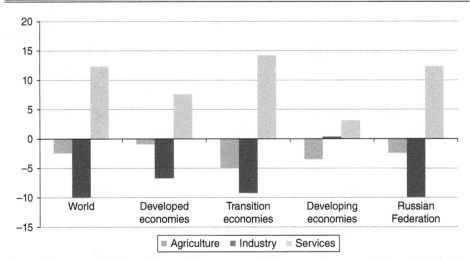

Figure 4.9 Contribution of economic sectors to GDP, change between 1992 and 2015 (%).
Source: UNCTADstat (https://unctadstat.unctad.org/EN/); UNCTAD (2017c).

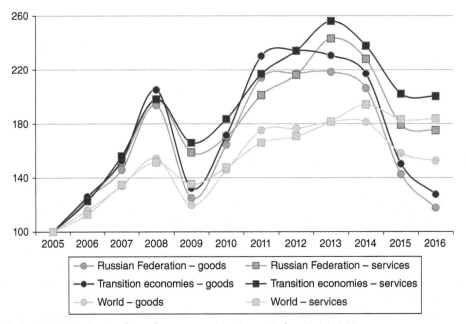

Figure 4.10 Services and goods exports, 2005–2016 (index: 2005=100).
Source: UNCTADstat (https://unctadstat.unctad.org/EN/); UNCTAD (2017c).

notably, between 2005 and 2016, trade in services in the Russian Federation has grown 5% annually, faster than trade in goods, which grew 1% annually (see Figure 4.10).

In the Russian Federation, between 2005 and 2016, the fastest growing categories of trade in services were telecommunications and ICT services (13% annual growth), personal, cultural and recreational services and financial services (both with 8%), other business services and charges for use of intellectual property (both with 7%) (see Figure 4.11).

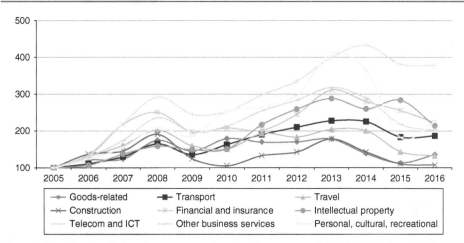

Figure 4.11   Russian Federation: exports of services by category, 2005–2016 (index: 2005=100). Source: UNCTADstat (https://unctadstat.unctad.org/EN/); UNCTAD (2017c).

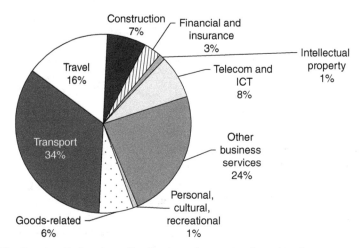

Figure 4.12   Russian Federation: distribution of exports of services by category, 2016 (%). Source: UNCTADstat (https://unctadstat.unctad.org/EN/); UNCTAD (2017c).

Some of these fastest growing categories are important because they entail activities with higher value added. This is the case of telecommunications and ICT, financial services and other business services. Furthermore, some of the fastest growing categories correspond to categories that have relevant contributions to national services exports in 2016. These include other business services (24% of national exports of services), telecommunications and ICT (8%) and construction (7%). Still, the services categories that contributed the most to national exports of services were transport (34%) and travel (16%) (see Figure 4.12).

This is reflected in the analysis of RCAs for categories of services exports. In 2016, the Russian Federation had RCAs in construction (3.9), transport (1.9) and other business services (1.0). These RCAs already existed in 2005, at the same level in other business services, a higher level in construction and a lower level in transport (see Figure 4.13).

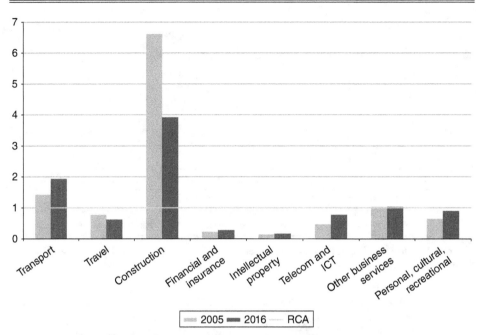

Figure 4.13 Russian Federation: RCAs in services by category, 2005 and 2016.
Source: UNCTADstat (https://unctadstat.unctad.org/EN/); UNCTAD (2017c).

Revealed Dimension of Trade in Services

Current balance of payments-related statistics capture only a part of services trade and do not reflect its full importance. Most importantly, there are data gaps and challenges related to some modes of services trade. Cross-border services trade data captures only a part of services trade, as services trade increasingly occurs with commercial presence (mode 3) and with the temporary movement of natural persons (mode 4). Nevertheless, while international transactions can sometimes be allocated to a single mode, a single transaction can also be composed of several modes. For example, architectural services may include mode 1 – delivery of design by email – and mode 4 if occasional visits to the clients' location are required.

Commercial presence is the most important mode of supply of services, as can be inferred from the ever-growing sales by foreign affiliates. If assumed that it also derives from its services component, the amount reached US$30 trillion in 2017, a 6% increase from 2016 but a decrease from US$37 trillion in 2015 (UNCTAD, 2016c). In 2013, 69% of services exports in the European Union were through mode 3. The temporary movement of people supplying services is particularly important in professional and business services, as well as in services related to agriculture, manufacturing and mining. Taking into account the sizeable amounts of remittances, mode 4 of supplying services is of substantial importance for developing countries. In 2018, worldwide remittance flows were US$689 billion, with US$529 billion flowing to developing countries (World Bank, 2019). In 2019 remittances are expected to grow by 3.5% and global remittances by 3.4%. In 2018 global remittances grew by 9%. The largest recipients of remittances include India (US$79 billion), China (US$67 billion), the Philippines (US$34 billion), Mexico (US$36 billion) and Egypt (US$29 billion). The global average cost of sending US$200 remittances remained stagnant at 7.2% in the third quarter of 2017, significantly higher than the SDG Goal target of 3%. In Sub-Saharan Africa it remained high, at 9.1%. The average costs of sending remittances to South Asia was the lowest, at 5%. The relevance of migration for the services sector is also underscored by the fact that around 71% of migrant workers are concentrated on services.

In addition to the direct effects of services on output, employment, FDI and trade, the services sector – and most notably the ISS – can provide intermediate inputs to all economic activities, including agriculture and manufacturing. Furthermore, services are bundled with goods, for example with manufacturing firms that also provide the distribution services or with the machinery industry where maintenance, repair and installation can be indispensable services to be sold with the good. These indirect effects of services imply that there is services value added included in output and exports in all economic sectors – the forward linkages of services. The significant differences between direct services exports and services' value added in exports from all sectors are also not captured in cross-border services trade data. This draws attention to the need to work across boundaries and overcome the silos between goods and services trade-related data and policymaking.

In addition to this, neither cross-border services trade data nor analyses of value added in gross exports capture the increasing importance of services activities within manufacturing companies. To add more value and innovation-related content to their products, to promote client relationships and to keep strategic business functions in-house, firms develop services activities themselves rather than outsourcing. Services inputs accounted for an estimated 37% of the value of manufacturing exports, but by adding services activities within manufacturing firms, that share increased to 53% and the contribution of services to overall exports was close to two thirds (Miroudot and Cadestin, 2017). This reveals the increased tradability of services, especially when they can be bundled with tradeable products.

More fundamentally, the intangible nature of services and services trade raises a particular challenge for data registry and collection. Moreover, services trade data is often not fully available for all countries. Despite important advances, there is still a lack of information regarding partner country data for services trade between developing countries, and data often lacks the level of disaggregation necessary for informed policymaking. Institutional challenges often arise because a broad array of institutions are usually involved in services trade in all four modes of supply, including national statistical office, tax authorities and social security agencies. This implies that the provision of valid statistics requires institutional cooperation. Harvesting this potential requires high-quality, reliable, timely, comprehensive and sufficiently disaggregated data on services trade flows to facilitate specific evidence-based policy-oriented actions. A focus on data is a required strategy to develop the right policies for the right services-led structural transformation It is relevant to have information on the sector, mode of supply and trade partner at transactional level (Box 4.1). The availability of data is a key element for measuring the achievement of SDGs.

Services, SDGs and Structural Transformation

Given the multifaceted contribution of services to the overall economy, poverty reduction and employment, there is a real opportunity for exploring a services-driven growth and development strategy. Indeed, achieving many of the goals and targets

Box 4.1   Siscoserv.

In Brazil, the Integrated System of Foreign Trade in Services and Intangibles (SISCOSERV) is a key tool for services classification, data collection and policy action. The system covers all services transactions between residents and non-residents and data collection encompasses the 4 modes of trade in services, with national and subnational levels of information. The effectiveness of SISCOSERV relies on assigning a high priority and political support to data availability and quality, mandatory reporting from economic agents associated to a strong institutional support, and in the country's experience in e-government and e-platforms. The implementation process also included training and awareness-raising initiatives focused on the private sector (Mashayekhi and Antunes, 2018). Released information includes all exports and imports of services and intangibles in multiple languages, including bilateral services trade profiles and an overview aiming to provide greater economic visibility to the services sector.

SISCOSERV helped different Brazilian authorities to identify services' export potential, supported market intelligence and trade promotion, enabled other public policies in favour of services exports and provided inputs for trade negotiations. Together with information disaggregated by mode of supply, which unveils business models adopted by companies, this contributes to international negotiations of trade in services, to government procurement in services and e-commerce agreements and to the management and monitoring of public policies. Information is shared between the Brazilian Revenue Agency and other supervisory bodies in operations against money laundering. Based on data from the system, specific statistics have been developed to support business strategies from services sectors, and a public–private initiative ("Services Export Leverage Forum") was launched to increase competitiveness through the identification of relevant measures that can be taken by both public and private actors to increase services exports.

under SDGs implicitly and explicitly relies on the universal access to basic and infrastructure services, which renders the 2030 Agenda for Sustainable Development essentially a services agenda. Many services activities with important social functions – health, financial, energy, transport and telecommunications – remain indispensable for the achievement of the SDGs. Essential and infrastructure services can make significant contributions to Goal 1 on ending poverty; Goal 2 on ending hunger; Goal 3 on health; Goal 4 on education; Goal 5 on gender equality (e.g. though financial inclusion); Goal 6 on water and sanitation; Goal 7 on energy; Goal 8 on economic growth and decent work; Goal 9 on infrastructure development, including financial services, telecommunications and information and communication technology (ICT) services; Goal 10 on reducing inequalities; Goal 11 on human settlement (transport services); and Goal 17 on means of implementation (e.g. ICT services).

The provision of intermediate inputs by the services sector facilitates productive and export processes to move forward in obtaining final or other intermediate products. This central role of services can be observed in all stages of productive processes, mainly in back-office – e.g. business services – and production stages – e.g. quality control, engineering services, security services – but also in establishment, pre-production, post-production and after-sales stages (Asia Global Institute, 2015).

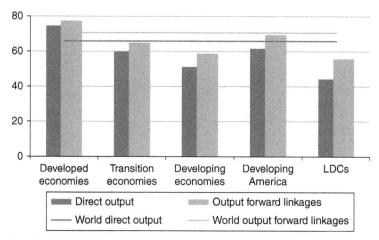

Figure 4.14   Share of services in total direct output and in total forward linkages in output by income level, 2011 (%).
Source: UNCTAD calculations based on the World Bank's Export Value Added Database (EVAD; https://datacatalog.worldbank.org/dataset/export-value-added-database).

Services also have an important role in creating linkages and coordination throughout production processes, providing the means for different activities to interact. This role can be easily found in infrastructure services, for example in telecommunication services that allow for cooperation between different activities and participants in the production process. It can also be identified in knowledge and technology-based services that have an intermediation function facilitating specialisation.

The services' value added incorporated in output and exports in all economic sectors reveals the real importance of the services sector for the economy at large and for development. While in 2011 services' direct output accounted for 74% of total output in developed economies and 51% in developing economies, services represented 77% of the value added in total output in developed economies and 59% in developing economies. In Latin America and the Caribbean, while services' direct output represented 62% of total output, services' value added accounted for 69% of the value added in total output (Figure 4.14). This value added in total output represents the forward linkages of services in output and the "servicification" of economies at all income levels.

As mentioned, direct exports of services in 2011 accounted for 25% of total exports in goods and service in developed economies and 14% in developing economies. Still, services represented 44% of the value added in total exports in developed economies and 32% in developing economies. In Latin America and the Caribbean, while direct exports of services represented 12% of total exports, services' value added accounted for 32% of the value added in total exports, an enormous difference of crucial importance for policymaking (Figure 4.15). The export of this services' value added within products of all economic sectors is referred to as "mode 5" of supply of services and is the reflection of servicification in international trade (Cernat and Kutlina-Dimitrova, 2014). The substantial differences between direct exports of services and of services' value added in exports from all sectors reveals the importance of services for improving export capacity. This mode 5 also

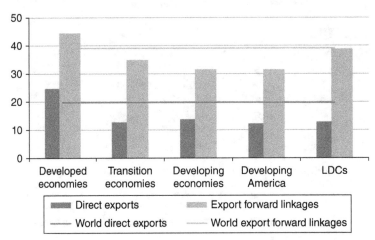

Figure 4.15 Share of services in total direct exports and in total forward linkages in exports by income level, 2011 (%).
Source: UNCTAD calculations based on EVAD (https://datacatalog.worldbank.org/dataset/export-value-added-database); UNCTAD (2017c).

confirms the increased tradability of services, especially when they are associated with inherently tradable goods and services. Global GDP gains from liberalising mode 5 services at a multilateral level could reach up to €300 billion by 2025 and world trade could increase by over €500 billion (Antimiani and Cernat, 2017).

These effects can induce efficiency and effectiveness and the reduction of productive and trade barriers and costs, and thereby contribute to more productivity and increased productive and export capacity. Opportunities may emerge for economic agents to join value chains supporting exports, including in some cases for micro, small and medium enterprises (MSMEs) (Box 4.2). Still, the participation in GVCs alone does not guarantee relevant development gains. In the apparel industry in the United States, 70% of the final retail price remains in the country, although as many as 56 different countries or regions contribute to this value chain. This is because high value-added services activities, such as design, distribution and marketing, continue to be concentrated in the United States (Durkin, 2017). On a different scale, similar examples of heterogeneity can be found in regional value chains. China and India have a preponderant role in value chains, with the foreign content of their exports amounting to 32 and 24%, respectively, of their gross exports.

By increasing productivity and productive and export capacity, services change relative prices in the sectors to which they contribute, thus impacting production, employment, investment, trade and consumption decisions related to those sectors. This creates services-led changes in the economic structure, where some sectors become more important by building on support from the services sector. The structural changes that derive from services may favour sectors which tend to have higher productivity, be more technological intensive or have more upgrading potential, leading to a services-led growth. The impacts that services can have on a positive structural transformation – through the diversification of production, development of new productive capacities and upgrading – expands the debate on development options (Jouanjean *et al.*, 2015). Services should no longer be considered

Box 4.2   Services and MSMEs.

MSMEs are important for development as they represent a meaningful share of the number of firms (95%), output (50%) and employment (60%), are sources of innovation and provide more opportunities for women and youth to participate in and contribute to economic growth (WTO, 2015). This importance is met by the challenges MSMEs face, such as the productivity gap between them and larger firms, wider in developing economies. The participation of MSMEs in international trade is minimal and focuses on low value-added production. Trade costs are higher for MSMEs due to lack of scale, including for example in access to information, financing and compliance with requirements. By providing inputs and linkages throughout production processes, services can improve their productivity, reduce trade barriers and costs and allow for their diversification and upgrading. Infrastructure services are particularly critical for MSMEs. For example, financial services are mentioned in both targets of SDGs that refer to MSMEs (8.3 and 9.3), and telecom and ICT services promote MSMEs' inclusion, inter alia, through digital financial services and e-commerce.

Services activities are also more amenable for MSMEs' participation in the economy and trade. Services activities are less dependent on economies of scale and are often less capital-intensive and more focused on other production factors. This democratisation of the economy by the services sector is also expanded as services can be providers of atomised inputs for different stages of broader productive processes. MSMEs can concentrate on producing such atomised services' inputs rather than face the challenge of producing the whole final product. The integration of services in broader productive processes and value chains also means that some costs are, to some extent, distributed by the several participants, such as reputational costs, costs of capital and costs of technology transfer. This facilitated participation can provide the incentives for the formalisation of many MSMEs and for informal workers to enter formal labour markets. This is also very important for development, as revealed by the increasing formalisation of the Brazilian economy since 2000, which appears to enhance growth, whereas in India the increase in informality reduces growth (de Vries *et al.*, 2012).

This also applies to MSMEs using online marketplaces to engage in e-commerce. In China, the e-commerce company Alibaba established a diverse ecosystem to enable trade through a network of services including its own e-payment system, which soon expanded to banking, investment and a clearing house for cross-border trade. SMEs account for a larger share of businesses trading through Alibaba than in non-ICT-enabled markets. Furthermore, Chinese companies trading through Alibaba can reach up to 98 export destinations, almost double that in non-ICT-enabled markets (Mashayekhi *et al.*, 2017).

These positive linkages need to be enabled by an environment which includes a developmental state that assigns adequate priority and mainstreams MSMEs' issues into national development policies, recognising their specificities; promotes coherence, institutional coordination and multi-stakeholder partnerships and MSMEs' association; and promotes skills upgrading and technology adoption in MSMEs to build their supply capacity. Trade policies need to address barriers, promoting trade facilitation in services; improve access to information, for example by domestic regulation and transparency provisions; and negotiate flexibilities for MSMEs. International cooperation is also relevant to build productive capacity in MSMEs, for instance by improving access to finance through Aid for Trade and the Enhanced Integrated Framework.

as a mere alternative in the absence of industrialisation or a tactic to improve export revenues, but as a transformative strategy for development which can also promote industrialisation.

The linkages between services and changes in the economic structure are very important for development, as was evidenced by structural changes from low- to high-productivity sectors in Asia leading to growth since 1990. Conversely, in Africa and in Latin America and the Caribbean structural changes had a different pattern, with workers displaced to lower-productivity activities including in services and the informal sector, and led to reduced growth. The challenge for Latin American countries is complex. On the one hand, they are more industrialised than countries in Africa, and openness has allowed industrial upgrading and increased efficiency. On the other hand, countries in Latin America were also more affected by globalisation, including by a contraction in the manufacturing sector, partly a result of China's increasing role in global manufacturing. This contraction forced a reallocation of resources across sectors, and globalisation has brought uneven outcomes in this regard (McMillan *et al.*, 2014). Therefore, the services sector is more likely to assume a supporting role in accelerating structural transformation in countries that have a dynamic manufacturing industry with fast productivity and income growth (UNCTAD, 2016b). For example, no less than one third of aggregate productivity growth is associated with the performance of the services sector in countries where manufacturing has grown rapidly, such as in Vietnam (Mendez-Parra, 2017).

In 2011, services' value added represented 23% of agricultural output in developed economies and 9% in developing economies, as measured by the sector's backward linkages. This can be even more meaningful in several manufacturing sectors. In textiles, for example, services' value added accounted for 27% of sectoral output in both developed and developing economies (Figure 4.16). Developing countries incorporate less services' value added than developed countries in many sectors, and are lagging behind in using the potential of services, particularly in agriculture

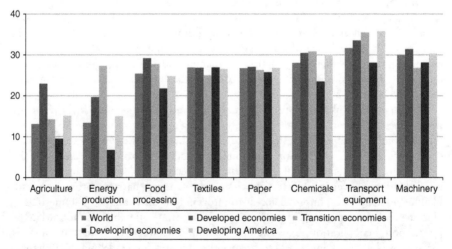

Figure 4.16 Participation of services in total backward linkages in output of selected sectors by income level, 2011 (%).
Source: UNCTAD calculations based on EVAD (https://datacatalog.worldbank.org/dataset/export-value-added-database); UNCTAD (2017c).

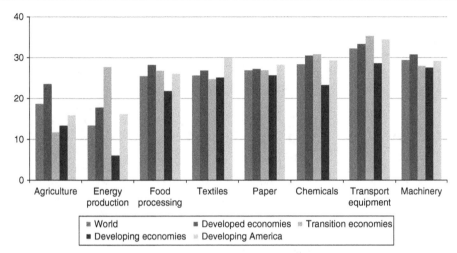

Figure 4.17 Participation of services in total backward linkages in exports of selected sectors by income level, 2011 (%).
Source: UNCTAD calculations based on EVAD (https://datacatalog.worldbank.org/dataset/export-value-added-database); UNCTAD (2017c).

and energy production. In Latin America and the Caribbean, most sectors incorporate more services' value added than in the developing countries' average. For instance, the value added of services represented 15% of agricultural output in this region. A similar scenario can be observed in exports. In 2011, services' value added represented 24% of agricultural exports in developed economies and 13% in developing economies. In textiles, services' value added accounted for 27% of sectoral exports in developed economies and 25% in developing economies. In Latin America and the Caribbean, sectoral exports incorporate more services' value added than in the developing countries' average. For example, the value added of services represented 16% of agricultural exports and 30% of textile exports in this region (Figure 4.17).

The services sectors that contributed more than others in 2011 to the world's total export value added are distribution (7%), transport (7%), financial and insurance services (5%) and ICT services (13%). Other business services are also key providers of inputs to all industrial sectors, and play an important role in sustaining innovation as they include knowledge-intensive activities such as professional services (Evangelista *et al.*, 2015). While transition and developing economies tend to incorporate more value added of distribution and transport services in total exports, developed economies use more value added of financial and insurance services and much more value added of ICT services. Developed economies embedded 18% of ICT services' value added in total exports, while transition and developing economies only incorporated 6 and 7% respectively (Figure 4.18). This is consistent with the analyses of direct exports (Table 4.2) and confirms the importance of ICT services to enable trade. The digital economy had a higher role in facilitating exports in Latin America and the Caribbean than in the average of developing countries, as 9% of ICT services' value added was embedded in total exports of the region, above the developing countries' average (Buiatti *et al.*, 2017).

Developed economies are more advanced in the use of ICT services' value added in agriculture and manufacturing exports than transition and developing economies.

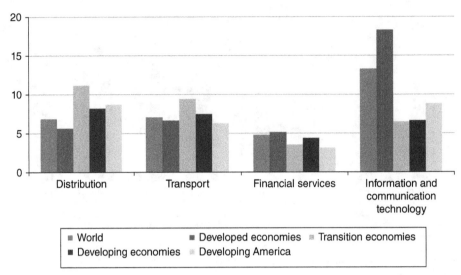

Figure 4.18   Share of selected services sectors in total forward linkages in exports by income level, 2011 (%).
Source: UNCTAD calculations based on EVAD (https://datacatalog.worldbank.org/dataset/export-value-added-database); UNCTAD (2017c).

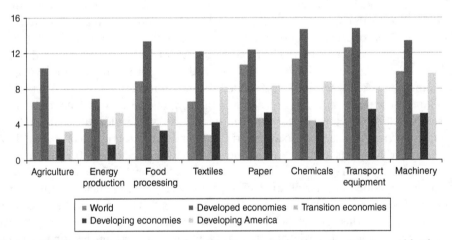

Figure 4.19   Share of information and communication technology services in total backward linkages in exports of selected sectors by income level, 2011 (%).
Source: UNCTAD calculations based on EVAD (https://datacatalog.worldbank.org/dataset/export-value-added-database); UNCTAD (2017c).

In 2011, agricultural exports incorporated 10% of ICT services' value added in developed economies, as compared to only 2% in both transition and developing economies. In Latin America and the Caribbean, agricultural exports incorporated 3% of ICT services' value added. As an example in manufacturing, in the same year exports of transport equipment incorporated 15% of ICT services' value added in developed economies, 7% in transition economies and 6% in developing economies. In Latin America and the Caribbean, ICT services' value added in exports of transport equipment was 8% (Figure 4.19). ICT services are also relevant to improved performance of services activities. ICT diffusion, among other factors, is especially associated with higher productivity of wholesale, retail and business services, and these are the sectors responsible for most of the lack of catch-up in labour productivity between Europe and the United States.

Policies and Regulation for Services-Led Structural Transformation

An ecosystem of enabling policies and regulations is required for the improvement of services performance and the promotion of a resulting economic transformation that favours sectors with higher productivity and value added. Market failures require economic regulation and thus the quality of policies and regulations is a key determinant of services performance (UNCTAD, 2018). Harnessing the potential benefits of trade and services for structural transformation requires sound, evidence-based policy, along with regulatory and institutional frameworks adapted to local conditions and introduced gradually. These are key components of services policy and are necessary to addressing domestic supply-side constraints, externalities and coordination issues in services, particularly infrastructure services; minimising inadvertent trade-restrictive effects; and determining services performance. They are especially important in ensuring efficient and competitive markets and available, affordable, convenient, equitable and quality infrastructure services (UNCTAD, 2012a). The effectiveness of such frameworks relies on achieving the necessary coherence between several policy areas, as well as between these areas and trade liberalisation. Elements of possible policy mixes and options in support of services sector development may be found in existing literature and national experiences and UNCTAD Services Policy Reviews (SPRs) (UNCTAD, 2012a)

In Africa, services provide inputs to exports related to agriculture, energy and manufacturing. Access to low-cost, high-quality services helps countries participate in local, regional and global value chains and to achieve social development objectives. This requires services trade policies, such as for adequate levels of openness and regulation. Successful structural transformation in rural areas requires investment incentives, productivity growth and risk management. Policy priorities may therefore include investment in deficient physical and institutional infrastructure, such as roads and electricity and telephone and internet access, as well as financial and agricultural extension services, with a focus on science, technology and innovation services to ensure the sustainability of growth decoupled from exhaustible natural resources (UNCTAD, 2012b). It is also necessary to encourage the emergence of rural financial institutions and products to help farmers and traders manage risk more efficiently, as financial market failures in rural areas generate problematic resource allocation patterns that perpetuate low productivity and ultra-poverty (World Bank, 2017). For example, Kenya's relative success in including services in a transformation strategy comprises the Vision 2030 strategy which contains clear objectives for tourism, retail trade, business process outsourcing and financial services sectors (Jouanjean *et al.*, 2015). Success factors also include determined public and private efforts in ICT-enabled services, significant public investments in ICT infrastructure and strong regulation, for instance for financial services.

In Asia, the services sector has been given particular attention given its linkages with a competitive manufacturing sector, as illustrated by the experience of China and India. In China, the process of economic transformation has had several industrial upgrade phases, which culminated after the country's accession to the World Trade Organization (WTO). The Government opted to mobilise limited resources to build special economic zones and industrial parks in which it provided competitive infrastructure and business environments. More general economy-wide reforms were introduced at a more gradual pace (Lin and Wang, 2014). In 2013, the pilot free trade zone in Shanghai deployed several reform measures to further improve the business environment and open up investments. A negative list for foreign investment was initiated in 2016 to test opening policies, comprised of 122 items, which will be shortened, following which the Shanghai free trade zone model will be expanded across China. The economy of India is mainly services intensive; 55% of economic activities are services intensive. While services and agriculture appear to have little interdependence, industry is also highly services intensive; 70% of its activities are related to services. The services sector is more growth-inducing than agriculture or industry, but this potential requires growth impulses from all sectors (Hansda, 2005).

In Latin America and the Caribbean more attention is being given to the services sector. For example, services in Brazil account for a significant part of the economy, including two fifths of the manufacturing value added, and have had important growth. Still, their productivity lags behind other sectors and they underperform in international markets, remaining focused on the domestic market. This derives from severe deficiencies in infrastructure, with transport, logistics and credit representing an important part of manufacturing costs. A stable and simplified policy and regulatory framework is also necessary to strengthen services and improve their contributions to the rest of the economy. Furthermore, there are inadequate competitive pressures for services and in several areas there are more restrictions towards foreign services providers than in other Latin American countries. The Brazilian government has undertaken several initiatives to open the market, some of them under discussion and others already launched. Foreign entry in tandem with a strong and supportive regulatory framework, public–private partnerships and evidence-based policymaking enabled by SISCOSERV will help to attract further investment and trade, providing competitive pressure, lowering production costs and increasing productivity in services activities and downstream in the whole economy. In Brazil, half of services imports are services offshored in relation to export contracts, confirming the importance of foreign providers for export capacity (OECD, 2016).

In Costa Rica, where exports of business services and ICT-related services are important, a strategy was devised to generate human capital aiming to allow exporters of these services to upgrade into higher value-added segments of the value chain. The strategy comprises providing vocational training, encouraging technical workers to pursue further education with time off for study and the reimbursement of university fees. Firms work with universities to design curricula to ensure that these address the needs of the sector. To improve English skills, the government has established bilingual public high schools, established the National English Plan aiming to provide intermediate or advanced level of English to high school graduates, and launched the Costa Rica Multilingüe – a not-for-profit organisation to improve communication skills for older people (Hernández et al., 2014).

Some cross-cutting lessons for effective regulatory and institutional frameworks are detailed in the following paragraphs (UNCTAD, 2015b). The horizontal and vertical coordination of sectoral policy initiatives is important in formulating a coherent overall national strategy for services sector development. The use of a single policy document for the services agenda favours the achievement of a coherent out-come. Services development strategies also need to be consistent with trade, investment, competition, industrial, macroeconomic and social policies. This is facil-itated by a multi-stakeholder approach to policymaking involving the private sector, such as coalitions of services industries. Regulatory design, which ensures policy objectives and avoids unnecessary restrictions, is a major component of ensuring coherence.

Sound institutions and good governance are also required so that through cross-ministerial and multi-stakeholder coordination, strategic objectives, priorities and strategies can be defined and resources – human, financial and other – allocated. To be effective, an inter-institutional coordination mechanism would need to enjoy endorse-ment at a high political level and be institutionalised with the requisite legal man-date, resources and capabilities. This presumes effective institutional capabilities and requires capacity-building support. In Peru, setting up an inter-institutional committee and translating the national agenda into a public instrument has catalysed inter-institutional coordination. Independent regulators are essential in ensuring neutral, effective and procompetitive regulation, and their national, regional and international cooperation is important for trade facilitation, infrastructure development and stan-dard recognition and harmonisation. Regional regulatory cooperation can lead to the development of regional standards and stronger regulatory cooperation in addressing issues such as roaming fees. In Central America, the Regional Technical Commission on Telecommunications coordinates the development and regulatory harmonisation of telecommunications in the region.

There is a need for an enabling productive, technology and business environment, based on coordinated supply-side measures. The development of productive clusters can promote cooperation and coordination among firms and create economies of scale to reduce operational costs and enhance competitiveness, with a view to achiev-ing better integration of higher value-added segments of regional and global value chains. Such policies are particularly supportive of MSMEs. Enhancing a national innovation system is also an important factor enabling the integration of firms in higher value-added segments of global value chains. The SPR of Peru recommended establishing a centre of technological innovation for software as a strategy for the development of computer-related services. Formalising the informal economy can help create an enabling environment, as informality affects many MSMEs, and for-malised MSMEs can create stronger linkages with the rest of the economy. Tax reforms reducing the tax burden on informal MSMEs and other incentives for for-mality, such as extending social protection coverage, can be pursued.

Labour skills development is required as a qualified workforce promotes knowledge and technology-intensive services. This calls for a sound education strategy, both at technical and at higher levels, that matches labour demand and provided skills and a strong interaction between the private sector, academia and policymaking bodies facilitating the identification of skills gaps and academic solutions. Agreements with foreign universities to allow academic exchanges and the promotion of international accreditations for national universities would strengthen academic programmes and their recognition. English language skills are of particular importance to reinforce labour supply, particularly in information technology-enabled services.

Evidence-based policymaking is also emphasised by SPRs to harvest the potential of services to structurally transform society by building on improved collection, treatment and analysis of services data. The availability of reliable data should be placed high on the national regulatory agenda (Box 4.1).

Sectoral Policy and Regulatory Issues

Telecommunication and ICT Services

Telecommunication and ICT services are essential for all economic activities, with digitisation allowing for increased productivity and greater efficiency as well as reduced production, transaction and trade costs, as exemplified in digital financial services, e-commerce and ICT-enabled trade in general. Their inputs strengthen the supply capacity of the overall economy and their coordinating role in production networks, together with important innovation in digital technology, has promoted tradability and the development of GVCs, with a relevant inclusive role for MSMEs. Telecom and ICT services are recognised in SDGs, implicitly through multiple references to technology and innovation, and explicitly in targets 9.c and 17.8. Still, progress in reducing the digital divide between developed and developing countries remains insufficient. While the number of mobile cellular subscriptions in low/middle-income economies has increased faster than the world average between 2007 and 2015, low/middle-income economies are still lagging behind in terms of the number of internet users and of fixed broadband subscriptions (Figure 4.20).

Regulatory and institutional frameworks remain critical to enable telecom and ICT services, connectivity and the transformative role of the digital ecosystem.

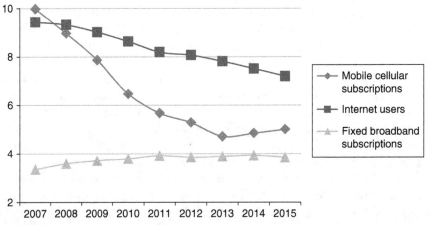

Figure 4.20 Difference between global and low/middle-income economies in number of subscriptions and level of use of selected telecommunications and ICT services, 2007–2015 (per 100 users or subscriptions).

Source: UNCTAD calculations based on the World Bank's World Development Indicators (WDI; https://datacatalog.worldbank.org/dataset/world-development-indicators); UNCTAD (2017c).

Promoting universal access is a key component of this broad objective, including by funding mechanisms for infrastructure and service uptake, provisioning grants, encouraging innovation and increasing demand, for example by extending digital literacy. In the Republic of Korea, for example, in 2014, internet access for 95% of households was facilitated by an informatisation promotion fund focused on ICT investments, including earmarking ICT-related profits, while new financing methods (such as "invest first, settle later") and government seed money attracted private investments.

Facilitating the investment and business environment, including by supporting tech clusters, is highly important. Regulators can play a role in public–private partnerships, by encouraging infrastructure and network sharing and spectrum pooling and using licence-based obligations. Ensuring competition is another key component of a strategy to enable the development role of the digital ecosystem. This includes measures facilitating market entry and licensing, encouraging non-discriminatory access and number portability, addressing high mobile termination rates and securing net neutrality. The growth of the Internet of Things and of mobile applications and services brings new challenges: improving connectivity; addressing spectrum, switching, roaming and numbering regulatory issues; and promoting interoperability (International Telecommunication Union, 2016). Moving from rigid rules to a light-touch regulatory approach would increase responsiveness to this innovative context, ensuring a sound and proportional approach to enable multiple development objectives. At the institutional level, sectoral regulators need to collaborate more in this environment of blurred intersectoral borders. The consumer should continue to be at the centre of regulatory concerns, including data and personal privacy issues, while moving to a digitally connected ecosystem.

In Paraguay, access limitations are compounded by high transport costs associated with its landlocked position. The country is dependent on neighbouring countries to interconnect with submarine cable networks. The National Telecommunications Plan addressed this issue by setting investment targets and promoting public–private partnerships for long-distance fibre optic cables that ensure broadband access. The strategy entails subsidies through the Universal Service Fund to install the necessary infrastructure. The competition law is recent but it also requires coordination with the National Telecommunications Commission (Comisión Nacional de Telecomunicaciones, CONATEL) (UNCTAD, 2015c).

Telecom and ICT services have been paramount to connect consumers and providers through digital means allowing for e-commerce and ICT-enabled trade, of both goods and services. This facilitates MSMEs and individuals to connect to new domestic and foreign markets and GVCs, for example through online marketplaces, promoting competition, consumer choice and increased trade. The increase of internet use in an exporting country is directly linked to the increase in the number and value of products traded. An e-commerce divide still persists and an enabling ecosystem needs to be implemented. This includes the efficient provision of ICT connectivity and other infrastructure such as energy, payment services and e-commerce platforms. Regulatory frameworks are needed to build the digital economy with security, availability, affordability, convenience and quality objectives.

Financial Services and Financial Inclusion

Financial services and financial inclusion facilitate transactions, mobilise savings and channel investment and credit for firms, including MSMEs, as well as households. Trade is increasingly important for the sector, with cross-border exports of financial services having reached US$540 billion in 2015, with an annual growth rate of 7% between 2005 and 2015. Developing economies grew faster in the same period, with a 12% annual growth rate. This is explained mostly by developing Asia, which accounted for 87% of developing economies' exports in financial services in 2015 and is the fastest growing region (13% annually between 2005 and 2015). Nonetheless, developed economies still accounted for 84% of global exports in 2015. Latin America and the Caribbean accounted for 9% of developing economies' exports in financial services in 2015 and grew 8% annually between 2005 and 2015.

Financial inclusion, defined as the effective access and use of affordable, convenient, quality and sustainable financial services from formal providers, needs to factor in the increased international provision of financial services. Financial inclusion is a central element of SDGs as acknowledged in several targets: 1.4, 2.3, 5.a, 8.3, 8.10, 9.2, 10.5 and 10.c. Access to financial services can also contribute to facilitated, speedier, safer and less costly remittances and to maximise the development role of remittances by facilitating options to invest these private funds in productive activities, social services and infrastructure (UNCTAD, 2013). This is important from a development perspective as a 10% rise in remittances may contribute to a 3.5% reduction in the share of people living in poverty (UNCTAD, 2015a).

Although progress has been made in recent years, a large variation in financial inclusion still exists in terms of income, region, gender and age. The share of adults in developed economies who have a financial services account is much higher than that in developing countries. The ratio of account penetration is higher in Asia and the Pacific and lower in the Middle East and North Africa and Sub-Saharan Africa. In 2014, 62% of adults had an account (as compared to 50% in 2011). In the same year, women still lagged behind, with the ratio being 58% (as compared to 47% in 2011), and this is particularly the case in South Asia. In 2014, the youth was also worse off, with 46% (as compared to 37% in 2011), and lagging behind more in Europe and Central Asia. In Latin America and the Caribbean in 2014, women, the poor, people with lower education and youth are all better off than in 2011, but worse off than the average of the entire population and worse off than the average of developing countries and the global average (Figure 4.21).

Policies with a supply-side focus regarding financial services include subsidies and mandatory requirements, such as universal services obligations, to enhance access and sound and proportional regulatory and institutional frameworks that address under- and oversupply, protect consumers, promote competition and pursue balanced objectives of financial inclusion, stability and integrity.

For example, in India, simplified branch authorisations and no frills accounts have been implemented, and in Mexico, simplified account requirements have been introduced to achieve inclusion through proportionality. Increasing levels of regulation and demand for reporting have led to the development of regulation technology, or regtech solutions, another example of the importance of digital services (Box 4.3). Demand-side policies include government use of financial services, support for information

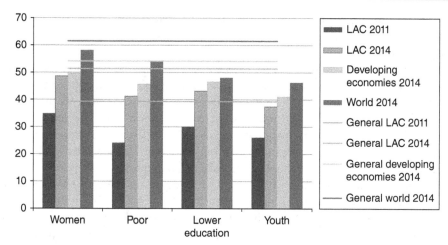

Figure 4.21 Financial services account owners, globally and in developing economies, by gender, income level, education level and age, 2011 and 2014 (%).
Source: UNCTAD calculations based on the World Bank's Global Findex Database (https://globalfindex.worldbank.org/).

Box 4.3   Regulation technology solutions.

Where there are more regulations and more demanding requirements, economic agents face greater compliance-related challenges. In developing countries in particular, managerial and operational impacts may be important in implementing regulations and in providing reports and evidence of compliance. As in many other areas of production processes, services can contribute to increasing the performance of firms towards regulatory frameworks. Technology services, notably software services, are increasingly important in addressing regulatory requirements; they allow for more agile and integrated solutions in implementing and reporting on regulatory compliance, in particular when big datasets need to be processed and analysed, such as in financial services. Related tools include those for management information and for conducting regulation gap analyses, training, monitoring and reporting, automating compliance tasks and reducing risks of non-compliance.

Source: Deloitte (2015).

---

availability – for instance by setting standards for disclosure and transparency – and improvements in financial literacy and consumer empowerment.

Increasing levels of regulation and demand for reporting have led to the development of regtech solutions, as another example of the importance of digital services.

It is necessary to apply best practices in risk management, including stronger know-your-customer (KYC) requirements, wider use of legal entity identifiers, more effective information sharing, clear know-your-customer's-customer (KYCC) rules, and anti-money-laundering/combating-the-financing-of-terrorism (AML/CFT) requirements. National identity schemes are beneficial to the implementation of these practices, particularly for the unbanked. In addition, it is crucial to apply a proportional approach and effective risk management, rather than risk avoidance, as in the case of de-risking. Demand-side policies include the government using financial services, supporting information availability – for instance by setting standards for disclosure and transparency – and improving financial literacy, capabilities and consumer empowerment.

The financial sector in Paraguay expanded at an average rate of 9% in the past ten years but has fallen short of achieving financial inclusion and facilitating the channelling of resources to MSMEs. The Central Bank is setting up a credit bureau to balance information asymmetry that contributes to increased financial spread, drafting a guarantee fund act and cooperating with the Secretariat of the Consumer Protection Office to launch financial education projects. In addition, the Central Bank created basic savings accounts that facilitate access to banking deposits by not requiring minimum amounts to open them or minimum average balances. The accounts can be opened without the physical presence of the client, through electronic media such as mobile telephones.

In Chile, importance has been given to financial services to raise and mobilise resources and encourage investment for structural transformation towards higher productivity sectors. The country has liberalised the financial sector, yet the Banco Estado, a state-owned commercial bank, has remained a key player in providing financial services to SMEs (UNCTAD, 2014a).

Financial services in Nicaragua are small and concentrated. The sector contains only seven active banks, four of which control over 90% of the market. After liberalisation and closure of the Development Bank, the supply of credit and other financial services did not spread to the majority of the population and MSMEs. Financial depth (total credit/GDP) was 27% in 2012, well below the 40–50% in other countries of similar size. Instead, financial institutions have focused on carefully selecting potential customers, offering mostly consumption and trade credit, rather than supporting investments and productive activities. The SPR of Nicaragua suggested that the existing public Banco Produzcamos, whose main objective is to support productive agricultural and industrial MSMEs, be transformed into a fully fledged development bank. The new development bank would preferably be endowed with a mixed capital base.

Digital financial services (DFS) play a key role in financial inclusion, building on ICT services to reduce infrastructure costs and increase coverage. In addition, DFS are more gender neutral and youth friendly and have positive externalities such as incentivising the use of banking services by establishing linkages and helping credit scoring by providing information on mobile money usage. Developing DFS requires an enabling environment and infrastructure readiness that addresses several challenges: the infrastructure gap, most notably regarding availability and reliability of energy and ICT services; data and personal privacy issues; fraud and security issues regarding data and payment systems; lack of technological skills; adequate agent networks; and interoperability. Digital liquidity is necessary for the sustainability of DFS and this is promoted by the provision of additional DFS, such as savings, credit and investment services. Proportional and inclusive regulation is necessary to involve inter alia digital illiterates, the poor, people in rural areas, migrants and MSMEs.

Transport and Logistics

Transport and logistics is pivotal in providing connectivity linking consumers and producers. It contributes to integrating markets within an economy and to integrating these domestic markets with the rest of the world, by facilitating exports and imports, as well as the movement of people. Improvements in transport infra-structure, logistics and cross-border trade facilities are instrumental for reducing delivery times and costs, and therefore for integration into GVCs and for deep-ening international trade. This is particularly important for developing countries that are worse off in terms of soft and hard transport infrastructure, and critical for landlocked developing countries. This is recognised by SDGs in targets 9.1 and 11.2. Despite recent improvements, Latin America and the Caribbean are lagging behind in the quality of trade and transport-related infrastructure. The same occurs with developing economies in general, particularly Sub-Saharan Africa (Figure 4.22). In addition, transport services are increasingly an ecosystem that integrates ancillary services such as banking, insurance, freight forwarding and others.

Policies for the transport sector have an important regional and international dimension, which has been centred on extending transport networks and cross-border connectivity. This increasingly requires linking national planning to interna-tional strategies, connecting transport corridors with present and future growth centres, promoting multimodality and prioritising trade facilitation, including through the elimination of non-tariff barriers (CUTS International, 2017). Cross-border efficiency is associated with the harmonisation or recognition of trans-port regulation, including vehicle and drivers permits and certificates, and the development of automated and streamlined one-stop cross-border posts as impor-tant trade facilitation measures (UNCTAD, 2014b). ICT services can also have a relevant transformative role in providing connectivity by improving transport ser-vices and trade facilitation. This comprises the ability to track and trace shipments, to manage and internationally synchronise schedules and information on inven-tories, and to automate and optimise utilisation rates, and overall logistic services (Kunaka *et al.*, 2013).

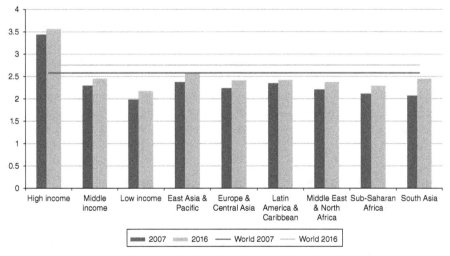

Figure 4.22 Logistics performance index related to quality of trade and transport-related infrastructure, by region and income level, 2007 and 2016 (index).
Source: UNCTAD calculations based on WDI (https://datacatalog.worldbank.org/dataset/world-development-indicators); UNCTAD (2017c).

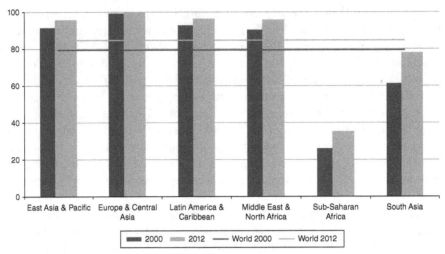

Figure 4.23   Access to electricity by region, 2000 and 2012 (%).
Source: UNCTAD calculations based on WDI (https://datacatalog.worldbank.org/dataset/world-development-indicators); UNCTAD (2017c).

Energy Services and Electricity Services

Energy services and electricity services are crucial to the prosperity of economies and to social welfare. The availability of electric supply is essential for both economic development and quality of life and it is a key requirement for human development (UNCTAD, 2017a). This is reflected in Goal 7 of SDGs on energy. Although many developing regions have achieved levels of access to electricity close to or above 90%, including Latin America and the Caribbean, the status of Sub-Saharan Africa, with only 35% of the population having access to electricity in 2012 (Figure 4.23), remains critical. An African regional policy with harmonised regulatory frameworks that, as in other regions, explores the potential of the regional dimension in the optimisation of supply is required. This involves creating common regional infrastructure, power interconnection and harmonisation of specifications, and common markets that facilitate cross-border trade of energy. As in other sectors, the digital ecosystem is important for energy services, by enabling smart power grids that improve power transmission efficiency and the monitoring and maintenance of delivery systems (International Telecommunication Union, 2016). Renewable energy and energy efficiency remain at the core of energy services strategies and SDG-compliant services policies.

International Trading System for Services Sector Development

National regulatory frameworks attending to legitimate public policy concerns are central for development aspirations and are a precondition to trade liberalisation. Given the overwhelming importance of both the direct contributions of the services sector, and their role in creating network linkages, enhancing productivity and promoting a services-led structural change growth, there is need to examine services trade restrictions to ensure they are not unnecessarily harmful for the development potential of the services sector. These can include the prohibition of

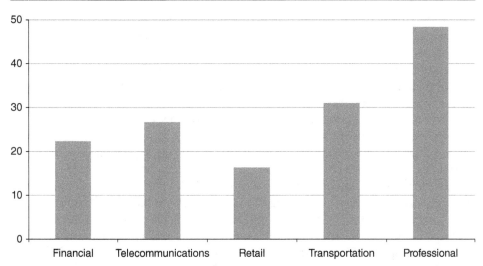

Figure 4.24 Services trade restrictions index average by services category (index).
Source: World Bank Services Trade Restrictions database (https://datacatalog.worldbank.org/
dataset/services-trade-restrictions-database); UNCTAD (2017c).
Note: Index values range from 0, signifying that the sector is completely open to trade, to 100,
signifying that the sector is completely closed.

foreign providers, limits on foreign ownership and on foreign personnel, or implicit
discriminations on qualification and licensing requirements. Restrictions in telecom are associated with fewer telephone lines and internet subscriptions; in financial services, restrictions are linked to less developed credit and insurance markets;
and in transport, restrictions are associated with longer journeys for containers.
Although some countries have reduced restrictions, mainly related to mode 3, there
are tighter restrictions on the temporary movement of people to provide services
through mode 4, such as quotas, labour market tests and durations of stay. Despite
its importance, services trade continues to face relevant restrictions, particularly in
mode 4, specifically professional services and transport (Figure 4.24).

Tackling restrictions requires proactive, appropriately combined and sequenced
trade policies to reform the services sector through its different dimensions,
including trade negotiations, services trade facilitation, market intelligence and
trade promotion. This multi-dimensional trade policy is relevant for the enabling
policy mix for services, including contributions for policy coherence and coordination;
sound regulatory and institutional frameworks; infrastructure development –
particularly of telecom and ICT services enabling digitisation; and for improving
endowments of skills. Trade policy thereby connects with industrial policy to promote efficiency, competition, innovation and enhanced productive and export
capacity in services. A "whole-of-supply-chain approach" is required to avoid policymaking in silos, while recognising the heterogeneity of services sectors (UNCTAD,
2017b). This catalyses the role of the services sector in inducing productivity and
structural transformation.

The type of trade rules that were required has evolved in the light of the changing
production patterns that have led international trade to go from the exchange of
products that are "packages of a single nation's productive factors, technology, social

capital, governance capacity, etc." to trade through supply chains which represent the same factors from several countries. GVCs embody complex cross-border flows of products, people, services, investment and information and therefore require complex rules to govern these flows. However, as GVCs have become more prevalent, with developing countries increasingly joining in these supply chains, certain topics, including in the area of services, are currently gaining more traction in the multilateral setting. Indeed, 21st-century trade characterised by GVCs requires ever more services, including infrastructure services.

Opening areas like services and digital trade may bring important benefits due to their direct and indirect cross-cutting contributions, and current high trade barriers. The growing digitisation of economic activities is allowing for new tradable goods and services and new ways of trading. While existing multilateral and regional trade rules already cover many aspects of digital trade, particularly services, there may be a need to update countries' specific commitments and to clarify and enhance rules in certain areas. In financial services in China, the value added of the financial intermediation sector could double with trade openness in that sector as labour, capital, technology and elasticity respond to liberalisation policies (Hsu and Melchor Simon, 2016).

Economies need to pursue a balanced growth strategy to capitalise on the growth-inducing and catalytic role of services. At the international level, efforts are needed to advance a global SDG-led services trade agenda in the international trading system to enable the transformative potential of services trade for development. In general, liberalisation policies require that the risks, costs and trade-offs that the reform agenda may entail for national regulatory autonomy and policy space are attended. This points to the adequate content, pace and sequencing of liberalisation so that regulatory and institutional frameworks are set in advance and retain the possibility to adapt to new challenges, including those from liberalised markets. It also calls for skills development, social safety nets and adjustment mechanisms, including by allowing countries to adequately revise and use rollback mechanisms on commitments (UNCTAD, 2017c). Support for developing countries remains paramount, for example through the use of inclusive rules of origin, preferential treatment, flexibilities, experimentation, capacity-building and aid for trade to build supply capacity, towards an effective international trading system. International cooperation at bilateral, regional and multilateral levels is also necessary, particularly to strengthen national regulatory frameworks.

Multilateral Trading System

Progressive services liberalisation has been pursued at the multilateral level under the WTO. Services negotiations were integrated into the Doha Round launched in 2001. The challenges to the multilateral trading system became apparent before and during the past two Ministerial Conferences held in Nairobi (MC-10) in December 2015 and Buenos Aires (MC-11) in December 2017. At MC-11, ministers did not confirm the primacy and validity of multilateralism. Since MC-11, tensions have been on the rise, looming particularly between the United States and China, and there is a threat of trade war, which although starting in the goods sector may affect also the services sector.

Box 4.4   Services-related preferential treatment and graduation
from the LDC category.

The Programme of Action for the Least Developed Countries for the Decade 2011–2020
aims for half the number of LDCs to meet the criteria for graduation by 2020, and target
17.11 of the SDGs aims to double their share in world trade by the same year. LDCs are
not yet on track to meet this target. Their share of merchandise exports in global exports
decreased from 1.1% in 2010 to 0.9% in 2015. Services exports from LDCs rose from
0.6% in 2010 to 0.8% in 2015. As LDC exports are still concentrated in a few primary
products, it is important to strengthen industrial and services productive capacity to promote economic diversification, including by addressing services trade barriers. A preliminary assessment of 23 services waiver notifications shows some preferences going
beyond Doha Development Agenda (DDA) offers and matching preferences in regional
trade agreements. A modal analysis reveals that there are several preferences under mode
4, but that the majority of these have limitations. A few notifications focus on preferential regulatory treatment, support for LDCs in conforming to domestic regulation and
meeting quality standards in foreign markets, a key avenue to providing meaningful and
effective preferences.

Sources: UNCTAD (2017c).

Lack of progress and uncertain prospects have contributed to intensified plurilateral and regional initiatives outside of the WTO. In an effort to retain relevance
for the multilateral level, countries have recently opted for a less ambitious agenda.
The main services-related outcome of MC-10 was the extension of preferential
treatment to services and services suppliers of LDCs for an additional four years
until 31 December 2030. Services are also relevant for graduation from the LDC
category (Box 4.4).

New efforts prior to MC-11 aimed to identify deliverables with regard to services,
namely domestic regulation disciplines; propose a trade facilitation agreement for
services; and address services aspects of e-commerce, investment facilitation, MSMEs
and plurilaterals. At MC-11 a series of joint statements were issued by some 70 countries on investment facilitation, MSMEs and e-commerce committing to undertake
discussion and work on these issues. It is unclear what these discussions will lead to.

There is an urgent need to effectively operationalise the development provisions
of the General Agreement on Trade in Services (GATS), such as Article IV and the
annex on telecommunications, to allow countries to implement proactive policies
necessary to explore the potential of services including the digital economy for structural transformation.

Domestic Regulations

The importance of disciplines for domestic regulations is one area where a clear link
appears possible with the growing importance of services for structural transformation and global value chains. GATS mandates WTO members engaging in negotiations to develop multilateral disciplines on domestic regulations for qualification
and licensing requirements and procedures and for technical standards, in order that

these instruments do not act as unjustifiable trade barriers. Following the long-term development of a comprehensive set of disciplines covering all issues in Article VI.4 on transparency, licensing, qualification and technical standards requirements and procedures, a more modest building-block approach has been adopted to focus on a few specific elements of the possible disciplines.

One proposal seeks to address the administration of requirements and procedures for licensing, qualification and technical standards. The aim is to simplify the steps required for suppliers applying for authorisation to supply services where WTO members have undertaken specific commitments, such as through the establishment of single windows. Another proposal addresses transparency, proposing that members provide the information necessary for services suppliers or persons seeking to supply a service to comply with the requirements for obtaining authorisation. A key element relates to the opportunity for interested persons to receive and comment on information before the entry into force of regulations. Two other proposals with regard to the development of measures raise concerns regarding policy space, as some provisions could impose constraints on developing countries, such as with regard to publications, information availability and enquiry points (not from member to member as in GATS, but from member to suppliers or persons seeking to supply a service).

Trade Facilitation Agreement for Services

WTO members have embarked on discussions regarding a proposal by India for a trade facilitation agreement for services. The premise for the proposal is the importance of ensuring a timely and cost-effective delivery of services for members and the related need to facilitate the movement of information, data, technology and natural and juridical persons to enable services trade in an increasingly globalised and digitised world, while easing the regulatory burden in providing the basis for the realisation of the full benefits of trade in services. The proposed agreement is intended to apply to all measures by members affecting trade in services in sectors in which specific commitments have been undertaken.

The proposed agreement includes several elements of domestic regulations related to publication, information availability and the administration of measures. The agreement also provides guidelines regarding fees and charges, the administration of economic needs tests and the recognition of qualification and licensing requirements. Several measures are proposed to facilitate the effective supply of services through different modes, such as the cross-border transfer of information by electronic means, facilitating consumption abroad, and provisions facilitating the movement of natural persons (for example through separate visa categories that correspond to each category of natural person in respect of which commitments have been undertaken, multiple entries and exemptions from social security contributions for natural persons engaged in the supply of services). The agreement models special and differential treatment provisions on the Agreement on Trade Facilitation. Conversely, some elements of the proposed agreement are challenged by its possible impact on developing countries, including provisions on transparency, cross-border flows of information and economic needs tests. Some proposals emphasise that the supply and consumption of services rarely involve a single mode in isolation and that a discussion of all modes is therefore necessary. Typically, modes 1 and 3 complement mode 4. This topic has traditionally been considered an area of particular interest for developing countries, yet their services suppliers face a variety of barriers in this area. Further discussions on mode 4 regional trade agreement practices have been proposed, including on access, pertinent regulatory disciplines and mode 4 commitments administered within broader regulatory frameworks, such as labour and immigration frameworks, where non-economic and non-trade policy objectives play a significant role. The progress on services facilitation has been limited.

Other WTO discussions concern investment facilitation, which may impact GATS and elements of the proposed trade facilitation agreement for services. The question of whether there is need to develop rules in this area has been raised. The proponents pursue some outcomes on this issue for MC-12, for example in the area of transparency.

Electronic Commerce

With regard to e-commerce, a group of countries has suggested examining developments in and potential constraints on e-commerce business opportunities, and the ways in which trade disciplines can facilitate the process. Proponents aim to ensure balance is preserved between further unlocking the potential of e-commerce and fulfilling legitimate regulatory objectives related to e-commerce, such as on data protection, privacy protection and cybersecurity. Such objectives may lead to controversial regulations, such as commercial presence and localisation requirements. It is therefore important to examine the need to develop rules in this area and determine the best technological and regulatory means of ensuring policy objectives.

At MC-11, the moratorium on e-commerce was extended to continue the practice of not imposing customs duties on electronic transmissions. There is a proposal to extend the moratorium at MC-12. Different proposals have been discussed focused on electronic signatures as one of the essential tools for e-commerce and electronic contracts and bank operations and on trade policy considerations and how digital technology is transforming the global economy. Several developing countries have emphasised the importance of e-commerce for development as well as the problem of digital divide. Related issues of interest to developing countries include empowering smaller businesses to use e-commerce and lower the costs of conducting trade (such as through access to logistics services); addressing infrastructure gaps (such as in broadband access) to enable e-commerce; and improving business and consumer access to various payment options, including payment through mobile telephones and cash-on-delivery options, to better enable them to conduct and access cross-border e-commerce.

Plurilateral and Regional Initiatives

Services have become a key feature of new-generation regional trade agreements oriented towards deeper and more comprehensive integration, with a strong regulatory focus, and addressing behind-the-border regulatory measures affecting services, investment and competition, such as the continental free trade area (Box 4.5) and the Trans-Pacific Partnership.

> **Box 4.5   Continental free trade area.**
>
> The continental free trade area negotiations, launched in June 2015 based on African Union Decision 569, aimed to achieve a comprehensive and mutually beneficial trade agreement by 2017. The first phase of negotiations covering goods and services was concluded and signed and the second phase is expected to cover investment, intellectual property and competition issues. Negotiators reached a trade in services agreement as well as agreeing on modalities for trade in services negotiations. Key principles of the negotiations included the following: negotiations shall be driven by member states of the African Union, regional economic commissions and customs territories; free trade agreements of regional economic commissions shall serve as building blocks for the continental free trade area; preservation of acquis; variable geometry; substantial liberalisation; and there shall be no a priori exclusion of any services sector or mode of supply of services in negotiations.

Following the withdrawal in January 2017 of the United States from the Trans-Pacific Partnership, the remaining members pursued the agreement with a minus one approach. In a marked departure from GATS, the investment chapter of the Trans-Pacific Partnership covers all investments, including in services, while the cross-border trade in services chapter encompasses the supply of services under modes 1, 2 and 4. The agreement also includes a chapter on regulatory coherence, defined as "the use of good regulatory practices in the process of planning, designing, issuing, implementing and reviewing regulatory measures in order to facilitate achievement of domestic policy objectives". The agreement reiterates the sovereign right to identify regulatory priorities, yet also promotes regulatory coherence as a means of facilitating increased trade and investment between the parties.

A trade in services agreement has been negotiated since 2012 between 23 members of the WTO, representing 70% of global services trade. Negotiations were expected to be concluded in 2016, yet there is increased uncertainty over the prospect. Participating countries have identified common criteria to evaluate the offers presented, including on commitments beyond GATS and commitments that match the best free trade agreements of countries. Particular attention is given to the level of commitments under mode 4, as well as the treatment of new services. Divergences have emerged related to certain issues such as the liberalisation of public services, data protection and the process for dealing with new services in schedules of commitments.

Conclusion

Services play a crucial role in support of economic and social transformation, and adequate regulation and international trade can generate further transformation opportunities, particularly for developing countries. Trade in services plays an important role in economic transformation, employment creation and value addition, enabling countries to diversify and upgrade their economies, including through integration into GVCs. There is a need for economies to pursue a balanced growth strategy to capitalise on the growth-inducing and catalytic role of services. It is also important to make a compelling case for the importance of services in structural transformation and in achieving the SDGs. Business is increasingly giving attention to the implementation of the SDGs in services sectors.

Maximising the positive contributions of services requires, as preconditions, fit for purpose policies, support to supply capacity upgrading and value added, adequate regulations and strong institutions as well as skill-building with a focus on technology and innovation together capable of creating an enabling environment for the services economy and trade. Evidence-based policymaking requires sound, timely and disaggregated data, including at the firm level. Human, regulatory and institutional capacity-building is fundamental to allowing developing-country producers and exporters to export, producers to use imported services inputs and policymakers to effectively regulate and develop services sectors. An inclusive and multi-stakeholder approach to services policymaking and public–private partnerships in services are needed to ensure policy and regulatory cooperation and coherence. The assessment and revision of national services economy and regulatory frameworks and strategies as well as monitoring of implementation of action plans are prerequisites for evidence-based, proactive polices aimed at services-led growth.

At the international level, efforts are needed to advance a global services trade agenda in the international trading system that is supportive of the SDGs, and includes preferential treatment, flexibilities, experimentation, adjustment mechanisms and support and capacity-building for developing countries, in order to unlock the transformative potential of services trade to spur growth and development. Adequately designing the content, pace and sequence of the liberalisation process, and coordinating this process coherently with the implementation of national policies and regulations, is essential to creating an enabling environment for trade in services. Complementary measures, such as strengthening productive capacity and regulatory and standards-related cooperation relating to services trade to create a more facilitative services trade environment, could also make an important contribution.

References

Antimiani, A. & Cernat, L. (2017) Liberalizing Global Trade in Mode 5 Services: How Much Is it Worth? Chief Economist Note, DG Trade. Brussels: European Commission.

Asia Global Institute (2015) The Role of Services in Global Value Chains. Paper presented at UNCTAD, Geneva, 17 September 2015.

Buiatti, C., Duarte, J.B. & Felipe Sáenz, L. (2017) Why Is Europe Falling Behind? Structural Transformation and Services' Productivity Differences between Europe and the U.S. *Working Paper Series* No. 2017/04, Cambridge: INET.

Cernat, Lucian & Kutlina-Dimitrova, Z. (2014) *Thinking in a Box: A "Mode 5" Approach to Services Trade.* Brussels: European Commission.

CUTS International (2017) *Facilitating Connectivity in the Bay of Bengal Region.* Jaipur: CUTS.

Deloitte (2015) Regtech Is the New Fintech: How Agile Regulatory Technology Is Helping Firms Better Understand and Manage their Risks. Retrieved from: https://www2.deloitte.com/content/dam/Deloitte/ie/Documents/FinancialServices/IE_2016_FS_RegTech_is_the_new_FinTech.pdf (accessed 2 July 2019).

Durkin, A. (2017) Jobs in Fashion You Didn't Know Were Connected to Trade. Retrieved from: https://tradevistas.org/jobs-fashion-didnt-know-connected-trade/ (accessed 2 July 2019).

Evangelista, R., Lucchese, M. & Meliciani, V. (2015) Business Services and the Export Performances of Manufacturing Industries. *Journal of Evolutionary Economics*, 25(5), 959–981.

Hansda, S.K. (2005) Sustainability of Services-Led Growth: An Input Output Exploration of the Indian Economy. Retrieved from: https://econwpa.ub.uni-muenchen.de/econ-wp/ge/papers/0512/0512009.pdf (accessed 2 July 2019).

Hernández, R.A., Martínez, J.M. & Mulder, N. (2014) *Global Value Chains and World Trade: Prospects and Challenges for Latin America*. Santiago: ECLAC.

Hsu, S. & Melchor Simon, A.C. (2016) China's Structural Transformation: Reaching Potential GDP in the Financial Services Sector. *China Finance and Economic Review*, 4(3). https://doi.org/10.1186/s40589-016-0027-x.

International Labour Organization (2017) *World Employment Social Outlook: Trends 2016*. Geneva: ILO.

International Labour Organization & World Trade Organization (2017) *Investing in Skills for Inclusive Trade*. Geneva: UNCTAD.

International Telecommunication Union (2016) *Trends in Telecommunication Reform 2016: Regulatory Incentives to Achieve Digital Opportunities*. Geneva: ITU.

Jouanjean, M.A., Mendez-Parra, M. & te Velde, D.W. (2015) *Trade Policy and Economic Transformation*. London: ODI.

Kunaka, C., Mustra, M.A. & Saez, S. (2013) Trade Dimensions of Logistics Services. *Policy Research Working Paper* No. 6332. Washington, DC: World Bank Group.

Lin, J.Y. & Wang, Y. (2014) China-Africa Cooperation in Structural Transformation: Ideas, Opportunities and Finances. *World Institute for Development Economics Research Working Paper* No. 46. Tokyo: United Nations University.

Mashayekhi, M. & Antunes, B. (2018) Trade, Migration and Development. In: *Handbook for Improving the Production and Use of Migration Data for Development*. Washington, DC: Global Migration Group, pp. 91–102.

Mashayekhi, M., Ito, T. & Antunes, B. (2017) Digital Economy and ICT Services-Enabled Trade, Box II.1. In: *World Economic Situation and Prospects 2017*. New York: United Nations, pp. 51–52.

McKinsey Global Institute (2017) *Jobs Lost, Jobs Gained: Workforce Transitions in a Time of Automation*. New York: McKinsey.

McMillan, M., Rodrik, D. & Verduzco-Gallo, I. (2014) Globalization, Structural Change, and Productivity Growth, with an Update on Africa. *World Development*, 63, 11–32.

Mendez-Parra, M. (2017) Trade in Services and Economic Transformation: Some Evidence. In: *Trade in Services and Economic Transformation*. London: ODI, pp. 11–12. Retrieved from: http://cadmus.eui.eu/bitstream/handle/1814/45504/SET-essays_2017_02.pdf?sequence=1&isAllowed=y (accessed 2 July 2019).

Miroudot, S. & Cadestin, C. (2017) Services in Global Value Chains: From Inputs to Value-Creating Activities. *OECD Trade Policy Papers*, 197. Paris: OECD.

OECD (2016) *Services and Performance of the Brazilian Economy: Analysis and Policy Options*. Paris: OECD.

UNCTAD (2012a) *Services, Development and Trade: The Regulatory and Institutional Dimension of Infrastructure Services*. New York and Geneva: United Nations.

UNCTAD (2012b) *Economic Development in Africa Report 2012*. New York and Geneva:, United Nations.

UNCTAD (2013) *Maximising the Development Impact of Remittances*. UNCTAD/DITC/TNCD/2011/8. New York and Geneva: UNCTAD.

UNCTAD (2014a) *The Least Developed Countries Report 2014*. E.14.II.D.7. New York and Geneva: United Nations.

UNCTAD (2014b) *Services, Development and Trade: The Regulatory and Institutional Dimension*. TD/B/C.I/MEM.4/5. New York and Geneva: UNCTAD.

UNCTAD (2015a) Access to Financial Services as a Driver for the Post-2015 Development Agenda. *Policy Brief* No. 35. New York and Geneva: UNCTAD.

UNCTAD (2015b) *Services, Development and Trade: The Regulatory and Institutional Dimension.* TD/B/C.1/MEM.4/8. New York and Geneva: United Nations.

UNCTAD (2015c) *Services Policy Review: Paraguay.* UNCTAD/DITC/TNCD/2014/2. New York and Geneva: UNCTAD.

UNCTAD (2016a) *Services, Development and Trade: The Regulatory and Institutional Dimension.* TD/B/C.I/MEM.4/11. New York and Geneva: UNCTAD.

UNCTAD (2016b) *Trade and Development Report.* New York and Geneva: UNCTAD.

UNCTAD (2016c) *World Investment Report 2016: Investor Nationality: Policy Challenges.* New York and Geneva: UNCTAD.

UNCTAD (2017a) *Report of the Multi-year Expert Meeting on Trade, Services and Development on its Fifth Session.* TD/B/C.I/MEM.4/15. New York and Geneva: UNCTAD.

UNCTAD (2017b) *Energy Services Toolkit.* UNCTAD/DITC/TNCD/2017/1. New York and Geneva: UNCTAD.

UNCTAD (2017c) *The Role of the Services Economy and Trade in Structural Transformation and Inclusive Development.* TD/B/C.I/MEM.4/14. New York and Geneva: UNCTAD.

UNCTAD (2018) *Survey of Infrastructure Regulators and Competition Authorities.* New York and Geneva: UNCTAD.

Vries, G. J. de, Erumban, A.A., Timmer, M.P. *et al.* (2012) Deconstructuring the BRICS: Structural Transformation and Aggregate Productivity Growth. *Journal of Comparative Economics*, 40(2), 211–227.

World Bank (2017) *Migration and Development Brief 27. Migration and Remittances: Recent Developments and Outlooks.* Washington, DC: World Bank Group.

World Bank (2019) Record High Remittances Sent Globally in 2018. Press release, 8 April. Retrieved from: https://www.worldbank.org/en/news/press-release/2019/04/08/record-high-remittances-sent-globally-in-2018 (accessed 23 July 2019).

World Trade Organization (2015) *Fostering the Participation of Micro, Small, and Medium Enterprises (MSMEs) in Regional and Global Markets.* JOB/GC/80. Geneva: WTO.

Chapter 5

Cities and Trade

Thomas Hoehn

Introduction

In this chapter I analyse the development of the global economy and its trading system through the perspective of cities as major centres of economic, social and cultural exchange which, I argue, represent important economic and political entities beyond the countries in which they are located. I discuss how international trade and trade policies have shaped the development of major cities and their economies and how these cities in turn have shaped and influenced the structure and development of global trade.

The analysis of the global trade economy through the lens of cities is perhaps unusual but is justified for several reasons and evidenced by the research surveyed in this chapter. The urban rather than national or international country perspective generates valuable insights into the observed pattern of economic development and helps us to understand the phenomenon of globalisation. Major cities produce unique products and services that are often traded on a global scale (such as banking, insurance, law and other business services) and support the international trading system. In the superleague of global cities, we find cities that have much more in common with each other than they do with other cities in their respective home countries. They are in this sense true representatives of globalisation (Sassen, 2011). While global cities generally do not form autonomous political entities and are not able to claim and exercise full sovereignty (with the exception of independent city states such as Singapore), they have nevertheless a political influence backed by their economic weight.

As the former Director-General of the World Trade Organization, Pascal Lamy, observed in a thoughtful speech at the Shanghai Expo in 2010:

The Handbook of Global Trade Policy, First Edition. Edited by Andreas Klasen.
© 2020 John Wiley & Sons Ltd. Published 2020 by John Wiley & Sons Ltd.

Cities have always provided the infrastructure which facilitates exchange. The market, the centre for trade in its many manifestations, has long been at the centre of the city. The place where people have come together – to do business, yes, but also to catch up on the news, to share a joke, to learn from others. The organization of cities and the pursuit of trade share a common fabric, man's desire to reach out to others, socially and commercially.

He went on to develop further analogies between the development of cities and trade:

> … there are other similarities between the development of trade and the growth of cities. The roots of both lie in the development of technology. Technological advances permitting greater agricultural productivity gave rise to surplus production which freed many people from the need to farm to survive. Occupational specialization created the conditions for city life and for the exchange of goods and services. (Lamy, 2010)

Today, more than half of the world's population lives in an urban environment, a milestone we passed a few years ago. As Glaeser (2011) observes, although we now mostly live in cities, the world's population could easily fit into an area the size of Texas – "each of us with our personal townhouse". According to research with colleagues at PricewaterhouseCoopers (2009), I estimated that in 2008 the world's largest 100 cities accounted for 30% of the global gross domestic product (GDP), with the top 30 cities alone accounting for 18% of the world's GDP. When measured by their economic output, the largest cities in the world appear to have an influence and weight that is comparable to those of many smaller or even mid-sized countries. The GDP of Los Angeles, for example, is larger than that of Australia or Poland, which themselves are only slightly larger than the city economies of Chicago, London or Paris. The world's leading city economies, Tokyo and New York, have a GDP about the same size as Spain (PricewaterhouseCoopers, 2009). These global cities are important trading centres and form a global network with many connections to each other (Table 5.1).

Table 5.1 GDP of the largest city economies compared to that of selected countries, 2008 (US$ billion)

Tokyo	1479	Russia	2288
New York	1406	Spain	1456
Los Angeles	792	Canada	1214
Chicago	574	Australia	672
London	565	Poland	672
Paris	564	South Africa	492
Osaka/Kobe	417	Colombia	396
Mexico City	390	Belgium	369
Philadelphia	388	Sweden	345
São Paolo	388	Switzerland	325

Source: PricewaterhouseCoopers (2009, Table 3.4).

Seen through the perspective of concentrated economic activity in a densely populated urban environment, we are able to analyse a large part of the global economy through a limited number of entities that share many common characteristics. This is not to say that all cities are the same, far from it. They are very different from each other and have unique features. Nevertheless, the 100 largest cities in the world share a large number of common economic features and are more similar than the 196 countries in the world, which range in terms of size from the very small countries of less than 100 square kilometres (San Marino, Monaco and the Vatican City) to the very large countries of nearly 10 million square kilometres or more (China, Canada, the United States and Russia).

What is striking about the GDP rankings of the world's largest cities is how the list is dominated by commercial and financial centres and not the cities that are the capitals of their countries. Of the top 30 global cities, only ten are the capitals of their countries. The other cities on this list are national and international trading hubs, such as New York, Chicago, Hong Kong, Singapore, Shanghai and Mumbai. Very often these cities are old port cities and have therefore been part of international and global trading orders for many centuries.

I would argue that cities have been important economic and political actors shaping the international trading system throughout history, whether as the capital city of a country (e.g. Paris), the centre of an empire (e.g. Rome and London), or the trading cities of the Hanseatic League which have helped to develop financing systems for global trade (e.g. Hamburg, Kiel and Lübeck). This was true in the past and is true today in the era of globalisation when, until recently, the nation state still reigned supreme. Take the case of the C40 group of cities, an informal network set up by the mayors of some of the world's largest cities only ten years ago, which now counts 91 affiliate member cities representing 25% of global GDP. The C40 has, within a short time, become an important force in the combat of climate change and now pursues a broader agenda covering finance, business and innovation.

In the following sections, I want to further develop these themes. First, I will summarise and discuss the definition of cities as places of opportunity and growth, before introducing the measurement concepts related to the size and structure of a city used in empirical studies. I will then provide short paired sketches of eight major trading cities that at some time in history have been or still are major commercial centres and seats of political power. The selection of the four city pairs of Venice/Florence, London/Tokyo, Chicago/Mexico City and Shanghai/Dubai is a subjective one but is informed by, and aimed at, highlighting the connection of cities throughout history to trade, economic development and globalisation. The next section analyses from a mainly economic perspective the success factors that determine the growth of cities, covering economic, political and institutional factors, including a review of the more recent literature of the new economic geography, which for the first time has brought together spatial economics and international trade theory to explain more coherently the structure and growth of cities. I then focus on the literature dealing with the role of global cities in a network of cities that support globalisation and define the new international economic order. This is followed by a discussion of the relationship between cities and their nation states, before I end with some concluding remarks about the role of cities in trade policy and suggestions for further research.

Definitions and Concepts

Why do cities exist? What defines a city? Cities are permanent human settlements characterised by a relatively large population, a high density of dwellings and an infrastructure that supports a multitude of economic, social and cultural activities. These activities do not happen only within a city's boundaries but also through interactions with its surrounding regions, trading partners and the rest of the world. As Pascal Lamy pointed out in a speech he gave in Geneva in 2006, in ancient Egypt times, the hieroglyph for a city or town consisted of a cross inside a circle, which could in his view be interpreted as a place of exchange within a protected space and a vision of the city that continues to be relevant today. Cities can thus be seen as the starting points and end points of trade networks that reach out into the neighbouring countryside and towards the world at large (Lamy, 2006).

Figure 5.1 (Crowe, 1995) illustrates this point with reference to four representations of a town or city in antiquity. Clockwise, from upper left, they are: an early Chinese ideogram for "village" (1300–612 BC), an Assyrian bas-relief depicting scenes of city life (c. 1600 BC), an Egyptian hieroglyph for "city" (3110–2884 BC), and an Icelandic drawing of the "heavenly city of Jerusalem" (13th century AD).

Trade and exchange apart, why do we choose to live in cities and cluster together in a dense and often heavily polluted and congested space where the richest and

Figure 5.1   Four representations of the town or city.
Source: Crowe (1995).

poorest people choose to live in close proximity to each other? What makes cities so attractive?

In short, the answer in my view is "opportunities". Cities offer people the opportunity to meet and exchange products and services, as well as to find like-minded souls and exchange ideas. People are drawn to cities by their promise of jobs and a career and to meet people who may share their views of the world and search for knowledge. In his book *The Triumph of the City*, Glaeser (2011) suggests that cities offer young people and poor immigrants the opportunity to better themselves and "create the clearest pathway from poverty to prosperity". He further argues that cities are our best invention, which makes us richer, smarter, greener, healthier and happier. This is a strong claim that is not without its critics, Mahatma Gandhi being one of the more prominent anti-urbanites, who said that "the true India is to be found not in its few cities, but in its 700,000 villages" (Glaeser, 2011).

A unique and critical voice in the literature on cities is that of Jane Jacobs, a celebrated author and neighbourhood activist from New York, who in the 1960s took it upon herself to challenge the urban planning orthodoxy of the time to argue that city planners often underestimate the importance of urban evolution through the act of living, or, in Jacob's words, to recognise that "cities have the capability of providing something for everybody, only because, and only when, they are created by everybody" (Jacobs, 1961). The city in her view is not simply made up of streets and buildings, but defined by the interactions among people that take place on the streets. Her view was that the art of keeping a city alive and allowing it to renew itself is to create the right balance between public and private spaces. Building on the view of the city as a place of opportunity, Jacobs in her later work (Jacobs, 1969) points to the city as a place for creativity and source innovation, that generates spillover effects which typically arise in a high-density environment rather than in quiet rural backwaters. As I will explain further below, these spillover effects can be internal to an organisation or external across organisations, industries and enterprises in a city where the exchange of ideas can happen spontaneously and in many different ways. Being a largely self-taught economist, she anticipated the new economic growth theory of the 1980s and 1990s (Romer, 1986) and was proven correct in the empirical work of Glaeser *et al.* (1992), who, using a dataset on the growth of large industries in 170 US cities between 1956 and 1987, found that local competition and urban variety, rather than knowledge spillovers within industries, drove growth, consistent with the theories of Jacobs (1969).

Smart Cities

A more modern concept that has received much attention in recent years is the notion of a smart city, sometimes also called a digital city, or a technology-enabled city, highlighting the role of digital technology in redefining the delivery of urban infrastructure and supporting sustainable growth. Townsend (2011) defines a smart city as a place where government, business and citizens are using digital technology to address timeless urban problems such as traffic congestion, pollution, crime, health service provision and disease control. Proponents of the concept of a smart city stress the fact that "cities now represent the core hubs of the global economy, acting as hives of innovation in technical, financial and other services" and that cities have to adapt to changes in information and communications technology (ICT) to realise the productivity and efficiency gains that have transformed the way businesses and corporations operate.

> Globalisation has led to the creation of a hierarchy of cities across the world within which cities compete for access to natural resources and skilled workers. Cities must not only create traditional employment opportunities, but also help create and attract new industries to their areas. To maintain and secure global competitiveness, cities today must tackle their own challenges while also maintaining growth. (The Climate Group *et al.*, 2011)

This technology-based concept of urban planning builds on similar ideas voiced by Jacobs half a century earlier and developed by economic geographers and urban sociologists in the 1990s. Through the concept of the smart city, technology can be seen as a turbocharger for places where innovation and creativity are fostered through the exchange of ideas and other spillover effects that rely on physical proximity and chance encounters.

The Boundary of a City – Urban Areas as a Geographic Concept

Cities are typically delineated with respect to the area and population over which a city government possesses political authority and has the responsibility to maintain its urban infrastructure, safeguard the safety of its citizens, and run schools, cultural institutions etc. Cities have administrative boundaries and within cities we find boroughs, districts and quarters that have their specific governance structures and responsibilities for the supply of local services and utilities. These city government structures and areas of competence of city councils can vary from city to city and from country to country. Some cities have developed political institutions that resemble those that operate at the national level and include the authority to tax its citizens, whereas other cities have a system of local administration under the tight control of a central or regional government.

Economists sometimes define the city more broadly and sometimes more narrowly. The core of a city – a narrow concept – is the central location for firms, government and other cultural institutions which offer jobs and services for people who live inside but also outside the city boundaries. Economists understand the city as a local labour market and proceed to define the city in terms of a functional urban area or region (FUR) within which the large majority of economic activities take place. A city may sometimes form the core of a metropolitan area containing a large population nucleus. In the definition of a metropolitan statistical area (MSA) of the US Management and Budget Office (2010), an MSA is made up of a principal city or core-based statistical area with a minimum population of 50,000 and adjacent communities that have a high degree of integration with that nucleus.

The economic definition of an FUR or an MSA is important when estimating the economic size and weight of a city. For example, in 2014 the city of Paris contained within its administrative boundaries a population of 2.2 million (INSEE, 2014), but estimates by UN Population Division (2014) put that figure at 10.46 million for the metropolitan population. The population estimates for London vary between 8.2

million for the 32 boroughs that make up the Greater London, the UN definition of 9.7 million (UN Population Division, 2014) and another estimate, by Brinkhoff (2017), which put the size of the London agglomeration at over 14 million in 2016.

With these examples, I want to demonstrate that our understanding and analysis of cities depend on estimates and assumptions and not always very clearly defined boundaries. While from an economic analytical perspective I prefer to rely on an economic definition of an agglomeration, either an FUR or an MSA, to measure a city's importance, I recognise that the political analysis may be better served by a definition based on the administrative boundaries over which a mayor or city council can wield political influence. The two perspectives do not necessarily coincide.

Another concept that is relevant to our discussion in this chapter is the sociological perspective, which focuses on understanding functions and processes among social and political groups in a city that determine power structures, social hierarchies and spheres of influence. Through this perspective, which has been successfully applied by city scholars such as Saskia Sassen in a number of books (e.g. Sassen, 1998, 2011, 2001), we come to understand and appreciate how major cities such as New York, Tokyo and London have become global cities that are critical elements of a new international trading system and have helped to shape and define globalisation. We will consider this perspective further when discussing globalisation and the role of cities.

Cities as Political and Commercial Centres in History

Many authors and historical scholars have told the story of the golden age of cities in history (e.g. Hall, 1998; Bairoch, 1988), and have traced their development through the ages. Athens, Florence, Rome and Venice as the classical cities of antiquity were known for their status as centres of trade and political power. These classical cities were also known for their role as sponsors of new forms of art, architecture and literature, developing new ideas in philosophy and concepts of citizenship (e.g. Athens), and exporting innovations in trade and finance (e.g. Florence and Venice). In 1700 there were nine great cities that together saw their combined population grow from 600,000 to over 2 million in 1700, all of them capitals (Amsterdam, Copenhagen, Dublin, Lisbon, London, Madrid, Paris, Rome and Vienna) and five of them port cities. In an analysis of a sample of 207 cities, Bairoch (1988) finds that "Port cities, many of which also had other, purely commercial functions, constitute after capitals the class of cities with the greatest growth: roughly 55% of them doubled or even tripled in population." Today, Paris, London, New York and Tokyo are by common consent the most prominent world cities (Taylor, 2002; Sassen, 2001), with New York "the paradigm of urbanity" (Glaeser, 2011). Like all great metropolitan centres, they owe their rise to the pre-eminence of trade and very often shipping.

There is a fascinating historical analysis regarding the development of cities between 1000 and 1800, the start of the Industrial Revolution. In their paper "Princes and Merchants: European City Growth before the Industrial Revolution", De Long and Shleifer (1993) demonstrate on the basis of a statistical analysis of historical population data for 112 cities in nine regions in Europe from 1050 to 1800 that absolutist city governments – the "princes" in the title of their article – are associated with low economic growth, as measured by population growth. This is in contrast to non-absolutist regimes, such as self-governing city states ruled by merchants' oligar-chies or cities in constitutional monarchies where the rulers were bound by law. In their basic regression analysis, the effect of living under an absolutist regime for cities of more than 30,000 was a population reduction of nearly 180,000 per century (with a standard error of 50,000 people per century). The authors interpret this result as evidence that "suggests that limited government allows for faster city growth because they tend to impose lower taxes and less destructive tax rates". For reference, the total population living in Western European cities of 30,000 or more in 1650 was 4.7 million. Their results suggest that with no absolutist rule in the previous 150 years, Europe would have had a population of 8 million by 1650.

I believe it is instructive to discuss at this point a sample of cities whose development is closely related to trade and other salient factors that allowed the city to grow and flourish. I have chosen four city pairs to illustrate different historical situations and offer a perspective on factors that have driven the growth of cities through trade, technological change, and political power and governance: Venice and Florence, London and Tokyo, Chicago and Mexico City, and finally Shanghai and Dubai.

Venice and Florence

Let us start our review of cities and trade in history with Venice, an artificial city built by exiles and refugees on the mudflats and swamps of a lagoon off the north Italian coast, which from the 8th century onwards was trading salt from its marshes and eventually rose to a pre-eminent position in Europe in the 13th and 14th centuries (Ackroyd, 2009). Together with Florence, Venice is one in a network of commercial cities that overcame the decline in urbanisation after the fall of the Roman Empire through trade with Byzantium, a city that during these centuries of recession and population decline in Europe enjoyed periods of prosperity and growth. As Bairoch (1988, pp. 144–115) observes: "practically all of the largest cities of the Italian peninsula fell into the category of commercial cities, since international trade played a decisive role in almost every one of them". In the same passage Bairoch states: "Therein lays the seeds of the growth of the Italian trade cities, those independent commercial city-states that were thereafter to contain the largest part of the urban population of Italy."

This view is confirmed by De Long and Shleifer (1993), discussed above, who claim that the Venetian and Florentine republics were merchant and burgher-ruled city states where "government was close to a committee for managing affairs in the common interest of the bourgeoisie – a class that had a very strong interest in rapid economic growth".

According to their analysis, illustrated in Table 5.2, the republics ruled northern Italy from 1050 to 1650, after which the Habsburgs dominated the region with pre-dictable effects (until the end of the period of analysis, 1800). This coincides with the end of their population growth and the relative decline of Venice and Florence from the 16th century onwards, a period when Amsterdam became the immediate succes-sor to Venice, yielding this position to London two centuries later. London was the first city to reach a population of circa one million by 1800, under a regime of a constitutional monarchy. The role of the Venetian city government and its highly

Table 5.2 Classification of Western European regimes governing cities 1050–1800

1050–1200	1200–1330	1330–1500	1500–1650	1650–1800
Prince (Norman d'Haute-villes)	Prince (Hohenstaufens and Angevins)	Prince (Aragonese)	Prince (Habsburgs)	Prince (Habsburgs)
Free (Investiture Struggle)	Free (Republics)	Free (Republics)	Prince (Habsburg domination)	Prince (Habsburg domination)
Free (feudal)	Free (constitution)	Free (constitution)	Prince (Habsburgs)	Prince (Habsburgs)
Prince (Medieval empire)	Prince (anarchy: Great Interregnum)	Prince (petty despots)	Prince (petty despots)	Prince (petty despots)
Free (feudal)	Free (constitution)	Free (constitution)	Free (Dutch republic)	Free (Dutch republic)
Free (feudal)	Free (constitution)	Free (constitution)	Prince (Habsburgs)	Prince (Habsburgs)
Prince (Normans)	Prince (Angevin empire)	Prince (Wars of Roses)	Prince (Tudors)	Free (constitution)
Free (feudal)	Free (feudal)	Free (Hundred Years' War)	Free (religious strife)	Prince (Bourbons)
Free (feudal)	Free (constitution)	Free (constitution)	Prince (Habsburgs)	Prince (Bourbons)

Source: De Long and Shleifer (1993, p. 683).

secretive committees is vividly described by the historical biographer of cities Ackroyd (2009), who points out the ambiguity, duplicity and ambivalences that characterised the workings of the Council of Ten, who had to swear and live by an oath of "jura, perjura, secretum prodere noli" ("swear, forswear, and reveal not the secret"). This at some point in time undermined the capability of the city to grow and became an impediment to progress.

London and Tokyo

The history of London and its rise to become the largest city in the world by the early 19th century cannot be told in this short sketch nor can we dwell here on what makes London one of the three leading global cities today, alongside New York and Tokyo (more about this later). What makes the history of both London and Tokyo interesting is the population explosion and economic developments in the late 17th century which occurred roughly at the same time in both cities. London, like other trading cities in Europe, grew from Roman origins and by 1520 was still a city with only 55,000 inhabitants, one of several European trading cities of similar size, and much smaller than Paris, which at that time had a population of 225,000. By 1700, Paris and London were the first metropolises that had a population close to 500,000.

In the case of London, the rise of the textile production century since the late 16th century was arguably a critical factor (Ades and Glaeser, 1995). The late 16th century also saw innovations in transport that increased London's role as a centre for (i) internal commerce through the humble four-wheel cart, which was a major innovation introduced in 1588, and (ii) external trade through advances in shipping and navigation technology. International trade grew further: first as a consequence of military success against Spain and the discovery of vast new markets in Asia and the Americas, second through a change in the political balance of power with a highly discriminatory tax policy introduced by the Stuart monarchs that favoured the capital over the provinces in a period of great political instability in the 17th century, and third through the introduction of the constitutional monarchy after the Glorious Revolution in 1688 (Ades and Glaeser, 1995).

The comparison of Tokyo and London is instructive. Ades and Glaeser (1995, p. 220) estimate that the population of Edo (Tokyo's old name) without military personnel in 1700 was between 500,000 and 1 million (the lower figure is ascribed by Ades and Glaeser, 1995, to Samson, 1963, and the higher figure to Seidensticker, 1980). Like London, it grew explosively through a combination of politics and trade from being a castle surrounded by a village to become the second-largest city in the world (after Peking). The growth of Edo came at the expense of other Japanese centres of commerce and trade such as Nagasaki and Osaka, when "the sheer power of the central Japanese government created such a disproportionate amount of employment, safety, and wealth in Edo that the city became an urban giant" (Ades and Glaeser, 1995).

Today, Tokyo is the largest city in the world, whether measured by the population of its metropolitan area (c. 36 million) or GDP (US$1479 billion; PricewaterhouseCoopers, 2009). Together with New York and London, it is one of the three leading global cities in the world, thanks to the growth in national and international producer services and finance in the past 30 years. The parallels with the earlier period of growth in the 17th century are striking, as they highlight the role of government in promoting the urban restructuring of Tokyo and supporting its evolution into a global city in the 1980s (Sassen, 2001). According to Sassen, in the mid-1980s, a profound transformation took place in Tokyo, with many old industrial districts in central areas of the city being rebuilt, thus changing the face of the urban landscape and with it the employment structure. Overall, the category of producer services increased by 71% in Tokyo from 1977 to 1985 (Sassen, 2001). She ascribes this development to a deliberate policy switch away from a "strategy of multi-polar, autonomous and sustainable development (Third Comprehensive Development Plan) that would promote dispersal of activities out of Tokyo to one of selective concentration of global economic functions such as finance, information services, and media in Tokyo (Fourth Plan)". A similar pattern can be observed for London from the 1960s onwards: a city that was an important centre for light manufacturing lost 800,000 jobs up to 1985, had a stagnant economy for 20 years, and, beginning in 1984, saw a new phase of rapid growth based on finance and producer services, with employment in these industries quickly overtaking that in manufacturing (Sassen, 2001).

Chicago and Mexico City

Chicago and Mexico City are two American cities that share some similarities while exhibiting some significant differences. Both cities are among the top ten largest cities in the world when measured by population and GDP. Chicago is the fourth-largest city economy in the world and more or less the same size as London. Mexico City, with a population the size of New York, ranks eighth in terms of GDP (PricewaterhouseCoopers, 2009). Both cities are major trading hubs in their respective countries or regions, but neither are major port cities, being located inland.

Historically, going back to the 19th century, Chicago at the shores of Lake Michigan was a major manufacturing centre and a trading hub of an enormous agro-industrial complex with its own financial services sector to support its regional business (Sassen, 2001). It owes its history to its geography and the technological revolution of rail transport. Mexico City, by comparison, is a very old city, arguably one of the oldest cities in the world, and a capital city of an ancient Aztec Empire in the 15th century. It became the major manufacturing city in Mexico and at one point supported over 50% of the country's manufacturing activities, representing a highly concentrated source both of demand and of supply in a domestic economy that for a long time was closed off from international trade. Both these cities, however, underwent massive structural changes in the 1980s, losing the headquarters of many large corporations and much of their manufacturing employment. In the case of Mexico City, this was correlated with the Mexican currency and debt crisis of 1982, which was followed by an effort to embark on a major programme of trade liberalisation that had a significant impact on the structure of Mexican industry and led to a decentralisation of manufacturing away from Mexico City. This phenomenon has been the subject of several economic studies, which will be reviewed in the following section on geography and trade.

What further makes the history of these two cities interesting and meaningful in the context of this chapter is the way in which both cities in their recent history transformed themselves into leading international centres of producer services, serving not only their historical hinterland but also increasingly a global market. This has led some analysts to argue that both cities have to be considered today as global cities, or at least world cities in formation. Taylor (2002), for example, ranks Chicago as a top ten full-service global city, just behind the top four of New York, London, Tokyo and Paris, and Parnreiter (2010) makes the case that Mexico City has become part of the cross-border network of global cities.

Shanghai and Dubai

According to Brook (2013), Shanghai and Dubai are both prime examples of "future cities", cities that "look as if they were not where they are". These cities, like the other two cities he describes in his book, Mumbai and St Petersburg, were built with a design that was purposefully disorienting in terms of its national geographic context. In each of these cities the development of trade played a crucial, if not an overriding, role.

Shanghai is located where the world's third longest river, the Yangtse, empties into the great Pacific Ocean, making it one of the great port cities of the world and "the gateway to the world for one tenth of humanity" (Brook, 2013). Not surprisingly, Shanghai is China's commercial and financial capital. Its rise to global pre-eminence is historically closely linked to trade and, more specifically, a series of government trade policy interventions that allowed it to prosper. As documented in Brook (2013), until the early 19th century international Chinese trade was conducted primarily and in a tightly controlled way through the port of the city of Canton (now Guangzhou) on the Pearl River Delta, 1000 miles south of Shanghai, and the major gateway for the export of tea and import of opium. When the emperor outlawed opium in 1839, the previously very important trade in opium was immediately affected, triggering a three-year trade war with the British which only ended with the peace of Nanjing in 1842. As part of the peace deal, Shanghai, together with four other Chinese cities, was opened up to trade. In the case of Shanghai, this implied the permission for foreigners to reside year-round in Shanghai and the introduction of the legal principle of "extra-territoriality", thereby avoiding the application of China's strict criminal code to foreign merchants in favour of the application of British law (Brook, 2013). Extending this principle to other areas of law led, among other things, to the creation of foreign-run zones called "foreign settlements and concessions" (e.g. British, French and American settlements), which even today still give the city a distinctly global look and feel through the Western-style buildings and country-specific architecture in each zone. Shanghai's extraterritorial status also meant that it became a very open city with a multitude of nationalities settling in the city and a booming economy. Major banks set up business in Shanghai, such as the Hong Kong and Shanghai Banking Corporation in 1865, which today is one of the world's largest banks. Like all booms, Shanghai's boom did not last, and the city's fortunes ebbed and flowed together with political upheavals, uprisings and revolutions in the 20th century.

It was only by the end of the 20th century that another opening up of Shanghai to international trade and finance occurred through the deliberate policy of the communist Chinese government, which transformed the fortunes of Shanghai by decree and a series of liberalizing policy initiatives designed to attract foreign talent and expertise, with notable success. With a metropolitan population of circa 15 million, PricewaterhouseCoopers (2009) ranks it 25th globally in terms of the 2008 GDP (about the same as that of Greece), but projects that the city will enter the top ten by 2025 with a GDP of US$692 billion, which would be about the same as the GDP of Switzerland in 2016.

Our final city mini-case study is Dubai. In Taylor's classification of world cities, Dubai is classed as a "world city in formation" (Taylor, 2002). It does not figure among PricewaterhouseCoopers' top 100 cities ranked by economic size. Yet it deserves to be analysed as a global trading and finance hub alongside other cities that are much larger. Dubai is estimated to have a population of 2.5 million (UN Population Division, 2014). According to Brook (2013), Dubai has a trading history of over 2000 years, being in a central location at the crossroads of Europe, Asia, Africa and the Middle East. The British East India Company sought to safeguard the region and struck a series of agreements with the local sheiks as early as 1820 to keep the region peaceful and the trade routes open, and this continued up to and throughout the 20th century, supported by a laissez-faire approach born of a trading port tradition.

Dubai is arguably a supply-side success story rather than the result of a demand-led economic development. With full independence from Great Britain (1971) and the discovery of oil in the 1960s, Dubai obtained an independent source of finance. Through a deliberate government policy, the city allowed for the influx of traders and guest workers from newly independent but protectionist/socialist India. This was accompanied by major infrastructure investments (which reached 25% of GDP) that, among other things, created Jebel Ali (1979) as the largest man-made port and saw the launch of Emirates Airways, the establishment of "free zones" where local laws did not apply, and the creation of the International Financial Centre in 2002. "As the locomotive built Daniel Burnham's Chicago, the jetliner built Sheikh Mohammed's Dubai" (Brook, 2013). Sheik Mohammed (in 1981 only aged 31) transformed Dubai in the 1980s from a regional trading hub into a global hub (with 96% of the population being foreign).

Geography and Trade

There is a long history of spatial economics and the analysis of location of economic activity, going back to Johann Heinrich von Thünen (1826/1966), a pioneer of economic geography, writing in the early 19th century (for an excellent overview of the early literature on spatial economics see Fujita *et al.*, 1999). He analysed optimal land use by farmers around a central town location, with daily foods such as vegetables being grown close to the town and cattle being farmed further away, thus integrating transports costs and land rents into his analysis. This very basic insight of a trade-off between transport costs and land rents is simple yet powerful and was translated by Alonso (1964) into an analysis of central business districts in urban areas, where farmers were replaced by commuters who had to make location decisions, taking into account the price of residential property and trading this off against commuting costs.

Another strand of economic location analysis focuses on the analysis of urban systems and the geographic size distribution of cities (Henderson, 1986, 1974). A third strand of analysis, central place theory, emphasises the external benefit of certain professions and industries being located in one central place, generating scale economies and increasing returns to scale, a concept going back to one of the giants of classical economics: Alfred Marshall (1920). Using the example of the city of Sheffield, Marshall explained the development of industrial districts in terms of three types of effects of increasing returns: (i) knowledge spillovers, (ii) the existence of thick markets in specialised skills, and (iii) the backward and forward linkages with input and output markets. Central place theory was developed by Christaller (1933/1966) and Lösch (1954) and emphasises the trade-off between scale economies and transportation costs to explain agglomeration effects and the distribution of cities and their hinterlands in an economy characterised by a hierarchy of "central places".

Much of this traditional type of economic geography of cities did not explicitly model or focus on international trade, and certainly did not capture explicitly the trade policy dimension. The economic analysis of cities was largely restricted to the analysis of land use, questions of migration of the rural population to urban centres, the process of urbanisation, and the size structure and distribution of cities within countries. This may seem surprising, as any analysis of cities as trading centres is by definition associated with international trade, whether it is trade with the national hinterland of a city or trade with other countries. The notion of transport costs determining the location of sources of supply of goods applies equally to internal transport costs and external costs of trade, whether these costs are transport costs or tariff costs. However, in this early period of location analysis the trade policy perspective did not matter. Location analysis did not include or deal with the costs of trading across national borders. Conversely, international trade theory, a traditional branch of economic theory, did not apply the concepts of transportation costs and economies of scale that are part of spatial theory and location analysis either. This only changed in the 1980s, when the new industrial economics literature developed these concepts in models of monopolistic competition and applied them, among others, to international trade (Helpman and Krugman, 1985) and economic growth and innovation (Grossman and Helpman, 1991). These seminal contributions and developments in economic thought paved the way for economists to go back and apply these concepts and models to the study of cities in what has become known as the new economic geography.

The contribution of the economic analysis of cities, integrating the new economic geography with international trade theory, is very much linked with the path-breaking work of Paul Krugman and others in the 1990s and developed further since then. In a series of articles, these authors sought to analyse the interaction between the development of a city and a country, linking this development to political and economic factors such as the decrease in costs of transport, the decrease in external tariffs and other trade barriers, as well as changes in political regimes and the stability of the political system in a country (see for example: Krugman, 1991a, 1991b; Krugman and Livas, 1996). In his Gaston Eyskens Lectures, Krugman (1991a) explained the emergence of a more unified discipline in economics as follows:

> About a year ago I more or less suddenly realized that I have spent my whole professional life as an international economist thinking and writing about economic geography, without being aware of it. By "economic geography" I mean "the location of production in space"; that branch of economics that worries about where things happen in relation to each other.

A good illustration of this type of analysis is the story of the explosive population growth and subsequent slowdown of Mexico City, a city that grew from a population of 1.5 million in 1940 to 8.5 million in 1970 and 18 million in the mid-1990s (Ades and Glaeser, 1995). This was the starting point for a seminal article by Krugmann and Livas (1996), who analysed explicitly the impact of the trade liberalisation on the decentralisation of the population and industrial activity in a country that was, prior to the conclusion of several bilateral and multilateral trade agreements, heavily focused on one giant urban centre that was both the most important market and the most important source of supply. In the case of Mexico, 40% of all manufacturing production was at some time concentrated in Mexico City. With trade liberalisation, the benefit of being close to the largest market was reduced, as imported goods at a lower cost became more readily available across the country. Trade with other countries, notably the United States, thus became more attractive. Starting in 1985, a number of reforms and trade agreements were swiftly implemented (culminating in 1993 with the conclusion of the North American Free Trade Agreement, or NAFTA), leading to a closer integration of the Mexican economy with its much larger neighbouring market of the United States. This natural experiment has attracted much attention in the economic literature and Krugman and Livas's theoretical paper is one that has focused on the effect of this event on the deconcentration of economic activity away from the capital city. They present a simplified model of the pull of centripetal forces of economies of scale in a large city, with commensurate forward and backward market linkages that operate against the pull of centrifugal forces due to land rents and commuting costs. What their model successfully does is to demonstrate how the lowering of trade and tariff barriers promoted the deconcentration process that fits the economic history of Mexico and Mexico City and illustrates the effect of protectionism and the explosive growth of Mexico City prior to trade liberalisation.

At the same time, Ades and Glaeser (1995) undertook an empirical cross-country analysis, supported by five case studies, which widened the analysis to include political factors in their analysis of the emergence of mega-cities. The data they collected and analysed related to urbanisation and population statistics for 1970, 1975, 1980 and 1985 in 85 countries, covering 100 agglomerations with a population of over 2 million in 1985. Their results indicate that an increase in the size of a country along with a decrease in population density tends to lower the growth rate of main cities, thus confirming the predictions of the Krugman and Livas model (Ades and Glaeser, 1995). Their results also demonstrate "that main cities are, on average, 42 percent larger if they are also capital cities". They claim that their results, while generally confirming the findings of Krugman and Livas (1996), add more explanatory power through the inclusion of models of government and political stability.

Table 5.3 summarises the findings of Ades and Glaeser (1995) with respect to the influence of politics on urban concentration. More recent studies have further tested the Krugman and Livas theory by improving on the empirical analysis and extending the model to include other cost factors such as communication costs. While not all studies were able to confirm the original findings, the work indicates how valuable it is to bring together the economics of trade and geography. Other studies have

Table 5.3 Urbanisation and political stability

STABLE DEMOCRACIES
Urban Concentration = 0.23 (0.032)
Number of Observations = 24

UNSTABLE DEMOCRACIES
Urban Concentration = 0.35 (0.07)
Number of Observations = 6

STABLE DICTATORSHIPS
Urban Concentration = 0.3 (0.03)
Number of Observations = 16

UNSTABLE DICTATORSHIPS
Urban Concentration = 0.37 (0.02)
Number of Observations = 3

Source: Figure 1, Ades and Glaeser (1995). Urban concentration is defined as the average share of urbanised population living in the main city from 1970 to 1985. Stable countries are defined as those whose average number of revolutions and coups is below the worldwide median. Dictatorships are countries whose average Gastil index for the period is higher than 3. Standard errors are in parentheses.

tried to evaluate the economic inequality effects at the city level that materialise in a globalising economy.

One paper that illustrates very well the empirical analysis of the relationship between trade liberalisation and urban concentration in developing countries is the paper in the *World Bank Economic Review* by Karayalcin and Yilmazkuday (2015) using more recent and detailed trade openness data. They measure trade openness on the basis of tariff measures controlled by policymakers rather than the traditional trade-to-GDP ratio used in older studies. They claim that their results are robust to many alternative estimation methods and consideration of alternative explanatory variables. They also refer to a similar approach adopted by Sanguinetti and Volpe Martincus (2009) to the analysis of trade liberalisation in Argentina, in terms of which careful analysis of a reduction of tariffs on an industry-by-industry basis over the period 1985–1994 confirmed the impact on location choices of industries away from Buenos Aires, which to date had been the absolutely dominant city in Argentina, with a share of the population of over 35% in 1985.

Figure 5.2, reproduced from the paper by Karayalcin and Yilmazkuday (2015), illustrates how the level of urban concentration, measured by the percentage of the urban population living in the largest city of a country, has tended to fall significantly in the period 1970–2000 in liberalising countries and significantly more so

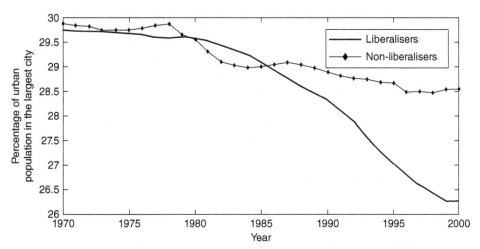

Figure 5.2 Urban population concentration under different trade policy regimes.
Source: "The Great Liberalization and the Percentage of Urban Concentration in the Largest City" (table) from Karayalcin and Yilmazkuday (2015).
Notes: The average percentage of urban population in the largest city for non-liberalisers has been normalised to the corresponding average value for liberalisers from 1970 to 1985 for comparison. Source: World Development Indicators.
The samples are as follows:
Liberalisers: Argentina, Australia, Bangladesh, Bolivia, Brazil, Chile, China, Colombia, Ecuador, Indonesia, India, Japan, South Korea, Sri Lanka, Mexico, New Zealand, Pakistan, Peru, Philippines, Thailand, Trinidad and Tobago, Taiwan, Uruguay, Venezuela.
Non-liberalisers: Algeria, Austria, Belgium, Canada, Côte d'Ivoire, Denmark, Finland, France, Germany, Ghana, Hong Kong, Iceland, Israel, Italy, Malaysia, Morocco, Nepal, Netherlands, Paraguay, Singapore, Spain, Sweden, Turkey, United Kingdom, United States.

than the ratio observed for non-liberalisers. In other words, the Uruguay Round of liberalisation has had a dramatic effect on the distribution of economic activity, particularly in developing countries that had adopted tariff-reducing trade policies. An interesting finding worth mentioning is that their theoretical model integrates intermediate goods in the analysis and allows the model to capture the reduction of international trade costs that are particularly relevant for border and port cities, thus refining the deconcentration analysis.

The new economic geography literature has provided further empirical evidence on the drivers of growth of cities that sheds light on the intimate relationship between cities and trade, and importantly, globalisation. The contribution of Glaeser *et al.* (1992) is an empirical test of the type of spillover effects that economists and urban theorists have claimed are at the heart of the success of cities and explain the positive effect of industries locating in a city in spite of high land rents, congestion and other costs of location in a dense urban environment. The authors collected data on employment growth across major industries in 170 US cities from 1956 to 1987 that permits the testing of two alternative theories of spillover effects: (i) the synergies derived from co-location and specialisation of industries in the same city (intra-industry synergies) argued, among others, by Marshall (1920), against the alternative, and (ii) the spillover effects that come from outside an industry, which Jacobs (1969) argued were at the heart of a city's attractiveness and ability to attract talent. Their analysis strongly supports industries' external spillover effects, as argued by Jacobs. They find that, as measured by relative employment growth, industries grow slower in cities where they are more heavily overrepresented. They cite the example of the metals industry growing strongly in Savannah, Georgia, where the industry was not heavily present in 1956, in contrast to Fresno, California, where the metals industry declined, having been overrepresented in 1956 (Glaeser *et al.*, 1992).

Overall, what these papers do is to highlight the importance of the international trading environment, changes in transport costs, national taxation systems and changes in trade policy for the economic development of cities. This serves as the basis for analysing other perspectives on cities and trade, namely the sociological and political perspectives which look at the role of global cities in the globalisation process.

Cities and Globalisation

So far, we have mainly discussed the relationship between trade and cities in the context of national trade policy measures. But what about the role of cities in the global context and the wider multilateral global trading system, and in particular the dominant trend towards the globalisation of business over the past 20–30 years? What is the contribution of academic research on cities in this area?

The answer in short is quite a lot! In particular, Saskia Sassen has over an extended period studied the interdependence of cities (Sassen, 1990), cities in the world economy (Sassen, 2011), the demand for labour in global cities (Sassen-Koob, 1984) and the mobility of labour and capital (Sassen, 1988). Her approach has primarily been a sociological one, developing the modern concept of the global city and amassing empirical evidence, in particular in her classic book *The Global City*, which first appeared in 1991, with a second edition ten years later, in which she discusses the emergence and significance of the three leading global cities of today, New York,

London and Tokyo (Sassen, 2001). In this book she develops seven hypotheses, which must be seen against three major economic trends. The major trends can be summarised as: (i) the globalisation of industry and commerce, (ii) the technological revolution in the information technology (IT) and communications industry, and (iii) the increase in international capital and labour mobility. Her seven hypotheses are:

1. The geographic dispersal of economic activities as a key factor in the growth and importance of central corporate functions;
2. The outsourcing of these increasingly complex central functions by global firms;
3. The freedom of global firms to locate where they see the greatest advantage;
4. The agglomeration economies that specialised service firms are able to exploit;
5. The importance for specialised service firms of international networks and affiliations;
6. The growing numbers of highly specialised high-level professionals and high-profit-making specialised service firms; and
7. The growing informalisation of a range of economic activities which find their effective demand in cities.

This is not the place to discuss Sassen's important book and analysis in detail, but it helps to illustrate her thesis with reference to the example of the growth of one of the major producer services for global firms where services are provided through offices in major cities, namely corporate legal services. In her book on global cities, Sassen provides a table (Sassen, 2001) illustrating the leading law firm in the year 2000 operating in a number of countries outside its home country, together with the percentage of lawyers operating outside the home country (Table 5.4).

I have updated the list with similar information for 2017 (Table 5.5), which ranks the top ten law firms by global revenues. The table also indicates the number of countries in which these firms operate and the number of lawyers on their books.

What these tables demonstrate is the predominance of global law firms from the United States and the United Kingdom and the growth of the geographic scope of their operations over the past 20 years. What these tables also illustrate is the

Table 5.4 Top ten law firms in 2000 ranked by number countries

Rank	Name	HQ	Lawyers % abroad	Number of countries
1	Baker & McKenzie	Chicago	80	35
2	White & Case	New York	47	24
3	Clifford Chance	London	62	20
4	Linklaters	London	n.a.	17
5	Allen & Overy	London	35	17
6	Freshfields	London	51	15
7	Skadden Arps	New York	8	11
8	Shearmann & Sterling	New York	25	9
9	Cleary Gottlieb	New York	33	8
10	Sullivan & Cromwell	New York	13	7

Source: *The Economist*, cited in Sassen (2001).

Table 5.5   Top ten law firms by revenues 2018

Rank	Name	HQ	Revenues (US$ billion)	Number lawyers	Number of countries
1	Latham Watkins	Los Angeles	2.82	2600	14
2	Baker McKenzie	Chicago	2.67	4700	47
3	Kirkland & Ellis	Chicago	2.65	2000	n.a.
4	Skadden Arps	New York	2.50	1700	22
5	DLA Piper	London/Chicago	2.47	n.a.	40
6	Dentons		2.21	7000	50
7	Clifford Chance	London	2.09	3300	26
8	Allen & Overy	London	2.06	2800	31
9	Jones Day	Cleveland	1.98	2800	18
10	Linklaters	London	1.95	2000	20

Source: Investopedia (2018).

increased importance of the international networks in major cities for one professional service sector, a picture that could easily be replicated for other producer services such as accounting and management consultancy. One of the drivers of this trend that Sassen sets great store by relates to the increase in capital and labour mobility, which she considers to be one of the chief characteristics of globalisation, where global cities act as hubs and magnets for globalising business and contribute to the international trading order through their specialisation in producer services.

While some major cities that we surveyed in our earlier section on cities in history have declined or disappeared, many have continued to grow and expand to become international centres of trade and finance and now form a network of interconnected global cities. The Globalisation and World Cities Research Network (GaWC) at the University of Loughborough prepared an Inventory of World Cities which classifies 122 cities with respect to their aggregate scores for business services (accounting, advertising, banking and law) at four different levels (Taylor, 2002):

1. *Alpha World Cities* (10): Full-service world cities, which include the four top-rated global cities of Tokyo, New York, London and Paris, as well as Chicago, Frankfurt, Hong Kong, Los Angeles, Milan and Singapore;
2. *Beta World Cities* (10): Major world cities, which include San Francisco, Sydney, Toronto, Zurich, Brussels, Madrid, Mexico City, São Paulo, Moscow and Seoul;
3. *Gamma World Cities* (35): Minor world cities; and
4. *Evidence of world city formation* (67).

Today these cities have more in common than in earlier times when their role was defined more closely by their local geography and their role within a country. Take the case of Mexico City, which has been extensively studied and of which Parnreiter (2010) argues:

> ... that in the 1990s Mexico City has become part of the cross-border network of global cities that constitutes the basic structure of today's world economy. As part of this network, Mexico City takes on global city functions such as controlling, managing and servicing processes of globalization.

Cities and Nations

At the beginning of this chapter, we defined cities as areas of high population density and concentration of economic activity, which since antiquity have owed their existence to trade. By measuring the economic output of the world's largest cities, we then demonstrated the economic power of those that are on par with major countries in terms of that economic power. We further placed the analysis of the growth of cities in a framework of economic geography and location analysis and surveyed the empirical literature that illustrated the impact of trade policy on a city's development, as well as on the deconcentration of economic activity within a country. In the previous section, we surveyed the burgeoning literature on the role of major and global cities in the context of globalisation, which emphasises the connectedness of global cities and their role as producer services hubs for global corporations.

In all this, we have focused on the city and less on the country in which the city is located and which provides the political and legal system in which it operates. The key role of the nation state in the economic development of a country and its cities and the emergence of the global trading system through the initiatives of national governments appears obvious and hardly worth emphasising. Some have argued that the 20th century should be regarded as the century of the nation state (Clark and Moonen, 2016; Waltz, 1999), with the global economy growing at sustained levels for a very long period and national governments building an impressive system of multilateral institutions engaged in the promotion of international conflict resolution, education, economic development and trade. More recently, however, with the onset of the new millennium, the emergence of globalisation as a driving force in the world economy (remember *The World is Flat* by Thomas Friedman, published in 2005), and in the wake of the Global Financial Crisis, some have argued that today is the era when nation states are "rapidly ceding sovereignty to alternative configurations of governance, power and influence" and "major 20th century institutions like the United Nations and the World Bank are paralysed" (Muggah and Florida, 2017). Or, as Clark and Moonen (2016) put it:

> One upshot of 21st century globalisation is that more countries have seen their leading city or group of cities become international commercial and corporate management hubs and visitor destinations, serving large customer and client markets in their wider regions beyond national borders. National policymakers find that these cities fundamentally alter the migration patterns of workers, set new business and service standards and have a major impact on the number and kind of international firms, capital and visitors that a nation attracts.

There are two sets of interesting questions here. One is whether the role of nation states and multilateral institutions made up of and supported by nation states is indeed declining and being usurped by other forms of governance, power and influence such as major cities and conurbations of mega-cities. The other question which is relevant in the context of this chapter is what role cities can and do play in actively shaping the international trading system and trade policy.

To answer the first question requires exploring the fundamental difference between a city and a nation and understanding what the relationship is between them. Paul Krugman provides a succinct answer. In his Gaston Eyskens Lectures held in

Brussels (Krugman, 1991a), he devoted his third lecture to the topic of regions and nations. He started with the observation that a nation is not a region or a single location like a city, which is characterised by spatial economic phenomena such as knowledge spillovers, labour market pooling advantages and the supply of intermediate goods and producer services. They all matter at the city level and determine the relationship between an urban core and its periphery and between cities in the global city network (as discussed in the previous section). By contrast, in his view, countries are collections of cities and regions that define themselves by the restrictions they impose on their citizens and business and this gives them a role in industry localisation, but the relationship does not operate in the opposite direction. In other words, cities are about trade and countries are about borders. In the words of Krugman (1991a):

> Nations matter – they exist in a modelling sense – because they have governments whose policies affect movements of goods and factors. In particular, national boundaries often act as barriers to trade and factor mobility.

Krugman then takes the example of the European Single Market 1992 Programme, where national governments decided to remove any remaining obstacles to internal trade in the European Union (EU) and make national borders obsolete. This was a major regional trade liberalisation project, where cities did not have a formal role in determining the removal of these restrictions although these were bound to have major economic consequences for the fortunes of London, Paris and Frankfurt as well as the regions of Europe. Another example that Krugman cites to make the point that countries do not necessarily define meaningful economic areas is that of the large manufacturing regions in the Northeast of the United States that arguably include parts of Ontario but not the states of Nebraska or Idaho. In the same vein, Vancouver and Seattle share more economic linkages than exist between Vancouver and Montreal.

This view is provocative and perhaps a gross simplification. But it does bring home the fact that, economically speaking, the role of countries in international trade is focused on and limited to shaping policies that facilitate trade by enterprises and movements of capital, intermediate goods and services across borders, but that the real action is happening in multinational corporations and global cities.

A more tempered and balanced critique of the notion that the nation state is dead and that we are now living in the age of cities has been put by Clark and Moonen (2016), who suggest that nation states have to rethink their traditional approach to cities, recognising the trends that have taken place and which require a more collaborative approach between cities and states. The three forces that they identify are: (i) metropolitanisation, (ii) systems of cities, and (iii) the internationalisation of multiple cities. The first trend is simply the emergence of very large city-regions and metropolitan areas everywhere in the world, which requires more cooperation, coordination and reform of governance, including redrawing the boundaries of a city. The second trend is related to our discussion in the previous section of the emergence of a heavily interconnected network of global cities and systems of cities, which often have complementary functions and specialisations which were previously constrained to national economies but can now be exploited internationally.

The third trend relates to the need for nation states to recognise the emerging capacities of multiple cities in the same nation to acquire international roles instead of only one global city being a country's gateway to the world. In their conclusions and recommendations Clark and Moonen suggest that:

> In the current cycle of globalisation, world cities have to develop the tools and the leadership to plan and guide their own success, but they also need national partners to help them achieve their competitive and citizen aspiration.

Given these trends and the analysis of the global role of cities, what about the role of cities as political actors? Do mayors have a political voice? Do they sit in a national parliament and have a voice in shaping the laws of countries? What is the role of the city in shaping and influencing trade policy and the global trading system? Are they represented in the global trade and development institutions such as the World Trade Organization (WTO), the United Nations Conference on Trade and Development (UNCTAD) and the World Bank? No, is the short answer. Membership of the WTO is the privilege of national governments. Cities and their political representatives are not part of the WTO and are not even partners or affiliates. Other international organisations such as the World Bank, the Caribbean Community (CARICOM) and the Economic Commission for Europe are affiliate members, observers or members of various trade policy initiatives and committees, but not cities. We look in vain for the name of the informal group of the world's largest cities, the C40, to appear anywhere. The influence of the C40 group of cities is mainly restricted to the promotion of environmental policies and knowledge sharing. Trade policy clearly remains the domain of national governments.

Still, there has been a significant increase in networks linking cities in the United States and across the world. Muggah and Florida (2017) claim that there are more than 200 of them. In the EU the Covenant of Mayors for Climate and Energy, launched in 2008, today includes 7755 European signatories, covering at least 250 million people. The signatories to the covenant have pledged actions to support the implementation of the EU CO_2 emissions reduction target of 40% by 2030. Similarly, in the United States, 392 so-called climate mayors, representing 69 million Americans, have affirmed their commitment to honour and uphold the Paris Agreement days after the US announcement of its withdrawal in 2017. Another example is the Global Parliament of Mayors which was launched in 2016 as a governance body of, by and for mayors from all continents to assert cities' right to self-government and empower cities to assume greater leadership and speak with a common voice. There are probably already more networks of cities than there are of nation states, though the former do not have nearly as much power.

But does this amount to a significant extension and strengthening of the formal role of cities in trade policy and economic policymaking generally? I am not sure this question can today be answered in the affirmative. These are attempts by major and global cities to become more involved in policy development, most prominently and successfully in the area of climate change and environmental policy, but I doubt whether the growth of the political and economic role of cities has led to a rapid decline in national sovereignty. In fact, what we currently observe in many democratic elections around the Western world is a nationalist backlash and resentment of a global elite that ironically typically resides in major cities. In the capital city and some other major commercial cities of a country we find the intellectual urban elite that shapes and disseminates ideas which ultimately find their way into a piece of legislation or government policy. Let us take the example of the network of producer services in global cities discussed in the previous section. The large accountancy and law firms all have their major offices in major cities and are frequently consulted and give advice on major new policy initiatives. Ditto major universities, which more often than not are located in major cities.

In conclusion, while I believe that the economic role of cities in trade and the development of the international trading system cannot be underestimated, the political role of cities should not be overestimated.

A Cities and Trade Research Agenda

In this chapter I have surveyed different strands of the economic, sociological, political and historical literature, analysing the relationship between cities and trade from different but always cities-based perspectives. I have tried to demonstrate how cities have been central to the growth and development of global trade and the world economy. Most recently, cities have become a critical factor explaining the phenomenon of globalisation through the emergence of an interconnected network of global cities. Trade policies have themselves been instrumental in the development of cities, as has been empirically demonstrated in a number of economic studies surveyed in this chapter and a historical case study review of four city pairs. While trade and trade-facilitating policy measures have been central to the growth of cities, these studies have also indicated how, contrary to popular belief, the opening up of a previously closed economy subject to a protectionist regime not only benefits the major cities in a country but also leads to a deconcentration of manufacturing activities in favour of other regions. This raises the interesting question of the political role of cities and whether cities should be more prominent in shaping a future trade policy agenda, particularly in a situation where in many countries more nationalist protectionist policies are being pursued and international treaties are being challenged and potentially weakened.

Regarding the scope for further academic research, it is fair to say that there have been major advances in the economic literature of the past 20 years, which has integrated economic geography with international trade theory. In another advance, the sociological literature has focused on themes such as globalisation and analysed cities as international or global systems of cities. Yet much of the empirical analysis is still undertaken on a regional or national basis. This is particularly true when it comes to international empirical economic analyses which require data on cities that is collected systematically. Here there is a research and information deficit. Countries have statistical offices and we are amply served with macroeconomic statistics on a regular basis. This is not true for cities, which, I have argued, are meaningful economic entities in their own right. Obtaining statistics would not take much effort. A few years ago, the World Bank started to take cities more seriously, moving away from the emphasis on rural poverty and development to trying to better understand the costs and benefits of urban development policies and climate change initiatives where cities play an important role (World Bank, 2009). Is this something that the WTO or the C40 could sponsor or contribute to?

The more important question is, however, whether cities should have a voice and be represented more in international trade bodies and organisations, given their economic importance in what some observers have called "the age of cities". This chapter does not provide the answer but suggests that the argument merits further discussion.

References

Ackroyd, P. (2009) *Venice: Pure City*. London: Chatto & Windus.

Ades, A.F. & Glaeser, E.L. (1995) Trade and Circuses: Explaining Urban Giants. *The Quarterly Journal of Economics*, 110, 195–227.

Alonso, W. (1964) *Location and Land Use: Toward a General Theory of Land Rent*. Cambridge, MA: Harvard University Press.

Arias, A.D.L. (2003) Trade Liberalisation and Growth: Evidence from Mexican Cities. *The International Trade Journal*, 17, 253–273.

Bairoch, P. (1988) *Cities and Economic Development: From the Dawn of History to the Present*. Chicago: University of Chicago Press.

Brinkhoff (2017) City Population – United Kingdom: Greater London. Retrieved from: https://www.citypopulation.de/php/uk-greaterlondon.php (accessed 4 July 2019).

Brook, D. (2013) *A History of Future Cities*. New York: W.W. Norton.

Christaller, W. (1966) *Central Places in Southern Germany*. Translated by Baskin, C.W. Englewood Cliffs: Prentice Hall. First published 1933.

Clark, G. & Moonen, T. (2016) *World Cities and Nation States*. Oxford: Wiley Blackwell.

Crowe, N. (1995) *Nature and the Idea of a Man-Made World*. Cambridge, MA: MIT Press.

De Long, J.B. & Shleifer, A. (1993) Princes and Merchants: European City Growth before the Industrial Revolution. *The Journal of Law & Economics*, 36, 671–702.

Friedman, T.L. (2005) *The World is Flat: A Brief History of the Globalized World in the Twenty-First Century*. London: Allen Lane.

Fujita, M., Krugman, P.R. & Venables, A.J. (1999) *The Spatial Economy: Cities, Regions, and International Trade*. Boston: MIT Press.

Glaeser, E. (2011) *Triumph of the City: How Our Greatest Invention Makes Us Richer, Smarter, Greener, Healthier, and Happier*. London: Macmillan.

Glaeser, E.L., Kallal, H.D., Scheinkman, J. *et al.* (1992) Growth in Cities. *Journal of Political Economy*, 100, 1126–1152.

Grossman, G.M. & Helpman, E. (1991) *Innovation and Growth in the Global Economy*. Cambridge MA: MIT Press.

Hall, P.G. (1998) *Cities in Civilization*. London: Weidenfeld & Nicholson.

Helpman, E. & Krugman, P. (1985) *Market Structure and Foreign Trade: Increasing Returns, Imperfect Competition, and the International Economy*. Cambridge, MA: MIT Press.

Henderson, J.V. (1974) The Sizes and Types of Cities. *American Economic Review*, 64, 640–656.

Henderson, J.V. (1986) Efficiency of Resource Usage and City Size. *Journal of Urban Economics*, 19, 47–70.

Hoornweg, D., Sugar, L. & Lorena Trejos, G.C. (2011) Cities and Greenhouse Gas Emissions: Moving Forward. *Environment and Urbanization*, 23, 207–227.

INSEE (Institut national de la statistique et des études économiques) (2014) *Populations Légales 2014 – Commune de Paris*. Retrieved from: https://www.insee.fr/fr/statistiques/2534314?geo=COM-75056 (accessed 4 July 2019).

Investopedia (2018) Retrieved from: https://www.investopedia.com/ (accessed 4 July 2019).

Jacobs, J. (1961) *The Death and Life of Great American Cities*. New York: Random House.

Jacobs, J. (1969) *The Economy of Cities*. New York: Random House.

Karayalcin, C. & Yilmazkuday, H. (2015) Trade and Cities. *World Bank Economic Review*, 29, 523–549.

Krugman, P. (1991a) *Geography and Trade*. Cambridge, MA: MIT Press.

Krugman, P. (1991b) Increasing Returns and Economic Geography. *Journal of Political Economy*, 99, 483–499.

Krugman, P. & Elizondo Livas, R. (1996) Trade Policy and the Third World Metropolis. *Journal of Development Economics*, 49, 137–150.

Lamy, P. (2006) Mastering Globalization: Contribution of the Cities. Speech presented to World Trade Organization, Geneva, 18 May 2006.

Lamy, P. (2010) The Role of Trade in the Rise of Merchant Cities. Speech presented to World Trade Organization, Shanghai, 22 July 2010.

Lösch, A. (1954) *The Economics of Location*. Yale: Yale University Press.

Marshall, A. (1920) *Principles of Economics*. London: Macmillan.

Muggah, R. & Florida, R. (2017) With Our Nation States on the Ropes, It's Time for Cities to Take the Lead. World Economic Forum. Retrieved from: https://www.weforum.org/agenda/2017/10/why-its-time-for-cities-to-take-the-lead (accessed 4 July 2019).

Parnreiter, C. (2010) Global Cities in Global Commodity Chains: Exploring the Role of Mexico City in the Geography of Global Economic Governance. *Global Networks*, 10, 35–53.

PricewaterhouseCoopers (2009) Which are the Largest City Economies in the World and How Might this Change by 2025? Retrieved from: http://pwc.blogs.com/files/global-city-gdp-rankings-2008-2025.pdf (accessed 4 July 2019).

Romer, P. (1986) Increasing Returns and Long-run Growth. *Journal of Political Economy*, 94, 1002–1037.

Sansom, G.B. (1963) *A History of Japan*. Stanford: Stanford University Press.

Sanguinetti, P. & Volpe Martincus, C. (2009) Tariffs and Manufacturing Location in Argentina. *Regional Science and Urban Economics*, 39, 155–167.

Sassen, S. (1988) *The Mobility of Labor and Capital: A Study in International Investment and Labor Flow*. Cambridge: Cambridge University Press.

Sassen, S. (1990) Economic Restructuring and the American City. *Annual Review of Sociology*, 16, 465–490.

Sassen, S. (1998) *Globalization and Its Discontents*. New York: New Press.

Sassen, S. (2001) *The Global City: New York, London, Tokyo*. Princeton: Princeton University Press.

Sassen, S. (2011) *Cities in a World Economy*. London: Sage.

Sassen-Koob, S. (1984) The New Labor Demand in Global Cities. In: Smith, M. (ed.) *Cities in Transformation*. Beverley Hills: Sage.

Seidensticker, E. (1981) *Low City, High City: Tokyo from Edo to the Earthquake*. New York: Knopf.

Taylor, P.J. (2002). The GaWC Inventory of World Cities. Retrieved from: http://www.lboro.ac.uk/gawc/rb/briefing5.html (accessed 4 July 2019).

The Climate Group, Accenture & University of Nottingham (2011) Information Marketplaces: *The New Economics of Cities*. Retrieved from https://www.theclimategroup.org/sites/default/files/archive/files/information_marketplaces_05_12_11.pdf (accessed 4 July 2019).

Townsend, A.M. (2013) *Smart Cities: Big Data, Civic Hackers, and the Quest for a New Utopia*. New York: W.W. Norton.

UN Population Division (2014). World Urbanization Prospects, the 2014 Revision. Available from: https://esa.un.org/unpd/wup/CD-ROM/ (accessed 4 July 2019).

US Management and Budget Office (2010) 2010 Standards for Delineating Metropolitan and Micropolitan Statistical Areas. Federal Register Vol. 75, No. 123, 28 June. Retrieved from: https://www.gpo.gov/fdsys/pkg/FR-2010-06-28/pdf/2010-15605.pdf (accessed 11 July 2019).

Von Thünen, J.H., Hall, P. & Wartenberg, C.M. (1966) *Der isolierte Staat. Von Thünen's "Isolated state"*. Translated by Carla M. Wartenberg, edited with an introduction by Peter Hall. Oxford: Pergamon. First published 1826.

Waltz, K.N. (1999) Globalization and Governance. *PS: Political Science & Politics*, 32, 693–700.

World Bank (2009) *World Development Report 2009: Reshaping Economic Geography*. Retrieved from: http://documents.worldbank.org/curated/en/730971468139804495/pdf/437380REVISED01BLIC1097808213760720.pdf (accessed 4 July 2019).

Chapter 6

Strategic Trade as a Means to Global Influence

Rebecca Harding and Jack Harding

Introduction

Since the 2008 Global Financial Crisis, the character of trade has changed. In the years before the crisis, world leaders spoke of trade almost exclusively in terms of its mutual economic benefits and as a tool for promoting global economic growth (Krueger, 2000; Clinton, 2000). For example, commentators spoke enthusiastically about the growth of South–South trade. There were investment opportunities, there was untold wealth in emerging markets, technology meant that we would share ideas, create a borderless world and even that fully fledged war would be a thing of the past. We talked about performance, integration and global citizenship with opportunities for all.

In the United States, every leader since Jimmy Carter has spoken of trade in these terms: in 1988 in his State of the Union address to Congress, Ronald Reagan stated that "protectionism is destructionism" (Reagan, 1988), George Bush Senior spoke in a presidential debate in 1992 of how free trade was linked to greater opportunities (Bush G. Sr., 1992). His successor, Bill Clinton, wrote in 1996 that "air trade among free markets does more than simply enrich America; it enriches all partners to each transaction" (Clinton, 1996). In January 2006, George W. Bush gave his State of the Union address and stated, "[k]eeping America competitive requires us to open more markets for all that Americans make and grow" (Bush, G.W., 2006). Bush's successor, Barack Obama, gave a speech in 2008 in Berlin where he declared "ogether, we must forge trade that truly rewards the work that creates wealth, with meaningful protections for our people and our planet. This is the moment for trade that is free and fair for all" (Obama, 2008).

However, in the years following the financial crisis, and in the past two years in particular, there has been a marked shift in the way states approach trade (Meyer

The Handbook of Global Trade Policy, First Edition. Edited by Andreas Klasen.
© 2020 John Wiley & Sons Ltd. Published 2020 by John Wiley & Sons Ltd.

and Garcia, 2018). To some this has been the demise of globalisation, while to others it has been directly triggered by changes in US policy (Noland, 2018), or, indeed, changes in UK policy (Lydgate and Winters, 2018). What is clear is that policy is shifting from multilateralism to bilateralism (Trommer, 2017). We contend that this is the result of more overtly nationalistic policies and based on the responses, in the US in particular, to populism which have arisen due to discontent with globalisation's capacity to provide the economic and welfare benefits to all that the "Trickle Down" theory of growth and development posited that it should (Aghion and Bolton, 1997).

The visible shift to bilateralism is corroborated by the way in which restrictive policy measures have been escalating. In 2016, the World Trade Organization (WTO) reported the highest monthly average increase in the number of protectionist measures by its members since 2011, with some 154 restrictive measures being introduced (WTO, 2016). Trade did decline in nominal value terms by some 15% between 2015 and 2016 but this was as much a function of the collapse of commodity prices as it was of trade restrictions – not least because over the same period there were 132 measures facilitating world trade, while the trade protectionist measures that were introduced were targeted at specific sectors by specific countries. Since trade in volume terms at least appeared to tick upwards in 2017, the longer-term economic effects of small-scale protectionism are minimal.

The Weaponisation of Trade

However, while it is too early to suggest that there has been a permanent shift in trade, the language of trade policy of late has been steeped in the rhetoric of war. Instead of global opportunities and wealth creation, politicians on both sides of the Atlantic have spoken of "protection", "security", "national interest", and "defence" in the context of trade. Former trade partners have been referred to as "enemies" with "unfair" protectionist policies against which it is natural for any politician to rail (Stracqualursi, 2017).

Since his election as the 45th US President, Donald Trump has conflated trade with foreign policy goals by explicitly linking discussions with China to the issue of curbing North Korea's nuclear programme and, in 2018, by linking unilateral tariffs on iron, steel and aluminium with specific tariffs on Chinese technology goods and, potentially, European cars with national security. The British Prime Minister, Theresa May, in her Article 50 letter to the President of the European Council triggering the United Kingdom's exit from the European Union (EU), suggested that a trade deal could be linked to UK participation in European security arrangements and, justifying the United Kingdom's arms sales to Saudi Arabia, declared that "they are important for us in terms of security, they are important for us in terms of defence and yes, in terms of trade" (May, 2017). This linguistic metamorphosis has altered how first-world states conceive of trade – its utility is now *publicly* seen as dual-purpose: to serve the national economic interest through promoting growth, but also to achieve foreign policy and military objectives abroad.

This *de facto* weaponisation of trade is clearly damaging, not just for the global economy with its reliance on multilateralism to support the principle of free trade, but also because it puts trade in a battlefield, not a boardroom. More nationalistic policies create an "us versus them" mentality which then becomes entrenched by more aggressive political rhetoric transforming trade irreparably from an economic tool into a political one.

This is not to argue that trade has hitherto been a purely economic phenomenon. Trade is clearly about more than just economics; it has an inescapable connection with politics principally as a result of the role it plays in creating power. This was the main argument proffered by Hirschman (1945) and forms the backdrop to our analysis here. His central argument is that trade is a means by which power is exerted over weaker nations and therefore is inherently "war-like" and political in nature.

After the financial crisis, trade has been wielded differently by states in their pursuit of political ends. Previous eras conceptualised trade as something that was *explicitly* economic and *implicitly* political – indeed much of the economic literature on trade policy and strategy focuses either on efficient tariffs regimes (Schroeder and Tremblay, 2015; Walker, 2015) or on corporate strategy (Rugman and Verbeke, 2017; Ghosh and Saha, 2015). Trade's connection to power and national interest has been viewed as secondary, even incidental, to the principal objective of mutually beneficial economic growth.

What makes this era substantively different from previous ones is that through more bellicose and nationalistic rhetoric, trade has become *explicitly* political and, in many cases, the preferred means in the pursuit of political ends. This, we contend, is an era of *strategic trade* and, as a result, we need to examine more closely its links with the theory of war and the theory of national strategy, not least because talk of trade wars in the national interest is now endemic.

This chapter is divided into two sections. The first section looks at our concept of strategic trade, its roots in globalisation and how the attempt to balance domestic and foreign policy goals through trade has had the unintended consequence of fuelling economic nationalism and, as a result, populism. The second section investigates the data behind strategic trade. This section examines trends in global and G20 (Group of Twenty) arms and dual-use goods trade. It then introduces a soft and hard power matrix based on this data for conceptualising each state's approach to foreign policy. It then moves on to examine the specific cases of Russian trade with Syria and UK trade with Syria and Saudi Arabia.

It is worth pointing out from the outset that this chapter is not an exposition of the economics of trade, nor is it an attempt to look at economic strategies towards trade. Rather, it is an exploration of how the role of trade has, largely through the rhetorical weaponisation of trade, shifted to become part of a more economically nationalist narrative.

Our central theme is clear: this shift from economics (intrinsic to multilateralism and the era of globalisation) to politics is not healthy for the global economy and yet this appears to be the direction in which the world is heading; our use of Hirschman's work is deliberate – he conflated trade, power and war to describe the link between trade and foreign relations in the run-up to World War II. This is an area that is only just beginning to be explored by economists in a theoretical sense and still relies heavily on a critical appraisal of the response of multilateral trade institutions such as the WTO to protectionism (Siles-Brügge and De Ville, 2015; Sheldon *et al.*, 2018). To ensure that we have shown the strategic use of trade in a variety of countries, we have given a general picture for the G20 countries, not just the ones that are currently exhibiting economic nationalism. However, we contend that the current change is so rapid and so dramatic that it is no longer adequate to restrict our theory or empirical analysis to economics alone. To understand the political economy of trade, we argue, we need also to understand its role in national strategy.

Strategic Trade

We begin with a discussion of strategic trade as we define it. Strategic trade was a phrase coined by Krugman (1986). For Krugman, it suggested that governments can catalyse resource reallocation to those sectors and businesses where economic rents (i.e. returns to capital and labour) are highest and protect them against foreign competition. He argued that trade was increasingly about taking national advantage of economies of scale and of the positive spillover effects (external economies) from technology and organisational learning. However, Krugman was writing in a period before the end of the Cold War and before the completion of the European Single Market. We argue that the free movement of capital, labour and ideas that defined the post-Cold War period has shifted the positive externalities of trade for technological and organisational purposes from the nation state to the multinational corporation (MNC) with three main effects.

First, it makes the real value in trade economically almost impossible to measure. Services and goods trade combine in one supply chain. This increases the value of trade even if volumes of goods traded themselves stay constant. Transactions within supply chains are hard to capture in trade statistics, and it is difficult to trace the value added and economic rents. This makes trade as a tool of national interest very difficult to gauge in economic terms. The consequence is that, just as we want to start to measure trade and trade performance nationally, trade growth itself has become unreliable – almost a Goodhart's Law[1] of international trade flows.

Second, it weakens the ability of domestic macroeconomic policy to capture the advantages of trade, either through currency manipulation or through tariffs and subsidies. Companies are able to shift their operations relatively swiftly to take advantage of favourable tax regimes and subsidies. As a result, the traditional policy levers can no longer deliver benefits at a domestic level.

Third, proportionately, it increases the power of nation states and trade blocs to form aggressive policies to disadvantage another nation politically (through sanctions) without doing lasting damage to their MNCs. This has the effect of creating global trade "enemies" – like Syria, Russia and Iran, or even China, from a Western perspective – and using them in public discourse to harness war-like rhetoric (US Government, 2017a) Therefore, given the nature of the modern era, we argue that the concept of strategic trade needs updating. Like Krugman, we also view trade as political. However, we see its utility as not only to benefit economic and social goals domestically, but also to promote national interests abroad in a military sense. Thus, our conceptualisation moves beyond his domestically focused framework and argues instead that trade is an integral component of state strategy.

This is a departure from the conventional view of trade. It is a revival of the link between foreign trade and power discussed by Hirschman, in the context of the build-up to World War II and by Findlay and O'Rourke (2007) in their analysis of inter-regional trade through history and its interface with economic and political power. It examines trade through the lens of strategic theory and what follows are three brief points on strategic theory to help clarify the argument.

First, strategy, like trade, is necessarily and inescapably linked with politics. The military theorist Liddell Hart (1967) defined it as "the art of distributing and applying military means to fulfil the ends of policy". However, in the context of the concept of strategic trade, nuclear strategist Gray's definition is more helpful: strategy is "the use made of (any) means by chosen ways in order to achieve desired political ends" (Gray, 2016).

Second, strategy is fundamentally about ends (or consequences), but it is not an end in itself. Instead, it should be understood as the *ways used* to achieve policy objectives. Conventionally, this refers to military means; however, as we will argue, there seems to be an emerging trend towards the use of trade to achieve policy objectives that just 15 years ago could have involved direct military action. Through the arms and dual-use goods trade, states are able to protect their strategic interests without direct military engagement. Trade in this manner is, to borrow British military strategist Liddell Hart's theory, an effective component of the "indirect approach" (Liddell Hart, 1967).

Third, strategies are a function of their cultural and social contexts. Therefore, in an era when the political will to engage with direct military action has been undermined by domestic discontent with protracted campaigns, trade becomes an attractive strategic option. To this end, the challenge is to reconcile a chosen strategy, in this context, trade, with the will of the people – this is done through public rhetoric.

Thus, trade can be aggressive, coercive, instrumental and political. In this sense, it is redolent of von Clausewitz's classic definition of war, first as the continuation of policy by another means, and second, through the supply of arms and ammunition to strategic partners, as an indirect "act of force to compel our enemy to do our will" (Clausewitz, 1832). In short, through language, the character of trade has changed from an *implicit* tool of coercion to the *explicit* means through which foreign policy objectives are achieved.

The question is why has there been such a shift in our approach to trade? And what are the consequences for domestic politics? The following section aims to answer these questions.

The Context of Globalisation

Arguably, globalisation has created the uncertainties we see now. As Stiglitz (2003) wrote, globalisation has put "new demands on nation states at the very same time that, in many ways, it has reduced their capacity to deal with those demands." The ever-closer integration of economies around the world put power into the hands of businesses to optimize capital and labour flows across borders. This challenged nation states to become multilateral in guaranteeing their economic security simply to support their business base, which itself meant that inequalities built domestically, while new entrants to the world trading system, such as China or South Korea, gained economic power (Stiglitz, 2017).

It is not that free trade and global movements of capital and labour are not intuitively a good thing. However, their benefits are not obvious to the general population who see lack of economic improvements in their own lives, and this has distanced the electorate from politics. The result is populism – or at the very least direct public scrutiny of the democratic legitimacy of international institutions, globalisation and its accompanying free movement of labour (immigration and the conflation with terrorism) and free movement of capital (perceived inequalities).

Trade is the logical route to connect both the national economic and the national strategic interest. Globalisation is both politicised and nationalised at the same time and nowhere has this been better captured than in the "Buy American, Hire American" executive order signed by Donald Trump in April 2017 (US Government, 2017b) or even the United Kingdom's "Exporting is Great" campaign (UK Department for International Trade, 2015). Trade policy at once becomes a tool to protect domestic interests and further strategic interests abroad. In short, it gives politicians a means of reconnecting with their electorates when traditional economic and foreign policy mantras have failed. It also, intentionally or otherwise, bolsters nationalist sentiments. The fact that US trade policy is so closely conflated with national security and, indeed, military ends corroborates the increasingly blurred lines between economic and military objectives in trade policy (Harding and Harding, 2017).

Globalisation itself has brought us to this point. It represented a paradigm shift: international activity and interactions changed the way in which politics, economics and society operated domestically. Because we are looking at this process in both economic and foreign policy terms, we are loosely grouping globalisation into four time-frames, starting with the transition to modernity and the nation state:

• *Imperialism and empire (1800–1945):* Like Baldwin's (2016) "old" globalisation, we see this as driven by a process of rapid technological change, the quest for new markets and territories abroad. This means that, far from being a period of relative stability, as Baldwin suggests, it is a period of power games and conflict centred around trade. The role of trade in creating power was central, because economics and politics are connected through its weapons: tariffs, exchange controls, sanctions and capital investment to name a few (Hirschman, 1945). The rise of the nation state during this period was the consequence of the modernity that came from the process of industrialisation and technological change (Gellner, 1983). Hirschman points out that the pursuit of influence can be focused as much on the *means* of creating power (for example through trade) as on the *ends* of power and national interest itself (Hirschman, 1945).

• *The Cold War (1945–1990):* Unlike Baldwin, we have separated out the Cold War period from the period of globalisation up to the end of World War II. The Cold War period is commonly, and perhaps erroneously, associated in the economics literature with the dominance of the nation state. However, the nation state evolved during the earlier phase, as Hirschman points out, to support trade. So, the main distinction between the second period and the pre-war period is that in the second, nation states built vast military-industrial complexes. In other words, the literature confuses the nation state with its military-industrial complex capable of fighting large-scale, industrial, even nuclear wars. Although supra-national organisations were present, bilateral relationships dominate both international relations and trade. In Hirschman's terms, this era represents trade dominated by mercantilism. Trade is an instrument of power because more of it implies greater wealth and, hence, influence. Because this wealth through trade is at the expense of the wealth of another nation, protectionist brinkmanship ran in parallel to the "war of nerves" (Hirschman, 1945) that was endemic to the Cold War.

- *"New" globalisation (1990–2014):* Following the collapse of the Soviet Union, the bipolar world order came to an end, leading to greater multipolarity in international relations. This forced a total re-evaluation of how states approached economic and foreign policy. The focus was on greater connectivity during the 1990s, the rise of "Western Liberalism" (Luce, 2017) and "new threats" such as small wars, insurgencies and counter-insurgencies (Kaldor, 1999). "New" globalisation is the term used by Baldwin to describe the shift in trade power to emerging nations through information and communications technologies and free movement of capital and labour. This concept is discussed in more detail in subsequent chapters, but what is important here is that while authors and commentators were claiming the "End of History" (Fukuyama, 1992), a new multipolar, multilateral order was also emerging – not necessarily driven through nation states, but which affected national interest nevertheless.

- *Political globalisation (approx. 2014 onwards):* It may seem premature to declare a new era after such a short period of time, but there are patterns of economic nationalism and foreign policy isolationism that are already evident. There is something different about this era in that neither economic nor military policies as they have evolved through globalisation appear to be serving the national, strategic interests as well as they did. In the wake of the Global Financial Crisis, the orthodox tools of economic management have been ineffectual in stimulating sustained economic growth. Further, protracted military interventions, most notably in Afghanistan and Iraq, have not yielded the level of success expected by policymakers. This, coupled with public discontent over the efficacy of military interventions, has seriously undermined the political will for direct military engagement with "boots on the ground". A case in point here is the decision not to intervene in Syria in 2013 following chemical weapons attacks in Ghouta – an attack that had flagrantly crossed Barack Obama's so-called Red Line. We contend that trade offers politicians another means of influence in an era when the efficacy of interventions and the public and political will for action have weakened while imperatives for economic growth have strengthened. The evidence that trade is used strategically is presented later in this chapter, but the fact that trade seems to be used as a weapon of war draws worrying parallels with the first phase of globalisation highlighted above.

The collapse of the Soviet Union also changed the way that economists and strategists looked at the world. Globalisation and the role of the global corporation dominated thinking alongside a narrow narrative on the mutual benefits of multilateral trade. Globalisation was seen in terms of cross-border technology transfer and the free movement of labour and capital. As such, it was a function of corporate strategy rather than economic policy. Up to 2014, export-led growth and globalisation were the mantras of politicians and business leaders alike, but since 2014, with trade failing to grow as expected, there has been a trend towards the promotion of national interest.

Simultaneously, a new body of literature on conflict emerged. There was the sense that "old" large-scale wars, that were a function of the military-industrial complex of the Cold War era and before, had given way to "new" or "fourth-generation" conflicts characterised by small-scale local conflicts, insurgency and counter-insurgency. Fourth-generation wars were seen as a function of the contradictory political pressures of globalisation; states had lost their "monopoly on the use of armed violence" (Lind, 1994) as non-state actors operating among the people began to dominate conflicts. For the nation states involved, protracted, relatively unsuccessful military campaigns, most recently in Afghanistan and Iraq, have eroded the public and political will for this type of multilateral engagement.

So, if the character of both war and globalisation has changed, how do nation states wield the same influence abroad and at home? We are witnessing a "political" phase of globalisation where trade becomes an instrument of foreign policy. Its appeal is that the *direct* military risks are one step removed, allowing states to influence outcomes *indirectly* without "boots on the ground". A weaponised narrative provides the vehicle for communicating and justifying this strategy to the public. However, the unintended consequence of the nationalist rhetoric has been the rise of populism.

Trade's Role in the Rise of Populism

In the past few years, politicians have created a sense in the voting population that most people have been excluded from the benefits of globalisation. Further, a wave of immigration across Europe, indeed the world, and the perception of a greater threat from terrorism have combined to generate so-called populism that, at least in some countries, has left global liberal democracy with its own crisis of legitimacy – a democratic deficit, even.

However, at its core, the rise of populism is a manifestation of the power that the people hold. It is a product of a lack of transparency in the actions of the policy elites and is a wake-up call to the dangers of ignoring the will of the people. Old politics says, "the economy stupid" and that captures the hearts and minds of a country's electorate. Populist politics is more subtle: "it's *our* economy stupid" means that the economic interests of the nation are paramount. The individual is at once a citizen of that nation and empowered by the economic nationalism that results. Whoever heard of public outrage at another country's trade surplus? Yet, this seems to be the sentiment expressed by the current US administration. Trade with the world is the way both to secure jobs at home and to feel pride in a nation's global status without feeling the threat of globalisation. And mixing trade deals rhetorically with, for example, greater expenditure on the North Atlantic Treaty Organization (NATO), the threat from North Korea, or the maintenance of European security, brings trade, power and the nation back together and back to the heart of the nationalism they evoke.

The resultant invocation of economic nationalism can be seen as an attempt to recapture the lost territory of global leadership and to win the hearts and minds of their electorates; the benefits of trade are being conflated with more nationalist agendas. In the words of one former intelligence official we interviewed, "trade is a useful weapon in a nationalist narrative". However, in an era of social media, where every political action has a public reaction, policy needs justification. In other words, it is no longer acceptable simply to export weapons to Saudi Arabia, we now need to justify those exports – and how better than through the language of "national interest" and "safety and security". This association with national interest through social media and global communications is what makes this era substantively different to previous ones.

All of this is problematic for state strategy and, in a sense, is at the heart of the current policy challenge. At an economic level, the third phase of globalisation removed the power to regulate trade (directly through tariffs or indirectly through non-tariff barriers like regulation). As a result, governments in the political phase find themselves without adequate control over their trade or current account deficits and, hence, with only limited influence over how the economy grows. Combined with the fact that central banks are largely independent, and have set monetary policy since the financial crisis to provide liquidity for growth, governments have effectively lost control of the real levers of macroeconomic policy, on the one hand to central banks and global capital flows and on the other to the largesse of global corporates. Appealing to the public's anti-globalisation and anti-corporate sentiments through trade and nationalism could simply be seen as a strategic manoeuvre by governments to re-establish their own power.

Populism appears to be both a cause and an effect of the rise of economic nationalism and weaponised language that is being used to promote national interests through trade. The policy response to uncertainty, and indeed fear, has been aimed at recalibrating the domestic influence of politics. This is a dangerous road: weaponised language creates enemies and, since trade is a traditional tool of grand strategy, it becomes a weapon. The warning to politicians, therefore, is to handle trade with care – to step back from the current rhetoric, which is too dangerous to be used loosely. In the words of one French advocate with whom we spoke, "For centuries, politicians had to win real wars to keep the 'enemy' in check. Now they have to do something else – so they are turning to trade and this weaponises both economic and foreign policy."

In other words, the type of war this politics now creates is based on trade as a proxy for power. Power is a strong word with negative as well as positive connotations. Trade plays a key role in creating hard and soft power and, more importantly, this is measurable through trade itself. The important point is that the more hard or soft power a country has through its economic and trade position, the more likely it is to use trade strategically. This is because the "strategic choices" open to a country in terms of its international relations are broader. The next section examines the observable state strategy in the trade data.

Strategic Trade in the Data: Trends in Arms and Dual-Use Goods Trade

Our focus is on the time period between 1996 and 2016 – broadly the two time frames associated most commonly with Baldwin's seminal definition "new" globalisation and with our "political" globalisation defined earlier. It shows that on the face of it there was a decline in the value of arms trade globally, but that trade in the "dual-use" sectors, which are more closely identified with strategic trade, increased. While this cannot be directly associated with an increase in military activity, since the goods are, by definition, for civilian purposes as well, it measures clearly the strategic intent of a nation state; in other words, the extent to which its soft power has hard power potential.

So how much did trade change during the period of globalisation? Was it really the case that trade grew, but the importance of the military-industrial complex declined? In other words, did trade in the goods directly associated with war actually decline? Certainly, on the face of it, that appears to be the case. Figure 6.1 shows arms trade as a percentage of total trade through the globalisation era (1996–2016).

Figure 6.1 shows two things: first, that arms trade as a share of global trade has fallen back since 1996, and second, that since 2008 it appears to be growing again, albeit in a more volatile way. The year 2015's percentage share of 0.21% of the value of world trade was the highest for 15 years, and while it would be a mistake to generalise from one year, 2016's value is considerable higher than that of 2008 and the same as that in 2000.

Nevertheless, it seems that globalisation did have some impact on the proportion of trade accounted for by arms. This does not mean that world arms trade has declined, however, and nor does it mean that arms trade is the only means through which goods that are used for military objectives are traded. Figure 6.2 shows the actual values of arms trade compared with dual-use goods trade between 1996 and 2016.

Dual-use goods are defined by the EU as goods, software and technology that have both civilian and military applications and/or can contribute to the proliferation of Weapons of Mass Destruction (WMD) (European Commission, 2018). Care

Figure 6.1 Arms trade as a share of world trade, 1996–2016 (%).
Source: Authors' interpretation of Coriolis Technologies data, 2018.[2]

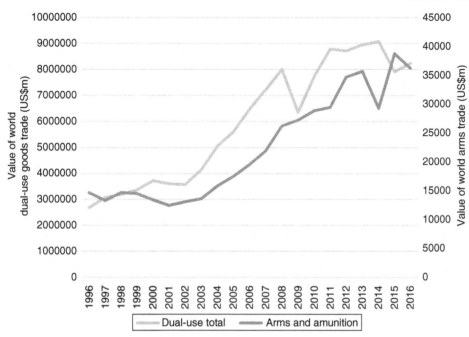

Figure 6.2   Value of arms and dual-use goods trade, 1996–2016 (US$ million).
Source: Authors' interpretation of Coriolis Technologies data, 2018.

should be taken in interpreting their value because, by definition, these goods can be used for civilian purposes and are not necessarily traded with a military objective behind them. Because of this, it is likely that the value presented here will marginally overestimate the amount of dual-use goods trade that is used militarily.

This does not detract from the importance of the chart since our analysis shows that dual-use goods arguably proxy for the strategic intent of a nation, not least because technology is a critical component of military hardware and many of these sectors have strong technology elements. Both arms and dual-use goods trade grew in value terms during the period of globalisation at a very similar rate. The only two exceptions are in 2009 and 2015. In these years, there was also a significant drop in commodity prices, which explains the drop in dual-use goods trade (since many apparently ordinary commodities are used for military purposes as well) while arms trade continued to grow in value terms. The substantial drop in arms trade in 2014 was not related to oil or other commodity prices, nor was it necessarily related to a sudden decline in violence. There was, however, a tightening of sanctions against Russia in 2014 while the anti-money-laundering (AML) and know-your-client (KYC) compliance backlash after the HSBC fines in 2012 also came into force in 2014. While the evidence is circumstantial, this seems more than coincidence.

Speculation aside, it is legitimate to conclude two things. First, arms trade is growing at a similar rate to dual-use goods trade globally. While arms trade has fallen back as a proportion of global trade, its growth in value terms has been substantial. Second, arms and ammunition are not the only routes through which materials used for military purposes are transmitted. While it is probable that dual-use goods data presented here overestimate the trade that is attributable purely to military objectives, the similar growth over the period to arms trade indicates that trade related to state strategy is both strong and growing. It may well be the case that world trade grew rapidly during the globalisation era. However, it is not the case that military-related trade declined, suggesting that some sectors within the dual-use goods sector in particular are not economic, but rather have a political or strategic purpose.

This means that we should re-examine the assumption that the nature of the nation state changed during the globalisation era. It stands to reason that if trade in what can only be described as strategic goods grew, there must have been countries for whom this trade was important. In other words, these countries still had power, not just in their overall trade (arguably reflecting their soft power) but also in their military trade, reflecting a harder, more strategic aspect to their trade.

To get to the real relationship between hard and soft power through trade, we need to take a proxy measure. Figures for dual-use goods, as already stated, overestimate the size of strategic trade in that they include goods that are equally used for civilian purposes. However, they proxy well for the overall size of trade that is associated with state strategy, in both economic and military terms. In other words, it is the trade that is important for strategic influence and power. More specifically, it tells us a lot about how the nature of strategy-related trade is changing since it includes, for example, telecommunications and security systems, nuclear materials and electronics.

Arms trade, in contrast, is directly linked to military activity, either directly in conflict or to deter against conflict. There are big differences in how imports and exports of each should be interpreted so we have taken total trade overall to give an overall indication of the importance of these sectors for each of the G20 economies.

For most of the G20, there are strong correlations between arms trade and gross domestic product (GDP) and between dual-use goods trade and GDP over the period of globalisation between 1996 and 2016 (Figure 6.3). The high correlations for most countries suggest that strategic trade has a strong association with economic growth. In itself this statement is unsurprising and, of course, says nothing about causality – simply that larger countries (here the G20 only) have larger sectors with strategic functions in both economic and political terms. In other words, the goods and services associated with a nation's defence are connected with its economic interests as well, for the G20 at least.

There are some noticeable cases where this is not the case, however. The first is the United Kingdom. Here, the correlation of arms with GDP is just 0.55 while for dual-use goods the correlation is 0.77. Although the United Kingdom's trade is overall highly correlated with GDP (0.94), this suggests that sectors that are not associated with strategy or defence are more closely correlated. It might be inferred from this that the United Kingdom's military and economic interests are more separated than they are, say, in the United States or even Germany and China. This may suggest a link to the importance of physical security as much as its link with GDP.

Second, Japan's arms trade is similarly weakly correlated with its GDP. This is unsurprising given that since 1954, Japan has had a Self-Defence Force, not an army. Since the end of World War II, Japan has maintained a strategic culture of overt pacifism; they have only been involved in one conflict (in Iraq, where they deployed 1000 troops in a non-combative role) and one United Nations (UN)-led anti-piracy

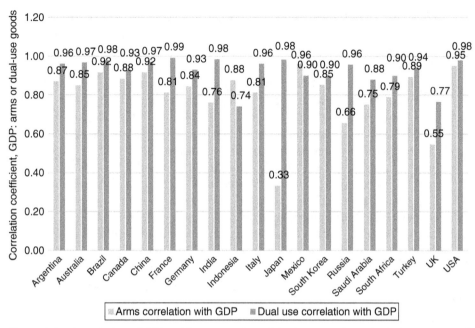

Figure 6.3 Correlation of GDP with arms trade and dual-use goods trade, 2000–2016 (coefficient value).
Source: Authors' interpretation of Coriolis Technologies data, 2018 & IMF data, 2018.

mission (Operation Ocean Shield). Therefore, if we assume that arms proxy for use in, or protection against, direct conflict, then the low correlation of arms with its GDP begins to make sense. However, this does not suggest that strategic trade is unimportant for Japan: the correlation between dual-use goods trade and GDP is strong. That is, Japan has robust strategic intent even if it does not use the goods for military purposes overtly.

Third, Germany and China are regarded as "soft" rather than "hard" powers in that their global power emanates from their overall economic presence proxied through trade. However, both of these countries have correlations between arms trade and GDP and between dual-use goods trade and GDP that are extremely high. The reasons behind this differ: despite all its soft-power rhetoric, China's military expenditure amounted to US$214 billion in 2015 (SIPRI, 2018). While this is half of the equivalent spent by the United States, it dwarfs expenditure by Germany, or indeed the United Kingdom.

Germany's case is interesting. Like Japan, its military has had a national defence remit since World War II. It also has constitutional restrictions on the use of force and against participation in "wars of aggression". In fact, it has been until recently unable to discuss the link between strategic interests, business and trade: when Horst Köhler, the then German President, stated in 2010 that Germany's involvement in Afghanistan was protecting its trade interests, the public outcry was so great that he had to resign. This may explain why the relationship between its arms trade and GDP is weaker than it is for China. However, the relationship is still very strong and this is because Germany is a major manufacturer and exporter of arms equipment as well as of dual-use goods. This cannot be classed as a military-industrial complex, however, since this, and its associated foreign policy, is constrained by its post-war constitution. As a result, this power has to be seen as economic. This explains the close correlation with GDP, but, unlike China, its power remains (at least for now) soft.

Similarly, India is highly militarised and its trade is highly strategic around core sectors such as iron and steel and technology. It has ongoing insurgencies in Jammu and Kashmir, a strong strategic nuclear programme, a strong military and air force and is constantly embroiled in a "war of nerves" with Pakistan. This is reflected in the relatively high arms trade–GDP correlation.

The rates of compounded trade growth in dual-use goods and arms trade shed some further light on why the rates of growth in India and Argentina are so high. Figure 6.4 ranks growth in countries' arms trade by their compound annualised growth rate (CAGR) for the period 1996–2006, since this shows the key changes between that first "pure globalisation" period and the second "financial crisis globalisation" of 2007–2016. As noted above, arms trade at a global level did not fall back in 2009, unlike other sectors, so this latter grouping is not distorted by the crisis.

By ranking the G20 growth based on the earlier time period, Figure 6.4 shows where arms trade is growing most from a modest or negative base. For example, Indonesia's arms trade growth was negative between 1996 and 2006 but has grown extremely rapidly in the second period between 2007 and 2016. Saudi Arabia's arms trade growth in the second period compared to the first is even more dramatic. Turkey's arms trade also shows more rapid growth in the second period, while Russia and India, albeit from a stronger growth base in the first period, have also shown greater growth in the second.

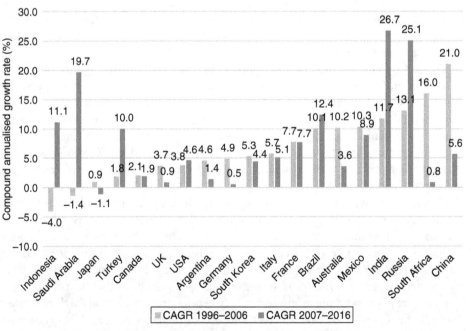

Figure 6.4   G20 arms trade growth, CAGR, 1996–2006 & 2007–2016 compared (%).
Source: Authors' interpretation of Coriolis Technologies data, 2018.

It would be misleading to classify India's or Indonesia's arms trade growth as the same as that for Saudi Arabia, Turkey or Russia. In these countries, arms trade is growing from a very low base, but this is not the case for Saudi Arabia or Russia and increasingly not the case for Turkey either. The growth in Saudi Arabia, Turkey and to a certain extent Russia's arms trade may be interpreted as reflecting tensions in the Middle East region and therefore could be a reflection of strategic intent.

China presents an interesting case. Its arms trade growth was particularly marked in the first period, as it built the military strength that we now see. This arguably reflects the multipolarisation and convergence of growth in the globalisation period that was discussed earlier. However, what is equally marked is the slow-down in growth (albeit from a larger base) in the second period from 2007. This may reflect the capacity of China to produce arms itself, since import growth slowed from an annualised rate of 22% in the first period to just over 7% in the second. It may also reflect the shift in China's state strategy towards demand-led growth and a pattern of consumption more consistent with a mid-income economy. Furthermore, it is signalling a more assertive foreign policy through its actions in the South China Sea and through the Belt and Road Initiative (BRI). These are both important in broadening its trade reach, securing energy supplies and increasing maritime influence (Asia Maritime Transparency Initiative, 2018).

All of this suggests that there is, for many countries, an intrinsic "hard power" within their trade relationships with other countries. We can see that all the big G20 powers, with the notable exception of Germany, have substantial arms trades that proxy for strategic "intent", and furthermore, that arms trade has grown rapidly throughout the period of globalisation.

This does not paint the whole picture, however. The problem is that we cannot generalise from the G20. China's military power is well proxied through its growth in arms trade because the increase has been substantial; indeed, China's recent military expenditure rivals that of the developed nation states like the United States, Germany, the United Kingdom and France. The growth in Germany's arms trade is worth a special mention in the context of the constitutional framework within which its foreign policy has been formulated in the post–World War II period. It is a large exporter of arms, showing that the influence it wields through strategic trade allows it to promote its strategic interests abroad without explicitly spending money on its own army or engaging them directly.

It is worth exploring the role that strategic trade plays in generating soft power in more detail. Based on the analysis so far, a suggestion might be that a less protectionist country has greater soft power since its economic strength is more closely tied to its trade performance (Figure 6.5).

Trade openness is the total trade-to-GDP ratio. The fastest growing nations in terms of trade openness are, perhaps unsurprisingly, Brazil, Russia, India, Turkey, Mexico and Saudi Arabia. Such growth has given these newly emerging trading nations their place in the G20, which is arguably a political as well as an economic grouping. But what is interesting about this chart is how the United Kingdom's trade openness has shrunk over the period while the United States' growth in trade openness, although greater, is lower than that of either China or Germany.

As always, this sort of finding should be handled with care. The United Kingdom's trade has been sluggish since the financial crisis and has struggled to get back to its

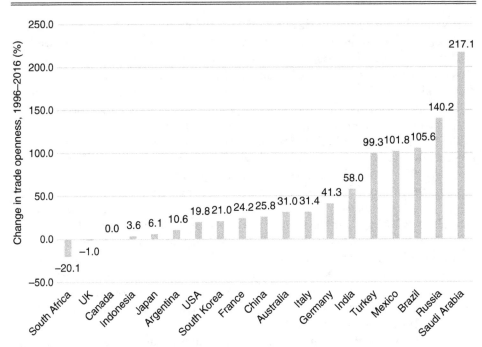

Figure 6.5   Change in trade openness, 1996–2016 (%).
Source: Authors' interpretation of Coriolis Technologies data, 2018, IMF 2017.
Note: The change for South Africa is between 2008 and 2016 because of lack of data for earlier years.

nominal levels in 2008, while GDP has grown because of strong domestic demand. The United Kingdom remains a more open economy than the United States or China, with a ratio of 42.3% of trade to GDP.

As hinted above, it is Germany that really exhibits the strongest soft power through trade, and this is important in a country whose foreign policy and military expenditure is constitutionally restricted. It is the most open economy of the G20 and the world's third-largest trading nation in terms of exports and imports, after the United States and China. However, the United States and China have large militaries that back up their otherwise "soft" power. Germany, although a significant strategic player, does not invest the proportion of its GDP in its military that other NATO members do. Yet the importance of its strategic trade means that its foreign policy and its trade policy are both clearly aligned with national interest. Furthermore, in the words of one senior politician, "We see, and increasingly the German public sees, that we need to take our soft power seriously, indeed take up the responsibility that we have both in NATO and in Europe for security, particularly once the United Kingdom is no longer part of the EU. But we can't invest in our military – not just because of German public opinion. Our GDP is huge – can you imagine the size of our army if we spent 2% of it on military? You might find that others have a problem with that as well."

Its role as the answer to the Kissinger Question – "Who do I call if I want to talk to Europe?" – has become accepted in the period since the financial crisis and the Eurozone crisis: European power has shifted from a Franco-German axis to Berlin. While some may attribute this to a conflict of underlying ideologies and economic philosophies (Brannermeier *et al.*, 2016), the truth is that Germany's economy has withstood the various crises since 2008 better than the French, and largely because of trade. This gives it a global soft power which, however reluctantly, it has had to accept as its duty, arguably to protect its national interests since Germany's future is bound with Europe for historical reasons (Green, 2016).

Conceptualising Hard and Soft Power through Trade

What all of this means is that we can construct a matrix of the G20 that shows the relationship between hard and soft power. This is a stylised representation but nevertheless provides a picture of how trade and hard and soft power are linked to the nation state. We put soft power on the vertical axis (from weak to strong) and hard power on the horizontal axis from weak to strong. Soft power is seen as a function of trade value and trade openness while hard power is proxied through the correlation between arms trade and GDP and dual-use goods as a share of total trade.

To be clear, we are using dual-use goods trade as a proxy for strategic intent in this context. We could perhaps have used military expenditure, but the point we are making is, as was shown in the case of Germany, military expenditure is only a partial picture of that strategic intent and, hence, dual-use goods trade is a better proxy.

This approach puts Germany, South Korea and Japan largely into the top left hand corner of the quadrant showing strong trade (soft power) but weaker actual hard power. The United States, in contrast, is at the top of quadrant showing both strong hard power and strong soft power: it is the world's second-largest trading nation (the largest importer) but it is not as open as, say, Germany. China is interesting to place: it is the world's largest trading nation and yet is quite closed, so it is away from the left quadrants. Its background hard power, represented through dual-use and arms trade, places it in the strong hard power quadrant, despite the fact that rhetorically and diplomatically it presents itself as a soft power. The United Kingdom is the hardest to place: it is the world's sixth-largest importer and tenth-largest exporter, meaning that its soft power is weaker than, say, the United States, howsoever open it may be.

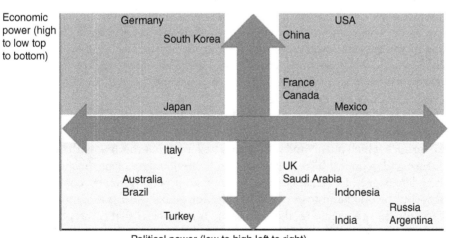

Figure 6.6 The trade-based soft–hard power matrix.
Source: Authors' interpretation.

Alongside this, the correlation between arms trade and GDP is weaker than for many other countries, although the proportion of trade accounted for by dual-use goods is the highest of the G20, suggesting "strategic intent" is inherent to its military-industrial complex. In other words, "strategic trade", for example with Saudi Arabia, helps it fight proxy wars without a direct engagement. This places it towards the centre of the matrix with a bias towards hard power.

Current and Future Challenges

There is, then, no real evidence that the trade power of the world's most established nation states has diminished over the period. We have used arms trade as a proxy for direct engagement and evidence of confrontational "hard" foreign policy observed in a country's trade statistics. Dual-use goods trade proxies for the "strategic intent" of a nation. Neither has diminished as a percentage of the size of a country's total trade over the period of globalisation, suggesting that similarly there is no evidence that either confrontational foreign policy or the strategic intent of the nation state has diminished through the period of globalisation. Indeed, its growth was at its fastest during the period when the globalisation hubris was at its greatest: before the financial crisis. More than this, it seems that countries like Turkey, Saudi Arabia, Russia and even Mexico and Brazil have seen substantial arms trade growth. Particularly for Turkey, Saudi Arabia and Russia, this reflects the tensions within the Middle East and Central European/Central Asian arena.

This leads us to conclude that there is no sense in which globalisation altered the strategic intent as a driver of the nation state's power. However, the rise of a country like China through the period of globalisation does provide evidence to the idea that the "Western" (for want of a better term) nations were so focused on the size of the Chinese market and the opportunities that arose from globalisation that they perhaps did not link that rising soft power with an equivalent rise in hard power too.

There are danger signs in the data as well. Russia, Turkey and Saudi Arabia have always had "hard power" largely in the form of arms and oil and gas but show signs of greater aspirations to "hard power" in their arms trade but not their dual-use goods trade. This suggests that these countries are driven by "conflict and confrontational" foreign policies and that these are at the base of the uncertainties and geopolitical conflicts we see now. That is, their strategic intent is driven to a greater extent by the fact that their trade is less diversified and, hence, driven by geopolitics and is intrinsically less predictable.

Trade generally, and strategic trade in particular, is intrinsically geopolitical in that it is about allocation and control of resources across borders. It is the mechanism through which power and influence are exerted, but this link with both political influence and geopolitical power is only now becoming explicit through the weaponised language that is being used. With that power, however, comes responsibility – on the one hand to provide stability for global businesses and on the other not to provoke others into retaliatory action. It is not clear that this is obvious to key policymakers around the world.

This is a reaction to the current uncertainties in the world that have themselves emerged as a result of the globalisation process. Ernest Gellner argued that the nation state, as a collection of institutions with shared cultural and social values (i.e.

nationalism), would logically emerge from the pre-industrial morass of loosely connected groups and interests whose actions were uncoordinated and random. The process of industrialisation itself created the modern nation state that marshalled resources, control and citizens around one identity (Gellner, 1983)

There is a resounding familiarity to this theme. Has globalisation not itself created loose collections of interest groups around religion, ideologies and territories that fight for recognition or domination of resources? Might this not be the reason why individuals themselves feel unaligned and displaced? And if this is the case, is a re-invocation of nationalism, through the weaponisation of trade, not the logical – if "irrational" (Fukuyama, 1992) – response?

This is not an attempt to build a conspiracy theory of world trade and nor are we apportioning any responsibility. We report simply on facts. Nation states control the institutions (even weapons) of trade (customs and excise, tariff and regulatory regimes and taxation, for example). It is not our intention to suggest that there is any direct involvement of a nation's military-industrial complex in any deliberate activity, but it is important to distinguish between what is observable strategic intent in the previous chapter and what might be called covert action in this.

Strategic Trade in Practice

Sanctions are a powerful tool of policy, and Iran and Syria, in different ways, show how these impact the overall trading position of the nation. Iran, for example, has had strong trade despite sanctions, because of its relationship with Turkey and Russia. Turkey acts as a conduit for sanctioned trade between Europe, Russia and the Middle East and this is reflected in the fact that its top import partners are Iraq, Iran, Saudi Arabia, Israel and Russia (Figure 6.7). The volatile trade with Iran since 2012 reflects the EU's embargo on Iranian oil, and the subsequent drop in trade with all partners, particularly marked since 2014, reflects the tightening of both AML and KYC as well as the drop in oil prices.

This is similarly reflected in Iran's trade with the world which, although substantial, has fallen back considerably since 2012 (Figure 6.8).

The impact of the EU's oil embargo on Iran's trade is particularly marked here. The pick-up in 2016 may simply be because of the slight improvement in commodity prices. It is unlikely that anticipation of the end of sanctions towards the end of President Obama's presidency would have had much impact on the overall trade figures. This is not least because US regulators still restrict trade finance relations with any Iranian bank that may have links to the nuclear programme and, while this remains the case, it is extremely difficult for banks elsewhere to facilitate trade directly if they wish to remain compliant with US regulations. Given the current US administration's position towards Iran, it is very unlikely that there will be any change in this position. This gives some indication of why nation states may want to have some, let's just say, less transparent trade partners.

Russia and the United Kingdom's Trade with Syria

A more detailed case study of Syria and its relationship with Russia and the United Kingdom reinforces this view of strategic trade. We see evidence, particularly in Russia's exports to Syria, of trade fuelling the conflict (Figures 6.11 and 6.12).

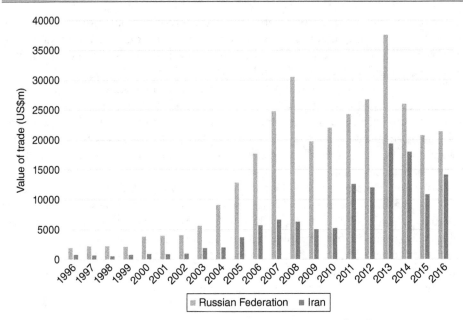

Figure 6.7   Turkey's imports from Russia and Iran, 1996–2016 (US$ million).
Source: Authors' interpretation of Coriolis Technologies data, 2018.

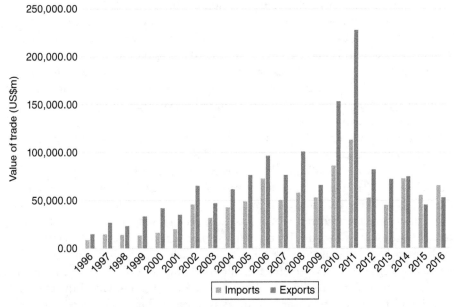

Figure 6.8   Value of Iran's trade, 1996–2016 (US$ million).
Source: Authors' interpretation of Coriolis Technologies data, 2018.

In 2011, widespread pro-democracy protests took place across the Middle East in
what became known as the Arab Spring. In Syria, these protests escalated after
Bashar al-Assad's forces opened fire on protestors. The protestors began arming
themselves in response and soon split into several rebel groups in violent opposition
to Assad's regime. As the war progressed, the conflict developed a sectarian element

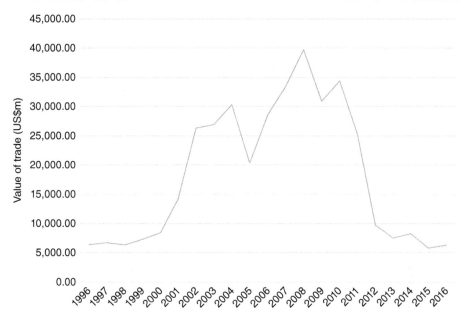

Figure 6.9 Value of Syria's total trade with the world, 1996–2016 (US$ million).
Source: Authors' interpretation of Coriolis Technologies data, 2018.

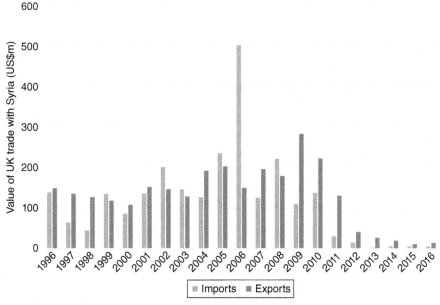

Figure 6.10 UK trade with Syria 1996–2016 (US$ million).
Source: Authors' interpretation of Coriolis Technologies data, 2018.

as Sunnis clashed with Alawites and Islamic State grew in influence. Since 2011, roughly 250,000 Syrians have lost their lives, millions have been displaced and their economy has all but collapsed as fighting has intensified. Sanctions against Assad also took their toll as members of the international community ceased trading with a regime they could not support. For example, Figure 6.10 shows how the United

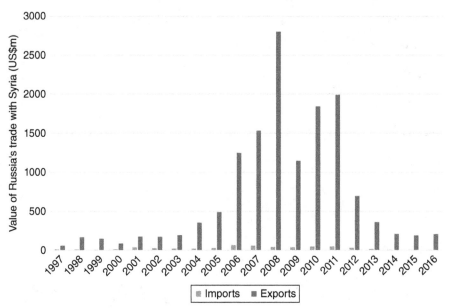

Figure 6.11   Value of Russia's trade with Syria, 1997–2016 (US$ million).
Source: Authors' interpretation of Coriolis Technologies data, 2018.

Kingdom's total trade with Syria severely declined between 2009 and 2016. In value terms, this was a drop from nearly US$400m in 2009, to just US$17m in 2016, or, as a percentage, a 95.5% reduction in trade.

However, trade with Syria has not disappeared completely (see Figure 6.11). In 2014, Jihad Yazigi wrote that the country had transitioned to a war economy and that goods entering the country were prolonging the conflict, with regime-controlled areas still enjoying "the provision of many basic state services" (Yazigi, 2014). Russia openly backs Assad and his campaign to regain control and, since 2010, they have provided the majority of these goods. As Figure 6.11 shows, Russia's trade increased by 9.6% between 2015 and 2016. By comparison, the United Kingdom's exports to Syria fell by 40% over the same period. Furthermore, instead of a drop in trade as civil war was breaking out, we see a 73.3% increase in Russia's exports to Syria between 2009 and 2011.

Russia's strategy in the Middle East revolves around keeping Assad in power; it would be incorrect to assume that this is because they are politically aligned, however. Rather, Russia has interests in protecting its naval base in Tartus; in January 2017, Russia signed a 49-year deal granting them full control of the base which is capable of hosting up to 11 warships and is in a key strategic location in the Mediterranean. Furthermore, by intervening in the region while the United States and NATO would not, Russia is sending a strong signal to current Middle Eastern regimes that *they*, not NATO, are the most reliable security actors in the region.

Russia's current strategy towards Syria is reflected in the goods Russia is exporting to Syria. Figure 6.12 looks at Russia's top ten exports to Syria in 2016 and compares these with their values in 2002 as evidence of Russia's changing strategy towards the country over the period.

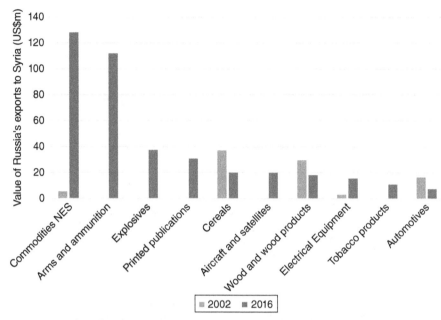

Figure 6.12 Value of Russia's top ten exports to Syria, 2002 and 2016 compared (US$ million). Source: Authors' interpretation of Coriolis Technologies data, 2018.

In 2016, US$128m of Russia's exports to Syria were in commodities NES (not elsewhere specified) while a further US$111m were in arms and ammunition and US$37m in explosives; this is compared with a total value of just US$5m in these sectors in 2002. Furthermore, within the sectors printed publications and electrical equipment are dual-use goods including instruction manuals and blueprints as well as electronic triggers for weapons systems. Meanwhile, Russia's trade in more benign sectors such as cereals, wood and wood products, and automotives fell from a total value of US$83m in 2002 to US$45.2m in 2016 – this is further evidence of Syria's war economy.

So, if Russia is protecting its interests by trading directly with the Syrian government, the next question to ask is how can the United Kingdom influence proceedings within Syria without direct military engagement or trading directly with them? The answer is to trade by proxy. In other words, to use neighbouring states as conduits to achieve their strategic objectives. The United Kingdom has had cordial relations with Saudi Arabia since 1932 when the Treaty of Darin was signed, and the country is viewed by the United Kingdom as one of the more stable and trustworthy countries in the region. Given this relationship and the country's advantageous strategic location, the relationship with Saudi Arabia is seen as integral to British security interests in the Middle East (Figure 6.13).

There are three striking aspects of Figure 6.13:

- Arms and ammunition trade was not in the top ten traded sectors in 2002 but by 2016 was the fourth-largest sector. This sector includes small arms and ammunition rather than components for sophisticated weapons systems which are found in other sectors, including aircraft and satellites and electrical equipment (the second- and fifth-largest export sectors in 2016).

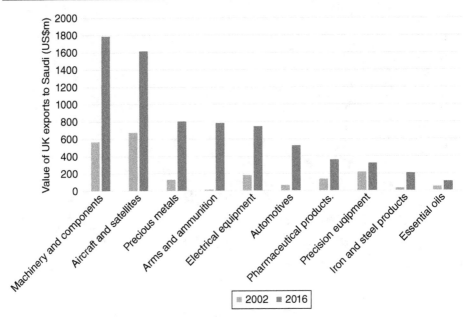

Figure 6.13   Value of the United Kingdom's top ten exports to Saudi Arabia, 2002 and 2016 compared (US$ million).
Source: Authors' interpretation of Coriolis Technologies data, 2018.

- The sectors all have high dual-use content: machinery and components, for example, includes computing, data storage and digital detection systems, while electrical equipment includes semiconductors and electronic monitoring systems. In other words, many of the products included in these sectors are associated with defence and security systems.
- The substantial increase in precious metal trade between 2002 and 2016 is largely the result of increased direct gold exports from the United Kingdom to Saudi Arabia. This sector includes precious metals used in high-end electronic equipment manufacture but is predominantly bullion.

It appears that Russia and the United Kingdom's respective policy positions in relation to the conflict in Syria are reflected in the trade data. We can see evidence of a change in strategy from both states over our time period, highlighted not only by trends in total exports but also by *what* is being traded, and with whom.

Yemen and Saudi Arabia – Arms-Length Conflicts?

Yemen, is another excellent example of how conflict in one states is fuelled by the actions of other states. The humanitarian crisis has been developing since 2015 when the conflict began. In April 2017, during Theresa May's trip to Saudi Arabia, she argued that the trade deals she had done with Saudi Arabia were in the United Kingdom's national and security interests. Similarly, President Trump's trade deal with Saudi Arabia was predominantly in arms and military equipment, again suggesting that there were strategic objectives in sealing it.

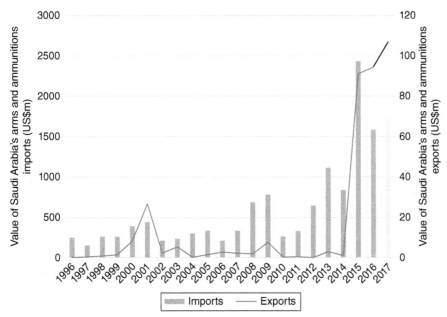

Figure 6.14   Value of Saudi Arabia's arms and ammunition trade, 1996–2017 (US$ million).
Source: Authors' interpretation of Coriolis Technologies data, 2018.
Note: 2017 is estimated.

Saudi Arabia does not report its trade in arms and ammunition with Yemen. Both countries have poor reporting and, as a result, we need to look at other countries' trade with Saudi Arabia. Figure 6.14 shows Saudi Arabia's trade with the world in this sector.

Two things are clear from this chart:

• There was a substantial increase in imports of arms between 2011 and 2013 and a proportionately substantial increase in exports of arms between 2012 and 2013. These dates are broadly consistent with the Arab Spring.
• The most marked increase in both exports and imports is between 2014 and 2015 – the precursor and start to the conflict with Yemen. Exports of arms continued to grow into 2016 and are projected to grow further in 2017. Although Saudi Arabia's imports of arms and ammunition look to have fallen back in 2016, the projections for 2017 suggest an increase again.

According to the Stockholm International Peace Research Institute (SIPRI), many of the arms deals include substantial intellectual property and knowledge transfer because they enable the partner in that deal to produce the weapons locally.

Focusing just on the arms and ammunition trade itself is crucial because of the relationship between small arms and ammunition and insurgencies and political instability. The trade is hard to regulate, however. Although it falls within the United Nations Arms Trade Treaty (ATT) of 2014, for example, the ATT itself does require the trade to be registered, but not reported. Loans, leasing and gifts of arms are excluded from the Treaty, and Saudi Arabia is not a signatory anyway. According to

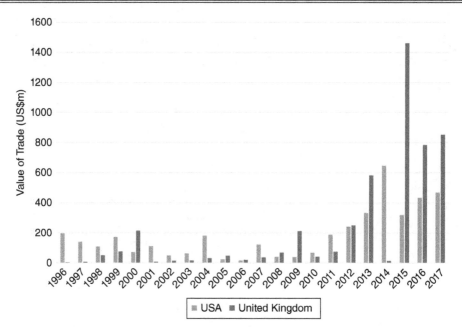

Figure 6.15 US and UK arms and ammunition trade with Saudi Arabia (US$ million). Source: Authors' interpretation of Coriolis Technologies data, 2018.

the UN itself, more than 80% of ammunitions trade is excluded from reliable export data (UN, 2018). In other words, neither the suppliers nor the end users of arms and ammunitions are reporting their usage or their trade.

Given this, it is instructive to look at countries where the trade *is* recorded: the United States and the United Kingdom are good examples here because both are signatories to the ATT, even though the United States has not yet ratified it.

Figure 6.15 speaks for itself. It shows a major increase in arms and ammunition exports from the United States to Saudi Arabia up to 2014. The United Kingdom's exports to Saudi Arabia increased to US$1.5 billion between 2014 and 2015 – more than twice the level of US arms exports. Both countries have increased their exports since 2011.

What is clear from this is that the arms and ammunition trade with Saudi Arabia is fuelling conflict in the region, both in Syria and in Yemen. But what is equally clear is that the reporting is poor and that the size and scale of arms and ammunitions trade is hard to capture fully. The United States, for example, has allegedly argued that ammunitions are hard to include in regulations because bullets are hard to track, but the important point here is that while used weapons and weapons parts can be passed over borders, only unused ammunition can be traded -- with terrible consequences for civilian populations.

Summary and Conclusions

One of the most difficult things to attempt is to mesh disciplines, data analysis and current news. The core messages become blurred. But our focus, we hope, has nevertheless been clear. We have aimed to demonstrate how the process of globalisation between 1998 and 2014 created an identity void for individuals who saw themselves as national rather than global citizens. Similarly, the relative failure of military engagements in the likes of Afghanistan or Iraq has demonstrated the limitations of national strategic power, not least because insurgencies and localised wars create long-term strategic problems beyond pure conflict – the wave of immigration globally being perhaps the most pressing.

The two combined have resulted in the populist backlash that was apparent in the form of the Brexit vote in the United Kingdom in June 2016, the election of President Trump and the sweep of populism across Europe, too. It has pitched individuals against individuals in the quest for a meaningful identity and given rise to many of the conflicts, in soft and hard power terms, that we have seen become more acute since the financial crisis. We have argued that the populism that has been a feature of elections and referenda in Europe and the United States since 2014 is a product of the latest stage of globalisation in that it has created the economic nationalism that has started to underpin policy, even in countries that are not explicitly or publically nationalist, like Germany or France. In contrast to the period of globalisation from the end of the Cold War until 2014, what is unfolding now is political and differentiates itself from previous stages because it has economic nationalism at its base and involves coercion through trade and strategic influence in foreign policy.

Clearly there is a lot we do not know about this emerging era – almost by definition. It is relatively new and its protagonists have populist agendas which may be volatile according to political events. The fact that Le Pen was defeated in France and that Theresa May did not win outright the election she called for in 2017 could perhaps be interpreted as a move away from the populism that has been so obvious in the public discourse. But populism has already been highly disruptive and has the potential to be highly disruptive in the future – both to the structure of multilateral "free" trade and to the way in which countries settle conflicts between each other.

Both trade institutions and the institutions through which the resultant national economic interests are protected are fundamental to government, society and, ultimately, the nation state. However, their enduring role in international politics since the collapse of the Soviet Union has meant that we tend to take them for granted; we assume that the national and supra-national organisations we have built in the postwar period will always be there. The WTO will provide the principles for free trade, the UN will act as a global peacekeeper, NATO will provide security and defence, and "Europe" will exist as a "special" trading partner even if, for example, the United Kingdom is outside of the EU. In short, in institutional terms, we can "have our cake and eat it". What is happening now is governments are distancing themselves from those institutions, calling their whole existence into question. They are doing this in the name of the people whose domestic and personal security they are seeking to protect. This may be a self-defeating approach since the people have an equal right to expect that, through the process of transition, those institutions will be protected.

However, the defining feature of the evolving political stage of globalisation is what we have called "strategic trade". That is, trade that serves a purpose of furthering strategic influence, both nationally and internationally. We argue that this trade is highly concentrated in strategic sectors, such as arms, electronics, communications technologies, aerospace, oil and gas. These are also sectors in which dual-use goods are found. These, by definition, can be used for military or civilian purposes but, as we argued, the definition of what is military and what is civilian is no longer clear. For example, cyber-defence systems are not necessarily built by individuals with formal military training and yet provide a "protection" against cyber "attacks." This means that the scale of dual-use goods trade itself is a good proxy for the strategic intent of a country.

Similarly, "strategic trade" wars are "indirect" wars and are the result of Western failures in recent conflicts. They use trade as a vehicle for coercion – either through orthodox trade wars (protectionism and sanctions) or through trade in specific sectors with specific countries. This does not directly involve conflict, but still bears the hallmarks of war in that they are politics by another means.

Notes

1   Goodhart's Law: after Charles Goodhart, who argued that when a measure becomes a target, it ceases to be a good measure.

2   The data here is for the years 1996–2016. This is because it includes the period of globalisation and runs to the latest available and complete United Nations data. While this runs the risk of appearing out of date, use of 2017 data would require estimations, and by using older data, it shows how trade has been literally weaponised throughout the period under investigation, quite apart from any influence of current rhetorical weaponisation. The evidence for strategic trade is drawn from a database of our own design that holds statistics on trade flows for 200 countries and 12,800 products. The unique nature of the database necessitates a brief discussion of the methods used. Official trade statistics are known to be asymmetric and often do not match bilateral flows of imports and exports: for example, imports to the United Kingdom from Germany should equal exports from Germany to the United Kingdom. In this example, the flows differ but not by much, so we take a simple average of the two numbers, both by sector and in the aggregate. Often, though, the differences are much bigger. In these cases we take one of two routes.

   If the difference is between 5 and 49%, we use statistical techniques to assess which country has the most reliable data and take an average of the two flows weighted more heavily towards the statistics of the more reliable country.

   If the difference is bigger, or one country does not report the statistics, we take the data from the best reporting country. This is a standard technique used by organisations such as the Organisation for Economic Co-operation and Development (OECD) and the WTO. We apply it to all countries and sectors (over one data point) using big-data techniques. It means that our database has far fewer gaps in it than alternatives because many countries, in the Middle East and Africa for example, do not report trade or do so infrequently. We use data from more reliable countries: Germany's imports data to measure Saudi Arabia's exports to Germany, for example. Our big-data approach is particularly helpful for exploring strategic trade products such as arms and dual-use goods, which are largely hidden in other databases. The database, which draws on data from the UN Comtrade Database and (for services) the UN, OECD and Eurostat, is publicly available through Coriolis Technologies. With such a data source, it was simple to then track changes in certain sectors across time and measure for the strategic intent of a state. For the purposes of this section, we used case studies with reliable data such as the G20. Our more in-depth case studies look at Russian trade with Syria compared with British trade with Syria and Saudi Arabia. Our findings in the data were supplemented with a series of elite interviews with leading economists, government officials and military and intelligence officers in order to understand how the data matched the reality.

References

Aghion, P. & Bolton, P. (1997) A Theory of Trickle-Down Growth and Development. *The Review of Economic Studies*, 64(2), 151–172.

Asia Maritime Transparency Initiative (2018). Retrieved from: https://amti.csis.org/maps/ (accessed 4 July 2019).

Baldwin, R. (2016) *The Great Convergence: Information Technology and the New Globalisation*. Cambridge, MA: Harvard University Press.

Brannermeier, M., James, H. & Landau, J-P. (2016) *The Euro and the Battle of Ideas*. Princeton: Princeton University Press.

Bush, G., Sr. (1992) *The Clinton-Bush-Perot Presidential Debates*. Retrieved from: http://www.ontheissues.org/Celeb/George_Bush_Sr__Free_Trade.htm (accessed 4 July 2019).

Bush, G.W. (2006) *State of the Union Address*. Retrieved from: http://www.ontheissues.org/Celeb/George_W__Bush_Free_Trade.htm (accessed 4 July 2019).

Clausewitz, von, C. (1832) *On War*. Abridged edition. Translated by Howard, M. & Paret, P. Introduction by Heuser, B. (2008). Oxford: Oxford University Press.

Clinton, B. (1996) *Between Hope and History: Meeting America's Challenges for the 21st Century*. New York: Random House.

Clinton, B. (2000) *Speech on China Trade Bill*. Retrieved from: https://www.iatp.org/files/Full_Text_of_Clintons_Speech_on_China_Trade_Bi.htm (accessed 4 July 2019).

UK Department for International Trade (2015) *Exporting is Great*. Retrieved from: https://www.export.great.gov.uk/ (accessed 4 July 2019).

European Commission (2018) Dual-Use Trade Controls. Retrieved from: http://ec.europa.eu/trade/import-and-export-rules/export-from-eu/dual-use-controls/index_en.htm (accessed 4 July 2019).

Findlay, R. & O'Rourke, K.H. (2007) *Power and Plenty: Trade, War, and the World Economy in the Second Millennium*. Princeton: Princeton University Press.

Fukuyama, F. (1992) *The End of History and the Last Man*. London: Penguin Books.

Gellner, E. (1983) *Nations and Nationalism*. New York: Cornell University Press.

Ghosh, A. & Saha, S. (2015) Price Competition, Technology Licensing and Strategic Trade Policy. *Economic Modelling*, 46, 91–99.

Gray, C.S. (2016) *Strategy and Politics*. Oxford: Routledge.

Green, S. (2016) *Reluctant Meister: How Germany's Past is Shaping its European Future*. London: Haus Publishing.

Harding, R. & Harding, J. (2017) *The Weaponization of Trade: The Great Unbalancing of Politics and Economics*. London: London Publishing Partnership.

Hirschman, A. (1945) *National Power and the Structure of Foreign Trade*. Berkeley: University of California Press.

Kaldor, M. (1999) *New and Old Wars: Organised Violence in a Global Era*. Cambridge: Polity Press.

Krueger, A.O. (2006) *Stability, Growth, and Prosperity: The Global Economy and the IMF*. Retrieved from: https://www.imf.org/en/News/Articles/2015/09/28/04/53/sp060706 (accessed 4 July 2019).

Krugman, P. (ed.) (1986) *Strategic Trade Policy and the New International Economics*. Cambridge, MA: MIT Press.

Liddell Hart, B. (1967) *Strategy: The Indirect Approach*. London: Faber and Faber.

Lind, W.S. (2004) Understanding Fourth Generation War. *Military Review*, 84(5), 12–16.

Luce, E. (2017) *The Retreat of Western Liberalism*. London: Little Brown.

Lydgate, E. & Winters, L. (2018) Deep and Not Comprehensive? What the WTO Rules Permit for a UK–EU FTA. *World Trade Review*, 1–29. doi:10.1017/S1474745618000186.

May, T. (2017) Theresa May Defends UK Ties with Saudi Arabia. BBC News (4 April). Retrieved from: http://www.bbc.com/news/uk-politics-39485083 (accessed 4 July 2019).

Meyer, T. & Garcia, F.J. (2018) Restoring Trade's Social Contract. *Michigan Law Review*, 116(78), 78–100.

Noland, M. (2018) US Trade Policy in the Trump Administration. *Asian Economic Policy Review*, 13(2), 262–278.

Obama, B. (2008) Global Trade Is Unsustainable if It Favors Only the Few. Retrieved from: http://www.ontheissues.org/2008/Barack_Obama_Free_Trade.htm (accessed 4 July 2019).

Reagan, R. (1988) State of the Union Message to Congress. Retrieved from: http://www.ontheissues.org/Archive/SOTU_RR_Free_Trade.htm (accessed 4 July 2019).

Rugman, A. and Verbeke, A. (2017) *Global Corporate Strategy and Trade Policy*. London: Routledge.

Schroeder, E. & Tremblay, V.J. (2015) A Reappraisal of Strategic Trade Policy. *Journal of Industry, Competition and Trade*, 15(4), 435–442.

Sheldon, I., Chow, D. & McGuire, W. (2018) Trade Liberalization and Institutional Constraints on Moves to Protectionism: Multilateralism versus Regionalism. Conference paper presented to American Economic Association, Philadelphia, 6 January 2018. Retrieved from: https://www.aeaweb.org/conference/2018/preliminary/1907?q=eNqrVipOLS7OzM8LqSxIVbKqhnGVrJQMlWp1lBKLi_OTgRwlHaWS1KJcXAgrJbESKpSZmwphFSSmg1hmSrVcMESbGEM (accessed 4 July 2019).

Siles-Brügge, G. & De Ville, F. (2015) The Transatlantic Trade and Investment Partnership and the Role of Computable General Equilibrium Modelling: An Exercise in "Managing Fictional Expectations". *New Political Economy*, 20(5), 653–678.

SIPRI (Stockholm International Peace Research Institute) (2018) SIPRI Military Expenditure Database. Retrieved from: https://www.sipri.org/databases/milex (accessed 4 July 2019).

Stiglitz, J.E. (2003) Globalization and the Economic Role of the State in the New Millennium. *Industrial and Corporate Change*, 12(1), 3–26.

Stiglitz, J.E. (2017) The Overselling of Globalization. *Business Economics*, 52(3), 129–137.

Stracqualursi, V. (2017) 10 Times Trump Attacked China and Its Trade Relations with the US. ABC News (9 November). Retrieved from: http://abcnews.go.com/Politics/10-times-trump-attacked-china-trade-relations-us/story?id=46572567 (accessed 4 July 2019).

Trommer, S. (2017) The WTO in an Era of Preferential Trade Agreements: Thick and Thin Institutions in Global Trade Governance. *World Trade Review*, 16(3), 501–526.

US Government (2017a) National Security Strategy of the USA. Retrieved from: https://www.whitehouse.gov/wp-content/uploads/2017/12/NSS-Final-12-18-2017-0905.pdf (accessed 4 July 2019).

US Government (2017b) Buy American, Hire American. Retrieved from: https://www.whitehouse.gov/the-press-office/2017/04/18/presidential-executive-order-buy-american-and-hire-american (accessed 4 July 2019).

United Nations (2018) Poorly Managed Ammunition – A Clear Driver of Conflict and Crime. Retrieved from: https://www.un.org/disarmament/convarms/ammunition/more-on-ammunition/ (accessed 4 July 2019).

Walker, J.T. (2015) Strategic Trade Policy, Competition, and Welfare: The Case of Voluntary Export Restraints between Britain and Japan (1971–2002). *Oxford Economic Papers*, 67(3), 806–825.

World Trade Organization (2016) Report Urges WTO Members to Resist Protectionism and "Get Trade Moving Again". Report to the TPRB from the Director-General on trade-related developments. Retrieved from: https://www.wto.org/english/news_e/news16_e/trdev_22jul16_e.htm (accessed 4 July 2019).

Yazigi, J. (2014) Syria's War Economy. *European Council on Foreign Relations, Policy Brief*. Retrieved from: www.ecfr.eu/page/-/ECFR97_SYRIA_BRIEF_AW.pdf (accessed 4 July 2019).

Part II Global Governance and International Institutions

Chapter 7

Is There a Future for Multilateral Trade Agreements?

Judith Goldstein and Elisabeth van Lieshout

Introduction

As the World Trade Organization (WTO) approaches its 25th birthday, its future is less certain than at any point in its history. While there is no move to dismantle the organisation, the initial expectation that the WTO would be the fulcrum for future international trade agreements has not been met. At best, we can say that its tenure has had mixed results. On one hand, the organisation continues to be an adjudication focal point, with nations using panel processes when there is contestation over rule interpretation. But on the other hand, and more problematic given the function of the organisation, the legislative arm of the WTO is moribund. If we were to compare the WTO with the tenure of its predecessor organisation, the General Agreement on Tariffs and Trade (GATT), the WTO would appear lacklustre. What happened?

This chapter examines the WTO, its history and its relevancy today to our understanding of trade agreements. The review examines the central norms of the system and compares trade liberalisation under the multilateral WTO with the more exclusive regional and/or preferential trade agreements (PTAs). This is a time of deep concern about the role of the WTO and the future of the trading order (Goldstein, 2017). Echoing sentiment heard in Washington, Debra Steger (2007), the first Director of the Appellate Body Secretariat of the WTO, has said the organisation is in need of "major surgery" (p. 495). T.N. Srinivasan (2005), long an advocate of open borders, has commented on the archaic nature of the nondiscrimination principal in the WTO, which, he claims, is touted as a fundamental principle while in practice it is rife with exceptions. Esty (2002) suggests that there is a fundamental legitimacy problem with the WTO that can only be solved via an expanded mandate into a set of fundamental economic issues, ranging from poverty alleviation to public health.

The Handbook of Global Trade Policy, First Edition. Edited by Andreas Klasen.
© 2020 John Wiley & Sons Ltd. Published 2020 by John Wiley & Sons Ltd.

Explaining why the crisis arose, and how it affects the future of the trade regime, is the task we undertake below. While some in Washington have suggested that the organisation has outlived its purposes, we counter with the observation that on the whole, member nations have complied with the significant commitments made in earlier negotiations and, in general, WTO members have resisted protectionist pressures. But there is little forward momentum in the organisation towards deeper or wider agreements, and recent actions by the United States suggest a loss of confidence in the rule-based system. Alan Wolff, the deputy director-general of the WTO, attributes this to a lack of US leadership: "Atlas, tired of his burden, shrugged," he explains (Wolff, 2017). No one, however, should sound the death knell for the WTO. For the European Union (EU), Brazil and China, for example, the WTO has provided "insurance" against ad hoc changes at the border. For them, the benefits from maintaining the organisation are great, and this benefit could give birth to collective leadership. Still, it is difficult to see a path to new global agreements, especially in absence of US stewardship. We suggest that the reluctance to further expand the institution is in part due to the difficulty of reconciling members' domestic constraints with perhaps the most important norm of the system, that is, non-discrimination.

We divide this chapter into four parts. Part one addresses the political consequences of GATT/WTO membership, focusing both on the rules and norms of the regime and on the explanation for why they have become less functional over time. Part two looks at its legislative success and compares that with agreements that have existed simultaneously, but have limited membership. In part three, we look at the effectiveness of the WTO as a forum for dispute settlement. Section four concludes with some general thoughts on the impact of a rise in populism and other stumbling blocks the WTO faces.

Trade Policymaking in the 21st Century

Our analysis is informed by three general observations on trade policymaking. First, looking at the literature, we find that too few scholars have paid attention to the negative distributional effects of trade agreements and how that interacts with constraints on policymaking in member states. As the 2016 US presidential election has shown, trade policy is an easy target for demagogues, in part because the idea of comparative advantage is one of the more opaque ideas to come out of economics. But it is more than the complexity of trade theory that has undermined support for trade. As Robert Driskill (2012) has observed, even economists, who are trained to ask questions of trade-offs, treat the promises of free trade as "akin to a zealous prosecutor's advocacy of a point of view" (p. 3). More caution and consideration of distributional effects is needed. Open markets may be good in the aggregate, that is, for the nation as a whole, but global forces are not kind to every individual. We need to better understand the more micro effects of trade agreements in order to understand when and why the WTO, and its agenda to further reduce impediments to trade, is supported by member nations.

Second, the literature focusing on dispute settlement points us to a more critical evaluation of the dispute settlement process in all trade agreements. While the WTO may have failed to legislate deeper trade agreements, it has been active in creating a forum for dispute adjudication. This has spurred a robust debate about the WTO as an international court, adding significant knowledge, and some optimism, to the possibility of solving disputes without endangering trade. Yet, the success of the courts may well be related to the failure of the legislative process. As nations fear an inability to renege in hard economic times, they become wary of signing new agreements that may be difficult to adhere to. The result is an efficient court and a broken legislative system.

Third, trade policymaking is best understood as a two-level game: nations cooperate in order to increase their aggregate welfare but the form and extent of cooperation reflects the aggregation of domestic political interests. These domestic interests vary across nations, a function of both their specific endowments and the incentives of social groups to organise. Political and economic analysts approach the "game" somewhat differently, and, in fact, Donald Regan (2015) has argued that the two approaches are contradictory. Political analysts, he argues, see trade agreements as a way to undermine political support for import competing groups. The reigning economic theory of trade agreements, by comparison, focuses on terms of trade manipulation. The difference, he says, is significant because in one, the purpose of tariff protection is to "affect domestic relative prices, in response to special-interest politics, [while] terms of trade manipulation aims to affect world prices, to increase national income" (p. 393). While not agreeing with this sharp distinction, this chapter chooses to set aside the terms of trade explanation for the WTO and instead focuses on the interaction between international rules set by the trading regime and the domestic preferences of signatories.

Those who focus on domestic governance report that regime members are constrained because pro-open border majority coalitions are often allusive. Instead, the distribution of social preferences is more often parochial and nationalistic (see Milner and Kubota, 2005, for an alternative perspective). Even in the United States, where there has been a common understanding that very high protective walls are bad for the economy, there has never been a consensus on free trade being the replacement policy. In this sense, the GATT/WTO system has always had tenuous roots. To the extent that open markets were assumed to lead to growth, and export interests remained powerful, nations were willing to cooperate on trade agreements. Today, not only is the pro-trade coalition harder to assemble, but there is also far less confidence that more openness will, in fact, lead to more growth.

The Rules and Norms of the Trading Regime

Since the WTO's creation, there have been no negotiating rounds successfully completed. This is not to say that the system is totally broken; as a forum for discussion, the WTO continues to tackle trade problems. However, larger issues, such as the current query of whether or not China is a market economy and how, for example, that influences dumping margins, are stumbling blocks. Moving from discussions to legislation is difficult, in part, because of a consensus norm. As the number and type of nations that entered the WTO expanded, interests diverged and consequential issues languished. To explain why the organisation chose a consensus norm as well as most contemporary trading rules, we need to return to the WTO's predecessor, the GATT. The WTO and contemporary PTAs incorporate GATT norms and rules into their own texts, and those GATT rules arose from a specific set of historical and political constraints that faced the organisation's founders, in particular the United States.

Origins of the rules and norms

Where did the rules come from? The explanation begins with US politics in the inter-war years. In 1932 a new majority Democratic Party inherited a high tariff wall, a remnant of the 1930 Smoot–Hawley tariff. Recognising that the closure of the US market to European goods contributed to an ensuing disorder in international financial markets and job displacement for their constituents, the traditional party of Southern exporters sought a change in policy. But given that party control in the United States is ephemeral, the new majority sought to guarantee their preferred trade policy against future legislative log rolls. Their method of assuring open trade in the Reciprocal Trade Agreements Act (RTAA) in 1934 was to shift institutional responsibility for trade treaties to the Executive branch (Bailey *et al.*, 1997; Goldstein and Gulotty, 2014). The form of this delegation to the President, however, was less radical than is often portrayed. Some scholars have argued that delegation removed Congress from tariff setting (Haggard, 1988); it is more accurate to see delegation as a change in form, and not a loss of control.

In the RTAA the President was given a "first mover advantage" in that he had authority to negotiate trade agreements, but the process was constrained by, and in the shadow of, congressional oversight. Legislation specified the upper limit of tariff reductions and a fixed period in which he could negotiate. In addition, Congress specified exactly how the reductions could occur. All tariff cuts by the United States needed to be met with reciprocal reduction by the other nation. Treaties needed to provide most-favoured-nation (MFN) treatment, meaning the United States would receive any future reductions in barriers its treaty partners offered to other countries. Further, any product subject to negotiation had to be authorised prior to negotiations and those negotiations had to be focused on the principal supplier of the good, the nation which was currently the largest source of imports of the product. Delegation required regular renewals, forcing the Executive to return to Congress to report on trade agreements and to ask for continued authority. To assure renewal, the President needed to maintain a pro-trade coalition in Congress, which was in no way assured. Mindful of the need to show results, the State Department worked diligently and was able to conclude 38 agreements.

As World War II entered its last phase, the United States was also involved in talks on a more inclusive body, the International Trade Organization (ITO), which was to be an international organisation regulating most aspects of commercial policy. In parallel and interrelated, the President continued to ask for congressional approval of his tariff-setting authority. But the timing was off; fearing political resistance in the upcoming 1948 renewal discussions, the State Department wanted earlier tariff talks in order to legitimate an expansion of negotiation authority. Attempting to finesse the timing issue, the United States had gained acceptance for an Interim Tariff Committee at the ITO's London Conference. Under that umbrella, the United States invited a set of other nations in 1946 to meet in Geneva to conduct bilateral tariff negotiations. Twenty-three nations came to Switzerland and over a nine-month period were able to agree to reduce particular tariffs. At the completion of the talks, a set of rules was attached on top of the new tariff schedules. This became the GATT. While thought at the time to be an interim agreement, the failure to create the ITO made these rules, which were modelled on the 38 earlier US agreements, the backbone of trade coopera-tion until the WTO's creation.

What explains the choice of rules that were institutionalised in the new GATT? Each was a rational response to a political problem faced by Congress at the time. The principal supplier rule purposefully focused negotiations on low-cost producers. But the principal supplier rule was not only about prices; it served the political function of providing, ex ante, information to legislators on whether or not products in their district would be in the reciprocal bundle and subject to import pressures. MFN merged America's multilateral aspirations with the principal supplier rule by assuring producers and their congressional representatives that MFN, which increased the potential entrants into the US market, would not lead to deeper price competition. Finally, the reciprocity rule assured equity in swaps, but more impor-tantly, it motivated exporters to political activity. In the past, few exporters had mobilised on tariff issues, creating a pro-protection bias. Bundling import cuts with export access allowed congressional representatives to advocate for the broader interests in their districts.

Reciprocity, MFN and principal supplier-based negotiations were well entrenched by the time the United States began talks on the trade regime, and thus it isn't sur-prising to see them in the early documents from the wartime conferences on the future of global trade (Chapter III of the First Session and Chapter IV of the Preparatory Committee's second session report). In these sessions, the United States demanded that tariff talks mimic the RTAA process, that is, that reductions would be reciprocal and thus mutually advantageous and MFN apply to both reductions in general and reductions in preferential rates. Negotiated rates would be bound and if reneged upon would need to be compensated in some other part of the tariff schedule. Exempted from these rules were previous preference agreements – they did not have to be granted MFN privileges. These included not only the British Imperial system but also Cuban-American preferences.

There was a fourth US contribution to the GATT framework whose importance is often overlooked: the accounting system used for reciprocal deals. In the GATT, reciprocity mandated that all trade deals be bilaterally balanced; because of the MFN rule, their effect was multilateral. The process of agreeing to a bilateral cut was iterated – nations produced a list of products on which they wanted their trading partner to grant them increased access, and the other nation responded with a list of offers of access. The two then sat down to balance what each wanted and received from the other. When a deal was struck, the nation received what was called an initial negotiation right (INR). The INR was a property right, derived from the original concession. If a nation rescinded on the bilateral deal at any time after the negotiations, the holder of the INR could demand that the other nation make them "whole" via a reduction on another product of equal value to their exporters. While third countries could be compensated, it was the original holder that had the guar-antee. These INRs created an unexpected path dependency, privileging prior partners over later negotiators. On one hand, the INR system stabilised deals, making it more difficult to renege; but on the other hand, it skewed the products and nations who held a "property right" and thus an investment in the GATT system.

These rule choices had long-lasting effects and remain the underlying norms of the system. Ironically, the features that explain early success became the Achilles heel of the WTO. Shifting patterns in both the direction and the type of world trade had the unanticipated effect of generating political challenges for the organisation.

Unintended consequences of the rules and norms

What was good for the domestic politics of the creators of trade agreements became counterproductive as time passed. Three problems emerged.

Interests. First, the GATT was mindful of the domestic constraints faced by leaders in committing to market liberalisation. This attention to domestic politics was eroded by the "hardening" of rules in both the WTO and some PTAs. In the GATT, nations were provided with many ways to renege, and centralised decisions were stipulated to be only by consensus. The "weakness" of the central regime was viewed positively by then current and potential members, and it encouraged expansion. But while each subsequent member of the GATT/WTO created a positive network effect making membership even more valuable, the organisation itself became less of a club of like-minded democratic nations (Gowa and Kim, 2005). Over time and as a result of the success of prior agreements, international trade moved from manufacturing items to services, and from commercial transactions to foreign direct investment. Nations' interests diverged. As behind-the-border policies replaced the earlier negotiations over border measures, non-governmental actors, such as labour and environmental groups, increasingly turned their focus on GATT/WTO policies. Non-governmental organisations (NGOs) participated independently and through national members, increasing the difficultly of crafting a consensus among the voting nations, even around technical issues.

Shifting interests of the members increasingly divided along North–South lines, especially with regulatory harmonisation after 1995. New rules required fundamental change in the domestic legal and regulatory regimes of the developing member states and were unpopular in their national capitals. In addition, as the rules became more demanding, compliance expectations grew, in part because the end of the Cold War fuelled ideological fervour in those who supported free markets. This expanded commitment to open markets then made salient the counter to pro-trade argument that harmonisation was leading to a "race to the bottom." By the end of the century, labour and environmental groups had all turned against trade agreements. Much of the wrath was oriented towards the WTO; from the perspective of leaders in national capitals, the WTO appeared to have turned a "deaf ear" to the changing political landscape they faced at home. They responded by negotiating PTAs, although these faced similar objections as groups demanded PTAs include more stringent commitments to protect constituent interests.

Norms. Second, the new entrants to the regime rejected the fundamental norms of the system, pushed by the United States, that were the backbone of early cooperation. As a negotiating system, the use of reciprocity for most of the 20th century was based on a mercantile notion of trade, that is, trade deals were bilateral and composed of equal swaps. Specific reciprocity and balanced bilateral trade is not a concept that adheres to basic notions of comparative advantage. Reciprocity with MFN, however, is diffuse – with the MFN rule, one's partners may be viewed as a group and there is less of an emphasis on equivalence (Keohane, 1986, p. 4). Specific reciprocity limits the range of possible trade swaps; diffuse reciprocity, as encased in MFN, is more inclusive, because it requires "a widespread sense of obligation" (p. 20).

From the start, parties to the GATT needed to believe in the underlying goal of universalising trade deals, even though they sought reciprocal swaps during negotiations. This belief was never realised, and by the 1960s both the use of specific reciprocity in trade rounds and the expectation of diffuse reciprocity in access to markets had been rejected by the developing world. At the request of the emerging market nations, Part IV of the GATT was legislated, stipulating that a set of member nations were no longer expected to give access to other GATT members' imports in return for access for their exporters. Further, a subset of nations now claimed a need for differential and special access to other members' markets, greater than that given to other regime members. But, even in the absence of the "revolt" from the developing world, MFN would have become problematic as the organisation moved into the realm of domestic regulatory harmonisation. If nations harmonised on strict standards, the developing world balked; if there was standardisation at lower levels, there was a cry of race to the bottom.

Also problematic for harmonisation attempts in the latter part of the 20th century was Article III of the GATT, which specified national treatment. While in origin, national treatment was to be a guarantee of non-discrimination, it undermined the internationalisation of production standards. Since the use of domestic taxes and/or regulations as a form of protectionism was illegal, it encouraged nations to use standards to influence investment and trade patterns. Some nations even began to give imports an advantage not given to domestic producers in order to incentivise foreign direct investment (FDI). While a somewhat simple concept – the prescription to treat all products, domestic or international, in the same manner – national treatment or "inland parity" proved unworkable in practice.

The conflict over universal norms became most obvious in the growing number of PTAs that came into effect in 1990s. While PTAs are consistent with the formal rules of the system (Article XXIV of the GATT), these agreements are inconsistent with the aspirations of the organisation's founders. By definition, these agreements are "preferential": concessions are given only to the other participants. To some extent, countries' ability to engage in preferential liberalisation is limited by the stipulation that such agreements must remove "substantially all" tariffs. This rules out the option of granting special access on an industry-by-industry basis. Still, PTAs are a challenge to the non-discrimination norm of MFN, and it is surprising that the institution explicitly allows such "mini-lateral" agreements.

Why would the GATT have allowed discrimination? Looking back, the primary proponents of the PTA provision in the GATT "contract" were colonial powers, in particular the United Kingdom, who wanted to maintain preferential market access to their former colonies. For other developed countries, the provision functioned as an insurance policy – they could not be sure how successful the GATT would turn out to be and needed certainty that other options would be available if the institution stalled. In a compromise, the rule became part of the original GATT; over time and with the creation of the European Economic Community (EEC), the exception became ingrained in international law. When progress in multilateral negotiations stalled, countries utilised the fall-back option they had created at the outset and began organising trade liberalisation on a smaller scale.

Flexibility.   Third, the founders of the WTO and the GATT had very different beliefs about the optimal specificity of trading rules. The GATT's founders sought "thin" and ambiguous rules; imprecision created space for countries to placate powerful domestic groups when necessary without endangering their general commitment to the regime. For the first 40 years, disputes were most often settled without formal procedures, a reflection of a shared vision of the purposes of the organisation. The GATT was purposefully a "member-driven" organisation with a small and ineffectual secretariat – centralisation and authority at the centre of the regime was not what the founders wanted.

Over time, flexibility became a problem. It granted new members licence to ignore the spirit of the rules. It encouraged "gray area" responses to problems, such as voluntary export restraints (VERs), to accommodate the needs of members. The fundamental rules of the system became rife with exceptions. It is not surprising that the response to this shirking in 1995 was to re-legislate in order to more clearly specify rules and then, relatedly, make it more difficult to break an agreement. From the perspective of the reformists, and in particular, the United States, Canada and the EU, it was the other members of the regime who were out of compliance, not them. As a result, there was consensus among the larger nations on the need for a more robust organisation, and the WTO treaty was, in fact, more specific, stricter and mandated universal adherence.

But there was an unanticipated effect. Even the early supporters found themselves in court over rule violations. Rule specificity and mandatory dispute settlement created a fear of accepting new commitments and signing on to new agreements. With countries facing the possibility of being forced to comply in full and regardless of domestic context, global consensus became harder to achieve and legislating liberalisation at a multilateral level ground to a halt. Some countries still continued to pursue a system with both more extensive and more strictly enforced rules and harmonisation, but they could only do so through smaller-scale agreements.

Legislating Liberalisation

How well has the trade regime's rules and norms served to open member markets? When assessing the success of trade cooperation, both multilateral and preferential, one crucial aspect must be the extent to which they have succeeded at both reducing barriers and increasing trade flows. An extensive empirical literature exists on the effects of both types of agreements, which we examine here.

Multilateral Cooperation

Trade barriers today are at historic lows. While nations, including the United States, continue to have heterogeneity in their tariff structure, overall, the average tariff of trading nations has been dramatically reduced in the post-World War II era. Focusing on tariff reductions, we see three different patterns in the degree of openness of

WTO members. This pattern holds for non-tariff barriers as well. High-income nations have average MFN tariffs that are low and bound; the emerging nations have higher rates but the rates are mostly bound; the developing world has rates that are higher and fewer of the rates are bound (see Table 7.1). The United States, as an example of the first category, has a tariff average slightly above 3%; only Australia among the high-income nations has a lower average tariff. India has the highest

Table 7.1 Tariff levels, 2012

WTO *member economy*	*MFN applied rate, simple average*[a,b]	*Binding coverage*[a,c]
G20 High-income		
Australia	2.7	97.1
Canada	4.3	99.7
European Union	5.5	100.0
Japan	4.6	99.7
Saudi Arabia	5.1	100.0
South Korea	13.3	94.6
United States	3.4	100.0
G20 Emerging		
Argentina	12.5	100.0
Brazil	13.5	100.0
China (2011)[d]	9.6	100.0
India	13.7	73.8
Indonesia	7.0	96.6
Mexico	7.8	100.0
Russia	10.0	100.0
South Africa	7.6	96.4
Turkey	9.6	50.3
Developing, other[e]		
Bangladesh (2011)[d]	14.4	15.5
Burma	5.6	17.6
DR of the Congo	[f]	100.0
Egypt	16.8	99.4
Ethiopia[g]	17.3	[h]
Iran (2011)[d,g]	26.6	[h]
Nigeria (2011)[d]	11.7	19.1
Pakistan	13.5	98.7
Philippines	6.2	67.0
Thailand	9.8	75.0
Vietnam	9.5	100.0

[a] Computed from Bagwell, Bown et al. (2015)
[b] Ad valorem rate
[c] Share of import products
[d] Data availability for 2011
[e] Developing countries with 2012 populations greater than 50 million
[f] Not available
[g] Observer only; non-WTO member
[h] Countries without bound rates

average tariff, at about 14%, among the emerging economies, and retains a number of unbound rates. In the developing world, the tariffs vary dramatically, from a low of 6% for the Philippines (with 67% bound) to 17% for Egypt (99% bound). Both reductions and binding of tariffs are consequential. Binding provides predictability or insurance that the tax would not capriciously be changed. Reviewing Table 7.1, it is apparent that while the 21st century is not about free trade, the world is far more open than at the inaugural meeting of the GATT. But still, how much of world trade today was made possible because of the creation of the GATT/WTO? On this question, there is much disagreement.

Until 2004, most analysts assumed that GATT/WTO membership explained both the liberalisation of trade in the post-war years and the resultant increase in bilateral trade. In that year, however, Rose (2004) penned a paper that suggested that membership was, in fact, not consequential. Using the value of bilateral trade from 1948 to 1999, and controlling for a host of factors in a gravity model, Rose found that while some factors were associated with the level of trade (such as membership in a currency union), GATT/WTO participation was not.

The Rose paper elicited much attention to both its method and its findings. Subramanian and Wei (2007) re-ran the data and, with a slightly different dataset and a tweak to the model, argued that membership in the GATT/WTO did account for an increase in world trade, by about 120%. They did acknowledge, however, that the increase was not uniform. Goldstein *et al.* (2007) and Tomz *et al.* (2007), also puzzled by the findings, re-ran the Rose data, using the same method but adding trade data from the pre-GATT days and including trade for nations that participated in the GATT while still part of a colonial structure. The expansion of the dataset was consequential, and now the GATT/WTO had a positive and significant effect on bilateral trade. Gowa and Kim (2005) also find a positive effect of the GATT on trade, but the increase is specific to trade between five states: Britain, Canada, France, Germany and the United States. Instead of seeing the GATT/WTO as having universal effects, they argue that the benefits were only for a privileged group of members. And most recently, Allee and Scalera (2012) look again at the data and find that countries that undergo rigorous accession processes are the nations more likely to experience an increase in trade flows.

Other scholars suggest that the WTO increases trade volume as a result of oversight by the dispute system. Bown (2004) and Bown and Reynolds (2015) examine variation in the outcome of specific dispute cases and trade flows. Bechtel and Sattler (2015), employing a matching approach, also find a positive effect of dispute settlement on bilateral trade, in fact, for both for the main participants and third parties. On average, Bechtel and Sattler (2015) claim that sectoral exports from complainant countries to the defendant increase by US$7.7 billion in the three years after a panel ruling, as compared to similar pairs of countries that did not undergo dispute settlement, which is not statistically different from the gains obtained by third parties. At the same time, exports to the defendant from pro-complainant third party countries increase by about US$6 billion, as compared to neutral third parties. Not only is the dispute system assuring the flow of trade, but they suggest the dispute decisions also have a spillover effect on third, and often smaller, nations.

In contrast, Chaudoin *et al.* (2016) report less promising results on disputes and trade flows. Rather than examining the relationship of dispute and trade at the dyadic level, they look at trade in disputed products from WTO members to respondent countries and disentangle the various categories of dispute settlement. They find that import values in respondent countries increase by less than 10% after a dispute, which is not statistically significant with country-year fixed effects. Only in cases that have been withdrawn do they find an increase in import values; disputes do not consistently and robustly increase trade flows when controlling for dispute characteristics, such as issue area, and country-specific respondent characteristics.

In addition, some scholars have suggested that membership may affect economic behaviour more broadly. Carnegie (2014), for example, argues that membership can forestall a hold-up problem between politically dissimilar pairs of countries. Employing a log-linear gravity model of trade, she asks whether the effect of WTO membership on trade is greater for dyads that are politically dissimilar, as measured by the difference in capability (power) and regime type and by their alliance status, relative to similar pairs of countries. Under different model specifications, her main finding – that WTO membership increases trade most for dissimilar country dyads – consistently holds. She further tests the causal mechanism by examining the effect of WTO membership on trade in goods that are contract-intensive and on fixed capital investment, areas in which political hold-up problems are most likely to occur.

Carnegie's findings support the idea that the WTO successfully constrains members from using trade policies as political leverage. Büthe and Milner (2008) find a similar virtue from signing any trade agreement. They suggest that trade institutions convey member states' commitment to liberal economic policies, mitigating time inconsistency problems and thereby increasing the flow of foreign direct investment. Membership reassures investors, and the monitoring and compliance mechanisms of the trade agreement raise the reputation costs of a violation. Their empirical findings show that the GATT/WTO and PTAs are positively associated with inward FDI, and the finding holds under different robustness checks, including an instrumental variables method.

As well as influencing FDI because of this reputation and information links, membership has been shown to constrain behaviour in other domains. Simmons (2000) explores the link between monetary and trade policy through a study of Article VIII obligations of the IMF. With respect to GATT membership, she hypothesises that the "GATT might encourage a country to maintain free and nondiscriminatory foreign exchange markets" (p. 596). She finds that GATT membership is negatively correlated with violations of Article VIII obligations, but the effect is not statistically significant at conventional levels. In a more recent study, Copelovitch and Pevehouse (2013) re-examine a potential link between GATT/WTO membership and exchange rate policy choices and, like Simmons, cannot find empirical support for the connection.

The relationship between WTO membership and the signing of a PTA, taken up below, is explored in numerous papers and with different conclusions. For example, Tobin and Busch (2010) employ a rare events logistic regression on a propensity score-matched dataset of 132 low- and middle-income host countries and 23 developed partner countries, seeking to explain PTA formation, controlling for GATT/WTO membership of the host country; Mansfield et al. (2002) also include GATT membership in exploring the effect of democracy on PTA formation during the period from 1951 to 1992. Contrary to the insignificant result found in Tobin and Busch (2010), Mansfield et al. (2002) find a statistically significant, positive effect of dyadic GATT membership on PTA formation. In a later paper, the reason for the relationship between GATT membership and PTA formation is explored (Mansfield and Reinhardt, 2003).

While there are convincing quantitative studies suggesting different degrees of GATT/WTO effect, there is still a lack of clarity of when and how the effect is manifest. As a result of a declassification of data on the specifics of trade rounds, a number of recent papers address this lacuna, beginning to provide these micro-foundations. Bagwell, Staiger *et al.* (2015), in an intensive study of the 1950 Torquay Round, connect the GATT's negotiating rules with a specific pattern of tariff reductions; Goldstein and Gulotty (2017) provide a similar exercise for the 1947 Geneva Round. Both analyses are based on tariff-level coding of offers, responses and the final outcome of the bargain, and both argue that the chosen rules and norms of bargaining were consequential for outcomes. In these two rounds, reciprocity in bargaining over tariff cuts was both a goal and an outcome, although there was less back-and-forth bargaining than had been assumed. Once offers and requests were made, nations tended to either reach agreement or move on to other products. If there was a modification, it was less likely to be on the requests than on the offers. Further, the offers were more or less in line with the principal supplier expectation and swaps were often on very narrow products. While there was some evidence of diffuse reciprocity, both papers find that most of the bargaining was bilateral and specific.

Preferential Cooperation

In the first decades of the GATT, use of preferential trade agreements was limited to regional organisations. The creation of the European Community (1957) was followed by the Central American Free Trade Area (1958), East African Community (1966), Southern Africa Customs Union (1969) and Caribbean Community (1973). Bilateral deals were rare and mostly confined to neighbours or countries with prior colonial ties. In the 1990s, the locus of trade negotiations shifted drastically to preferential, mostly bilateral, deals. Figure 7.1 shows the rapid change in the number of new trade agreements signed each year. Since the completion of an agreement between Japan and Mongolia in June 2016, all WTO members are party to at least one bilateral and/or regional trade agreement. A total of 294 such agreements have been formally notified to the WTO, but over 800 preferential trade agreements have been signed (Dür *et al.*, 2014).

Which sets of countries are most likely to engage in such a trade agreement? Magee (2003) examined a cross-section of country pairs in 1998 and find that dyads with larger trade volumes, who are similar in size, and are both democracies are the most likely to have created a trade agreement. In a similar study, Baier and Bergstrand (2004), using cross-sectional data from 1996, find that PTAs are more likely between pairs of countries who are closer to each other in distance, who are more remote from the rest of the world, who are larger and similar in economic size, whose capital–labour ratios are different from one another, and whose capital–labour ratios are more similar to the rest of the world. Both papers point out that these findings are consistent with the claim that trade agreements are more likely to arise where the benefits of such agreements would be larger.

More recent papers have focused on the idea of cross-PTA externalities. Countries may consider not just direct relationships when choosing which agreements to negotiate, but also the existence of deals between other countries. Egger and Larch (2008) find that generally, the establishment or expansion of a PTA increases the probability

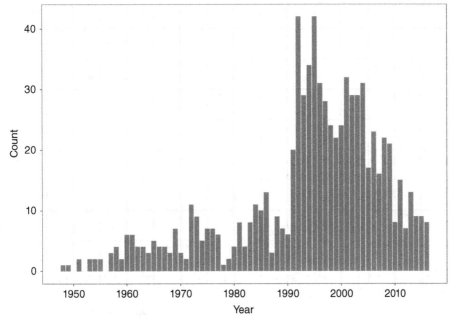

Figure 7.1 Number of PTAs created by year.
Source: Dür *et al.* (2014).

of other countries either joining the agreement or creating one of their own, although the probability of either response decreases with distance. Similarly, Baldwin and Jaimovich (2012) argue that trade agreements are "contagious" and that the rapid spread of PTAs is partially due to "defensive" agreements. If a pair of countries creates a PTA, this creates incentives for all third-party countries to also negotiate a PTA with those two states in order to avoid the discrimination imposed by the original PTA.

PTAs work to liberalise trade in a number of ways. The constraints of Article XXIV of the GATT, which specifies that preferential agreements must remove "substantially all" tariffs, mean that many agreements involve a significant slash in tariffs. In post-1990 bilateral agreements, on average over 95% of remaining tariffs are removed; this is especially striking when taking into account that these tariffs had often been maintained over the course of up to eight rounds of GATT negotiations. Some regional groupings have formed full free trade areas, with no internal barriers, or customs unions, where external barriers are also collectively set. PTAs also frequently cover issues beyond tariffs, in some cases going substantially beyond commitments made in the GATT. The most common topics of agreement include liberalisation of services trade, competition policy, sanitary and phytosanitary measures, technical barriers to trade, intellectual property rights and investment protection (Dür *et al.*, 2014).

Whether the liberalisations entailed in PTAs also resulted in increased trade is a persistent topic of debate, and for a long time no clear consensus existed. More recent work has pointed to a variety of challenges to properly estimating these types of trade flows, and has developed more sophisticated methods for such analysis. The effects of trade agreements are usually assessed using gravity models, where the existence of a PTA is one of the predictors of dyadic trade. In a meta-analysis of papers employing the gravity model, Cipollina and Salvatici (2010) find an overall result equivalent to a 40% increase in trade when a pair of countries has a PTA. This effect of PTAs seems to grow stronger over time, suggesting that more recent deeper agreements may be having a larger impact. However, the authors note there is substantial variation in estimates across papers, which has added to uncertainty about the existence and size of PTA effects. Cipollina and Salvatici attribute this heterogeneity in part to a variety of mistakes in econometric specification.

One challenge in estimation is that trade agreements are not exogenously assigned. Whether or not a pair of countries has a PTA is an endogenous consequence of their current trade flows and related characteristics. Therefore, simply including a variable for PTA in a broader model may fail to capture the true effect of that agreement (Magee, 2003; Baier and Bergstrand, 2007). As discussed above, previous work had identified that PTAs are more likely to arise where they would have the largest trade effects, thus where the current trade flows are small relative to their potential level. This may create a downwards bias on the estimates of the effects of PTAs. Baier and Bergstrand (2007) address this using a panel approach, and find a much larger effect than previous studies. They estimate that a PTA doubles bilateral trade after ten years.

Another line of research has been to unpack the heterogeneous effects of PTAs. One type of heterogeneity is between different types of agreements. Magee (2008) finds that free trade areas have the largest effect in the short run, while customs unions have a larger long-run effect. Agreements which are preferential but do not fully remove barriers have the smallest effect. Dür et al. (2014) analyse the difference in trade effects based on agreement depth. They operationalise this depth as either an index or a latent trait based on their classification of the commitments included in different agreement chapters. Their results suggest the positive effects found of PTAs on trade are primarily due to deep agreements, with shallow agreements having a much smaller impact. Baier et al. (2014) look at the effects on the intensive margin (existing trade flows becoming bigger in quantity) versus the extensive margin (trade in new dyads, industries, products or firms) and find that the effects on the intensive margin occur sooner while the change in the extensive margin is a longer-term consequence. Most recently, Anderson and Yotov (2016) and Baccini et al. (2016) find that effects are highly varied by industry and firm productivity. The largest and most productive firms experienced expanded sales, especially subsidiaries of multinational corporations, but this has also led to an increase in market concentration.

Aggregate data on the effects of PTAs have been supported by the more detailed analyses of single agreements. For example, Trefler (2004) studies the 1987 US-Canada FTA and finds that while on the one hand, the deal lowered Canadian manufacturing employment by 5% (up to 10% in the most impacted industries), on the other hand it raised manufacturing labour productivity by 6% (up to 15% in the most impacted industries). Bustos (2011) argues that Mercosur, and particularly the reduction in Brazil's tariffs, induced Argentinean firms to invest in technology improvement, leading to an increase in overall productivity. Caliendo and Parro (2015) examine the effects of the North American Free Trade Agreement (NAFTA), and find an increase in interbloc trade of 41%, 11% and 118% for the United States, Canada and Mexico, respectively. They also estimate welfare effects of the agreement, and conclude it increased US welfare by 0.08%, raised Mexican welfare by 1.13% and actually decreased Canada's welfare by 0.06%.

To summarise, based on current evidence it seems that both multilateral and preferential trade cooperation have contributed to increases in global trade flows. However, negotiating progress in the WTO has halted while the creating of further PTAs continues apace, suggesting the future of trade legislation may lie outside of the WTO. Yet, legislating is only one of the roles of the institution. We turn to the analysis of dispute settlement. The judicial system created in the WTO treaty has spurred in-depth analysis of all aspects of adjudication, explaining who files, who wins and even who is "in the room" and why. For both critics and supporters, the rise of judicial authority has been an unexpected development in the trade regime.

The WTO as a Judicial Institution

The Function of the Courts

In theory and practice, the founders of the trade regime understood that there needed to be oversight and a sanctioning system to undermine the incentive of members to abrogate inconvenient agreements. Given the lack of any centralised policing powers, the dispute settlement system needed to be self-enforcing. As a result, the GATT system encouraged both arbitration and mutual recognition of, and thus adjustment to, trade shocks. GATT47 granted the secretariat neither oversight of infractions nor judicial power. The original wording in Article XXIII was a very thin set of procedures in cases where the parties could not agree even after consulting on a violation. The need for some judicial procedures was acknowledged in 1947, but how that was to be done was relegated to the Annex and customary, rather than a set of specific practices. Over time, that Annex became more detailed, covering issues on how to create an adjudication panel, and included rules on notification, the selection of panel members and the role of member governments. Under pressure, the GATT secretariat created a separate legal division in the early 1980s, and the staff participated in the writing of a series of understandings among the members on the structure, timing and rules for the resolution of disputes. In 1989, the last vestige of the old order was eliminated, namely the right to veto an inconvenient decision for domestic reasons.

In its most stripped down version, the GATT/WTO dispute settlement mechanism (DSM) remained constant over time. A complaint by a member mandated consultation with the aggrieved party. There was the expectation of some joint, mutually acceptable agreement. In the absence of a consensus, the parties could ask for a decision from a panel of experts on whether or not there was a breach and the extent of the damages. If ruled against, the offending party was expected to change its policy, and if that did not occur, retaliation was within the rights of the hurt party. After 1995, most parties asked the appellate body of standing judges to re-examine the panel's findings.

With the creation of the WTO, the number of disputes that went to panels increased dramatically. The result has been more clarity on policy, and a form of "common law", reinforced by decisions by the appellate body. But because of both increasing complexity and the appellate stage, cases take longer to adjudicate and may actually encourage "foot dragging". According to Rachel Brewster (2011), instead of the new system encouraging compliance, the DSM created a remedy gap. Respondent states could violate trade rules for several years without facing trade retaliation, undermining the incentive for early settlement.

The WTO's dispute system has engendered considerable interest and differences of opinion on its efficacy. There are different interpretations of the rise in the number of cases, to over 500 now. Some argue this signals easier access, especially for developing countries, which has undermined the asymmetry in economic power. Critics suggest that too much litigation is a sign of failure, since nations are not self-regulating.

Interpreting the Dispute Settlement Mechanism

The new WTO and binding dispute settlement were initially interpreted through the lens of what appeared in the 1990s as a more general shift in interstate relations towards legalisation. Legalisation, or the increase in the degree of obligation, precisions and delegation found in international agreements, seemed to characterise not only the WTO but other agreements which allowed for an increase in the autonomy of courts (Alter, 1998; Burley and Mattli, 1993; See *Annual Review of Law and Social Science* Vol. 7). The increased autonomy of WTO courts also gained attention because of the vastly expanded legislative domain after 1995, in particular the expansion of jurisdiction because of the single undertaking (which eliminated the previous "a la carte" set of obligations) and the regulation of behind-the-border production in the Agreement on Trade-Related Aspects of Intellectual Property Rights (TRIPS) (see Barton *et al.*, 2006).

Twenty-five years later, the scholarly community continues to debate the virtues of this increased judicialisation in light of the WTO mandate. For some it is the source of WTO strength; for others, it has undermined cooperation. The heart of the issue rests with the concept of "efficient breach". According to Schwartz and Sykes (2002), the role of the WTO dispute system is not to punish violations through deeper penalties but to assure that unilateral sanctions will not spiral out of control. The role of the DSM is to set the "price" of an efficient breach, that is, allow defection when the cost of compliance is higher than the cost of non-compliance. The standard for an efficient DSM is that it deters, not punishes. In equilibrium, we should see cases decreasing in line with the clarification of what is, and what is not, a punishable breach of the rules, because, as Maggi and Staiger (2011) suggest, the role of the DSM is to complete and clarify aspects of the WTO's "incomplete contract".

Although the new DSM is often said to be binding, the compliance mechanism remains self-enforcing: nations comply because of the potential of a sanction hurting a powerful domestic exporter and/or a fear of a reputational externality. But how much of a sanction is necessary, and, as Pelc and Urpelainen (2015) ask, when is it acceptable for a nation to buy their way out of a violation? More generally, there is still a lack of consensus on the degree to which domestic flexibility will either encourage compliance or, alternately, lead to shirking. To better understand whether or not the current system of rules is efficient, we need to explore not only when and why nations comply but also how exceptions are viewed as signals to domestic actors (Pelc, 2016).

Rosendorff (2005) and Rosendorff and Milner (2001) present a logic for why the DSM's design is consistent from an efficient breach perspective, focusing on granting nations increased flexibility by legitimating a system of temporary escape from rules (Rosendorff 2005). Goldstein and Martin (2000) and Gilligan *et al.* (2010), however, are less sure about the optimality of the constraints imposed by the WTO's rules, including the fail-safe escape clause mechanism. Goldstein and Martin (2000) argue that legalisation increases the clarity of the effects of a rule violation, and as such, can have the unintended effect of mobilising the wrong domestic groups. Anti-trade groups, when mobilised, undercut the ability of leaders to both sign and adhere to inconvenient trade obligations. Gilligan *et al.* (2010) concur but offer a different logic. Strong courts, they argue, can create a disincentive for states to reveal information, undermining pre-trial arbitration and making brinkmanship and conflict more likely without the intervention of the court. Alter (2003) also implies that too much international litigation may actually undermine support for the international legal system.

Like Rosendorff (2005) and Rosendorff and Milner (2001), Kucik and Reinhardt (2008) present evidence that suggests that the escape provisions are, in fact, efficient. Similar to Carnegie (2014), they see the escape rule as solving a time inconsistency problem; at some future moment a nation may need to renege because of changed circumstance. Thus, "counter to intuition, formal provisions for relaxing treaty commitments can actually boost cooperation relative to what would otherwise be possible" (p. 478). Focusing on anti-dumping cases, Kucik and Reinhardt support the WTO's level of flexibility. After accounting for a host of selection issues, they find that states with legislated anti-dumping provisions are more likely to join the GATT/WTO and to bind their tariffs.

Assessing the Dispute Settlement Mechanism

The assessment of the DSM is ultimately an empirical issue and there is a large number of studies that provide insight into who files and who wins cases. Not surprisingly, the findings have been quite diverse. In 2000, Busch and Reinhardt argued that the WTO dispute procedures still lacked enforcement power and therefore its success depended on "its ability to encourage bargaining in the shadow of weak law" (p. 160). A few years later, Iida (2004) looked at the cases and found that the dispute system had partially done what was expected, pointing in particular to a decline in unilateralism by the United States. Since the fear of American unilateralism was a key reason that many of the regime's members were willing to accept a reformed DSM, this could be interpreted as a strong metric of success. Still, a review of the many scholarly papers on the DSM reveals that effectiveness is often in the eye of the beholder.

First, a set of authors looks at domestic political characteristics to explain initiation and outcomes. For example, Rickard (2010) collects data on democracies and electoral institutions as explanation for the variation in case behaviour. She finds that majoritarian systems, like the United States, are on average less likely to comply and are more constrained by particular segments of the electorate. Using data on complaints filed at the GATT/WTO over illegal narrow transfers, she finds that having a majoritarian system significantly increases the probability of a nation violating an obligation. Chaudoin (2014) also looks at domestic constraints but focuses on the timing of disputes, which he argues varies with the political and economic conditions in the defendant country. Complainants are more likely to find international arbitration appealing when there is a high probability that the case will mobilise pro-compliance domestic audiences. This will be more likely at particular moments, for example during an election year or when there is some shift in the domestic economy. Using data on potential disputes against the United States, Chaudoin finds that trading partners of the United States are more likely to file complaints during election years with a low unemployment rate.

Second, authors such as Davis and Shirato (2007) have used industry characteristics as an explanation for dispute initiation and thus outcomes. Focusing on Japan and its production profile, they find that industries characterised by many product lines and rapid product turnover face higher opportunity costs of filing an objection and are less likely to request dispute resolution. Using data on potential cases for WTO litigation in Japan, they show the importance of a number of industry-level variables, including industry size, past political contributions and concentration. Third, many authors have suggested that the variation in cases filed and case outcomes resides in the size and strength of one or both of the parties. Richer nations may be at an advantage in being able to utilise the system in a manner not available to the emerging or developing economies. Although developing countries can build procedural power by forming coalitions, high-capacity members hold positional strength, or structural power, at the WTO (Elsig 2006). Guzman and Simmons (2005) explain that there are significant costs to litigation and monitoring and Kim (2008) and Bown (2005) find that judicialisation has provided disproportionate benefits to those with greater institutional capacity.

The cost of litigation has elicited considerable attention. For example, while recognising that there may be a fixed and high cost to litigation, a number of papers have implied that developing nations can affect dispute outcomes by either participating as third parties (Busch and Reinhardt, 2006; Johns and Pelc, 2014) and/or learning how to strategically use the system. Davis and Bermeo (2009) argue that the cost of litigation is largely a function of information; countries spend resources in the process of fact-finding, which is specific to each case, but they also pay a significant amount of fixed cost in the process of getting acquainted with WTO rules and procedures. Having experience in WTO adjudication reduces such fixed costs for governments and their domestic producers. Examining dispute initiation for 75 developing countries between 1975 and 2003, they find that prior experience, either as a complainant or a respondent, increases the probability of dispute initiation. In the same vein, Conti (2010) finds that the relative experience between the complainant and respondent influences the manner in which the dispute unfolds. Experience seems to predict whether or not a nation settles or goes to panel. His data shows that early settlement is more likely in cases where the complainant has been involved in more disputes relative to respondents, while the odds of going to a panel increases when respondents have more experience. Prior experience in WTO litigation may also have spillover effects on dispute initiation in other trade courts. In examining the determinants of formal dispute initiation in regional forums among South American countries from 1996 to 2008, Gomez-Mera and Molinari (2014) find that prior dispute experience at the WTO influences dispute initiation at the regional level.

Figure 7.2 shows the use of the DSM over time. It is noteworthy that the number of requests for consultation by an aggrieved party has started to shift downward. Given the increase in politicisation of trade in just about all WTO member nations, how should we interpret the relative decline? Is the decline indicative of a clarification of a previously underspecified contract and thus better information on the potential outcome of a case or is the decline simply an indicator that nations comply, even in hard economic times? Maggi and Staiger (2016) argue the former, that is, that there has been judicial learning and rule clarification by the courts. They find that the probability of a new dispute or a ruling is related to the accumulation of article-specific, directed-dyad-specific and complainant-specific rulings. But while

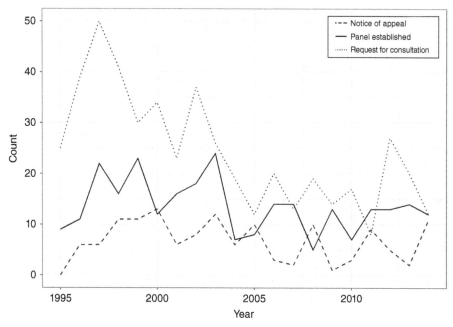

Figure 7.2   Number of WTO disputes by year.
Source: Overview of the State of Play of WTO Disputes – Annual Report 2014.

they find that the specificity of rulings matters, they find only weak empirical evidence of what they call general-scope learning (the impact of the total number of rulings regardless of issue area and disputant characteristics is only weakly supported). The lack of a general finding casts some doubt on the argument that governments are getting "smarter" about the DSM process.

The other explanation, that decline is evidence of more compliance, is also problematic, according to a recent paper by Kucik and Pelc (2016). In this study, these authors look directly at trade policy choices, focusing on behaviour during the Great Recession, 2008–2011. Their conclusion is that the more rigorous and ambitious the nation's accession agreement, the more likely it was to be shirked during this period. Countries, in hard times, took "action to protect the interests of domestic producers, in spite of their stated commitments to liberalise" (p. 393). Their data suggests that leaders do respond to domestic political and economic pressures, even in the shadow of a binding dispute system. It may be that some nations, in particular those who recently acceded to the WTO, worry less about another country taking them to court than about the domestic pressures that emanate from an economic shock. While not undermining what we know about the institutionalisation of the WTO court procedures, it does suggest that we need a deeper understanding of when and why the courts, and the general membership, are more forgiving of nations' inability to comply with obligations.

Dispute Settlement in PTAs: Is Small Better?

The vast majority of preferential agreements include some form of dispute settlement within their text; Dür *et al.* (2014) find dispute provisions are present in 87% of agreements. However, there is substantial variation in the design of these settlement procedures, and scholars have asked what explains the kind of rules countries choose to include. Smith (2000) argues that states form preferences over the level of legalism in their agreements based on the relative cost of diminished policy discretion against the benefits of increased compliance, which depends on their economic stake in the agreement, their relative power compared to other parties, and the depth or intensity of the proposed deal. Empirically, he demonstrates for a group of 62 agreements signed before 1995 that treaties involving larger states have a lower level of legalism in their dispute settlement.

Jo and Namgung (2012) update and extend Smith's argument. They argue regime type plays an important role, with democracies being more likely to choose moderately strict dispute settlement, and show that trading partners emulate each other and adopt similar legal templates. Allee and Elsig (2016) move beyond the concept of legalism in explaining variation in DSMs. They argue that mechanism design is a response to both the depth of the agreement and the diversity of its membership, as these factors will increase the need for a way to resolve disputes. They find that agreements which entail a greater degree of policy change (in terms of trade liberalisation, market access and harmonisation) generally contain stronger dispute settlement provisions, and that DSM strength also increases in number of members. Moreover, they identify that agreements with a power imbalance, either North–South agreements or those involving the United States, also have stricter dispute rules.

Most countries with trade agreements are simultaneously members of the WTO. This means that when an issue arises, countries have the option of bringing a dispute either to the WTO or through the DSM included in their PTA (or in some cases multiple PTAs) with this particular partner. This phenomenon of "forum shopping" leads Busch (2007) to ask what drives countries' decisions when facing the choice of where to raise a trade dispute. He argues that it depends in part on where they expect to obtain the most favourable ruling, but the decision is also influenced by whether and where the state would like to set a precedent through the case in question. There is concern that forum shopping could create a less efficient system of dispute resolution. Davis (2009) argues that overlapping dispute settlement institutions could potentially arrive at contradictory rulings, which could undermine compliance by increasing uncertainty. However, she notes that overlapping institutions may also increase compliance if reputational consequences transcend across forums, as this would increase the cost of being found in violation. In a detailed case study on a long-running dispute on the tariff on bananas, Alter and Meunier (2006) concur, showing that the existence of multiple overlapping institutions may create significant legal complexity in what could otherwise be a simple dispute.

To a certain extent, the concern about both the design and the overlapping of PTA dispute settlement may be a moot point. Disagreements between pairs of countries who share a trade agreement arise regularly, but the overwhelming majority of such disputes are brought to the WTO rather than to a panel appointed through the PTA. Most of the disputes that do occur outside of the WTO are in large regional bodies such as NAFTA and Mercosur. So far, no explanation exists as to why countries choose to include but not utilise DSMs in their preferential agreements, and no quantitative studies exist exploring why countries choose WTO or PTA dispute resolution in a particular instance. This relative lack of use of non-WTO dispute settlement options presents an important puzzle for future research (Kim, 2017). It also demonstrates that the WTO has a crucial role it will continue to hold, even in absence of further legislative successes. The presence of a central institution for countries to resolve their disagreements, whether about WTO rules or outside agreements, may prove central to the continued stability of the international trade regime.

General Conclusions

The future of the WTO remains uncertain. Internally it has been unable to resolve its legislative gridlock, and externally it faces direct competition in the form of preferential trade agreements. Its most important member, the United States, has become its greatest critic, not only flouting the rules but undercutting judicial appointments. One prominent explanation for these challenges is shifts in domestic public opinion. Alan Blinder (2016) inked a blog post noting that, "this [is] an unpropitious time for rational discourse" on the subject of international trade. Trade in general, regional trade agreements and the WTO are all being blamed for a host of economic problems, most of which have little to do with the agreements. A *Washington Post*-ABC News Poll (2016) taken in May, not long after the Blinder post, found that 53% of respondents believed that trade took away jobs; two months earlier, 65% had responded that US trade policy should be more restrictive in order to protect jobs (Bloomberg Politics Poll, 2016). European public opinion is equally negative. Even though the job "churn" is rarely a result of a trade agreement, the public's perception is that trade and job prospects are interconnected. While those who benefit from globalisation, the more educated, continue to support open borders, the shift in the labour market that has resulted from technological innovations and declining productivity is more often seen as a result of some external public policy. (For explanations of trade attitudes see e.g. Hiscox, 2002; Scheve and Slaughter, 2004; Mayda and Rodrik, 2005; Pandya, 2010.) These attitudes make the prospect of pursuing global efforts to further liberalise trade unattractive for most political leaders. But while public attitudes may be the most visible of the constraints on trade policymaking, this is not the only problem that confronts the WTO. This review suggests another three central problems.

First, the inability to legislate may be tied to the increasing precision of international law. Gilligan *et al.* (2010) have provided such a logic. A number of other scholars have argued that states are more likely to sign and abide by agreements when they think their partners will challenge them if they do not (Davis, 2012). But whether or not the current WTO dispute settlement system allows efficient breach remains an open question. To the extent that nations feel constrained by existing law, they will fear any new obligations. And as Kucik and Pelc (2016) illustrate, in hard economic times, nations fail to adhere to promises made when their economy was booming. More generally, the Kucik and Pelc (2016) finding of rule violations suggests two possible interpretations of the relationships between the courts and the legislative impasse today. By one interpretation, the ability of nations to escape a rule in hard economic times is evidence that nations are not overly bound by WTO obligations. The DSM is allowing efficient breach. The other interpretation, however, is that post-WTO, nations have increasingly recognised that economic shocks do require reneging and therefore continue to fear the potential of DSM punishment. In either case, nations would be wary of any new obligations given uncertainty about the level of acceptable breach.

A second stumbling block to new legislation may be the norms of the regime and, in particular, the norms that regulate internal decision-making. Steinberg (2002) argues that the original choice of the GATT founders to grant each member "sovereign equality" is a substantial impediment to the legislative process. Reviewing the history of past rounds, he concludes that the rule has always been understood to be impractical and, historically, legislating in the GATT/WTO depended upon joint action between the United States and Europe and not a more general agreement among members. The transatlantic partnership, he finds, created an "invisible weighting"; cooperation depended upon agreement between Brussels and Washington (pp. 354–355). The absence of reform in decision-making may explain the failure of the most recent Doha Round of negotiations. As the interests of the developed and developing countries have diverged and the shared sense of purpose that facilitated consensus in the early years of the GATT has eroded, the organisation has found consensus an elusive goal.

A third set of scholars focus less on the courts or the voting system and instead focus on the expansion of the agenda. The first 50 years of the trade regime focused on the binding and reduction of tariffs. With success, the WTO turned its attention to a set of non-tariff barriers. But the problems they now seek to solve are of a different nature; they are behind the border and are more likely to elicit attention from domestic audiences. The new issues range from FDI to the environment to competition policy. All require domestic actors to change their regulatory regimes in a manner that is fundamentally disruptive to politics at home. Making those changes was difficult, more so because simultaneously with a push for deeper liberalisation through regulatory reform came the demand for more inclusive and transparent negotiations. Not surprisingly, transparency has made cooperation even more problematic by increasing the number of domestic veto players.

As a most general conclusion, we find that it is wrong to assume that the popular malaise about the virtues of trade is a function of something the WTO did or did not accomplish. The current fear of deeper liberalisation may well reflect the success of the multilateral system, not its failure. The GATT/WTO has been extremely efficacious in facilitating the transnational opening of borders to the movement of goods and services. Few international organisations can claim credit for having influenced the policies of member states to this degree. Still, this success occurred in an era in which multilateralism was valued. Today, with rising nationalism and populism, multilateralism has become anachronistic. In this political climate, it is hard to imagine domestic support for any more rounds and/or a greater harmonisation of trading rules. But even if so, history will record the 20th and perhaps the 21st centuries as ones in which the GATT/WTO system was profoundly important.

References

Allee, T.L. & Elsig, M. (2016) Why Do Some International Institutions Contain Strong Dispute Settlement Provisions? New Evidence from Preferential Trade Agreements. *Review of International Organizations*, 11(1), 89–120.

Allee, T.L. & Scalera, J.E. (2012) The Divergent Effects of Joining International Organizations: Trade Gains and the Rigors of WTO Accession. *International Organization*, 66(2), 243–276.

Alter, K.J. (1998) Who Are the Masters of the Treaty? European Governments and the European Court of Justice. *International Organization*, 52(1), 121–147.

Alter, K.J. (2003) Resolving or Exacerbating Disputes? The WTO's New Dispute Resolution System. *International Affairs*, 79(4), 783–800.

Alter, K.J. & Meunier, S. (2006) Nested and Overlapping Regimes in the Transatlantic Banana Trade Dispute. *Journal of European Public Policy*, 13(3), 362–382.

Anderson, J.E. & Yotov, Y.V. (2016) Terms of Trade and Global Efficiency Effects of Free Trade Agreements, 1990–2002. *Journal of International Economics*, 99, 279–298.

Baccini, L., Pinto, P.M. & Weymouth, S. (2016) The Distributional Consequences of Preferential Trade Liberalization: Firm-Level Evidence. *International Organization*, 71(2), 373–395.

Bagwell, K., Bown, C.P. & Staiger, R.W. (2015) Is the WTO Passé? *World Bank Group Policy Research* No. 7304.

Bagwell, K., Staiger, R.W. & Yurukoglu, A. (2015) Multilateral Trade Bargaining: A First Look at the GATT Bargaining Records. *NBER Working Paper* No. 21488.

Baier, S.L. & Bergstrand, J.H. (2004) Economic Determinants of Free Trade Agreements. *Journal of International Economics*, 64(1), 29–63.

Baier, S.L. & Bergstrand, J.H. (2007) Do Free Trade Agreements Actually Increase Members' International Trade? *Journal of International Economics*, 71(1), 72–95.

Baier, S.L., Bergstrand, J.H. & Feng, M. (2014) Economic Integration Agreements and the Margins of International Trade. *Journal of International Economics*, 93(2), 339–350.

Bailey, M.A., Goldstein, J. & Weingast, B.R. (1997) The Institutional Roots of American Trade Policy: Politics, Coalitions, and International Trade. *World Politics*, 49(3), 309–338.

Baldwin, R. & Jaimovich, D. (2012) Are Free Trade Agreements Contagious? *Journal of International Economics*, 88(1), 1–16.

Barton, J.H., Goldstein, J.L., Josling, T.E. & Steinberg, R.H. (2006) *The Evolution of the Trade Regime: Politics, Law, and Economics of the GATT and the WTO*. Princeton: Princeton University Press.

Bechtel, M.M. & Sattler, T. (2015) What Is Litigation in the World Trade Organization Worth? *International Organization*, 69(2), 375–403.

Blinder, A.S. (2016) Five Big Truths About Trade. *The Wall Street Journal* (21 April). Retrieved from: http://www.wsj.com/articles/five-big-truths-about-trade-1461280205 (accessed 4 July 2019).

Bloomberg Politics National Poll (2016) Retrieved from: http://assets.bwbx.io/documents/users/iqjWHBFdfxIU/rXX28ED96saU/v0 (accessed 4 July 2019).

Bown, C.P. (2004) On the Economic Success of GATT/WTO Dispute Settlement. *Review of Economic Statistics*, 86(3), 811–823.

Bown, C.P. (2005) Participation in WTO Dispute Settlement: Complainants, Interested Parties, and Free Riders. *World Bank Economic Review*, 19(2), 287–310.

Bown, C.P. & Reynolds, K.M. (2015) Trade Agreements and Enforcement. *World Bank Group Policy Research* No. 7242.

Brewster, R. (2011) The Remedy Gap: Institutional Design, Retaliation, and Trade Law Enforcement. *George Washington Law Review*, 80(1), 102–158.

Burley, A.M. & Mattli, W. (1993) Europe Before the Court: A Political Theory of Legal Integration. *International Organization*, 47(1), 41–76.

Busch, M.L. (2007) Overlapping Institutions, Forum Shopping, and Dispute Settlement in International Trade. *International Organization*, 61(4), 735–761.

Busch, M.L. & Reinhardt, E. (2000) Bargaining in the Shadow of the Law: Early Settlement in GATT/WTO Disputes. *Fordham International Law Journal*, 24(1), 158–172.

Busch, M.L. & Reinhardt, E. (2006) Three's a Crowd: Third Parties and WTO Dispute Settlement. *World Politics*, 58(3), 446–477.

Bustos, P. (2011) Trade Liberalization, Exports and Technology Upgrading: Evidence on the Impact of MERCOSUR on Argentinean Firms. *American Economic Review*, 101, 304–340.

Büthe, T. & Milner, H. (2008) The Politics of Foreign Direct Investment into Developing Countries: Increasing FDI through International Trade Agreements? *American Journal of Political Science*, 52(4), 741–762.

Caliendo, L. & Parro, F. (2015) Estimates of the Trade and Welfare Effects of NAFTA. *Review of Economic Studies*, 82(1), 1–44.

Carnegie, A. (2014) States Held Hostage: Political Hold-up Problems and the Effects of International Institutions. *American Political Science Review*, 108(1), 54–70.

Chaudoin, S. (2014) Audience Features and the Strategic Timing of Trade Disputes. *International Organization*, 68(4), 877–911.

Chaudoin, S., Kucik, J. & Pelc, K. (2016). Do WTO Disputes Actually Increase Trade? *International Studies Quarterly*, 60(2), 1–13.

Cipollina, M. & Salvatici, L. (2010) Reciprocal Trade Agreements in Gravity Models: A Meta-analysis. *Review of International Economics*, 18(1), 63–80.

Conti, J.A. (2010) Learning to Dispute: Repeat Participation, Expertise, and Reputation at the World Trade. *Law Social Inquiry*, 35(3), 625–662.

Copelovitch, M.S. & Pevehouse, J.C.W. (2013) Ties That Bind? Preferential Trade Agreements and Exchange Rate Policy Choice. *International Studies Quarterly*, 57(2), 385–399.

Davis, C.L. (2009) Overlapping Institutions in Trade Policy. *Perspectives on Politics*, 7(1), 25–31.

Davis, C.L. (2012) *Why Adjudicate? Enforcing Trade Rules in the WTO*. Princeton: Princeton University Press.

Davis, C.L. & Bermeo, S.B. (2009) Who Files? Developing Country Participation in WTO Adjudication. *Journal of Politics*, 71(3), 1033–1049.

Davis, C.L. & Shirato, Y. (2007) Firms, Governments, and WTO Adjudication: Japan's Selection of WTO Disputes. *World Politics*, 59(2), 274–313.

Driskill, R. (2012) Deconstructing the Argument for Free Trade: A Case Study of the Role of Economists in Policy Debates. *Economics & Philosophy*, 28(1), 1–30.

Dür, A., Baccini, L. & Elsig, M. (2014) The Design of International Trade Agreements: Introducing a New Dataset. *Review of International Organization*, 9(3), 353–375.

Egger, P. & Larch, M. (2008) Interdependent Preferential Trade Agreement Memberships: An Empirical Analysis. *Journal of International Economics*, 76(2), 384–399.

Elsig, M. (2006) Different Facets of Power in Decision-Making in the WTO. *NCCR Working Paper* No. 2006/23.

Esty, D.C. (2002) The World Trade Organization's Legitimacy Crisis. *World Trade Review*, 1(1), 7–22.

Gilligan, M., Johns, L. & Rosendorff, B.P. (2010) Strengthening International Courts and the Early Settlement of Disputes. *Journal of Conflict Resolution*, 54(1), 5–38.

Goldstein, J. (2017) Trading in the Twenty-First Century: Is There a Role for the World Trade Organization? *Annual Review of Political Science*, 20, 545–564.

Goldstein, J. & Gulotty, R. (2014) America and Trade Liberalization: The Limits of Institutional Reform. *International Organization*, 68(2), 263–295.

Goldstein, J. & Gulotty, R. (2017) Opening Markets: Rules, Norms and Bargaining in Trade Treaties. Working paper. Retrieved from: https://siepr.stanford.edu/sites/default/files/publications/602wp_1.pdf (accessed 20 July, 2019)

Goldstein, J. & Martin, L.L. (2000) Legalization, Trade Liberalization, and Domestic Politics: A Cautionary Note. *International Organization*, 54(3), 603–632.

Goldstein, J.L., Rivers, D. & Tomz, M. (2007) Institutions in International Relations: Understanding the Effects of the GATT and the WTO on World Trade. *International Organization*, 61(1), 37–67.

Gomez-Mera, L. & Molinari, A. (2014) Overlapping Institutions, Learning, and Dispute Initiation in Regional Trade Agreements: Evidence from South America. *International Studies Quarterly*, 58(2), 269–281.

Gowa, J. & Kim, S.Y. (2005) An Exclusive Country Club: The Effects of the GATT on Trade, 1950–94. *World Politics*, 57(4), 453–478.

Guzman, A.T. & Simmons, B.A. (2005). Power Plays and Capacity Constraints: The Selection of Defendants in WTO Disputes. *Journal of Legal Studies*, 34(2), 557–598.

Haggard, S. (1988) The Institutional Foundations of Hegemony: Explaining the Reciprocal Trade Agreements Act of 1934. *International Organization*, 42(1), 91–119.

Hiscox, M.J. (2002) Commerce, Coalitions, and Factor Mobility: Evidence from Congressional Votes on Trade Legislation. *American Political Science Review*, 96(3), 593–608.

Iida, K. (2004) Is WTO Dispute Settlement Effective? *Global Governance*, 10(2), 207–225.

Jo, H. & Namgung, H. (2012) Dispute Settlement Mechanisms in Preferential Trade Agreements: Democracy, Boilerplates, and the Multilateral Trade Regime. *Journal of Conflict Resolution*, 56(6), 1041–1068.

Johns, L. & Pelc, K.J. (2014) Who Gets to Be In the Room? Manipulating Participation in WTO Disputes. *International Organization*, 68(3), 663–699.

Keohane, R.O. (1986) Reciprocity in International Relations. *International Organization*, 40(1), 1–27.

Kim, I.S. (2017) Political Cleavages within Industry: Firm-Level Lobbying for Trade Liberalization. *American Political Science Review*, 111(1), 1–20.

Kim, M. (2008) Costly Procedures: Divergent Effects of Legalization in the GATT/WTO Dispute Settlement Procedures. *International Studies Quarterly*, 52(3), 657–686.

Kim, S.M. (2017) An Expressive Nature of International Law: The Case of Preferential Trade Agreements. Stanford University working paper (unpublished).

Kucik, J. & Pelc, K.J. (2016) Over-Commitment and Backsliding in International Trade. *European Journal of Political Research*, 55(2), 391–415.

Kucik, J. & Reinhardt, E. (2008) Does Flexibility Promote Cooperation? An Application to the Global Trade Regime. *International Organization*, 62(3), 477–505.

Magee, C.S. (2003) Endogenous Preferential Trade Agreements: An Empirical Analysis. *Contributions in Economic Analysis & Policy*, 2(1), 1–19.

Magee, C.S. (2008) New Measures of Trade Creation and Trade Diversion. *Journal of International Economics*, 75(2), 349–362.

Maggi, G. & Staiger, R.W. (2011) The Role of Dispute Settlement Procedures in International Trade Agreements. *Quarterly Journal of Economics*, 126(1), 475–515.

Maggi, G. & Staiger, R.W. (2016) Learning by Ruling: A Dynamic Model of Trade Disputes. Working paper. Retrieved from: https://law.yale.edu/system/files/area/workshop/leo/leo16_maggi.pdf (accessed 4 July 2019).

Mansfield, E.D. & Reinhardt, E. (2003) Multilateral Determinants of Regionalism: The Effects of GATT/WTO on the Formation of Preferential Trading Arrangements. *International Organization*, 57(4), 829–862.

Mansfield, E.D., Milner, H.V. & Rosendorff, B.P. (2002) Why Democracies Cooperate More: Electoral Control and International Trade Agreements. *International Organization*, 56(3), 477–513.

Mayda, A. & Rodrik, D. (2005) Why Are Some People (and Countries) More Protectionist Than Others? *European Economic Review*, 49(6), 1393–1430.

Milner, H.V. & Kubota, K. (2005) Why the Move to Free Trade? Democracy and Trade Policy in the Developing Countries. *International Organization*, 59(1), 107–143.

Pandya, S.S. (2010) Labor Markets and the Demand for Foreign Direct Investment. *International Organization*, 64(3), 389–409.

Pelc, K.J. (2016) *Making and Bending International Rules: The Design of Exceptions and Escape Clauses in Trade Law*. Cambridge: Cambridge University Press.

Pelc, K.J. & Urpelainen, J. (2015) When Do International Economic Agreements Allow Countries to Pay to Breach? *Review of International Organizations*, 10(2), 231–264.

Regan, D.H. (2015) Explaining Trade Agreements: The Practitioners' Story and the Standard Model. *World Trade Review*, 14(3), 391–417.

Rickard, S.J. (2010) Democratic Differences: Electoral Institutions and Compliance with GATT/WTO Agreements. *European Journal of International Relations*, 16(4), 711–729.

Rose, A.K. (2004) Do We Really Know That the WTO Increases Trade? *American Economic Review*, 94(1), 98–114.

Rosendorff, B.P. (2005) Stability and Rigidity: Politics and Design of the WTO's Dispute Settlement Procedure. *American Political Science Review*, 99(3), 389–400.

Rosendorff, B.P. & Milner, H. (2001) The Optimal Design of International Trade Institutions: Uncertainty and Escape. *International Organization*, 55(4), 829–857.

Scheve, K. & Slaughter, M.J. (2004) Economic Insecurity and the Globalization of Production. *American Journal of Political Science*, 48(4), 662–674.

Schwartz, W.F. & Sykes, A.O. (2002) The Economic Structure of Renegotiation and Dispute Resolution in the World Trade Organization. *Journal of Legal Studies*, 31(1), S179–S204.

Simmons, B.A. (2000) The Legalization of International Monetary Affairs. *International Organization*, 54(3), 573–602.

Smith, J.M. (2000) The Politics of Dispute Settlement Design: Explaining Legalism in Regional Trade Pacts. *International Organization*, 54(1), 137–180.

Srinivasan, T.N. (2005) Nondiscrimination in GATT/WTO: Was There Anything to Begin with and Is There Anything Left? *World Trade Review*, 4(1), 69–95.

Steger, D.P. (2007) The Culture of the WTO: Why It Needs to Change. *Journal of International Economic Law*, 10(3), 483–495.

Steinberg, R.H. (2002) In the Shadow of Law or Power? Consensus-Based Bargaining and Outcomes in the GATT/WTO. *International Organization*, 56(2), 339–374.

Subramanian, A. & Wei, S. (2007) The WTO Promotes Trade, Strongly But Unevenly. *Journal of International Economics*, 72(1), 151–175.

Tobin, J.L. & Busch, M.L. (2010) A BIT is Better Than a Lot: Bilateral Investment Treaties and Preferential Trade Agreements. *World Politics*, 62(1), 1–42.

Tomz, M., Goldstein, J.L. & Rivers, D. (2007) Do We Really Know That the WTO Increases Trade? Comment. *American Economic Review*, 97(5), 2005–2018.

Trefler, D. (2004) The Long and Short of the Canada-U.S. Free Trade Agreement. *American Economic Review*, 94(4), 870–895.

Washington Post-ABC News Poll. (2016) *Clinton and Trump Widely Unpopular with American Voters*. (23 May). Retrieved from: https://www.washingtonpost.com/page/2010-2019/WashingtonPost/2016/05/22/National-Politics/Polling/release_426.xml?uuid=v4d0jh_REeaCwqfcsxMofQ&tid=a_inl (accessed 4 July 2019).

Wolff, A. (2017) Lecture on the Future of the World Trading System, American University, 8 November, 2017. Retrieved from: https://www.wto.org/english/news_e/news17_e/ddgra_08nov17_e.htm (accessed 20 July 2019).

World Trade Organization (2014) Overview of the State of Play of WTO Disputes – Annual Report 2014. Retrieved from: https://docs.wto.org/gtd/WTOdispute/64A1_e.pdf (accessed 22 July 2019).

Chapter 8

Finance That Matters: International Finance Institutions and Trade

Steven Beck and Alisa DiCaprio

Introduction

The global trade finance gap is estimated at US$1.5 trillion. This number was first calculated in 2013 in an effort to shed light on the geography of underserved markets (DiCaprio *et al.*, 2017). It tells us that even in the absence of crisis – when global trade finance flows are fully functioning – small and medium-sized enterprises (SMEs) and firms in frontier markets are not able to access the finance they need to trade. This perspective enables us to see the public good features of what is generally considered to be a private sector operation.

High risk ratings in developing countries make it difficult for the private financial sector to support trade in challenging markets. And if suppliers are not willing to assume direct buyer payment risk, potential trade does not get realised. For these reasons, multilateral developments banks (MDBs) have become active in trade finance. MDBs are regional or international institutions owned by multiple governments that seek to promote economic development globally or regionally. In contrast to private financial institutions, MDBs are mandated to assume country risk in challenging markets and are able to act on a cross-border scale. This mandate has enabled MDBs to create value that other public and private institutions cannot achieve.

MDB activity in trade finance is relatively new and reflects two changes in the way they engage with the private sector. The first shift was a gradual move towards private sector lending. Historically, MDBs have pursued the goal of poverty reduction via sovereign lending. The move into trade finance reflected a global trend towards engaging with the private sector. Greater private sector engagement reflected greater awareness among MDBs that the private sector was an important partner and could promote development objectives while pursuing purely commercial outcomes.

The Handbook of Global Trade Policy, First Edition. Edited by Andreas Klasen.
© 2020 John Wiley & Sons Ltd. Published 2020 by John Wiley & Sons Ltd.

A second shift was precipitated by the Global Financial Crisis (GFC) in 2008. This led some MDBs to take a more activist role in global regulation of trade finance. As part of this, they developed several new data sources which shed light on the development impacts of trade finance and have continued to impact global trade well beyond their original scope. The participation of MDBs in trade finance has become deeper over time. During the early days, most trade finance programmes involved only guarantees. Today, MDB trade finance offerings include risk participation and funded products. As open account has become more prominent, development banks have also begun to offer supply chain finance products to help close gaps.

Even as MDBs have evolved their offerings to meet changing demands in the market, trade finance itself has been relatively inflexible. The instruments available for cross-border transactions have changed little over the past 100 years. But this will all change in the next ten years. In an effort to understand the role of MDBs, we also cover the fundamental technological adjustments that are happening in trade. This allows us to explore how technology will impact the relationship between trade finance and development going forward.

Our objective in this chapter is to detail the development impacts of trade finance as the basis for discussion of the role MDBs have played in these markets. Since other chapters cover trade finance, we focus on the three ways that MDBs have reduced friction in global trade finance markets.

The next section describes the defining moment of modern trade finance. The GFC brought trade finance into the popular lexicon. It was also the first time that data generation in this sector began to uncover global patterns of trade finance shortfalls. The following section examines these shortfalls through a development lens. Specifically, it examines which populations are impacted and how local banks fit in. The next section then describes the critical role played by MDBs to drive positive developmental impacts of trade finance. This covers both their role and the instruments at their disposal. The following section looks more closely at the concept of additionality. This includes some key benefits only MDBs can confer given their role at the intersection of the public and private sectors. The last section covers new trends in trade finance that are disrupting the sector completely, including digitalisation and blockchain. It highlights the important role that MDBs and other international institutions are playing in facilitating this transition.

How the Global Financial Crisis Changed Everything

Trade finance gaps are more than just the result of a crisis. We know for example that trade decreases with weaker contracting environments in either the exporting or importing country (Schmidt-Eisenlohr, 2013). And there is evidence that inadequate levels of trade finance will reduce both the total volume of a firm's exports and the variety of goods it produces (Contessi and deNicola, 2013). Related to this, finance shortfalls can limit firms to participation in only low value-added stages of production (Manova and Yu, 2012).

While trade finance shortfalls are not a new phenomenon, it took the GFC in 2008 to turn the world's spotlight on the issue. When trade volumes plunged and banks were in crisis, we first learned that no one had any data with which to guide policy response.

Gaps exist for numerous reasons, not exclusive to trade finance. At the bank-to-bank level, banks don't have (i) the country limit/appetite; (ii) the counterparty limit/appetite; (iii) the anti-financial crimes risk appetite. At the bank-to-firm level, banks (i) don't have sufficient and reliable information on credit and performance risks of SMEs; (ii) don't want to take financial crimes risk for relatively low compensation; (iii) aren't comfortable with SMEs' financials and collateral.

The cost and availability of trade finance is variable across many measures. However, access to finance remains a persistent challenge for both emerging markets and SMEs. For emerging markets, trade finance is constrained via four channels: low or non-existent country risk ratings, weak banking systems, lack of credit, and regulatory infrastructure. For SMEs, constraints also include the high price of capital, and inability to meet bank requirements. .

The relationship between trade finance and trade outcomes gained particular attention during the GFC. The decline in world trade flows (and especially manufacturing flows) was greater than the decline in world gross domestic product (GDP). The contraction of trade finance is one of the primary explanations of the magnitude of the trade shock.

SMEs and emerging markets were particularly hard hit during the GFC as a result of the scarcity of capital among many banks. This led to financial institutions focusing on core clients in strategic markets at the expense of SMEs and developing countries. While the crisis has subsided, these populations remain underserved and represent market segments and regions with proportionally high market gaps for trade finance.

While it was immediately obvious that trade finance was constrained during the GFC, the lack of data obscured the extent to which trade finance frictions were responsible for the decline in merchandise trade. In 2008/2009, The World Trade Organization (WTO) convened several Trade Finance Expert Group meetings to coordinate action against plummeting trade volumes. Policymakers need statistics to help direct policy decisions, but none were available to help guide an official response to the crisis in trade finance. Calls from the private sector for massive government and multilateral action to enhance financial support for trade were not underpinned by hard data.

Data Limitations Make Targeting Difficult

Trade finance gaps are difficult to measure for three reasons. The first is data collection – few banks have a single point of acceptance for trade finance proposals, so any value given for how much is requested is an estimate and probably a relatively inaccurate one. The second is data reporting – few banks are able or willing to release exact numbers of trade finance proposals that were funded as this is proprietary. The third reason is that where there are estimates of the proportion of proposals that were rejected, these do not account for the quality of the proposals. Equilibrium trade finance is not one where all requests for finance are granted. Some proposals are inappropriate, or do not meet minimum requirements.

The lack of data about global trade finance trends is a development problem in itself. The reason is that solutions to trade finance gaps can only be bluntly targeted due to lack of data. Even the Bank for International Settlements offers only an "interpretive characterisation" of the size of the global market for trade finance.

There is no single dataset that can be repurposed for trade finance questions. Papers in this area have been creative with data, using either single firm data (Antras and Foley, 2015; Bricongne *et al.*, 2012), bank-specific data (Neipmann and Schmidt-Eisenlohr, 2017) or firm survey data (Ahn *et al.*, 2011). Broadly datasets are unavailable for two reasons. One is confidentiality. For example, default rates are only shared in a highly aggregated form. We can see a disconnect in some regions between very low default rates and high rejection rates. But without country-level data, it is difficult to properly target capacity-building or guarantee programmes. Another reason that data is unavailable is that collection can be expensive and time-consuming. Banks' information systems may not be harmonised internally, so collecting data is difficult. Under reporting requirements for MDB guarantee programmes, banks share the aggregate number of funded transactions that go to SMEs. This would be a more informative breakdown if it showed whether SME lending increases are the result of new SMEs opening credit lines, or a static group of SMEs receiving additional credit volumes.

The Asian Development Bank (ADB) survey on trade finance gaps and their impact of growth and jobs has collected data on a global basis since 2013. While data is not comparable between years, it provides useful descriptive statistics about the sector. Over the past five years, we have learned several facts about trade finance. Better data has enabled us to understand both where markets are not being served, and the behaviours of firms who do not receive sufficient trade finance.

First, emerging markets in Asia and the Pacific face the greatest shortfalls. Rejection rates are higher and firms are more dependent on trade finance in order to trade in those markets. Second, the tighter regulatory environment has exacerbated a trend of banks scaling down their trade finance operations in developing countries. Third, most SMEs that are rejected for a transaction do not try again. Those that execute the transaction do so using informal sources of finance. Fourth, 60% of trade finance transactions that do not receive trade finance become failed transactions, which represents a significant amount of forgone growth and job creation.

Asia's Experience in the Global Financial Crisis

In Asia, the relative health of commercial banks was good in 2008 as a result of improvements following the 1997 Asian Financial Crisis. In addition, the region had experienced a rising tide of intra-regional trade, which provided some temporary protection from the GFC.

Banks in Asia's relatively developed emerging markets (the People's Republic of China [PRC], India, the Republic of Korea, Malaysia and Thailand) are more integrated into the global financial system than banks in developing Asian countries (Bangladesh, Nepal, Pakistan and Vietnam) and were therefore more susceptible to systemic global crisis. Banks in more developed emerging markets had trouble acquiring funding in general, including for trade finance. Pricing for trade finance doubled and fluctuated wildly during the height of the crisis, including for imports to Asia (required for export production).

At various intervals during the crisis, Asia suffered from a lack of US dollars to support trade. Approximately 80% of international trade is conducted in US dollars and insufficient dollars placed a major strain on Asia's ability to conduct trade.

US banks that had dollars (US Treasury programmes were important to ensure sufficient liquidity) were reluctant to lend to their correspondent banks around the world at the height of the crisis because they didn't know which institution would go bankrupt next; the interbank market was closed. This overreliance on one currency poses risks to the international trade system, as has been seen at various intervals during the crisis. Interest in the renminbi as a potential alternative settlement currency rose as a result.

Another impact of the GFC for Asia stemmed from the inability to get payment obligations from banks (such as letters of credit) guaranteed. These guarantees are critical to trade. The fact that most Asian banks were not in jeopardy and were in much better condition than US and European banks was lost. Trust and confidence in financial institutions everywhere evaporated at the height of the crisis, so did the interbank system of guarantees that are so important to trade. But even in the best of times, banks in many of the ADB's developing member countries have trouble securing guarantees, hence the existence of persistent market gaps.

Much of Asia was, and to a lesser extent remains, dependent on export markets in the United States and Europe. As a result of the crisis, and ensuing recessions in traditional export markets, many Western buyers were performing poorly or going bankrupt. This resulted in a considerable rise in non-performing loans in many export-dependent Asian developing countries, and this has had an adverse impact on Asia's banking sector.

While Asia's finance sector was generally healthy, it was not immune to significant weaknesses in the West's financial system. At the height of the crisis, the ability of banks to provide Asian companies with finance to support trade was severely impaired.

Development Impacts of Trade Finance Shortfalls

Trade finance shapes export opportunities. The networks that define cross-border commerce all entail some form of finance. This means that for countries where trade finance functions well, it enables firms which would otherwise be considered too risky to link into global value chains and thus contribute to employment and pro-ductivity growth. Exporters in developing countries are particularly affected due to their reliance on bank-intermediated trade finance. Trade-driven growth is a common development goal, but it requires trade finance to mitigate risk and enable cross-border payments – especially for non-traditional exporters including SMEs.

There are several characteristics that impede trade finance in developing countries. Most significant are low country ratings and underdeveloped financial markets. These impact both sides of the bank-to-bank relationships that underpin a substantial por-tion of global trade. For international commercial financial institutions, risk factors lead to a situation where most have not established bank limits or even country limits in many of the ADB's developing member countries (without these limits, it is difficult to price risk and, therefore, most banks will be unwilling to enter deals). For financial institutions in developing countries, capacity limits mean they lack the correspondent networks, credit limits and access to international capital markets that would enable them to extend more support for trade. In addition to low country ratings and weak banking systems, liquidity constraints due to low domestic savings capacity and poor access to international capital markets are another reason that availability of trade finance may not meet demand in growing economies. This is not an issue for markets such as the PRC, where household savings rates are near 30%, but in countries where savings are much lower, this is a concern.

The relationship between trade finance and trade is clearly understood. It has been shown both that sufficient trade finance has a positive impact on trade (Auboin *et al.*, 2016), and that insufficient trade finance has a negative impact (Amiti and Weinstein, 2011). Other chapters in this volume will cover this relationship in depth.

In this section, we take the relationship between trade and trade finance as given and explore the question of what happens to countries and clients who are rationed. But before we jump in, we need to be clear about why advances in this field have been so limited since the GFC.

Trade Finance and SMEs

Trade finance falls among the major constraints to business as reported by SMEs. This is a problem globally, but is more acute in developing countries where financial markets are underdeveloped. There are clear transmission channels between a lack of trade finance and firm development. Market failures in financial markets fall disproportionally on SMEs. These firms are impacted more by the higher cost of screening and higher interest rates from banks (Beck and Demirgüç-Kunt, 2006; Stiglitz and Weiss, 1981).

Seventy-one percent of SMEs report that when a bank declines to finance a trade transaction, they do not seek alternative financing for that transaction. While some of these transactions are then self-financed, the DiCaprio *et al.*'s 2017 "Trade Finance Gaps, Growth, and Jobs Survey" suggests that many of them do not go forward. It may be that some of these were low-quality transactions, unlikely to come to fruition in any case. We will take a closer look at what data is available to surmise to what extent this may be the case.

While some transactions may be unbankable, there seems little doubt that most of the high rejection rates faced by SMEs screen out potentially viable transactions. Bankers surveyed by the ADB study estimated that only 20% of transactions rejected by financial institutions were unambiguously unbankable. Surveyed firms reported that relationships between banks and SMEs in both Africa and Asia are underdeveloped and therefore potentially profitable transactions go unfinanced.

By the numbers, both African and Asian SMEs report similar reasons behind trade finance rejections – insufficient collateral or guarantee (33% vs. 25%) and lack of existing business relationship (13% vs. 17%). This suggests that even where firms are able to fulfil documentary requirements, and submit a sound proposal, they are not receiving finance.

Rationed firms may scale their trade portfolios more slowly. Firms that have secured formal bank-intermediated finance should be able to access finance on better or cheaper terms in the future. In addition, trade finance is critical to introduce and scale up export sales. Li and Wilson (2009) show that trade finance increases the propensity of SMEs to become exporters. At early levels of trade, trade costs may be absorbed internally. But as exports increase in volume, trade finance becomes critical. The firms under consideration in this chapter are formal, active in trade and have already secured banking relationships. These characteristics suggest that in the universe of SMEs, they are already the most productive (LaPorta and Shleifer, 2014) and likely to promote growth (Torm and Rand, 2012). They may also signal that the firm has reached a certain level of financial management and capacity. Trade finance may indicate their exploration of new products or markets.

The underlying assumption for the global focus on SME finance is that by promoting SME trade finance, employment will increase. This is backed up by two empirical regularities. First, SMEs employ the majority of the global workforce. The median employment share of SMEs across countries is 67% (Ayyagari et al., 2011). Second, exporting firms grow faster than non-exporters in terms of number of employees (Dinh et al., 2010). Intuitively, it follows that by enabling SMEs to export more, employment will expand.

But empirically, this link is indirect and not easy to establish. Endogeneity is an issue since bigger firms get more finance, thus rationed firms have lower employment. The literature offers some evidence about the trade finance-employment links from episodes of credit crunches – specifically, that employment levels at firms associated with unhealthy banks fall more than those at firms associated with healthy banks (Chodorow-Reich, 2014). In another effort to describe this relationship, firms surveyed by the 2017 ADB study (DiCaprio et al., 2017) indicated that a 10% increase in the availability of trade finance would result in a 1% increase in employment.

Another feature of this employment relationship is the argument that SMEs which receive trade finance are likely to produce higher quality employment. This results from both the selection of firms into trade finance and also the standards faced by firms in international markets. SMEs in developing economies are often informal. Informal firms, by definition, are not required to follow labour laws. SMEs in the formal sector are at least nominally subject to domestic laws.

There are social benefits from an equitable distribution of trade finance among small and large firms, among urban and rural firms and among female- and male-owned firms. There are also social benefits from extending trade finance to markets where it is scarce.

Trade Finance and the Important Role of Local Banks

There is one actor that impacts both inclusion and trade: local banks. Local or regional banks may have closer relationships with clients, but less ability to service them as they demand more sophisticated instruments. In addition, local banks may not have the ability to comply with the regulatory requirements of confirming banks.

At the transaction level, bigger banks are associated with greater volumes of proposed trade finance and higher rejection rates. However, cancelled correspondent relationships significantly differ by region (higher in Africa, Asia and Latin America) and type of bank (higher in banks that only operate in one country rather than regionally or globally).

In such cases, lack of financing may at some point limit trade expansion, as either banks are inhibited by regulators from providing the necessary working capital to accompany the development of their client's trade activity (for example if foreign exchange regulation prohibits inter-bank borrowing with non-resident entities), or simply because they do not have the experience of handling trade finance instruments, which is hence left to the foreign customer/supplier's bank. Strengthening the capacity of local banks to provide adequate trade finance flows can be a real challenge in developing and least-developed countries.

This highlights the multi-level nature of trade finance constraints faced by SMEs in developing countries and particularly Asia. Bank density in Asia and the Pacific is below the world average. This matters because banking concentration has been shown to have a particularly negative impact on SMEs (Ryan *et al.*, 2014). Thus, options are limited by the lack of banking relationships. If the original bank rejects the transaction, SMEs – which are unlikely to have diversified banking relationships in low-density regions – are unlikely to have a second option.

The level of risk a bank will accept on behalf of a client depends on internal allocations of risk exposure. Client risk is generally allocated on a bank-wide level then broken down by different lines of businesses (Office of the Comptroller of the Currency, 2015). Because trade finance is cross-border, the measurement of risk will include country, bank and client risk. Where risk is high for any of these measures, trade finance availability will drop. Where data is unavailable, it is difficult or impossible to price financial instruments in those markets.

Evidence that the private sector has difficulty assessing and taking risk comes from several sources. First, shortfalls in trade finance are concentrated geographically. In some countries, trade finance instruments may not be available at all. This can result from an underdeveloped regulatory regime. This makes the legality of different instruments unclear. It can result from foreign exchange controls; for example, there are at least 28 countries where letters of credit (L/Cs) are required as a way to facilitate foreign exchange controls (Ahn, 2014).

In addition, there is regional variation by payment terms. There are three types of payment methods: pre-shipment, post-shipment and L/Cs. The decision by a corporate to choose one or the other depends on conditions in both the source and the destination country. Conditions include contract enforceability (Antras and Foley, 2015; Schmidt-Eisenlohr, 2013), account receivable controls (Ahn, 2014) and depth of the financial sector, among others.

Finally, there are countries where a lack of correspondent banking relationships mean that trade finance cannot be directly contracted between banks. The risk of the transaction may be low, but there is simply no way for the two banks to interact directly using today's messaging protocols.

A Brief History of Trade Finance Operations in MDBs

MDBs play an important intermediary role in international trade and trade finance. In international trade, intermediation is critical to facilitate activities in markets that are difficult to penetrate (Ahn *et al.*, 2011) and where there is a need to ensure the credibility of honest behaviour (Olsen, 2010). Often, these are developing countries, and countries with limited experience with cross-border commerce. These are also the countries where MDBs are most active.

Multilateral development banks were originally created to support post-war and post-colonial reconstruction in various regions of the world following World War II. Although there is considerable overlap today, each was designed differently with different objectives, shareholders and financing models.

Trade finance was not a focus of any of these institutions in the 1950s and 1960s when they were founded. Trade finance programmes were initiated in the 2000s, following the successful launch by the European Bank for Reconstruction and Development (EBRD) of a trade finance programme. Their initiation reflected a more fundamental shift in focus from government-driven provision of public goods to efforts to harness the private sector to accomplish development goals. The trade finance programmes have been a key enabler in this shift.

We begin by taking a step back to look at the reasons the MDBs were founded. The objectives and roles of MDBs have changed over time. A key feature has been a shift towards private sector engagement. This shift precipitated and enabled trade finance programmes.

What Are MDBs?

MDBs are international organisations that represent a collectivity of members where decision-making authority is delegated from individual states to the organisation (Trachtman, 2014). In the case of the ADB, there are 65 shareholder governments, 45 of which represent developing economies in the region. Not all shareholders are regional. The two largest shareholders of the ADB are the United States and Japan, with roughly 15.7% each, followed by China at 6.5% and India at 6%.

Traditionally, MDBs are sovereign lenders (that is, lending goes to governments, not private actors). This remains true today. The EBRD, created in 1991, is somewhat unique in that it was designed to work exclusively with the fledgling private sector in Central and Eastern Europe following the collapse of the Soviet Union. The ADB was created in 1966 and focused exclusively on sovereign support until little more than a decade ago. The ADB's Trade Finance Program is one of the bank's largest lines of business. While the ADB's private sector operations continue to grow exponentially, about 70% of the ADB's lending still goes to public sector projects, mostly involving loans to governments for infrastructure. The size and focus of private sector operations varies by institution. All major MDBs provide a wide range of products, including guarantees, loans, equity and technical assistance for infrastructure projects and transactions with local financial institutions.

The six major MDBs are the World Bank Group, the EBRD, the ADB, the African Development Bank (AfDB), the Inter-American Development Bank (IADB) and the Islamic Development Bank. Over time there have been numerous other, smaller and more narrowly focused banks.

The two more recent multilateral banks – the Asian Infrastructure Investment Bank (AIIB) and the New Development Bank (originally called the BRICS Development Bank) – focus on infrastructure, and both are headquartered in the PRC. The AIIB expects to lend to Asia and beyond, while the New Development Bank lends in member countries. Both were established in 2015/2016. These efforts resulted from the rise of emerging markets to prominence and the complexities (some would say hesitation of existing MDBs) involved in increasing their voting shares.

The ADB is the largest of all regional banks. It was established in December 1966. In 2016, its equity tripled to around US$53 billion from US$18 billion with the merger of the hard loan window, known as Ordinary Capital Resources, and the soft loan Asian Development Fund. The latter will become a 100% grant operation. This reform has significantly increased the ADB's capacity, and other MDBs are considering it as a future model. MDBs exist to fill gaps that the private sector and local governments are not able or willing to fill. In MDB parlance, MDBs seek to provide "additionality" where there is maximum development impact. For example, long-term infrastructure project finance is a classic form of MDB activity.

As the global economic landscape has changed, the objectives of and needs for MDBs have changed (Ahluwalia *et al.*, 2016). Many countries in Eastern Europe have fully graduated from EBRD programmes. China, for example, has become a significant donor to developing countries in its own right. Chile and Mexico are now part of the Organisation for Economic Co-operation (OECD) and when the ADB was established, Singapore and South Korea were developing economies. In addition to graduation, the rise of middle-income countries has also required that MDBs adapt their role and what is considered "additional" and impactful.

Prior to the GFC, there was talk in some quarters about whether MDBs still served a useful purpose. Prior to the crisis, some took the view that the private sector did not need public sector support to address challenges in international development.

Why Were MBD Trade Finance Programmes Established?

There are two important features of the intermediary role played by MDBs in trade finance. The first is that their participation in markets that are perceived as risky has been shown to have a positive impact on the risk exposure that investors were willing to bear (Wezel, 2004). The second is that they are acting to fill gaps in markets where perception of risk does not reflect reality. Trade finance has been shown to have default rates of between 0.02 and 0.05% on a global industry basis, including the most poorly rated developing countries.

Trade finance is inherently intermediated. When markets function well, the intermediation by banks is sufficient to guarantee the credibility of the firm. This leads to a natural progression whereby repeated interactions between the buyer and the seller ultimately open up new opportunities for finance, including open account. However, in low-rated markets where contract enforcement is weak, and local banks themselves do not yet have sufficient repeated interactions with foreign banks to signal their suitability as a trusted counterparty, another level of intermediation is critical. This is the space occupied by MDBs' trade finance programmes. They facilitate trade by conferring their reputation to facilitate repeated interactions with financial institutions in uncertain markets. MDBs also play a counter-cyclical role in ensuring liquidity in periods of market volatility.

The involvement of the major MDBs in trade finance started with the EBRD, which created the first trade finance programme (TFP) in 1999. Trade was viewed as an important pillar of private sector development, and the EBRD's trade finance programme sought to work with banks to both support trade and strengthen the private banking sector. The EBRD provided guarantees, loans and training to banks to support trade. Other MDBs soon followed by duplicating the EBRD's trade finance programme in most every respect: the ADB established its TFP in 2004, the International Finance Corporation (IFC; private sector part of World Bank Group) and the IADB in 2005 and the International Islamic Trade Finance Corporation

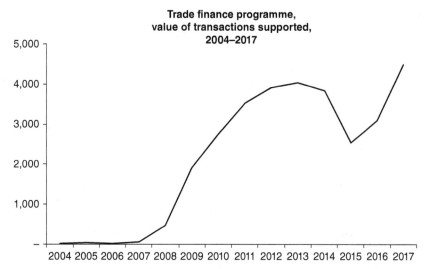

Figure 8.1   Growth of supported transactions, 2004–2017 (US$ million).
Source: ADB Trade Finance Program unpublished data, 2018.

(ITFC, part of the Islamic Development Bank group) in 2008. The AfDB started a trade finance programme more recently in 2013. Collaboration and support between most major MDBs on trade finance is relatively strong.

The ADB's Trade Finance Program was established in 2003 and ramped up in the wake of the GFC. In 2009, the ADB Board of Directors increased the amount of risk the Trade Finance Program could assume to US$1 billion at any one time, from the original limit of US$150 million that was approved in 2003. The ADB's Trade Finance Program has grown exponentially. In 2017, the ADB's Trade Finance Program supported more trade than in any other previous year – over 3500 trade transactions valued at US$4.5 billion – and required the higher programme limit to meet market demand. Among the 21 countries where it operates, its four most active markets are Bangladesh, Pakistan, Sri Lanka and Vietnam.

Instruments Offered by MDBs

There are three ways in which trade finance programmes promote development through trade finance operations: providing guarantees and liquidity, building commercial (local, regional and international) bank capacity and mobilising private sector resources.

Each of the programmes offers a range of guarantees and loans through partner banks to support trade. Guarantees provided to banks (these banks would be confirming payment risk for their exporting clients) cover the risk of non-payment from other banks obliged to pay for goods on behalf of their importing clients. MDB guarantees also provide cover to international and regional commercial banks providing other commercial/local banks with loans to support their clients' short-term trade requirements (pre- and post-shipment finance).

In addition to guarantees, MDBs provide local banks directly with loans used to support clients' (in developing countries) import and export finance requirements.

The ADB was the first to introduce an unfunded risk participation product (RPA); the IFC soon followed. Risk participations are similar to guarantees. One differentiating feature is the RPAs often operate on a portfolio, rather than transaction-by-transaction, basis, which creates efficiencies for all concerned when managing and acquiring country and counterparty exposure. The AfDB also adopted an RPA product. The IFC innovated a funded RPA and the ADB recently created its own version.

Collectively, the MDB programmes, since their inception, have supported over US$100 billion in trade through over 80,000 transactions. MDB trade finance programmes are market driven, meaning that if their commercial bank clients don't need their support and aren't willing to pay market rates for guarantees and loans, the programmes won't be used. In light of this, one can argue that the value of trade supported by the MDBs truly represents a (narrow) closing of market gaps for trade finance. As mentioned above, the ADB's "Trade Finance Gaps, Growth, and Jobs Survey" suggests that over 60% of trade finance transactions rejected by commercial banks do not end up being realised. That represents a significant drag on growth and job creation and points to the importance of MDBs closing gaps in this space and the contribution to development.

In addition to the trade finance products mentioned above, which are focused exclusively on bank intermediated support for trade and only assume bank risk, the IFC and ADB have sought to complement these efforts by creating Supply Chain Finance Programs (SCFP). SCFPs, which often share risk with commercial banks, support open account transactions and, unlike TFPs (which only take bank risk), assume risk on buyers, sellers and distributors in a (cross-border) supply chain.

MDB SCFPs are relatively new – the IFC was the first to create one in 2010, followed by the ADB in 2013 – and have not reached any kind of scale compared with trade finance programmes. MDBs are by nature wholesale banks, not designed to undertake transactions directly with smaller entities (including SMEs) due to their limited capacity on the ground, which makes due diligence and monitoring of thousands of SME risks not practicable. Moreover, MDBs do not want to replace private financial institutions, but seek to complement their efforts and enhance their ability to operate in areas deemed important for development.

In line with this thinking, MDBs use mobilisation of private sector funds (also called co-financing) as an important metric. The ADB's TFP, for example, attracted US$2.8 billion in co-financing in 2017 from insurance companies and banks to support trade in developing Asia – mostly Bangladesh, Pakistan, Vietnam and Sri Lanka, but also Mongolia, Uzbekistan, Armenia, Georgia and other ADB developing member countries. As development banks increase their trade finance operations in hard-to-reach countries, they gather a large amount of information about risks and opportunities. This information is shared to enable the industry to assess and assume risk in challenging markets. This has resulted in the private sector establishing limits for new markets to support trade.

In some cases, such information has helped and encouraged commercial banks to establish country and credit limits for the first time in countries like Mongolia and Bangladesh. The ADB conveys its risk assessment results with partner banks in countries of operation to help the banks improve their financial standing and operations.

MDB trade finance guarantees enable the private sector to safely develop experience, and credit histories in new markets. This leads the private sector to close market gaps. Ultimately, the end goal for trade finance programmes, indeed for all MDBs, should be to "crowd in" the private sector to a point where gaps narrow such that MDBs are no longer required.

Beyond Banking: Additionality from MDBs' Position between the Public and Private Sector

In the previous section, we looked at the history and mechanics of the trade finance products offered by MDBs. In this role, MDBs are similar to commercial banks – they offer different types of products that facilitate trade. However, as intermediaries, their role goes beyond this function. They are not only intermediaries between counterparties, but MDBs intermediate between the public and private sector as well. But beyond simply providing guarantees and liquidity, MDBs play two other critical roles: sharing information and building local capacity for banks and regulators.

In addition to closing market gaps by executing guarantee and loan transactions, the ADB's Trade Finance Program has implemented softer initiatives that have delivered impact beyond the market role assumed by product offerings.

ICC Trade Finance Register

At the height of the GFC, there was great concern that Basel III would exacerbate market gaps for trade finance. There was a general view that while Basel III was necessary, its treatment of trade finance would create unintended consequences. The ADB's Trade Finance Program shared this concern.

Through the WTO's Trade Finance Expert Group, the ADB proposed that the public and private sector work together to create a "trade finance register" that would create statistics to demonstrate to Basel, and others, that trade finance carries a relatively low probability of loss and that regulatory requirements should be more appropriately calibrated for trade finance. After conducting research into the concept and finding an appropriate home for the register, at the International Chamber of Commerce (ICC), the ADB funded and created the pilot ADB-ICC Trade Finance Register.

The ADB-ICC Trade Finance Register mobilised the private sector to create a statistical database on loss and default rates for the trade finance industry worldwide. The Register collected data from banks on over 5.2 million trade finance transactions. This dataset, which spanned 2004–2009, including the GFC, found a probability of default below 1% and an ever lower loss rate.

The information was presented to Basel and underpinned what eventually triggered a change in Basel III guidelines on trade finance. This served to change Basel regulatory treatment of trade finance, resulting in the freeing up billions of dollars to support trade in emerging markets globally. The Finance Register underpinned three changes Basel made to regulations on trade finance:

- The one-year maturity floor for self-liquidating trade finance instruments has been removed, reducing capital charges when calculating risk-weighted assets. Banks were initially obliged to set aside capital for tenors of no less than 360 days, while trade finance deals are often at tenors of less than 180 days.

- Basel decided that short-term, self-liquidating letters of credit and guarantees would receive a credit conversion factor of 20% and 50%, respectively, rather than 100%. This has further reduced banks' capital charge.
- The Basel Committee waived the sovereign floor. Now that the floor is waived, banks can be rated better than the sovereign (where the bank is domiciled) which, in some cases, has better capital implications for financial institutions assuming risk on those banks and intermediating trade.

Having played its development role in establishing the Register, the ADB has left it to the ICC and its private financial institution members to fund the Register, now called the ICC Trade Finance Register, and to develop future reports. That said, the ADB, through the Trade Finance Program, remains engaged in the process to work closely with the ICC. Since the initial register report, one has been released by the ICC every year, each becoming more robust and granular.

While the statistical work the ADB initiated is important to underpin a substantive dialogue with regulators to loosen requirements for trade finance and therefore close related market gaps, this information also encourages the private sector to assume more trade finance risk in challenging markets. For example, one of the largest insurance companies informed the Trade Finance Program's work on the Register, demonstrating the low probability of loss, was the single greatest factor in it deciding to enter the credit insurance business for trade finance. As a result, more capacity to support trade in higher-risk countries is brought to the market, helping to close gaps and therefore create economic growth and jobs

ADB Survey on Trade Finance Gaps, Growth and Jobs

The ADB's "Trade Finance Gaps, Growth, and Jobs Survey" was initiated in 2013 as part of the process to help fill this knowledge gap. These surveys collected, for the first time, information on the reasons for and sizes of gaps in trade finance. They also related those gaps to economic growth and job creation outcomes.

The ADB is the only institution that offers a global gap estimate. Other institutions report direction of trends in pricing for certain instruments, activity levels or rejection rates of the sample population. The ADB is also the only institution that highlights the causes of gaps in addition to their existence. By surveying both providers and users, it allows us to gain a richer understanding of sources and dynamics of bottlenecks. This enables us to show that while some are systemic and require changes at the global level, others are manageable via existing channels (e.g. knowledge sharing).

Third, the ADB survey explores the link between trade finance, jobs and growth. This is done via a question in the User Survey about how additional finance inputs would contribute to these outputs.

Measuring trade finance gaps is difficult to do with precision, but it is also a critical exercise that highlights the ongoing shortfalls that limit trade and growth. In 2017, the ADB estimated a global trade finance gap of around US$1.5 trillion. This number is notable both for its size and for the relatively consistent regional distribution that has held over the four years of the survey.

In the following three sections, we break down this global number by region and client group. Efforts to understand the size and dynamics of the global trade finance market only began following the 2008 GFC. In 2008, it was clear that credit had stopped and it was dragging trade with it. Both firms and banks were reporting an inability to finance existing transactions. But at that moment in time, there was no obvious indicator that policymakers could use to understand what was happening and how to respond.

Two prominent, but one-off surveys were subsequently produced to estimate the volume and change in the availability of trade finance. The first was done by the Committee on the Global Financial System (CGFS) and the Bank for International Settlements (BIS), which compiled an extensive array of sources, most of which use 2011 data (BIS, 2014). The estimated value is calculated from national data of different CGFS members plus L/C figures from the Society for Worldwide Interbank Financial Telecommunication (SWIFT). Crosschecks are done with data from the ICC Trade Register. Bank-intermediated trade finance was projected globally to be approximately between US$6.5 and 8 trillion, US$2.8 trillion of which are L/Cs. This is the first, and so far only, attempt to estimate the size of trade finance markets globally. Another comprehensive survey was done by the International Monetary Fund (IMF) along with the Banker's Association for Finance and Trade and the International Financial Services Association (BAFT-IFSA) that surveyed 63 banks (IMF, 2011). This data illustrated the beginnings of a recovery by 2011. A total of 17.1% of respondents reported having received more trade finance in 2011 than in 2010, with the most notable change seen in emerging Asian countries, which include the PRC and India.

The ADB also initiated a study in response to this lack of data for policymakers during the GFC. The objective was to provide a comprehensive understanding of trade finance flows and their impact on firm behaviour, including productivity, job creation and growth. While the main interest is in Asia, because of the nature of cross-border trade, the survey was launched on a global basis. There are two survey instruments – a user and a provider survey. In the 2017 survey (DiCaprio et al., 2017), 515 financial institutions participated. This represented more than 100 countries and covered all of the global banks, as well as a cross-section of regional and local banks. The data has been collected for three periods; however, this is not a panel dataset since respondents vary from year to year.

The ADB estimates unmet global demand for trade finance in order to underscore the persistence of shortfalls even as global flows have recovered. The trade finance gap is estimated using the value of rejected proposed trade finance transactions, as reported by responding banks and weighted to match a global distribution.

Capacity-Building through Due Diligence

Since MDBs are often the first movers into new and uncertain markets, their efforts to fill financing gaps for economic growth involve the provision of technical assistance to upgrade skills in the public and private sectors, and to create structures (including the provision of guarantees) through which partnerships are formed with international investors and banks.

To onboard participating banks, MDBs undertake a thorough and rigorous due diligence process, covering credit, governance and anti-financial crimes capacity. In addition to due diligence at the front end, MDB trade finance programmes monitor participating bank risk, at a minimum through annual due diligence, on an ongoing basis.

The due diligence process delivers significant development impacts in frontier economies. Commercial banks may have never been through such a process. Simply going through the information required and how information needs to be reported helps local banks understand what potential correspondent banks, international investors and (over time) rating agencies will require.

Central banks also build capacity in this process. This is due both to the sharing of due diligence methodology used on domestic commercial banks and to shared findings from the process. This is a particularly important feature of MDB engagement since the regulatory environment directly impacts both risk and availability of trade finance.

Capacity-building through the due diligence process enables the MDB itself to gain a better understanding of the banking system and individual banks in that market. This can be shared globally with the international financial community to reduce uncertainty about frontier markets and mitigate the risk involved in establishing trade finance relationships. Over time, this role of sharing the public good of development knowledge has become a more important part of the role of MDBs (Ravallion, 2016).

What Will Trade Finance Look Like Tomorrow

This chapter would not be complete without a look forward. The next 10 years are unlikely to look much like the last 20. Technology is disrupting the sector. And the primary disruptor is blockchain. There is little doubt that blockchain technology will change global trade. The question, however, is how it will impact some of the most intractable issues in trade finance.

Trade finance has a long history. Documented intermediation in trade goes at least as far back as the 11th-century Maghribi traders (detailed in Greif, 1993). As trade finance has progressed from simple promissory notes into more complicated risk mitigation instruments, this has enabled trade to happen with parties that were further removed from one another and has expanded trade volumes. Yet, trade finance today looks a lot like trade finance yesterday. It is a bank-intermediated product intended to play two roles – providing working capital in support of international trade transactions, and reducing payment risk (BIS, 2014).

Trade tomorrow will look different for three reasons. The first reason is that trade is changing. This is the result of physical changes such as 3-D printing (which will change what is traded and what is owned), logistical changes such as ecommerce, and organisational changes such as the reorganisation of global supply chains in what is being called the fourth industrial revolution.

The second reason is that digitalisation has become global. Trade finance standards have recognised this. MT798, Bank Payment Obligations and the electronic Uniform Customs and Practice for Documentary Credits (eUCP) are all sets of rules that enable electronic documentation in trade finance.

While both of these developments are changing demand and availability for trade finance, they are not fundamentally changing the process. The reason goes back to the cross-border and confidential nature of trade finance. It is also hindered by the number of actors and documents involved in a trade. By one estimate, a letter of credit transaction has 15 documents, 19 steps, and 65 data fields in addition to repeated checking and verification.

In 2015, financial institutions began exploring blockchain technology. By 2018 there were go-live strategies for products spanning L/Cs, factoring and open account. By changing trade finance from a process where finance is depending on the matching of documents to one where there is a single source of truth shared by all participants in the trade process, this will change the point at which finance can become available, as well as payment cadence and verification cost.

Two Lessons from Digitalisation

While blockchain will clearly change trade finance, will it impact the trade finance gaps that hold back growth and job creation? The progress of digitalisation and fintech on gaps provides us with some insight into the challenges going forward.

The first challenge is that financial institutions need to develop some basic infrastructure before fintech can advance to a point where it provides meaningful solutions for transparency and financial inclusion. We need fintech not only to reduce cost, but also to make transparency and performance-related due diligence more efficient and reliable.

A second challenge is that efficiency improvements alone will not improve development outcomes. One of the conclusions of the ADB's 2017 "Trade Finance Gaps, Growth, and Jobs Survey" (DiCaprio *et al.*, 2017) is that there is little evidence to support the idea that fintech is reducing gaps. No question, where implemented, it's reducing cost and gaining efficiency; those are good outcomes, but we can now see that reducing cost is not the boon to inclusion and to SME finance that we once thought.

Blockchain has one fundamental difference with earlier digital innovations. To date, efforts to modernise trade finance have had limited traction due to the decentralised nature of trade. Even as individual entities or even sectors digitalised, applying centralised solutions resulted in multiple disconnected digital islands that could not communicate and which trapped assets. The difference is that blockchain technology is decentralised.

If we look at the three major bank-reported reasons for trade finance gaps, each of them has the potential to be addressed by blockchain solutions (DiCaprio and Jessel, 2018). Profitability of trade finance can be improved through a single source of verified information, automated processes and oracles. Regulatory concerns can be eased by introducing transparency for real-time auditing, and lack of information through consensus and attestations.

All of these can help the public and private sector narrow trade finance gaps. But alone it's unlikely that blockchain will close them. Even if less cost is involved in supporting SMEs, a financial institution won't get involved if it can't get comfortable, in an efficient and reliable way, with anti-money-laundering/know-your-customer (AML/KYC) risks on the transparency side, and performance type risks.

Three Initiatives to Create Infrastructure to Link Fintech with Development

To address the challenges above, the trade finance community has gone forward with several initiatives. Each is intended to connect the digital islands that resulted from prior digitalisation efforts. These cover the lack of standards, the absence of a common global identity method and the legal environment around fintech and digitalisation.

The first initiative aims to develop digital standards for trade. The idea is to identify existing standards – many co-exist and overlap – and choose or merge the most appropriate one(s), then seek buy-in from all component parts of the supply chain, and then drive industry-wide adoption.

The second is a global harmonised identity for all companies, large and small. Mandated by the G20 (Group of Twenty), the Financial Stability Board created in 2014 the Global Legal Entity Identifier (GLEIF) system. GLEIF is a non-profit entity overseen by more than 70 regulators that created a system capable of issuing unique identifiers inexpensively.

Behind the unique identity is verification of (i) who's who, (ii) who owns whom, and (iii) who owns what. The benefit to all companies in the world having a GLEIF is clear on the transparency (AML/KYC) front. But more than that, it is critical infrastructure required to mine large pools of metadata for information pertaining to the specific (small) company on which a financial institution is conducting due diligence.

Without reliable identifiers, the metadata that blockchain will introduce, create and uncover may be impossible to navigate. Identifiers will enable financial institutions to find information on SMEs – performance risk, commercial dispute risk, credit risk, money-laundering risk – efficiently and inexpensively. GLEIF provides an essential piece of infrastructure for the future economy; it helps to advance blockchain fintech to a stage where it can have meaningful benefits for society.

A third initiative focuses on the legal side. Without rules accepted by courts, there will always be a certain level of reluctance to embrace digitisation. Formed in 1919 in the absence of a global system of rules to govern trade, the ICC created in 1936 an industry standard that would become known as the Incoterms (International Commercial Terms) rules, which has become accepted by courts all over the world.

We are in the same situation today as we were pre-1936 with respect to trade digitisation. The ICC Banking Commission has a strong role to play in filling a void of acceptable rules. Creating digital standards for trade and rules for digitisation and achieving global adoption of one harmonised legal identity for companies will create the infrastructure required to move fintech further. It's only that way that we will be able to use this technology to solve real problems in transparency and inclusion. There is an important role for MDBs to play, harnessing the public and private sectors to create the infrastructure necessary for technology to take hold and make a meaningful difference.

Conclusion

Market gaps for trade finance are dampening economic growth, job creation, development and our ability to achieve the Sustainable Development Goals. MDBs have an important role to play in closing these gaps. Through guarantees and loans, MDB trade finance programmes have closed more than US$10 billion of the gap over the past decade. In addition to executing transactions in difficult markets, mostly supporting SMEs, MDB trade finance programmes have developed important statistical work which, among other things, has proven low default rates for trade finance and impacted the regulatory environment, freeing up billions of dollars in capital to support trade. By sharing valuable information, MDBs have drawn the private sector more into developing countries where market gaps are proportionally largest. Moving forward, MDBs can play an important role developing basic infrastructure to infuse blockchain and other technology into trade finance. As technology advances, MBDs have the incentive and mandate to introduce resources to meet development goals. Beyond cost-cutting, these technologies, if steered responsibly, have the potential to generate information about SMEs that could make real gains on market gaps adversely affecting development.

References

Ahluwalia, M., Summers, L. & Velasco, A. (2016) *Multilateral Development Banking for this Century's Development Challenges*. Washington, DC: Center for Global Development.

Ahn, J. (2014). Understanding Trade Finance: Theory and Evidence from Transaction-Level Data. *IMF Working Paper*. Retrieved from: https://www.imf.org/external/np/seminars/eng/2014/trade/pdf/ahn.pdf (accessed 8 July 2019).

Ahn, J., Khandelwal, A. & Wei, S.-J. (2011) The Role of Intermediaries in Facilitating Trade. *Journal of International Economics*, 84(1), 73–85.

Amiti, M. & Weinstein, D. (2011) Exports and Financial Shocks. *Quarterly Journal of Economics*, 126(4), 1841–1877.

Antras, P. & Foley, F. (2015) Poultry in Motion: A Study of International Trade Finance Practices. *Journal of Political Economy*, 123(4), 853–901.

Auboin, M., Smyth, H. & Teh, R. (2016) Supply Chain Finance and SMEs: Evidence from International Factoring Data. *WTO Staff Working Paper* ERSD-2016-04. Retrieved from: https://www.wto.org/english/res_e/reser_e/ersd201604_e.pdf (accessed 20 July 2019).

Ayyagari, M., Demirguc-Kunt, A. & Maksimovic, V. (2011) Small versus Young Firms across the World: Contribution to Employment, Job Creation, and Growth. *World Bank Policy Research Working Paper* No. 5631.

Beck, T. & Demirguç-Kunt, A. (2006) Small and Medium-Size Enterprises: Access to Finance as a Growth Constraint. *Journal of Banking and Finance*, 30, 2931–2943.

BIS (2014) Trade Finance: Developments and Issues. *CGFS Papers* No. 50. Retrieved from: https://www.bis.org/publ/cgfs50.pdf (accessed 8 July 2019).

Bricongne, J., Fotagne, L., Taglioni, D. & Ward, V. (2012) Firms and the Global Crisis: French Exports in the Turmoil. *Journal of International Economics*, 87, 134–146.

Chodorow-Reich, G. (2014). The Employment Effects of Credit Market Disruptions: Firm-Level Evidence from the 2008–2009 Financial Crisis. *Quarterly Journal of Economics*, 129(1), 1–60.

Contessi, S. & DeNicola, F. (2013). What Do We Know about the Relationship between Access to Finance and International Trade? *Federal Reserve Bank of St. Louis Working Paper* 2001-054B. Retrieved from: https://s3.amazonaws.com/real.stlouisfed.org/wp/2012/2012-054.pdf (accessed 20 July 2019).

DiCaprio, A. & Jessel, B. (2018) Does Blockchain Make Trade Finance More Inclusive? *Journal of Financial Transformation*, 47, 35–44.

DiCaprio, A., Kim, K. & Beck, S. (2017) 2017 Trade Finance Gaps, Growth, and Jobs Survey. Mandaluyong: Asian Development Bank. *ADB Briefs* No.83.

Dinh, H., Mavridis, D. & Nguyen, H. (2010) The Binding Constraint on Firms Growth in Developing Countries. *World Bank Policy Research Working Paper* No. 5485.

Greif, A. (1993) Contract Enforceability and Economic Institutions in Early Trade: The Maghribi Traders' Coalition. *American Economic Review*, 83(3), 525–548.

International Monetary Fund (2011) Trade Finance Monitor: IMF/BAFT-IFSA 6th Annual Trade Finance Survey. Retrieved from: http://baft.org/docs/news-archive-2012/imf_survey_results_aug_2011.pdf (accessed 20 July 2019).

LaPorta, R. & Shleifer, A. (2014) Informality and Development. *Journal of Economic Perspectives*, 28(3), 109–126.

Li, Y. & Wilson, J. (2009) Trade Facilitation and Expanding the Benefits of Trade to SMEs. World Bank background paper. Retrieved from: https://pdfs.semanticscholar.org/8efe/0f188f79c441d30c2da1d1e384d00ce29c3c.pdf (accessed 8 July 2019).

Manova, K. & Yu, Z. (2012). Firms and Credit Constraints along the Global Value Chain: Processing Trade in China. *NBER Working Paper* No. 18561. Retrieved from: https://www.nber.org/papers/w18561.pdf (accessed 8 July 2019).

Neipmann, F. & Schmidt-Eisenlohr T. (2017) No Guarantees, No Trade: How Banks Affect Export Patterns. *Journal of International Economics*, 108, 338–350.

Office of the Comptroller of the Currency (2015) *Trade Finance and Services: Comptroller's Handbook*. Washington, DC: OCC.

Olsen, M. (2010) *Banks in International Trade: Incomplete International Contract Enforcement and Reputation*. Harvard University job market paper. Retrieved from: https://pdfs.semanticscholar.org/a970/f4d98b1e05b290251c4ef16400fd7dea251b.pdf (accessed 8 July 2019).

Ravallion, M. (2016) The World Bank: Why It Is Still Needed, and Why It Still Disappoints. *Journal of Economic Perspectives*, 30(1), 77–94.

Schmidt-Eisenlohr, T. (2013) Towards a Theory of Trade Finance. *Journal of International Economics*, 91, 96–112.

Stiglitz, J. & Weiss, A (1981). Credit Rationing in Markets with Imperfect Information. *American Economic Review*, 71(3), 393–410.

Rand, J. & Torm, N. (2012) The Benefits of Formalization: Evidence from Vietnamese Manufacturing SMEs. *World Development*, 40(5), 983–998.

Ryan, R., O'Toole, C. & McCann, F. (2014) Does Bank Market Power Affect SME Financing Constraints? *Journal of Banking and Finance*, 49(C), 495–505.

Trachtman, J. (2014) The Economic Structure of the Law of International Organizations. *Chicago Journal of International Law*, 15(1), 162–194.

Wezel, T. (2004) Does Co-financing by Multilateral Development Banks Increase "Risky" Direct Investment in Emerging Markets? Evidence for German Banking FDI. *Deutsche Bundesbank Discussion Paper* No. 02/2004.

Chapter 9

How Banking Regulators and Trade Ministers are Singing from Different Songbooks

Diana Smallridge and Jennifer Henderson

Introduction

Trade is a fundamental human activity. That societies have bourgeoned throughout history through their commercial trade transactions is well known; the evidence of trade substantially contributing to social and economic outcomes, standards of living and degrees of economic inclusiveness is apparent around the globe. While some barriers in global trade corridors are difficult to remove, it is generally appreciated that the removal of excess protectionist policies will expand opportunities, contribute to employment and enrich lives. International trade is also strongly connected with a well-developed and properly functioning financial environment. Policies that are geared towards facilitating a sound financial system, and those that encourage trade, benefit every level of society, from consumers to micro, small and medium-sized enterprises (MSMEs), mid-caps, large corporates and multinationals. Generating growth through trade is an essential part of the policy strategy of many economies. Export-oriented countries benefit from the improved allocation of scarce resources, the successful use of capacity, greater economies of scale and the advantages of sharing know-how, as well as more innovation. Although some developing economies have been relative latecomers to benefit from globalisation and international trade, they also have significantly profited from open markets and the prevention of protectionist measures in recent decades.

This chapter delves into the current global environment of trade finance. Its primary purpose is to examine the impact that banking regulations have had on those financial institutions serving small and medium-sized enterprises (SMEs), women-led enterprises and emerging economies. This chapter argues that the mismatch in mandate between trade ministers and financial regulators, with each singing from a different songbook, creates some policy conflict and opens up new market gaps.

The Handbook of Global Trade Policy, First Edition. Edited by Andreas Klasen.
© 2020 John Wiley & Sons Ltd. Published 2020 by John Wiley & Sons Ltd.

Does this mean that regulators should compromise on their standards or trade ministers should ignore the business realities of their local companies? In the face of regulatory-led trade finance gaps, trade ministers can: first, work with domestic regulators to influence international regulatory bodies, and ensure regulation is sufficiently nuanced to uphold the highest standard without unnecessarily truncating trade; and second, work with local regulators to ensure that, as national regulation moves towards international standards, it is clear and easily understood by local and international banks and businesses. Further, where regulatory-led trade finance gaps emerge, trade ministers and other policymakers must be solution-focused. Therefore, this chapter also provides an overview of potential remedies offered through current and evolving technological advances and, more significantly, via multilateral and national development bank interventions. In light of this, though regulation has contributed to market gaps, the future of trade finance and the diffusion of its development impact (increased employment, GDP growth etc.) are promising.

Working towards this conclusion, this chapter is split into five sections. The first section presents an overview of the current context of trade and trade finance. The second section outlines the general mandate of trade ministers in the face of current global economic trends. Then, the following section describes the current global regulatory movements. The fourth section looks at the real economy impact of post-Global Financial Crisis (GFC) regulations. Finally, the last section discusses the road ahead and potential solutions offered through the spread of technologies, and efforts of multilateral and national development banks.

The Current Context of Trade and Trade Finance

Background to the Current Global Economic Environment

In the early and mid-2000s, prior to the 2008 GFC, the world witnessed considerable growth in trade flows, rising from US$6.3 trillion to US$15.6 trillion between 2000 and 2008 (Ramachandran *et al.*, 2017a). From around 1950 to 1990, merchandise trade was growing 1.5 times faster on average than world real gross domestic product (GDP), and between 1990 and 2008 it had accelerated further, becoming twice as fast as world real GDP (WTO, 2017a). New markets were opening up, financing for trade was steadily more available and regulation was fairly non-complex. However, patterns and trajectories changed following the GFC – markets collapsed and trade dropped sharply. By 2016, the ratio of trade growth to world GDP growth had reached a low of 0.6:1 (WTO, 2017a). Unlike previous modern economic crises, the GFC began within the financial sector due to the unravelling of overvalued assets. It moved quickly to affect trade and investment: many banks' ability to finance trade dried up as they could no longer access capital or did not have available risk capacity. Trade then took a hit as it could not be financed, and trade flows collapsed. During the course of the crisis, governments intervened with large fiscal stimulus packages and monetary easing to bring back confidence in financial markets, create growth and secure jobs. In line with the G20 (Group of Twenty) global plan for recovery and reform, G20 governments also committed US$250 billion of support for trade finance (in the form of credit guarantees and trade insurance), US$130 billion of which was set aside for developing countries

(WTO Secretariat, 2016). Indeed, the response by both policymakers and regulators has been lasting: governments backed financial systems, lending regulations tightened and new supervisory structures, bodies and agreements were established to reduce the probability of any future systemic collapse.

Now, a decade after the beginnings of the crisis, the global economic outlook is slightly more positive. While the International Monetary Fund (IMF) *World Economic Outlook* recorded global growth at 3.6% in 2018 (an increase from 3.1% in 2016 and 3.5% in 2017), the 2019 projection fell to 3.3% (IMF, 2018; IMF, 2019). Yet, though the world is a very different place now than it was ten years ago during the beginnings of the GFC, a hangover from the crisis remains. Low to zero-interest environments became the norm following the GFC to help speed up recovery; weak investment and productivity growth have lingered in both advanced and developing economies. Meanwhile, despite the G20's efforts to ignite the trade finance market, the pre-crisis, or "normal", flows in major trading routes did not emerge until 2012 and remain unsteady; developing countries have yet to experience a return to normality. If there was a sense of accomplishment among global leaders after seeing modest growth and a brief high in trade flows of US$18.1 trillion around 2012, it was perhaps short-lived as trade flows contracted to near pre-crisis levels (US$15.8 trillion) in 2016 (Ramachandran *et al.*, 2017a). In addition, even though the decline in the value of trade finance activities was not as severe as the fall in merchandise trade, the availability of trade finance around the world has suffered ever since 2008. Brief periods during which bank-intermediated trade finance increased during the GFC (some quarters of 2008–2009) presumably reflect a heightened risk aversion among exporters and importers that led them to seek solutions which allow them to shift some risks on to banks, rather than the industry's recovery (WTO, 2010). Global trade growth in 2016 was the weakest since the GFC, with goods trade stagnant for most of the year (Engel and Reis, 2018). Just as global trade flows reached their lowest level in 2016, revenues in trade finance declined from US$41 billion in 2014 to US$36 billion in 2016 (Ramachandran *et al.*, 2017b).

Stagnation in trade growth has been attributed to various factors: a cyclical inventory drawdown across advanced economies, shrinking import levels in China and major commodity exporters, an exacerbating low-inflation environment etc. Meanwhile, some of the decline in trade finance revenues might have been attributable to the shift to simpler and cheaper trade finance products. Notably, however, trade restrictions reached a post-crisis high in 2016. During that year, G20 countries took more trade-restrictive measures than trade-facilitating ones. Between 2008 and 2016, the World Trade Organization (WTO) recorded 2978 trade-restrictive measures on members (WTO Secretariat, 2016). Of those measures, only 240 had been removed by mid-October 2016, and the overall share of G20 imports affected by restrictions has continued to rise (WTO Secretariat, 2016). This tone of trade restriction, sanctions and tariffs is very much present in the 2018 trade policies of the United States. Some restrictions can be viewed as imperative: they might serve short-term public policy objectives without being overly protectionist, i.e. protect infant industries, avoid dumping and prevent illicit flows of goods across borders. Excess restrictions and regulations, on the other hand, create cost and complexity; they are a barrier to economies reaching their full potential.

Nevertheless, though global trade growth remained slow between 2016 and 2017 – at only 2.4% (IMF, 2017a), it was faster in 2017 than in the five previous years, and trade volumes are forecast to recover in 2018. The Boston Consulting Group (BCG) developed a trade finance model that explores the evolution of trade flows and estimates that trade flows will grow at an annual rate of about 4% (6.5% in a bull scenario, 1.9% in a bearish market) to reach a peak of US$24 trillion by 2026 (US$30 trillion in a bullish market, US$20 trillion in a bear scenario) (Ramachandran et al., 2018b).

The Current State of Trade Finance

The importance of trade finance has been well documented. The WTO and others suggest that as much as 80% of annual global merchandise trade is enabled through some form of trade financing (WTO Secretariat, 2016). This includes traditional trade finance such as documentary letters of credit (L/Cs) and documentary collections, as well as supply chain finance (SCF) and a range of risk mitigation/trade insurance solutions. Trade finance is crucial for trading partners in order to bridge the time lag between export order and payment for goods and services produced. Factors such as transaction volume and credit period can considerably increase costs of financing or make it difficult for firms to negotiate with banks for their financing needs. Exporters and investors operate in a global environment characterised by heterogeneous political and legal systems, economic conditions and cultural behaviour. Therefore, internationally active companies are exposed to numerous challenges and several dimensions of risk: political risk, commercial risk, legal risk and currency exposure, as well as cross-cultural risk, which trade finance helps manage or mitigate. Typically, major risks in international business arise from non-payment for political or commercial reasons. Commercial risks include payment defaults by the buyer or insolvency leading to full write-offs or temporarily uncollectable receivables. Political risk refers, for example, to war, riots or a payment moratorium imposed by the government.

Just as the BCG's Trade Finance Model sees trade flows increasing, it also predicts that trade finance revenues will grow to US$45 billion by 2021 (Ramachandran et al., 2017b). Hence, growth rates in trade finance revenues are projected to slightly outpace flows. In the 2017 survey by the International Chamber of Commerce (ICC) of 255 banks covering 98 countries, over 65% of respondents reported that topline revenues for their business had increased or remained unchanged in the past year (Zakai and Thompson, 2017), while the ICC's more recent (2018) survey to 251 respondents in 91 countries revealed that the majority of respondents expected revenues to rise in both traditional and supply chain trade finance (ICC, 2018). At the same time, prices of trade finance products have remained broadly stable (Ramachandran et al., 2017a). Increased revenues might be partially bolstered by positive technological trends giving ease to international communication and access to information on counterparties (which in turn also increases confidence in non-documentary trade). Yet, in the ICC's survey, over one third of respondents said that implementing some form of technology solution or capability is not on their agenda (ICC, 2018). In addition, concerns have been raised to suggest that the current global financial and regulatory environment is not favourable for trade finance. These are discussed in later sections of this chapter, but broadly they are twofold. First, capital adequacy requirements have made it more expensive to conduct trade finance business and have translated directly into balance sheet constraints that compound those constraints related to risk appetite. Second, as compliance costs have surged post-GFC there is some evidence that banks are passing on certain compliance-related costs to customers or cutting off certain customer segments entirely.

As discussed by Beck and DiCaprio in Chapter 8 of this book, there is strong evidence of market gaps in the ability and willingness of the private sector sources of finance to address trade finance needs. In simplest terms, a market gap can be defined as a type of market failure whereby exporters or importers have unmet demand for trade finance because there is insufficient supply of finance, due to either lack of capacity or lack of risk appetite of the finance providers. Depending on the reasons, market gaps may be widespread or very specific to a company or a sector or a country. Today, market gaps in trade finance are particularly visible in asymmetries between demand-side needs of SME clients, as well as banks themselves (particularly in emerging markets), which do not have available trade lines to service their clients – big and small. However, a significant portion of these market gaps have arisen, not because the demand side is un-creditworthy or has unviable requests; rather, these can be described arguably as "regulatory" market gaps. SMEs report they lack access to trade finance in advanced and emerging economies alike. In a 2016 survey of 2664 UK exporting firms, 24% recorded they faced difficulty in obtaining trade finance or credit insurance (Auboin and Di Caprio, 2017). Similarly, studies in the United States indicate that SMEs across sectors have struggled to obtain finance for conducting cross-border trade – up to 46% in the services sector (Auboin and Di Caprio, 2017). However, the lower end of the market faces the greatest problems to obtain affordable finance, affecting smaller companies in developing economies the most. Indeed, emerging market SMEs share similar challenges to their counterparts in advanced economies, such as weak creditworthiness or limited collateral (WTO Secretariat, 2016). But the barriers they face are often compounded by characteristics of the local financial institutions available to them; tending to be smaller, less sophisticated in process, product range and technology, and limited in access to important banking relationships as well as knowledge of handling trade finance instruments, emerging market banks have their own difficulties.

Without the provision of trade finance, smaller firms are not able to gain access to global value chains that are critical for private sector employment and growth. The African Development Bank (AfDB) released a report in 2014 after investigating the market for bank-intermediated trade finance, and estimated that the value of unmet demand for trade finance in Africa was as much as US$120 billion (AfDB, 2014a). Meanwhile, latest survey results and analysis by the Asian Development Bank (ADB) point to a gap in global trade finance in the range of US$1.5 trillion annually – much of it in emerging markets, particularly developing Asia and the Pacific (DiCaprio et al., 2017). This is substantial, even though it suggests a US$100 million decrease from the previous year. According to the ADB's 2017 study, which gathered data from 515 banks from 100 countries and 1336 firms from 103 countries, the Asia and Pacific region faces some of the greatest shortfalls in trade finance. It makes up 46% of trade finance proposals globally and yet it accounts for close to 40% of total rejections (DiCaprio et al., 2017). The ICC (2018) reports similar levels of unmet demand for trade finance: Asia Pacific registering rejection rates upwards of 20% and the Middle East, Africa and Central and Eastern Europe each showing rejection rates circa 17% among banks surveyed. The same survey found MSMEs to be most frequently rejected (close to 40% of proposals) in comparison to mid-caps or large corporates (ICC, 2018). A breakdown of the proportion of rejected proposals out of proposed transactions by type in a 2017 ICC report shows that the highest is supply chain finance (16%), followed by commercial L/Cs (12%), guarantees (12%), standby L/Cs (10%) and collections (5%) (Kim *et al.*, 2017).

Example: Trade Finance in Africa

The global balance of trade shifted after the GFC – Europe and the United States declined while emerging economies relatively expanded. Africa's traditional industrialised export partners faced decline, while trade volumes between Asia and Africa and Asian investment in Africa rose rapidly – the value of Sino-African trade grew by an average rate of 14% a year in 2000–2012 (AfDB, 2014b). As the global economy has rebounded and liquidity levels have improved since the GFC, shifting dynamics within Africa – urbanisation, population growth and improving political stability – have enabled many countries within the continent to become drivers of global economic growth.

However, Africa still lags behind. It has the world's highest proportion of low-income countries, accounts for a small proportion of global trade and has an estimated trade finance gap of US$120 billion (Sénéchal, 2018). Lacking affordable trade finance, the region has not been able to take full advantage of the opportunities that the changing global economic landscape has offered. It also is yet to fully exploit trade opportunities with neighbouring emerging economies, and importantly, intra-African trade remains a relatively small proportion of total African trade.

Even though a report by the AfDB in December 2014 revealed that 72% of responding African banks expect to increase their trade finance activities in the immediate future (AfDB, 2014a), Society for Worldwide Interbank Financial Telecommunication (SWIFT) data revealed that Africa experienced the highest decrease (12.99%) in trade finance traffic of all regions in 2016 compared to the previous year (Garg, 2017). Moreover, drawing from input by the AFDB and other multilaterals, Sénéchal (2018) notes that African banks cite insufficient risk capital (21%), insufficient limits from international correspondent banks (18%) and regulatory and compliance restrictions (16%) among their biggest constraints to growth. In light of this, there are still many obstacles to overcome. Low economic growth combined with weaknesses in the African banking sector – such as low US dollar liquidity, regulation compliance, limited capital and the inability of local banks to assess the credit-worthiness of potential borrowers – create a bottleneck to increased access to trade finance, particularly for SMEs (WTO Secretariat, 2016).

In addition, trade finance default rates have remained higher in Africa than in the rest of the world – estimated at 5% in comparison with a global average of less than 1%, while the average default rate of SMEs in Central Africa is as high as 31% (Drammeh, 2017). Given this, it is unsurprising that the most frequently cited reasons why banks reject the trade finance requests of clients are weak client creditworthiness

(36%) and insufficient client collateral (30%) (Drammeh, 2017). These findings corroborate earlier studies by the AfDB and others.

Going forward, as long as these market gaps persist, economic development in Africa will be stymied. Innovative solutions are needed, as traditional approaches will not suffice.

Supply- and Demand-Side Challenges

Various organisations and groups have explored the barriers faced by potential clients in accessing trade finance and the key limiting factors among providers in fulfilling trade finance needs. Risk tolerance and perception has been a major force in shaping supply-side trade finance gaps. Surveys issued to financial institutions in 2016 showed that both anti-money-laundering/know-your-customer/counter-terrorism financing (AML/KYC/CTF) regulations and Basel III regulatory requirements were viewed as major impediments to their ability to service trade finance gaps; 79.2% of respondents expressed agreement that AML/KYC/CTF is a barrier (nearly half stated they "strongly agree") and 71% of respondents affirmed Basel III was a barrier (Kim *et al.*, 2017). Again, financial institutions in the ADB's 2017 trade finance survey indicated that the foremost reason applicants were rejected related to KYC concerns (29.3%) (DiCaprio *et al.*, 2017). Insufficient collateral or information (21%), unsuitability for financing (20%) and low bank profits (15%) were also frequently cited reasons for banks' and private providers' rejection of trade finance proposals (DiCaprio *et al.*, 2017). Most recently, the TFX and ICC's 2018 export finance survey suggested a large proportion (54%) of export financiers (banks and corporates) felt that legal and regulatory hurdles were holding them back from doing business in new markets; fear of corruption (42%) and sanctions (35%) were also of concern (Thompson, 2018). Similarly, low country credit ratings and low credit ratings of issuing banks (each over 70% of respondents) have also been cited as key barriers among institutions in extending trade finance (Kim *et al.*, 2017). Affirmed by 23% of banks, the ICC's 2018 survey showed that an unacceptable risk profile – especially for banks based in the Middle East and Latin America – was a primary reason for application rejection (ICC, 2018). This has likely resulted in consolidation away from perceived high-risk (potentially high-cost) segments of the market.

As was observed in the ADB's study, trade finance transactions that were rejected by respondents on the grounds of low profitability or for lacking information or collateral were likely considered workable (but undesirable) propositions. Therefore, these types of rejections may be fundable by alternative financial arrangements or financial institutions. It is more ambiguous as to whether firms rejected on KYC concerns may actually represent viable businesses. It is possible that the trade finance provider considered the expense associated with completing the necessary due diligence on the applicant simply too prohibitive, or it might be that the applicant truly failed to provide evidence to support its activities were anti-financial crimes. As will be discussed in later sections, increased pressure and compliance costs associated with KYC and AML regulations, paired with heightened capital requirements in the banking sector, create an incentive for trade finance providers to avoid low-value transactions (SMEs) and build a portfolio around bigger, more cost-effective applicants. In a world where both the cost of due diligence on transactions in new markets, and the stakes for entering a new market and failing to properly address regulatory requirements are extremely high, it is likely that any lack of clarity or shortfall in information available will generate a more pronounced risk aversion. It is worth noting that widespread consensus regarding the challenges around due diligence costs has resulted in increased global efforts to establish and promote KYC utilities, such as the SWIFT KYC register, and the emergence of various technologies that establish digital identities. This will be explored in greater detail later.

Meanwhile, on the demand side, it would seem that trade finance gaps appear to be exacerbated by a lack of awareness and familiarity among companies – particularly SMEs – about the many types of trade finance products and innovative alternatives such as supply chain financing, bank payment obligations and forfaiting. The WTO's 2016 study on trade finance and SMEs (WTO Secretariat, 2016) suggested that greater financial education would help overcome major demand-side barriers contributing to trade finance gaps. The ADB's 2017 trade finance survey (DiCaprio et al., 2017) also sheds light on the main market segments facing demand-side challenges and thus contributing to development and market failures in trade finance industry. Consistent with surveys that the ADB has undertaken in previous years, it finds that SMEs and mid-caps continue to represent the greatest market segments underserved by trade finance; these businesses face more challenges than large corporates in accessing every type of trade finance mechanism. Banks report that 74% of rejections are towards SMEs and mid-caps (DiCaprio et al., 2017). In addition, women – who are primarily owners of smaller businesses – are 2.5 times more likely than men to have 100% of their proposals rejected by banks (DiCaprio et al., 2017). Following rejection, they are also less likely to find alternatives (ADB, 2016). A case in point: it is estimated that over 70% of women-led SMEs are either unserved or underserved financially (Women's World Banking, 2014). There may be a myriad of reasons for this, including sociocultural biases as well as economic. According to a recent Goldman Sachs study, the credit gap for women-led businesses is an unmet opportunity of approximately US$285 billion (Stupnytska et al., 2014). The study defines the value of the credit gap as formal financing that is needed but not available. This formal financing is assumed to be debt that would be included on a company's balance sheet, such as loans, overdrafts, trade financing, leasing and factoring. According to the study, if credit gaps for women-led SMEs were closed by 2020 across the developing world, then growth rates in per capita incomes would exceed 110 basis points on average (Stupnytska et al., 2014).

Perhaps one of the most revealing statistics on the negative impact of enduring trade finance gaps was found when participating firms in the ADB's 2017 trade finance survey were asked what happened to the trade transaction after rejection. Close to 60% of responding businesses indicated that they were unable to execute the transaction when their application for trade finance was rejected (DiCaprio et al., 2017). Given that businesses of every size category (SME, mid-cap and large) consistently report that trade finance would enable their businesses to generate more employment and growth (over 86%), the cumulative lost economic opportunity here is substantial (DiCaprio et al., 2017).

Future of Trade Finance

The ICC describes trade financing as critical for "opening access to a new market with a new trading relationship, on the basis of competitively priced financing and when necessary, on a largely risk-mitigated basis" (ICC, 2017, p. 87). Various stakeholders at national and international levels have an interest in seeing trade finance gaps minimised and international and intra-regional trade flourish. It is in the best interest of national governments, multilateral institutions and development banks to work in harmony and alongside international advocacy and regulatory organisations and committees.

Going forward, the vast majority of respondent banks in the ADB's 2017 survey reported that greater integration and harmonisation of rules, standards and regulations in trade finance would reduce market gaps and lead to more support for SMEs and higher economic growth (Kim *et al.*, 2017). Policymakers need to find the right balance for policies that encourage risk-taking and boost output and investment, while also avoiding financial stability risks and exacerbating domestic and global imbalances. However, within a country, these two policy interests are typically considered within different domains and responsibilities and therefore seldom are they considered together. The following sections explore the imperatives generally held by trade ministers and then banking regulators to suggest that, while national and international actors in these two realms have shared interests, recent developments in financial regulation have a negative bearing on trade finance and therefore trade expansion.

Trade Ministers and Regulators

Overview

The impetus around commercialisation and trade expansion is strong in every country. Trade ministers (or other ministers where, in some countries, the ministries of trade, economy and industry are combined) are keenly engaged in seeing trade opportunities for their exporters open up and pursuing policies that ensure the basic enabling environment to foster growth is in place. Whether at the highest strategic multilateral policy level via the WTO or supporting an individual trade mission, the job description of a trade minister is clear – encourage trade.

It may also be that trade objectives are more specific than just overall growth in trade flows. Trade ministers may be seeking to diversify trade partners (e.g. reduce Canada's reliance on trade with the United States), or enhance trade flows between specific partners (e.g. the Organisation of Islamic Cooperation (OIC) seeks to expand intra-OIC trade; COMCEC, n.d.). Or, it may be that countries are seeking to move up the value chain and shift to greater value-added imports (e.g. African commodity producers seeking to produce the refined products rather than shipping raw materials offshore). Within each country, specific trade objectives are articulated, with a view towards greater benefit to local companies. Ensuring access to financial support for these trade objectives is not necessarily considered as part of the strategy. A trade minister might recognise if aspects of regulation were to have unintended consequences on trade, or generate barriers among underserved segments, but is not necessarily positioned to influence what is championed by national regulators.

Example: Uganda's National Development Plan, and the Roles of Trade Minister and Regulators

Take Uganda, for example: expansion of trade (particularly exports that are higher in the value chain), regional integration through trade and the promotion of a rule-based open trading system are key elements in its National Development Plan (NDP II). Like other emerging economies, Uganda's NDP II commits it to undertake a variety of trade and trade-facilitation measures, as well as measures to ensure its financial systems adhere to international regulatory standards. Therefore, it includes the removal of internal tariffs, non-tariff and technical barriers to trade, harmonisation of standards etc. It also outlines objectives around, inter alia, improving private sector competitiveness and increasing market access for Uganda's goods and services in regional and international markets (Government of Uganda, 2015). Accordingly, the mission statement of Uganda's Ministry of Trade and Industry is "to develop and promote a competitive and export-led private sector through accelerating industrial development for economic growth" (MTIC, 2017). The means by which the private sector would obtain necessary financing to import or progress upwards in the commercialisation continuum and become active exporters, is left unstated. However, inter alia, it would require a stable financial system (established through harmonised standards) and banks that are knowledgeable of, and prepared to undertake, the private sector's risks. Meanwhile, the Bank of Uganda (BoU) is the country's primary agent for upholding financial rules and supervising the financial sector. It has a mandate to foster macroeconomic and financial system stability (Bank of Uganda, 2018). In doing this it takes into consideration international standards, for example Basel III, and seeks to ensure financial institutions carry out their normal function of intermediating funds between savers and investors, and facilitating payments (Bank of Uganda, 2018). Much like the banking regulators of other economies, it is not within the BoU's purview to be concerned about which market segments the financial institutions are choosing to facilitate payments for (provided they are not facilitating financial crimes or generating instability in the financial sector). That is to say, so long as the local banks are intermediating funds correctly from a regulatory perspective, the BoU would not necessarily be concerned if, for example, perfectly "clean" (non-money-laundering) SMEs, women-business owners and exporters were underserved or excluded from bank transactions. Hence, though both regulators and trade ministers have important roles to play in national development, they sing from different songbooks

General Observations

At the same time, regulators cannot lower their standards, and any regulatory deviation from international AML and KYC standards may see the country sanctioned or quickly cut off from international financial flows – thus generating an even more adverse effect on trade. In addition, even though both financial regulators and trade ministers are answerable for ensuring a country's economic prosperity and long-run stability, they have different reporting lines.

Nevertheless, going forward it is important that trade ministers and those involved in public policy understand the areas of regulation that regulators are demanding of financial institutions, and the impact these regulations have on trade finance. With this, trade ministers, regulators and those involved in public policy can coordinate to see trade-led national development without compromising on regulatory standards. Financial regulators have a voice in shaping international financial architecture; with obligations to a combination of "supra-national" governing structures, formal networks and bodies – such as the Basel Committee within the Bank for International Settlements, the International Organisation of Securities Commissions (IOSCO) and the Financial Action Task Force (FATF) – they have a role in ensuring that regulation is appropriately nuanced and doesn't unjustly constrain their economy's development. Trade ministers must work with local regulators and those who shape public policy to see that, as national regulation moves towards international standards, it is clear and easily understood by local and international banks and businesses. They are also responsible for carrying their national government's development agenda forward to international networks, such as the G7, G8, and G20, as well as in working groups and panels of the WTO.

The Doha Ministerial Conference, in November 2001, saw trade ministers launch the Doha Development Agenda, which placed development issues and the interests of developing countries front and centre in the WTO's work. At the WTO's most recent (December 2017) Ministerial Conference in Buenos Aires (MC-11), 87 members issued a joint statement declaring their intention to focus on addressing obstacles faced by MSMEs in trade. Leading up to this, a working group of representatives from 30 counties submitted a draft ministerial decision calling for the establishment of a work programme under the General Council focusing on the needs of MSMEs – recognising MSME access to trade finance and opportunities fundamentally influences a country's development and prosperity. Consultations are ongoing on this matter, but the link between MSME access to finance and regulatory challenges was drawn; a work programme centred on "ways to promote a more predictable regulatory environment for MSMEs", among other things, was proposed (WTO, 2017b, p. 2). The shape this takes, and the extent to which regulators will be brought into the design and outworking of such a programme, is yet to be shown.

Financial Regulators

Three Areas of Regulation

The requirements banking regulators are expecting of financial institutions broadly fall into three areas: (i) capital, leverage and liquidity parameters as stipulated in the Basel Accords; (ii) AML and CTF measures; and (iii) sustainable banking. Like other financial sector mechanisms, trade finance benefits from policies that promote financial stability. However, the implementation of these regulations can be costly and complex for domestic banks and can have negative effects on trade finance and generate market gaps.

Since the GFC in 2008, banking regulation has expanded and intensified around the world. The Basel Committee on Banking Supervision has been at the centre of these developments, with the set of reforms it released under the third Basel Accord (Basel III) in response to the deficiencies in financial regulation revealed by the financial crisis. Basel III has ushered in significant regulatory changes to international banking rules; tougher capital, leverage and liquidity requirements are the key pillars of the new standards (Basel Committee on Banking Supervision, 2017). It sets parameters for both the quality and the quantity of capital held by banks, and defines liquidity rules to ensure banks have sufficient high-quality liquid assets to withstand a period of economic stress (Mnuchin and Phillips, 2017). Importantly, these regulations reduce incentives for banks to build up high-risk, highly leveraged balance sheets. Legislators around the world began phasing in the rules at varying times from 2013, and they are due to be fully realised by 2019 (Basel Committee on Banking Supervision, 2017). The most recent (December 2017) updates – referred to as Basel IV by market participants – are to go into effect in January 2022. Though Basel III regulations are internationally recognised, until they are fully phased in there remains some inconsistency in application across nations, with some applying Basel III while others are still applying II. With December's updates going into effect by 2022, discrepancies and time lags in application of regulation across trading partners are likely to continue.

The second area on which regulators in recent years have become increasingly focused is the mitigation of financial crimes such as money laundering or terrorism financing. Recommendations and standards set by the FATF – an inter-governmental body that aims to promote effective implementation of legal, regulatory and operational measures for combating money laundering, terrorist financing and other related threats (FATF, 2017) – have been adopted to different degrees by regulators around the world. To wit, pressures to mitigate illicit financial flows have intensified, and AML and CTF procedures, laws or regulations have placed banks under intense scrutiny and compliance obligations (Kaminski and Robu, 2016). Financial institutions providing credit or allowing customers to open accounts are required to complete comprehensive due-diligence assessments of their customers and counterparty banks to stop the practice of generating income through illegal actions. These AML rules have therefore led to a significant focus on KYC as well as KYCC (know-your-customers'-customer), KYCS (know-your-customers'-supplier) and KYT (know-your-transaction). As touched on earlier, recent surveys reveal that among various impediments to trade finance, increasing compliance and regulatory burdens are of foremost concern to banks.

Third, a movement is afoot to institutionalise the concept of *sustainable banking* into regulatory regimes. Just as Basel III is designed to protect financial system stability and AML/CTF requirements are in place to protect financial institutions' integrity, sustainable banking regulations are intended to protect (and enhance) the environmental and social (E&S) dynamics in which a financial institution operates (IFC, 2017a). The International Finance Corporation (IFC) summarises sustainable banking policy as generally relating to:

> i) the financial sustainability of the financial institution and its client-companies, so that they can continue to make a long-term contribution to development; ii) the economic sustainability of the projects and companies that the financial institution finances; iii) environmental sustainability through the preservation of natural resources; and iv) social sustainability through focus on improved living standards, poverty reduction, concern for the welfare of communities, and respect for key human rights. (Grigoryeva *et al.*, 2007, p. 9)

The IFC was one of the first financial institutions to embrace the paradigm of sustainable banking. Its standards, along with the World Bank Group sector-specific

"Environmental Health and Safety Guidelines" (2018), were foundational for developing the Equator Principles, a voluntary set of principles/risk management framework for determining, assessing and managing environmental and social risk in projects (IFC, 2017b). First adopted by ten international banks in 2003, the Principles are now applied by 43 financial institutions, covering 80% of global project finance (Grigoryeva *et al.*, 2007). Other voluntary – but prominent – banking sector sustainability frameworks include the United Nations Environment Programme Finance Initiative (UNEP FI) Statement of Commitment by Financial Institutions; the London Principles of Sustainable Finance; and the World Business Council for Sustainable Development Financial Sector Statement. Currently, it is among emerging economies that the concept of sustainable banking has had considerable uptake (IFC, 2017a). Perhaps this is because though the definition is still evolving, it tends to overlap with and reinforce commonly held national development goals (as well as the Sustainable Development Goals). Indeed, recognition that the financial sector's business relationships are exposed to E&S risks, and a view that sustainability practices should be integrated into the financial sector's internal processes, has led national governments to establish country-level sustainability frameworks (IFC, 2017b). For this reason, the requirement to undertake E&S evaluations and impact assessments is becoming a component of pre-screening for credit transactions.

What Does this Regulation Mean for Banks Providing Trade Finance?

These areas of regulation – Basel III, AML/CTF and sustainability policy – have various implications. In general, their effects on financial institutions relate to profitability and risk tolerance. The decisions that institutions make in response to such effects will dictate the aggregate impact on the trade finance industry.

First, since their publication in 2010, certain elements of the Basel III reforms have been highlighted by actors in the trade finance industry as having, potentially, adverse effects on the ability of banks to provide trade finance in a cost-effective fashion (Basel Committee on Banking Supervision, 2017; Tavan, 2013; Brandi *et al.*, 2014). Initially, concern was raised that Basel III was not sufficiently nuanced to reflect the nature of trade finance products. Specifically, it is very unlikely that trade finance assets, which tend to be low-risk and highly collateralised, will contribute to financial system instability; yet, Basel III requires banks to take them into account in capital and leverage calculations (Thieffry, 2016). The ICC's Trade Register indicates that default and loss rates for traditional trade finance products are very low. For example, the probability of default on all trade finance assets is low: from 0.03% on export L/Cs and 0.07% on import L/Cs, to 0.22% on loans for imports/exports and 0.24% for performance guarantees (ICC, 2018). When first developed, Basel III treated the risk weighting of trade finance assets the same as other riskier assets. By this design, there are incentives for banks to favour riskier transactions because a bank could use its resources to gain a higher rate of return for the same level of regulatory capital, given that the same risk weights apply to different risk-level transactions. In light of this, the Basel architecture has evolved with time to accommodate the nuances of trade finance and mitigate these unintended consequences (Nixon *et al.*, 2016). Nevertheless, some concerns remain around the asset value correlation to be used in capital calculations for trade finance, and inflows permitted for trade finance in the liquidity coverage ratio (Thieffry, 2016). In addition, it has been suggested that capital-constrained banks may have incentives to reduce their balance sheets by divesting short-term commitments such as trade finance, as it is one of the easiest ways to downsize. Notably, a 2016 ICC study revealed that roughly two thirds of respondent banks said that the implementation of Basel III regulations had affected their cost of funds and liquidity for trade finance (ICC, 2016a). Therefore, while progress has been made, it will be important that industry professionals continue to collect data that adequately captures any impacts of the regulation on the provision of trade finance, and coordinate with trade ministers and domestic regulators to dialogue with the Basel Committee.

Second, with the onus to perform extensive customer due diligence and E&S assessments on the financial institution, compliance costs in the financial sector have swelled and led banks to look for means to minimise their expenses. Estimations of financial firms' average costs to meet their obligations vary. It has been cited as on average around US$60 million, with some firms spending upwards of US$500 million on compliance with KYC and customer due diligence (Thomson Reuters, 2016). A LexisNexis survey of banks across the six Asian markets estimated that AML compliance budgets reached US$1.5 billion annually (LexisNexis, 2016). It seems that since the financial crisis, costs have continued to trend upwards: 82% of the survey respondents saw overall AML compliance costs increasing in 2016, and one third projected that costs will continue to rise by 20% or more (LexisNexis, 2016). Connected with this, since 2009 the role of compliance within banks has evolved. Formerly, compliance departments featured as an enforcement arm associated with the legal function and were charged with disseminating regulations and internal bank policy (Kaminski and Robu, 2016). Compliance activities were primarily of an advisory capacity; now the role of compliance is expansive. "Best practice" has risk and compliance units not only performing regular assessments of the state of overall compliance, but actively involved in the broader risk control environment (Kaminski and Robu, 2016). Inter alia, personnel within these units are creating internal standards for risk, managing risk processes via the generation of scorecards and methodologies, developing and enforcing standards for effective risk mediation, establishing training programmes related to risk, ensuring that the first line of defence is effective, and providing a view on clients' transactions and products based on predefined risk-based rules. All this is invariably matched by increased resources devoted to compliance and higher KYC costs. Indeed, among financial institutions in Asia, personnel costs are attributed as by far the largest portion (81%) of AML compliance spending (LexisNexis, 2016). In addition, to add perspective, 1 in 6 employees at JPMorgan Chase, America's biggest bank, now work directly on "controls" – a figure reached after jumping from 24,000 in 2011 to 43,000 in 2015 (*The Economist*, 2017). Overall, KYC processes, periodic screening etc. are estimated to account for 33% of AML compliance costs (LexisNexis, 2016).

Meanwhile, the penalties for non-compliance have risen considerably in recent years and there have been a number of high-profile enforcement actions. In 2014, the UK regulator alone issued £1.5 billion in fines – a considerable increase from the £474 million it issued in the year before (Thomson Reuters, 2015). Global figures vary on the amount banks and other financial institutions have paid in fines and settlements for failing to identify and address money laundering, market manipulation, terrorist financing etc. One study found that between 2013 and 2015 financial institutions had been fined more than US$10 billion worldwide for failing to meet AML rules for KYC (Thomson Reuters, 2015). Meanwhile a 2017 Boston Consulting Group report values the amount paid by banks in fines since 2008 at US$321 billion (Grasshoff *et al.*, 2017). Less quantifiable is the reputational damage they incurred. Hence, not desiring to be subject to such fines, banks have accordingly deepened their investment in customer due diligence, as discussed. They have also, however, adjusted their risk tolerance for certain clients and markets, and terminated certain correspondent banking relationships deemed too risky – a phenomena that will be discussed in detail later. Related to this, inconsistencies in regulation across borders add cost and complexity for banks dealing with relationships under different regulatory bodies, causing them to re-evaluate the business case for their involvement in certain transactions and markets (Starnes *et al.*, 2016). In general, because the cost of compliance is already high, incentives are low among banks to incur potential additional costs associated with due diligence on transactions in far-off emerging economies where national credit ratings are poor and transactions details may be opaque.

In a different vein, though sustainable banking regulations add compliance costs for financial industry participants, they present a fundamental difference; the Basel Accords and regulation regarding AML, KYC and CTF demand compliance that moves financial institutions to process *conformance* with pre-determined acceptable risk thresholds. The intention behind regulation around sustainable banking, on the other hand, is process *performance* to create long-term value (IFC, 2017b). In this sense, though three forms of regulation have been discussed in this section, the former two, without devaluing their importance, present obstacles to successful trade finance, while the latter creates opportunity. The scope of responsibility among financial institutions (particularly in emerging markets) is widened via the introduction of sustainability regulations. Broadly, their adoption requires a blend of adjusted risk management perspectives, and a focus on "green" loan origination (IFC, 2017b). The former relates to managing social and environmental risks at both a strategic and a transaction level; the latter is proactive – it involves identifying opportunities for innovative (green/sustainable) product development (IFC, 2017b). The IFC's Sustainable Banking Network (SBN) – a voluntary community developed in 2012 of financial regulators, banking associations and environmental regulators – is at the of centre of sustainable banking progress by supporting green/sustainable policy formation and implementation in member countries. Notably, of the SBN's 32 member countries, there have been examples of both regulatory-led transitions to sustainable banking (Bangladesh, China, Indonesia, Morocco, Peru and Vietnam) and industry-led transitions via banking associations (Colombia, Ecuador, Kenya, Mexico, Mongolia, Turkey and South Africa) as well as cases where regulation has developed through collaboration among those involved in policy and industry (IFC, 2017a).

The broadening reach of banking regulations is a critical development for the global financial sector to become immunised against the contagion seen in the GFC. However, arguably there are and will continue to be some unintended consequences of these regulations for the economy. That these are unintended consequences has everything to do with the policymakers – the banking regulators on the one hand

and the trade ministers on the other – not coordinating their approaches to establish a robust financial system hand in hand with an accessible one.

Real Impacts: The Consequences for The Real Economy

De-Risking

Banks are managing more risks. This is a good thing. The surge of regulatory activity in recent years has built greater resiliency into the global financial system. Nevertheless, as discussed in the previous section, it comes at a cost. Banks face increases in capital reserve requirements and in compliance costs. Where, formerly, banks premised business decisions on credit risk and quality, banks now rely on lengthy on-boarding processes in efforts to mitigate operational risk associated with environmental and social factors, financial crimes etc. As a result, compliance costs among banks are at unprecedented levels. The outcome: "de-risking". De-risking refers to banks terminating or restricting their relationships with clients or categories of clients to avoid risk (World Bank, 2015). Specifically, the FATF defines de-risking as: "the phenomenon of financial institutions terminating or restricting business relationships with clients or categories of clients to avoid, rather than manage, risk [...]. De-risking can be the result of various drivers, such as concerns about profitability, prudential requirements, anxiety after the Global Financial Crisis, and reputational risk" (FATF, 2014). Its impact falls on both direct customers and correspondent banks. Correspondent banking, which can be broadly defined as the provision of banking services by one bank (the "correspondent bank") to another bank (the "respondent bank"), is essential for customer payments, especially across borders, and for the access of banks themselves to foreign financial systems (IMF, 2017b). The ability to make and receive international payments via correspondent banking is vital for businesses' and individuals' cross-border payments, foreign currency settlements and access to foreign financial systems.

The effects of increased regulation on correspondent banking relationships (CBRs) post-financial crisis have been well documented over the past five years. In 2014, the IFC captured the sentiments of both correspondent and respondent banks through a survey issued to members of its Global Trade Finance Program (GTFP), a programme providing risk mitigation solutions to global banks to build their capacity to service emerging markets and thus facilitate trade. The survey showed 60% of correspondent banks had not increased their overall lines for emerging market banks over the past six months (Starnes et al., 2017). Where CBRs had dropped, rising compliance costs and country or counterparty bank risk factors were cited as the primary reasons. The persistence of these challenges is evidenced in more recent surveys. The IFC's 2017 survey on correspondent banking, issued to over 300 banking clients in 92 countries, revealed that over one quarter of participants in Europe, Central Asia, Latin America and the Caribbean experienced decreases in their CBRs (Starnes et al., 2017). At over one third, the impact in Sub-Saharan Africa recorded by survey participants is even more pronounced (Starnes et al., 2017). The IFC's Global Trade Finance Program (GTFP) clients in emerging markets identified various and costly compliance requirements and stress in CBRs among their biggest challenges in 2017 (Sénéchal, 2018). Indeed, the compounded challenges of local regulators and cross-border correspondent banks imposing further (and often dissimilar) compliance requirements; reductions in the number of active CBRs; reductions of line limits; and limited alternatives are regularly cited as the main barriers in local banks' ability to serve customers today (IMF, 2017b).

In addition, surveys issued by the IFC to respondent banks in 2015 and again in 2016 revealed that the participants' expectation for CBRs to decrease in availability had risen from 3% to over 20% within a year (Starnes *et al.*, 2017). Meanwhile, a 2016 IFC survey of 210 emerging market banks illustrates the levels of pessimism among emerging market banks regarding the availability of correspondent lines. Indeed, of those surveyed, the percentage that indicated they had a negative outlook on CBR availability had increased from zero to 27% (Starnes *et al.*, 2016). This is unsurprising, given the findings of numerous other global bank surveys, such as the Institute of International Finance (IIF) and Ernst & Young's (EY) annual survey of banks in October 2016, whereby over 48% of banks stated they had exited or were planning to exit business lines, and 27% said they were leaving specific countries (IIF and EY, 2016). Or, for example, a 2015 World Bank survey on regulatory bodies and local banks, which revealed that three quarters of large correspondents had reduced their correspondent relationships and that 95% stated concerns about AML/CTF risks for terminating and/or restricting foreign CBRs (World Bank, 2015). Again, in a 2016 survey by the ICC of 375 banks in 109 countries, the percentage of banks claiming to having experienced termination of correspondent banking lines due to compliance measures came to 35% (ICC, 2016b). Globally, the decline is CBRs between 2009 and 2015 has been estimated at 25% (Accuity, 2017). SWIFT examined messaging data relevant to correspondent banking between 2011 and 2015. Looking at 204 jurisdictions, it confirmed a decrease in the number of active correspondents in over 120 of them, and over 40 of those experienced a decline exceeding 10% (Garg, 2017).

Though de-risking is a global phenomenon, it appears to be concentrated towards certain markets and customer segments. Where CBRs have been terminated, it has tended to be where relationships are considered higher risk, less profitable or unproductively complex. International banks – increasingly concerned about AML and CTF risk – are de-risking at times from entire countries where there is a lack of transparency over local banks' activities and compliance strategies (Starnes *et al.*, 2016). In a joint survey by the Association of Certified Anti-Money Laundering Specialists (ACAMS) and LexisNexis, 40% of surveyed banks said they intended to leave specific geographic areas (LexisNexis and ACAMS, 2015). The two most frequently cited reasons why were: (i) that the segment was no longer within the firm's risk appetite (56%); and (ii) that the cost of compliance made the segment unprofitable (51%) (LexisNexis and ACAMS, 2015). Emerging markets, where some surveyed banks have stated they terminated over 60% of their CBRs, are the most harmed by this (IMF, 2017b). Additionally, where relationships have remained, many banks have set new minimum activity thresholds, passing on higher costs to respondents, or pressured respondents to limit their exposure to certain "high-risk" categories of customers (World Bank, 2015). Often these "high-risk" customers have been small and medium-sized companies.

Impact on SMEs

Where the cost of due diligence is equally high, or comparable, for SME clients as it is for larger corporates, there is less incentive for a bank to maintain low-return SME relationships. As mentioned earlier, this is an issue for SMEs globally, not only in emerging economies. Even though the global financial system has largely returned to pre-financial-crisis levels of liquidity, the availability of finance is skewed towards multinationals and large corporates; MSMEs are consistently constrained in access to credit (Stein *et al.*, 2013). In a world where more than 90% of companies are SMEs, the impact of this is tangible. In emerging markets, where SMEs contribute greatly to exports and account for almost 40% of GDP and as many as four out of every five new jobs, the consequences are immense (WTO Secretariat, 2016). Entrepreneurs are faced with even greater challenges in their efforts to progress in commercialisation, their growth stunted without adequate access to finance. Close to 70% of MSMEs in emerging markets lack access to credit (Stein *et al.*, 2013) and the IFC and McKinsey have estimated their global financing gap to be in the range of US$2.6 trillion (Starnes *et al.*, 2017). The impact of trade finance shortages on the ability of SMEs to link into global trade flows has been well substantiated. Insufficient access to trade finance among exporters leads to reduced exports and turnover as a result of foregone sales to foreign customers. In one study, of 3000 exporting firms from 52 countries, respondents indicated that turnover decreased as much as 30% on average as a consequence of limited access to trade finance (CBI, 2013). In theory, successful national development strategies around improving SME access to trade finance should generate a positive development impact. Specifically, SMEs employ the majority of the global workforce (the median employment share of SMEs across countries is 67%; Auboin and Di Caprio, 2017). In addition, exporting firms grow and hire new employees at a faster rate than non-exporters (Auboin and Di Caprio, 2017). Therefore, enabling SMEs to export more should increase employment. Woman-owned SMEs tend to hire more women – yet, as already discussed, they are the most credit-constrained (Stupnytska *et al.*, 2014). Therefore, one can also conclude that improving trade finance to this particular group can also expand employment among women. As trade ministers continue to look for ways to improve MSME opportunities and access to trade finance – particularly in light of the WTO MC-11's recent focus on MSMEs – mechanisms to overcome the interplay of financial regulation and de-risking should not be ignored.

Least Connected Countries

Of further concern, and linked to what has already been discussed, is the possibility of new forms of financial exclusion arising as an unintended consequence of regulators and international banks managing financial crime-related risks. As highlighted by the IMF, though it may be rational by cost–benefit analysis for an individual bank to cease some of its CBRs, the aggregate withdrawal by many banks from CBRs could have a systemic impact and result in some countries being disconnected from the global financial system (IMF, 2017b). The concept of *least connected countries (LCCs)* is used in discussion around internet connectivity. Yet, when examining data on the decline of CRBs, it might be suitable to talk about the least connected countries in the context of global trade.

A 2015 World Bank survey showed financial exclusion resulting from global de-risking has been particularly felt by smaller developing economies in Africa, the Caribbean, Central Asia, Europe and the Pacific (World Bank, 2015). Small Island Developing States (SIDS), such as in the Caribbean, appear to be the most affected by declines in CBRs. Trade is well recognised as a fundamental driver of development and economic growth, but for some Caribbean small states, trade is equivalent to almost 100% of GDP (CaPRI, 2016).

At least 16 banks across five countries in the Caribbean region have lost all or some of their correspondent relationships (Boyce and Kendall, 2016). Banks' de-risking in the Caribbean and terminating CBRs puts the region in a position of disproportionate vulnerability. In addition, SIDS often rely on imports for critical goods such as food, medical supplies, oil, primary resources etc. Hence, the reduction of CBRs not only limits export potential but inhibits some economies' access to fundamental production inputs and other goods for living (Starnes *et al.*, 2016). In addition, while regulators dictate AML and CTF requirements in order to ensure financial institutions in their jurisdiction are not involved in illegal financial flows, if CBR flight is the impact of these regulations, then – perhaps ironically – there might be an increase in the risk of money laundering and terrorist financing. In particular, as the availability of CBRs declines, the risk increases that businesses or individuals, who have become excluded from the financial system, will seek less regulated and less transparent channels to conduct transactions.

Banking regulations have naturally changed the way banks operate. This is all to be expected. What has not been sufficiently anticipated is the impact on access to finance, particularly access to trade finance, for small firms, small banks and small countries. Without access to trade finance, trade opportunities evaporate, trade flows shrink and economic growth stalls. Hence, access to trade finance becomes a development problem.

Example: Belize

In the past two years, the Central Bank of Belize has lost three of its five CBRs – including one that was used to process selected wires for banks that lost CBRs. At one stage, some 22 CRB accounts (out of 31) were terminated by major global banks across Belize's commercial and offshore banks (IMF, 2017b). Thereby a mere two of 11 domestic and international banks in Belize had full banking services with their CBRs (IMF, 2017b). Some were unable to process US dollar wire transfers. Four banks lost credit card settlement accounts in New York, and were forced to process credit card transactions through brokerage accounts or through a large credit card company (CaPRI, 2016).

The flight of CBRs in Belize has had a considerable impact on its trade relations. CBRs enable cross-border payment services, which are vital to international trade. As trade is a high proportion of its GDP (2000–2015, 7.5% of average foreign direct investment net inflows) relative to other countries, de-risking that limits CBRs is thus particularly liable to affect Belize on metrics such as poverty levels, unemployment and economic growth (CaPRI, 2016).

Cumulatively, the impact of the loss of CBRs on Belize's international trade volumes remained difficult to detect based on the data available at the time. Most CBRs actually remained in place until late 2015 or early 2016 (IMF, 2017b). Its adverse effects can be seen in the hikes in wire transfer fees and in processing time, and in decreases in the rate of deposits in Belize's banking system during this time period. At worst, a scenario analysis undertaken by the IMF found that a loss of 70% of CBRs would generate a drop in real GDP of up to six percentage points in the next five years (Starnes *et al.*, 2017).

Solutions entertained by the authorities have included: (i) increasing fees for CBR services; (ii) channelling more business volume to a more concentrated number of correspondent banks through collective action; (iii) processing cross-border payments through a US-licensed special purpose vehicle; and (iv) providing CBR insurance policies (CaPRI, 2016).

The Road Ahead

Avoiding the widening of regulatory market gaps and the risks of financial exclusion among emerging markets requires coordinated efforts between the public and private sector. Promising steps towards overcoming regulatory gaps have already been made in each sector.

Supply Chain Finance

Over time the dominant mechanisms of trade finance have shifted. Since 2014 the trade finance product mix has shifted from traditional documentary trade finance products (e.g. L/Cs) into simpler, cheaper open account transactions. Certainly, traditional forms of trade finance remain important and relevant; there was some evidence of a heightened use of traditional mechanisms vis-à-vis newer "open account" mechanisms at the peak of the GFC (ICC, 2017). Yet, increasingly trade is conducted on open account terms, and therefore enabled through techniques of supply chain finance (SCF), which provides working capital and off-balance-sheet financing. Where traditional trade finance mechanisms focus on financials and collateral (two areas in which SMEs tend to be weaker), SCF assesses performance history and the "stickiness" of relationships in a supply chain; therefore, it enables a different approach to risk assessment, often more accessible to SMEs (DiCaprio *et al.*, 2017).

As more buyers have moved to purchasing goods on open account, the ability for SMEs to obtain local bank financing only on the basis of purchase orders has been greatly reduced. This lack of financing is a major deterrent to having SMEs join global supply chain linkages and move up the value chain. Therefore, supply chain financing has offered an attractive and viable option. Nearly 80% of respondents surveyed by the ICC in the 2017 "Survey on Trade Finance and Supply Chain Finance" expressed the view that traditional forms of trade finance will exhibit little or no growth, or decline outright year-on-year going forward (ICC, 2017). However, recent data gathered by the ICC relating to flows enabled through traditional trade finance suggest it still accounts for upwards of US$1.5 trillion in annual merchandise trade (about 10%; ICC, 2017). While, SCF offers a promising solution for bringing SMEs into international trade, it is not sufficient by itself to overcome the challenges of regulatory market gaps.

The Role of Technology

As regulatory demands have increased, new technology solutions from the private sector to minimise the burdens of compliance have emerged. Digitalisation and, in particular, financial technologies (fintech) offer to reduce the time, cost and complexity of financial transactions and cross-border money transfers. On the supply side, among banks and trade finance providers, fintech ranges from new "disruptive" technologies like distributed ledger technology (DLT; block chain and others), to technologies that offer interoperability (open-sourced, real-time global payment systems), to technologies that capture and sort big data, and others. The recent report by Boston Consulting Group and SWIFT estimates that over three to five years digital trade finance can cut costs by between US$2.5 billion and US$6 billion (35%; Ramachandran *et al.*, 2017b). The report further highlights three key areas of digital innovation that will drive cost reduction: (i) intelligent automation (e.g. artificial intelligence programmes and optical character recognition); (ii) collaborative digitisation (e.g. e-docs); and (iii) emerging digital solutions (e.g. DLT). This corroborates findings in the ADB's most recent trade finance survey, whereby 80% of banks responded that they expect digitalisation will reduce the cost of complying with regulatory requirements and due diligence (DiCaprio *et al.*, 2017). Perhaps some of the most talked about in the trade finance industry are ones that leverage DLT, as they, through immutability mechanisms and shared ownership, fundamentally alter the transparency of financial flows and provide a permanent and fully accessible history of all information entered into the ledger. While we are still at the cusp of their integration into the financial industry, their potential for reducing the time and cost of KCY, KYCC and KYT assessments while increasing the accuracy of these, such AML and CTF processes, is enormous.

In 2014 SWIFT released the KYC Registry. This and other data utilities employ interoperability technology to deliver a central repository of up-to-date due diligence documents and data on banks (IMF, 2017b). Though less "disruptive" than DLT, it also has offered a faster and more cost-effective solution for bank's KYC obligations. This said, over one third of the 251 respondents to the ICC's 2018 trade finance survey said they do not use a KYC utility due to cost, operational implications and the complexity of technical integration (ICC, 2018). Meanwhile, several of the largest global banks (including Barclays, Citigroup, UBS, Santander and Deutsche Bank) are beginning to experiment with different DLT applications and other fintech solutions to overcome the various AML/CTF challenges. Fintech will enable banks to form a more accurate and unique risk appetite for certain markets and customer segments. Interestingly, the ADB's 2017 survey found that 66% of institutions – particularly smaller banks – expect digitisation to enhance their ability to assess SME risk (DiCaprio *et al.*, 2017). However, rejection rates of SMEs remain elevated. Until the adoption of digitalisation is more widespread among financial institutions, and the technical integration costs and operational barriers associated with fintechs are overcome, it is all too tempting to establish a blanket risk threshold for a given customer type, and thus exclude potentially viable transactions.

Digitalisation and advances in technology also present new modes of doing business, potential cost savings and other efficiencies for exporters. Demand-side fintech solutions have been defined in the ADB's recent survey as crowdfunding, peer-to-peer (P2P) lending and debt-based securities. While trade finance providers appear to be embracing the benefits of digitalisation in their provision of trade finance, the potential for fintechs to bridge demand-side deficiencies appears to be less known. Only around 20% of all surveyed firms in the ADB's most recent "Trade Finance Gap, Growth, and Jobs Survey" reported using digital finance platforms (DiCaprio et al., 2017). Among those firms, 38% also received bank finance (i.e. they used fintech to diversify their financing), and P2P lending is the dominant type of fintech used. Interestingly, the ADB's survey showed that woman-led firms (77%) are more likely to use demand-side fintech (DiCaprio et al., 2017).

In addition, a new subset of fintech companies, known as "regtech" have surfaced, posing innovative technological solutions to regulatory requirements across industries, including financial services. Their focus includes: improved automation and linking of manual processes; improved data quality; the creation of a holistic view of data; the automation of data analysis; self-learning technology; and the generation of reports that are meaningful and relevant to regulators (Martín et al., 2016). Their promise: cost-effective, timely and flexible mechanisms to increase trade surveillance, financial crime risk monitoring, AML, customer profiling and conduct risk monitoring. Fintechs and regtechs may encourage banks to grow their correspondent banking networks, and therefore, help reduce global trade finance gaps and reconnect those least linked into the financial system. The direction and depth with which these advances in digitisation and technology will influence the trade finance industry over the next few years is not assured. Nevertheless, as fintech and regtech solutions gain traction, the marginal cost and effort required to serve clients will fall and banks will be provided with a greater opportunity to look to SMEs to build scale (Ramachandran et al., 2017a). Hence, it will be important for industry players to work together to ensure that the value offered by digitalisation is leveraged to achieve greater financial inclusion. This will require trade ministers, regulators, banks, customs, shipping, logistics and fintech companies to work together to inform new regulatory, legal and technical standards.

The Role of Development Banks

Multilateral Development Banks (MDBs) and international development finance institutions are actively pursuing methods to reduce the adverse impacts of de-risking. The World Bank, IFC, IMF and other regional development banks have been active in engaging and facilitating international dialogue on the dimensions and implications of de-risking. Moreover, as per the first item of the Financial Stability Board's (FSB) 2015 action plan for addressing the decline in CBR, various multilaterals have sought to gather data and conduct surveys to better understand the issue (Starnes et al., 2017). In regions particularly impacted by the withdrawal of CBRs, multilateral development banks have engaged industry associations and other regional bodies in advocacy efforts and sought to find solutions or embark on policy-based courses of action to ensure access to trade, cross-border payments and other critical services. For example, the Caribbean Development Bank (CDB) has worked alongside regional bodies such as the Caribbean Community (CARICOM) and local groups such as the Jamaica National Building Society (JNBS) to address the decline in CBRs (IMF, 2017b). Moreover, as pressures mount on major commercial banks to add regulatory capital, the integral role that MDBs play of keeping supply chains financed through trade finance programmes (TFPs), is increasingly apparent. Just as there is evidence to suggest that public sector support through MDB trade facilitation programmes helped to stabilise trade finance markets during the financial crisis, so too do they remain relevant today post-crisis.

As discussed by Beck and DiCaprio in the previous chapter of this Handbook, not only do TFPs facilitate short-term guarantees to confirming banks, covering both the commercial and political risks of international trade credit transactions emanating from issuing banks, some MDBs also provide revolving credit facilities directly to specified companies and banks. In doing so, these programmes try to address the lack of availability of trade finance for countries with little access to international markets and/or no or low international ratings, and for small transactions. They also aim at increasing the capacity of local banks and traders to handle themselves in trade finance operations through training. Gaps specifically exist for smaller transactions in countries with little access to international markets and/or no or low international ratings. In such countries, even where the banking system might be sound, local financial institutions do not find partners to share the relatively limited risk of financing or guaranteeing short-term trade transactions. Therefore, by providing short-term guarantees to banks covering commercial and political risks of international trade credit transactions emanating from local banks, MDBs play a crucial role in financing trade. Over 75% of bank respondents indicated that the TFPs of multilateral development banks – such as the European Bank of Reconstruction and Development (EBRD), ADB and Inter-American Development Bank (IDB), among others – were narrowing trade finance gaps, according to a 2016 ADB survey (ADB, 2016). In 2017, MDBs helped facilitate over US$30 billion worth of trade in countries with the greatest trade finance shortfalls (ICC, 2018). More generally, these programmes have proven effective for addressing market gaps – be they cyclical gaps which emerge during crises; or regulatory-driven structural gaps relating to transaction size; or regulatory-driven structural gaps relating to country or bank size/creditworthiness.

The Role of National Development Banks

National Development Banks (NDBs) can prove important players. They play a potentially crucial role in bridging market gaps and supporting segments of the market in local economies that have been shut out by commercial banks. Some of the main features that allow NDBs to make valuable contributions to addressing trade finance gaps and mitigating the effects of de-risking include their (i) development mandate; (ii) ability to mobilise; (iii) risk appetite level; and (iv) understanding of financial rules (Smallridge, 2013).

Development Mandate: NBDs exist to meet a public policy need. They are mandated to deliver to their shareholder (usually a public sector governing authority) a return on investment in both financial and socio-economic development terms. In other words, they must seek to generate a financial return as well as a "development dividend". Those which operate in the area of trade (Eximbanks and export credit agencies) look for economic impact of their intervention. Therefore, they operate in market gaps and meet the needs of areas of the economy that are underserved by private sources of finance. Where gaps exist in trade finance, NDBs may be well positioned to provide various forms of trade credit or risk-sharing activities with the private sector.

Ability to Mobilise: Typically, NDBs have strong relationships with the development finance community, bilateral and multilateral development finance institutions (DFIs) and borrowers. As such, they are well positioned to mobilise resources in order to serve a development financing need. In a number of countries, NDBs are the main financial player with access to hard currency borrowings as well as grants and non-reimbursable technical assistance resources. It is not in the nature of NDBs to compete. They seek to "crowd in" private financial intermediaries and be "additional" (i.e. support transactions that would not be financed otherwise). Similarly, they look to generate "demonstration effects". This means that NDB's look to lead other market participants to change their behaviour. MDBs, bilateral DFIs and foreign export credit agencies use NDBs as financial intermediaries and in turn NDBs usually look to increase their capital via credit lines from these actors.

Risk Taker: NDBs tend to have strong relationships with local private sector financial institutions and are well attuned to the myriad of factors influencing domestic markets. They understand the risks and barriers that local financial institutions encounter in providing trade finance. Moreover, as a financial institution, NDBs are risk takers. Their development mandate usually gives them a higher risk appetite than a commercial bank and thus leads them to accept certain risks that private sector entities cannot or will not take. Therefore, they are able to go down market to smaller transactions and be a trade finance player for smaller transactions/market segments (such as the women-led SMEs discussed earlier). They are also able to step in and assume the role of "collateral provider" by providing a guarantee.

Understanding of Financial System: NDBs are first and foremost financial institutions and are therefore in the business of financing and risk taking. Moreover, they are designed to work with the grain of their local financial system. Some are required to operate under the same bank supervision rules as their respective domestic commercial banks; others – overseen instead by a specific governing body – are not. Nevertheless, by virtue of being an agent for executing national development strategies, NDBs have a unique relationship with bank supervisors, occupying a seat at the same table when it comes to public policy.

In general, MDBs and NDBs can expand their range of instruments to fill trade finance gaps and further support banks and underserved markets (SMEs) in emerging economies, for example, through the provision of trade credit insurance or risk-sharing activities with the private sector. MDBs can also provide technical assistance to help affected countries strengthen their regulatory and supervisory frameworks to meet relevant international standards. Table 9.1 summarises some of the ways development banks can play an important role in addressing regulatory-driven market gaps.

MDBs and NDBs can support domestic banks to utilise technology to improve their due diligence processes, timeliness and the quality of information provided for correspondent banks and thus mitigate further decline of CBRs. Many local banks use manual processes in on-boarding new customers and when monitoring the

Table 9.1   Importance of development bank contributions

Areas an MDB/NDB can contribute	Examples
Facilitating policy dialogue	• Facilitate policy dialogue between regulators, trade minister and domestic financial institutions with a view to demystify regulation, exploring unintended consequences and moving towards greater harmonisation between countries • Enhance support to emerging market regulators in developing compliance regulations
Financing	• Provide additional capital and liquidity by investing directly in and with correspondent banks to sustain and/or expand their CBRs • "Fill the gap" through innovative product offerings and trade finance programmes
Capacity-building	• Provide technical assistance to local banks to improve the transparency of their KYC, AML and CFT processes and meet the standards of international counterparts • Provide training on international and local compliance regulations
Technology investment	• Invest in, and promote, innovative technologies that are able to address challenges associated with access to finance in emerging economies
Reduce information barriers	• Support the development of central registries for respondent customer data • Support the development of national identity registries for KYC due diligence

business relationships against potential money-laundering or terrorism-financing risks. This is a slow process and unlikely to instil confidence among correspondent banks as to the quality of the respondent bank's risk management processes. As an initial step, supporting these banks to implement a simple level of digitalisation – for example in account documentation – would help streamline compliance and reduce the customer due diligence in the long run. It would obviate the pressure on local banks to go as far as investing in comprehensive new fintechs and regtechs themselves.

Conclusion

The road ahead is uncertain. Global banks and the largest financial institutions are stepping in to take a lead on the development of these "disruptive" technologies. Time will tell what is truly disruptive and what is merely trending as these technologies become mainstream and genuinely facilitate new ways of doing business and communicating across borders. Commercial banks, lenders, MDBs and NDBs need to keep up with the technology curve because it will offer opportunities to improve business efficiency, transparency and so forth. However, the promise of new opportunities presented by advances in technology must be tempered with an understanding that new technologies also present new risks, new systems, integration challenges and legal questions. Given this, there is not a quick-fix plug to place in the

US$1.5 billion trade finance gap. The coordinated efforts of industry stakeholders, MDBs and NDBs are required.

Alongside this, national trade ministers and bank supervisors – each with their own missions and mandates – are well-advised to work together on considering and weighing the implications of regulation on their local economies to ensure that authentic, but underserved, businesses and exporters have an opportunity to flourish.

References

Accuity (2017) Derisking and the Demise of Correspondent Banking Relationships. Retrieved from: https://s3-eu-west-1.amazonaws.com/cjp-rbi-accuity/wp-content/uploads/2018/04/18170221/0037_Accuity_Derisking-and-the-demise-of-correspondent-banking-relationships-%E2%80%93-A-research-report-by-Accuity-Report.pdf (accessed 8 July 2019).

African Development Bank (2014a) *Trade Finance in Africa*. Abidjan: African Development Bank.

African Development Bank (2014b) *Fostering Development Through Trade Finance*. Abidjan: African Development Bank: Trade Finance Division.

Asian Development Bank (2016) Global Trade Finance Gap Reaches $1.6 Trillion, SMEs Hardest Hit. Retrieved from: https://www.adb.org/news/global-trade-finance-gap-reaches-16-trillion-smes-hardest-hit-adb (accessed 8 July 2019).

Auboin, M. & DiCaprio, A. (2017) Why Do Trade Finance Gaps Persist: And Does it Matter for Trade and Development. *World Trade Organization Working Paper* ERSD-2017-01 / *Asian Development Bank Institute Working Paper* No. 702. Retrieved from: https://www.adb.org/sites/default/files/publication/236486/adbi-wp702.pdf (accessed 8 July 2019).

Bank of Uganda (2018) What We Do. Retrieved from: https://www.bou.or.ug/bou/about/what_we_do.html (accessed 8 July 2019).

Basel Committee on Banking Supervision (2017) Consultative Document Guidelines: Sound Management of Risks Related to Money Laundering and Financing of Terrorism. Bank for International Settlements. Retrieved from: https://www.bis.org/bcbs/publ/d405.pdf (accessed 8 July 2019).

Brandi, C., Schmitz, B. & Hambloch, C. (2014) The Availability of Trade Finance: A Challenge for Global Economic Governance. German Development Institute briefing paper. Retrieved from: https://www.die-gdi.de/uploads/media/BP_1.2014.pdf (accessed 8 July 2019).

Boyce, T. and Kendall, P. (2016) Decline in Correspondent Banking Relationships: Economic and Social Impact on the Caribbean and Possible Solutions. Caribbean Development Bank Policy Brief.

Caribbean Policy Research Institute (CaPRI) (2016) The Correspondent Banking Problem: Impact of De-Banking Practices on Caribbean Economies. Caribbean Policy Research Institute, Report No. 154. Retrieved from: https://capricaribbean.org/sites/default/files/public/documents/report/the_correspondent_banking_problem.pdf (accessed 8 July 2019).

Centre for the Promotion of Imports from Developing Countries (CBI) (2013) *Access to Trade Finance: First-hand Perspectives on Bottlenecks and Impacts for SME Exporters in the South*. The Hague: Ministry of Foreign Affairs of the Netherlands.

COMCEC (Standing Committee for Economic and Commercial Cooperation of the Organization of the Islamic Cooperation) (n.d.) Cooperation Areas: Trade. Retrieved from: http://www.comcec.org/en/cooperation-areas/trade/ (accessed 8 July 2019).

DiCaprio, A., Kim, K. & Beck, S. (2017) 2017 Trade Finance Gaps, Growth, and Jobs Survey. Mandaluyong: Asian Development Bank. *ADB Briefs* No. 83.

Drammeh, L. (2017) Access to Trade Finance for SMEs and First-Time Clients of Banks in Africa – From the Perspective of Financial Institutions. In: Malaket, A.R., Broom, D., Evans, M. *et al.* (eds.) *2017 Rethinking Trade and Finance*. Paris: International Chamber of Commerce, pp. 204–207.

Engel, J. & Reis, J.G. (2018) Global Economic Outlook: Protectionism and Reform Complacency Could Imperil a Sustained Recovery. In: Malaket, A.R., Broom, D., Evans, M. *et al.* (eds.) *2018 Global Trade – Securing Future Growth*. Paris: International Chamber of Commerce, pp. 25–31.

Financial Action Task Force (2014) FATF Clarifies Risk-based Approach: Case-by-Case, Not Wholesale De-risking. Retrieved from: http://www.fatf-gafi.org/publications/fatfgeneral/documents/rba-and-de-risking.html (accessed 8 July 2019).

Financial Action Task Force (2017) Who We Are. Retrieved from: http://www.fatf-gafi.org/about/ (accessed 8 July 2019).

Garg, H. (2017) SWIFT Trade Finance Traffic: 2016 Statistics. In: Malaket, A.R., Broom, D., Evans, M. *et al.*(eds.) *2017 Rethinking Trade and Finance*. Paris: International Chamber of Commerce, pp 88–99.

Government of Uganda (2015) *Second National Development Plan (NDP II) 2015/16–2019/20*. Retrieved from: https://consultations.worldbank.org/Data/hub/files/consultation-template/materials/ndpii-final11.pdf (accessed 8 July 2019).

Grasshoff, G., Mogul, Z., Pfuhler, T. *et al.* (2017) Global Risk 2017: Staying the Course in Banking. Boston Consulting Group. Retrieved from: http://image-src.bcg.com/BCG_COM/BCG-Staying-the-Course-in-Banking-Mar-2017_tcm9-146794.pdf (accessed 8 July 2019).

Grigoryeva, E., Morrison, N., Mason, C.H.J. & Gardiner, L (eds.) (2007) *Banking on Sustainability: Financing Environmental and Social Opportunities in Emerging Markets*. Washington, DC. International Finance Corporation. Retrieved from: http://documents.worldbank.org/curated/en/434571468339551160/pdf/392230IFC1Bank1tainability01PUBLIC1.pdf (accessed 8 July 2019).

Institute of International Finance & Ernst and Young (2016) Eighth Annual global IIF/EY Bank Risk Management Survey: Restore, Rationalise, and Reinvent. Retrieved from: https://www.ey.com/Publication/vwLUAssets/ey-eighth-annual-global-eyiif-bank-risk-management-survey/$FILE/ey-eighth-annual-global-eyiif-bank-risk-management-survey.pdf (accessed 19 July 2019)

International Chamber of Commerce (2016a) 2016 Rethinking Trade Finance. ICC Report No. 878E.

International Chamber of Commerce (2016b) ICC Trade Register Report 2016: Global Risks in Trade Finance. Retrieved from:http://image-src.bcg.com/Images/ICC_Trade%20Register%20Report_2016_WEB2_tcm9-140866.pdf (accessed 8 July 2019).

International Chamber of Commerce (2017) ICC Global Survey on Trade Finance and Supply Chain Finance 2017. In: Malaket, A.R., Broom, D., Evans, M. *et al.* (eds.) *2017 Rethinking Trade and Finance*. Paris: International Chamber of Commerce, pp. 66–87.

International Chamber of Commerce (2018) ICC Global Survey on Trade Finance: Where Banks Stand on Strategy and Operations. In: Malaket, A.R, Broom, D., Evans, M. *et al.* (eds.) *2018 Global Trade – Securing Future Growth*. Paris: International Chamber of Commerce, pp. 41–59.

International Finance Corporation (2017a) Impact of MDB Trade Facilitation Programs: Regional Insights. In: Malaket, A.R, Broom, D., Evans, M. *et al.* (eds.) *2017 Rethinking Trade and Finance*. Paris: International Chamber of Commerce, pp. 168–189.

International Finance Corporation (2017b) Greening the Banking System: Experiences from the Sustainable Banking Network. Input Paper for the G20 Green Finance Study Group. International Finance Corporation and Sustainable Banking Network. Retrieved from: https://www.ifc.org/wps/wcm/connect/413da3f3-f306-4e99-8eee-679768463130/SBN_PAPER_G20_02102017.pdf?MOD=AJPERES (accessed 8 July 2019).

International Monetary Fund (2017a) *World Economic Outlook: Seeking Sustainable Growth: Short-Term Recovery, Long-Term Challenges.* Retrieved from: https://www.imf.org/en/Publications/WEO/Issues/2017/09/19/world-economic-outlook-october-2017 (accessed 8 July 2019).

International Monetary Fund (2017b) Recent Trends in Correspondent Banking Relationships — Further Considerations. Retrieved from: https://www.imf.org/~/media/Files/Publications/PP/031617.ashx (accessed 8 July 2019)

International Monetary Fund (2018) *World Economic Outlook, April 2018: Cyclical Upswing, Structural Change.* Retrieved from: https://www.imf.org/en/Publications/WEO/Issues/2018/03/20/world-economic-outlook-april-2018 (accessed 5 July 2019).

International Monetary Fund (2019) *World Economic Outlook, April 2019: Growth Slowdown, Precarious Recovery.* Retrieved from: https://www.imf.org/en/Publications/WEO (accessed 19 July 2019)

Kaminski, P. & Robu, K. (2016) Compliance in 2016: More than Just Following Rules. McKinsey & Company. Retrieved from: https://www.mckinsey.com/business-functions/risk/our-insights/compliance-in-2016-more-than-just-following-rules (accessed 8 July 2019).

Kim, K., DiCaprio, A. & Beck, S. (2017) Analysis of Global Trade Finance Gaps. In: Malaket, A.R., Broom, D., Evans, M. *et al.* (eds.) *2017 Rethinking Trade and Finance.* Paris: International Chamber of Commerce, pp. 102–109.

LexisNexis (2016) *Uncover the True Cost of Anti-Money Laundering & KYC Compliance.* LexisNexis Risk Solutions. Retrieved from: https://www.lexisnexis.com/risk/intl/en/resources/research/true-cost-of-aml-compliance-apac-survey-report.pdf (accessed 8 July 2019).

LexisNexis & ACAMS (2015) Current Industry Perspectives into Anti-Money Laundering Risk Management and Due Diligence. Retrieved from: https://www.acams.org/money-laundering-risk-management-survey/ (accessed 19 July 2019)

Martín, A., Casadas, V., Hernanz, I. *et al.* (2016) RegTech, The New Magic Word in FinTech. BBVA Research. Retrieved from: https://www.bbvaresearch.com/wp-content/uploads/2016/03/Banking-Outlook-Q116_Cap6.pdf (accessed 8 July 2019).

Mnuchin, S.T. & Phillips, C.S. (2017) A Financial System That Creates Economic Opportunities: Nonbank Financials, Fintech and Innovation (Executive Order 13772 on Core Principles for Regulating the United States Financial System). US Department of the Treasury. Retrieved from: https://home.treasury.gov/sites/default/files/2018-07/A-Financial-System-that-Creates-Economic-Opportunities---Nonbank-Financi....pdf (accessed 8 July 2019).

MTIC (Uganda Ministry of Trade, Industry and Cooperatives) (2017) About Us. Retrieved from: http://www.mtic.go.ug/index.php?option=com_content&view=article&id=14&Itemid=125 (accessed 8 July 2019).

Nixon, K., Spoth, C. & Strachan, D. (2016) *Navigating the Year Ahead: Banking Regulatory Outlook 2017.* Deloitte: Center for Regulatory Strategy Americas. Retrieved from: https://www2.deloitte.com/content/dam/Deloitte/us/Documents/regulatory/us-banking-regulatory-outlook-2017.pdf (accessed 8 July 2019).

Ramachandran, S., Porter, J., Kort, R. *et al.* (2017a) Digital Innovation in Trade Finance (white paper). Boston Consulting Group and SWIFT. Retrieved from: https://www.swift.com/sites/default/files/resources/swift_bcg_swiftfocus_white_paper.pdf (accessed 8 July 2019).

Ramachandran, S., Porter, J., Hanspal, R. & Harwood, K. (2017b) Evolving Trade Flows and Trade Corridors, Reconfiguration of Global Supply Chains and Sourcing Patterns. In: Malaket, A.R, Broom, D., Evans, M. *et al.* (eds.) *2017 Rethinking Trade and Finance.* Paris: International Chamber of Commerce, pp. 52–65.

Sénéchal, T. (2018) Multilateral Development Banks: No Letup on Expansion. In: Malaket, A.R., Broom, D., Evans, M. *et al.* (eds.) *2018 Global Trade – Securing Future Growth.* Paris: International Chamber of Commerce, pp. 91–108.

Smallridge, D., Buchner, B., Trabacchi, C. *et al.* (2013) The Role of National Development Banks in Catalyzing International Climate Finance. Inter-American Development Bank. Retrieved from: https://unfccc.int/sites/default/files/jj_gomez.pdf (accessed 8 July 2019).

Starnes, S., Kurdyla M. & Alexander, A.J. (2016) De-Risking by Banks in Emerging Market – Effects and Responses for Trade. International Finance Corporation. Retrieved from: https://www.ifc.org/wps/wcm/connect/3dc1cc57-2ab3-4eab-8018-f93203d5a00b/EMCompass+Note+24+De-risking+and+Trade+Finance+11-15+FINAL.pdf?MOD=AJPERES (accessed 8 July 2019).

Starnes, S., Kurdyla, M., Prakash, A. *et al.* (2017) De-Risking and Other Challenges in the Emerging Market Financial Sector: Findings from IFC's Survey on Correspondent Banking. International Finance Corporation. Retrieved from: http://documents.worldbank.org/curated/en/895821510730571841/pdf/121275-WP-IFC-2017-Survey-on-Correspondent-Banking-in-EMs-PUBLIC.pdf (accessed 8 July 2019).

Stein, P., Ardic, O.P. & Hommes, M. (2013) Closing the Credit Gap for Formal and Informal Micro, Small, and Medium Enterprises. International Finance Corporation. Retrieved from: https://www.ifc.org/wps/wcm/connect/4d6e6400416896c09494b79e78015671/Closing+the+Credit+Gap+Report-FinalLatest.pdf?MOD=AJPERES (accessed 8 July 2019).

Stupnytska, A., Koch, K., MacBeath, A. *et al.* (2014) Giving Credit Where Is Due: How Closing the Credit Gap for Women-Owned SMEs Can Drive Global Growth. Goldman Sachs. Retrieved from: https://www.goldmansachs.com/insights/public-policy/gmi-folder/gmi-report-pdf.pdf (accessed 8 July 2019).

Tavan, D. (2013) The Banker: Basel III Reshapes Trade Finance. Retrieved from: http://www.thebanker.com/Transactions-Technology/Trading/Basel-III-reshapes-trade-finance (accessed 8 July 2019).

The Economist (2017) A Decade After the Crisis, How Are the World's Banks Doing? Retrieved from: https://www.economist.com/news/special-report/21721503-though-effects-financial-crisis-2007-08-are-still-reverberating-banks-are (accessed 8 July 2019).

Thieffry, C. (2016) Basel III and Commodity Trade Finance: An Update. *Journal of International Banking Law and Regulation*, 31(3), 124–132.

Thompson, M. (2018) TXF-ICC Export Finance Survey: Profits Hold Up Amid Mixed Views on the Market. In: Malaket, A.R., Broom, D., Evans, M. *et al.* (eds.) *2018 Global Trade – Securing Future Growth*. Paris: International Chamber of Commerce, pp. 75–90.

Thomson Reuters (2015) Regulatory Changes and Stiffer Fines are a Call to Action for Smarter KYC & AML Compliance. Originally retrieved from: https://blogs.thomsonreuters.com.

Thomson Reuters (2016) Know Your Customer Surveys Reveal Escalating Costs and Complexity. Retrieved from: https://www.thomsonreuters.com/en/press-releases/2016/may/thomson-reuters-2016-know-your-customer-surveys.html (accessed 8 July 2019).

Women's World Banking (2014) Global Best Practices in Banking Women-Led SMEs. Women's World Banking and European Bank of Reconstruction and Development. Retrieved from: https://www.ebrd.com/documents/gender/global-best-practices-banking.pdf (accessed 8 July 2019).

World Bank (2015) Withdrawal from Correspondent Banking: Where, Why, and What to Do about It. Finance and Markets Global Practice, The World Bank Group. Retrieved from: http://documents.worldbank.org/curated/en/113021467990964789/pdf/101098-revised-PUBLIC-CBR-Report-November-2015.pdf (accessed 8 July 2019).

World Bank Group (2018) Environmental Health and Safety Guidelines. Retrieved from: www.ifc.org/ehsguidelines (accessed 19 July 2019).

World Trade Organization (WTO) (2010) The Trade Situation in 2009–10. Retrieved from: https://www.wto.org/english/res_e/booksp_e/anrep_e/wtr10-1_e.pdf (accessed 5 July 2019).

World Trade Organization (WTO) (2017a) Overview of Developments in the International Trading Environment. Trade Policy Review Body, World Trade Organization. Report No.

WT/TPR/OV/20. Retrieved from: https://www.wto.org/english/news_e/news17_e/trdev_04dec17_e.pdf (accessed 5 July 2019).

World Trade Organization (WTO) (2017b) Joint Ministerial Statement: Declaration on the Establishment of a WTO Informal Work Programme for MSMEs. Ministerial Conference Proceedings: Buenos Aires, 10–13 December 2017. Report No. WT/MIN(17)/58, p. 2. Retrieved from: https://docs.wto.org/dol2fe/Pages/SS/directdoc.aspx?filename=q:/WT/MIN17/58.pdf (accessed 5 July 2019).

World Trade Organization Secretariat (2016) Trade Finance and SMEs: Bridging the Gaps in Provision. Retrieved from: https://www.wto.org/english/res_e/booksp_e/tradefinsme_e.pdf (accessed 5 July 2019).

Zakai, H. & Thompson, M. (2017) Export Finance Market Trends. In: Malaket, A.R., Broom, D., Evans, M. *et al.* (eds.) *2017 Rethinking Trade and Finance*. Paris: International Chamber of Commerce, pp. 138–147.

Chapter 10

Trade and Illicit Flows: A Case Involving the United States, China and Mexico

Nikos Passas

Introduction

Despite several major US domestic and international initiatives since 9/11, there remain significant opportunities for criminals and terrorists to evade efforts to detect and intercept their illicit activities within the global flows of money, people and goods. Financial controls, in particular, have been stepped up to try to address serious crime and security challenges. These controls are embedded within a national and international legal and institutional infrastructure that has been developed to combat proliferation activities, money laundering, terrorism finance, corruption, tax evasion and sanctions violations. Nonetheless, even if all countries and jurisdictions were to fully embrace and effectively apply the measures that are now in place, there would still be a general lack of transparency and traceability in the commercial transactions associated with the movement of goods (Passas, 2012, 2011, 2006). There also remain significant shortcomings with the current US and international cargo security programmes that rely on rudimentary intelligence-based targeting tools and an extremely limited number of non-intrusive inspections and even fewer physical examinations of cargo containers (Cassara, 2016; Flynn, 2008; Flynn 2012; Bakshi *et al.*, 2011; Young, 2017). Consequently, criminals and terrorist groups have been able to hide very high levels of illicit money flows by exploiting the limited monitoring of commercial trade through false invoicing, diversion and other fraudulent practices (Baker *et al.*, 2014; Bindner, 2016; DeKieffer, 2005; Passas, 1994; Passas and Nelken, 1993; Zdanowicz, 2009; Zdanowicz *et al.*, 1995). Additionally, currency, narcotics, weapons and other contraband continue to be smuggled within international cargo shipments (Erickson 2015; OECD, 2018).

National and international security, as well as private sector profitability, increasingly depend on making not just financial global flows visible and traceable, but the

The Handbook of Global Trade Policy, First Edition. Edited by Andreas Klasen.
© 2020 John Wiley & Sons Ltd. Published 2020 by John Wiley & Sons Ltd.

flows of trade as well. Inter alia, this requires enhancing the analytical capabilities to support the work of inspectors and investigators as well as the deployment of new technological tools that can validate the legitimacy of goods moving through the global transportation system. The goal should be to develop the means to reliably verify the contents of trade flows, thereby deterring trade-based money laundering and supporting efforts to detect and interdict contraband. Unfortunately, the current practices by law enforcement and regulatory agencies including Customs and Border Protection (CBP), Immigration and Customs Enforcement (ICE) and the Financial Crimes Enforcement Center (FinCEN) fall well short of this goal. While improvements have been made on integrating various databases and enhancements have been made to the software that supports data-mining, there remain large data gaps that preclude assembling a detailed picture against which the detection of irregularities can be done efficiently and effectively. Since many analysts and investigators have limited confidence in the efficacy of new data-mining and decision-support tools, they end up relying on time-honoured methods for identifying suspicious transactions. While these methods may work for catching common criminals, they are no match for the latest tactics of sophisticated offenders and terrorist groups.

Despite well-documented shortcomings of data- and intelligence-based targeting tools, most cargo moves through the international trade system and across US borders without being subjected to inspection. This is true even though a 2007 US law mandates that 100% of US-bound cargo be subjected to non-intrusive scanning at the overseas port of loading. According to testimony by Kevin McAleenan, the then Assistant Commissioner for CBP's Office of Field Operations, before the House Subcommittee of Border and Maritime Security on 6 February 2012, the total number of containers inspected overseas in 2011 prior to shipment to the United States was just 45,500. This represents 0.5% of the 9.5 million manifests that CBP stated that the agency reviewed overseas in advance of loading. If the 45,500 number is divided by 365 days and the 58 Container Security Initiative (CSI) ports where US inspectors have been deployed overseas, the result is that these inspectors are examining with their foreign counterparts, on average, 2.15 containers per day per port before they are loaded on carriers bound for the United States (Flynn, 2012). Upon arrival in the United States, only 1–3% of containers are being subjected to some form of non-intrusive scanning to confirm if the contents match the declared cargo manifests. As the continuing occurrence of smuggling, trade fraud and cargo theft makes clear, there remains a long way to go in securing global supply chains against illicit trade (Oxford Economics, 2018). This includes preventing the scenario of transportation conveyances being used as a weapon of mass destruction (WMD) delivery device (Bakshi *et al.*, 2011).

With sobering implications for North American security, Mexican criminal groups have been particularly adroit at capitalising on the myriad shortcomings of US efforts to monitor and police global trade flows. The power of these organisations is undermining governance in Mexico through corruption and violence. Drugs and arms are big business, and Mexican traffickers have had little trouble in laundering their ill-gotten gains in ways that damage the Mexican economy. Their schemes include variations on what is known as black market peso exchange (BMPE), which was first developed by Colombian traders in the 1960s and then used by drug traffickers for money laundering (Dellinger, 2008; US Congress, 1999).

As early as 2000, law enforcement officials found evidence that Mexican drug traffickers were using non-bank financial institutions to send dirty money to China to purchase goods such as clothing items. These goods were exported to Mexico through the US in-bond system. After the goods arrived in the United States for trans-shipment to Mexico, the process was manipulated at the border to falsely declare the cargo to be US-manufactured goods, thus avoiding the very high Mexican Customs duties applied to many Chinese imports. These goods were then sold within the Mexican economy at discounted rates, providing traffickers with "clean" pesos for their illicit proceeds. These schemes have benefited from the nominal oversight by US authorities of outbound commercial trade flows into Mexico as well as the limited effort by Customs authorities on both sides of the border to fully exploit proven technological tools and applications for better detecting fraudulent shipments (Wilkinson and Ellingwood, 2011).

This study illustrates the fragmented, unsystematic and wasteful way in which trade integrity is approached not only in Mexico and the United States but also globally. It is consistent with the view that efforts to counter illicit trade are inadequate even though data exists, software for big data analytics is available and expertise can be found to make optimal use of these resources (Passas, 2016). The study uncovered preliminary evidence, gathered from active and retired law enforcement officials, of substantial outflows of US dollars to China through money service businesses (MSBs) that suggest remitters and agents engaged in purposeful actions to reduce the risk their transactions would be identified as suspicious by government authorities. The study also identifies ways that existing data and technologies could be improved upon to help reveal ongoing conspiracies, identify likely offenders and support the seizure of criminal assets to the extent that strong investigative clues, hints and leads can be produced by the suggested approach, so that both government and private sector leaders will be able to undertake a more comprehensive and systematic approach to preventing criminal and terrorist groups from exploiting global trade flows for nefarious purposes. This study also finds that, given the significant limitations of current intelligence-based analytical tools, efforts to improve those tools should be made in parallel with more widely deploying technologies that can support the monitoring and non-intrusive scanning of cargo and conveyances.

The chapter proceeds as follows. It first outlines the methods and data used for the study. It then provides some information about the processes that have been developed by US Customs authorities for detecting and intercepting criminal activities within trade movements. It then proceeds to examine the vulnerabilities of trade-based money laundering in cargo flows across the US–Mexican border. It then provides evidence of transaction irregularities revealed by this study that suggest that trade-based money laundering involving China, the United States and Mexico is ongoing, while also identifying additional problem areas that warrant close attention by US and Mexican authorities. The chapter concludes with some recommended next steps to address the serious issues highlighted by the study.

Methods and Data

The study began with a review of open-source materials and interviews with enforcement officials in Washington, DC, and Arizona. Data for financial flows from and to the southwest US states via non-bank financial institutions were collected by the

Arizona Attorney General's office and shared with Northeastern University according to terms governed by a Memorandum of Understanding. Specifically, the focus was on fund transfers from three US states (Arizona, California and Texas) to China. The objective was to identify irregularities in US–China flows outside the banking sector where trade finance and related transactions are normally done. Finally, a sample of private sector data on import/export activities was collected from the commercially available Port Import/Export Reporting Service (PIERS) database that tracks information on US imports and exports to assess the likelihood that goods exported from China to Mexico were moving through the US in-bond system to Texas where they could potentially be compromised before they were sent on to Mexico.

Detecting and Intercepting Criminal Activities within Legitimate Trade Movements

After 9/11, the two groups of officials that made up the then-US Customs Service inspectors and agents were split into separate agencies that were incorporated into the new Department of Homeland Security. The inspectors were placed within CBP, where they were assigned oversight of the arrival and payment of duty on cargo. The agents were placed in ICE. While the responsibilities of inspectors and investigators remained relatively unchanged, their activities ended up becoming more isolated from each other. Ironically, while the attacks of 9/11 resulted in efforts intended to strengthen collaboration and information-sharing across the intelligence community, the CBP/ICE split had just the opposite outcome, disrupting longstanding intra-agency collaborative arrangements between inspectors and agents.

For instance, once the US Customs Service was broken apart, agents in ICE lost their capacity to directly access the automated commercial data systems operated by CBP. CBP inspectors, in turn, do not have routine access to the Data Analysis & Research for Trade Transparency System (DARTTS), a proprietary system developed to create a common interface for a variety of entry-related documents including Automated Manifest System (AMS), Automated Commercial System (ACS), Custom and Border Protection Form 7501 (goods "Entry Summary"), Currency and Monetary Instrument Reports (CMIR), Currency Transaction Reports (CTR), Foreign Bank and Financial Accounts Reports (FBAR), Suspicious Activity Reports (SARs), Form 8300 (Reporting Domestic Currency Transactions) and a wide collection of import and export data provided to the United States by other countries. At present, DARTTS is mainly distributed to a select group of criminal investigators. Additionally, the division of data and tools ended up fragmenting established control systems, potentially raising the risk of abuse.

While post-9/11 organisational changes had the unintended effect of eroding the ability of inspectors and agents to closely collaborate, several new initiatives were launched to enhance the capacity of Customs authorities to better detect and intercept dangerous contraband. Of greatest concern was the risk that terrorists might smuggle a WMD or nuclear-related materials into the United States concealed within the legitimate trade system. To provide more time to evaluate the risk that a cargo shipment might be present within a shipment, CBP began requiring that manifest data be transmitted electronically 24 hours before the cargo was loaded on a ship destined for the United States from an overseas port. In 2009, CBP began requiring additional information pertaining to cargo brought to the United States by vessels under the Importer Security Filing "10+2" Program. These data were then transmitted to the US National Targeting Center-Cargo to decide on whether the cargo might pose a risk and therefore should be examined. A total of 58 ports from around the globe have agreed to participate in the CSI whereby US Customs inspectors are deployed overseas to work with their counterparts to inspect cargo identified as high risk.

The Vulnerability of the In-Bond System on the US–Mexican Border

Mexican crime thrives on the profits from sales of illicit narcotics in the United States. This brings with it the attendant challenge of repatriating these earnings into Mexico. Law enforcement and media reports (Coleman, 2006; Holmes, 2012) suggest that Mexican traffickers have devised sophisticated money-laundering operations that exploit trade transactions associated with the flows of legitimate commercial products. Indeed, it is likely that illicit flows first identified by US and Mexican authorities a decade ago continue largely unabated today. The most recent mutual evaluation of Mexico's anti-money-laundering efforts is insufficient and undermined by corruption (Financial Action Task Force [FATF] and Financial Action Task Force on Latin America [GAFILAT], 2018). Specifically, what is known as the black-market peso exchange (Dellinger, 2008; James et al., 1997) or trade-based money laundering (FATF, 2006; Liao and Acharya, 2011) may be at the centre of the traffickers' money-laundering activities. These schemes involve the use of crime proceeds from across the United States to place orders for goods produced in China and other countries. These goods are then sent to Mexico or neighbouring countries and sold so as to generate pesos that appear to be derived from legitimate commercial activity. The basics of trade-based money laundering have been described in the following way.

"Instead of smuggling the money the old-fashioned way, by simply carrying it south in bags and trucks, teams of money launderers working for cartels use dollars to purchase a commodity and then export the commodity to Mexico or Colombia. Paperwork is generated that gives a patina of propriety. Drug money is given the appearance of legitimate proceeds from a trade transaction. By turning their mountain of proceeds into tomatoes, say, or bolts of Chinese fabric shipped and resold in Mexico, cartels accomplish two goals at once: They transfer earnings back home to pay bills and buy new drug supplies while converting dollars to pesos in a transaction relatively easy to explain to authorities. Long used by Colombian cartels, the scheme is becoming more popular with Mexican traffickers after new efforts to combat laundering by restricting the use of dollars. Those restrictions, plus proposed limits on cash purchases of big-ticket items such as houses and boats, make it less attractive for traffickers to hold trunks full of US cash. After many years of using dollars to buy luxury items and pay their suppliers and dealers, cartel capos have suddenly found themselves in need of pesos. Trade-based money laundering solves that problem" (Wilkinson and Ellingwood, 2011).

One way that drug traffickers have been able to get their cash into the financial system is to deposit it in multiple transactions via the non-bank financial sector in bundles under US$10,000. These smaller deposits are made to avoid triggering cash transaction reports that financial institutions are required to make to US authorities. Wire transfers can then be combined overseas to purchase textiles, toys, perfumes and other goods in Asia. A case involving the Angel Toy Corporation in Los Angeles illustrates this money-laundering scheme, which involved the collection and structured deposit of the proceeds of illegal drug sales to purchase goods from China. In this instance, the goods were shipped from China to South America, to be sold in retail outlets, from where the proceeds were passed on to the criminal entrepreneurs (Wilkinson and Ellingwood, 2011).

Mexican traffickers may also be exploiting the in-bond process that allows goods that originate outside of North America to move through the United States for delivery in Mexico. The normal routine for an in-bond shipment is for cargo to move unmolested through a trans-shipment country. However, along the Texas border with Mexico, in-bond shipping containers arriving by train from the US West Coast are offloaded on the Texas side of the border. Then, Customs bonded *cartmen* transfer them to local warehouses. *Cartmen* are subjected to a mandatory background screening by CBP and issued a licence. They are required to post a bond that will automatically be drawn upon to pay a penalty should CBP find that there has been a violation of any prescribed procedures and protocols when carrying transit cargo from one Customs location to another (e.g. from a railhead to a port). The risk of this penalty is to provide an incentive for *cartmen* to maintain constant custody and control over a shipment. However, at the common warehouse, the seal applied to the container door is broken, and the goods are then removed from the original container in which they were shipped and reloaded for movement across the border by truck.

According to interviewees, the rationale for this cumbersome repacking procedure is that it is supposed to facilitate the inspection and confirmation of the contents of the imported goods in order to ensure that they match what is described in the cargo documentation. This procedure has been advanced as a necessary contingency for lowering the risk of major delays and fines that Mexican importers face when the Mexican Customs inspection process identifies discrepancies between the shipment and the associated documentation.

The procedure of repacking in-bond container shipments on the US–Mexican border creates a significant opportunity for fraud. For one thing, the supporting paperwork provided to Mexican Customs officials could potentially be altered to declare the goods as originating in the United States instead of China. In this way, the shipment can take advantage of the terms of the North American Free Trade Agreement (NAFTA) that has fuelled a tremendous upsurge in trade between the United States and Mexico over the past quarter century. NAFTA allows for goods that originate in Mexico, Canada and the United States to be shipped within North America without incurring Customs duties. By fraudulently declaring overseas imports to be "Made in the USA", traffickers can sell the goods in Mexico at a considerable discount. Beyond the laundering of illicit profits, this illicit activity causes two other negative effects. First, the Mexican government is deprived of revenue. Second, legitimate companies who produce similar products in Mexico, or import them and pay the required duties, are placed at a competitive disadvantage when their goods must go up against those merchants.

In short, Mexican traffickers are able to take advantage of the lax oversight of in-bond shipments by US authorities to relabel Asian imports as US goods and export them duty-free to Mexico. The scale of the opportunity is likely to be considerable since each year ocean containers with billions of dollars of in-bond shipments arrive by rail in Laredo, Texas, and other border areas. Once these goods are unloaded at common warehouses and then transported by the local truckers for the short trip across the border into Mexico, they are unlikely to receive any scrutiny by US Customs inspectors.

But it should be possible to reduce this vulnerability since illicit flows invariably leave traceable marks that should raise red flags for law enforcement. For example, shippers might be making different declarations about the contents of the same shipment to authorities in the originating, transiting and final jurisdictions. If those declarations are shared and compared among Mexican, US and Chinese authorities, irregularities and discrepancies will be revealed. It would be a simple matter of (i) checking that goods stamped as exported do indeed cross the border; (ii) cross-checking declarations/export documents presented to Mexican Customs authorities about US-origin fabrics and other goods; and (iii) reviewing the declared US exporters to ensure they are legitimate traders. Additionally, data held by private sector entities involved in shipping the goods can be analysed to assist in detecting anomalies; for example, Union Pacific Railroad maintains records showing the arrival time of the in-bond containers that it transports to Laredo from the West Coast and the recipient who assumed custody of the shipment.

This important vulnerability could also be addressed by ending the practice of unloading in-bond shipments from their original container at the US side of the border and reloading them for shipment by truck into Mexico. The contents of a sealed container can be confirmed as not having changed while in transit by subjecting the container to scanning via non-intrusive inspection technology.

More close monitoring of trade flows can be an important complement to other anti-money-laundering efforts. Indeed, any effort to combat the financial crimes that facilitate serious crimes or sophisticated terrorism requires a comprehensive approach that simultaneously takes on the "challenge of three global flows": financial, commercial and informational (Passas, 2017). While significant efforts have been made to better police financial flows and to bolster the transparency and accountability of informational flows, much work remains to be done toward strengthening the integrity of physical movement of commercial flows within the international trade system. This is especially the case with the in-bond system.

Our Approach

There are several sources of data that are being routinely incorporated into efforts to better manage the risk of misconduct through trade. These include Bank Secrecy Act (BSA) financial data, arrival and departure data as declared to CBP by traders, investigation reports, criminal records and foreign government data (including Mexico). With the development of DARTTS, Customs agents and inspectors are provided with access to all these databases. In addition, Customs officials have new means to evaluate financial data that support tracking commercial and financial transactions and the movements associated with imported goods using common identifiers, such as the importer number.

Nonetheless, our study has found that there are ordinary business data that are not being used by Customs authorities, even though these data could help them make more accurate predictions of what shipments arriving in the United States could be compromised and therefore should warrant an inspection. For instance, data routinely collected by ocean carriers used to manage their cargo-handling operations could support efforts to more closely monitor the movement of cargo and identify irregularities. These data can help to develop baseline patterns of "normal" cargo movement. Such baselines can make it relatively straightforward to identify trading anomalies in much the same way as an air traffic controller can spot flights that deviate from established flight patterns. This provides a way for an investigator to develop leads. It should be possible for a third party, such as a university, to develop a system to receive, securely store and analyse business data that could then be used by inspectors and agents to develop patterns and spot anomalies.

To test this hypothesis, we set out to gather data about trans-Pacific shipments of cargo destined for Mexico via the US in-bond systems. Specifically, we received private sector data from two sources. First, we partnered with the Arizona Attorney General's office and obtained the complete dataset of financial flows collected by that office from six non-bank MSBs. Second, we obtained a small sample of commercial data provided by the PIERS. Analysis of this data appears to substantiate that trade-based money laundering is taking place using US MSBs to send funds to China to purchase Chinese low-cost goods that move through the US in-bond process so as to take advantage of the vulnerabilities in that system to enter Mexico while evading duties and tariffs.

Analysis of MSB Data and Findings

Several years ago, the southwest region of the United States organised a Southwest Border Anti-Money-Laundering Alliance that began collecting the complete set of remittances from and to the United States made through MSBs within Arizona, California and Texas. The Arizona Attorney General's office provided us with data from 3 January 2005, to 29 June 2012 for analysis. These records included information from six companies that we have designated as C1, C2, C3, C4, C5 and C6. The records include information on the sender, payee, amount, date, recording agent and paying agent, country, sender identification number, occupation, address and phone, and payee occupation. In total, the data filled 70 fields.

The Arizona Attorney General's Office relies on a consulting company to organise the MSB data it receives. An early challenge we faced in subjecting the data to analysis was that we found several problems with the reliability and accuracy of some of the fields, especially with respect to country codes, names of transaction parties, telephone numbers, sender identification numbers and addresses. We suspect (and interviewees agree) that some of these data inaccuracy problems may have arisen as a result of remitters and agents who showed little interest in ensuring transmitters provided complete and accurate information even though that information is central to the capacity for authorities to detect suspicious transactions.

One common problem was that first and family names were not in separate fields to allow proper sorting and retrieval of the information. For instance, the Arizona database listed within a single column the first name, the middle name, the last name and generational suffixes such as "senior" or "junior". It also included forms of salutation such as Mr, Mme, Miss etc. There were also problems of consistency when it came to ethnic names such as Spanish names that may include both the father's family name and the mother's family name. Some of the names were also entered in different versions (shorter and longer ones, different sequences and complete versus incomplete names). The fields were rife with typographical errors, or in some cases, fields were left totally blank.

We encountered similar problems with variations in the information provided in the address field. Many times, the telephone numbers were either empty or the entry contained random numbers, probably to avoid giving the correct information. For example, there was sometimes just the area code, or a series of zeros or simply sequential numbers such as 123, 123 – 456 – 7890, which limits the utility of the field.

There were also problems with the way country codes were entered to include inconsistencies both within and across the data provided by the six remitting companies. These included people's names added to country code field or strange combinations of numbers such as "Jesus", "Maria", "B1", "85586".

The identified problems affected the majority of the funds destined to China. We, therefore, had to create routines and clean up the data on a sample basis. Once this was done, it improved the usefulness of the data dramatically. For instance, we were able to identify when variations of the same name were used with the telephone number. We were also able to identify when multiple senders used the same telephone number. Ideally, similar routines and methods could be replicated by the Southwest Border Anti-Money Laundering Task Force to clean up the entire database.

One of our first steps was to do a financial volume analysis by examining total volumes and the destinations for the MSB companies. In doing this we found that the MSB designated as C5 dealt mainly with South America, and when aggregated, senders were below US$200,000 for the entire period. C4 dealt mostly in 16 countries in South America, with Mexico being the main destination. C3 dealt also with 16 countries, with Mexico again being the top declared destination or paying agent location. We found that the total amount sent to Mexico was over US$1 billion between 2005 and 2012. C1 was the largest operator, with a total of 23 million records. The top destination was again Mexico, where the total amount sent was US$7 billion during the period we examined.

C1 is the most interesting part of the database for our case study because it both illustrates problems with the data and has the largest volumes around the world. Most importantly, it is the only MSB in the database with financial flows to China. Therefore, for our purposes, it made sense to focus mostly on C1 data.

The total amount wired via C1 to China in the study period was US$1,156,566,352.61 in 597,517 transactions or an average just above US$1935 per transaction. In addition, US$421,231,818.71 went to "CN" (also China) in 228,923 transactions (average US$1840/ transaction), US$20,023,520.46 went to "Hong Kong" in 11,319 transactions (average of US$1769/transaction) and US$9,074,981.70 went to "HK" (also Hong Kong) in 5797 transactions (average of US$1565.46/transaction). Finally, US$408,648.91 was wired to Macau in 377 transactions (average of US$1083.94/ transaction). In short, the data demonstrated that a considerable amount of money is going to China in small transactions from the Southwest United States through C1.

Given that money going to China was our main interest, the next questions we wanted to answer were who has been placing funds into the financial system and sending them to China, how many of these transactions were made by the same people and what sort of irregularities could be spotted in the data. In trying to accomplish this task, one obstacle we faced was that the sender names were often missing. For instance, we found that there were nine transactions for a total of US$447,267.57 that did not list the sender names. Another obstacle was that there were clearly erroneous entries made in the records, such as "133100". Given the obligation of remitters and all MSBs to properly record identifiers for transacting parties, these practices reflect a heedless carelessness that suggests that transactions may have a suspicious origin. In some cases, there was a name but it was mistakenly placed in a different field in the database.

Once we identified the senders, we listed them by volume. This revealed that some senders were making hundreds of transactions over the period. The total value of each of these senders' transactions was often over half a million dollars. The individual transmissions averaged from more than US$1000 to just under US$7000 per transaction (amounts below the US$10,000 level avoid triggering a mandatory report by the MBS).

These patterns are irregular for businesses, both because legitimate importers would not use this payment vehicle and because the amounts are too structured in small pieces, which translates into the sender paying fees for making each of these many small transactions. If the funds were indeed legitimate, it does not seem likely the senders would be willing to incur these extra costs. This prompted an inquiry into the payees for these transactions, which showed lower amounts for each payee, showing that senders have been transferring funds to more than one payee over this period.

The next step was to see whether searching by the payee phone numbers would yield a better aggregator. This revealed that the phone data were extremely poor and problematic: in just one entry, for example, there were missing numbers for US$390 million and 203,543 transactions. When we narrowed the analysis to total amounts over US$500,000 in the study period, we found that hundreds of millions of dollars flow through the system to China (and other places as well) with the authorities never receiving proper information on the sender's telephone number. As we inquired more into the recipients of funds in China, our analysis revealed that the payee designated as AS25 had the highest total amount, with a value of US$1,319,943.00 and a count number of 272.

The next step was to see how much open access information we could gather on these recipients. We were able with simple online searches to track down several of them, who happened to have trading businesses. AS25 turned out to be located in Guangdong Province and has a website with company profile, contact (with the phone number we had in our data) and other details.

In another example, we found information on an individual who listed a Los Angeles, California, address and with a business listed as "China Manufacturer – T-Shirts – Apparel". In yet another example, we located information on multiple entities linked to an individual who was listed as operating a furniture company in Guangdong and Los Angeles as well as several technology companies in Shenzhen. In short, the data identified that the largest recipients of the funds appear to be traders in China, as hypothesised.

Going back to the top payee in China, AS25, we were able to link him with two senders from the United States, one of whom used two ways of entering the name field. Moreover, we found that AS25 had been using multiple telephone numbers entered in the data for different sets of transactions. Further analysis of several China payees showed that many of them were traders and used multiple telephones, multiple senders and numerous transactions in small amounts. This way of doing business makes no logical or commercial sense. The amounts and partners are too fragmented into a few thousand or hundred dollars per transaction with identifiers that are inconsistent, incomplete or missing altogether, and to reiterate, the very use of MSBs for trade purposes is unusual and costly.

To summarise, the Arizona database provided valuable insights that are suggestive that considerable funds are being moved by remitters to China to undertake trade-based money-laundering schemes. The data also point to numerous additional irregularities.

The first pattern noted was that tens of millions of dollars were going to stored value cards. In other instances warranting further inquiry, we found several senders using different telephone numbers. Some of them were Asian, but the practice goes beyond China. The extent of structuring that was going on by senders with no name entered was also found to be quite remarkable. Finally, even when a known commercial name was entered, questions can be raised with respect to the excessive number of transactions used at MSBs for very small sums, even when the total amount was in the millions.

PIERS Data

We requested PIERS data for Los Angeles in-bond shipments of goods originating in China. We received these data covering one month (January 2010), for which there were a total of 11,229 records in total. The main issue we wanted to confirm was the movement of textiles and similar goods from China through the in-bond process.

Small as the size of this sample is, the data confirm that clothing and other items do come to Los Angeles from China and go through the in-bond process, the majority of which then go to Texas, as hypothesised.

Several of the shipments go to Laredo, Texas, but much higher volume is going to Dallas, Houston and El Paso, with a smaller amount going to San Antonio and other cities.

We were not able to gain access to Customs declarations made to Mexican authorities. For this reason, we were not able to document that these in-bond fabric shipments were re-characterised as originating from the United States. A follow-on study that includes data from Mexican Customs officials could confirm this. It is important to note that the financing used in the trade-based money-laundering schemes identified in this study differs from the kinds of transactions that the banking sector normally uses in financing trade. In a legitimate trade transaction, the bank requires that contracts be signed overseas that specify the goods to be purchased, the destination of where they will be sold and the means that will be used to move the goods. These requirements are made because banks do not want to be duped into providing funds for "phantom shipments". In other words, the bank needs to be satisfied that the goods exist before it agrees to serve as the financial backer for the purchase of those goods. Further, the bank will not make payment until it is provided with the bills of lading and Customs entry documentation since it wants to be sure that the goods are not being held up by Customs authorities, but are available to be sold into the economy.

In short, for legitimate trade transactions, it is customary for importers and their bankers to be involved in the purchase of cargo from start to finish. The cargo would be picked up at the supplier site, transported to a port, loaded on a ship, moved by ship to the destination port, unloaded and delivered to the purchaser. In some instances, the goods might be put into the in-bond system for trans-shipment through the United States to the border region for importation into Canada or Mexico. All these transactions would be fully documented. For in-bond shipments, the banks would be waiting for the document showing the movement of the container across the border into Mexican territory and would likely require that Mexican Customs documents be submitted as well to verify that the goods were on their way to their intended destination. At that point, the banks would release the funds to support payment of the trade transaction. In short, when normal trade financing is involved, banks end up ensuring that there is a clean trail of documentation as a condition of underwriting the transaction.

However, when large trade purchases are being made by bundling small transactions transmitted by US-based MSBs to China, such purchases will not involve bankers looking over the importer's shoulder. Without this check in the system, a dishonest importer can more easily alter the documentation after it arrives in the United States. Normally goods moving as a part of the in-bond system would require a declaration to the Mexican authorities that the goods originated outside North America. But for the trade-based money-laundering scheme outlined in this study, the documentation can be changed to falsely declare that the goods originated from the United States without there being an auditable paper trail at a financial institution that could prove otherwise. Lacking such a basis to challenge the false declaration, Mexican Customs authorities are compelled under NAFTA rules to allow the goods into the Mexican economy without having to pay heavy Customs duties.

Next Steps

Even by drawing on a relatively small set of commercial data sources, limited in their quality, size and time duration, the study was able to uncover evidence of suspicious transactions that suggest trade-based money laundering is exploiting gaps within the US non-bank financial sector and shortcomings in the oversight of the import and in-bond system. This is taking place despite the stepped-up efforts since the attacks of 11 September 2001 to enhance the monitoring and analysis of trade data to identify anomalies that might point to supply chain security risks. Specifically, the study findings show that there are substantial flows of money moving out of the southwest region of the United States by way of MSBs. These money flows are being structured into small amounts that are well below levels that trigger a reporting requirement by the MSB. The aggregated transactions result in large amounts of money finding their way to recipients in China in ways that make no commercial sense given the fees involved. These recipients appear to include Chinese exporters who ship goods such as textiles to Mexico by way of Los Angeles and via the

US in-bond system. These shipments may not be showing up in Mexican statistics as Chinese imports. Instead, because banks are not providing financing and serving as intermediaries for these transactions, it is likely that dishonest importers are manipulating the importation process and falsely declaring to Mexican Customs authorities that the goods have originated from the United States and therefore are not subject to duties. The findings of this study also revealed additional irregularities that point to other possible fraudulent activities that warrant investigation by law enforcement authorities.

The implications of the above are threefold. First, Customs authorities have been overlooking important sources of business data that could support their efforts to more effectively detect and intercept illicit activities involving international trade flows. Second, national security officials should re-evaluate the extent to which they are relying on the current targeting capabilities of Customs authorities to identify cargo that may pose a threat. A system of controls that Mexican and US criminal organisations appear to be successfully working around to repatriate their illicit drug profits is hardly up to the task of detecting a sophisticated terrorist conspiracy intent on smuggling a WMD into the United States via the global supply chain. This leads to the third implication: a renewed effort should be made to identify and integrate new technologies that can more closely monitor and verify the contents of international trade flows.

A great deal can be accomplished towards making trade flows more transparent by simply ensuring that data are entered correctly by mandated reporters through closer monitoring of the data's quality. Also, existing data sources could be better organised and additional sources of business data could be used to provide a more comprehensive picture of all the transactions associated with a given trade flow. Collectively, these sources could be integrated into software-based analytical systems that are used by Customs inspectors and investigators looking for clues of illicit activities. The Document Archiving, Reporting, and Regulatory Tracking System (DARRTS) system can integrate all such data, as well as financial data, and enable comparisons and analysis indicating where manufacturers in the United States understate or overstate the quantity of goods they are exporting to Mexico. The DARRTS system could also be refined to support the analysis of other evidence of trade-based fraud, such as irregular pricing and the use of similar or other names to engage in nominee trade.

The goal should be to develop as detailed a picture of legitimate flows as possible, thereby creating a baseline for identifying anomalous behaviour that indicates the likelihood of illicit flows. When analysts who understand shadow financial and commercial activities evaluate anomalies, they can develop leads for investigations. These investigations are likely to result in significant asset seizures that, in turn, can help provide additional resources to fund advance training and the development of new applications to support the sustainable and long-term success of control efforts against serious crime and security threats.

Systematic comparisons should also be made between the documentation that US authorities possess for exportation of in-bond goods from the United States and the documentation that their Mexican counterparts received for the importation of goods in Mexico. Such routine reconciliation of data would allow for the detection of in-bond shipments from Asia that are fraudulently characterised as goods that originate from the United States. This study suggests that if US and Mexican enforcement agents perform this analysis, they will find, for instance, that textiles that are manufactured in China are being routinely imported into Mexico as having been "Made in the USA". Cross-border reconciliation would also detect blatant discrepancies in the reporting of quantity and value of goods.

Finally, there should be much closer monitoring of border warehouses and businesses repackaging in-bond shipments. These entities should be required to provide data on when they assume custody of in-bond goods and how and when they are loaded on "over-the-road-trucks" to move into Mexico. An even better solution would be to eliminate this procedure altogether. In-bond shipments could be scanned by using non-intrusive technology at the overseas port of loading and/or at the US port of arrival. When these goods arrive at the US–Mexican border, they could be scanned again so that US and Mexican authorities can compare the images. There should be no reason to break the seal of a bonded shipment at the US border if the images do not reveal evidence of tampering during trans-shipment.

Conclusion

Much can and should be done to improve the current efforts to detect and intercept criminal and security threats involving global supply chains. Too much commercial data is left unexamined, scattered among databases and subjected to fragmented analysis across different agency units. Adequate resources have not been allocated to harness new technologies that can make global trade flows far more visible and accountable. This reality should be a substantial cause for concern for policymakers, law enforcement agents, national security officials and civil society.

At the same time, this study points to the still largely untapped expertise that lies outside the US government that could and should be enlisted in enhancing global supply chain security. The private sector can be engaged to make their legitimate transactions more transparent so that they can be more closely monitored. Academic institutions such as Northeastern University can collect commercial and open-source data, and integrate and analyse that data to find anomalous behaviour that might point to criminal and security risks. Universities can serve as honest brokers by entering into agreements with the appropriate safeguards that allow them to undertake research by acquiring, developing, storing, updating and maintaining sensitive databases from both private and public sources across national boundaries. This research can support the development of information and control approaches that enhance private–public collaborations. Academic institutions can also assist by providing the kind of advanced training that government analysts increasingly need to do their jobs.

In a nutshell, the data needs to be systematically reviewed and analysed as follows: Most governments maintain online computer systems that are used to control the flow of goods into and leaving their respective countries. The control is typically designed to ensure the admissibility and classification of goods with the aim of accurate revenue collection and the denial of entry of goods deemed to be hazardous, unsafe or illegal. In addition, goods that can cause economic destruction of local industries require further review.

The documentation produced in the performance of these duties is usually processed (where personal and propriety information is stripped) and made available to the public.

This results in four classes of records:

1. *Inbound* manifest/movement transactions: Goods arriving by road, rail, sea and air; usually provided as manifest data detailing the who, what, where and when of goods shipped and received. These records are supplied by the carriers and shippers of such goods.

2. *Import* declarations: Goods declared to the government as entering the economy, becoming part of the goods and services of the country, where the importer performs his legal responsibilities. These documents are usually provided to the public in a form whereby individual transactions are treated to remove the particulars of individual transactions and grouped by some means that accurately reflects the totals of the import transactions.

3. *Outbound* manifest/movement transactions: Goods departing by road, rail, sea and air; usually provided as manifests detailing the who, what, where and when of goods shipped and departing. These records are supplied by the carriers and shippers of such goods.

4. *Export* declarations: Goods declared to the government as leaving the economy, becoming part of the goods and services of another country. These documents are usually provided to the public in a form where the individual transactions are treated to remove the particulars of individual transactions and grouped by some means that accurately reflects the totals of the export transactions. These types of export records are collected for and maintained for statistical purposes mainly because few countries collect duty and taxes on exportations.

The databases mentioned above are either released directly to the public by the concerned governments at their respective official websites (US import and export data can be found on websites maintained by the US Department of Commerce and International Trade Commission) or, for other countries, they may be available at the revenue producing or statistical agencies' websites.

In the case of manifest data, there are several large firms that specialise in collecting these public data. Each firm has its own niche market and processes the data offered by the governments to satisfy their customers. PIERS is available for a fee and was the source of the manifest data reviewed in this report. Similar data are collected, by PIERS and others, from other countries and are commercially available.

Other types of data are available, such as port and ship loading information. It should be noted, there are currently no commercial sources of such data, which is the heart and soul of the shipping companies' business.

In the past, the US government looked to industry to maintain documentation (supply chain correspondence) normally prepared in the course of business in lieu of providing entry documents. This approach assumed that government officials would need such data only to support investigations. Because the events of September 2011 highlighted the need to better assess the risk a cargo shipment might pose *prior* to arrival, US Customs officials began demanding that data be presented to them in advance.

Collection and analysis of these data files could provide a system, when processed by off-the-shelf computer programs, which could illuminate threats and trends deleterious to the welfare and security of the country.

This chapter attempted to review some of the above records and compare that information with records of the movement of money through a non-banking system under scrutiny. In the end, reducing the risk of global trade flows being exploited to cause harm is a mission we must all share. Hence, it is important to move beyond government-centric approaches to policing global supply chains. There is much that civil society, academia and the private sector can contribute towards enhancing cargo security. An important stepping-off point is for Customs authorities to acknowledge that significant gaps exist in their current capabilities to detect and intercept illicit and dangerous goods. They should also frankly declare that they would welcome this assistance and collaboration. As noted before the US Congress,

> The answer to all of these challenges can be found by simply addressing the opportunities we have been missing up to now. As noted, all the necessary data is not in one place but does exist. Hawala is not only a problem but also an intelligence asset and resource if properly handled. Agencies that gather useful information can be encouraged to share it. Open-source data is available for analysis. The private sector and academia can assist with additional data, collection in a secure environment, analysis and feedback to both government and business with red flags and guidance. Our view is blurred thus unnecessarily. It is like having a 4K TV that we use for analog programs instead of creating the feed for a high-definition picture of the global illegal trade and finance. The means are there to create it. (N. Passas written statement and testimony at the US Congress Committee on Financial Services, Task Force to Investigate Terrorism Financing, 2016)

References

Baker, R., Clough, C., Kar, D. *et al.* (2014) Hiding in Plain Sight: Trade Misinvoicing and the Impact of Revenue Loss in Ghana, Kenya, Mozambique, Tanzania, and Uganda: 2002–2011. Global Financial Integrity. Retrieved from: http://um.dk/en/danida-en/partners/research/other//~/media/UM/English-site/Documents/Danida/Partners/Research-Org/Research-studies/Hiding%20In%20Plain%20Sight.pdf (accessed 11 July 2019).

Bakshi, N., Gans, N. & Flynn, S. (2011) Estimating the Operational Impact of Container Inspections at International Ports. *Management Science*, 57(1), 1–20.

Bindner, L. (2016) Illicit Trade and Terrorism Financing. Center for the Analysis of Terrorism. Retrieved from: http://cat-int.org/wp-content/uploads/2017/03/Interim-note-Illicit-trade-and-terrorism-financing-Dec-2016.pdf (accessed 11 July 2019).

Cassara, J.A. (2016) *Trade-Based Money Laundering: The Next Frontier in International Money Laundering Enforcement*. Hoboken: John Wiley & Sons.

Coleman, R. (2006) US and Brazilian Stings Nab Trade-Based Laundering Ring. *Money Laundering Alert* (August).

DeKieffer, D. (2005) Trade Diversion as a Fund Raising and Money Laundering Technique of Terrorist Organizations. Unpublished paper.

Dellinger, L. (2008) From Dollars to Pesos: A Comparison of the US and Colombian Anti-Money Laundering Initiatives from an International Perspective. *California Western Law Journal*, 39, 419ff.

Erickson, J.L. (2015) *Dangerous Trade: Arms Exports, Human Rights, and International Reputation*. New York: Columbia University Press.

Financial Action Task Force (2006) Trade Based Money Laundering. Financial Action Task Force, OECD. Retrieved from: https://www.fatf-gafi.org/media/fatf/documents/reports/Trade%20Based%20Money%20Laundering.pdf (accessed 11 July 2019).

Financial Action Task Force & Financial Action Task Force on Latin America (El Grupo de Acción Financiera de Latinoamérica) (2018) Anti-Money Laundering and Counter-Terrorist Financing Measures: Mexico. Fourth Round Mutual Evaluation Report. FATF and GAFILAT. Retrieved from: https://www.fatf-gafi.org/media/fatf/documents/reports/mer4/MER-Mexico-2018.pdf (accessed 11 July 2019).

Flynn, S. (2008) Overcoming the Flaws in the U.S. Government Efforts to Improve Container, Cargo, and Supply Chain Security. Hearing on Container, Cargo and Supply Chain Security: Challenges and Opportunities before the Homeland Security Appropriations Subcommittee, US House of Representatives, 2 April. Retrieved from: http://opim.wharton.upenn.edu/risk/library/2008-04-02_Flynn_ImprovingContainerSecurity.pdf (accessed 11 July 2019).

Flynn, S. (2012) The New Homeland Security Imperative: The Case for Building Greater Societal and Infrastructure Resilience. Hearing on The Future of Homeland Security: Evolving and Emerging Threats before the Committee on Homeland Security and Governmental Affairs, US Senate, 11 July, pp. 114–124. Retrieved from: https://www.hsdl.org/?view&did=729192 (accessed 11 July 2019).

Holmes, C. (2012) Mexico Threat Assessment: Strategy and Countermeasures. *Southwest Border Anti-Money Laundering Alliance*, August.

James, A.C., Doody, A.J. & Passic, G. (1997) The Colombian Black Market Peso Exchange. Statement before the Subcommittee on General Oversight and Investigations Committee on Banking and Financial Services, US House of Representatives, 22 October.

Liao, J. & Acharya, A. (2011) Transshipment and Trade-Based Money Laundering. *Journal of Money Laundering Control*, 14(1), 79–92.

OECD (2018) Illicit Financial Flows: The Economy of Illicit Trade in West Africa. OECD. Retrieved from: https://www.oecd.org/development/accountable-effective-institutions/Illicit-Flows-Economy-of-Illicit-Trade-in-West-Africa.pdf (accessed 11 July 2019).

Oxford Economics (2018) Combatting Illicit Trade. Retrieved from: http://www.oxfordeconomics.com/publication/download/300615?__hstc=30812896.2d3fcf2f99a265337744294b740e0787.1554076800139.1554076800140.1554076800141.1&__hssc=30812896.1.1554076800142&__hsfp=3733277192 (accessed 11 July 2019).

Passas, N. (1994) European Integration, Protectionism and Criminogenesis: A Study on Farm Subsidy Frauds. *Mediterranean Quarterly*, 5(4), 66–84.

Passas, N. (2006) Setting Global CFT Standards: A Critique and Suggestions. *Journal of Money Laundering Control*, 9(3), 281–292.

Passas, N. (2011) Terrorist Finance, Informal Markets, Trade and Regulation: Challenges of Evidence in International Efforts. In: Lum, C. & Kennedy L.W. (eds.), *Evidence-Based Counterterrorism Policy*. New York: Springer, pp. 255–280.

Passas, N. (2012) Financial Controls and Counter-Proliferation of Weapons of Mass Destruction. *Case Western Reserve Journal of International Law*, 44(3), 747–763.

Passas, N. (2016) Collective Action for Trade Transparency against Financial Crime. *Translational Criminology*, (Spring), 16–18, 26.

Passas, N. (2017) Security Threats and Illicit Flows: What they Hide and How to Control Them. Paper presented at Dangerous Ties: How to Fight the New Networks of Terror and Crime, German Council on Foreign Relations (DGAP), Berlin.

Passas, N. & Nelken, D. (1993) The Thin Line Between Legitimate and Criminal Enterprises: Subsidy Frauds in the European Community. *Crime, Law and Social Change*, 19(3), 223–243.

United States Senate Caucus on International Narcotics Control (1999) The Black Market Peso Exchange: How US Companies Are Used to Launder Money: Hearing before the

Senate Caucus on International Narcotics Control, One Hundred Sixth Congress, First Session, 21 June 1999. Washington, DC: US Government Publishing Office. Retrieved from: https://www.govinfo.gov/content/pkg/CHRG-106shrg60125/html/CHRG-106shrg60125.htm (accessed 11 July 2019).

United States House of Representatives Committee on Financial Services, Task Force to Investigate Terrorism Financing (2016) Trading with the Enemy: Trade-Based Money Laundering Is the Growth Industry in Terror Finance: Hearing before the Task Force to Investigate Terrorism Financing of the Committee on Financial Services, US House of Representatives, One Hundred Fourteenth Congress, Second Session, 3 February 2016. Washington, DC: US Government Publishing Office. Retrieved from: https://www.hsdl.org/?abstract&did=806585 (accessed 11 July 2019).

Wilkinson, T. & Ellingwood, K. (2011) Cartels Use Legitimate Trade to Launder Money, US, Mexico Say. *Los Angeles Times* (19 December). Retrieved from: https://www.latimes.com/world/la-xpm-2011-dec-19-la-fg-mexico-money-laundering-trade-20111219-story.html (accessed 19 July 2019).

Young, A. (2017) *Trade-Based Money Laundering: Overview, Issues, Perspectives.* Hauppauge: Nova Science.

Zdanowicz, J.S. (2009) Trade-Based Money Laundering and Terrorist Financing. *Review Of Law & Economics*, 5(2), 855–878.

Zdanowicz, J.S., Welch, W.W. & Pak, S.J. (1995) Capital Flight from India to the United States Through Abnormal Pricing in International Trade. *Finance India*, IX(3), September.

Part III Global Trade and Regional Development

Chapter 11

Regional Integration: The Next Wave

Marion Jansen, Sebastian Klotz, and Jasmeer Virdee

Introduction

The nature and extent of trade has changed over time as transport technologies, production technologies and the rules of trade have evolved. As briefly discussed by Goldstein and van Lieshout in Chapter 7 of this Handbook, the multilateral trade rules currently governing world trade are a relatively recent phenomenon from a historical perspective. The General Agreement on Tariffs and Trade (GATT) celebrated its 70th anniversary in 2017. Before the existence of the GATT, international trade was largely governed by bilateral treaties among a limited numbers of players and by power relationships resulting from colonialism. The shift in global power relationships in the aftermath of World War II opened the door for a new set of rules for trade that ended up being multilateral in nature. Following the 70th anniversary of the GATT, international trade relationships may undergo another set of changes, as they are exposed to three types of pressures concurrently:

- the rise of China as a major global player;
- the appearance of a new "industrial revolution", due to the fast development of the digital economy; and,
- the increased complexity of trade rules as further liberalisation increasingly implies the need to move "behind the border".

In this chapter, regional integration is discussed within the context of these three phenomena. The second section gives a short and broad-brush historical overview of regional integration with a focus on the past century and the interplay between multilateral and regional trade rules. Then, section three examines the surge of so-called mega-regionalism in the light of the relationships between three major trade "blocks":

The Handbook of Global Trade Policy, First Edition. Edited by Andreas Klasen.

Northern America, the European Union (EU) and China. The interaction between different "domestic" policy areas and international trade is the subject of the following section, which also discusses the advent of the digital economy and its impact on trade rules. Finally, section five ventures into the future by asking what the next wave of regional integration may look like.

Regional Integration within a Multilateral Framework

Early Trade Policy

Throughout history trade has mostly occurred within relatively small geographic regions, and for good reason. The main constraints faced by early traders were primitive transportation and communication technologies, combined with poorly maintained or entirely absent infrastructure. One of the earliest recorded direct inter-regional trading relationships was between the Sumerians in Mesopotamia and the Harappan civilisation of the Indus Valley in around 3000 BCE (Possehl, 2002).

Perhaps the first example of regional trade on a scale modern observers would find familiar was during the height of the Roman Empire, between 26 and 180 AD (the dates chosen here are the generally accepted span for the so-called Pax Romana, a period of relative peace and prosperity experienced by the Roman Empire). During this period, vast amounts of grain, olive oil and wine were produced and shipped across the Empire. Even so, trade was heavily controlled by the state, with tariffs applied to goods moving between provinces and strong regulations on ship-owner associations which executed much of this trade. Indeed, it would be misleading to characterise trade in this period as efficiency maximising; for the Romans, trade was about maintaining control and power rather than promoting commercial links, increasing productivity or stimulating investment (Bang, 2007). This would be the lens through which trade policy would be viewed until the European Enlightenment.

In the 18th and 19th centuries, the contributions of both Adam Smith and David Riccardo to economics challenged prevailing mercantilist theories. Adam Smith was the first to articulate the principles of absolute advantage in the context of international trade in his seminal 1776 publication *An Enquiry into the Nature and Causes of the Wealth of Nations*. Around 40 years later, David Ricardo would refashion these ideas into what is now referred to as the law of comparative advantage. As also discussed by Höppner in Chapter 2 of this Handbook, comparative advantage, which focuses on the opportunity costs of producing goods instead of absolute costs, is the basis for the free trade consensus among economists today.

These arguments helped precipitate the so-called first wave of regionalism in the second half of the 19th century (Mansfield and Milner, 1999). Under Britain's lead, a broad network of bilateral trade agreements were signed, starting with the Anglo-French free trade agreement of 1860 (although commonly referred to as the "Anglo-French treaty", the proper name is the Cobden–Chevalier Treaty, after its originators). However, when these bilateral free trade agreements came up for renewal in the 1890s, many European nations decided against prolonging previous agreements. Despite being near the peak of her power and prestige, Britain could do little to stop this drift away from free trade ideals, partly because she had already abolished most of her tariffs and consequently was left with little bargaining power.

The United States and Latin America remained relatively protectionist in this period, while Asian, African and other countries were being forced into trade agreements *via* so-called gun-boat diplomacy (World Trade Organization, 2007). In the early 20th century, Britain herself became split on the issue of free trade when the conservative party argued in favour of reintroducing tariffs. Economic fragmentation in Europe increased at the turn of the century, and combined with strained foreign relations between major European powers, set the conditions for World War I, and the economic turmoil that followed.

Trade policy in the inter-war years

World War I was fought on an industrial scale. It led to a severing of trading relationships between enemies, and a shift of production to war materials damaging lower priority trading relationships (Horowitz, 2004). In the aftermath of the World War I, the resulting structural changes shifted the economic balance towards industries in favour of continued protection. A lack of leadership prevented a reciprocal dismantling of wartime trade restrictions. As a result, European nations looked to their colonial holdings as markets for their products rather than to each other. In the British Commonwealth, for example, by 1925 preferential *ad valorem* tariffs had grown by 9% since the end of World War I. In some senses, the Imperial Preference system developed by Britain in the 1930s can be considered the first expression of regionalism on a truly global scale.

What little trust existed in the international trading system evaporated with the passage of the US Smoot–Hawley Tariff Act in 1930. The protectionist measures introduced by the world's biggest creditor with the largest trade surplus stoked retaliatory action. Agricultural prices plunged and a long depression set in similar to that experienced in the 1870s. Europe suffered greatly, being still heavily dependent on agriculture.

The United States attempted to correct course with the adoption of the Reciprocal Trade Agreements Act of 1934. However, undoing the damage of the Smoot–Hawley Tariff Act proved slow and difficult (Irwin, 2017). In the end, it came too late to help stem rising disillusionment in Europe, and the world was set on course for war once again.

The Failure of the ITO and the Establishment of GATT

In the aftermath of World War II, the victorious powers were determined not to return to beggar-thy-neighbour trade policies. Indeed, as soon as the war began to turn against the axis powers, conferences discussing the architecture of post-war international cooperation were held. At the United Nations Monetary and Financial Conference, better known as the Bretton Woods Conference, the Monetary Fund and the International Reconstruction Development Bank were formalised (United States, Department of State, 1944). However, even though the elimination of tariffs and restrictions on trade was seen as important, it was not viewed as an immediate priority (Irwin, 1993). Therefore, it was not until 1946 that an international conference was held to discuss the creation of a multilateral trade body, known as the International Trade Organization (ITO).

The ITO was designed to have the power to create rules over a wide variety of aspects of economic policy, including employment, business practices and international investment. However, business groups in the United States refused to support an organisation with weak protections on foreign investment and provisions for commodity price stabilisation (Narlikar *et al.*, 2012). At the same time, the United States and Britain clashed over the elimination of the Commonwealth's Imperial Preferences (World Trade Organization, 2007).

The United States was in favour of non-discrimination without exception, and while Britain did not disagree with American goals, they disagreed on the timing of US plans, fearing their beleaguered economy would suffer greatly if tariffs fell before Britain could secure itself on a firmer economic footing (Zeiler, 1997). Although the United States eventually backed down, the ITO was effectively killed off when in 1950 US President Truman announced his administration would not put the charter to Congress.

Regionalism under GATT

GATT Article XXIV

The GATT was originally intended to serve as an interim agreement until the ratification of the ITO. When it became clear that the ITO would not be ratified, the GATT became the primary vehicle through which liberalisation efforts would be coordinated. The GATT was signed by 23 countries in 1947, and came into force on 1 January 1948. The overall objective of the GATT was to reduce tariffs and the use of quotas. A cornerstone of the GATT system was the principle of non-discrimination or the most-favoured-nation (MFN) rule. However, exceptions to the MFN rule were written into the GATT from an early stage (World Trade Organization, 2007). Interestingly, although scholars have traditionally attributed these exceptions to a desire on the part of the United States to facilitate European integration and keep the British from abandoning the talks, this is not the full story. At the time, US officials had secretly entered into trade negotiations with Canada, which they wanted GATT rules to accommodate (Chase, 2006). Ironically, no such treaty was ever signed or ratified, leaving behind only the ambiguous terminology of Article XXIV. However, within these exemptions the genesis of regionalism as we understand it today would form.

GATT Article XXIV gives exceptions from the obligation of the MFN principle to customs unions and free trade areas as long as they meet certain criteria. The main criteria are transparency, that a "substantial part of trade" between territories is covered in the liberalisation effort, and neutrality vis-à-vis third parties.

Regionalism in the 1960s and 1970s

The first major regional trade agreement (RTA) to be reviewed under Article XXIV was Part IV of the 1957 Treaty of Rome, which established a preferential treatment between European Economic Community (ECC) members and their overseas countries and territories (the Treaty of Rome was signed in March 1957. The founding ECC members were Belgium, France, Italy, Luxembourg, the Netherlands and West Germany). The working group charged with reviewing the agreement quickly stalled on a fundamental issue: what constituted a customs territory or free trade area? Here it is instructive to quote Article XXIV:8(b) from the GATT.

> A free-trade area shall be understood to mean a group of two or more customs territories in which the duties and other restrictive regulations of commerce [...] are eliminated on substantially all the trade between the constituent territories in products originating in such territories. (World Trade Organization, 1947)

But what constitutes *substantially all the trade* or *other restrictive regulations of commerce*? The working group was not able to reach clear conclusions, which may have partly been due to political considerations, but also because GATT Article XXIV was designed to be intentionally vague on these issues. Both these concerns would preoccupy subsequent RTA examinations and demonstrated the weakness of GATT rules on regional arrangements. In the end, the GATT sanctioned Part IV of the Treaty of Rome by granting a waiver to GATT rules, as the politics of the day trumped legal considerations. Interestingly, there was some enthusiasm to follow the ECC's example and set up free trade areas centred on the United States. Japan probed the possibility of a free trade agreement with the United States in 1960, but the United States remained indifferent to such ideas (Bhagwati, 1992).

In the following years, developing countries, encouraged by the example of European countries, sought to create free trade areas of their own to stimulate indus- trialisation. However, given strong state control of many of the sectors under discussion, the talks came to nothing as negotiations centred on industry-trade allo- cations rather than liberalisation (Bhagwati, 1992).

Regionalism builds up steam

Regionalism in the post-World War II era thus remained confined to European coun- tries for a few decades. That changed when the United States, then a key defender of multilateralism, entered talks first with Israel and then, more significantly, with Canada, in the 1980s. Negotiations conducted in the following years concluded with the signing of the United States' first major post-war free trade agreement, the 1988 Canada–United States Free Trade Agreement (CUSFTA). Soon after, Mexico approached the United States on signing a bilateral agreement. Canada, fearing it would lose its recently won preferences, asked to join the talks. The three parties first sat down in 1990, and on 1 January 1994 the North American Free Trade Agreement (NAFTA) came into force. NAFTA eliminated tariffs on over 97% of the parties' tariff lines, representing more than 99% of intra-trade by volume (World Trade Organization, 2000). NAFTA set the stage for an explosion of RTAs and preferential trade agreements (PTAs) starting in the mid-1990s.

A Surge in Preferential Trade Agreements

The establishment of the World Trade Organization (WTO) ushered in a new era of multilateral trade cooperation. This development was accompanied, however, by a new wave of regionalism in the form of a surge of bilateral investment treaties (BITs) and regional trade agreements (Mansfield and Milner, 1999). The terminology can be confusing. For instance, in some cases "PTAs" refer to preferential trade agreements while in others to preferential trade arrangements (preferential trade arrangements are unilateral trade preferences as well as other non-reciprocal preferential schemes granted a waiver by the General Council). In this section, we use the more generic term PTA (preferential trade agreements) as we discuss reciprocal bilateral, plurilat- eral and regional agreements.

By 2016, almost 650 PTAs had been signed (Figure 11.1; Dür *et al.*, 2014). A large share of PTAs are between countries in the Americas and Europe. Agreements bet- ween countries in Asia and countries in Europe, the Americas and Africa also account

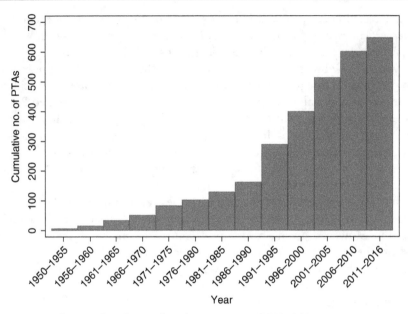

Figure 11.1 Evolution of preferential trade agreements, 1950–2016.
Source: Authors' illustration based on the Design of Trade Agreements (DESTA) database (Dür *et al.*, 2014).

for a substantial share of PTAs. The number of PTAs signed among Asian countries has increased over the past ten years. However, the growth rate of intra-African PTAs has been somewhat stagnant since the early 2000s.

Why do countries sign PTAs?

There is a rich body of research that assesses the economic and political reasons of why countries enter into bilateral, plurilateral and regional PTAs. On the domestic side, governments might join PTAs to accommodate interest groups in the exporting as well as importing industries. Beyond the important role played by these key industries and other interest groups, states' domestic institutions and the type of electoral system have been found to affect a country's interest in joining PTAs (Mansfield and Milner, 2015).

From an international economic perspective, PTA ratification is thought to be motivated by strategic interaction and the competition for market access. As exporters face trade diversion from the exclusion from a PTA concluded by other countries, they push their governments into signing an agreement with the country in which their exports are threatened. This contagion effect accelerates the spread of PTAs known in the literature as the Domino Theory of Regionalism (Baldwin and Jaimovich, 2012; Baldwin, 1993).

Another body of literature suggests that the proliferation of PTAs is related to "slow multilateralism", i.e. the stagnation of the Doha Round, and other shortcomings of the WTO system (Bhagwati, 1993, 2008; Krugman, 1993, 1991). On the one hand, member countries of the WTO may have little incentive to join PTAs because they already benefit from multilateral openness and liberalisation. On the other hand, WTO members might be especially interested in joining PTAs as this may increase their (block) bargaining power at the WTO. A PTA may also allow them to achieve negotiation outcomes that are unlikely to be feasible when being negotiated with a large number of countries with different interests. In fact, a PTA may also serve as a means to discriminate against certain WTO members while being compliant with WTO law. A forth reason, that may gain relevance in these turbulent times, is that countries sign PTAs as an insurance against a faltering WTO system (Mansfield and Milner, 2015; Mansfield and Reinhardt, 2003).

EU and United States at the centre of the spaghetti bowl

The rapid growth of PTAs has resulted in a dense network of partly overlapping (double) PTAs – the so-called spaghetti bowl of trade agreements (Pauwelyn and Alschner, 2014; Figure 11.2). The EU is the leading signatory of PTAs and plays a central role in the global PTA network. Figure 11.2 also illustrates the variability of

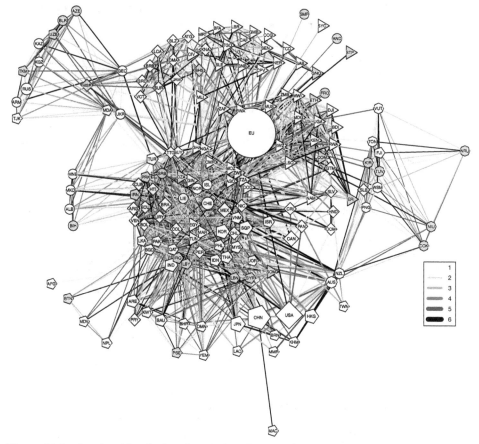

Figure 11.2 Spaghetti bowl of preferential trade agreements, 1950–2016.
Source: Authors' illustration based on the Design of Trade Agreements (DESTA) database (Dür *et al.*, 2014) and the World Bank Development Indicators (World Bank, 2018).
Note: The size of each marker is proportional to the country's exports of goods and services (current US$) in 2016. The marker's shape indicates a country's region (Africa – triangle, Americas – square, Asia – pentagon, Europe – circle, Oceania – octagon). The marker's colour indicates a country's WTO membership status (White – WTO member, grey – not WTO member). Thin and grey ties present shallow PTAs, dark and thick ties present deep PTAs.

PTA design in terms of scope and depth. A depth indicator developed by Dür *et al.* (2014) captures the degree of tariff reductions as well as substantive cooperation in areas such as services trade, investments, standards, public procurement, competition and intellectual property rights (IPRs). The result of this work showed that the EU's PTAs have the highest average depth (Hofmann *et al.*, 2017).

The large majority of deep agreements were signed after 1995. Prior to this, less than a quarter of PTAs included substantive provisions on services, investment, IPRs, public procurement, competition, technical barriers to trade (TBT) or sanitary and phytosanitary (SPS) measures. Over the years, this has changed. Now, more than three in four PTAs include substantive provisions on these policy areas. However, regional differences remain. The largest share of PTAs that contain substantive provisions on services and investment is found in the Americas, as reflected in Table 11.1. European agreements lead the way in the other policy areas, including IPR, public procurement, TBT and SPS. Overall, countries seem to put a particular emphasis on these policy areas when signing intercontinental agreements.

PTAs become deeper and more flexible

These regional differences in PTA design are the focus of a growing body of literature. In a recent contribution, Rohini (2016) collects a number of subject-specific studies on: market access provisions (Crawford, 2012), rules of origin (Abreu, 2016), anti-dumping rules (Rey, 2016), safeguard provisions (Crawford *et al.*, 2016), SPS (Jackson and Vitikala, 2016), TBT (Molina and Khoroshavina, 2015), services (Pierre, 2016), IPRs (Valdes and McCann, 2016) and dispute settlement (Chase *et al.*, 2013). It is interesting to note that not only the depth of PTAs has changed over time. As PTAs have become more ambitious, countries have also started to include more flexible measures and op-out clauses which allow them to react to changing domestic conditions or international challenges without leading to a *de jure* breach of an agreement (Baccini, Dür *et al.*, 2015).

In the short run, such flexibility measures mainly include tariff transition periods. Long-term flexibility measures include escape clauses as well as anti-dumping and anti-subsidies provisions. Figure 11.3 illustrates the co-evolution of depth and

Table 11.1 Preferential trade agreements with substantive provisions on different policy areas, by region, 1950–2016

	No. of total PTAs	Services (%)	Invest-ment (%)	IPR (%)	Procure-ment (%)	Competition (%)	TBT (%)	SPS (%)	Dispute (%)
Africa	38	21	32	8	0	8	37	32	76
Americas	161	51	60	26	29	17	48	47	80
Asia	82	46	44	28	22	16	45	44	79
Europe	163	48	52	63	64	16	60	75	91
Oceania	7	43	29	0	29	0	29	14	100
Inter-continental	197	63	65	49	52	34	63	68	89

Source: Authors' calculations based on the Design of Trade Agreements (DESTA) database (Dür et al., 2014).

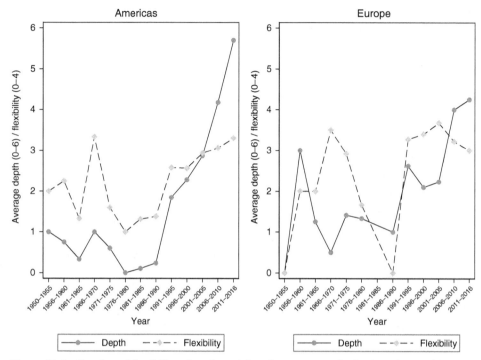

Figure 11.3   Depth and flexibility of preferential trade agreements in the Americas and Europe, 1950–2016.
Source: Authors' illustration based on the Design of Trade Agreements (DESTA) database (Dür *et al.*, 2014).
Note: The depth index ranges between 0 and 6, the flexibility index between 0 and 4.

flexibility in the PTAs signed since 1950, for the Americas and Europe. Both indices have experienced a significant increase since the early 1990s. This is the case across the different regions, albeit the increase is most substantial in PTAs signed among countries in the Americas and Asia as well as across continents.

PTA provisions strongly influenced by WTO legal language

There is a longstanding debate as to whether the proliferation of PTAs is a stepping stone or a stumbling block to multilateralism and the WTO. Some studies regard rising regionalism as a threat to the multilateral trading system (Bhagwati, 2008, 1993; Krugman, 1993, 1991; Winters, 2015). While there continue to be sceptics, much of the more recent literature finds that the relationship between the WTO and PTAs is complementary and dialectical (Lejárraga, 2014; Cottier *et al.*, 2015; Allee *et al.*, 2017a).

The WTO Agreement on Trade-Related Aspects of Intellectual Property Rights (TRIPS), for instance, grew out of two PTAs: the Paris Convention on the Protection of Industrial Property and the Berne Convention on the Protection of Literary and Artistic Works. The WTO General Agreement on Trade in Services (GATS), in contrast, has not been influenced by previous PTAs but rather had considerable influence on the design and structure of subsequent PTAs (Cottier *et al.*, 2015).

In a comprehensive study of 292 recent PTAs, Allee *et al.* (2017a) examine the WTO–PTA relationship systematically. The authors find that around 90% of PTAs

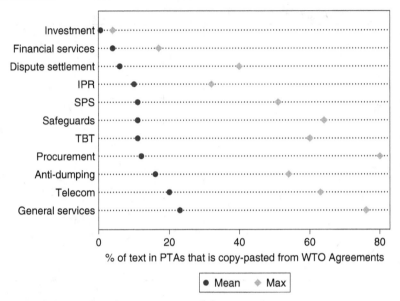

Figure 11.4 Preferential trade agreements and the WTO Agreements.
Source: Authors' illustration based on Allee *et al.* (2017a).

engage the WTO with explicit references and do so across the majority of chapters. A sizeable majority of PTAs that do not explicitly refer to the WTO are PTAs where at least one signatory is not a WTO member. The authors further find that PTAs do not only refer to the WTO – they copy-paste sizeable parts in verbatim. As illustrated in Figure 11.4, this methodology is particularly dominant in PTAs' services chapters. On average, 23% of text is copy-pasted from the GATS. In some instance, more than three quarters of text is adopted.

The Surge of Mega-Regionalism

The WTO and its rules have been influential to the design of PTAs around the globe. Two other initiatives that have significantly shaped the landscape of (mega-) regionalism are the EU and NAFTA. The competitive interdependence of the big trading communities on either side of the Atlantic has characterised trade policies, and trade politics, since the 1950s. The end of the 20th century witnessed the rise of China as a major trading partner, with a market that has the potential to outgrow both the EU and the United States. With the rise of China, the Pacific became the centre of interest for trade flows and deals.

Europe: The European Union

The first steps towards a "European Federation" were made on 18 April 1951 when Belgium, France, Germany, Italy, Luxembourg and the Netherlands signed the Treaty of Paris to establish the European Coal and Steel Community (ECSC). The relevance of steel in the forging of the EU is worth noting, given the current pressures on China to reduce its volume of steel production.

The ECSC came into force on 23 July 1952 with the primary objective to support the modernisation and conversion of the coal and steel sectors. Beyond increasing efficiencies, accelerating the reconstruction process and eliminating discrimination in intra-regional coal trade, the choice of the coal and steel sectors was highly symbolic as the pooling of French and German resources was intended to mark the end of the rivalry between the two nations. The ECSC created a set of institutions including a High Authority, Council, Parliamentary Assembly and Court of Justice, which would ultimately be copied to a significant degree in the later European Communities.

On 25 March 1957, the same six countries signed the Treaty of Rome to set up the European Economic Community (EEC) and the European Atomic Energy Community (EAEC). When the EEC entered into force on 1 January 1958, the European integration project was extended to include general economic cooperation including the elimination of customs duties between member states; the establishment of an external common customs tariff; the introduction of common agricultural (CAP), transport and commercial policies; the creation of a European Social Fund; the establishment of the European Investment Bank and the development of closer relations between the member states.

Ten years after the signing of the Treaty of Rome, the Brussels Treaty (1957) entered into force with the objective to streamline the European institutions. The Treaty created a single Commission and a single Council to serve the then three European Communities of the ECSC, EEC and EAEC.

After the entry into force of the Single European Act in 1987, the Maastricht Treaty (formally the Treaty on the European Union, TEU) of 1993 marked another milestone, as it prepared for the European Monetary Union and introduced elements of a political union in the form of three pillars: common economic, social and environmental policies; common foreign and security policies; and justice and internal affairs. The EEC became the European Community to reflect the fact that the community no longer dealt with economic matters only.

The TEU marked a significant step towards European integration. The Treaty of Amsterdam, which entered into force on 1 May 1999, made further substantial amendments to the TEU. The member states agreed to devolve certain powers from their national governments to the European Parliament, existing EU institutions were reformed in preparation for the arrival of future member countries and a High Representative for EU Foreign Affairs and Security Policy was introduced. The Treaty of Nice (2003) and the Treaty of Lisbon (2009) further reformed the European institutions to enable them to efficiently accommodate the new member states.

Since the Treaty of Rome, the European Communities (and since 1993 the European Union) has expanded both its member states and its external trade and partnership relations. Denmark, Ireland and the United Kingdom joined in 1973, followed by Greece (1981) and Portugal and Spain (1986), as well as Austria, Finland and Sweden (1995). In 2004, Cyprus, the Czech Republic, Estonia, Hungary, Latvia, Lithuania, Malta, Poland, Slovakia and Slovenia joined, followed in 2007 by Bulgaria and Romania. With many of the now-member states, the EU had signed PTAs prior to their accession. Since its early days, the EU has also followed an active, and increasingly deeper, PTA policy with other partners around the world (Figure 11.5).

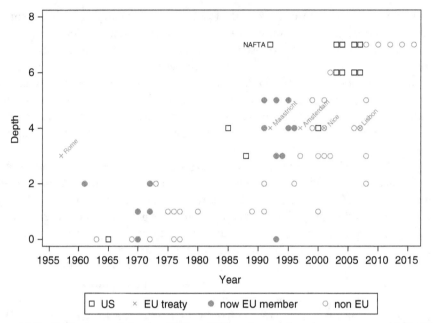

Figure 11.5 Evolution and depth of EU and US preferential trade agreements, 1950–2016.
Source: Authors' illustration based on the Design of Trade Agreements (DESTA) database
(Dür *et al.*, 2014).
Note: Filled circles show EU accession treaties. Empty circles show PTAs between the EU and
non-EU countries.

The United States was a firm supporter of a tightly integrated post-war Europe.
However, the progressing integration and the expansive drive for PTAs with countries all around the world also caused some concern on the other side of the pond.

North America: North American Free Trade Agreement

During the 1960s and early 1970s, three events/policies were particularly relevant to
the formulation of US trade policy: the accession of the United Kingdom, Denmark
and Ireland to the European Communities; the pursuit of PTAs with the remaining
countries of the European Free Trade Association (EFTA); and the PTAs with the
Mediterranean countries. The enlargement of the European Community entailed the
expansion of the CAP which, in turn, was feared to increase the level of trade barriers to the fifth-largest market for US agricultural products – the United Kingdom.
US agriculture exporters were equally concerned about the European Community's
PTAs with Israel in 1964 and Spain in 1970 as these agreements were likely to divert
trade at the expense of US agriculture exporters. As a reaction to European trade
policies, the United States even demanded a "standstill agreement" that would stop
the "proliferation" of PTAs beyond Europe as well as the consultations with the
EFTA countries (Dür, 2010).
    Another major concern of the US administration was the European push towards
standardisation, harmonisation and mutual recognition of technical regulations with
limited concerns for third-country considerations. The United States hoped to use

the WTO Tokyo Round (1973–1979) to achieve an agreement that would allow it to monitor standard-setting in the European Community. The Community, in contrast, attempted to convince the United States to accept international standards. While the parties found some compromise in the Tokyo Agreement of Technical Barriers ("Standards Code"), the different regulatory systems and approaches towards standard-setting continue to be a hot-button issue until this day.

The European Community continued to push for the completion of the internal market. In 1985, it published a white paper that contained some three hundred proposals for the elimination of physical (border formalities, quotas), technical (standards, public procurement rules) and fiscal (taxation) barriers within the Community. Starting in 1987, and gathering speed in 1988 and 1989, the aim was to implement the single market programme (SMP) by 1992.

This big push for further integration did not go unnoticed on the other side of the Atlantic. In fact, the US administration's reaction to the SMP even entailed the setting up of an interagency task force focusing on the external effects of a deeper integrated Europe in 1988. As a response to the US trade deficit with European and other countries, the US Congress also pivoted away from free trade towards fair and strategic trade (Nollen and Quinn, 1987) – terminology that is popular with the current US administration.

On 1 January 1989, CUSTFA entered into force. Influenced by the 1965 Auto Pact, CUSFTA was a comprehensive agreement that provided national treatment; the elimination of tariffs, duty drawbacks and most quantitative restrictions, export taxes and other export measures. It also afforded reciprocal access to government procurement and services, relaxed most foreign investment restrictions and facilitated temporary immigrations entry for business purposes. CUSFTA was an important model for NAFTA, which entered into force on 1 January 1994.

While there are many economic, political and social considerations that led to the decisions of the three countries to sign a North America-wide FTA, it is hard to argue that the accelerating integration of the EU did not play a part. As pointed out by Schott (2004), NAFTA was also a way for the United States to convince its recalcitrant GATT partners, and in particular the EU, to resurrect the then stalled WTO Uruguay Round by demonstrating that the United States was prepared to achieve freer trade through regional agreements if it proved impossible to do so multilaterally in Geneva.

With its 22 chapters and economic size, NAFTA is often regarded as the first comprehensive mega-regional PTA. Of course, the regional integration efforts in North America did not go unnoticed in the EU either. In the years immediately after NAFTA's entry into force in 1994, EU trade with Mexico declined significantly, from 10.6% of Mexico's total trade in 1991 to 6.5% in 1999 (Gantz, 2009). The EU's response to NAFTA was clear-cut. Pierre Defraigne, then Deputy Director-General in the Commission's Directorate-General for Trade, stated the dynamic clearly:

> In order not to be evicted from the NAFTA market, the EU immediately started a FTA negotiation with Mexico. (Defraigne, 2002)

As illustrated in Figure 11.5, in the subsequent years the EU and the United States engaged in a race for increasingly deep PTAs, partly in a tit-for-tat manner. For instance, the EU signed a PTA with Mexico six years after NAFTA while the United States signed a PTA with Jordan, only three years after the EU did. The United States and the EU were also simultaneously negotiating with Chile, resulting in an EU–Chile PTA in 2002 and a US–Chile PTA in 2003. After the United States signed PTAs with Colombia and Peru in 2006, the EU signed a PTA with the two countries in 2012. Similarly, the EU signed a PTA with the Republic of Korea in 2010, only three years after the United States did.

The EU and NAFTA: Templates for (Mega-) Regionalism

Signing PTAs with countries and regions all over the world is driven by economic, social and political considerations. No doubt, preferential market access plays an important role. However, for trade heavyweights such as the United States and the EU, signing PTAs is also a way of strategically diffusing their regulatory systems and shaping the design of future regional integration initiatives.

Both the European model and the NAFTA model have become templates for subsequent PTAs (in many of which the EU or United States were not signatories) and therefore directly and indirectly shaped the evolution of regionalism over the years (Baccini, Haftel *et al.*, 2015). The EU presents an institutions-based integration model in which powerful bodies and institutions are created to reinforce the integration process. These agreements tend to cover non-trade issues, but the legal language is kept relatively vague and leaves it to the created institutions to enforce the commitments. The NAFTA model, by contrast, promotes rules-based integration. Trade and non-trade commitments as well as their enforcement are more precisely formulated, which limits the need to create further institutions.

Based on a cluster analysis on almost 600 PTAs and their provisions on services, investment, IPRs, public procurement, competition, TBT, SPS measures and dispute settlement, Baccini, Haftel *et al.* (2015) identified a clear pattern. Whether a PTA is closer to the EU or the NAFTA model is found to be influenced by the PTA signatories' political relationship with the EU and the United States, respectively. Furthermore, the choice between the templates depends on the nature and objective of the PTA to be signed. Plurilateral agreements that aim to integrate a number of markets, such as for instance the Central American Common Market (CACM), the Caribbean Community (CARICOM), the Andean Community and the Economic and Monetary Community of Central Africa, are closer to the EU than to the NAFTA model. Many of the bilateral agreements, in particular those signed by the United States, Chile, Japan and Mexico, show significant parallels to NAFTA.

Despite its impact on the world of bilateral, plurilateral and regional PTAs, NAFTA has become the focus of criticism – including within the US administration. On 18 May 2017, the United States began renegotiating NAFTA with the primary objective to eliminate the country's trade deficit with its northern and southern neighbours. On 30 November 2018, the NAFTA parties signed the United States–Mexico–Canada Agreement (USMCA), sometimes referred to as NAFTA 2.0.

Transpacific: Trans-Pacific Partnership (TPP)

The 1990s were an eventful time for trade policy – the WTO Uruguay Round was concluded and NAFTA established. At the same time, the leaders of the Asia-Pacific Economic Cooperation (APEC) signed the Bogor Declaration (1994) calling for free trade in the Pacific region by 2020. China became a WTO member in 2001. At the time, it was the world's fourth-largest merchandise exporter. A few years later it had risen to number two, behind the EU and ahead of Japan and the United States.

In October 2015, 12 Pacific-Rim countries signed the Trans-Pacific Partnership (TPP). The TPP originally evolved out of the Trans-Pacific Strategic Economic Partnership Agreement by New Zealand, Singapore, Chile and Brunei in 2005. The United States, Australia, Peru and Vietnam joined the talks in 2008, followed by Malaysia in 2010 and Canada and Mexico in 2012. Japan was the last country to join the TPP negotiations, in 2013.

Given its geographic and economic scope, the TPP presented a mega-regional PTA that could have become a new standard for future trade negotiations at the plurilateral or even multilateral level. Therefore, the country or the countries that had the greatest hand in writing the TPP could see their influence magnified if the contents of the TPP become the standard legal text and spread into future agreements. The United States clearly saw the TPP through this lens, as its then President Barack Obama stated in the 2 May 2017 issue of the *Washington Post*:

> The world has changed. The rules are changing with it. The United States, not countries like China, should write them. (McGlone, 2017)

Allee and Lugg (2016) look at the 74 previous PTAs that TPP members have signed and calculate the share of text copied into the final TPP draft. NAFTA plays a surprisingly small role. This is not to say that the United States did not rely on previous PTAs though. In fact, Allee and Lugg (2016) find that the language of previous US PTAs is disproportionally prominent in the TPP compared to other TPP drafters' past PTAs. Ten of the PTAs that match the TPP most closely are previous US PTAs. Some bilateral PTAs, such as, for instance, those with Bahrain, Oman and South Korea, have almost half of their contents copied into the TPP.

This becomes even more evident when zooming into the different issue areas (see Figure 11.6). For instance, on average 80% of the investment chapter is copied from previous PTAs, and 88% of the investment chapter corresponds to the investment chapter of the US–Oman PTA. Figure 11.6 illustrates that the TPP relies strongly on previous PTAs among the member states and that the treaty is to a large extent "Made in America", as proclaimed by US authorities in 2016.

Despite the influential role of the United States in shaping the TPP and potentially future regional trade initiatives, the Trump administration decided to withdraw from the agreement on 23 January 2017. The 11 remaining members reached a partial agreement on 11 November 2017 for a Comprehensive and Progressive Agreement for Trans-Pacific Partnership (CPTPP).

Transatlantic: CETA and TTIP

With the United States' trade negotiation activity turning towards the Pacific, the EU made further efforts to intensify its ties across the Atlantic. Negotiations with Canada on a Comprehensive Economic and Trade Agreement (CETA) started in 2009 and CETA was signed in 2016. The idea of a free trade agreement between the United States and the EU had been discussed since the 1990s but formal

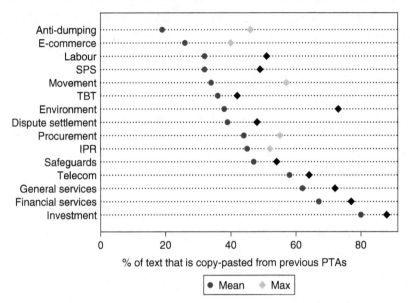

Figure 11.6   Trans-Pacific Partnership and previous preferential trade agreements.
Source: Authors' illustration based on Allee and Lugg (2016). The marker is black if this maximum amount of text was copied from a previous US PTA and grey if it was copied from a previous PTA of another TPP member.

negotiations on the so-called Transatlantic Trade and Investment Partnership (TTIP) between the United States and the EU only started in 2013. They were put on halt again in 2016.

Both the CETA and the TTIP agreements had the ambition to be innovative models for future trade deals. Only the future will tell whether this will be the case. What is clear already, however, is that neither agreement was drafted in a void and both do rely, to varying degrees, on legal text from previous agreements. In the case of CETA, Allee *et al.* (2017b) find that the agreement is indeed more forward-looking than backward-looking, and that relatively little of its treaty text is recycled from past trade agreements – certainly when compared to the TPP. As illustrated in Figure 11.7, this varies by issue area, and there are exceptions. In the case of the procurement chapter, for instance, 79% of the text was adopted from the EU–Singapore agreement.

Similar to CETA, TTIP was envisaged to become a template for future trade agreements and therefore a shaping factor for the future of regionalism. A comprehensive study on TTIP does not exist as the negotiations were stalled before a common draft was reached. However, Elsig and Klotz (2019) rely on the US and EU draft proposals to assess the extent to which the two parties rely on previous agreements when designing their TBT and SPS chapters. For both issue areas, the authors find that the US negotiators rely, on average, more on their previous PTAs than the EU negotiators. Interestingly, the TPP plays a fairly limited role in the US draft proposal for TTIP, even though it is an agreement largely written by the United States. In contrast, the European draft proposals for the TBT and SPS chapters of TTIP rely heavily on CETA text (Figure 11.8 and Figure 11.9).

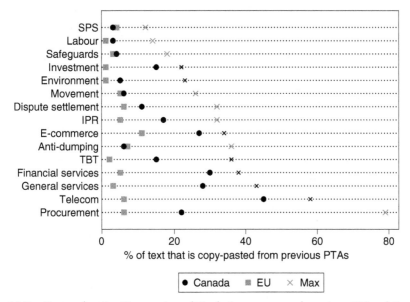

Figure 11.7 Comprehensive Economic and Trade Agreement and previous EU and Canadian preferential trade agreements.

Source: Authors' illustration based on Allee *et al.* (2017b).

Note: Max shows the maximum amount of text copied from a previous PTA. The marker is black if this maximum amount of text was copied from a previous Canadian PTA and grey if it was copied from a previous EU PTA.

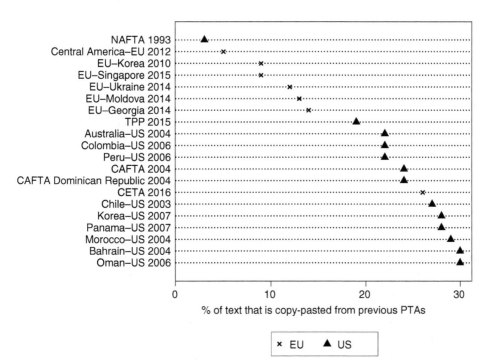

Figure 11.8 TBT in EU and US draft proposals for the Transatlantic Trade and Investment Partnership (TTIP).

Source: Authors' illustration based on Elsig and Klotz (2019).

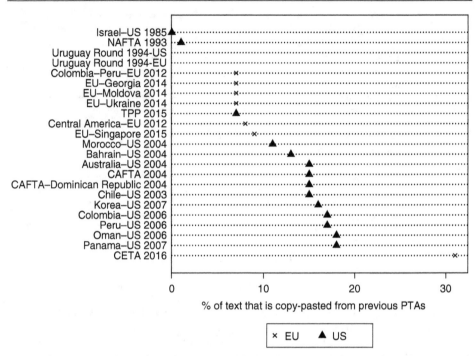

Figure 11.9   SPS in EU and US draft proposals for the Transatlantic Trade and Investment Partnership.
Source: Authors' illustration based on Elsig and Klotz (2019).

Asia and beyond: Belt and Road Initiative

The previous section illustrates that recent years have experienced the rise of mega-regionals on either side of the Atlantic as well as the Pacific. Beyond this, new forms of mega-regionalism are evolving – the most prominent one is the Belt and Road Initiative that has been undertaken on the initiative of China.

Like the EU and the United States, China has been actively negotiating PTAs, and several have been ratified since China's entry in the WTO. A preliminary textual analysis confirms that earlier EU and US PTAs are also influential to the design of Chinese PTAs (Figure 11.10). US PTAs had a stronger influence on China's PTAs with Anglo-Saxon countries like Australia and New Zealand and its PTAs with Latin American countries like Chile and Costa Rica. The influence of EU PTAs, instead, is stronger in China's PTAs with the EFTA countries Iceland and Switzerland, but also with the Eastern European country Georgia and with the Asian country Korea. China borrowed significantly from the EU PTA with Korea (2010) when it designed its own agreement with Korea in 2015. While not shown in Figure 11.10, the textual analysis of Chinese PTAs also indicates that the Europeans adopted considerable parts of Chinese PTAs when designing their agreements with Vietnam (2016) and Singapore (2018).

One of the most striking aspects of regional integration as pursued by China is, however, that the focus may not be on designing joint rule books. China's best known and by far most ambitious initiative, the Belt and Road Initiative (BRI), is an ambitious plan for greater regional integration without predefined rules. Representing a political vision to foster cooperation and connectivity between China and BRI

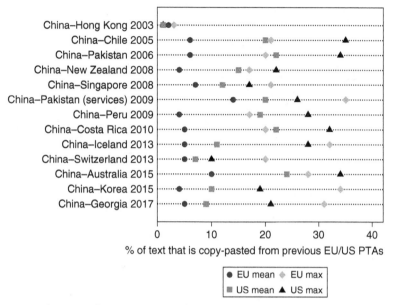

Figure 11.10   Chinese and previous EU and US preferential trade agreements.
Source: Authors' calculation and illustration based on PTAs identified in the Design of Trade
Agreements (DESTA) database (Dür *et al.*, 2014).

members, the initiative is different from conventional trade agreements or regional
cooperation mechanisms (International Trade Centre [ITC], 2017). The emphasis is
on strengthening physical infrastructure (railways, ports, energy pipelines and special
trade zones) as well as soft infrastructure (such as institutional foundations for trade
and investment flows, i.e. easing customs processes). While the BRI is not a free trade
agreement, the expansion of infrastructure, finance and information technology (IT)
links across countries is likely to facilitate trade further, provided that soft (regulatory)
infrastructure is upgraded simultaneously with hard (physical) infrastructure.

Invoking historical imagery of ancient China's naval expeditions and trading
routes, the BRI aims to establish two new routes. The land-based "Silk Road
Economic Belt" links: China and Europe *via* Central Asia and Russia, and China and
the Middle East *via* Central Asia. The sea-based "Maritime Silk Road" connects
China with Southeast Asia, the Middle East, Europe and Africa (Figure 11.11).

China's President Xi Jinping unveiled the initiative in 2013 during his visits to
Central Asia and the Association of Southeast Asian Nations (ASEAN), and in 2015,
China's National Development and Reform Commission (NDRC), Ministry of
Foreign Affairs and Ministry of Commerce jointly issued the Vision and Actions Plan
on the BRI.

The BRI can potentially enhance interconnectivity in a geographical area
accounting for roughly 70% of the world's population, 55% of world's gross
domestic product (GDP) and 75% of known energy reserves. However, the geographic composition of BRI has not been clearly defined. Any country with an
interest in the initiative can potentially join it. This contrasts sharply with existing
treaty-based integration efforts, where the geographical scope, partner countries,
strategy, principles and rules were clearly defined at the outset.

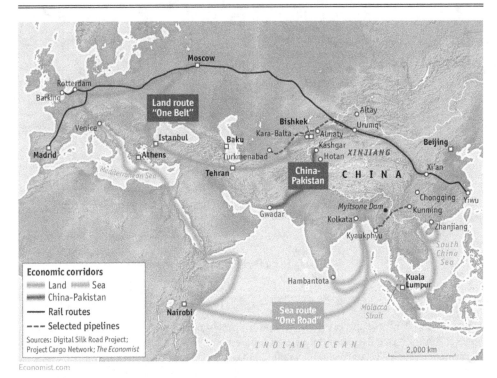

Figure 11.11   Routes of the Belt and Road Initiative.
Source: *The Economist* (2017).

The BRI calls for a massive infrastructure push to enhance the connectivity among the countries on the proposed Belt and Road routes. It aims to deliver greater energy and power interconnections as well as a more secure and efficient network of land, sea and air passages across the key routes. Its influence is already evident in China's overseas investment flows, with investment related to the BRI rising twice as fast as total outward foreign direct investment (FDI) in 2015.

According to the China Development Bank, some 900 projects at an estimated cost of US$890 billion are currently under way or planned. For instance, in January 2017, the first direct train from China to the United Kingdom arrived in London carrying 44 containers of clothes and consumer goods. It took 15 days to travel 12,000 km across ten countries, half the time it would have taken by sea.

China and its neighbouring countries have an urgent need for basic infrastructure. Data from the Asian Development Bank (ADB) show that Developing Asia will need to invest US$26 trillion from 2016 to 2030, or US$1.7 trillion per year, to maintain its rapid growth and respond to climate change. Of the total investment needs over the period, US$14.7 trillion will be for power, US$8.4 trillion for transport, US$2.3 trillion for telecommunications and US$800 billion for water and sanitation. The Asia-Pacific region's infrastructure investment gap is estimated to equal 2.4% of projected GDP in 2016–2020, with the gap at 5% of projected GDP if China is excluded.

A number of government and multilateral funds were created recently to reduce this funding gap and finance Silk Road projects, although some of these are not exclusively directed towards the BRI. They include: the Asian Infrastructure

Investment Bank (AIIB) with a capital stock of US$100 billion; the US$100 billion BRICS New Development Bank and the US$40 billion Silk Road Infrastructure Fund (SRF); China Development Bank, with a capital stock of US$16.3 billion; ASEAN Infrastructure Connectivity Fund, with a capital stock of US$20 billion; and Maritime Silk Road Bank with a capital stock of US$810 million. The Export-Import Bank of China is also expected to make major contributions – it lent more than US$80 billion in 2015.

But even taken together, these official and multilateral financing channels will not be able to meet the funding needs of BRI projects and, more broadly, bridge the investment gap in the Asia-Pacific region. Hence, it is critical to facilitate participation of the private sector and institutional investors, such as international pension funds, insurers and sovereign wealth funds, to complement public funds. Challenges for investors in the BRI will be as diverse as the BRI countries covered by the initiative, which range from Singapore to Syria.

According to its vision document, the BRI initiative goes beyond infrastructure to include closer coordination of economic development policies, harmonising technical standards, removing investment and trade barriers, establishing free trade areas and deepening financial integration. Although it remains to be seen how the BRI will evolve, it is already clear that it represents a new approach towards regional trade integration as it appears to prioritise the reduction of transport costs over the reduction of transactional costs like those related to tariffs.

New Players, Shifting Priorities?

The second half of the 20th century has been characterised by a high level of activity in designing multilateral and preferential trade rules, driven by the WTO and also by the two major trading powers of the period: the EU and the United States. One important difference between the EU and US approaches to integration is the way in which their agreements deal with behind-the-border measures. The EU approach puts a stronger emphasis on harmonisation and mutual recognition of standards and regulations than the US approach. The creation of joint bodies or institutions also plays an important role in the EU approach towards integration. In their respective PTAs, the EU and the United States have sought (and often succeeded) to transmit their preferred approaches to integration.

The rise of China has significantly, if not entirely, upset this race for influence and market access between the EU and the United States, a race that was still ongoing but taking place in a rather friendly manner and following a well-understood script. China has upset this race in at least two ways: by representing a third global power that is seeking influence and market access through PTAs, and by giving an entirely new importance to infrastructure investments thus upsetting the script that the EU and the United States were used to.

New Themes: Preferential Trade Agreements in the Driver Seat

The 11th Ministerial Conference of the WTO in Buenos Aires took place 16 years after the start of the Doha Round of negotiations. No significant progress has been made to conclude that round. Yet the world of trade continues to evolve, and policymakers need to find ways to deal with these changes. Two changes are of particular importance in this context: the rapid development of the digital economy, and the recognition that trade, investment and other financial flows are much more intertwined than originally expected.

The rise of the digital economy confronts trade policymakers with fundamental and often new questions regarding the borders between merchandise and services trade, the nature of data flows and the technologies, regulations required to protect individual consumers and also the security of nations. The dazzling speed at which the digital economy evolves stands in stark contrast with the slowness of multilateral trade negotiations.

The gradual opening of markets for trade flows after World War II was accompanied, at the end of the 20th century, by a rapid opening of markets for capital flows. One of the results was the increased role of value chain trade that for many industrialised countries now represents two thirds of all trade. With trade liberalisation at the multilateral level, investment through a myriad of BITs and taxation still being a matter of purely national rules, governments ended up losing the ability to tax large chunks of capital. This became painfully clear in the aftermath of the Global Financial Crisis when state funding was needed to intervene in a recessionary economic environment. Governments needed to act rapidly in the context of a slow-moving multilateral trading system that has no clear mandate for either investment or taxation.

The 11th Ministerial Conference of the WTO witnessed the introduction of the themes "e-commerce" and "investment facilitation" in the WTO agenda, but in an ambiguous and explicitly plurilateral way. Rule setting has in the meantime progressed but in different forums. New legal language for e-commerce and digital trade is emerging in bilateral and regional agreements, supported by active and innovative unilateral rule-making in this area. The investment theme has been brought into numerous integration agreements as a separate chapter, and international collaboration on tax rules has progressed rapidly through G20 (Group of Twenty) initiatives and at the Organisation for Economic Co-operation and Development (OECD) level.

Investment

Trade and investment are the drivers of the global economy. The share of trade in GDP has steadily increased from 13% in 1970 to 29% in 2016. The growth of net investment outflows as a share of GDP is much more volatile (see Figure 11.12). While foreign investment accounts for a smaller share of GDP, it has been growing six times as fast as income and two times as fast as trade (van Marrewijk, 2017). The increase in global investment flows has been accompanied by a rise in regulatory initiatives to protect foreign investors.

The bumpy multilateral road

Although the 1948 Havana Charter already recognised the relationship between trade and investment and encouraged work on multilateral rules for FDI, it took the multilateral system until 1994 to agree on an international set of rules. The 1994 Uruguay Round Agreement contains two legal texts dealing explicitly with investment: the Agreement on Trade Related Investment Measures (TRIMS) and the

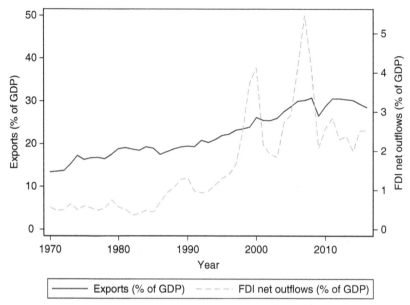

Figure 11.12 Evolution of exports and outward foreign direct investment, 1970–2016.
Source: Authors' illustration based on the World Bank Indicators database (World Bank, 2018).

GATS. The latter, however, only concerns investment in the field of services as it falls under the GATS concept of "mode 3 services trade" (services trade through commercial presence). Furthermore, TRIPS is of relevance for investment.

It appeared clear from the outset that this set of rules may not be sufficient, and 1995 witnessed the start of negotiations on a Multilateral Agreement on Investment (MAI) under the auspices of the OECD. The MAI draft text, however, became subject to widespread criticism, in particular from civil society, and negotiations were stopped in 1998. In 2017, investment found its way back on the WTO agenda. At the 11th Ministerial Conference in Buenos Aires, 70 WTO members, recognising the links between investment, trade and development, announced plans to pursue structured discussions with the aim of developing a multilateral framework on investment facilitation.

International rules for investment: going bilateral

BITs began to mushroom in the early 1990s. For developing countries, BITs were a way to attract investment. Investors from developed countries used BITs to seek protection for their investments in foreign countries. More recently, developing countries also regard BITs as a way to protect their regulatory policy space from international arbitration excesses (Forere, 2017). The historical nature and purpose of BITs also explains why the vast majority of BITs are signed between countries from different continents. Over the past three decades, more than 6000 BITs have been signed and resulted in a dense, intricate network in which Germany, China, Switzerland, the United Kingdom and France play central roles (see Figure 11.13 and Figure 11.14).

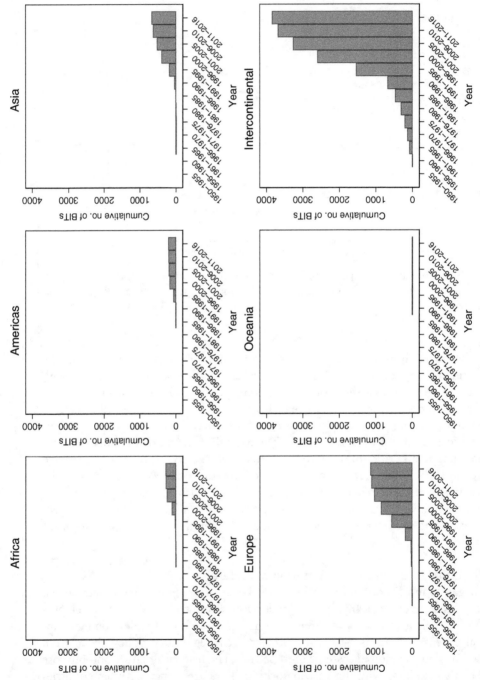

Figure 11.13 Evolution of bilateral investment treaties by region, 1950–2016.
Source: Authors' illustration based on the UNCTAD International Investment Agreement database (UNCTAD, n.d.).

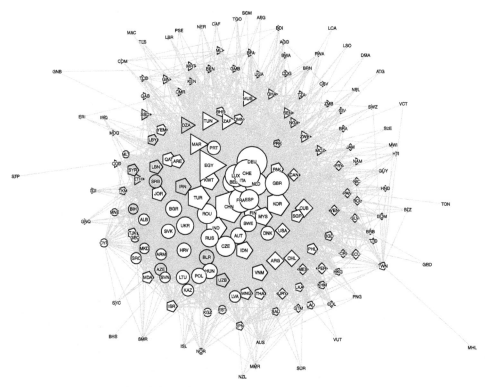

Figure 11.14 Network of bilateral investment treaties, 1950–2016.
Source: Authors' illustration based on the UNCTAD International Investment Agreement database (UNCTAD, n.d.).
Note: The size of each marker represents the total number of a country's bilateral investment treaties. The marker's shape indicates a country's region (Africa – triangle, Americas – square, Asia – pentagon, Europe – circle, Oceania – octagon). The marker's colour indicates a country's WTO membership status (White – WTO member, grey – not WTO member).

Investment chapters in preferential trade agreements

More and more, however, bilateral investment is also governed in PTAs. As illustrated in Figure 11.15, investment chapters that go beyond the governance of services have increasingly been included in trade agreements since the early 2000. In recent years, almost 75% of trade agreements have included an investment chapter that goes beyond services. Only a minority of agreements are explicitly based on existing BITs. Evidence suggests that the inclusion of investment and trade provisions under one legal umbrella is beneficial for the country receiving FDI inflows as it supports domestic value addition to trade within international value chains (ITC, 2017).

The large majority (more than 70%) of these agreements grants MFN and national treatment (NT) for foreign investments. Around half of recent agreements still include explicit restrictions on the temporary movement of businesses and natural people. Similarly, most of the PTAs that include investment chapters also include an investor–state, and increasingly state–state, dispute settlement mechanism. Maybe surprisingly, only a low share of less than 10% of recent PTAs includes an explicit reference to TRIMs.

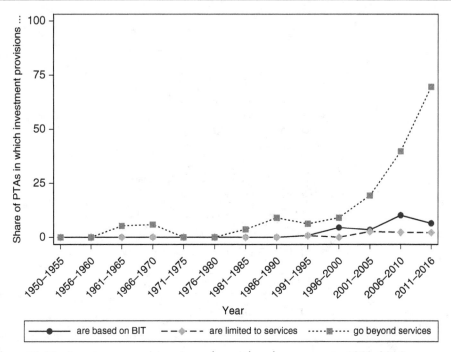

Figure 11.15   Investment provisions in preferential trade agreements, 1950–2016.
Source: Authors' illustration based on the Design of Trade Agreements (DESTA) database
(Dür et al., 2014).

Taxation

Taxation of business: bilateral agreements

Double taxation treaties (DTTs), which prevent excessive or double taxation of multinational companies, also affect trade flows. DTTs have emerged as international
legal instruments concluded between two or more countries primarily to relieve
juridical double taxation, considered one of the most visible obstacles to FDI (Egger
et al., 2006).

Double taxation is when two or more countries levy tax on the same declared
income. In such cases, a multinational company pays tax on the same corporate
income twice, in two different countries – once to the tax authorities of the foreign
country which is host to the economic activity, and once to the tax authorities of the
home country, where the parent company is headquartered.

Bilateral DTTs, now totalling more than 3000 worldwide, have remained outside
of the network of PTAs and mega-regional trade pacts (Hufbauer and Moran, 2015).
Only half of DTT relationships are also covered by a BIT (UNCTAD, 2015). Mirroring
the spread of BITs around the world (Neumayer and Spess, 2005), DTTs first grew
quickly between developed countries and then expanded in the 1980s and 1990s to
accords between developing and developed countries. By 2008, these accounted for
more than 50% of DTTs signed (UNCTAD, 2009).

Most bilateral DTTs are based on either United Nations or OECD Model Tax
Conventions, thus the WTO plays no substantial role in this area. In practice, DTTs
can mitigate legal and fiscal uncertainty for foreign investors about how overseas

profits from their investments will be taxed (Neumayer, 2007). Yet, the evidence on whether DTTs actually affect FDI turns out to be mixed (IMF, 2014). There are growing fears, however, that DTTs will lead to major tax revenue losses, especially for developing countries. Moreover, the complex network of DTTs at a global level may offer the opportunity for multinational companies to avoid taxes.

Moving towards multilateral solutions

One aspect that opens doors to tax evasion is related to the fact that tax authorities do not necessarily know which assets tax payers hold in different jurisdictions. Concerns about this lack of transparency led to the creation of the Global Forum on Transparency and Exchange of Information for Tax Purposes in 2000. The Global Forum has a self-standing dedicated Secretariat, based in the OECD Centre for Tax Policy and Administration. The Global Forum has notably supported the creation of the Common Reporting Standard (CRS), developed in response to the G20 request and approved by the OECD Council in 2014. The CRS calls on jurisdictions to obtain information from their financial institutions and automatically exchange that information with other jurisdictions on an annual basis.

Even in the case of full transparency, tax differences across countries provide multi-nationals with an arbitrage opportunity allowing them to minimise tax payments. While there are many ways in which firms can shift profits to low-tax locations, the use of internal, or transfer, prices is seen as one of the most significant (OECD, 2012). This is

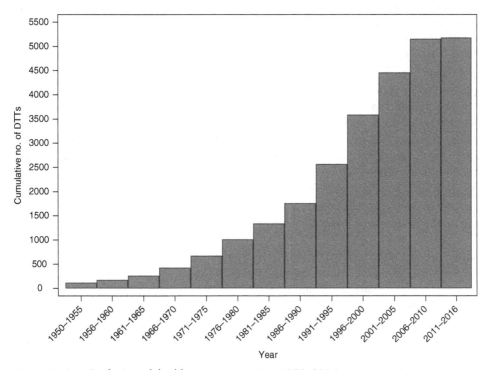

Figure 11.16 Evolution of double taxation treaties, 1950–2016.
Source: Authors' illustration based on the UNCTAD Investment Policy Hub database (UNCTAD, n.d.).

achieved by having an affiliate in a low-tax location charge high transfer prices for what it sells to an affiliate in a high-tax jurisdiction – in essence, inflating revenues where taxes are low and costs where taxes are high (Davies *et al.*, 2018). Such behaviour need not be illegal, yet the result is that profits are artificially shifted towards low-tax locations.

A multilateral legal platform for the taxation of transnational corporations' income is currently being explored by the OECD's Base Erosion and Profit Sharing (BEPS) Project and upon initiative of the G20 (OECD, 2013). In June 2017, over 70 countries signed the Multilateral Convention to Implement Tax Treaty Related Measures to Prevent Base Erosion and Profit Shifting. The so-called Multilateral Instrument (MLI) includes signatories from all continents and all levels of development. The MLI offers concrete solutions for governments to close the gaps in existing international tax rules by applying the results from the OECD/G20 BEPS Project into bilateral tax treaties worldwide. The MLI modifies the application of thousands of bilateral tax treaties concluded to eliminate double taxation.

Digital Trade

As discussed by Gröning, de la Rubia and Straubhaar in Chapter 3 of this Handbook, the digital economy is an increasingly important part of world trade. As early as 1998, the WTO adopted a first definition of the related term, "electronic commerce", understood as the "production, distribution, marketing, sale or delivery of goods and services by electronic means" (World Trade Organization, 1998). Twenty years on, there is consensus that digital trade encompasses digitally enabled transactions in trade in goods and services which can be either digitally or physically delivered, and which involve consumers, firms or governments (González and Jouanjean, 2017).

The liberalisation of digital trade presents similar challenges for policymakers who want to increase the benefits from trade whilst maintaining the possibility to pursue "other legitimate policy objectives". One particularity of digital trade is that the national and international rule books have to be designed from scratch. Whilst regulations in areas such as food safety have sometimes existed for over 500 years, rules to guarantee public security, enforcement of national law, national security, privacy, consumer protection and freedom of speech in the context of free data flows have often been designed from scratch. The risk of designing regulations that act as protectionist barriers is therefore real. At the same time, serious gaps in national and individual protection (at commercial, physical health and private levels) can arise, if regulation is absent or too weak.

Multilateral initiatives: early start, slow progress

As the key policy player in modern global trade, the WTO has established a system of agreements regulating international trade. To differing degrees, these treaties also extend to digital trade. The GATT, the GATS and its Annex on telecommunications services, TRIPS and the Information Technology Agreement (ITA) as well as its subsequent extension at the Nairobi Ministerial Conference (ITA-II) are the major treaties that are relevant to the governance of digital trade.

The WTO Work Programme on Electronic Commerce, established in 1998, sets out responsibilities for WTO bodies in e-commerce-related areas. While the latest initiative of the WTO, the Trade Facilitation Agreement (TFA) promotes electronic procedures to facilitate trade, it does not include e-commerce as an explicit part of the WTO negotiations on trade facilitation.

There are a number of challenges the WTO faces with regards to the governance of digital trade, including challenges regarding definitions (e.g. Fleuter, 2016) and challenges regarding classifications (e.g. Wu, 2017). In addition to this, a myriad of challenges need to be addressed in order to define the interface between trade liberalisation and relevant regulatory frameworks and in order to operationalise desired market opening. In preparation for the 11th Ministerial Conference of the WTO in Buenos Aires in December 2017, members submitted papers and proposals to reflect their interests with regards to these issue areas. The EU *et al.* paper (World Trade Organization, 2017) provides an interesting structure for thinking about digital commerce in the context of the multilateral trading system (the here-called EU *et al.* paper was circulated at the request of the delegations of Canada, Chile, Colombia, Côte d'Ivoire, the EU, the Republic of Korea, Mexico, Montenegro, Paraguay, Singapore and Turkey). In particular, it distinguishes between disciplines related to regulatory frameworks and disciplines guaranteeing open markets.

In the first category, the paper distinguishes between regulatory frameworks to address transparency, consumer confidence and trade facilitation. The explicit reference to consumer confidence is interesting in itself as it is not a theme that past trade negotiations have tended to give such a prominent role. The paper mentions consumer protection, cybersecurity, privacy protection and unsolicited communications as specific concerns. The trade facilitation header features a number of topics that are of quite technical nature, like the recognition of e-signatures, addressing e-payment and the role of technical standards.

Regarding the opening of markets, the paper makes the distinction between explicit commitments to liberalise trade in relevant services (e.g. telecom, professional services) and goods on the one hand and measures to ensure openness on the other hand. Disciplines regarding the cross-border flow of data, access to source code and localisation requirements fall under the second category according to the EU *et al.* paper.

Fundamental differences exist among WTO members on many of the topics mentioned in the previous paragraphs. In some cases, members are not even certain whether they are willing to negotiate the items. At the 2017 Ministerial Conference, members therefore merely agreed to continue to work under the Work Programme on Electronic Commerce, and no substantial progress was made in negotiations at the multilateral level. An important subgroup of 71 members, however, said they would initiate exploratory work towards future WTO negotiations on trade-related aspects of electronic commerce, with participation open to all WTO members. The group accounts for around 77% of global trade but excludes one of the most important players: China.

Rule-making in regional integration initiatives: progress with hurdles

In parallel with discussions at the multilateral level, a number of mega-regional initiatives, such as the Trade in Services Agreement (TISA), TTIP, CETA, the Regional Comprehensive Economic Partnership (RCEP) and TPP, have made significant progress in developing definitions (e.g. "digital product", "electronic transmission", and "personal information") and agreeing on provisions regarding market-opening commitments and relevant regulatory framework. To varying degrees, these agreements also include provisions on the intermediary liability of internet platforms, the use of cryptographic technologies or algorithms, the disclosure of source code of digital products, data localisation and geo-blocking, network neutrality and cyber espionage (e.g. Wu, 2017).

Progress on rule-making has therefore been more rapid at the regional rather than at the multilateral level, with the caveat that most of these regional initiatives represent ongoing negotiations or negotiations that have been put on hold. The only agreement that is currently operational is CETA, the agreement between Canada and the EU. This agreement contains a separate chapter on electronic commerce. Interestingly, out of the seven articles in this chapter, one deals with "trust and confidence in electronic commerce", stipulating that each party "should adopt or maintain laws, regulations or administrative measures for the protection of personal information of users engaged in electronic commerce and, when doing so, shall take into due consideration international standards of data protection of relevant international organisations of which both Parties are a member". The importance of the protection of personal information is thus explicitly recognised in the legal text.

Design of regulatory frameworks: catching up rapidly

As mentioned before, given the novelty of relevant technologies, regulatory frameworks for areas like cybersecurity and protection of private information were virtually non-existent at the national level until very recently. Regulators are, however, rapidly catching up, at least in the three main trading economies discussed in this chapter: China, the EU and the United States. Whilst the United States – home to some of the most important players in the digital world – maintains its traditional "hands off" stance when it comes to regulating markets, the level of regulatory activity has been high in the EU.

The EU has been one of the major promoters of privacy and data protection, affecting the global digital policy landscape in particular through the EU General Data Protection Regulation (GDPR) and the Privacy Shield between the United States and the EU. The EU adopted the GDPR in 2016 and it came into force in May 2018. The EU regulation affects the way private companies and organisations handle EU citizens' data. The GDPR is intended to harmonise data protection laws in EU member states. It also gives EU citizens much more control over their data, for example, by allowing users to move data (portability), or to demand the erasure of their data (right to be forgotten). At the same time, it imposes strict and onerous obligations, requiring companies, regardless of where they are based, to adhere to compliance requirements and standards of security.

China's cybersecurity law came into force in June 2017 and also contains explicit provisions regarding the protection of private information. Interestingly, the law contains a separate provision regarding restrictions on the transfer of "sensitive" personal information and business data overseas.

The EU also has an instrument dealing with the overseas sharing of data. The so-called Privacy Shield was adopted in 2016 and addresses the sharing of data across the Atlantic Ocean – the major data highway in the world – between the EU and the United States. The Privacy Shield is an attempt to reconcile differences in how the EU and the United States regulate data protection in cases in which data of

EU citizens are hosted in the United States. The Shield imposes stronger obligations on US companies and the US government to protect EU citizens' personal data and requires the US government to more robustly enforce the new provisions and monitor their implementation.

New Themes, New Partners?

At the writing of this chapter, discussions and negotiations on investment, taxation and digital trade are ongoing at the bilateral, regional and plurilateral level. As a matter of fact, positions on these matters are in many cases not yet clearly defined at the national level. It is therefore hard to predict where ongoing discussions and negotiations will lead. It is, however, interesting to note that entirely new spaces for synergies, compromise but also disagreements appear to be opening up.

The theme of investment is actively pursued at the WTO, albeit at the plurilateral level. It is the subject of new legal proposals, like the one for a Multilateral Investment Court by the EU. It is also the object of negotiations between two of the three main global players, as the EU and China are negotiating a Comprehensive Agreement on Investment.

Digital trade is a top theme on most countries' national policy agenda and is actively discussed and negotiated in different international forums. One of the main challenges in this field is how to define the interface between domestic regulation and international flow of digital products and data. As has been the case in the context of goods trade (e.g. relevant for TBT and SPS provisions), the US and EU positions are not entirely aligned in this matter, the United States rather taking a "hands-off" approach whilst regulatory activity at the EU level is high. China finds itself at the other extreme of the spectrum, being considered to maintain a "digital wall". In this context, it is interesting to note that the EU and Japan agreed in July 2018 to recognise each other's data protection systems as "equivalent", thus creating the world's largest area of safe data flows.

Last but not least, the theme of taxation has also entered the sphere of international negotiations after the financial crisis of 2007–2009, with the most prominent initiative, the Multilateral Convention to Implement Tax Treaty Related Measures to Prevent Base Erosion and Profit Shifting, being supported by the OECD.

From Mega-Regionalism to Mega-Multilateralism?

Whilst the second half of the 20th century has been marked by impressive progress on the multilateral trade agenda, the first two decades of the 21st century have taken a distinctive regional or plurilateral character. Since the creation of the multilateral trading system after World War II, regional integration has progressed in parallel with global integration. Indeed, multilateral trade rules have from the outset left space for preferential integration within their framework. Regional economic spaces like the EU and NAFTA could therefore be created and develop in full compliance with the WTO system.

As argued in this chapter, the interplay between the EU and the United States has played a fundamental role in shaping the dynamics and nature of the development of PTAs. This interplay also fundamentally shaped discussions and negotiations at the WTO. Agreements like the TBT Agreement and the SPS Agreement have very much arisen out of transatlantic differences in attitudes towards food safety.

With the success of early multilateral trade negotiation rounds to bring down tariffs, attention of discussions, negotiations and increasingly also disputes has shifted towards questions of how to deal with non-tariff measures. The Uruguay Round put issues like (trade-related) investment measures and (trade-related) IPRs on the negotiating table. Themes like labour, environment and competition policy entered and exited the discussions in different ways.

As this chapter shows, all these themes have been taken up in PTAs over the years. It can be argued that this is increasingly the case and that PTAs have significantly deepened the trade agenda. It is nevertheless the case that WTO discussions tended to be the stage setter for legal responses to new challenges in the realm of international trade. GATT rules also fundamentally influenced legal design in PTAs.

The beginning of the 21st century has arguably been marked by the recognition that the interaction of rule setting in trade with other domestic policy areas is even more complex than acknowledged so far. Two important construction sites on "trade and" matters have been added to the list for policymakers. The first one concerns the relationship between trade and finance. The Global Financial Crisis has brought the relationship between markets for goods and services on the one hand and financial markets on the other hand to the forefront of public attention. Matters of trade and matters of finance and taxation have traditionally been dealt with by different ministries and within different international frameworks yet are fundamentally interconnected. The second one concerns the development of new technologies and the need to create new rules for phenomena like e-commerce and data flows at the national and international level. The speed of technological development requires a speedy response.

Under pressure to deliver responses to complex challenges, changes in the membership of the WTO have at the same time made it more difficult to agree on common rules. If, in the second half of the 20th century, it was impossible to come to a deal at the WTO without an agreement between the two main players, the United States and the EU, the system now has a third player that cannot be avoided: China. China is, however, at a different level of development than the United States and the EU. In addition, though cultural differences between the United States and the EU exist and are significant, the differences between the old couple and the new player are probably starker. Those differences matter when it comes to questions regarding the balance between risk and technological progress, regarding the relationship between finance and trade and more generally regarding the need to balance trade prerogatives against other "legitimate policy objectives".

The jury is out as to where these new challenges will bring the multilateral trading system in the medium to long term. At the time of writing, the following three phenomena are worth highlighting:

- Regional agreements have traditionally relied on WTO legal text, but rule-making in new areas – like digital trade – is now increasingly being driven by legal innovation in preferential treaties. Preferential treaties now set the stage, rather than multilateral ones, which may create a real incentive for large players to influence regional rule setting with their views.

- Two players have been particularly active when it comes to "innovative" rule setting: the EU and China. The EU stands out because of its initiatives in the areas of trade and standards/regulation and because of the headway it has made in the area of digital trade. China has turned the post-World War II approach towards trade liberalisation upside down by putting a significantly stronger emphasis on infrastructure than on trade rules in its Belt and Road Initiative.
- The Global Financial Crisis has triggered unprecedented international interest in taxation rules for multinationals and, through the G20, put the OECD at the forefront of international actors in this field. The organisation that failed to bring the MAI negotiations to an end is now successfully handling the BEPS aspect.

Together, these three phenomena suggest that innovation in rule-making for trade has shifted to the regional level and that multilateral collaboration efforts on international economic law have shifted away from the WTO towards forums like the OECD. What does this imply for the role of the WTO as a rule setter for global trade?

The past two decades of the 20th century witnessed an unprecedented increase in trade and investment flows, largely driven by China's integration in the global economy. This integration was strongly facilitated by China's entry into the WTO. Future jumps in global trade and investment activity will not be the consequence of enlargements of the WTO family as most nations of the globe are already members.

Any new impulses will either come from the WTO deepening existing agreements or expanding into new areas, or from a deepening of regional integration. The latter is already happening, implying that regional integration initiatives increasingly incorporate new fields of international economic law like digital trade and investment. Innovation in international trade law is therefore more likely to come from the side of regional initiatives in the coming decades rather than from the side of the WTO.

In the meantime, multilateral activity in the field of international economic law is not dead but has shifted towards other fields of economic law, most notably taxation. This is a field that is highly "trade-related" and indeed has come to the forefront of policymakers' attention because of the tax avoidance strategies of multinational enterprises. The relevance of tax policies for trade is also recognised in the GATT. Like other national policies (e.g. labour market policies), tax policies have nevertheless never been dealt with directly under the WTO framework.

It remains to be seen whether the multilateral trading system manages to absorb these new regional initiatives and connect to "trade-related" multilateral initiatives. For the time being, the initiation of a number of plurilateral initiatives on small and medium-sized enterprises, investment facilitation and e-commerce within the WTO framework may put the multilateral system in a good position to get back in the driver's seat once major global trade players feel that it is time to return to the multilateral negotiating table.

References

Abreu, M.D. (2016) Preferential Rules of Origin in Regional Trade Agreements. In: Acharya, R. (ed.) *Regional Trade Agreements and the Multilateral Trading System.* Cambridge: Cambridge University Press, pp. 58–110.

Allee, T., Elsig, M. & Lugg, A. (2017a) The Ties between the World Trade Organization and Preferential Trade Agreements: A Textual Analysis. *Journal of International Economic Law*, 20(2), 333–363.

Allee, T., Elsig, M. & Lugg, A. (2017b) Is the European Union Trade Deal with Canada New or Recycled? A Text-as-Data Approach. *Global Policy*, 8(2), 246–252.

Allee, T. & Lugg, A. (2016) Who Wrote the Rules for the Trans-Pacific Partnership? *Research & Politics*, 3(3). https://doi.org/10.1177/2053168016658919.

Baccini, L., Dür, A. & Elsig, M. (2015) The Politics of Trade Agreement Design: Revisiting the Depth-Flexibility Nexus. *International Studies Quarterly*, 59(4), 765–775.

Baccini, L., Haftel, Y.Z. & Dür, A. (2015) Imitation and Innovation in International Governance: The Diffusion of Trade Agreement Design. In: Dür, A. & Elsig, M. (eds.) *Trade Cooperation: The Purpose, Design and Effects of Preferential Trade Agreements*. Cambridge: Cambridge University Press, pp. 134–164.

Baldwin, R. (1993) A Domino Theory of Regionalism. *CEPR discussion paper*. Retrieved from: https://www.researchgate.net/publication/5192440_A_Domino_Theory_of_Regionalism (accessed 10 July 2019).

Baldwin, R. & Jaimovich, D. (2012) Are Free Trade Agreements Contagious? *Journal of International Economics*, 88(1), 1–16.

Bang, P.F. (2007) Trade and Empire In Search of Organizing Concepts for the Roman Economy. *Past & Present*, 195(1), 3–54.

Bhagwati, J. (1992) Regionalism versus Multilateralism. *The World Economy*, 15(5), 535–556.

Bhagwati, J. (1993) Regionalism and Multilateralism: An Overview. In: de Melo, J. & Panagariya, A. (eds.) *New Dimensions in Regional Integration*. Cambridge: Cambridge University Press, pp. 22–51.

Bhagwati, J. (2008) *Termites in the Trading System: How Preferential Agreements Undermine Free Trade*. Oxford: Oxford University Press.

Chase, C., Yanovich, A., Crawford, J.-A. & Ugaz, P. (2013) Mapping of Dispute Settlement Mechanisms in Regional Trade Agreements – Innovative or Variations on a Theme? WTO *Staff Working Paper* ERSD-2013-07. Retrieved from: https://www.econstor.eu/bitstream/10419/80057/1/749852216.pdf (accessed 10 July 2019).

Chase, K. (2006) Multilateralism Compromised: The Mysterious Origins of GATT Article XXIV. *World Trade Review*, 5(1), 1–30.

Cottier, T., Sieber-Gasser, C. & Wermelinger, G. (2015) The Dialectical Relationship of Preferential and Multilateral Trade Agreements. In: Dür, A. & Elsig, M. (eds.) *Trade Cooperation: The Purpose, Design and Effects of Preferential Trade Agreements*. Cambridge: Cambridge University Press, pp. 465–496.

Crawford, J.-A. (2012) *Market Access Provisions on Trade in Goods in Regional Trade Agreements*. WTO *Staff Working Paper* ERSD-2012-20. Retrieved from: https://www.econstor.eu/bitstream/10419/80055/1/729502015.pdf (accessed 10 July 2019).

Crawford, J.-A., McKeagg, J. & Tolstova, J. (2016) Mapping of Safeguard Provisions in Regional Trade Agreements. In: Acharya, R. (ed.) *Regional Trade Agreements and the Multilateral Trading System*. Cambridge: Cambridge University Press, pp. 230–315.

Davies, R.B., Martin, J., Parenti, M. & Toubal, F. (2018) Knocking on Tax Haven's Door: Multinational Firms and Transfer Pricing. *The Review of Economics and Statistics*, 100(1), 120–134.

Defraigne, P. (2002) New Regionalism and Global Economic Governance. *UNI/CRIS e-Working Paper* W-2002/2.

Dür, A. (2010) *Protection for Exporters – Power and Discrimination in Transatlantic Trade Relations, 1930–2010*. Ithaca: Cornell University Press.

Dür, A., Baccini, L. & Elsig, M. (2014) The design on International Trade Agreements: Introducing a New Dataset. *Review of International Organizations*, 9(3), 353–375.

The Economist (2017) The Belt-and-Road Express: China Faces Resistance to a Cherished Theme of its Foreign Policy. (4 May). Retrieved from https://www.economist.com/

china/2017/05/04/china-faces-resistance-to-a-cherished-theme-of-its-foreign-policy (accessed on 22 July 2019).

Egger, P., Pfaffermayr, M. & Winner, H. (2006) The Impact of Endogenous Tax Treaties on Foreign Direct Investment: Theory and Evidence. *Canadian Journal of Economics/Revue canadienne d'économique*, 39(3), 901–931.

Elsig, M. & Klotz, S. (2019) Behind-the-Border Measures and the New Generation of Trade Agreements: TBT and SPS Compared. In: Francois, J. & Hoekman, B. (eds.) *Behind-the-Border Policies: Assessing and Addressing Non-Tariff Measures*. Cambridge: Cambridge University Press, pp. 246–276.

Fleuter, S. (2016) The Role of Digital Products Under the WTO: A New Framework for GATT and GATS Classification. *Chicago Journal of International Law*, 17(1), 152–177.

Forere, M.A. (2017) Move Away from BITs Framework: A Need for Multilateral investment Treaty? *WTI Working Paper* No. 15/2017. Retrieved from: https://www.wti.org/media/filer_public/eb/4a/eb4ae7db-3f2b-483d-9151-0ae41bdaf2a0/working_paper_no_15_2017_forere.pdf (accessed 10 July 2019).

Gantz, D.A. (2009) *Regional Trade Agreements – Law, Policy and Practice*. Durham: Carolina Academic Press.

González, J.L. & Jouanjean, M.-A. (2017) Digital Trade – Developing a Framework for Analysis. *OECD Trade Policy Papers* No. 205. doi:10.1787/524c8c83-en.

Hofmann, C., Osnago, A. & Ruta, M. (2017) *Horizontal* Depth: A New Database on the Content of Preferential Trade Agreements. World Bank, *Policy Research Working Papers*. doi:10.1596/1813-9450-7981.

Horowitz, S. (2004) Reversing Globalization: Trade Policy Consequences of World War I. *European Journal of International Relations*, 10(1), 33–59.

Hufbauer, G. & Moran, T. (2015) Investment and Trade Regimes Conjoined: Economic Facts and Regulatory Frameworks. Retrieved from: http://e15initiative.org/wp-content/uploads/2015/09/E15-Investment-Hufbauer-and-Moran-Final.pdf (accessed 10 July 2019).

International Monetary Fund (2014) Spillovers in International Corporate Taxation. Retrieved from: https://www.imf.org/external/np/pp/eng/2014/050914.pdf (accessed 10 July 2019).

International Trade Centre (2017) SME Competitiveness Outlook 2017 – The Region: A Door to Global Trade. Retrieved from: http://www.intracen.org/uploadedFiles/intracenorg/Content/Publications/smeco17.pdf (accessed 10 July 2019).

Irwin, D. (1993) The GATT's Contribution to Economic Recovery in Post-war Europe. Board of Governors of the Federal Reserve, *International Finance Discussion Papers* No. 442. Retrieved from: https://www.federalreserve.gov/pubs/ifdp/1993/442/ifdp442.pdf (accessed 10 July 2019).

Irwin, D. (2017) *Clashing over Commerce: A History of US Trade Policy*. Chicago: University of Chicago Press.

Jackson, L.A. & Vitikala, H. (2016) Cross-Cutting Issues in Regional Trade Agreements: Sanitary and Phytosanitary Measures. In: Acharya, R. (ed.) *Regional Trade Agreements and the Multilateral Trading System*. Cambridge: Cambridge University Press, pp. 316–370.

Krugman, P. (1991) The Move Towards Free Trade Zones. *Economic Review*, 76(6), 5–25.

Krugman, P. (1993) Regionalism versus Multilateralism: Analytical Notes. In: de Melo, J. & Panagariya, A. (eds.) *New Dimensions in Regional Integration*. Cambridge: Cambridge University Press, pp. 58–79.

Lejárraga, I. (2014) Deep Provisions in Regional Trade Agreements: How Multilateral-Friendly? *OECD Trade Policy Papers* No. 168. Retrieved from: https://www.oecd-ilibrary.org/docserver/5jxvgfn4bjf0-en.pdf?expires=1562749850&id=id&accname=guest&checksum=36CDAD9DE579F6C2E4B443A3A3A9D588 (accessed 10 July 2019).

Mansfield, E.D. & Milner, H.V. (1999) The New Wave of Regionalism. *International Organization*, 53(3), 589–627.

Mansfield, E.D. & Milner, H.V. (2015) The Political Economy of Preferential Trade Agreements. In: Dür, A. & Elsig, M. (eds.) *Trade Cooperation: The Purpose, Design and Effects of Preferential Trade Agreements*. Cambridge: Cambridge University Press. pp. 56–81.

Mansfield, E.D. & Reinhardt, E. (2003) Multilateral Determinants of Regionalism: The Effects of GATT/WTO on the Formation of Preferential Trading Arrangements. *International Organization*, 57(4), 829–862.

van Marrewijk, C. (2017) *International Trade*. Oxford: Oxford University Press.

McGlone, P. (2016) President Obama: The TPP Would Let America, not China, Lead the Way on Global Trade. *Washington Post* (2 May). Retrieved from https://www.washingtonpost.com/opinions/president-obama-the-tpp-would-let-america-not-china-lead-the-way-on-global-trade/2016/05/02/680540e4-0fd0-11e6-93ae-50921721165d_story.html?noredirect=on&utm_term=.d4de0a7bf18a (accessed 13 July 2019)

Molina, A.C. & Khoroshavina, V. (2015) TBT provisions in Regional Trade Agreements: To what extent do they go beyond the WTO TBT Agreement? *WTO Staff Working Paper* ERSD-2015-09. Retrieved from: https://www.econstor.eu/bitstream/10419/125799/1/845006401.pdf (accessed 10 July 2019).

Narlikar, A., Daunton, M. & Stern, R.M. (2012) *The Oxford Handbook on the World Trade Organization*. Oxford: Oxford University Press.

Neumayer, E. (2007) Do Double Taxation Treaties Increase Foreign Direct Investment to Developing Countries? *The Journal of Development Studies*, 43(8), 1501–1519.

Neumayer, E. & Spess, L. (2005) Do Bilateral Investment Treaties Increase Foreign Direct Investment to Developing Countries? *World Development*, 3(1), 31–49.

Nollen, S.D. & Quinn, D.P. (1987) Free Trade, Fair Trade, Strategic Trade, and Protectionism in the US Congress, 1987–88. *International Organization*, 48(3), 491–525.

OECD (2012) *Dealing Effectively with the Challenges of Transfer Pricing*. Paris: OECD Publishing.

OECD (2013) Action Plan on Base Erosion and Profit Shifting. Retrieved from: https://www.oecd.org/ctp/BEPSActionPlan.pdf (accessed 10 July 2019).

Pauwelyn, J. & Alschner, W. (2014) Forget About the WTO: The Network of Relations between PTAs and "Double PTAs". In: Dür, A. & Elsig, M. (eds.) *Trade Cooperation: The Purpose, Design and Effects of Preferential Trade Agreements*. Cambridge: Cambridge University Press, pp. 497–531.

Pierre, L. (2016) Services Rules in Regional Trade Agreements: How Divers or Creative Are They Compared to the Multilateral Rules? In: Acharya, R. (ed.) *Regional Trade Agreements and the Multilateral Trading System*. Cambridge, Cambridge University Press, pp. 421–494.

Possehl, G. (2002) Indus Mesopotamain Trade: The Record in the Indus. *Iranica Antiqua*, XXXVII, 326–342.

Rey, J.-D. (2016) Do Regional Anti-dumping Regimes Make a Difference? In: Acharya, R. (ed.) *Regional Trade Agreements and the Multilateral Trading System*. Cambridge: Cambridge University Press, pp. 157–229.

Rohini, A. (2016) Regional Trade Agreements: Recent Developments. In: Acharya, R. (ed.) *Regional Trade Agreements and the Multilateral Trading System*. Cambridge: Cambridge University Press, pp. 1–18.

Schott, J.J. (2004) Free Trade Agreements: Boon or Bane of the World Trading System? In: Schott, J.J. (ed.) *Free Trade Agreements: US Strategies and Priorities*. Washington, DC: Institute for International Economics, pp. 3–19.

UNCTAD (2009) *World Investment Report 2009: Transnational Corporations, Agricultural Production and Development*. New York: United Nations. Retrieved from: https://unctad.org/en/Docs/wir2009_en.pdf (accessed 22 July 2019).

UNCTAD (2015) *World Investment Report 2015: Reforming International Investment Governance*. New York: United Nations. Retrieved from: https://unctad.org/en/PublicationsLibrary/wir2015_en.pdf (accessed 22 July 2019).

UNCTAD (n.d.) Investment Policy Hub: International Investment Agreements Navigator. Retrieved from: https://investmentpolicy.unctad.org/international-investment-agreements (accessed 22 July 2019).

United States, Department of State (1944) *Proceedings and Documents of the United Nations Monetary and Financial Conference.* Washington, DC: United States Printing Office. Retrieved from: https://fraser.stlouisfed.org/files/docs/publications/books/1948_state_bwood_v1.pdf (accessed 10 July 2019).

Valdes, R. & McCann, M. (2016) Intellectual Property Provisions in Regional Trade Agreements: Revision and Update. In: Acharya, R. (ed.) *Regional Trade Agreements and the Multilateral Trading System.* Cambridge: Cambridge University Press, pp. 497–607.

Winters, L.A. (2015) The WTO and Regional Trading Agreements: Is It All Over for Multilateralism? University of Sussex, *Working Paper Series* No. 82-2015. Retrieved from: https://www.sussex.ac.uk/webteam/gateway/file.php?name=wps-82-2015.pdf&site=24 (accessed 10 July 2019).

World Bank (2018) World Development Indicators. Retrieved from https://datacatalog. worldbank.org/dataset/world-development-indicators (accessed 28 August 2018).

World Trade Organization (1947) *The General Agreement on Tariffs and Trade. World Trade Organization. Retrieved from*: Available from: https://www.wto.org/english/docs_e/legal_e/ gatt47_01_e.htm (accessed 10 July 2019).

World Trade Organization (1998) Work Programme on Electronic Commerce. Retrieved from: https://www.wto.org/english/tratop_e/ecom_e/wkprog_e.htm (accessed 10 July 2019).

World Trade Organization (2000) Draft Report on the Examination of the North American Free Trade Agreement. Retrieved from: https://docs.wto.org/dol2fe/Pages/FE_Search/FE_S_S009-DP.aspx?language=E&CatalogueIdList=1399&CurrentCatalogueIdIndex=0&FullTextHash= 371857150&HasEnglishRecord=True&HasFrenchRecord=True&HasSpanishRecord=True (accessed 22 July 2019).

World Trade Organization (2007) *World Trade Report 2007: Six Decades Of Multilateral Trade Cooperation: What Have We Learnt?* Geneva: WTO.

World Trade Organization (2017) Work Programme on Electronic Commerce: Trade Policy, the WTO and the Digital Economy. JOB/GC/116/Rev2, JOB/CGT/4/Rev.2, JOB/SERV/248/ Rev.2, JOB/IP/21/Rev.2 and JOB/DEV/42/Rev.2.

Wu, M. (2017) Digital Trade-Related Provisions in Regional Trade Agreements: Existing Models and Lessons for the Multilateral Trade System. Retrieved from: http://e15initiative. org/wp-content/uploads/2015/09/RTA-Exchange-Digital-Trade-Mark-Wu-Final-2.pdf (accessed 10 July 2019).

Zeiler, T. (1997) GATT Fifty Years Ago: US Trade Policy and Imperial Tariff Preferences. *Business and Economic History,* 26(2), 709–717.

Chapter 12

United States: What to Expect from a Protective US Trade Policy

Erdal Yalcin, Gabriel Felbermayr, and Marina Steininger

Introduction

With the inauguration of the new US President, protectionism in the world of international trade appears to have reached a new level. The United States is currently the world's largest single market, in which the US citizens earn one of the highest worldwide per capita incomes, of US$58,000. Due to its economic size, economic policy measures, in particular trade policies, have a far-reaching impact on global economic developments. The consequences of a protectionist US trade policy may not only be limited to economic dimensions, but can also have important political and social implications.

Against this background, this chapter quantifies the economic consequences of US protectionist trade aspirations. Our analysis focuses on trade policy scenarios, which have been communicated by the current US administration as potential new trade policies. We draw on the results of a recent study of the ifo Institute conducted on behalf of the Bertelsmann Foundation (Yalcin, Steininger et al., 2017). In the first simulation, a retraction from the North American Free Trade Agreement (NAFTA) is considered. The study then illustrates the potential consequences of a "border tax adjustment" (BTA) policy. Finally, further measures to protect the US market are simulated by presuming an increase in American duties. The study presents robust quantitative results that can be expected if an increasingly protectionist US trade policy were to be implemented.

Growing Protectionism

In our comprehensive analysis we reveal that the United States actually levies relatively low tariffs compared to its trading partners (see Figure 12.1).

The Handbook of Global Trade Policy, First Edition. Edited by Andreas Klasen.
© 2020 John Wiley & Sons Ltd. Published 2020 by John Wiley & Sons Ltd.

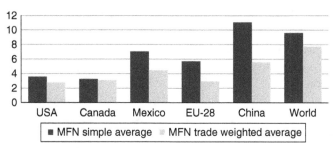

Figure 12.1   Average most-favoured-nation tariff by country, 2015 (%).
Source: World Integrated Trade Solutions (https://wits.worldbank.org/).

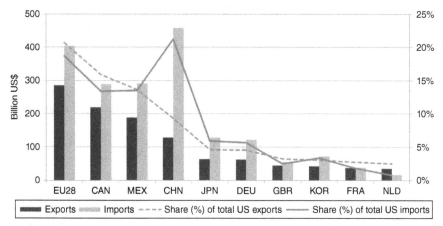

Figure 12.2   US trade balance with its top ten trading partners, 2015.
Source: Baci World Trade Database (http://www.cepii.fr/cepii/en/bdd_modele/presentation.
asp?id=1).

At the same time, it is clear that in parallel with this liberal tariff policy, the United States has run a high trade deficit for many years, especially in goods trade.

This macroeconomic imbalance can be observed with eight of the ten top US trading partners (see Figure 12.2). Considering these two phenomena – low tariffs and high trade deficits – it initially seems understandable that US political stakeholders regard the present trade structure as unfair. Moreover, US jobs are particularly concentrated in industries that suffer from America's open stance. These interest groups unsurprisingly see the isolation of the US market as an effective cure.

Moreover, in the wake of the Global Financial Crisis in 2008 and the resulting economic stagnation in the post-Doha Round within the World Trade Organization (WTO), leading trading nations such as the United States or the EU strived to conclude new regional trade agreements (RTAs) to advance progress in global trade liberalisation in individual regions. These agreements included the Transatlantic Trade and Investment Partnership (TTIP), aimed at improving economic relations between the EU and the United States, and the transpacific trade agreement between the United States and a multitude of Pacific countries (Trans-Pacific Partnership, TPP). Prevailing literature suggests that free trade agreements (FTAs) lead to a reduction of tariffs and non-tariff barriers (such as the mutual recognition of product standards; see e.g. Bergstrand *et al.*, 2015). In the mid-1990s, 30 trade agreements were ratified each year. This rate fell to 26 during the financial crisis, and since 2011 the average number of ratified FTAs has fallen to 10 (Figure 12.3). At this point, it is important to mention that these new agreements are deeper and farther reaching than their predecessors and include, for example, public procurement, services and regulatory chapters.

The ratification of FTAs can help to foster growth through structural reforms, for example, which are needed in times when the competitiveness of the industrial countries is eroded, especially compared to that of advanced developing countries like China or India. Thwarting such initiatives may not be a good idea. The relative gridlock of the ratification of new trade agreements certainly cannot be considered responsible for the rise of the protectionist era; available data shows that the global trend towards explicit protectionist measures has been growing for several years. Trade protection measures, such as anti-dumping tariffs, tariffs, quotas or other protective duties implemented for a certain number of product lines, are a good indication.

Admittedly, these measures are regulated through international trade laws and might even be justified, but they still occur in terms of protectionist aspirations. The share of product lines affected by such protective measures increased from approximately 0.5% in 1990 to 2.5% in 2015.

With the appointment of Donald Trump as the new US President, an "America first" attitude reached new dimensions. As illustrated above, in terms of its global tariff rates, the United States can be considered a very open economy due to its relatively low tariffs. This country has reduced tariffs both within NAFTA and within the WTO to a relatively low level compared to its respective trading partners. If non-tariff barriers are taken into consideration, however, this statement needs to be qualified. Examining non-tariff trade protection, the United States proves to be an increasingly protectionist country – especially in recent years. In recent years, the number of regulatory trade barriers, on the US import side, has increased considerably. Figure 12.4 shows the development of an increasingly protectionist attitude on the part of the United States. In 2009, only 126 protectionist measures were evident. In 2017 the number rose to almost 1200 discriminatory measures.

Compared to the remaining G20 countries, the United States is by far the most protectionist country, as it implements the highest number of non-tariff barriers (see Figure 12.5; the darker the shaded area, the higher the number of US protectionist measures against the respective region).

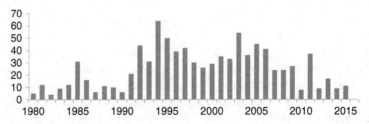

Figure 12.3 Number of FTAs ratified since 1980.
Source: WTO Regional Trade Agreements Database (http://rtais.wto.org/UI/PublicMaintain RTAHome.aspx).

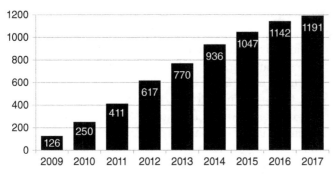

Figure 12.4 Number of US discriminatory measures since 2009.
Source: Global Trade Alert data (https://www.globaltradealert.org/).

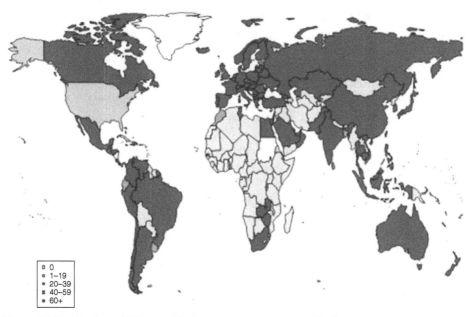

Figure 12.5 Number of US protectionist measures per country (in force).
Source: IMF (2016).

Empirical studies show that in recent years it is not an increase in tariffs but an increase in non-tariff barriers that is responsible for creating welfare losses. The protectionist measures adopted by the United States may therefore have serious consequences. The increasingly reluctant US attitude towards international trade might have ramifications that go beyond the economy to impact on politics and society across the globe. More specifically, the United States has put the already very advanced trade agreement negotiated with both the EU and the trans-Pacific countries on hold: TTIP and the TPP are not being implemented for the time being. Official papers on the foreign trade strategy of the US President suggest renegotiating old agreements if goals such as lowering the trade deficit are not achieved. The new US government has announced a renegotiation of NAFTA, and in addition, the Korean agreement and the conditions for China's WTO membership are also candidates for increasing US protectionism. The main goals of this protectionism include new job creation in the United States, lowering the trade deficit and a domestic economic upswing. But this "Buy American" approach misjudges the fact that the trade balance is more dependent on the saving and investment decisions made by US citizens than on trade policy. In these latter points, US attention is particularly focused on Germany and China.

In recent years, China has played a particularly important role in US trade relations with the rest of world. After China joined the WTO in 2001, in particular, US trade with the country surged dramatically. This development was the driving force behind the steadily growing US trade deficit with China. US import value from China now exceeds 3.5 times that of US exports to China. Over the years, a persistent US trade deficit has not only existed with China; the United States is currently running a sizeable trade deficit with eight out of its ten most important trading partners (see Figure 12.2). These partners include Japan and Germany, which export twice as much to the United States as they import. Within the EU, trade relations with the United States are predominantly characterised by trade surpluses.

The US administration is currently examining trade relations with all foreign countries and is evaluating whether the trade practices are "fair" from a US perspective. If trade practices by foreign countries are classified as non-competitive or unfair, the US administration plans to restrict their access to the US market. Specifically, the taxation of goods in America is to be reformed to the disadvantage of imported, foreign value added. This is to be achieved by, among other things, a so-called BTA. The fact that the United States in particular is showing an increasingly reserved attitude towards international trade weighs particularly heavily.

As illustrated, on the one hand, the United States is a relatively open economy with regard to tariffs, both within NAFTA and with the rest of the world; on the other hand, it is highly protectionist in the form of non-tariff barriers. Although the US service sector is increasingly moving into trade surpluses, political dissatisfaction with long-run adjustments is understandable. High trade deficits in goods trade, coupled with high import volumes from China and Europe, raise the question of how these developments are compatible with the low level of job creation in traditional industries in the Midwestern United States. Thus, the call for a correction of these imbalances via a protectionist trade policy is initially understandable. Nevertheless, a protectionist trade policy is very unlikely to address these economic imbalances. The threats of worldwide counteractive protectionist measures will not only harm key US trading partners, but will predominantly threaten the stability of the global economy.

Quantitative Analysis: ifo Trade Model

The essential objective in the following analysis is to quantify all of the trade effects that can take place in the course of a policy intervention. First, the direct response of trade flows to an increase in tariffs; and second, general equilibrium effects, such as price adjustments for consumers and the indirect increase in production costs. Trade protectionism can certainly benefit individual stakeholders while being to the disadvantage of a majority of economic agents. The quantification of general equilibrium welfare effects is therefore of particular interest to avoid any political misguidance.

The underlying ifo Trade Model is a computable general equilibrium (CGE) model which falls into the class of New Quantitative Trade Theory (NQTT) models.

This means that the estimation of parameters (essentially trade elasticities and the trade cost effects of the agreement in question) is conducted on the same data that are used as the baseline for the simulation exercise. However, the theoretical basis of the model is very standard and comparable to other CGE models. It is a stochastic, multi-sector, multi-country Ricardian model of the type developed by Eaton and Kortum (2002), extended to incorporate rich value chain interactions by Caliendo and Parro (2015), broadened to include non-tariff barriers by Aichele *et al.* (2014, 2016) and described in general terms by Costinot and Rodriguez-Clare (2014).

The pioneering work by Eaton and Kortum (2002), in particular the characterisation of technology as a random variable, allows us to obtain analytical results which make sure that the estimation of model parameters can be carried out in a consistent way based on a specific equilibrium relationship obtained from the model itself (the gravity equation). The estimation procedure is described in Aichele *et al.* (2016); note, however, that this paper provides more aggregate results than those shown in the present study.

Like all other well-known CGE models that are used for trade policy analysis, the ifo Trade Model assumes perfect competition and full employment; it requires detailed data on sectoral value added and production, trade flows of goods and services, input–output relations between domestic and foreign sectors and technological input coefficients (treating cost shares as constant assuming Cobb–Douglas technologies) as inputs. In a similar way to almost all other CGE models, these data come from the Global Trade Analysis Project (GTAP). We use the newest available dataset (GTAP 9.1), which refers to the year 2011. We use the model to update the data such that it reflects the trade policy landscape as observed in 2016.

The ifo Trade Model is a general equilibrium model which simultaneously quantifies the effects of trade policy scenarios on sectoral trade flows, value added, employment, wages, tariff income, gross domestic product (GDP), prices and other variables of all countries involved. Thus, trade diversion effects are fully accounted for. For example, US protectionism could lead to a redirection of European car parts imports away from sources such as the United States towards Asia. These diversion effects are the root cause for the fact that the welfare effects of FTAs are generally ambiguous for the parties engaged in negotiating them and also for the countries remaining outside of the agreement. The same argument holds for reverting trade agreements. The model allows for a very rich pattern of domestic and international sourcing patterns. This means that an expansion of economic activity in one country can lead to increased exports of third countries, which counteract the trade diversion effects.

The model provides static level effects on real income and trade. Potential dynamic effects of trade liberalisation, e.g. on the innovation activities of firms, are not taken into account. In other words, we provide a lower bound for the potential effects of a protectionist US trade policy. However, this does not imply that the static effects would result instantaneously after the increase in trade protection.

Another caveat worth mentioning is that the ifo Trade Model, like almost all other CGE models, does not explicitly include rules of origin. This means that the model may generate too little trade diversion, since goods originating from third countries may enjoy preferential treatment when used as inputs in the parties' production systems. Note, however, that at the level of sectoral aggregation used in the model, the share of third-party value added in exports is beyond the critical thresholds of 50% in almost all cases.

One important advantage of the ifo Trade Model is that one can calculate the effects of trade policy changes without knowing the level of trade costs. This is an enormous advantage, because trade costs other than tariffs would be very difficult to quantify and any quantification would come with substantial uncertainties. However, one needs to have information about the expected changes in sectoral trade costs to model the effects of, for example, a protectionist United States. This is relatively easy when talking about tariffs, since they can be directly observed. The only complication here is to aggregate tariffs up to the level of detail in the model (57 industries) and how to deal with specific tariffs and tariff quotas. We use the data provided by GTAP, which already solves these problems. How to deal with changes in non-tariff trade barriers is more involved. We follow the recent trade literature in order to identify non-tariff barrier changes based on structural gravity equations.

The ifo model has a number of attractive properties for our purpose:

- It has a detailed subdivision of sectors, with a maximum of 57 sectors. It has more than 20 agriculture and food processing subsectors.
- The model is estimated and specified at the country level, with 140 countries. Hence any pattern of FTAs can be analysed, and the United States appears individually and not as part of some aggregate (NAFTA etc.).
- The model captures international production networks so we can analyse "trade in value added". For aquaculture and the food industry in Norway, for instance, about 70–80% of the gross value of production is represented by input goods and services (see e.g. Melchior and Sverdrup, 2015). For services, such input–output effects are of huge importance and the model is constructed to take them into account.
- The model is data-based. Since all parameters are estimated on exactly the baseline data that describes the status quo, we have information about the variance–covariance structure of the estimated parameters. So, in principle, we can calculate exact confidence intervals for all of the endogenous model outcomes, computing time being the only restriction. Other approaches, which use parameter estimates from external data sources, cannot provide this type of analysis. Hence, we can tell how likely the predictions are, based on real data.

Scenarios

This subsection presents the actively communicated US trade policies that may potentially be implemented by the current US administration. Additionally, an isolation of the US market – as far as possible under the WTO agreement – is simulated. Due to uncertainties in the potential design of a US protectionist policy, it is necessary to quantify different scenarios. A detailed analysis and description of counterfactual policies can be retrieved from the recent ifo study on the consequences of Trump's protectionist aspirations (Yalcin, Felbermayr *et al.*, 2017).

Scenario No. 1: withdrawal from NAFTA
The first scenario considers the expected economic consequences of a partial reintroduction of US trade barriers with NAFTA countries. To this end, it considers possible

tariff adjustments and non-tariff barriers between the NAFTA countries. Countries like Germany could be indirectly affected due to the weakening of demand from NAFTA members due to protectionism. Sectors heavily reliant on this region's trade in particular may face negative consequences. However, third countries may also stand to profit from a decrease in trade between NAFTA members through trade diversion effects. The German automotive industry could, for example, act as a substitute for initial US demand from Mexico or Canada in this scenario.

Scenario No. 2: protectionist US trade policy with respect to the rest of the world

In principle, it is possible for the United States to introduce an even stronger protectionist trade policy by systematically raising tariffs on all traded goods of all WTO trading partners. The first sub-scenario assumes a one-sided US tariff increase of 20 percentage points. Simultaneously, WTO members increase their tariffs towards the United States, thus simulating tariff retaliation in response to the increased US import duties. In addition to the tariff increases of the previous scenario, the second sub-scenario includes a simultaneous 20% increase in non-tariff barriers (NTBs) against all US trading partners and vice versa.

Scenario No. 3: introduction of border tax adjustment

In 2016, the US representatives Paul Ryan and Kevin Brady introduced a new tax reform. They suggested a decrease in the federal tax on corporate profits from today's 35% to 20%, enabling investments to become completely deductible and making international revenues subject to the BTA. Concrete exports are tax deductible, while imports have to be added. Consequently, the system would tax consumption more heavily than production, making it equivalent to the European system of value-added taxes. It thereby offsets the disadvantage of (non-deductible) equity as opposed to deductible foreign capital. The US administration wants to tax domestic consumption instead of domestic production by increasing tariffs on imports and dispensing exports from taxation. Implicitly, such a tax policy means that US imports are subject to a protective tariff. The introduction of such a trade policy could affect not only foreign suppliers, but also US citizens. It is therefore of general interest that such a tax policy is evaluated quantitatively. This quantitative analysis shows which countries stand to gain from this trade policy and which will lose out. By assuming a flexible exchange rate, the US trade balance can be expected to remain largely unchanged, and any changes will be confined to welfare parameters, like changes in tax revenues and terms-of-trade conditions. Effects can nevertheless be expected across sectors and trading partners.

Results

As already described, the ifo Trade Model is able to show the trade diversion and creation effects arising due to a counterfactual change in trade policies. Table 12.1 shows the top ten US exporting destinations and the respective initial value of exports in million US dollars. Furthermore, the table shows the resulting percentage changes of US exports for each of the scenarios. Table 12.2 is built similarly to Table 12.1 and shows the US import side.

Table 12.1 Change in bilateral US exports with top ten trading partners

Rank	Importing country	Value of initial US exports (US$ million)	NAFTA	WTO (only tariff change)	WTO (tariff and NTB change)	BTA
					Change in exports (%)	
					with retaliation	
1	Canada	289,808	−11.4	−48.6	−73.7	−6.1
2	Mexico	176,284	−9.8	−55.6	−77.8	−6.9
3	China	110,369	−1.2	−48.0	−76.9	−7.5
4	Germany	79,446	−0.8	−34.7	−73.8	−7.5
5	UK	73,643	−1.3	−41.6	−76.0	−4.1
6	Japan	63,598	−1.2	−48.7	−75.3	−5.4
7	Ireland	60,924	−0.1	−12.5	−61.9	−6.2
8	France	57,650	−2.0	−38.4	−76.4	−5.3
9	Netherlands	47,883	−1.3	−30.4	−72.1	−7.0
10	Korea	43,853	−1.1	−45.0	−75.0	−7.1
	Total	1,917,773	−3.52	−38.54	−73.45	−5.87

Source: ifo Trade Model, Aichele *et al.* (2016).

Table 12.2 Change in bilateral US imports with top ten trading partners

Rank	Exporting country	Value of initial US imports (US$ million)	NAFTA	WTO (only tariff change)	WTO (tariff and NTB change)	BTA
					Change in imports (%)	
					with retaliation	
1	Canada	348,576	−21.2	−34.0	−57.0	−5.8
2	China	344,939	1.5	−37.3	−59.3	−6.7
3	Mexico	265,531	−13.7	−37.4	−58.6	−6.7
4	Germany	134,374	3.2	−32.4	−62.0	−5.0
5	Japan	120,174	4.1	−38.5	−60.8	−6.1
6	UK	85,289	2.1	−17.2	−61.3	−0.5
7	Korea	77,881	3.5	−34.0	−61.3	−5.4
8	France	49,168	1.6	−21.5	−61.1	−1.6
9	Italy	44,966	2.0	−33.4	−59.4	−5.1
10	India	36,474	2.2	−32.1	−55.0	−5.0
	Total	2,395,728	−2.82	−30.85	−58.80	−4.70

Source: ifo Trade Model, Aichele *et al.* (2016).

As a result of the protectionist US policies implemented against the other NAFTA members, exports from the NAFTA members decrease the most (−21% of exports from Canada and −14% of exports from Mexico). Exports from the other most important US export destinations increase slightly by between 1.5 and 3.5% (see Table 12.2, NAFTA scenario). On aggregate, however, US exports decrease by 3.5%, meaning that the positive trade diversion effect towards third countries like Germany or France cannot compensate for the decrease in trade with Canada and Mexico (see Table 12.1, NAFTA scenario). This picture looks quite similar for the import side, because trade diversion effects resulting from the resolution of NAFTA induce an increase in US imports from non-NAFTA members, mainly from China, Japan and Germany. At the same time, however, imports from NAFTA countries decrease by 21% (Canada) and 14% (Mexico), as already mentioned above. Overall, US imports decrease, which shows that the negative effects dominate (see Table 12.2, NAFTA scenario).

A protectionist US trade policy with respect to the rest of the world, as simulated in the next two depicted scenarios (WTO scenarios, only tariff change and tariff plus NTB change), would have larger effects on the US trade structure than the NAFTA scenario. This outcome is reasonable, because a protectionist trade policy would not only affect the trade structure with NAFTA members, it would also influence trade relations with all other remaining WTO members. Overall, US exports would decrease by 73.5% in the case of higher tariffs and non-tariff barriers (Table 12.1). The change in bilateral exports is relatively homogeneous across all top ten US export destinations. Only exports to Ireland are less negatively impacted than those to other countries, which can be ascribed to the high rate of service trade (e.g. financial transfers) between the United States and Ireland. The effects on US imports look fairly similar, although the percentage changes are a little bit smaller. In total, US imports would decrease by 58.8% (NTB plus tariff change, WTO scenario), as shown in Table 12.2. When only tariffs are treated and not NTBs, US imports decrease by 30.85%. The aggregate effect of the BTA causes a small decline in total US exports (–5.87% in Table 12.1) and imports (–4.7% in Table 12.2). In relative terms, US trade declines homogeneously across all partner countries.

Changing trade patterns through protectionism do not solely affect the import and export structure, but also impact the sectoral output of a country. On that account, the next two tables illustrate the changes in US sectoral value added. The percentage change featured in these tables gives an indication of the amount of pressure a sector is exposed to in times of rising protectionism. Table 12.3 shows the initial US value added for all goods in millions of US dollars, its initial share, the percentage changes and the change in million US dollars that occur in the counterfactual scenarios. The US mining industry (5.3%), wood and wood products (0.9%), print and reproductive media (1%), rubber and plastic (0.5%), processed metals (0.1%) and electrical machinery (1.7%) increase their sectoral value added in the case of the end of NAFTA.

Nonetheless, this does not compensate for the losses in the remaining sectors. Among others, the US agricultural sectors suffer from the potential termination of the NAFTA: crops decreases its sectoral value added by 0.1%, food and beverages by 0.2% and the fishery sector loses 5.9%. Similar to the trade picture, the WTO protectionist scenarios influence the United States to a larger extent than is the case in the NAFTA scenario.

For most US sectors the strongest decrease occurs when WTO member countries retaliate against the protectionist measures of the United States. The sectoral value-added changes increase with the growing extent of protectionism (WTO scenario increase of tariffs and/or NTBs). The vehicles sector "other means of transport" faces a decrease of 27.1%, followed by the "water transport" sectors (–20.5%). In nominal terms, the sectoral value added in wholesaling (excluding vehicles) only drops by 8.86%; yet this decline amounts nominally to US$93 billion, which represents the greatest absolute sectoral contraction in the United States (see Table 12.4). But there are also sectors like the computer and electronical machinery sectors that can expect

Table 12.3 Change in sectoral value added of US manufacturing and agricultural sectors

	Initial value added	Share of value added	Change of sectoral value added, different scenarios							
			NAFTA		WTO				BTA	
					only tariffs		tariffs and NTBs			
	US$ million	%	%	US$ million	%	US$ million	%	US$ million	%	US$ million
Crop and animal production etc.	177,155	1.02	-0.1	-195	-5.64	-9993	-7.28	-12,890	-2.12	-3,760
Forestry and logging	23,752	0.14	-1.9	-444	-0.12	-29	4.10	973	-2.13	-507
Fishing and aquaculture	14,505	0.08	-5.9	-852	-0.43	-63	3.52	510	-1.99	-289
Mining and quarrying	455,588	2.62	5.3	24,299	0.62	2,824	5.48	24,945	-0.88	-4,006
Food, beverages and tobacco	243,253	1.40	-0.2	-406	-2.54	-6,172	-3.93	-9,550	-1.74	-4,244
Textiles, wearing apparel and leather	27,698	0.16	-1.3	-349	11.47	3,177	31.76	8,796	-3.21	-890
Wood and products of wood and cork	28,805	0.17	0.9	255	-0.57	-165	0.95	274	-1.31	-377
Paper	55,730	0.32	-0.2	-135	-4.68	-2,609	-4.88	-2,721	-1.99	-1,111
Printing and reproduction of recorded media	38,301	0.22	1.0	365	-2.92	-1,118	-5.24	-2,007	-0.96	-369
Coke, refined petroleum	182,719	1.05	-2.8	-5,134	-6.94	-12,672	-8.75	-15,988	-2.39	-4,373
Chemicals and chemical products	267,111	1.54	-0.3	-873	-4.91	-13,108	-3.21	-8,570	-3.18	-8,493
Basic pharmaceutical products and preparations	95,467	0.55	-1.4	-1,361	-2.25	-2,150	1.87	1,785	-3.11	-2,966
Rubber and plastics	75,501	0.43	0.5	405	-2.79	-2,105	-1.17	-886	-2.21	-1,671
Other non-metallic minerals	46,791	0.27	-0.4	-169	-2.04	-953	-1.37	-642	-1.79	-840
Basic metals	60,861	0.35	-0.2	-127	-0.82	-497	8.21	4,998	-1.39	-845
Fabricated metal	147,060	0.85	0.1	202	-3.83	-5,630	-2.81	-4,127	-1.67	-2,459

Computer, electronic and optical products	269,400	1.55	-0.8	-2,213	5.30	14,275	21.32	57,433	-4.81	-12,971
Electrical equipment	54,138	0.31	1.7	918	6.77	3,663	24.02	13,002	-4.19	-2,267
Machinery and equipment; repair and installation	175,012	1.01	-1.7	-2,932	-3.49	-6,100	0.98	1,708	-4.07	-7,124
Motor vehicles, trailers and semi-trailers	141,160	0.81	2.0	2,820	2.53	3,575	10.19	14,390	-3.16	-4,463
Other transport equipment	127,798	0.74	-0.2	-292	-20.43	-26,105	-27.12	-34,657	-5.73	-7,321
Furniture and other manufacturing	105,839	0.61	-2.8	-2,956	0.84	887	4.61	4,879	-3.04	-3,213

Source: ifo Trade Model, Aichele *et al.* (2016).

Table 12.4 Change in sectoral value added of US services sectors

	Initial value added	Share of value added	NAFTA		WTO — only tariffs		WTO — tariffs and NTBs		BTA	
	US$ million	%	US$ million	%	US$ million	%	US$ million	%	US$ million	%
Electricity etc.	272,719	1.57	574	0.2	-2,991	-1.10	-5,691	-2.09	-948	-0.35
Water collection, treatment and supply	9,317	0.05	18	0.2	-128	-1.38	-75	-0.80	-14	-0.15
Sewerage, waste collection etc.	43,150	0.25	-39	-0.1	-1,910	-4.43	-3,965	-9.19	2,315	5.37
Construction	665,785	3.83	1,880	0.3	-3,131	-0.47	-15,269	-2.29	-3,904	-0.59
Wholesale etc. of motor vehicles and motorcycles	254,916	1.47	2,073	0.8	-2,076	-0.81	-2,339	-0.92	-783	-0.31
Wholesale trade (except motor vehicles & motorcycles)	1,044,655	6.01	2,186	0.2	-28,246	-2.70	-92,604	-8.86	-20,843	-2.00
Retail trade (except motor vehicles & motorcycles)	815,874	4.69	3,017	0.4	-4,648	-0.57	-16,533	-2.03	-4,737	-0.58
Land transports and transport via pipelines	240,382	1.38	278	0.1	-7,335	-3.05	-18,126	-7.54	-3,527	-1.47
Water transport	18,593	0.11	13	0.1	-902	-4.85	-3,805	-20.46	-806	-4.33
Air transport	84,344	0.49	-219	-0.3	-4,957	-5.88	-9,409	-11.16	-2,807	-3.33
Warehousing and support activities for transportation	106,151	0.61	125	0.1	-3,243	-3.05	-10,364	-9.76	-856	-0.81
Postal and courier	57,439	0.33	42	0.1	-2,017	-3.51	-7,393	-12.87	-624	-1.09
Accommodation and food	487,443	2.80	158	0.0	-3,747	-0.77	-11,363	-2.33	-2,244	-0.46
Publishing	210,656	1.21	472	0.2	-3,893	-1.85	-19,168	-9.10	-4,070	-1.93
Motion picture, video and television	200,183	1.15	248	0.1	-3,616	-1.81	-14,193	-7.09	-2,816	-1.41
Telecommunications	326,912	1.88	800	0.2	-4,084	-1.25	-15,747	-4.82	-2,603	-0.80
IT services etc.	338,229	1.95	838	0.2	-6,543	-1.93	-10,192	-3.01	-1,914	-0.57

Financial services	488,092	2.81	0.2	1,143	−1.98	−9,650	−8.12	−39,616	−1.41	−6,875
Insurance etc.	734,910	4.23	0.2	1,741	−1.59	−11,710	−3.92	−28,789	−0.65	−4,772
Real estate	2,059,168	11.85	0.3	5,559	−0.56	−11,598	−2.66	−54,805	−0.54	−11,056
Legal and accounting	693,747	3.99	0.2	1,160	−2.12	−14,717	−3.74	−25,935	−0.28	−1,961
Architecture and engineering etc.	448,150	2.58	0.3	1,361	−2.47	−11,075	−4.56	−20,456	−0.92	−4,105
Scientific research and development	140,414	0.81	0.2	275	−2.23	−3,131	−5.37	−7,543	−1.06	−1,490
Administration and support services	672,085	3.87	0.1	866	−3.07	−20,612	−1.56	−10,483	−0.26	−1,766
Public administration and defence etc.	2,277,285	13.10	0.3	5,895	−0.52	−11,794	−2.69	−61,351	−0.66	−15,097
Education	192,773	1.11	0.2	446	−0.76	−1,465	−2.70	−5,206	−0.72	−1,389
Human health and social work	1,227,402	7.06	0.3	3,587	−0.35	−4,344	−2.27	−27,805	−0.66	−8,076
Other services	458,561	2.64	0.2	1,136	−0.76	−3,494	−2.63	−12,052	−0.50	−2,301

Source: ifo Trade Model, Aichele *et al.* (2016).

an increase in sectoral value added (Table 12.3). The last scenario, the adjustment of the border tax, shows a relatively homogeneous decrease in value added across all manufacturing and agricultural sectors. Most US service providers gain homogeneously between 0.1 and 0.8% in value added in the case of the dissolution of NAFTA. Only a few sectors, such as air transport (–0.3%), are confronted with a decrease in their value added (Table 12.4). In general, the value-added changes for services change less heterogeneously across sectors than in the goods sectors.

The revocation of NAFTA would do considerable economic damage to its member countries: the United States (–0.22%), Mexico (–0.96%) and Canada (–1.54%), as shown in Table 12.6. With the exception of Luxembourg (0.06% in Table 12.5) and Norway (0.09% in Table 12.6), it would hardly change real income for third countries (see again Tables 12.5 and 12.6). The same applies to real wage changes.

In the case of increased protectionism against all WTO members and vice versa, the real income and real wages of the WTO members incur losses from increasing tariffs and non-tariff barriers. Mexico (–3.42%) and Canada (–3.85%) experience disproportionate declines, and the US real income would shrink by 2.32% (Table 12.6). For some countries, retaliation might compensate for the economic losses in the case of unilateral US protectionist policies. In the case of Germany, this would imply a 0.40% loss of GDP (Table 12.5), while China's GDP would only drop by 0.34% (Table 12.6). But one can see that retaliatory trade policy measures by WTO members against the United States do not improve the economic situation in any country, making it a "lose-lose" scenario. In general, this can be attributed to the strong dependency of domestic economies on the US market. Individual countries can nevertheless reduce their potential losses by taking countervailing measures (like increasing tariffs), but not a single country can fully compensate for the loss of gross household income and real wages incurred. Vengeance should therefore not be a main response to threatened, discriminatory US policies. Instead, a prior containment of protectionist policies is highly advisable.

Contrary to the intentions of the US government, the introduction of the BTA causes a negative US real income change of 0.67% (in Table 12.6). Taiwan (–1.45%), Luxembourg (–1.3%), Norway (–1.1%), Germany (–0.86%), the Netherlands (–0.74%) and South Korea (–0.73%) suffer even greater losses from the BTA than the United States itself. On average, Europe experiences an increase in its gross household income of 0.04%, as the BTA positively affects gross household income for the majority of EU28 countries. These changes are nevertheless quite small and therefore coincide with the prevailing views expressed in the literature on this topic.

The US real wage is also hardly affected by its implemented BTA (Table 12.6) and the EU28 effects are quite diverse. There are countries like Austria (0.03%), Belgium (0.52%), France (0.46%) and Britain (0.75%) that stand to gain in real wages. Germany (–0.22%) and Denmark (–0.05%), on the other hand, will suffer from US protectionist policies (Table 12.5).

Conclusion

Our analysis shows that the US administration's promise to create more jobs and investment in the United States through the presented trade policies is a fallacy. In all of the simulated scenarios, an isolation of the US market would primarily have a

Table 12.5 Real income and real wage changes for EU28 countries

	Real income changes (%)				Real wage changes (%)			
	NAFTA	WTO (only tariff change)	WTO (tariff and NTB change)	BTA	NAFTA	WTO (only tariff change)	WTO (tariff and NTB change)	BTA
		with retaliation				*with retaliation*		
Austria	0.01	-0.09	-0.20	-0.15	0.00	-0.12	-0.22	0.03
Belgium	0.02	-0.09	-0.72	0.34	0.01	-0.28	-0.80	0.52
Bulgaria	0.00	-0.04	-0.12	0.78	0.01	-0.07	-0.12	0.67
Cyprus	-0.02	-0.02	0.00	1.02	0.00	-0.05	0.02	0.95
Czech Rep.	0.02	-0.03	-0.13	-0.67	0.01	-0.09	-0.19	-0.16
Germany	0.03	-0.14	-0.40	-0.86	0.00	-0.21	-0.43	-0.22
Denmark	0.02	-0.11	-0.28	-0.50	0.00	-0.13	-0.30	-0.05
Spain	0.02	-0.01	-0.06	0.27	0.02	-0.07	-0.09	0.29
Estonia	0.01	-0.04	-0.14	0.24	0.00	-0.09	-0.17	0.31
Finland	0.00	-0.09	-0.32	0.31	0.00	-0.14	-0.35	0.35
France	0.00	-0.04	-0.25	0.48	0.00	-0.12	-0.29	0.46
UK	0.00	-0.10	-0.43	0.76	0.01	-0.24	-0.50	0.75
Greece	-0.01	-0.01	-0.08	0.88	0.01	-0.02	-0.04	0.84
Croatia	0.00	-0.06	-0.15	0.40	0.00	-0.11	-0.19	0.41
Hungary	0.03	-0.06	-0.32	-0.40	0.01	-0.12	-0.36	0.02
Ireland	0.00	-0.78	-3.60	-0.46	-0.03	-0.76	-3.00	0.70
Italy	0.01	-0.07	-0.19	-0.10	0.00	-0.10	-0.20	0.03

(Continued)

Table 12.5 (*Continued*)

	Real income changes (%)				Real wage changes (%)			
	NAFTA	WTO (only tariff change)	WTO (tariff and NTB change)	BTA	NAFTA	WTO (only tariff change)	WTO (tariff and NTB change)	BTA
		with retaliation				*with retaliation*		
Lithuania	0.04	-0.13	-0.17	-0.43	0.03	-0.16	-0.18	0.02
Luxembourg	0.06	-0.47	-2.31	-1.36	0.00	-0.41	-1.79	0.10
Latvia	-0.01	-0.04	-0.08	0.61	0.00	-0.08	-0.09	0.54
Malta	0.01	-0.09	-0.46	0.71	0.00	-0.17	-0.50	0.66
Netherlands	0.04	-0.05	-0.60	-0.74	0.00	-0.25	-0.70	0.05
Poland	0.01	0.00	-0.09	-0.11	0.00	-0.04	-0.12	0.05
Portugal	0.00	-0.04	-0.10	0.57	0.00	-0.07	-0.10	0.52
Romania	0.01	-0.02	-0.07	0.36	0.00	-0.05	-0.10	0.37
Slovakia	0.02	-0.05	-0.13	-0.38	0.01	-0.11	-0.17	-0.05
Slovenia	0.01	-0.03	-0.04	-0.39	0.00	-0.05	-0.07	-0.02
Sweden	0.01	-0.07	-0.27	-0.02	0.00	-0.11	-0.31	0.22

Source: ifo Trade Model, Aichele *et al.* (2016).

Table 12.6 Real income and real wage changes for non-EU28 countries

	Real income changes (%)				Real wage changes (%)			
	NAFTA	WTO (only tariff change)	WTO (tariff and NTB change)	BTA	NAFTA	WTO (only tariff change)	WTO (tariff and NTB change)	BTA
		with retaliation				with retaliation		
Australia	0.01	-0.05	-0.25	0.22	0.00	-0.17	-0.33	0.22
Brazil	0.00	-0.06	-0.24	0.36	0.00	-0.18	-0.29	0.32
Canada	-1.54	-1.20	-3.85	0.70	-1.44	-2.73	-4.73	0.75
Switzerland	0.02	-0.11	-0.50	-0.56	-0.01	-0.16	-0.46	0.04
China	0.01	-0.17	-0.34	-0.60	0.00	-0.19	-0.31	-0.25
Indonesia	0.01	-0.11	-0.23	0.01	0.00	-0.14	-0.24	0.04
India	0.01	-0.06	-0.14	0.24	0.01	-0.10	-0.16	0.24
Japan	0.01	-0.11	-0.29	0.26	0.01	-0.21	-0.34	0.22
Korea	0.05	-0.16	-0.61	-0.73	0.01	-0.33	-0.66	-0.18
Mexico	-0.96	-1.10	-3.42	0.30	-0.90	-2.31	-4.00	0.34
Norway	0.09	-0.10	-0.24	-1.10	0.03	-0.13	-0.29	-0.25
Russia	0.04	-0.08	-0.12	-0.34	0.02	-0.10	-0.14	-0.03
Turkey	0.00	-0.08	-0.24	0.14	0.00	-0.16	-0.28	0.22
Taiwan	0.03	-0.25	-0.74	-1.45	0.00	-0.39	-0.70	-0.50
USA	-0.22	-0.30	-2.32	-0.67	-0.23	-1.43	-2.93	0.04

Source: ifo Trade Model, Aichele *et al.* (2016).

negative impact on the US economy itself in the long term. It is also clear that a protectionist trade policy would most likely lead to a worldwide policy of retaliation against the United States. In such a scenario, the threat of economic damage is again particularly pronounced for the United States.

Clearly, there is need to support US workers forced to reorient themselves as a result of intensified competition due to trade. However, these challenges should be addressed with policy instruments that do not distort trade (e.g. public support for training programmes). At the same time, countries like China and Germany have to ask themselves whether their present trade surpluses are sustainable in the long term. While, in the case of Germany, this criticism should be relativised, because the surpluses are not induced by politics but can be explained, for example, by demographic ageing and the high saving rate that goes with it, the case of China is different. The relatively high level of isolation of the Chinese market and the simultaneous increase in overcapacity in individual industries, such as the steel sector, are leading to unfair trade with the United States and are encouraging a rash political response there. Finally, it should also be pointed out that in the service industries – in which the United States still has a high competitive advantage – the United States generally runs a trade surplus.

Overall, our comprehensive analysis clearly discourages the United States from pursuing the protectionist trade policy announced by their new administration for its own sake. Seeking new forms of cooperation with its main trading partners, like China, Germany and the NAFTA partners, would be a far more sensible strategy. First steps in this direction are to be found, for example, in the "Global Forum" for the global reduction of steel overcapacity and dumping. Such new coordination platforms are becoming increasingly necessary and help to identify new issues that can subsequently be tackled by existing international institutions like the WTO on a larger scale.

Finally, the United States is the architect of the global, rule-based, multilateral trading system. The country has consistently pushed ahead with the three pillars of the international economic system – the World Bank, the International Monetary Fund and the World Trade Organization. It is time for leading industrial countries to support the United States in this endeavour in order to avoid a throwback in free trade. Here, beneficiaries of the US post-war policy, such as Germany, Europe and Japan, need to recognise that they bear a special responsibility and step up to this challenge.

References

Aichele, R., Felbermayr G. & Heiland, I. (2014) Going Deep: The Trade and Welfare Effects of TTIP. *CESifo Working Paper* No. 5150.

Aichele, R., Felbermayr G. & Heiland, I. (2016) Going Deep: The Trade and Welfare Effects of TTIP Revised. *ifo Working Paper* No. 219.

Bergstrand, J., Larch, M. & Yotov, Y. (2015) Economic Integration Agreements, Border Effects, and Distance Elasticities in the Gravity Equation. *European Economic Review*, 78, 307–327.

Caliendo, L. & Parro, F. (2015) Estimates of the Trade and Welfare Effects of NAFTA. *Review of Economic Studies*, 82, 1–44.

Costinot, A. & Rodriguez-Clare, A. (2014). Trade Theory with Numbers: Quantifying the Consequences of Globalization. In: Gopinath, G., Helpman E. & Rogoff, K. (eds.) *Handbook of International Economics*, Vol. 4, pp. 197–262.

Eaton, J. & Kortum, S. (2002) Technology, Geography, and Trade. *Econometrica*, 70(5), 1741–1780.

International Monetary Fund (IMF) (2016) *World Economic Outlook, October 2016. Subdued Demand: Symptoms and Remedies*. Retrieved from: https://www.imf.org/~/media/Websites/IMF/imported-flagship-issues/external/pubs/ft/weo/2016/02/pdf/_text.ashx (accessed 22 July 2019).

Melchior, A. & Sverdrup, U. (2015) *Interessekonflikter i norsk handelspolitikk* [Conflicts of Interest in Norway's Trade Policy]. Oslo: Universitetsforlaget.

Yalcin, E., Felbermayr, G. & Steininer, M. (2017) Global Impact of a Protectionist US Trade Policy. *ifo Forschungsberichte*, 89. Retrieved from: https://www.econstor.eu/bitstream/10419/176886/1/ifo_Forschungsberichte_89_2017_Yalcin_etal_US_TradePolicy.pdf (accessed 22 July 2019).

Yalcin, E., Steininger, M. & Felbermayr, G. (2017) Global Impact of a Protectionist US Trade Policy. *ifo Forschungsberichte* 89. Munich: ifo Institute.

Chapter 13

Trade and Developing-Country Exporters: The Case of Latin American and Caribbean Countries

Banu Demir

Introduction

International trade involves a variety of risks: commercial risks, product risks, political risks, risks arising from freight transport and credit risks. Depending on the financing terms, the exporter faces the risk of the importer failing to make the payment, and the importer faces the risk of the exporter failing to deliver the goods. Longer transit times increase both the risk of damage and the need for working capital. Those risks are further aggravated because trade partners are located in different countries with different jurisdictions. This makes resolving international trade disputes far more difficult than resolving domestic business disputes, as illustrated by the following anecdote from Demir (2014).

> An interesting anecdote involves an Istanbul-based producer of textiles, which exported knitted dresses to an importer located in Italy. The freight forwarder broke the rules of the contract and delivered the goods to the importer before the payment was made. Upon receiving the shipment the importer claimed that the goods were not in accordance with the descriptions and specifications in the order and thus refused to pay. The exporter filed a lawsuit against the freight forwarder in Turkey, and the latter against the importer in Italy. The Italian court decided that the importer should make the payment to the exporter. But the importer claimed it did not have the means to do so, as it was liquidating. The Turkish court, on the other hand, decided that the freight forwarder should make the payment to the exporter. The exporter received the payment, but five years after the date of the shipment. (p. 1)

It is widely believed that international trade transactions involving developing-country exporters or importers are riskier than those involving developed-country firms for a number of reasons. First, developing countries are usually characterised

The Handbook of Global Trade Policy, First Edition. Edited by Andreas Klasen.

by high political risks and economic instability. Second, assessing customer and credit risks when they are not located in developed countries (e.g. members of Organisation for Economic Co-operation and Development [OECD]) is more difficult, if not impossible. For instance, it is easier to access information about the finances of potential buyers when they are located in developed countries. Third, developing countries usually have shallow and poorly regulated financial systems – which increase the opportunities for potential money-laundering activities. Therefore, for a transaction involving firms from developing countries, both parties must evaluate the potential commercial as well as political risks before they agree on the terms of the contract.

All the factors listed above increase the need for bank-intermediated trade finance instruments in developing countries, which include letters of credit (L/Cs) and documentary collections (non-bank-intermediated financing [payment]) terms, against open account and cash-in-advance terms. Under open account terms, payment is due after goods are delivered to the destination (usually 30 to 90 days) – this payment term places the risk of the transaction with the exporter. Under cash-in-advance terms, the importer pre-pays and receives the goods later; this payment term places the risk of the transaction with the importer.

L/Cs are the most widely used bank-intermediated trade finance instruments that are issued by the importer's bank (issuing bank). These instruments not only reduce payment risks associated with international trade transactions but also provide working capital needs required to directly support international trade. Figure 13.1 shows how L/Cs work. The issuing bank promises to make the payment to the beneficiary (exporter) upon the verification of the fulfilment of the conditions stated in the L/C. When the exporter receives the L/C, it presents it to its local bank (advising bank), together with all necessary documents. The exporter can request its bank to confirm the L/C, in which case the exporter's bank (now the confirming bank) also commits to make the payment if the issuing bank fails to transfer the payment on due date. With a standard L/C, payment is guaranteed by the importer's bank, provided that delivery conditions specified in the contract have been met. A deferred

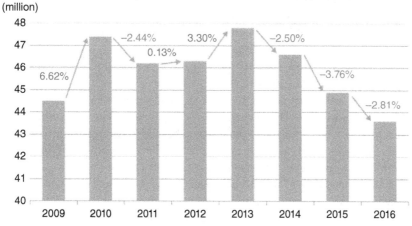

Figure 13.1 Evolution of the volume of L/Cs or issue of a documentary credit.
Source: ICC (2017).

L/C, in addition to providing payment guarantee, also delays payment for a specified amount of time after shipment or submission of the documents. In countries with well-functioning financial markets, there exist money-market instruments linked to L/Cs (e.g. bankers' acceptance), which can be used by exporters to cover their working capital needs. (A bankers' acceptance is a time draft drawn on and accepted by a bank. It is widely used in international trade. In a typical bankers' acceptance transaction, which is linked to an L/C, the bank commits to pay the exporter a specific amount at a specified date. The exporter can sell the bankers' acceptance at a discounted price on a secondary market and thus obtain short-term financing).

Trade financing is usually characterised as short-term and self-liquidating, and it provides working capital to exporters and/or importers. Consider the following example in Rhee (1989): a Bangladeshi garment exporter receives an L/C worth US$100,000 from a US-based importer, which specifies delivery in three months. The exporter requires working capital to pay for wages, rent, raw materials and so forth, until the receipt of the payment, which is generally made after the goods are delivered to the importer and is conditional on the confirmation of their quality, as specified in the contract. The time lag between production and payment also depends on the type of the L/C. If it is a sight L/C, then the exporter only needs pre-shipment financing. On the other hand, a deferred L/C would give the importer a grace period for payment, implying that the exporter would need pre- as well as post-shipment financing. The need for short-term financing would also be felt by domestic-input suppliers if the exporter uses domestic intermediate inputs in the production of the exported product. In that case, the suppliers (indirect exporters) would need working capital to manufacture the required inputs. If, for instance, the garment exporter is unable to self-finance or obtain trade credit, it would seek financing from domestic banks, which would then ask for collateral. In the case that the exporter is not able to supply collateral, or the bank does not have sufficient foreign exchange holdings – both of which are quite likely to happen in a developing country – the country would lose a valuable export opportunity. Here, the problem arises because the local bank is extremely risk-averse, and/or it does not have the required resources to provide trade financing to the exporter. This example explains why the provision of trade finance was identified, in April 2007, by the World Trade Organization (WTO) Task Force on Aid-for-Trade as an important supply-side issue to be addressed in developing countries. To this end, the WTO has been supporting initiatives by global financial institutions, regional development banks and domestic export credit agencies to increase the availability of trade finance in developing countries.

In some cases, it may be difficult to cover the underlying risks associated with international trade transactions through the terms of payment. The trading partners may fail to reach an agreement on the terms of payment due to various country- or relationship-level factors. In those cases, the exporter should explore other options that would help minimise the risk of the underlying transaction. One of the options available to firms in some countries is to use the products offered by export credit insurance markets, in which both private institutions and government agencies participate. While export insurance provided by private institutions usually covers short-term transactions, that provided by government agencies covers longer-term obligations. National export credit agencies have been established in about 40 countries. They provide financial support to domestic exporters in the form of, for instance, direct credits, interest rate support, credit guarantees or insurance, with an aim to enhance their competitiveness in international markets. In 1978, some OECD members produced a number of standards under the Arrangement on Officially Supported Export Credits to govern the provision of officially supported export credits in the participating states. The arrangement provides "a framework for the orderly use of officially supported export credits" to "foster a level playing field for official support … in order to encourage competition among exporters based on quality and price of goods and services exported rather than on the most favourable officially supported financial terms and conditions". The participants in the arrangement as of October 2017 are Australia, Canada, the European Union, Japan, Korea, New Zealand, Norway, Switzerland and the United States.

As it reduces risks and provides working capital to trading firms, the availability of trade finance is believed to be an important factor that improves domestic firms' competitiveness in international markets. Without access to financing, firms cannot meet foreign demand. The academic literature suggests that the need for bank-intermediated trade finance instruments increases as the quality of contract enforcement decreases in source or destination countries and as the time lag between production and sales increases. Since contract enforcement is generally weaker in developing countries, the need for traditional trade finance instruments is expected to be higher for transactions that involve developing-country firms. However, bank-intermediated trade finance markets in developing countries are shallow, and trade finance gaps are not uncommon – which represents a bottleneck for developing-country firms that engage in international trade.

This chapter poses the following question: What is the significance of bank-intermediated trade finance for developing-country exporters and importers? To answer this question, it will rely on currently available survey data on trade finance practices, as well as insights and findings of the recently growing literature on trade finance. The geographical focus of the chapter is Latin American and Caribbean countries.

Trade-Related Developments in Latin American and Caribbean Countries

As of 2016, exports and imports for Latin America and the Caribbean amounted to US\$816,075 million and US\$818,074 million, respectively. The United States and China are the major export destinations of the region. While the region exports (and imports) a large variety of products, primary commodities dominate the composition of exports. Commodity exports as a share of total exports of goods and services accounted for 55% for Caribbean countries, 23% for Central America, and 76% for South America during 2014–2015 (UNCTAD, 2017). For the entire region, the amount of commodity exports as a share of gross domestic product (GDP) was close to 10% during the same period.

Latin American and Caribbean countries benefitted from a sharp increase in commodity prices in the early 2000s, which led to a significant rise in their exports. Nevertheless, more recently, decreases in global commodity prices and slowdowns in external demand (particularly in the United States) have hurt the region's exports. In general, the region's heavy reliance on commodity exports makes it vulnerable to fluctuations in commodity prices (boom-bust cycles) and hurts growth stability.

Therefore, export diversification has gained importance as a development strategy for the region.

As in other developing countries, diversifying trade by switching to more sophisticated manufacturing products and participating in global value chains have been important items on policy agendas in Latin American and Caribbean countries. Achieving this goal requires improvements in a number of areas, including transportation infrastructure, logistics services and access to finance for domestic firms. According to the results of a survey conducted by the World Bank among firms located in 14 developing countries, access to pre-export financing was a major obstacle for exports after September 2008 (Malouche, 2009). In particular, the share of firms declaring access to pre-export financing an obstacle was relatively high for Latin American and Caribbean countries: 78% for Peru, 27% for Chile and 18% for Brazil.

Trade Finance Practices in Latin American and Caribbean Countries

Survey Data

There are no comprehensive data on the size of the bank-intermediated global trade finance markets. While an estimated 80% of global merchandise trade uses some form of trade finance (Auboin, 2009), only 10% of merchandise trade is estimated to be supported by traditional (bank-intermediated) trade finance instruments, e.g. L/Cs (International Chamber of Commerce [ICC], 2017). The rest is mostly financed on open account terms (supplier trade credit), which places transaction-related risks almost entirely with the exporter. It is worth noting that these figures are not "hard numbers". For instance, a report published in 2014 by the Committee on the Global Financial System (CGFS), which was established by the Bank for International Settlements (BIS), estimates that about one third of global trade is supported bank-intermediated trade finance instruments. According to this report, the volume of trade finance transactions amounts to about US$8–10 trillion annually. Surveys conducted by the International Monetary Fund (IMF) and the Banker's Association for Finance and Trade–International Financial Services Association (BAFT-IFSA) (2009, 2010, 2011) report an even larger estimate of the intensity of the use of trade finance: respondent banks estimate that banks provide financing for 40% of global trade – an estimate that assigns bank-intermediated trade finance a much greater role in facilitating global trade flows. On the regional front, for instance, the value of the bank-intermediated trade finance market in Latin America is estimated to be about US$40 billion (IDB, 2016).

The intensity of trade finance, i.e. volume of bank-intermediated trade finance markets as a share of the value of international trade flows, varies considerably across regions and even countries within a region. For instance, it was about 30% in Hong Kong Special Administrative Region in 2011, compared to 56% in the Republic of Korea. On the other hand, the ratio was below 25% in Brazil in the same year. How much a country's exporters or importers rely on trade finance instruments depends on a number of factors that are related to the characteristics of source and destination countries (e.g. bilateral distance between them, contractual frictions and so forth) and type of goods traded, as well as characteristics of exporting and importing firms. Those factors will be discussed in detail in the next subsection.

The only readily available data with a wide country coverage on the use of trade finance instruments in international trade is published by the ICC. The data are based on a global survey that the ICC has been conducting on trade finance trends among banks every year since the Great Recession (2009). The geographical coverage of the survey is wide: the latest one, released in 2017, was based on respondents from 98 countries. Nearly half of respondents were located in Western Europe or developing Asia (including China and India), broadly reflecting the geographical distribution of global trade flows. On the other hand, respondents located in Central America and the Caribbean, together with South America, accounted for fewer than 8% of the total number of respondents.

The ICC publishes the results from the global survey on trade finance, together with the Society for Worldwide Interbank Financial Telecommunication's (SWIFT's) trade finance volume statistics. The latter is a useful data source to analyse the actual usage of traditional trade finance instruments, i.e. L/Cs. As illustrated in Figure 13.1, the volume of L/Cs has generally been declining since 2010, posting a 2.8% decline between 2015 and 2016. While this downward trend is observed in all regions in 2015–2016, Latin American and Caribbean countries posted a significantly larger annual decrease in SWIFT trade finance traffic compared to other regions. This pattern resembles that of the value of trade flows originating from or destined for Latin America and the Caribbean during the same period (WTO, 2017). Figure 13.2 shows, unsurprisingly, that there exists a strong positive correlation between the annual growth rate of the region's international trade flows and that of its SWIFT traffic. Needless to say, this pattern does not necessarily reflect a causation, as the relation holds in both directions: trade drives demand for trade finance, and the availability of trade finance drives trade.

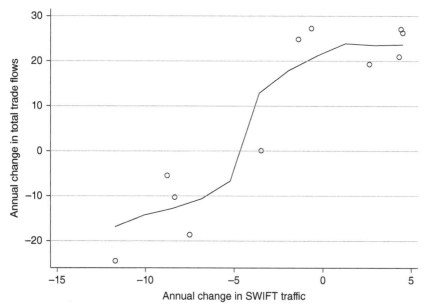

Figure 13.2 Volume of international trade and SWIFT traffic in Latin America and the Caribbean (2005–2016).
Source: Author's calculations based on data obtained from ICC (2017) and WTO (2017).
Note: Each circle represents a year between 2005 and 2016.

Countries in the Latin American region differ from other developing countries, particularly those of the Asia-Pacific region, in their reliance on traditional trade finance instruments when trading across borders. The volume of L/Cs sent by the Latin American region in 2016 was less than 95,000, compared to more than 3 million L/Cs sent by the Asia-Pacific region. The region lags even further behind the other regions in terms of the volume of L/Cs received: the number of L/Cs received by the Latin American region in 2016 was less than 41,000, which places the region with the second lowest L/C volume after Africa (ICC, 2017). Overall, the region's share in global trade finance exposure, measured in terms of the volume of SWIFT messages, is considerably less than its share in global trade flows (BIS, 2014). Given the lack of detailed micro-level data on the use of trade finance instruments, e.g. firm- or bank-level data, it is not possible to understand whether the reason behind this pattern is lack of demand for bank-intermediated trade finance instruments by firms, or banks' unwillingness to provide financial support for international trade transactions in those countries.

The annual global survey on trade finance conducted by the ICC also informs us about trade finance gaps which occur when the demand for trade financing by firms exceeds its supply by financial institutions. The financing gap in the global trade finance market is estimated at US$1.9 trillion annually (Malaket, 2015).

In the latest ICC survey, 61% of participating banks reported that there was more demand than supply of trade finance. Western Europe accounted for the largest share (18.4%) of the global value of proposed trade finance transactions. While China alone accounted for 15% of global demand, the share of Central and South American countries (including the Caribbean region) was only 5.7%. This, together with the low rejection rates of proposed trade finance transactions relative to many other regions (see Figure 13.3), suggests that lack of demand could, at least partly, explain the low intensity of the use of traditional trade finance instruments in the Latin America and the Caribbean region.

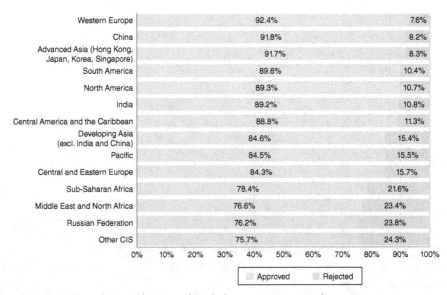

Figure 13.3 Approval rates of proposed trade finance transactions by region.
Source: ICC (2017).

On the supply side, holding trade finance assets seems attractive for banks, as these assets bear relatively small risks compared to, for instance, corporate lending. This holds for a number of reasons: (i) trade finance instruments usually have short maturity; (ii) they are of a self-liquidating nature; and (iii) they are secured against tangible collateral. Since trade finance lending is typically backed by the goods being traded, future receivables or other debt instruments, the payment is first used for repayment of any outstanding debt (Grath, 2014). As reported by the ICC (2017), the expected loss of import/export L/Cs is only 0.02%. This figure is significantly smaller than the expected loss of lending to small and medium-sized enterprises (SMEs) (0.14%) and to large enterprises (0.06%). Given such a low-risk profile, it is surprising to observe that trade credit intensity is quite low in many developing countries. Banks' abilities to provide trade finance depend on their refinancing options in foreign currency. This might be an important challenge for banks in developing countries. Another widely accepted reason for low levels of trade credit intensity is the high cost of compliance arising from stringent financial regulation.

The potential adverse effects of stringent financial regulations on the provision of trade finance has become a prevalent debate in policy circles. According to the results of the latest ICC global survey on trade finance, those concerns are well grounded. Participating banks identified anti-financial crimes and Basel III regulatory requirements as the top two most important barriers to providing trade finance (see Figure 13.4). Regarding the former, complying with banking regulatory requirements (e.g. Basel III) appears as a barrier to providing trade finance since increasing capitalisation might reduce the amount of capital available for trade finance. Regarding the latter, banks must be vigilant and incur costs to adapt to changing sets of regulations related to, for instance, anti-money laundering, trade sanctions and so forth.

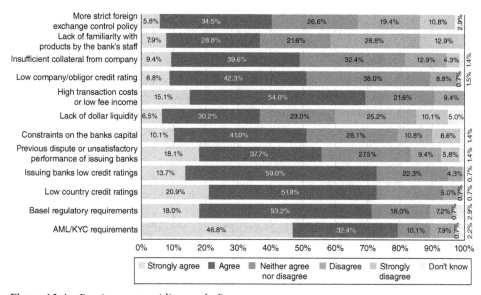

Figure 13.4   Barriers to providing trade finance.
Source: ICC (2017).
Note: AML and KYC stand for "anti-money laundering" and "know your customer", respectively.

Recently, there has been a growing concern among financial institutions about the potentially harmful effects of the proposed amendments to the Basel IV framework on the provision of trade finance in developing countries. The proposed changes are expected to result in a tightening of minimum capital requirements associated with trade finance instruments. Given that banks' profit margins are low on trade finance instruments, any increase in capital requirements would discourage banks from providing trade finance.

On the policy front, there has been a discussion whether, or to what extent, governments should take action to reduce the observed trade finance gap in developing countries. The answer to this question depends on whether the observed gap arises from reduced demand for trade finance (e.g. lower import demand) or insufficient supply of trade finance (e.g. miscalculation of financial risks). The gap can only be reduced by government intervention if it arises from insufficient supply. Nevertheless, it is often not easy to identify the underlying factors behind an observed trade finance gap.

Customs Data

As previously mentioned, an important challenge in exploring the factors that determine the use of bank-intermediated trade finance instruments is that detailed international trade data on payment methods are not widely available. Turkey is one of the countries which report detailed international trade data disaggregated by payment methods (see also Demir *et al.*, 2017; Demir and Javorcik, 2018). In this section, I will present some patterns of the use of different payment methods in Turkey's trade with Latin American and Caribbean countries. While it is not possible to generalise the patterns observed for the region's trade with Turkey, they might still be useful for understanding how the region differs from others, such as East Asia and Pacific, in terms of its reliance on bank-intermediated trade finance instruments.

During the 2004–2011 period, the share of Latin American and Caribbean exports to Turkey on L/C terms was 21%. The corresponding figure for the region's imports from Turkey was 27%. Nevertheless, these aggregate figures hide heterogeneity in the use of L/Cs across industries. Figure 13.5 presents Latin American and Caribbean (LAC) exports to and imports from Turkey on L/C terms at the industry level (two-digit Harmonised System [HS]). While the share of L/C-based exports is zero in more than ten two-digit HS industries, the share is almost 100% in ores, slag and ash (HS code 26). There is also considerable industry heterogeneity in the use of L/Cs for Latin American and Caribbean imports from Turkey. The figure also shows that reliance on L/Cs at the industry level differs between exports and imports. This could be explained by differences in the characteristics of exporters/importers between the two countries.

Figure 13.6 compares the reliance of Latin American and Caribbean countries on L/Cs in their international trade transactions with Turkey to East Asia and Pacific (EAP), OECD, and non-OECD countries during the 2004–2011 period. When exporting to Turkey, the region uses L/Cs more intensively than EAP countries (and OECD countries). This could be partly explained by differences in the industry composition of trade between the two regions: Latin American and

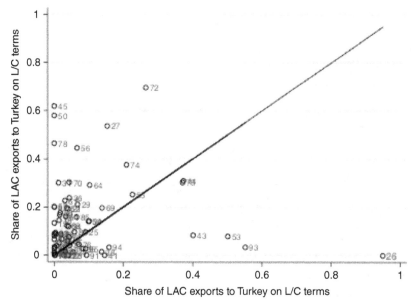

Figure 13.5 L/C-based exports to and imports from Turkey.
Source: Turkish Statistics Institute (n.d.).

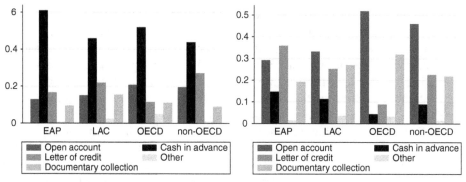

Figure 13.6 L/C-based exports to (left) and imports from (right) Turkey.
Source: Turkish Statistics Institute (n.d.).

Caribbean countries' exports to Turkey are concentrated in commodities, while EAP countries' exports are mainly concentrated in more sophisticated manufacturing products. Figure 13.7 also shows that open account transactions dominated Latin American and Caribbean countries' imports from Turkey during the 2004–2011 period. On the other hand, L/C was the most widely used payment method for EAP countries' imports from Turkey during the same period. It is worth noting that both regions use documentary collection terms heavily when importing from Turkey. While documentary collection is a more secure payment method than open account and cash in advance, it does not provide payment guarantee. Under documentary collection, banks intermediate the transaction by handling the payment and transaction-related documents.

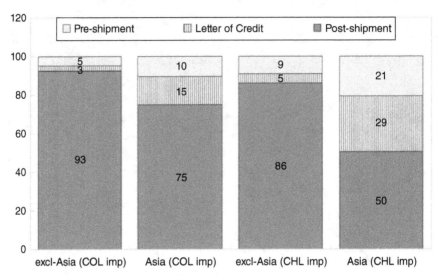

Figure 13.7 Distribution of Colombian and Chilean imports across financing terms by region, 2011 (% of total import value).
Source: Ahn (2014).
Note: COL and CHL stand for Colombia and Chile, respectively.

Academic Literature

Recently, there has been growing academic interest in the relationship between finance and international trade and finance. Given the focus of the chapter, it would be useful to survey the existing literature under three main headings: (i) impact of financial constraints on international trade; (ii) role of financial intermediaries in facilitating international trade transactions; and (iii) determinants of the choice of payment methods in international trade. When possible, country-level studies with a particular focus on Latin American countries will be discussed in detail.

The first strand of literature examines the impact of credit constraints on firms' abilities to engage in international trade. Most of the earlier literature studied the relationship between countries' level of financial development and their volumes of international trade. For instance, Beck (2002) finds that countries with more developed financial markets have higher levels of manufactured exports as a share both of GDP and of total merchandise exports, and they post higher trade balances in manufactured goods compared to countries with less developed financial markets. Do and Levchenko (2007) point out the importance of considering the potential simultaneity between the level of financial development and international trade. They show empirically that countries with comparative advantages in industries that rely more on external finance have more developed financial markets compared to those countries with comparative advantages in less financially intensive industries. To illustrate the economic significance of the mechanism, the authors compare Greece and Spain, which were respectively at the 25th and 75th percentile of the distribution of their measure of external finance dependence on exports over the period 1970–1999. While the main export categories of Greece were apparel and food products, those of Spain were transport equipment and machinery. Using the ratio of private credit to GDP as a measure of financial development, the estimates obtained by Do and Levchenko (2007) imply that if Greece moved up to the 75th percentile of the distribution of external finance dependence of exports, its private credit as a share of GDP would double: from an average of 35% during the same period to 68% – which is only slightly below the corresponding figure for Spain (74%).

More recent literature focuses on the role of financial friction in international trade. On the theoretical front, Chaney (2016) presents a model with liquidity-constrained exporters. In the model, firms have to pay fixed costs to start exporting, as in Melitz (2003). The ability to pay the fixed costs associated with exporting requires a certain level of liquidity, and thus only firms with sufficient liquidity are able to export. Chaney's model has important implications for developing-country exporters, as they typically do not have access to well-functioning financial markets to obtain liquidity in their domestic countries. On the empirical front, one of the earliest papers that show the importance of financial constraints for international trade is Manova (2008). Using data for a panel of 91 countries over the 1980–1997 period, the paper shows that shocks to the cost of capital, driven by equity market liberalisations, increase exports more in industries that are characterised by higher reliance on external financing or smaller shares of collateralisable assets. In particular, equity market liberalisation increases exports in the industry at the 75th percentile of the external capital dependence distribution by 43 percentage points more than exports in the industry at the 25th percentile of the distribution (external capital dependence is defined as the ratio of capital expenditures minus cash flow from operations to capital expenditures for the median firm in an industry). The importance of financial market conditions for international trade is empirically confirmed in another paper by Chor and Manova (2012), which studies the pattern of detailed US imports (disaggregated by country of origin and industry) during the Great Recession. Their results suggest that countries with tighter financial markets, proxied by the level of interbank rate, exported less to the United States during the recent financial crisis, and the effect was more significant in industries that rely more on external financing or have fewer collateralisable assets. (Some papers, on the other hand, argue that the bulk of the fall in international trade during the Great Recession was due to lack of demand and, in particular, a sharp decline in tradable goods – see e.g. Levchenko et al., 2010; Eaton et al., 2016 – instead of lack of trade finance available to firms as a result of adverse financial market conditions). A number of papers show more direct evidence of the impact of access to finance on export performance using micro-level data. Using detailed survey data on about 5000 Italian firms, Minetti and Zhu (2011) show that credit-rationed firms are less likely to participate in exporting and, conditional on exporting, their export sales are significantly lower. More interestingly, their results suggest that export sales are more responsive to credit constraints than domestic sales.

Another strand of literature studies the role of financial intermediaries in international trade. While some of the papers in this literature use aggregate data, the more recent papers use highly detailed matched bank-firm-level datasets. Auboin and Engemann (2014) use Berne Union data on export credit insurance and estimate that a 1% increase in international trade credit for a given country generates a 0.4% increase in its real imports, and the effect remains broadly unchanged between crisis and non-crisis periods. Using syndicated loan data from Loan Analytics for the 1990–2007 period, Hale et al. (2013) show that the intensity of bilateral trade increases as new bilateral international banking links are established between the trade partners. In another paper, Michalski and Ors (2012) find that financial integration across state borders, driven by deregulations of interstate banking entry restrictions, facilitates bilateral trade flows between US states – which is consistent with the hypothesis that financial intermediation facilitates trade across (country or state) borders.

Niepmann and Schmidt-Eisenlohr (2017a) use SWIFT data, which cover about 90% of global L/C transactions, to unearth new empirical patterns related to the use of L/Cs in international trade. First, they report that the share of global trade financed with L/Cs is 13% – which is comparable to the figures reported by Ahn (2014) for Chile and by Demir *et al.* (2017) for Turkey. Second, the frequency of zeros for the share of L/C-based bilateral trade is quite prevalent, particularly for trade partners located in Sub-Saharan Africa. This could be due to shortage of supply of trade finance in those countries. Third, the use of L/Cs increased during the Great Recession, which highlights the role of bank-intermediated trade finance in reducing risks in more uncertain environments and times. Finally, larger transactions are more likely to be settled on L/C terms, indicating the importance of fixed costs associated with obtaining L/Cs. In the presence of fixed fees, obtaining an L/C becomes profitable only for large transactions.

An important contribution to the empirical literature that relies on micro-level data on trade and financial intermediation is Amiti and Weinstein (2011). They use matched bank-firm-level data from Japan for the period 1990–2010 to unearth the mechanisms through which financial intermediation affects international trade. The richness of the dataset allows them to disentangle shocks to the supply of credit from shocks to the demand for credit. The authors find that firms borrowing extensively from financially unhealthy banks perform worse in their export markets. The effect is economically significant: one third of the decrease in Japan's trade-to-GDP ratio in the 1990s can be explained by the poor financial health of the main banks of large Japanese exporters. Regarding the potential channels, both the provision of working capital and insurance against default risk matter.

Ahn (2013) empirically investigates the importance of trade finance channels for the substantial decrease in international trade during the Great Recession. In particular, he uses matched importer-exporter data from Colombia, which also informs about payment methods, and exploits variations in L/C-based transactions for a given exporter-importer across issuing banks. The exceptionally detailed dataset used in the paper allows for controlling for demand-related factors for each exporter-importer in the estimation, leading to a cleaner identification of the causal effect of trade-finance-related shocks on international trade. The empirical results show that banks that had been hit by larger adverse liquidity shocks reduced their supplies of L/Cs to a larger extent, resulting in a larger reduction in imports by Colombian firms. The estimates imply that the trade finance channel accounts for about 40% of the decrease in imports by L/Cs in Colombia.

In a more recent paper, Paravisini *et al.* (2015) use highly detailed transaction-level export data from Peru to investigate whether negative shocks to access to credit contributed to the decline in Peruvian exports during the Great Recession. Their results suggest that the negative credit supply shocks experienced by Peruvian banks during the recent financial crisis account for about 8% of the drop in the country's exports in the same period. While both papers point to the importance of access to credit for firms' competitiveness in international markets, the estimate in Paravisini *et al.* (2015) is significantly smaller than the one reported by Amiti and Weinstein (2011) using Japanese data. The difference in the estimated impact of credit constraints on exports between the two studies could be partly explained by differences in empirical settings. According to Paravisini *et al.* (2015), the main driver behind declining Peruvian exports during the Great Recession was the drop in demand for Peruvian goods by the rest of the world.

As mentioned earlier, due to data limitations, little is known about how international trade finance choices are made by firms. On the theoretical front, Schmidt-Eisenlohr (2013) propose a simple model that answers the following question: Which trade-offs does a firm face when choosing between different payment contracts? The model covers the two key features of trade finance: (i) time lag between production and sales, and (ii) commitment problems arising from pre-financing by one of the trade partners, which generates default risk. In such a setting, the model shows that financial conditions (e.g. cost of borrowing) and the quality of contract enforcement in both source and destination countries matter for the choice of payment methods in international trade. In particular, the model predicts that open account financing (trade credit extended by the exporter to the importer) becomes more attractive if cost of financing and quality of contract enforcement in the destination country are high relative to the source country. Similarly, cash-in-advance becomes more attractive if the cost of financing and quality of contract enforcement in the source country are high relative to the destination country. L/C financing almost eliminates the moral hazard problem on both sides, but it is costly. Thus, it becomes more attractive if the quality of contract enforcement in both countries is low and L/C fees are low in the source country.

The result that weak contract enforcement matters for the choice of financing terms in international trade has important implications for developing countries. Those countries are generally characterised by weak rule of law and contract enforcement. This can be seen in Table 13.1, which presents the ranking of the country groups according to the quality of contract enforcement, as published by the World Bank (Doing Business, 2017). As expected, the quality of contract enforcement is the highest in OECD high-income countries. The countries in South Asia and Sub-Saharan Africa rank the lowest, and Latin American and Caribbean countries rank around the middle among 190 countries. Both the time and the cost for resolving a commercial dispute through a court are considerably high in those countries compared to OECD countries. This implies, according to the predictions of Schmidt-Eisenlohr (2013), that trading with developing-country firms might require bank guarantees or L/C financing. Therefore, lower L/C fees and/or cost of borrowing could boost international trade to/from those countries.

In another paper, Antràs and Foley (2015) use export transactions data from a large US poultry firm and rationalise the empirical patterns that they observe in a dynamic extension of the model developed by Schmidt-Eisenlohr (2013). They show that the length of the relationship between the trading partners also matters for the choice of financing terms in international trade: establishing a long-term relationship with an importer through repeated interaction reduces the incidence of cash-in-advance financing. In particular, when the value of cumulative transactions between

Table 13.1 Contract enforcement by country groups (2017)

	Contract Enforcement DTF	Rank	Time (days)	Cost (% of claim value)	Quality of judicial processes index (0–18)
OECD high income	66.76	47	577.8	21.5	11.0
Europe & Central Asia	65.38	51	489.9	26.2	10.0
Middle East & North Africa	54.21	106	638.5	24.4	5.9
Latin America & the Caribbean	53.13	107	767.1	31.4	8.4
East Asia & Pacific	53.09	102	565.7	47.3	7.9
Sub-Saharan Africa	48.14	128	656.8	44.0	6.5
South Asia	43.48	142	1101.6	29.6	7.0

Source: Doing Business (2017).
Note: DTF stands for "distance to frontier". The enforcing contracts indicator in the second column combines information presented in columns (4) and (5), namely the time and cost for resolving a commercial dispute through a local first-instance court, as well as the quality of judicial processes index, which is presented in the last column and measures whether each economy has adopted a series of good practices that promote quality and efficiency in the court system.

a seller and a customer increases from below US$25,000 to above US$5 million, the share of transactions on cash-in-advance terms decreases from 59% to about 11%. Antràs and Foley (2015) also document that bank-intermediated trade financing (comprised of L/Cs) is used relatively more often when trading with new customers than with old ones. One implication of this empirical finding is that access to trade finance is also an important factor for export diversification in terms of trade partners. In particular, it allows firms to establish new trade links and explore new destinations when they face reduced demand in their existing export destinations. As the relationship progresses, trade partners develop trust through repeated interactions so that they can switch to other forms of payment methods, particularly open account.

Other factors related to destination or source country and trading partners also affect the choice of financing terms. For instance, using detailed international trade data disaggregated by financing terms and exploiting an exogenous shock to market competition, Demir and Javorcik (2018) show that an increase in the level of market competition leads exporters to provide more trade credit to their buyers (i.e. increase in open account financing). Their results imply that competitive shocks faced by firms in their export markets affect their profits not only through reduced prices but also through the additional costs of providing trade credit. There is also anecdotal evidence that suggests competition matters for the choice of financing terms in international trade, and firms might provide export financing to gain edges in more competitive markets. For instance, the Trade Finance Guide, published by the International Trade Administration in the US Department of Commerce in November 2012, advices US exporters that providing trade credit "may help win customers in competitive markets" (p. 11), and asking for cash-in-advance financing "could, ultimately, cause exporters to lose customers to competitors who are willing offer more favorable payment terms to foreign buyers" (p. 5).

Ahn (2014) presents a portrait of the pattern of financing terms in international trade for two countries, Colombia and Chile, using detailed data from 2011. In both countries, the share of open account financing is above 80% of the total value of import transactions. The share of imports on L/C terms, on the other hand, is as low as 5% for Colombian imports and 10% for Chilean imports. These figures imply that Colombian and Chilean firms significantly rely on exporter financing (trade credit) when sourcing goods across borders. Nevertheless, the patterns show some degree of variation across regions of origin. As illustrated in Figure 13.7, open account financing is used significantly less by both Colombian and Chilean importers when sourcing from Asian countries. The decrease in the share of open account financing when importing from Asian countries can be explained, to a large extent, by increases in the use of L/C financing. The author explains this finding referring to the self-liquidating nature of trade credits, which makes open account financing relatively less expensive compared to the other methods of financing. If accounts-receivable financing is weaker in Asian countries, one could expect to observe a smaller share of open account financing when sourcing from those countries. An alternative explanation is that the relatively long distance between Asian countries and Colombia/Chile increases the default risk and working capital needs, which could lead trade partners to use L/C financing instead of open account financing.

In another paper, Ahn (2011) develops a model of trade finance, which predicts that adverse shocks to costs of trade financing would hurt trade partners with short relationships, i.e. those that do not know each other well. The mechanism is more pronounced for transactions that take place under post-shipment terms, e.g. open account. In the same paper, Ahn presents evidence that supports the mechanism. In particular, he uses Colombian customs data to understand the effect of increases in the cost of obtaining trade financing on trade by payment method during the 2008 financial crisis – a period characterised by high cost of trade financing. He finds that imports of Colombian firms from foreign partners – with which with they had longer relationships, or which were located in countries with more intense trade relationships with Colombia – fell less.

One of the challenges faced by researchers who study trade finance is disentangling demand and supply factors affecting the extent of the use of trade finance instruments. This is an important issue for understanding the drivers behind the observed trade finance gaps (as discussed in the previous section). Three recent papers address this challenge. Niepmann and Schmidt-Eisenlohr (2017b) use data on US banks' trade finance claims disaggregated by country to study whether shocks to the supply of L/Cs affect US exports. Their results indicate heterogeneous response of exports to L/C supply shocks, depending on the characteristics of the destination country and business cycle: they find statistically and economically significant effects only for smaller and riskier destination countries, and the estimated effects more than double during crisis times. Their estimates imply that, on average, a one-standard-deviation shock to the supply of L/Cs issued by US banks reduces the growth rate of US exports to a given country by 1.5 percentage points. Demir et al. (2018), on the other hand, use detailed international trade data disaggregated by financing terms and exploit the mandatory adoption of the Basel II framework in its standardised approach by all banks in Turkey on 1 July 2012 to investigate whether changes in banks' risk-based capital requirements affect firm-level exports. The adoption of the Basel II framework in Turkey affected the cost of holding L/Cs by changing risk weights used to adjust for counterparty bank risk to meet the Basel-mandated capital requirements. The empirical results suggest that firms decreased (increased) their reliance on L/Cs when exporting to countries for whose banks the risk weights (i.e. the cost of LCs) increased (decreased) after the Basel II adoption. However, changes in risk weights introduced by the Basel II framework did not affect the firm-level export growth, indicating that the regulatory change had a composition effect only.

Role of Multilateral Development Banks

As discussed earlier in this chapter, private financial institutions in the developing world often fail to meet the demand for trade finance by local firms because, for instance, the information networks, through which banks gather information about the creditworthiness of their customers, are either weak or non-existent. This implies that private banks in developing countries remain risk-averse and provide trade financing only to those firms that have enough collateral – which is expected to constitute a small share of firms in such countries. Given this background, it is not surprising that many multilateral development banks (MDBs) highlight trade financing as an important item on their policy agendas. As also discussed by Beck and DiCaprio in Chapter 8 of this Handbook, their aim is to reduce trade finance gaps in developing countries, which are often structural. MDBs provide guarantees, extend short-term loans to local financial institutions or use risk-sharing structures to support trade finance in countries in which they operate.

One important advantage of MDBs over private lenders is that they usually offer more favourable terms, e.g. lower interest rates and longer payment periods, to their borrowers thanks to their high international ratings arising from strong capital positions, as reflected by their financial ratios. Financial support provided by such MDBs is particularly valuable for developing countries, as the cost of capital faced by their private financial institutions is quite high. MDBs provide guarantees, loans, and similar products to support trade in developing countries. Trade finance programmes are run by five major MDBs: the European Bank for Reconstruction and Development (EBRD), the International Finance Corporation (IFC), the Asian Development Bank (ADB), the Inter-American Development Bank (IADB) and the African Development Bank (AfDB).

As expected, the IFC, a member of the World Bank Group, has the widest geographical coverage and appears to be the largest provider of trade finance support among others. The amount of financial support provided by the IFC to support global trade has reached US$145 billion and has covered thousands of firms in more than 90 countries across all regions. The IFC runs multiple programmes to support trade finance. Under the Global Trade Finance Program, the IFC helps private banks in improving their capacity to provide trade financing by offering confirming banks partial or full guarantees to cover payment risks on banks located in developing countries. These guarantees apply to L/Cs, trade-related promissory notes and bills of exchange, bid and performance bonds, advance payment guarantees and supplier credits for the import of capital goods. Thus far, the value of guarantees issued by the IFC under the Global Trade Finance Program has amounted to US$53 billion since its inception in 2005. The Latin American and Caribbean region is a significant beneficiary of the support provided under this programme. It has supported more than US$14 billion in trade flows in countries located in the region, and this accounts for about a quarter of the programme's global volume. More importantly, about 50% of the transactions supported under the Global Trade Finance Program in the region have involved local small or medium-sized companies.

As a response to the Global Recession and its impact on global trade, the IFC launched another support programme, the Global Trade Liquidity Program, in 2009. The programme aims to fill the persistent gap in trade finance in developing countries by "mobilizing funded and unfunded financing and channelling credit for trade transactions to targeted sectors and regions". The programme either uses a risk-sharing structure which channels funding to local banks through international banks, or creates lines of credit for local banks. Thus far, the Global Trade Liquidity Program has supported more than US$53 billion in global trade volume and benefited thousands of small and medium-sized companies engaging in international trade located in a large number of developing countries. During the first three years of its implementation, the amount of Latin American and Caribbean trade supported under the Global Trade Liquidity Program, on average, accounted for 38% of the programme's global volume.

Regional development banks have also been active in supporting global trade. The ADB appears to be the largest one among them in terms of the value of trade finance support provided. While it is relatively small in terms of the total number of transactions supported and their value, the support provided by the IADB per transaction is larger (US$4.1 million) than the corresponding figure for others. This might arise from, for instance, differences in the industry/product composition of trade across regions.

Trade finance support provided by the IADB falls under its *access2Trade* (or *access2Markets*) product lines, which aim to improve firms' access to trade finance and trade-related infrastructure in Latin America and the Caribbean by providing guarantees, extending loans, and offering trade- finance-related technical assistance.

The IADB launched a successful programme entitled the Trade Finance Facilitation Program in 2005 to provide sources of trade finance for the financial sector in Latin America and the Caribbean. In particular, it aims to (i) promote development and economic growth in the region through the expansion of trade financing; (ii) broaden the sources of trade finance available for firms in the region and support their internationalisation strategies; (iii) support global and intra-regional integration through trade; and (iv) provide liquidity in periods of market volatility – which highlights the counter-cyclical role of the programme. The programme provides financial products (e.g. credit guarantees and loans), technical assistance to local banks and knowledge creation (e.g. publications, face-to-face training programmes). The guarantees provided under the programme cover up to 100% of political and commercial risks.

Local financial institutions and international financial intermediaries participate in the Trade Finance Facilitation Program but assume different roles. First, any private or public local financial institution (without a sovereign guarantee) in one of the IADB's 26 member countries can participate in the programme as *issuing banks* under the guarantee programme and/or as *borrowers* under the loan programme. The Trade Finance Facilitation Program not only allows the participating local financial institutions to expand their trade finance funding sources, but also allows them to improve their creditworthiness in international markets and reduces the collateral requirements asked by international banks – which become an important obstacle to engaging in trade financing in particular during volatile times. Second, any international or regional financial institution (with or without a sovereign guarantee) can participate in the programme as *confirming banks* under the guarantee programme and/or as *participants* under the loan programme. Currently, the programme is participated in by more than 300 global financial intermediaries from more than 60 countries. The benefits provided by the programme to those institutions include the establishment of new correspondent banking relationships, access to the IADB's detailed credit analysis and reduction of capital-provisioning requirements.

As of June 2015, the Trade Finance Facilitation Program covered 102 financial intermediaries in 21 countries, and supported US$2.96 billion in trade flows under the guarantee programme and extended US$1.8 billions' worth of loans under the loan programme in Latin America and the Caribbean (the latter figure is the sum of loans disbursed directly by the IADB, B loans and co-loans). The programme supported internationalisation of more than 4000 small or medium-sized companies. The largest beneficiaries of the Trade Finance Facilitation Program are Brazil, Guatemala and Argentina.

Discussion and Conclusions

This chapter posed the following question: What is the significance of bank-intermediated trade finance for developing-country exporters and importers? The geographical focus of the chapter is Latin American and Caribbean countries. It is widely believed that the availability of trade finance is an important factor that affects firms' competitiveness in international markets. Foreign sales rely more on trade finance than domestic sales, for a number of reasons: the longer time lag between production and sales increases working capital needs; trade partners are subject to different jurisdictions, which increases uncertainty; and there are additional (fixed and variable) costs associated with exporting compared to selling domestically. If none of the trade partners is willing to provide pre-financing and to bear the risk associated with a given transaction, the transaction does not take place. Such burdens could be at least partly eliminated if banks intermediate between exporters and importers. The academic literature suggests that the need for bank intermediation in international trade increases as the quality of contract enforcement decreases in source or destination countries and as time lag between production and sales increases. Given that contract enforcement is generally weaker in developing countries, the need for bank-intermediated trade is expected to be higher for transactions that involve developing-country firms. However, bank-intermediated trade finance markets in developing countries are shallow, and trade finance gaps are not uncommon – which represents a bottleneck for developing-country firms that engage in international trade. According to banking surveys, the main reason behind the shortage of trade finance supply is the high cost of compliance arising from stringent financial regulations.

There is considerable heterogeneity in terms of the intensity of the use of trade finance instruments across developing countries. For instance, the usage of bank-intermediated trade finance instruments, e.g. L/Cs, is significantly higher in Asia than in countries in other regions such as Latin America and the Caribbean. This pattern could be explained by a number of factors, including geographical remoteness (i.e. bilateral distance to major trade partners) and types of products traded. According to the academic literature, bank-intermediated trade finance is used more intensively when shipping longer distances, exporting to or importing from countries with weak contract enforcement, underdeveloped financial markets and high political or economic risks. On the demand side, assuming that the United States is a major trade partner, Latin American and Caribbean countries may demand less trade finance: the United States is located relatively nearby, and its contract enforcement quality is high. Indeed, the low rejection rates of proposed trade finance transactions for the Latin American and Caribbean region, as reported by the annual ICC surveys, indicate that low demand, rather than low supply, could explain the low intensity of the use of traditional trade finance instruments in the region. Nevertheless, the proposed changes in the banking regulations under the Basel IV framework, which might increase banks' costs of providing trade finance, may lead to a decrease in the supply of trade finance in Latin America and the Caribbean, as in other regions.

The question arises regarding what the future of trade financing in developing countries looks like. Supply chain finance, which is also known as reverse factoring or approved trade-payable finance, is usually mentioned as an important innovation in the global trade finance market, and it is particularly relevant for developing-country firms. Supply chain finance is not a loan; it allows a supplier to sell its receivables to a bank before maturity at a discount once they are approved by the buyer (see Figure 13.8). Its main benefits include transition from paper-based transactions to electronic invoicing and using transaction-level data to assess the creditworthiness of potential borrowers (Saleem *et al.*, 2017).

Supply chain finance offers potential benefits to all stakeholders: large companies and their small trade partners, as well as financial institutions. While supply chain finance allows the supplier to obtain cash before the maturity date, it also allows the buyer to pay later. By doing so, supply chain finance optimises cash flows along a supply chain by letting buyers optimise working capital and allowing suppliers to

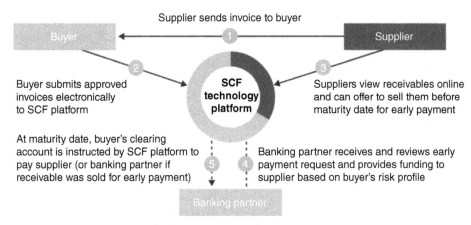

Figure 13.8   How does supply chain finance work?
Source: McKinsey & Company (2015).

obtain additional cash flow. The bank deals directly with the buyer instead of relying on the creditworthiness of the supplier. The market for supply chain finance is currently populated by "fintechs", which provide software-based services to support such operations. The size of the supply chain finance market was US$2 trillion as of 2015, and it has been growing at an annual rate of 20% since 2010 (McKinsey & Company, 2015). An important driver behind the fast growth of the supply chain finance market in the past few years has been the tightening of the banking regulations under the Basel framework, which has increased the cost of providing traditional trade finance instruments by banks and has made them less attractive.

While the supply chain finance market in Latin American countries has taken off recently, it is still not widely used, except in Mexico and Brazil for a number of reasons (Treasury Management International, 2015). First, given that the benefits from supply chain finance in terms of cash flow optimisation increase with the size of firms, the average size of Latin American firms (except those located in Mexico and Brazil) does not justify paying the cost of initiating supply chain finance programmes. Second, international banks have been reluctant to invest in Latin American countries to establish supply chain finance programmes because the diversity of legal and financial regulations within a region simply makes such investment costly and unprofitable. Third, buyers' credit quality is not significantly higher than that of suppliers in Latin American countries. This matters as the main principle behind the supply chain finance method relies on the difference in the credit quality between suppliers and buyers. It becomes profitable only when the buyer's credit quality is sufficiently higher than the supplier's. With the increased awareness of the benefits from optimising cash flows along a supply chain, the use of supply chain finance programmes has been increasing. As in other developing countries, supply chain finance appears to be the future of trade finance in the Latin American and Caribbean region.

References

Ahn, J. (2011) A Theory of Domestic and International Trade Finance. *IMF Working Paper* 11/262. Retrieved from: https://www.imf.org/external/pubs/ft/wp/2011/wp11262.pdf (accessed 10 July 2019).

Ahn, J. (2013) Estimating the Direct Impact of Bank Liquidity Shocks on the Real Economy: Evidence from Imports by Letters-of-Credit in Colombia. *IMF Technical Report*. Retrieved from: https://pdfs.semanticscholar.org/3e11/ed77476171850aa925e9b92ffcaea80da34b.pdf (accessed 10 July 2019).

Ahn, J. (2014) Understanding Trade Finance: Theory and Evidence from Transaction-Level Data. *IMF Working Paper*. Retrieved from: https://www.imf.org/external/np/seminars/eng/2014/trade/pdf/ahn.pdf (accessed 10 July 2019).

Amiti, M. & Weinstein, D.E. (2011) Exports and Financial Shocks. *Quarterly Journal of Economics,* 126(4), 1841–1877.

Antràs, P. & Foley, C.F. (2015) Poultry in Motion: A Study of International Trade Finance Practices. *Journal of Political Economics*, 123(4), 853–901.

Auboin, M. (2009) Boosting the Availability of Trade Finance in the Current Crisis: Background Analysis for a Substantial G20 Package. *CEPR Discussion Paper* No. 35. Retrieved from: https://cepr.org/sites/default/files/policy_insights/PolicyInsight35.pdf (accessed 10 July 2019).

Auboin, M. & Engemann, M. (2014) Testing the Trade Credit and Trade Link: Evidence from Data on Export Credit Insurance. *Review of World Economics*, 150(4), 715–743.

Bank for International Settlements (2014) *Trade Finance: Developments and Issues.* Basel: BIS.

Beck, T. (2002) Financial Development and International Trade: Is There a Link? *Journal of International Economics*, 57(1), 107–131.

Chaney, T. (2016) Liquidity Constrained Exporters. *Journal of Economic Dynamics and Control*, 72, 141–154.

Chor, D. & Manova, K. (2012) Off the Cliff and Back? Credit Conditions and International Trade during the Global Financial Crisis. *Journal of International Economics*, 87(1), 117–133.

Demir, B. (2014) Trade Financing: Challenges for Developing-Country Exporters. *CESifo Forum*, 15(3), 34–38.

Demir, B. & Javorcik, B. (2018) Don't Throw in the Towel, Throw in Trade Credit. *Journal of International Economics*, 111, 177–189.

Demir, B., Michalski, T. & Ors, E. (2017) Risk-Based Capital Requirements for Banks and International Trade: Evidence from Basel 2 Implementation In Turkey. *Review of Financial Studies*, 30(11), 3970–4002.

Do, Q.T. & Levchenko A.A. (2007) Comparative Advantage, Demand for External Finance, and Financial Development. *Journal of Financial Economics*, 86(3), 796–834.

Eaton, J., Kortum, S., Neiman, B. & Romalis, J. (2016) Trade and the Global Recession. *American Economic Review*, 106, 401–438.

Grath, A. (2014) *The Handbook of International Trade and Finance.* London: Kogan Page.

Hale, G., Candelaria, C., Caballero, J. & Borisov, S. (2013) Bank Linkages and International Trade. Federal Reserve Bank of San Francisco, Working Paper 2013-14.

Inter-American Development Bank (2016) Evaluation of IDB Group's Work through Financial Intermediaries: Trade Finance. Retrieved from: https://publications.iadb.org/publications/english/document/Evaluation-of-IDB-Group-Work-through-Financial-Intermediaries.pdf (accessed 10 July 2019).

International Chamber of Commerce (2017) *Rethinking Trade and Finance.* Paris: ICC.

International Monetary Fund–Bankers' Association for Finance and Trade (2009) *IMF-BAFT Trade Finance Survey: A Survey among Banks Assessing the Current Trade Finance Environment.* Washington, DC: IMF.

International Monetary Fund–Bankers' Association for Finance and Trade (2010) *IMF-BAFT Trade Finance Survey: A Survey among Banks Assessing the Current Trade Finance Environment.* Washington, DC: IMF.

International Monetary Fund–Bankers' Association for Finance and Trade (2011) *IMF-BAFT Trade Finance Survey: A Survey among Banks Assessing the Current Trade Finance Environment.* Washington, DC: IMF.

International Trade Administration (2012) Trade Finance Guide. US Department of Commerce. Retrieved from: http://build.export.gov/build/idcplg?IdcService=DOWNLOAD_PUBLIC_FILE&RevisionSelectionMethod=Latest&dDocName=eg_main_043219 (accessed 10 July 2019).

Levchenko, A., Lewis, L. & Tesar, L. (2010) The Collapse in International Trade during the 2008–2009 Financial Crisis: In Search of the Smoking Gun. *IMF Economic Review*, 58, 214–253.

Malaket, A. (2015) Leveraging Supply Chain Finance for Development. International Centre for Trade and Sustainable Development and World Economic Forum. Retrieved from: http://e15initiative.org/wp-content/uploads/2015/09/E15-Finance-and-Development-Malaket-Final.pdf (accessed 10 July 2019).

Malouche, M. (2009) Trade and Trade Finance Developments in 14 Developing Countries Post September 2008. *World Bank Policy Research Working Paper* No. WPS5138. Retrieved from: https://openknowledge.worldbank.org/bitstream/handle/10986/4329/WPS5138.pdf?sequence=1&isAllowed=y (accessed 10 July 2019).

Manova, K. (2008) Credit Constraints, Equity Market Liberalizations and International Trade. *Journal of International Economics*, 76, 33–47.

McKinsey & Company (2015) *Supply-Chain Finance: The Emergence of a New Competitive Landscape*. New York: McKinsey.

Melitz, M. (2003) The Impact of Trade on Intra-industry Reallocations and Aggregate Industry Productivity. *Econometrica*, 71(6), 1695–1725.

Michalski, T. & Ors, E. (2012) (Interstate) Banking and (Interstate) Trade: Does Real Integration Follow Financial Integration? *Journal of Financial Economics*, 104(1), 89–117.

Minetti, R. & Zhu, S.C. (2011) Credit Constraints and Firm Export: Microeconomic Evidence from Italy. *Journal of International Economics*, 83(2), 109–125.

Niepmann, F. & Schmidt-Eisenlohr, T. (2017a) International Trade, Risk and the Role of Banks. *Journal of International Economics*, 107(C), 111–126.

Niepmann, F. & Schmidt-Eisenlohr, T. (2017b) No Guarantees, No Trade: How Banks Affect Export Patterns. *Journal of International Economics*, 108, 338–350.

Paravisini, D., Rappoport, V., Schnabl, P. & Wolfenzon, D. (2015) Dissecting the Effect of Credit Supply on Trade: Evidence from Matched Credit-Export Data. *Review of Economic Studies*, 82(1), 333–359.

Rhee, Y.W. (1989) Trade Finance in Developing Countries. *World Bank Policy and Research Series* No. 5. Retrieved from: http://documents.worldbank.org/curated/en/172971468765928790/pdf/multi-page.pdf (accessed 10 July 2019).

Saleem, Q., Hommes, M. & Sorokina, A. (2017) Technology-Enabled Supply Chain Finance for Small and Medium Enterprises is a Major Growth Opportunity for Banks. *EMCompass*, Note 39. World Bank Group. Retrieved from: http://documents.worldbank.org/curated/en/104991502947116592/pdf/118730-BRI-EMCompass-Note-39-Supply-Chain-Financing-PUBLIC.pdf (accessed 10 July 2019).

Schmidt-Eisenlohr, T. (2013) Towards a Theory of Trade Finance. *Journal of International Economics*, 91(1), 96–112.

Treasury Management International (2015) Economic Clouds Bring Out the Sun for Supply Chain Finance in Latin America. Retrieved from: https://www.treasury-management.com/article/4/339/2847/economic-clouds-bring-out-the-sun-for-supply-chain-finance-in-latin-america.html (accessed 22 July 2019).

Turkish Statistics Institute (n.d.) Retrieved from: http://www.turkstat.gov.tr/VeriBilgi.do?alt_id=39 (accessed 22 July 2019).

United Nations Conference on Trade and Development (2017) International Trade Statistics. Retrieved from: https://unctadstat.unctad.org/wds/ReportFolders/reportFolders.aspx?IF_ActivePath=P,15912&sCS_ChosenLang=en (accessed 22 July 2019).

World Bank (2017) *Doing Business*. Washington, DC: World Bank. Retrieved from: https://www.doingbusiness.org/content/dam/doingBusiness/media/Annual-Reports/English/DB17-Report.pdf (accessed 22 July 2019).

World Trade Organization (2017) World Trade Statistical Review 2017 Retrieved from: https://www.wto.org/english/res_e/statis_e/wts2017_e/wts2017_e.pdf (accessed 22 July 2019).

Chapter 14

Sailing Against the Storm of Protectionism: The Role of the EU in Shaping Global Trade Policy

Lucian Cernat and Omar Alam

Introduction

For many decades, the European Union (EU) has been playing a leading role in shaping global trade flows and the rules governing them. Taken as a whole, the block of 28 EU member states is the world's largest exporter and importer of both goods and services, the largest foreign direct investor and the most important destination for foreign direct investment (FDI). This scale makes the EU the largest trading partner for about 80 countries and the second most important partner for another 40 (European Commission, 2015a, p. 7).

As a main engine for growth and prosperity, trade is arguably the EU's most significant link to the world beyond its borders. Since it was introduced by the Treaty of Rome in 1957, the common EU trade policy became the EU's oldest instrument for influencing foreign relations. Today, Article 207 of the Treaty on the Functioning of the European Union (TFEU) (European Union, 2012a) establishes the common trade policy as an exclusive EU competence.

EU Trade Policy: Importance for European Growth and Prosperity

Trade, Growth and Competitiveness

Far from being just an instrument for its external relations, trade is also a fundamental tool for promoting the EU's internal objectives. For instance, the EU's latest trade strategy – the 2015 "Trade For All: Towards A More Responsible Trade And Investment Strategy" (European Commission, 2015a) – considers free trade agreements (FTAs) fundamental for the creation of European growth and prosperity. Indeed, trade has never been more important for the EU economy. The recent global economic crisis brought about the realisation that trade could be a stabilising force

The Handbook of Global Trade Policy, First Edition. Edited by Andreas Klasen.

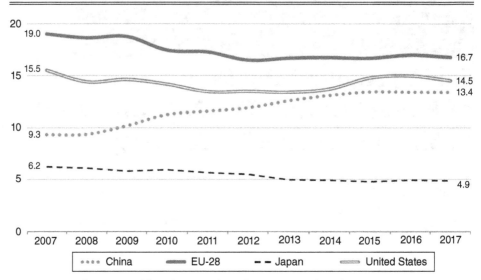

Figure 14.1   Share in world trade in goods and services in selected countries (%).
Sources: European Commission (2018g), p. 21.
Coverage: excluding intra-EU trade.

in times of economic hardship, by channelling demand from other parts of the world with higher growth back to Europe at a time when domestic demand remained frail. Trade also emerged as one of the few avenues for bolstering economic growth without weighing down on already constrained public finances.

Trade also fosters growth through the supply side of the economy. Opening up the EU economy to trade and investments helps increase the efficiency of European economies through better allocation of resources thanks to the principle of comparative advantage. Long-term evidence from EU countries demonstrates that a 1% increase in openness of the economy is associated with a 0.6% increase in labour productivity (European Commission, 2015b, p. 3). Moreover, trade has a multiplier effect on the EU economy, as advances in business competitiveness are multiplied when products and services are able to compete in world markets.

Within EU policymaking circles, there is also an increasing acknowledgement that Europe's future prosperity rests on its ability to trade with the rest of the world. The fact that by 2020 90% of world gross domestic product (GDP) growth will come from outside the EU has become a common mantra in Brussels. Despite the European continent not being at the epicentre of future growth, European companies are highly competitive at the global level, making the EU exceptionally well placed to benefit from increased international engagement.

Trade and Jobs

With an increasingly interdependent global economy and the proliferation of global value chains, global trade has become a progressively more significant source of jobs for Europeans. In fact, the contribution of exports to employment in the EU has been increasing over time. The European Commission's "Report on the Implementation of the Trade Policy Strategy Trade for All" estimates that in 2011 around 1 in 7 EU jobs (or 31 million) depended, directly or indirectly, on extra-EU trade – two thirds more

Table 14.1   EU employment supported by the extra-EU exports of each member state, 1995–2011 (in thousand jobs)

	1995	2011	2011–1995	2011/1995
Austria	359	832	473	131%
Belgium	417	812	396	95%
Bulgaria	541	586	45	8%
Cyprus	34	46	12	35%
Czech Republic	469	763	294	63%
Germany	3,477	7,478	4,001	115%
Denmark	389	578	189	49%
Estonia	71	83	13	18%
Greece	151	366	215	142%
Spain	683	1,508	825	121%
Finland	304	455	151	50%
France	2,079	2,736	657	32%
Hungary	457	793	336	74%
Ireland	200	732	531	265%
Italy	2,141	3,099	958	45%
Lithuania	222	245	23	11%
Luxembourg	44	373	329	753%
Latvia	151	132	–19	–13%
Malta	16	40	24	148%
Netherlands	954	1,306	352	37%
Poland	767	1,622	855	112%
Portugal	220	369	149	68%
Romania	794	1,279	485	61%
Sweden	673	969	296	44%
Slovenia	120	138	18	15%
Slovakia	137	239	102	74%
UK	2,749	3,583	834	30%
EU-27	18,620	31,163	12,542	67%

Source: Rueda-Cantuche and Sousa (2016).

than in 1995 (see Table 14.1 for a breakdown by member states) (European Commission, 2017a, p. 3; Rueda-Cantuche and Sousa, 2016). On average, each €1 billion increase in exports supports an additional 14,000 jobs across member states. In addition, these jobs are generally more productive, more qualified and better paid than in the rest of the economy (European Commission, 2015b, p. 2).

Moreover, these employment benefits are spread across EU member states, as trade by one EU country is also linked to job creation in other European countries. For instance, German exports outside of the EU account for more than 6 million jobs in Germany. Another 870,000 German jobs depend on other EU countries' trade with the rest of the world and similarly, German exports outside the EU create more than 1.3 million jobs in the rest of the EU. When considering all EU exports, about 1 in 6 German jobs depend on trade (European Commission, 2015c). When looking at the whole of the EU, in 2011 on average 83.8% of the jobs supported by extra-EU exports were found in the exporting member state, while the remaining 16.2% were related to spillovers. In the same year, a total of 5 million jobs were dependent on exports of other member states, representing 2.2% of total EU employment. Furthermore, the share of spillover-associated jobs has increased over time, denoting an increasingly integrated EU economy.

Similarly, the importance of investment for job creation should not be overlooked. After all, the EU remains the world's biggest foreign investor and recipient of FDI. Foreign-owned companies accounted for almost 8 million EU jobs in 2014 (equivalent to approximately 15% of total jobs) (Eurostat, 2018a, 2018b). On average, these jobs are also more productive, more qualified and better paid than in the rest of the economy. Additionally, international investment serves to further integrate the EU in GVCs, contributing to generating growth and jobs while also helping spread best practices and technologies (European Commission, 2015b, p. 5).

Trade Benefits for All: SMEs and Consumer Benefits

The expansion of European small and medium-sized enterprises (SMEs) into international markets is an important EU policy objective that can significantly benefit the European economy. Facilitating the internationalisation of EU SMEs is part of the objectives set out by the European Commission. FTAs help SMEs wishing to enter international markets outside the EU. SMEs exporting to these markets are already benefiting due to reduction in direct or indirect trade-specific barriers. This has been specifically indicated as a main priority for EU trade policy since the 2010 "Trade, Growth and World Affairs" Commission trade strategy (European Commission, 2010a). This strategy highlights that EU trade policy does provide tangible benefits to EU large companies and SMEs alike. By eliminating protective tariffs abroad or reducing the cost of non-tariff measures, the access to international markets is facilitated.

The rationale to prioritise SMEs in the EU trade strategy is also borne out from trade statistics. As can be seen in Figure 14.2, both the number and the share of exporting SMEs in the total number of exporters has been growing in recent years, from 81% in 2011 to 83% in 2015. Apart from their relative growing share in total exporting firms at EU level, in absolute terms, the export value of SMEs increased by 2% between 2011 and 2015 and the number of SMEs increased by 6%.

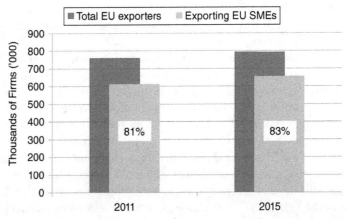

Figure 14.2 Number of EU exporting firms and the share of SMEs, 2011 and 2015. Source: Authors' calculations based on Eurostat data.

For certain EU member states, the importance of SMEs for their export performance is crucial. In the case of Italy for instance, around 90% of the total number of Italian exporting firms are actually SMEs and they generate almost 50% of the value of Italian extra-EU exports. For several other EU member states (e.g. Spain, Belgium, Portugal, Hungary, Latvia, Estonia) the role of SMEs in terms either of share of the number of exporting firms or of value of exports is equally, if not more, important. In 11 EU members states, SMEs accounted for 90% or more of the total number of exporting enterprises in 2015.

But trade benefits do not stop at promoting the competitiveness of EU SMEs. The positive effect of trade on per capita income has been testified by a number of studies (Feyrer, 2009; Rueda-Cantuche and Sousa, 2016). There is also some degree of consensus within the academic literature that trade affects consumers via a number of channels, including productivity gains and sectorial reallocation of production affecting employment, wages and prices. There are also a number of indirect gains, such as increased growth rates, product quality and variety. These consumer benefits are estimated to be strongest for the poorest households (Cernat *et al.*, 2018, p. 2). Low-income families typically spend a larger share of their budget on consumer goods. For this reason, lower import prices due to slashed tariffs are proportionally more important for them (Fajgelbaum and Khandelwal, 2016).

The increased competition brought about by FTAs lowers the prices of goods, incentivising firms to adjust their prices and decrease production costs by increasing cost-efficiency (e.g. by investing in research and development). While mark-ups are generally seen to fall as import competition increases, it is unclear whether this is due to the elimination of the market power or the creation of negative profits (see Tybout, 2001). In this context, the yearly gains resulting from trade agreements for the average EU consumer are in the range of €600 (EPRS, 2017).

Overall, thanks to all EU trade policy initiatives at the multilateral, bilateral and unilateral level, about 76% of imports enter the EU duty free, for the benefit of consumers and industries across Europe. In a report assessing the consumer benefits from EU trade liberalisation since the Uruguay Round, the Directorate-General for Trade (DG Trade)'s Chief Economist and Trade Analysis Unit estimated that the total annual tariff savings for all EU households amount to approximately €60 billion (if pre-Uruguay Round tariffs continued to apply to today's imports, i.e. the costs consumers would incur if they wished to keep their current lifestyle and consumption patterns if tariffs were to go to back to pre-Uruguay levels). This would mean that without these benefits EU households would have to pay on average €55 more every year just for "food and non-alcoholic beverages". It is also important to note that a single purchase of an imported product that previously was covered by import duties, for instance a car or a mobile phone, can far exceed these annual tariff savings (Cernat *et al.*, 2018).

Excursus: Trade, Global Value Chains and Income Inequality

While global income inequality has decreased since the early 1990s (Milanovic, 2012), especially due to reductions in wage inequality in emerging countries such as China and India, most developed countries have seen their wage inequality rise in this period (OECD, 2014, 2015).

The vast majority of existing studies on trade and income inequality focus on the extent to which trade has contributed to the observed increases in income inequality in some countries. However, there seems to be no consensus on the nature of this relationship, with some studies finding trade has an effect on income inequality, whereas others conclude it does not.

A recent OECD study (Lopez Gonzalez *et al.*, 2015) approaches the issue from a different angle. In the context of the most recent wave of globalisation, denoted by an increasing participation in global value chains (GVCs), the data suggests that there is an inverse relationship between participation in GVCs and wage inequality. That is to say, countries which engage more widely in GVCs through offshoring – i.e. using foreign value added to produce exports – are found to have lower levels of wage inequality. Specifically, the gap between wages of low- and high-skilled workers appears reduced as the wages of low-skilled workers rise faster than those of high-skilled workers. While the empirical analysis captures only relative changes in returns for those in employment, these general effects are found to be robust even when using alternative measures of inequality that account for the income of the unemployed.

Overall, GVC participation is found to have a small effect on the distribution of wages and, when it has, it can reduce wage inequality when it relates to GVC participation of low-skilled segments of the labour force. It must also be noted that offshoring high-skill tasks leads to increases in wage inequality as wages for higher-skilled workers rise. However, the data suggests that low-skilled tasks are traded more intensely within GVCs, which helps explain the small, albeit positive, effect of GVC participation in reducing income inequality (Lopez Gonzalez *et al.*, 2015). Based on these findings, one can conclude that the increased GVC participation facilitated by the EU's vast network of free trade agreements also contributes to the reduction of income inequality.

Spreading the Benefits of Trade

The EU has the widest range of FTAs in the world, and the number is only set to grow. The challenge is now to ensure they make a difference for all. Despite all the positive economic effects of trade, the EU seeks to ensure that the benefits from trade are shared equally among all stakeholders, including SMEs and consumers. This includes using trade policy to make sure trade and sustainable development (TSD) chapters feature more prominently within EU trade agreements.

In an independent study on the consumer welfare effects of trade agreements implemented by the EU between 1993 and 2013, Berlingieri *et al.* (2018) found that consumers in the EU's 15 founding member states benefited from an increase in welfare primarily due to a rise in the quality of imported products while prices remained largely unaffected. The authors suggest that trade agreements saved EU consumers approximately €24 billion per year over two decades. However, the same study notes that high-income countries (such as Benelux, the United Kingdom and Ireland) saw a much stronger increase in quality (and consequently, larger consumer benefits) than other EU countries. The new EU trade strategy seeks to address these differences, ensuring that the benefits of trade are shared equally among all stakeholders.

For instance, the cost of entering a new market is disproportionately high for SMEs compared to larger firms (the same is true for access to information about market opportunities). Moreover, the utilisation rates of trade agreements vary wildly across member states.

In additional to these tangible gains for consumers, there is a growing realisation of the fact that external trade can – and should – be used to promote fundamental European values. For instance, one area which is increasingly being focused on by policymakers is mainstreaming gender issues within the EU's external trade policy. A study by DG Trade's Chief Economist and Trade Analysis Unit found that in 2011, almost 12 million women in the EU had jobs thanks to the exports of goods and services to the rest of the world. However, a gender gap to the disadvantage of women still exists, largely due to the concentration of female employment in the less export-oriented sectors, notably in services (Rueda-Cantuche and Sousa, 2017). This has encouraged European policymakers to integrate provisions aimed at promoting gender equality within the context of EU trade agreements.

"Trade for All": Not Only for Europeans

The EU is committed not only to using its common trade policy to generate growth and jobs in Europe, but also to supporting countries around the world in achieving sustainable development. After all, the name of the EU's most recent trade strategy – "Trade for All" – is an indication of the will to ensure that the benefits of trade are spread equally not only within the EU, but also beyond its own borders.

The EU has a long tradition of granting preferential access to exports from developing countries into its market through its unilateral trade schemes (GSP, GSP+ and EBA – covered in greater depth in the following sections). They are primarily aimed at promoting economic development in beneficiary countries by offering them preferential access to the EU markets, thereby providing them with a competitive advantage vis-à-vis exports from other countries. Ultimately, an increase in the exports of developing countries results in a stimulus to their global economic activity and development (European Commission, 2015d, p. 13). One additional benefit of these schemes is they also allow EU consumers to enjoy greater benefits from trade by paying lower or no duties on their purchases, potentially saving them substantial amounts of money.

Recent EU Trade Policy Achievements

In view of the numerous benefits to be derived from open, free and fair global markets as outlined above, the EU strives to promote free trade in a multitude of ways as part of its "Trade for All" strategy, from tackling barriers to trade and investment to expanding its ever-increasing network of free trade agreements at the bilateral, unilateral and multilateral levels.

Tackling Barriers to Trade and Investment

The role of the EU in promoting trade and investment to sustain European growth is all the more important in the current global context of rising protectionism. This trend is testified by recent data in the EU's Market Access Database, which compiles data on the trade barriers reported by European businesses and member states: an unprecedented 67 new barriers to trade in 39 different third countries were registered in 2017, bringing the total stock of active trade and investment barriers against EU exporters to a historical record of 396. Russia remains the country with most trade restrictions, with China, Indonesia and India trailing closely behind. The trade flows potentially affected by all the new barriers registered in 2017 amount to more than €23 billion (this is a conservative estimate, as it excludes services, horizontal and other measures of difficult quantification), representing 1.2% of all EU exports in the same year (European Commission, 2018e). In this context, it is no coincidence that "implementation" and "enforcement" were identified as key priorities in the Commission's current trade strategy.

As a response to this rise in protectionism, the EU has ramped up its efforts to facilitate market access in three principal ways: strengthening coordination among stakeholders and EU institutions; improving the prioritisation of barriers; and enhancing communication and awareness-raising. By using all tools available in its toolbox – which include dispute settlement, the use of the Trade Barriers Regulation, diplomatic démarches and the introduction of an overarching European Economic Diplomacy Initiative – the EU was able to significantly improve market access for European businesses. In 2017 alone, 45 barriers were either partially or fully removed in 13 different sectors – including services, automotive, aircraft, machinery, ICT and electronics, pharmaceuticals, agrifood, iron and steel among others – as well as horizontally. Conservative estimates suggest that the removal of these barriers generates an additional €4.8 billion extra exports on a yearly basis – which is in the same order of magnitude as many EU FTAs. Moreover, the extra exports generated by the removal of trade barriers between 2014 and 2016 were roughly twice the value of those tackled between 2012 and 2013, the last time the Commission performed such an analysis using the same methodology (see Figure 14.3) (European Commission, 2018e). This is an indication of the fact that as the barriers to trade increase due to a more protectionist global environment, so does the EU's commitment to ensure enhanced market opening.

Bilateral Agenda: A New Generation of EU FTAs

As part of its efforts to improve market access for European businesses, the EU has also been pursuing an ambitious bilateral negotiating agenda, based on the principle of reciprocity while still taking into account the economic realities of its partners.

The last half decade has been the most prolific ever for the EU in terms of concluding FTAs with the rest of the world. Currently, the EU has over 40 FTAs in force with countries in virtually all continents (see Figure 14.4). However, the increased number of partnerships is not the only way the EU has recently strengthened its bilateral trade agenda. Responding to today's trends and greater economic complexity, the EU has moved from "traditional" FTAs focused on tariff reductions and trade in goods, to a new generation of FTAs. These aim to unlock the untapped potential of trade in services, public procurement, investment and regulatory cooperation. Additionally, these agreements seek to use the trade platform to promote sustainable development in line with European values. In this

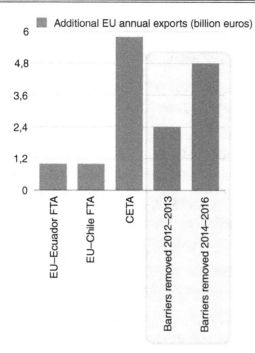

Figure 14.3 Additional EU annual exports, select FTAs and removed trade barriers.
Source: Authors' elaboration based on information available on DG TRADE website
(http://ec.europa.eu/trade/).

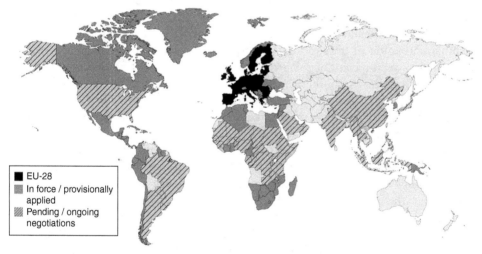

Figure 14.4 EU trade and investment relations.
Source: Authors' elaboration based on information available on DG TRADE website
(http://ec.europa.eu/trade/).

context, the EU is committed to including a chapter on TSD in trade agreements,
to harness globalisation to promote a value-based trade agenda. These TSD
chapters – part of the EU's attempt to link the EU's policies to the attainment of the
17 Sustainable Development Goals (SDGs) – are built around three pillars:
economic, environmental and social.

Trade with southern and eastern neighbourhoods

As part of the EU Stabilisation and Association Process (SAP) and the European Neighbourhood Policy (ENP) to promote peace, stability and economic prosperity in the EU's neighbouring regions, the EU has progressively concluded bilateral FTAs – referred to as "Stabilisation and Association Agreements" (SAA) – with each of its partners in the Western Balkans: Albania (2009), the former Yugoslav Republic of Macedonia (2004), Montenegro (2010), Serbia (2013), Bosnia and Herzegovina (2015) and Kosovo (2016). The SAAs are adapted to the specific situation of each partner country and, while establishing a free trade area between the EU and the partner concerned, they also identify common political and economic objectives and serve as the basis for the implementation of the EU accession process. The SAAs have established a free trade area over a transitional period which has now ended for all but Kosovo (2026). In the framework of the SAP, in 2000 the EU also granted autonomous trade preferences to all the Western Balkans. These preferences, which were last renewed in 2015 until end of 2020, allow nearly all exports to enter the EU without customs duties or limits on quantities. This preferential regime has contributed to an increase in the Western Balkans' exports to the EU (European Commission, 2018f).

In addition to this, the EU has also established three trade areas with Georgia, Moldova and Ukraine, known as the Deep and Comprehensive Free Trade Agreements (DCFTA) which are part of broader Association Agreements (AA). While the agreements with Georgia and Moldova have been in full effect since July 2016, the DCFTA with Ukraine entered provisional application in January 2016. These DCFTAs go further than traditional FTAs by offering partner countries a framework for modernising their trade relations and creating economic development by opening markets through the incremental removal of customs tariffs and quotas, and through an extensive harmonisation of laws, norms and regulations in various trade-related sectors, creating the conditions for aligning key sectors of their economies to EU standards.

With regards to its southern neighbourhood, the EU has implemented several Euro-Mediterranean Association Agreements with FTA provisions, which govern trade relations with countries of the Southern Mediterranean (with the exception of Libya and Syria): Algeria, Egypt, Israel, Jordan, Lebanon, Morocco, Palestine and Tunisia. In addition to this, the EU has been in negotiations with Morocco and Tunisia for a DCFTA, since March 2013 and October 2015, respectively. The Commission has also been mandated to start DCFTA negotiations with Jordan and Egypt, once these countries are ready.

The existing FTAs with Mediterranean countries generally provide reciprocal liberalisation of all trade in industrial goods and, to varying degrees, of agricultural and fisheries products. However, these FTAs typically include elements of asymmetry in favour of the Mediterranean partners, so as to stimulate the economic development of the region and closer integration with the EU internal market.

The EU–South Korea FTA

In addition to being the first EU FTA with an Asian country, the bilateral agreement with the Republic of Korea ushered in a new generation of EU FTAs, going further than any previous EU agreement in lifting trade barriers. After entering provisional application in 2011, it has formally been in force since December 2015. In addition to being the first EU agreement explicitly linking trade with labour and environmental regulations, the EU–Korea FTA contains several other groundbreaking features. Import duties covering 98.7% of traded value were eliminated within five years, and the agreement foresaw an (at the time) unprecedented liberalisation of trade in services across all modes of supply. The agreement also foresees provisions on intellectual property (including on geographical indications), competition, public procurement and regulatory transparency. The EU–South Korea FTA was also the first to include specific measures to tackle non-tariff barriers (NTBs) to trade in the automotive, electronics, pharmaceuticals and chemicals sector (European Commission, 2010c).

July 2017 marked the 6th anniversary of the implementation of the EU–South Korea FTA. Between 2010 and 2016, EU goods exports to South Korea benefited from an increase of almost 60%, turning the EU's €11.6 billion trade in goods deficit in 2010 into a €3.1 billion surplus by 2016. EU services exports also saw an increase of almost 50% between 2010 and 2015, whereas outward FDI stocks increased by nearly 60%. On the other hand, EU imports of services and inward FDI stocks both increased by approximately 33% (European Commission, 2018d).

The EU–Canada Comprehensive Economic Trade Agreement

The EU and Canada signed the Comprehensive Economic Trade Agreement (CETA) on 30 October 2016. It was ratified by Canada in February 2017 shortly after receiving approval from member states in the Council and from the European Parliament. This allowed for the provisional application of the agreement on 21 September 2017. As it is a so-called mixed agreement, thus not an exclusive competence of the European Commission, it will be fully applied only once national (and in some cases, regional) parliaments give it the green light.

The deal is already bringing considerable advantages to the EU, as European companies are enjoying the best treatment that Canada has ever offered to any trading partner. The agreement removes duties on 98% of products the EU trades with Canada, saving EU businesses approximately €590 million a year in customs duties. Based on a computable general equilibrium (CGE) simulation carried out for DG Trade by BKP Consulting, the gains deriving from tariff elimination, FDI liberalisation for goods and services bindings will result in an estimated annual increase in bilateral trade of at least 8%, roughly equivalent to €12 billion a year by 2030, split about evenly between the two parties. CETA will also contribute between €1.7 and 2.1 billion to the EU GDP on an annual basis (European Commission, 2017b).

One of the most innovative features of CETA is the inclusion of an ambitious chapter on public procurement that will open new business opportunities for EU companies looking to bid for public contracts in Canada at all levels. Based on the admittedly limited available data on public procurement in Canada, it is estimated that CETA will open up an extra €32 billion per year of the Canadian public procurement market, potentially bringing in €540 million a year in new contracts to European companies (European Commission, 2017b).

The EU–Singapore Free Trade Agreement

On 16 December 2012, the EU and Singapore announced the conclusion of negotiations on an EU–Singapore Free Trade Agreement (EUSFTA), the first of its kind with any Association of Southeast Asian Nations (ASEAN) country and the second, after South Korea, with any Asian county. Negotiations were launched in 2010 and completed four years later. In 2015, the Commission sought an opinion from the Court of Justice of the EU (CJEU) to determine which provisions of the EUSFTA fall within the EU's exclusive or shared competences, and which remain competences of member states. In 2017, the CJEU concluded that, in its 2014 form, the EUSFTA also covered shared competences (CJEU, 2017). This led to the Commission's decision in April 2018 to split the EUSFTA into two separate agreements: one strictly on trade liberalisation, which is of exclusive EU competence, and one on investment protection, for which the EU shares competence with its member states.

The EUSFTA essentially eliminates all tariffs on goods, addresses a number of NTBs (related to both technical regulations and sanitary and phytosanitary measures), opens up mutual access to procurement markets, contains enhanced provisions on Geographical Indications (GIs) and binds level of market access for services. Lower bound estimates (due to data limitations, NTB reductions and other non-quantifiable provisions were not included in the model) for the potential benefits of the EUSFTA resulting from a CGE analysis are of €550 million over a ten-year period, with EU exports to Singapore rising by €1.4 billion (European Commission, 2013).

The EU–Japan Economic Partnership Agreement

On 8 December 2017, the EU and Japan concluded negotiations to create the world's largest economic area through an Economic Partnership Agreement (EPA), four years after EU member states approved the European Commission's mandate to start negotiations. While agreement in principle was announced at the end of the EU–Japan Summit on 6 July 2017, the text of the agreement was presented by the Commission to the Council on 18 April 2018. It was subsequently signed on the occasion of the EU–Japan Summit in Tokyo on 17 July 2018 by Presidents Jean-Claude Juncker and Donald Tusk, and Japanese Prime Minister Shinzo Abe, marking the first step in the ratification process at the EU level. Following ratification by the European Parliament and the Japanese Diet, the agreement entered into force on 1 February 2019 after receiving the green light from the European Parliament and Member States. It is the most ambitious bilateral trade agreement ever negotiated by both parties, encompassing approximately 30% of global GDP and 40% of the value of global trade – and as much as 70% in high-tech sectors such as pharmaceuticals and aeronautics (Angelescu, 2018).

Since the start of negotiations in 2013, the Agreement has grown in scope and depth, hence the designation of EPA. Nonetheless, as with other recent EU trade agreements, the partnership with Japan extends far beyond just trade matters. The Agreement includes an ambitious TSD chapter, and is the first to explicitly make commitments under the United Nations Framework Convention on Climate Change (UNFCCC) and the Paris Agreement.

As part of the agreement, the EU has liberalised 99% of tariff lines and 100% of imports, with Japan liberalising 97% of tariff lines and 99% of imports (the somewhat lower liberalisation from the Japanese side is explained by the sensitivity of the agricultural sector, compensated by significant Japanese efforts to address non-tariff measures). In addition to its sheer breadth, the major achievement of the EU–Japan EPA is represented by the efforts made to address many non-tariff measures that had constituted a concern for EU companies, as the complexity of Japanese technical requirements and certification procedures often hinders the export of European products to Japan. This is especially relevant for the automotive sector, as the Agreement ensures that Japan and the EU conform to the same international standards on product safety and environmental protection, signifying that European car manufacturers will not require re-certification when exporting to the Japanese market.

Based on a CGE simulation carried out by DG Trade, the reduction of tariffs and NTBs covered by this agreement is expected to add €33 billion to EU GDP by the time the Agreement is expected to be fully implemented in 2035 (compared to a baseline situation with no agreement). This would represent a GDP increase of approximately 0.14%. For the EU, the Agreement would constitute a positive overall outcome as it would lead to considerable gains in sectors that are not always the principal beneficiaries of EU trade policy, for instance the agriculture, beverage, textile, apparel and leather sectors. These are also sectors with the highest participation of SMEs (European Commission, 2018a).

Beyond its economic value, the rapid finalisation of the EPA is clearly a strategic response to current geopolitical developments. Given the emergence of protectionist trends, the EU and Japan sought to signal their commitment as guarantors of global free trade. In this regard, it is no coincidence that the EPA negotiations intensified after the United States' withdrawal from the Trans-Pacific Partnership (TPP).

The EU–Mercosur FTA

After a long period of protracted negotiations, the European Union and Mercosur states – Argentina, Brazil, Paraguay and Uruguay – reached in June 2019 a political agreement for an ambitious, balanced and comprehensive trade agreement. The EU–Mercosur region-to-region agreement will remove the majority of tariffs on EU exports to Mercosur, making EU companies more competitive by saving them €4 billion worth of duties per year. EU–Mercosur trade is of considerable economic importance: over 850,000 jobs in Europe already depend on EU exports to Mercosur (European Commission, 2019a).

This FTA will help boost exports of EU products that have so far been facing high and sometimes prohibitive tariffs. Those include cars (tariff of 35%), car parts (14–18%), machinery (14–20%), chemicals (up to 18%), pharmaceuticals (up to 14%), clothing and footwear (35%) or knitted fabrics (26%). The EU agrifood sector will benefit from slashing existing Mercosur high tariffs on EU export products: chocolates and confectionery (20%), wines (27%), spirits (20–35%) and soft drinks (20–35%). The agreement will also provide duty-free access subject to quotas for EU dairy products (currently 28% tariff), notably for cheeses. Agrifood exporters of over 350 products protected in Europe by Geographical Indications (GIs) will also be now protected in the Mercosur market (European Commission, 2019b).

The agreement will open up new business opportunities for companies selling under government contracts, and for service suppliers in the information technology, telecommunications and transport sectors, among others. It will simplify border checks, cut red tape and limit the use of export taxes by Mercosur countries. Smaller companies on both sides will also benefit thanks to a new online platform providing easy access to all relevant information.

While delivering significant economic benefits, the agreement also promotes high standards. The EU and Mercosur commit to effectively implement the Paris Climate

Agreement. A dedicated sustainable development chapter will cover issues such as sustainable management and conservation of forests, respect for labour rights and promotion of responsible business conduct.

The EU–Mexico Global Agreement

In 1997, Mexico was the first Latin American country to sign an Economic Partnership, Political Coordination and Cooperation Agreement with the EU. The Agreement, which came into force in 2000, also covered political dialogue and cooperation in addition to trade relations (hence why it is also referred to as the EU–Mexico Global Agreement). The trade provisions in the Global Agreement were further developed into a comprehensive FTA covering trade in goods and trade in services, which came into force in 2000 and 2001, respectively.

Given the considerable age and outdated features of the Agreement, EU and Mexican leaders decided to explore the prospects for a comprehensive update to the Global Agreement on occasion of the EU–Community of Latin American and Caribbean States Summit of 2013. The parties reached an agreement in principle on the Agreement's trade provisions in April 2018, two years after the start of the negotiations. Once the remaining technical issues are ironed out and the updated agreement is approved by the European Parliament and Council of the European Union, it will replace the existing EU–Mexico Global Agreement.

The updated Global Agreement will remove virtually all tariffs on trade in goods, including in the agricultural sector. For 98% of goods there will be no duties from the moment the Agreement becomes effective. For the remaining items, customs duties will either be based on a quota or phased out over time. Simpler customs procedures will benefit EU industry, thanks to improvements related to technical requirements and fewer formalities relative to product certifications for compliance with Mexican standards. Under the revised agreement, Mexico has also committed to opening its public procurement market to EU companies more than it has to any of its other trading partners (European Commission, 2018b).

The Agreement underpins the EU's bolstered commitment to a value-based trade policy agenda thanks to a comprehensive trade and sustainable development chapter – now a mainstay in all recent EU trade agreements. One of the cutting-edge and innovative features of the Agreement is the unprecedented inclusion of provisions to fight corruption, with specific measures aimed at curbing bribery and money laundering (European Commission, 2018b).

Unilateral Measures

A key component of the Commission's "Trade for All" strategy involves using unilateral trade preferences as enablers to promote universal values of human rights, social justice and environmental protection. Currently the EU has three such tools in its unilateral toolkit under the so-called Generalised Scheme of Preferences (GSP) scheme, which grant developing countries preferential market access in varying degrees to support the expansion of their exports. In 2016, a total of €62.6 billion of imports entered the EU under these trade preferences, representing savings of €4.4 billion for businesses involved in imports from developing countries. However, the preferential imports represented just 4% of EU imports from the rest of the world (totalling €1717 billion for that year, according to IMF Direction of Trade Statistics data; IMF DOTS, n.d.). The relative importance of the unilateral schemes for EU trade in general therefore remains quite limited. However, for some of the beneficiary countries, the share of preferential exports to the EU is very significant, which helps explain the leverage the EU has been able to garner to promote human rights thanks to the conditionality of its trade preferences. By promoting economic development in beneficiary countries, these schemes also contribute to creating employment and lifting people out of poverty. (European Commission, 2018c).

Based on a micro-econometric analysis of a large dataset containing detailed tariff information at the six-digit product level, a study by the European Commission's Directorate-General for International Cooperation and Development was able to isolate the causal impact of unilateral preferences on growth of exports. The highly robust results indicate that the EU's GSP preferences have significantly increased the exports of developing countries to the EU. On average, the three unilateral measures have increased exports of the products covered by up to 5% (these aggregate results mask vast differences across different country groups, GSP schemes and individual product groups). The same study finds robust evidence that GSP preferences have increased the likelihood that beneficiary countries begin exporting a covered product to the EU, and that this effect is particularly large for least developed countries (LDCs) (GSP preferences increase the likelihood of exporting a covered product by 25% for LDCs) (European Commission, 2015d, pp. 17–18).

GSP General Arrangement

In 1971, the EU pioneered the introduction of a preferential initiative at the unilateral level which was in line with the United Nations Conference on Trade and Development (UNCTAD) proposal for a GSP (UNCTAD II, 1968) and the World Trade Organization (WTO) "Enabling Clause" which allows exception to the most-favoured nation (MFN) principle. It is the oldest EU trade regime contributing to the promotion of human rights, though it underwent substantial modifications through the years. The 1994 GSP Regulation was the first to allow for the possibility of suspending trade preferences in cases of forced labour. The revised GSP Regulation of 2001 made reference to the eight fundamental Conventions of the International Labour Organization (ILO). It was revised again in 2005 before the current regulation was adopted in 2012, entering into effect two years later (European Union, 2012b).

Under the current provisions, the GSP General Arrangement reduces import duties for approximately 66% of all EU tariff lines for low-income or lower-middle-income countries that do not benefit from other preferential trade access to the EU market. The GSP General Arrangement, of which 23 countries and territories are currently beneficiaries, remains an important tool to stimulate growth in developing countries by facilitating their exports to the EU.

GSP+

More recently, the EU introduced a GSP+ scheme which essentially removes all duties to the same 66% of tariff lines liberalised by the standard GSP (as opposed to just reducing the tariffs) for countries deemed "especially vulnerable in terms of their economies' diversification and import volumes" (European Commission, 2016e). In return, these developing countries are required to ratify and implement 27 core international conventions on human and labour rights, environmental protection and good governance. Currently, there are ten beneficiaries under the GSP+ scheme.

Everything but Arms

Finally, in 2001 the EU introduced a scheme for duty-free and quota-free access to the EU Single Market for all products except arms and armaments, aptly named "Everything but Arms" (EBA). A country may benefit from EBA status if it is listed as an LDC by the UN Committee for Development Policy. Unlike under the Standard GSP, countries do not lose EBA status by entering into an FTA with the EU. However, they can lose EBA status in some exceptional circumstances, such as in case of "serious and systematic violation of principles" laid down in fundamental human rights and labour rights conventions (European Union, 2012b). In 2016–2017, there were a total of 49 EBA beneficiaries.

In its assessment of the economic benefits in developing countries generated by EU trade regimes, the European Commission found that preferences have had an especially large impact on LDCs, which are also beneficiaries of the EBA scheme. Exports of a product granted duty-free access to the EU market through this measure benefitted from a 10% growth on average, approximately two times higher than the average across all countries, as well as twice the export increase for products under the GSP General Arrangement and GSP+ scheme (European Commission, 2015d, p. 17).

Trade and values: the "conflict minerals" example

On 1 January 2021 a new law will come into full force across the EU – the Conflict Minerals Regulation. It aims to help stem the trade in four minerals – tin, tantalum, tungsten and gold – which sometimes finance armed conflict or are mined using forced labour. As the world's largest trading bloc, the EU is a major market, so the regulation marks a big step in tackling the trade in conflict minerals. In politically unstable areas, the minerals trade can be used to finance armed groups, fuel forced labour and other human rights abuses, and support corruption and money laundering. These so-called conflict minerals can end up in everyday products such as mobile phones and cars or in jewellery. It is difficult for consumers to know if a product they have bought is funding violence, human rights abuses or other crimes overseas.

The new EU legislation will help break the link between conflict and the illegal exploitation of minerals and thus make sure that trade supports other efforts aimed at helping local communities and mine workers.

Multilateral and Plurilateral Initiatives

In recent years, multilateral and plurilateral achievements were mainly made at the WTO level. They include the agreements on modernising customs procedures and freeing up trade in the information technology (IT) sector as well as trade in services and environmentally friendly products.

The Trade Facilitation Agreement

Progress towards reducing costs of trade was made thanks to the recent Trade Facilitation Agreement (TFA), which came into force on 22 February 2017 following ratification by two thirds of WTO members. It is geared towards modernising customs procedures, containing provisions for expediting the movement, release and clearance of goods, building on relevant articles (V, VIII and X) of the General Agreement on Tariffs and Trade (GATT) 1994. The TFA establishes measures for effective cooperation between customs and other appropriate authorities on trade facilitation and customs compliance issues. The Agreement also includes special and differential treatment (SDT) provisions that allow developing countries and LDCs to determine when they will implement individual provisions of the Agreement and to identify provisions that they will only be able to implement upon the receipt of technical assistance and support for capacity-building.

WTO economists estimate that the TFA will reduce trade costs by 14.3% on average. Based on their results from a CGE model, full implementation of the TFA would increase global trade by between US$750 billion and US$1 trillion per year, with the greatest gains in LDCs. Results from their gravity model estimations are even more optimistic (WTO, 2015). While the TFA will benefit all signatories, the Agreement is an attempt to spread the benefits of trade to stakeholders that have traditionally been more excluded from trade, namely small businesses and less developed countries.

The Agreement on Government Procurement

In 1994, several WTO members, including the EU, signed the Agreement on Government Procurement (GPA), the only legally binding agreement in the WTO on the subject of government procurement. At present, the Agreement has 19 parties comprising 47 WTO members. Signatories undertake to provide national treatment and non-discrimination to goods, services and suppliers of other signatories, ensuring equal chance to compete for government contracts above specified threshold values. All participants are required to put in place domestic procedures through which aggrieved private bidders can challenge procurement decisions and obtain redress in the event such decisions are found to be inconsistent with the rules of the Agreement (European Commission, 2012). A revised Agreement with an updated set of tender rules and increased market access commitments entered into force in April 2014, two years after it was signed. The new GPA extends the scope of the initial Agreement to include numerous government entities and new services and areas of public procurement activities.

Excursus: public procurement

The issue of public procurement is featuring more prominently in trade negotiations both at the bilateral level in FTAs, and at the plurilateral level in the context of the WTO. This trend is driven primarily by an increased awareness of the economic importance of government procurement markets and of their latent potential from a trade perspective. International commitments have thus far been narrow in scope and coverage, despite the fact that the size of government procurement accounts for a double-digit share of GDP in most developed economies. In the EU alone, government procurement reached almost €2 trillion or 13.4% of EU GDP in 2016 (Kutlina-Dimitrova, 2018, p. 1).

Concurrently with the increasing importance of public procurement in bilateral trade agreements, protectionist measures in international public procurement have also been on the rise. During the recent financial crisis, many governments intervened to support their domestic economies through stimulus packages, some of which included domestic preferences for public procurement – the so-called home bias (Stone *et al.*, 2015; Evenett, 2009). What is more, a recent analysis of trends in discriminatory procurement practices based on the Global Trade Alerts (GTA) database (the GTA database tracks newly introduced *de jure* protectionist interventions around the world, including in the area of public procurement) shows that these protectionist measures have continued to rise steadily even after the financial crisis (Kutlina-Dimitrova, 2018).

Given the current international trade environment in which tariff duties are globally low and efforts to reduce NTBs in goods and services trade have not been particularly successful, the prospect of further liberalising public procurement is gaining relevance from a trade policy perspective. This is supported by recent empirical literature, for instance by Kutlina-Dimitrova (2017) and Dixon *et al.* (2017), who show that there are significant benefits to be enjoyed by extending the scope and coverage of the GPA or from getting rid of buy-American provision in the United States.

Expansion of the Information Technology Agreement

In June 2012, the EU and five other WTO members launched negotiations to expand the MFN-based plurilateral Information Technology Agreement (ITA) concluded at the WTO Ministerial Conference in 1996. At the time, the ITA was the most significant tariff liberalisation agreement negotiated in the WTO after its establishment, as it led to the elimination of import duties on a vast array of high-tech products, including computers, telecommunication equipment, semiconductors, software and scientific instruments, as well as most of these products' parts and accessories.

Since the first agreement came into force, ITA membership has increased significantly while the product coverage has remained unchanged, despite the exponential development of the IT sector in these years. In this context, the sub-group of ITA members agreed upon the expansion of product coverage during the 10th Ministerial Conference of the WTO in Nairobi in December 2015. The ITA expansion covers approximately 9–13% of current world trade, with around 90% of trade in these products occurring among ITA members.

Aside from the EU, the Agreement covers 23 other members and eliminates all tariffs for 201 different products. A CGE product-level analysis carried out by DG Trade's Chief Economist Unit found that total EU exports of goods and services increased by between €5.0 billion and €8.3 billion thanks to the Agreement. As EU imports were not seen as being significantly affected, the ITA expansion has had a positive effect on the overall EU trade balance (European Commission, 2016b).

In addition to these concluded trade deals, the EU is currently engaged in negotiating two other agreements at the WTO level: the Environmental Goods Agreement, and the Trade in Services Agreement.

The Environmental Goods Agreement

Since July 2014 the EU and 16 other members of the WTO have been negotiating an Environmental Goods Agreement (EGA) which seeks to remove trade barriers for products that play an important role in environmental protection and the mitigation of climate change. These include products that directly contribute to clean and renewable energy, resource efficiency, sustainable waste management and combatting air, water and noise pollution. The EU's ambition is for the agreement to eventually include services related to exports of environmental goods and NTBs, such as investment restrictions or local content requirements. Once a sufficient number of members is reached to have an agreement, the benefits of this plurilateral initiative will be applied to all WTO members on the basis of the MFN principle (European Commission, 2016c).

The EGA has the potential to become a pioneering agreement that demonstrates how trade policy can positively contribute to environmental sustainability, globally supporting green industries and helping meet the climate and energy targets agreed on in the Paris Climate Agreement. In addition to being congruous with the EU's push for the inclusion of TSD chapters in its trade agreements, the EGA would also serve to boost the European economy as the EU is the world leader in trade of environmental goods and boasts a very dynamic "green" industry.

The Trade in Services Agreement

The Trade in Services Agreement (TiSA) is a trade agreement currently being negotiated by 23 members of the WTO, including the EU. Taken together, the participating countries account for approximately 70% of world trade in services. All of TiSA's negotiated provisions are compatible with the WTO General Agreement on Trade in Services, including scope, definitions, national treatment, market access and exceptions.

From the standpoint of the EU, TiSA is intended to be a precursor to a multilateral agreement on services that would be integrated into the WTO once a sufficient number of signatories is reached. The Agreement is seen as an important tool to increase the EU's share of services trade by tackling existing barriers. In fact, services account for approximately 70% of EU GDP and employment, though the sector only represents around 25% of external trade (European Commission, 2016d). Whereas there is no formally set deadline for ending negotiations, they have been on hold since November 2016, and are expected to resume once there is a more favourable political context.

Future Challenges for EU Trade Policy

Improving Market Access Implementation and Enforcement

Given the recent expansion of the EU's network of preferential trade agreements, obtaining the greatest amount of benefits from FTAs is one of the European Commission's main priorities. The Commission's latest "Trade for All" strategy makes explicit reference to the need for effective implementation and enforcement of FTAs, making commitments to produce an annual report on FTA implementation (European Commission, 2015a).

A study by Nilsson (2016) examining data gathered by EU delegations from competent authorities in a selection of partner countries found that the preference utilisation rate (PUR) of EU exports in these markets was about 75% in 2013. The PUR to a partner country market is defined as the ratio of preferential exports of the good to the destination country over the value of preference eligible exports, i.e. products covered by the agreement not facing zero MFN duties (see Nilsson, 2016, p. 221). While this constitutes a significant increase from the 63% recorded for 2009, this means that approximately a quarter of EU exports in 2013 did not make full use of the preferential tariffs that exporters could have benefitted from. Despite these figures suggesting that EU exports use preferences moderately well, the aggregate data hide significant differences between member states. Moreover, partner countries generally display higher PURs for their exports to the EU than vice versa. These findings were largely confirmed by a study carried out by the National Board of Trade Sweden and UNCTAD (2018). Building on the data used by Nilsson covering 2009–2013, they find that on average partner country exporters use the EU's FTAs by 23 percentage points more at a relative level (see Figure 14.5).

In a recent Chief Economist Note by the European Commission's Directorate General for Trade, Nilsson and Preillon (2018) were able to quantify the cost of the foregone duty savings for EU exporters in 2016. They found that duty savings of EU exports under FTAs amounted to €11.5 billion in this year, though and additional €3.5 billion could have been saved, had the FTAs been fully utilised.

These findings suggest there is still ample room for improvement in terms of bolstering market access for European companies. Consequently, EU policymakers have doubled down on their commitment to facilitate the effective implementation of EU FTAs and to enable their utilisation by EU economic operators – with particular regard for SMEs. In this context, the Commission is currently in the process of analysing the underlying reasons why existing EU preferences are not fully utilised and

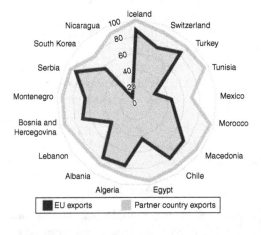

Free Trade Agreement	EU exports (%)	Partner country exports (%)	Difference (p.p.)
Iceland	88	98	−10
Switzerland	72	91	−19
Turkey	83	91	−8
Tunisia	26	95	−69
Mexico	44	69	−25
Morocco	51	96	−45
Macedonia	75	92	−17
Chile	80	91	−11
Egypt	44	94	−50
Algeria	77	87	−10
Albania	78	86	−8
Lebanon	39	83	−44
Bosnia and Hercegovina	69	93	−24
Montenegro	65	92	−27
Serbia	84	91	−7
South Korea	57	76	−19
Nicaragua	4	89	−85
TOTAL	67	90	−23

Figure 14.5 Preference utilisation rates in EU FTAs (2009–2013 average), in percent, chronological order by year in force.
Source: National Board of Trade Sweden & UNCTAD (2018), p. 14.

provide targeted assistance to economic operators. Some of these efforts include upcoming information campaigns specifically targeting SMEs, as well as the provision of a rules-of-origin tool and an online "one-stop shop" for market access information by integrating and enhancing existing tools.

Given the complex setting and diversity of stakeholders involved, improving market access implementation and enforcement will be a major challenge for the EU trade policy in the coming years. In addition to being labour intensive, such an endeavour will require close coordination between the European Commission, member states, business organisations and EU delegations abroad. However, the data suggests that enhancing market access and maximising the benefits of existing trade agreements holds great potential for the EU, thus warranting the allocation of additional resources.

Facilitating Trade for Small and Medium-Sized Enterprises

EU trade policy initiatives are already helping a large number of EU SMEs reach international markets outside the EU. However, there is potential for an even larger number of EU SMEs to trade internationally. This is because barriers specific to individual SMEs, the sector in which they operate and other barriers outside the SMEs' control can prevent them from reaching international markets. Even those firms already targeting markets outside the EU could enhance their performance in international markets. Most EU exporting firms continue to have a narrow export strategy. The data available from the Eurostat Trade by Enterprise Characteristics (TEC) database suggests that 60% of all exporting firms (including SMEs) depend on exports to only one or two extra-EU markets (Eurostat, 2014).

Despite exporting SMEs representing a large share of total exporting enterprises outside the EU, they represent a small share of the millions of existing SMEs in the EU (Gagliardi *et al.*, 2013). So indeed, the relatively few SMEs successfully exporting outside the EU could be considered as the "happy few". This highlights another important fact: given that a small share of EU SMEs account for one third of "direct" exports outside the EU in value, there could be a large untapped potential for the European economy if more SMEs were to target international markets outside the EU. A survey conducted on behalf of the European Commission has already pointed out a positive correlation between SMEs being internationally active (importing and/or exporting) and those achieving a higher turnover and employment growth (European Commission, 2010b). The role of GVCs and the ability of SMEs to leverage their GVC participation to become successful exporters is also important. One empirical study, based on a sample of Italian exporting firms, found a positive correlation between the participation of SMEs in GVCs and the propensity to become an exporter (Giovannetti *et al.*, 2014).

Revamping Key Performance Indicators

Building a strong set of key performance indicators would also allow for the creation of synergies between multiple EU trade policy objectives. For instance, many SMEs, notably in the processed food and beverage sector, are exporters of products protected by the EU geographical indications provisions in FTAs. Many recent EU FTAs clearly identify a well-defined list of protected GIs, out of thousands of existing EU GIs. For instance, in CETA, Canada has agreed to protect 143 GIs – distinctive food and drink products from specific towns or regions in the EU. They include products like Roquefort cheese, balsamic vinegar from Modena and Dutch Gouda cheese. Many of these products are among the EU's top EU food and drink exports. Producers are often small or medium-sized businesses in rural communities. Canada will protect these traditional European products from imitations in much the same way as the EU does. Having in place the necessary key performance indicators to measure the evolution of exports under these 143 GIs covered in CETA would allow a better monitoring and implementation strategy to maximise the benefits of EU trade policy in terms of both SME exports and GI exports. Similarly, such key performance indicators in other top priority areas for the EU trade negotiations (such as services and public procurement) would also allow policymakers at EU and member state level to better assist interested EU exporters to make the most out of the trade agreements. The recently reinforced Market Access Strategy and the planned improvements in the business-friendly tools made available for EU companies to successfully navigate the various FTA provisions will further expand the benefits from EU trade policy for the EU economy. For instance, the DG Trade Chief Economist team has estimated that the barriers removed in 2012 and 2013 by the European Commission as part of its Market Access Strategy had resulted in 2.4 billion euros of additional trade flows in 2014. This is equivalent to the annual EU trade increases generated by small FTAs such as the EU–Colombia FTA (European Commission, 2016a).

Facilitating Mode 5 Services Exports

The importance of facilitating the indirect exports of services (mode 5 services) along the strong value chains of EU manufacturing exporters is also a future challenge for trade policy, in a world where new digital technological advances redefine national comparative advantages and global competitiveness (Internet of Things, 3-D printing, artificial intelligence, blockchain and other trade-related high-tech solutions). The fact that "services in boxes" (mode 5 services) account for an important share of total services trade implies that virtually all protectionist measures discriminating against goods trade also indirectly affect a considerable part of the total value of services trade. For instance Nordås and Kim (2013) highlight the importance of the quality of the services inputs in promoting export competitiveness of manufacturing sectors while Miroudot and Cadestin (2017) provide extensive evidence of how manufacturing firms increase bundle services with the goods they produce. Already in 2011, the jobs associated to mode 5 services exports represented as much as 40% of the total EU employment supported by exports (up from 31% in 1995). In absolute terms, 8 million mode 5 jobs (representing 26% of the total exports-supported employment in the EU) were supported by EU exports. Moreover the data also show that this "servicification" of the employment base of manufacturing exports is increasingly spanning borders as EU exporters rely on global supply chains also for services inputs. In 2011 around 38% of foreign jobs supported by EU manufacturing and primary goods exports were found in services (Rueda-Cantuche, Cernat & Sousa, 2018).

If the share of mode 5 services in the total value of a manufactured product is somewhere between 30 and 40%, this means that any new discriminatory measures (increase in tariffs, subsidies, NTBs etc.) reducing the trade flows in that particular product will also have a negative impact on intermediate services providers along the supply chain for the manufacturers involved in producing the final product being exported. Moreover, the services provider may be in fact in a different country than the one exporting the manufactured product subject to protectionist measures, thus rendering the process of assessing the implications of protectionist measures imposed by a particular country rather complex.

Another element specific to trade in services is the interlinkages between the various modes of supply. Even if mode 3 services (commercial presence) generated by the activity of foreign affiliates of services companies abroad are the most important mode of supply, very often the activities of these foreign affiliates require exports and imports of services via mode 1 and 4 that are complementary to their main activity in the host country. Therefore, discriminatory measures that apply directly on mode 1 or 4 may have a significant harmful effect on mode 3 services trade. For this reason, protectionist tendencies that seem to affect a growing number of products and services may in fact lead to a compounded negative effect on world trade.

Enhancing Trade Policy Communication

Finally, although the EU trade policy has a clear surplus in terms of the net economic benefits for the EU economy and society as a whole, it has a communication deficit. Trade economists have not been able to communicate effectively the benefits from trade to politicians and voters (Blinder, 2018). In the current environment dominated in recent months by a resurgence in populist and protectionist policies, a successful trade policy communication needs to address the wider set of stakeholders: businesses, trade unions, non-governmental organisations (NGOs), local politicians and ultimately EU voters. The positive benefits of global trade are abstract, part of the "invisible hand" logic, whereas the opponents of trade are very vocal and use simple, visual and often distorted messages on social media to appeal to people's emotions. So, better communication on all main channels, and increasingly so under new social media, should be part of EU trade policymaking, to ensure the legitimacy of policy objectives in the eyes of EU citizens. A successful communication strategy about the benefits of trade for the EU society has to allow its messages to resonate personally with people. Trade benefits are often like a "misty imperceptible rain" which voters or consumers will not notice directly, unless prompted with factual, relevant information. A successful social media communication on trade therefore needs to be based on new Trade Policy 2.0 logic: for social media messages to be impactful, the main traditional narrative of EU trade policy based on macroeconomic indicators needs to be complemented by a wider set of detailed firm-level factual, local and more visible metrics. In this way, each and every individual (be it a consumer, a worker, an entrepreneur, an NGO activist or a local politician) can understand the economic case for trade in a way that resonates with them. It is about more direct messages that can speak to politicians who care about local impact, to individual consumers or to workers affected by (or afraid of) globalisation.

Using Trade to Benefit all Europeans

Last but not least, EU trade policy objectives need to be well embedded in the overall set of EU policies aimed at ensuring that the future looks bright to all Europeans. In this respect, the concerns of many that globalisation and further trade integration will widen social inequality in Europe need to be properly addressed. The recent decision by the European Commission to strengthen the functioning of the European Globalisation Adjustment Fund (EGF) goes in the right direction. Launching the EGF, Commission President Barroso stated: "The fund will express the Union's solidarity towards those severely and personally affected by trade-adjustment redundancies. In this way, it will provide a stimulus to respond appropriately and effectively to the adverse impact of market opening. The fund will help workers made redundant back to work because we want a competitive, but also a fair EU." (European Commission, 2006). A decade later, Commissioner Thyssen remained equally resolute: "The Globalisation Fund is Europe's main instrument to show solidarity with those harmed by the crisis and it has proven its worth over the years" (European Commission, 2016a). The issues that led to the creation of the EGF have not faded away. Quite the contrary. The current political context brought these issues even more acutely to the fore. Anti-trade opinions and the claims of trade-related negative effects on labour are not just regularly in the pages of newspapers, but are also one of the main issues (alongside migration and income disparity) that influenced the current political situation.

A general reflection on the social impacts of globalisation that has been recently expressed by the European Commission, signed by Vice-President Dombrovskis and Commissioner Thyssen, mainly focuses on "how to adapt our social models to current and future challenges and galvanise Europe's social spirit" (European Commission, 2017a).

Despite having a relatively small budget, little political visibility and somewhat complex procedures, the EGF has delivered tangible results for tens of thousands of workers across Europe. The reinforced EGF will continue to play its positive role as part of the wider "policy mix" that will allow Europe to remain open to trade and benefit from the opportunities offered by the global economy.

References

Angelescu, A. (2018) EU-Japan Partnership Agreements Herald New Era of Closer Cooperation. European Council on Foreign Relations (ECFR). Retrieved from: https://www.ecfr.eu/article/commentary_eu_japan_partnership_agreements_herald_new_era_of_closer_coopera# (accessed 12 July 2019).

Berlingieri, G., Brienlich, H. & Dhingra, S. (2018) The Impact of Trade Agreements on Consumer Welfare – Evidence from the EU Common External Trade Policy. *Journal of the European Economic Association*, 16(6), 1881–1928.

Blinder, A.S. (2018) Why Economists Like Free Trade but Politicians Don't. *Boston Globe* (20 April). Retrieved from: https://www.bostonglobe.com/opinion/2018/04/19/why-economists-like-free-trade-but-politicians-don/9XWtOBGdtVuh1KI2WA2AqM/story.html (accessed 12 July 2019).

Cernat, L., Gerard, D., Guinea, O. & Isella, L. (2018) Consumer Benefits from EU Trade Liberalisation: How Much Did We Save Since the Uruguay Round? European Commission, DG Trade, *Chief Economist Note*, 1. Retrieved from: http://trade.ec.europa.eu/doclib/docs/2018/february/tradoc_156619.pdf (accessed 12 July 2019).

Court of Justice of the European Union (2017) The Free Trade Agreement with Singapore Cannot, in Its Current Form, Be Concluded by the EU Alone. Press Release No. 52/17. Retrieved from https://curia.europa.eu/jcms/upload/docs/application/pdf/2017-05/cp170052en.pdf (accessed 12 July 2019).

Dixon, P.B., Rimmer. M.T. & Waschik, P.G. (2017) Macro, Industry and Regional Effects of Buy America(n) Program: USAGE Simulations. *Center of Policy Studies (CoPS) Working Paper* No. G-271. Retrieved from: https://www.copsmodels.com/ftp/workpapr/g-271.pdf (accessed 12 July 2019).

European Commission (2006) Commission Proposes up to €500 Million per Year for a New European Globalisation Adjustment Fund to Support Workers. Press release, Brussels, 1 March. Retrieved from: http://europa.eu/rapid/press-release_IP-06-245_en.htm?locale=en (accessed 21 July 2019).

European Commission (2010a) Trade Policy as a Core Component of the EU's 2020 Strategy. Retrieved from: http://aei.pitt.edu/38021/1/COM_(2010)_612.pdf (accessed 20 July 2019).

European Commission (2010b) Internationalisation of European SMEs – Final Report. Retrieved from: https://ec.europa.eu/docsroom/documents/10008/attachments/1/translations/en/renditions/pdf (accessed 12 July 2019).

European Commission (2010c) EU-South Korea Free Trade Agreement: A Quick Reading Guide. Retrieved from: https://eeas.europa.eu/sites/eeas/files/tradoc_145203.pdf (accessed 12 July 2019).

European Commission (2012) WTO Agreement on Government Procurement ("GPA"). Originally retrieved from: http://trade.ec.europa.eu/doclib/docs/2012/march/tradoc_149240.pdf.

European Commission (2013) *The Economic Impact of the EU-Singapore Free Trade Agreement*. Luxembourg: European Commission Publications Office. Retrieved from: https://publications.europa.eu/en/publication-detail/-/publication/318c4136-6404-4a72-bd2b-6eb6a3dc413b/language-en (accessed 12 July 2019).

European Commission (2015a) *Trade for All: Towards a More Responsible Trade and Investment Policy*. Luxembourg: European Commission Publications Office. Retrieved from http://trade.ec.europa.eu/doclib/docs/2015/october/tradoc_153846.pdf (accessed 12 July 2019).

European Commission (2015b) How Trade Policy and Regional Trade Agreements Support and Strengthen Economic Performance. Retrieved from http://trade.ec.europa.eu/doclib/docs/2015/march/tradoc_153270.pdf (accessed 12 July 2019).

European Commission (2015c). Trade and Jobs: Germany. Retrieved from: http://ec.europa.eu/trade/policy/in-focus/trade-and-jobs/germany_en.htm (accessed 12 July 2019).

European Commission (2015d) *Assessment of the Economic Benefits Generated by the EU Trade Regimes towards Developing Countries*. Luxembourg: European Commission Publications Office. Retrieved from: http://trade.ec.europa.eu/doclib/docs/2015/july/tradoc_153595.pdf (accessed 12 July 2019).

European Commission (2016a) Report from the Commission to the European Parliament and the Council on Trade and Investment Barriers. Retrieved from: http://trade.ec.europa.eu/doclib/docs/2017/june/tradoc_155642.pdf (accessed 12 July 2019).

European Commission (2016b) *The Expansion of the Information Technology Agreement: An Economic Assessment*. Luxembourg: European Commission Publications Office. Retrieved from: http://trade.ec.europa.eu/doclib/docs/2016/april/tradoc_154430.pdf (accessed 12 July 2019).

European Commission (2016c) The Environmental Goods Agreement (EGA): Liberalising Trade in Environmental Goods and Services. Retrieved from: http://trade.ec.europa.eu/doclib/press/index.cfm?id=1116 (accessed 12 July 2019).

European Commission (2016d) Trade in Services Agreement (TiSA) Factsheet. Retrieved from: http://trade.ec.europa.eu/doclib/docs/2016/september/tradoc_154971.doc.pdf (accessed 12 July 2019).

European Commission (2016e) Report on the Generalised Scheme of Preferences Covering the Period 2014–2015. Retrieved from: http://trade.ec.europa.eu/doclib/docs/2016/january/tradoc_154180.pdf (accessed 21 July 2019).

European Commission (2017a) *Report on the Implementation of the Trade Policy Strategy Trade for All: Delivering a Progressive Trade Policy to Harness Globalisation.* Luxembourg: European Commission Publications Office. Retrieved from: https://publications.europa.eu/en/publication-detail/-/publication/4f819c97-e3a6-11e7-9749-01aa75ed71a1/language-en (accessed 12 July 2019).

European Commission (2017b) *The Economic Impact of the Comprehensive Economic and Trade Agreement (CETA): An Analysis Prepared by the European Commission's Directorate-General for Trade.* Luxembourg: European Commission Publications Office. Retrieved from: http://trade.ec.europa.eu/doclib/docs/2017/september/tradoc_156043.pdf (accessed 12 July 2019).

European Commission (2018a) *The Economic Impact of the EU-Japan Economic Partnership Agreement. An Analysis Prepared by the European Commission's Directorate-General for Trade.* Luxembourg: European Commission Publications Office. Retrieved from: http://trade.ec.europa.eu/doclib/docs/2018/july/tradoc_157116.pdf (accessed 12 July 2019).

European Commission (2018b) New EU-Mexico Agreement: The Agreement in Principle. Retrieved from: http://trade.ec.europa.eu/doclib/docs/2018/april/tradoc_156791.pdf (accessed 12 July 2019).

European Commission (2018c) Report on the Generalised Scheme of Preferences Covering the Period 2016–2017. Report from the European Commission to the European Parliament and the Council, COM(2018) 36 final. Retrieved from: http://trade.ec.europa.eu/doclib/docs/2018/january/tradoc_156536.pdf (accessed 12 July 2019).

European Commission (2018d) Trade Policy: South Korea. Retrieved from: http://ec.europa.eu/trade/policy/countries-and-regions/countries/south-korea/ (accessed 12 July 2019).

European Commission (2018e) Report from the Commission to the Parliament and the Council on Trade and Investment Barriers. Retrieved from: http://trade.ec.europa.eu/doclib/docs/2018/june/tradoc_156978.pdf (accessed 12 July 2019).

European Commission (2018f) Trade Policy: Western Balkans. Retrieved from: http://ec.europa.eu/trade/policy/countries-and-regions/regions/western-balkans/ (accessed 12 July 2019).

European Commission (2018g) DG Trade Statistical Guide: June 2018. Retrieved from: http://trade.ec.europa.eu/doclib/docs/2013/may/tradoc_151348.pdf (accessed 21 July 2019).

European Commission (2019a) EU–Mercosur Trade in Your Town: Towns and Cities Across the EU Export to Mercosur. Retrieved from: http://ec.europa.eu/trade/policy/in-focus/eu-mercosur-association-agreement/eu-mercosur-in-your-town/ (accessed 22 July 2019).

European Commission (2019b) EU and Mercosur Reach Agreement on Trade. Press release, Brussels, 28 June. Retrieved from: http://trade.ec.europa.eu/doclib/press/index.cfm?id=2039 (accessed 22 July 2019).

European Parliamentary Research Service (2017) Benefits of EU International Trade Agreements. EPRS, European Value Added in Action Briefing. Retrieved from: http://www.europarl.europa.eu/RegData/etudes/BRIE/2017/603269/EPRS_BRI(2017)603269_EN.pdf (accessed 12 July 2019).

European Union (2012a) Consolidated Version of the Treaty on the Functioning of the European Union. Retrieved from: https://eur-lex.europa.eu/legal-content/EN/TXT/PDF/?uri=CELEX:12012E/TXT (accessed 12 July 2019).

European Union (2012b) Regulation (EU) No 978/2012 of the European Parliament and of the Council of 25 October 2012 Applying a Scheme of Generalised Tariff Preferences and Repealing Council Regulation (EC) No 732/2008. *Official Journal of the European Union* L303/1. Retrieved from: https://eur-lex.europa.eu/legal-content/en/TXT/?uri=CELEX:32012R0978 (accessed 12 July 2019).

Eurostat (2014) Trade by Enterprise Characteristics Database (TEC). Retrieved from: https://www.oecd.org/sdd/its/trade-by-enterprise-characteristics.htm (accessed 12 July 2019).

Eurostat (2018a) Foreign Control of Enterprises by Economic Activity and a Selection of Controlling Countries (from 2008 onwards) [fats_g1a_08]. Retrieved from: http://appsso.eurostat.ec.europa.eu/nui/show.do?dataset=fats_g1a_08&lang=en (accessed 12 July 2019).

Eurostat (2018b) Employment in Foreign Controlled Enterprises [egi_em1]. Retrieved from: http://appsso.eurostat.ec.europa.eu/nui/show.do?dataset=egi_em1&lang=en (accessed 12 July 2019).

Evenett, S. (2009) The Emerging Contours of Crisis-Era Protectionism. In: Evenett, S. (ed.) *Broken Promises: A G-20 Summit Report*. London: Centre for Economic Policy Research, pp.15–24. Retrieved from: https://www.globaltradealert.org/reports/download/38 (accessed 12 July 2019).

Fajgelbaum, P. & Khandelwal, A. (2016) Measuring the Unequal Gains from Trade. *The Quarterly Journal of Economics*, 131(3), 1113–1180.

Feyrer, J. (2009) Distance, Trade, and Income – The 1967 to 1975 Closing of the Suez Canal as a Natural Experiment. *NBER Working Paper* No. 15557. Retrieved from: https://www.nber.org/papers/w15557.pdf (accessed 12 July 2019).

Gagliardi, D., Muller, P., Glossop, E. *et al.* (2013) A Recovery on the Horizon? Annual Report on European SMEs 2012/2013. Final Report. Retrieved from: https://www.escholar.manchester.ac.uk/api/datastream?publicationPid=uk-ac-man-scw:212438&datastreamId=FULL-TEXT.PDF (accessed 12 July 2019).

Giovannetti, G., Marvasi, E. & Sanfilippo, M. (2014) Supply Chains and the Internationalization of SMEs: Evidence from Italy. *Robert Schuman Centre for Advanced Studies Research Paper* No. RSCAS 2014/62. http://dx.doi.org/10.2139/ssrn.2441121.

International Monetary Fund Direction of Trade Statistics (n.d.) Retrieved from: https://data.imf.org/?sk=9D6028D4-F14A-464C-A2F2-59B2CD424B85 (accessed 20 July 2019).

Kutlina-Dimitrova, Z. (2017) Can We Put a Price on Extending the GPA? First Quantitative Assessment. European Commission, DG Trade, *Chief Economist Note*, 1. Retrieved from: http://trade.ec.europa.eu/doclib/docs/2017/march/tradoc_155456.pdf (accessed 12 July 2019).

Kutlina-Dimitrova, Z. (2018) Government Procurement: Data, Trends and Protectionist Tendencies. European Commission, DG Trade, *Chief Economist Note*, 3. Retrieved from: http://trade.ec.europa.eu/doclib/docs/2018/september/tradoc_157319.pdf (accessed 12 July 2019).

Lopez Gonzalez, J., Kowalski, P. & Achard, P. (2015) Trade, Global Value Chains and Wage-Income Inequality. *OECD Trade Policy Papers* No. 182. Retrieved from: https://www.oecd-ilibrary.org/docserver/5js009mzrqd4-en.pdf?expires=1562930578&id=id&accname=guest&checksum=4E61114A47DBFBB219A9466E022571C6 (accessed 12 July 2019).

Milanovic, B. (2012) Global Income Inequality by the Numbers: In History and Now – An Overview. *World Bank Policy Research Working Paper* WPS6259. Retrieved from: http://documents.worldbank.org/curated/en/959251468176687085/pdf/wps6259.pdf (accessed 12 July 2019).

Miroudot, S. & Cadestin, C. (2017). Services in Global Value Chains: From Inputs to Value-Creating Activities. *OECD Trade Policy Papers* No. 197. Retrieved from: https://www.oecd-ilibrary.org/deliver/465f0d8b-en.pdf?itemId=%2Fcontent%2Fpaper%2F465f0d8b-en&mimeType=pdf (accessed 12 July 2019).

National Board of Trade Sweden & UNCTAD (2018) *The Use of the EU's Free Trade Agreements: Exporter and Importer Utilization of Preferential Tariffs*. Retrieved from: https://unctad.org/en/PublicationsLibrary/EU_2017d1_en.pdf (accessed 12 July 2019).

Nilsson, L. (2016) EU Exports and Uptake of Preferences: A First Analysis, *Journal of World Trade*, 50(2), 219–252.

Nilsson, L. & Preillon, N. (2018) EU Exports, Preferences Utilisation and Duty Savings by Member State, Sector and Partner Country. European Commission, DG Trade, *Chief Economist Note*, 2. Retrieved from: http://trade.ec.europa.eu/doclib/docs/2018/june/tradoc_156931.pdf (accessed 12 July 2019).

Nordås, H. & Kim, Y. (2013) The Role of Services for Competitiveness in Manufacturing. *OECD Trade Policy Papers* No. 148. Retrieved from: https://www.oecd-ilibrary.org/the-role-of-services-for-competitiveness-in-manufacturing_5k484xb7cx6b.pdf?itemId=%2Fcontent%2Fpaper%2F5k484xb7cx6b-en&mimeType=pdf (accessed 12 July 2019).

OECD (2014) All on Board, Making Inclusive Growth Happen. Retrieved from: https://www.oecd.org/inclusive-growth/All-on-Board-Making-Inclusive-Growth-Happen.pdf (accessed 12 July 2019).

OECD (2015) *In It Together: Why Less Inequality Benefits All. Overview of Inequality Trends, Key Findings and Policy Directions.* Paris: OECD. Retrieved from: https://www.oecd.org/els/soc/OECD2015-In-It-Together-Chapter1-Overview-Inequality.pdf (accessed 12 July 2019).

Rueda-Cantuche, J. & Sousa, N. (2016) EU Exports to the World: Overview of Effects on Employment and Income. European Commission, DG Trade, *Chief Economist Note*, 1. Retrieved from: http://trade.ec.europa.eu/doclib/docs/2016/february/tradoc_154244.pdf (accessed 12 July 2019).

Rueda-Cantuche, J. & Sousa, N. (2017) Are EU Exports Gender Blind? Some Key Features of Women Participation in Exporting Activities in the EU. European Commission, DG Trade, *Chief Economist Note*, 3. Retrieved from: http://trade.ec.europa.eu/doclib/docs/2017/june/tradoc_155632.pdf (accessed 12 July 2019).

Rueda-Cantuche, J., Cernat, L. & N. Sousa (2018) Trade and Jobs in Europe: The Role of Mode 5 Services Exports. *International Labour Review*, 158(1), 115-136.

Stone, S., Messent, J. & Flaig, D. (2015) Emerging Policy Issues: Localization Barriers to Trade. *OECD Trade Policy Papers* No. 180. Retrieved from: https://www.oecd-ilibrary.org/emerging-policy-issues_5js1m6v5qd5j.pdf?itemId=%2Fcontent%2Fpaper%2F5js1m6v5qd5j-en&mimeType=pdf (accessed 12 July 2019).

Tybout, J.R. (2001) Plant- and Firm-level Evidence on New Trade Theories. *NBER Working Paper* No. 8418. Retrieved from: http://www.nber.org/papers/w8418.pdf (accessed 12 July 2019).

UNCTAD II (1968) Proceedings of the United Nations Conference on Trade and Development, Second Session, Volume I. Retrieved from: https://unctad.org/en/Docs/td97vol1_en.pdf (accessed 21 July 2019).

World Trade Organization (2015) *World Trade Report 2015 – Speeding up Trade: Benefits and Challenges of Implementing the WTO Trade Facilitation Agreement.* Geneva: World Trade Organization. Retrieved from: https://www.wto.org/english/res_e/booksp_e/world_trade_report15_e.pdf (accessed 12 July 2019).

Chapter 15

Trade, Global Value Chains and Inclusive Growth in Asia and the Pacific

Yasuyuki Sawada, Cyn-Young Park, [1]Fahad H. Khan, and Cindy Jane Justo

Introduction

Even as traditional markets have faltered, developing Asia, the world's fastest growing region, has emerged as a growth pole in the world economy (Lee and Hong, 2012; Park, 2011). In the region, policies promoting export-oriented industrialisation while mobilising high savings have bolstered growth, outperforming the industrialised economies and other parts of the developing world.

In developing Asia and the Pacific region, real gross domestic product (GDP) grew 6.7% annually on average during 1960–2016, nearly double the 3.5% world average. The region's real GDP in constant 2010 dollars climbed from about US$449 billion in 1960 to US$17.1 trillion in 2016, an increase of more than 38 times, compared with about seven times for the world economy during the same period. By 2016, developing Asia accounted for 22.1% of world GDP, and 30.0% with Japan included. Most economies in the region have moved up the development ladder to reach middle income (Asian Development Bank [ADB], 2017a; Table 15.1), with dramatic improvements over a wide range of economic and social indicators. Average real income per capita rose from US$949 in 1960 to US$6035 in 2016 (Figure 15.1) and people living below the US$1.90-a-day poverty line fell from 68.1% in 1981 to 8.8% in 2013 (Figure 15.2). Average literacy increased from 91.0% in 2000 to 93.1% in 2010, people with access to clean drinking water reached 93.3% from 81.2% in 2000 and urbanisation increased from 20.8% in 1960 to 40.7% in 2016.[2]

In this dramatic economic transformation, open trade and investment have played a critical role in the past half century, leading to the acceleration of output growth and, in turn, boosting incomes, especially for lower-income groups and people in remote and otherwise marginal areas. Multilateralism underpinned Asia's international trade policy, a recognition of the benefits of open trade and investment regimes.

The Handbook of Global Trade Policy, First Edition. Edited by Andreas Klasen.
© 2020 John Wiley & Sons Ltd. Published 2020 by John Wiley & Sons Ltd.

Table 15.1 Income distribution of economies in Asia and the Pacific

Income classification	1987	1997	2007	2017
High income	Australia Brunei Darussalam Hong Kong, China Japan New Zealand Singapore Taipei, China	Australia Brunei Darussalam Hong Kong, China Japan Republic of Korea New Zealand Singapore Taipei, China	Australia Brunei Darussalam Hong Kong, China Japan Republic of Korea New Zealand Singapore Taipei, China	Australia Brunei Darussalam Hong Kong, China Japan Republic of Korea New Zealand Palau Singapore Taipei, China
Upper-middle income	Republic of Korea	Malaysia Palau	Fiji Kazakhstan Malaysia Palau	Armenia Azerbaijan People's Republic of China Fiji Kazakhstan Malaysia Maldives Marshall Islands Nauru Samoa Thailand Tonga Turkmenistan Tuvalu
Lower-middle income	Fiji Kiribati Malaysia Papua New Guinea Philippines Samoa Thailand	People's Republic of China Fiji Georgia Indonesia Kazakhstan Kiribati Maldives	Armenia Azerbaijan Bhutan People's Republic of China Georgia India Indonesia	Bangladesh Bhutan Cambodia Georgia India Indonesia Kiribati

	Tonga Vanuatu	Marshall Islands Federated States of Micronesia Papua New Guinea Philippines Samoa Solomon Islands Sri Lanka Thailand Tonga Uzbekistan Vanuatu	Kiribati Maldives Marshall Islands Federated States of Micronesia Mongolia Philippines Samoa Sri Lanka Thailand Timor-Leste Tonga Turkmenistan Vanuatu	Kyrgyz Republic Lao PDR Federated States of Micronesia Mongolia Myanmar Pakistan Papua New Guinea Philippines Solomon Islands Sri Lanka Timor-Leste Uzbekistan Vanuatu Vietnam
Low income	Afghanistan Bangladesh Bhutan Cambodia People's Republic of China India Indonesia Lao PDR Maldives Myanmar Nepal Pakistan Solomon Islands Sri Lanka Vietnam	Afghanistan Armenia Azerbaijan Bangladesh Bhutan Cambodia India Kyrgyz Republic Lao PDR Mongolia Myanmar Nepal Pakistan Tajikistan Turkmenistan Vietnam	Afghanistan Bangladesh Cambodia Kyrgyz Republic Lao PDR Myanmar Nepal Pakistan Papua New Guinea Solomon Islands Tajikistan Uzbekistan Vietnam	Afghanistan Nepal Tajikistan

Source: World Bank (n.d.a).
Note: Income classifications are based on the World Bank's analytical classifications and estimates of GNI per capita calculated using the Atlas method. Lao PDR = Lao People's Democratic Republic.

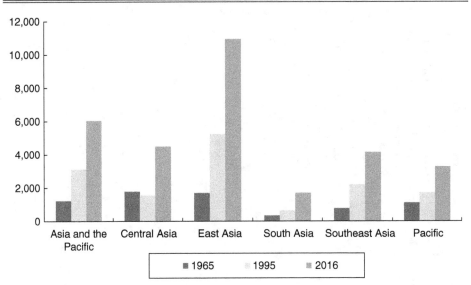

Figure 15.1   Real GDP per capita (constant 2010 US$).
Source: ADB calculations using data from World Bank (n.d.b).

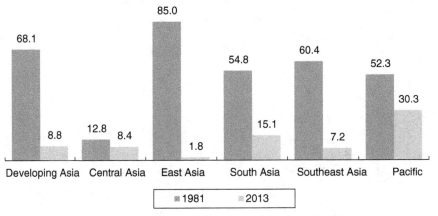

Figure 15.2   Population below US$1.90-a-day poverty line, by subregion (2011 PPP).
Source: World Bank (n.d.c).
Note: PPP means purchasing power parity.

This was guided by the World Trade Organization (WTO) Framework and General Agreement on Tariffs and Trade (GATT), and open regionalism supported by unilateral liberalisation for several decades. Outward-oriented development strategies in the Asian countries characterised international trade and investment policies (Harrison and Rodriguez-Clare, 2010; James *et al.*, 1989; World Bank, 1993).

In the years since the Global Financial Crisis (GFC), however, trade growth has fallen behind GDP growth, after outpacing it for many decades. While this was in part due to the uncertain global economic environment, structural factors were also at play as the cross-border production sharing model matured (Constantinescu *et al.*, 2015), with many economies, most notably the People's Republic of China (PRC), transitioning away from export-led growth towards domestic consumption and from manufacturing sector-led growth to service sector-based growth. The recent rise of protectionist talk and measures further threaten open trade and multilateral solutions.

Under this "new normal", Asia must find new ways to both sustain growth and make it more inclusive. The 2030 Agenda for Sustainable Development Goals (SDGs) emphasises inclusivity through a pro-growth, pro-poor and non-discriminatory approach, anchored on the principle of leaving no one behind. Apart from the obvious link between trade and economic growth, trade helps enhance productivity growth and broaden people's access to more economic opportunities. Trade policy can be steered to cater to the needs of the most vulnerable groups in society by aiming to tackle poverty. Regional trade and economic integration can be further strengthened, and the full potential of services trade remains untapped.

Given the important role of the regional trade–foreign direct investment (FDI) nexus in promoting sustained high and inclusive growth (Harrison and Rodriguez-Clare, 2010), this chapter first reviews various aspects of (and cross-relationships between) trade, global value chains (GVCs) and inclusive growth. Then it will identify areas where trade potential can be maximised, and discuss policies to realise potential trade outcomes for inclusive growth.

Trade and Investment as Engines of Growth and Development

Asian Trade and Investment in a Comparative Context

International trade has grown remarkably over the past five decades. Between 1960 and 2017, the value of global merchandise trade increased more than a 100-fold to US$35.8 trillion, growing at an average of 9.0% a year (Figure 15.3). This expansion was backed by significant reductions in trade costs through liberalisation of policy regimes and greater physical connectivity through improving logistics (Redding and Turner, 2015).

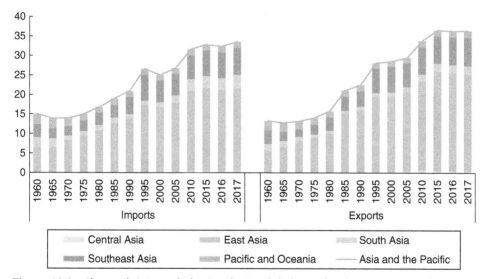

Figure 15.3   Share of Asia and the Pacific in global merchandise imports and exports, 1960–2017 (%).
Source: ADB calculations using data from World Trade Organization (n.d.a).

The rise of Asian trade has been even more spectacular, increasing more than 300-fold at an annual average growth rate of 10.7% over the same period. The share of Asia's imports in the global total doubled to 33.6% between 1960 and 2017 (Figure 15.3). Exports grew more rapidly over the same period – Asia's share in the world total almost tripling, from 13.3 to 36.4% – with the region becoming a net exporter around 1990. East Asia has driven much of Asia's integration with the world economy, accounting for a fifth of global merchandise imports and a quarter of exports in 2017.

The region's meteoric trade performance was enabled by trade-promoting FDI, demonstrating the strong complementarity between trade and investment in the context of factory-Asia, especially since the turn of the current century (Figure 15.4). Between 1970 and 2016, FDI inflows to the region increased more than 200-fold to reach US$491.7 billion. The region's share in global FDI inflows increased from 14.9 to 28.2% (Figure 15.5) as inward FDI to Asia and the Pacific increased faster than to the rest of the world. The region's status as a magnet for FDI was also largely driven by East Asia, which attracted more than half of total inward FDI to Asia throughout this period.

The role of trade and investment as engines of growth and development has been well documented in the literature (Harrison and Rodriguez-Clare, 2010). Indeed, it is international trade and FDI that have fueled the rise of Asia and the Pacific. Open trade and investment regimes allowed countries to access cheap inputs, facilitating technological transfer from advanced economies and the upgrading of labour force skills, in turn enabling the development of new industries and sectors.

Dynamically shifting comparative advantage also drove the process. Labour-intensive economies achieved industrial upgrading and capital-intensive production structures through investment in human capital and adoption of advanced foreign technologies. With Japan leading the way in the 1960s, the region followed the flying wild geese model of Akamatsu (1962), first by the newly industrializing economies (NIEs), then by the Association of Southeast Asian Nations (ASEAN) economies (James et al., 1989; World Bank, 1993), and further expanded throughout East and Southeast Asia through product fragmentation and regional value chains with the PRC becoming a main hub in the 1990s (Monetary Authority of Singapore, 2016).

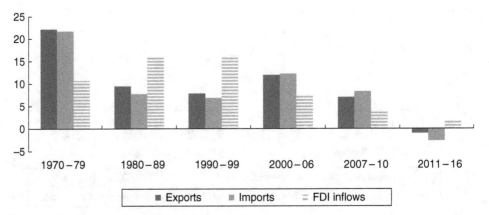

Figure 15.4 Merchandise trade and FDI growth.
Source: ADB calculations using data from World Trade Organization (n.d.a); United Nations Conference on Trade and Development (n.d.a).

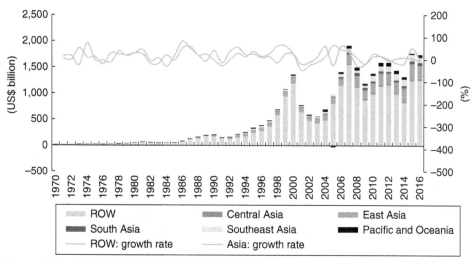

Figure 15.5   Total FDI inflows.
Source: ADB calculations using data from United Nations Conference on Trade and Development (n.d.a).
ROW = rest of the world.

The cross-border sharing of production was facilitated by multinationals in search of lower production costs through an extensive network of global and regional value chains characterised by the compartmentalisation of production process into discrete stages, wherein intermediate goods cross borders multiple times before final assembly rather than being manufactured from start to finish in a single location.

Initially, multinationals from outside the region were central to driving trade in parts and components through cross-border production sharing. However, the main phase of the great trade and investment expansion in developing Asia starting in the 1980s, especially after the Plaza Accord of 1985, was propelled by manufacturing-based regional value chains spawned initially by Japanese and subsequently Korean multinationals across developing Asia, mainly through "green-field" investments that entailed building assets from the ground up as opposed to acquiring existing ones (ADB, 2016a).

While Asia and the Pacific has benefitted greatly from trade and investment linkages outside the region, it has forged even stronger linkages within, driven by the internationalisation of Asian multinationals (Figure 15.6). From just under 30% in 1960, the intra-regional share of Asia's total trade has steadily increased over the past few decades to reach 38% in 1980, and 57% in 2016. East Asia has been the biggest source of intra-Asian trade flows, accounting for a fifth of intra-regional trade in 2016. At the same time, the intra-regional share of total inward FDI to Asia increased from 40 to 57% during 2001–2016.[3]

Following Japan and the NIEs, linking to value chains became a successful export-oriented development strategy subsequently followed by many economies in the region. For instance, Malaysia and Thailand first attracted multinationals into labour-intensive industries – such as food processing, shoes and garments – generating widespread employment, and subsequently moved into higher value-added segments of the value chain through successful industrial and investment promotion

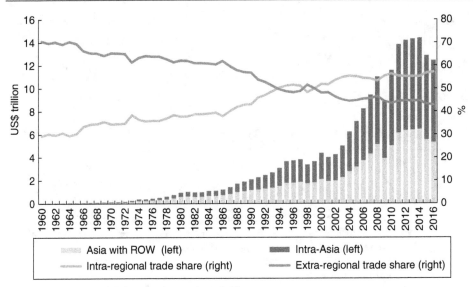

Figure 15.6 Asia and the Pacific total trade flows.
Source: ADB calculations using data from International Monetary Fund (n.d.a).
Note: Total trade refers to the sum of exports and imports. ROW = rest of the world.

policies. The eastern seaboard of Thailand and the Penang export hub in northern Malaysia are notable examples. As these economies moved up the value chain, the downstream segments of the production process were then further relocated to neighbouring economies, including Cambodia, Lao People's Democratic Republic and Vietnam (Athukorala, 2017).

The PRC example is perhaps the most remarkable instance of trade-and-investment-driven growth. Since the liberalisation reforms in the 1980s, the country has become the prime destination for both Asian and global multinationals and emerged as a hub for labour-intensive final assembly, in the process generating the widespread employment that pulled 853 million people out of poverty in the past three decades. Trade's share in PRC GDP increased from 19.9% in 1980 to 32.9% today.

More recently, subregions which had previously lagged behind, notably South Asia and Central Asia, are aiming to intensify participation in international production sharing. One of the examples to follow is Bangladesh, where the ready-made garment industry thrives because small and medium-sized enterprises (SMEs) have become part of international production networks as sub-contractors for large multinationals.

In fact, since 2001, Asia's trade growth has been largely steered by the developing economies of the region, which accounted for 71–83% of the region's total trade volume during 2001–2016. Data show that since accession to the WTO in 2001, which bolstered the PRC's position in the global economy, the PRC alone has accounted for 16–33% of the region's trade.

However, despite its role as an engine of economic growth since the 1960s, trade growth in Asia and the Pacific as elsewhere has slowed markedly since the GFC. After having outpaced GDP growth since 1970s (except for a brief period in the 1980s when the growth of trade in agriculture goods decelerated sharply), trade has

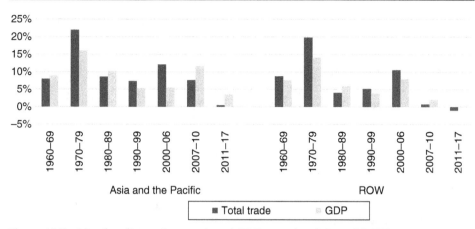

Figure 15.7 Merchandise trade growth and GDP growth – Asia and ROW.
Sources: ADB calculations using data from World Trade Organization (n.d.a); World Bank
(n.d.b); International Monetary Fund (n.d.a).
Note: Total trade refers to the sum of exports and imports. Data are in current US dollars.
ROW = rest of the world.

expanded at a lower rate than GDP since the GFC (Figure 15.7). A brief revival in
2009–2010 remained short-lived, with trade growth falling below GDP growth
again in 2012, and remaining sluggish since then, and even contracting in absolute
terms in 2015.

A host of structural and cyclical factors have played a role in the slowdown. To a
significant extent, the fall in trade growth was prompted by weak export demand
following the GFC and the sluggish economic recovery since then. But it also reflected
structural changes in the composition of economic activity, with a shift in demand
away from tradable goods, especially commodities and durable manufactured goods,
towards services. Moreover, deceleration in the pace of trade liberalisation, a decline
in the expansion of GVCs as PRC has moved up the value chain and weaker investment
have all played a role. At the same time, the prognosis for future FDI flows remains
uncertain in view of a 6% contraction in inward FDI to the region in 2016.

In the context of the uncertain global economic environment – the trade growth slowdown now compounded by increasingly inward-oriented trade policies in some advanced
economies – it has become ever more important for economies in the region to reinforce
the regional trade–FDI nexus to promote sustained high and inclusive growth.

What Drives GVC-linked FDI in Asia and the Pacific?

Multinationals play an especially critical role in investment flows (Antras & Yeaple,
2014). Not only are they the main organisers and coordinators of GVCs, but they
also serve foreign markets through relocation of the production process as an
alternative to trade. Understanding the factors that lead multinationals to set up
operations in a certain location and engage in trade-oriented activities is important
for many reasons.

Multinational-led GVC expansion drove the largest growth in world trade relative
to GDP, starting from 1980s until the GFC. Engagement in GVCs matters for growth.

Countries with the fastest growing GVC participation experienced GDP per capita growth rates 2 percentage points above the global average between 1990 and 2010 (UNCTAD, 2013). In fact, expanding GVC is known to contribute to productivity growth by prompting innovation and technological intensity as well as by leveraging economies of scale and specialisation (Asian Development Bank, 2018). Within the Asian sample, countries with per capita GDP growth above the median had higher GVC participation, in terms of both trade and FDI, than countries whose growth rate was below the median (Table 15.2).

ADB (2016a) investigates the factors that influence a multinational's decision to serve the domestic market instead of concentrating on trade-oriented activities using data on the global ultimate headquarters of multinationals and their overseas subsidiaries that both import and export at the same time.[4] The traditional determinants of that decision, within a country and in industry sectors, can be grouped broadly into comparative advantage, integration, institutions and responses to policy.

Using this data, some salient stylised facts are uncovered. Based on the number of affiliates that both import and export, PRC is the largest host for GVC-linked FDI (GVC-FDI) in Asia, whereas Japan is the most popular source. Moreover, the manufacturing sector still attracts multinational corporations (MNCs) most extensively engaged in GVC-FDI in Asia. The PRC and Vietnam attract the greatest share of foreign-owned affiliates (out of the total affiliates operating in these countries) in the manufacturing sector (92%).

Moreover, Asian MNCs are engaged in GVC-FDI more than MNCs from outside the region. However, this effect is mainly driven by Japanese- and Republic of Korean-owned affiliates. PRC- and Indian-owned multinationals are also increasingly engaging in GVC-linked activities in the region. The most popular destination for PRC-owned multinationals is Vietnam, and for Indian multinationals it is Singapore.

Table 15.3 presents an exhaustive list of averaged country characteristics for two groups of foreign-owned affiliates: those engaged in international trade and those that exclusively serve the local market of operation. Country characteristics can be grouped into variables related to integration, comparative advantage, institutional environment (both governance and business environment) and policy.

Some differences are striking. First, foreign-owned affiliates engaged in international trade are located in countries with substantially lower costs to export and import, as measured by a range of metrics from the World Bank's World Development

Table 15.2   Engagement in the GVC and growth

	Low	*High*	*Observations*
GVC-trade	2.1%	3.3%	8
GVC-FDI	2.8%	3.6%	27
FDI intensity	2.5%	3.4%	12

Source: ADB (2016a).
Note: Annual average growth rate of real GDP per capita, for 2000–2010, median among countries in each group. Low/high FDI intensity refers to countries with sales of foreign plants, as a share of total sales, below/above the median share across countries. Low/high GVC-FDI refers to countries with a fraction of foreign plants that export below/above the median share across countries. Low/high GVC-trade refers to countries with domestic value added (DVA) shares above/below the median across countries.

Table 15.3 GVC-FDI and average country characteristics

	Imports & exports	Only domestic sale
Integration variables		
Trade restrictiveness index	0.05	0.05
Burden of customs process	4.43	4.77
Cost to export (US$ per container)	577	752
Cost to import (US$ per container)	622	804
Number of documents to export	6.74	5.24
Number of documents to import	5.35	5.83
Logistics performance index	3.48	3.57
Quality of port infrastructure	4.55	4.93
Applied tariff rate	3.53	2.48
RTAs	0.34	0.36
BITs	0.55	0.38
BITs, investor-state dispute mechanism	1.9	1.7
DTTs	0.91	0.78
Comparative advantage variables		
Real GDP per capita (rgdpl)	13,006	24,227
Capital-labor ratio (K/L)	76,379	156,101
Average years of schooling	7.61	8.73
Log rgdpl, host relative to source	−1.32	−0.75
Log K/L, host relative to source	−1.51	−0.78
Institutional variables		
Rule of law	−0.09	0.68
Regulatory quality	0.05	0.76
Government effectiveness	0.27	0.87
Control of corruption	−0.05	0.69
Political stability	−0.29	0.23
Voice and accountability	−0.95	0.12
Policy Variables		
Days required to enforce a contract	390	353
Number of processes to register a business start-up	6.6	4.45
Cost of business start-up procedure (% of GNI)	8.6	4.7
Days to get electricity	57.9	58.9
Days required to register property	27.1	16.4
Days required to start business	17.1	8.2
Time spent dealing with government regulations	0.9	0.9
Hours required to prepare and pay taxes	304	168
Private credit (% of GDP)	0.46	0.91
GVC-trade variables		
DVA share	0.72	0.79
FVA share	0.21	0.16
Export upstreamness (overall)	1.97	2.2

Source: ADB (2016a).
Note: "Time spent dealing with government regulations" is measured in percentage of senior management time. Integration variables (except for RTAs, BITs and DTTs) and institutional variables are from the World Bank (World Governance Indicators and World Development Indicators). DVA share and FVA shares refer to the domestic and foreign – value added, respectively, as a share of gross exports, at the bilateral level. BIT = bilateral investment treaty, DTT = double taxation treaty, DVA = domestic value added, FVA = foreign value added, GDP = gross domestic product, GNI = gross national income, GVC = global value chain, RTA = regional trade agreement.

Indicators and Ease of Doing Business indicators. This has important implications for the role greater integration and trade facilitation measures play in promoting GVC-FDI, and enabling economies to link to international production networks.

Second, regarding comparative advantage motives, plants engaged in international trade are located in poorer countries, and in countries with abundant unskilled labour. Moreover, these host countries are at a substantially lower development stage, and have less capital than the countries from which the plants come.

Third, the institutional variables capturing governance of the host economy are, on average, lower where foreign affiliates that trade are located. The relationship with variables on "doing business" is similar. This is intuitive, as firms care more about the "rule of law" when their activities are directly linked to the domestic market. If their main activity is to export, the institutional environment may matter less – particularly as affiliates may be "shielded" from the regulatory and business environment of the host economy through special legislation and special economic zones (SEZs). On the flip side, multinationals may wish to avoid stringent domestic regulations, creating a "race to the bottom" among economies competing to attract GVC-FDI. Greater regional cooperation in harmonising the tax and regulatory environment, for example, would help.

SEZs have been widely employed in developing Asia as an instrument of trade and investment policy, and have enabled many of the region's economies to integrate with GVCs, especially in the labour-intensive manufacturing sector. Table 15.4 shows the number of SEZs and the amount of GVC-FDI in developing Asian countries: even if the number of observations is low, more SEZs are associated with more GVC-FDI. In contrast, regional trade agreements do not seem to play a major role in attracting GVC-FDI, perhaps because of competing considerations on trade creation and diversion, and complexities in rules of origin. The presence of bilateral investment treaties (BIT) – particularly with provisions to settle disputes – and a double taxation treaties (DTT) does seem to matter.

Fourth, trade-oriented foreign affiliates are mostly located in economies where exports are concentrated in more downstream activities with less domestic and more foreign value added, indicating that developing Asia is still mostly a hub for final assembly.

Finally, greater domestic production fragmentation (i.e. the strength of input–output linkages among the industries of parents and their affiliates) also helps to

Table 15.4   Special economic zones and GVC-FDI

	Number of SEZ	SEZ per km²	GVC-FDI (%)
Bangladesh	8	0.00006	10
Cambodia	14	0.00008	41
India	199	0.00007	47
Kazakhstan	10	0.000004	100
PRC	1,475	0.00016	82
Philippines	312	0.001041	66
Sri Lanka	12	0.00019	36

Source: ADB (2016a).
Note: The number of SEZs is for 2014. GVC-FDI refers to the fraction of foreign affiliates in the country that exports.

attract more GVC-FDI. In other words, industries and countries with more scope for production fragmentation attract more GVC-FDI.

In sum, the descriptive analysis indicates that while seemingly disadvantageous, a low development stage can continue to be leveraged to attract FDI, which can help link the lagging economies to GVCs. Labour abundance can also draw in GVC-FDI, further supported by lowering trade barriers. Developing countries can also attract more GVC-FDI by fostering richer linkages between domestic industries. The Penang export hub in Malaysia is an example of an area that first attracted multinationals into labour-intensive industries, and subsequently moved into higher value-added segments of the value chain through a successful investment promotion strategy and a rich network of domestic vendors (Athukorala, 2014). This could hold particular relevance for those economies that have yet to adequately connect their domestic industries to international production networks.

Growth and Trade-Related Policy Implications

Trade, Inclusive Growth and Female Empowerment

As discussed in the previous section, over the past five decades, trade openness has led to the acceleration of output growth which, in turn, has provided opportunities for upward income mobility, especially for lower-income groups and geographically challenged economies in the region.

Yet, the region remains home to half of the world's poorest people, poverty reduction has slowed and inequality has widened. And compared with the period before the 2008 GFC, potential economic growth has slowed significantly, particularly in the past few years.

To ensure continued prosperity and equitable and sustainable development, Asia will need to work on structural reforms that draw more people into the workforce, lift productivity and invest more in infrastructure and connectivity, while being mindful of the climate change/environmental impacts of all economic activities.

Free and open trade plays an important role in achieving the SDGs. It facilitates access to new markets and increased production, and trade liberalisation enables job creation, technological transfer, skills upgradation, knowledge production and innovation and institutional development. Along with adequate and efficient trade policies, these gains can contribute to other development-friendly outcomes and support the SDGs. Leveraging regional cooperation and integration also complements national development strategies, bolsters economic resilience and sustainable growth and enables wider sharing of benefits.

Trade Can Deliver Quality Jobs and Improved Employment Outcomes

The SDGs notably see job creation as the primary channel to realise inclusive growth.[5] SDG 8 "promote[s] sustained, inclusive and sustainable growth, full and productive employment, and decent work for all" by raising "economic productivity through diversification, technological upgrading and innovation, including through a focus on high-value added and labor-intensive sectors". Goal 8 also emphasises that policy measures must support productive capacities, employment generation and innovation if growth is to be inclusive.

Trade can help achieve the SDG employment targets. In aggregate, trade has a positive impact on welfare, which can lead to job creation (Vandenberg, 2017). However, trade and trade processes have different effects on labour supply, the movement of workers between economic sectors and the quality of jobs.

Gains from trade happen when economies produce goods and services for which they have a comparative advantage. Specialisation can advance welfare across a whole economy and, in turn, increase economic growth and demand for labour. Countries with liberal trade regimes proved to have lower unemployment rates than others (Dutt et al., 2009; Felbermayr et al., 2011; Moore and Ranjan, 2005). In the PRC, for example, manufacturing employment related to exports increased by 2.3 million in only four years (from 15 million in 2004 to 17.3 million in 2008) after WTO accession (Cai and Du, 2014).

Trade may also raise employment quality when trade competition encourages companies to formalise employment, an SDG aim, which incentivises workers and can raise productivity. And international buyers are increasingly keen to purchase from ethical producers who compensate workers adequately. However, trade can also pressure companies to cut costs by shifting to lower-paid casual employment, especially when human resources are abundant.

Empirical studies tend to prove that welfare gains from trade – such as by raising incomes and improving working conditions through the reinforcement of labour standards and penalising discriminatory practices – can also help reduce egregious forms of employment, such as child and forced labour (Edmonds and Pavcnik, 2004; ADB, 2017b, 2017c).

That said, trade openness causes some sectors and companies to expand and others to shrink in a process that creates demand for labour in some sectors while making jobs redundant in others. For instance, Hong Kong, China, has seen employment move from manufacturing to services as comparative advantage has shifted, with changes more pronounced in wages than in employment numbers (Vere, 2014). Indonesia similarly illustrates adjustments caused by trade, but jobs have been lost in more labour-intensive export sectors with weak export performance but strong barriers to investment (Aswicahyono et al., 2014). Another example is the PRC, where competition in manufacturing has caused job losses in the north (Vandenberg, 2017).

As shown in Figure 15.8, accompanying trade expansion is a reduction in labour force participation rates in many economies of Asia and the Pacific. For one, shocks created by trade competition and the inevitable adjustments brought by trade processes in economies as they undergo structural transformation affect labour force dynamics.

A complex range of supply- and demand-side factors significantly shape and transform the dynamics of this relationship too. On one hand, Asia's shifting demographics, as the working-age population declines, has hurt labour supply. On the other, technology and trade have reduced demand for less skilled, labour-intensive sectors, principally manufacturing.

Falling labour income shares
Technology and global integration through trade have been key drivers of falling labour income shares (IMF, 2017). Moreover, integration, more specifically participation in GVCs, typically implies offshoring of labour-intensive tasks, and thus can lower labour shares in tradable sectors (Dao et al., 2017).

Figure 15.8a   Log of trade and aggregate labour force participation rate.
Source: World Bank (n.d.b); International Labour Organization (n.d.a).

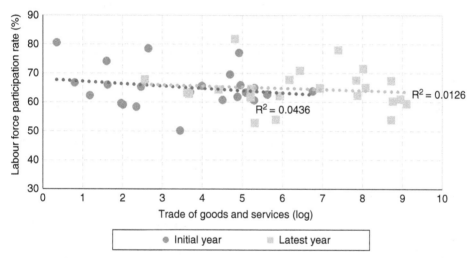

Figure 15.8b   Scatterplot of trade in goods and services (log) and labour force participation rates (%).
Source: World Bank (n.d.b); International Labour Organization (n.d.a).
Note: Initial year refers to 1990–1995 and latest year refers to 2011–2016. Log of trade in goods and services is the log of the sum of exports and imports in constant 2010 US dollars.

Data show that the share of national income paid to workers had been falling since the 1990s after being stable for many decades. The decline is most pronounced in low-income and lower-middle-income economies where labour income shares are now about 13 and 12 percentage points, respectively, lower than they were in the 1970s to 1990s. By subregion, South Asia, Central Asia and the Pacific and Oceania saw the sharpest declines, with labour shares falling between 12 to 22 percentage points since the 1970s (Figure 15.9).

The income share of labour indicates the bargaining power of the labour force and of the contribution of economic progress to the economic well-being of the labour force (Acemoglu, 2003; Bentolila and Saint-Paul, 2003; Krueger, 1999; Milberg and Winkler, 2013; Rodrik, 1998). By and large, the declining labour income shares tend to prove that while trade integration and technological advancement benefit economies, ensuring that welfare gains from trade are distributed more broadly is still a work in progress. In the face of rising anti-globalisation sentiments,

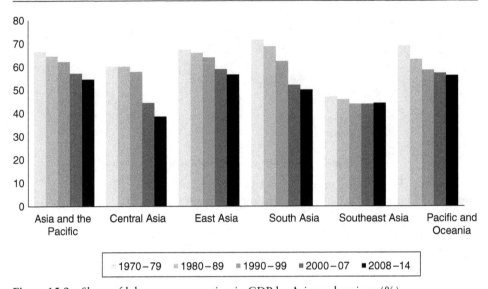

Figure 15.9 Share of labour compensation in GDP by Asian subregions (%).
Source: World Bank (n.d.b); Penn World Tables Version 8.0 (n.d.a).
Note: Figures are in current national prices converted to US dollars using official exchange rates.

it is increasingly important to find ways to make trade-driven growth inclusive especially for the marginalised segments such as women and smaller firms.

GVCs Widen Women's Options

Expanding and deepening GVCs have reinforced the specialisation, compartmentalisation and agglomeration of economic activities – all of which can influence women's work in a variety of ways.

Asia and the Pacific economies mostly conform to a global labor force participation rate (LFPR) convergence trend between women and men, with some exceptions. Within subregions, South Asia has the lowest LFPR for women and East Asia the highest (Figure 15.10). Narrowing gaps in LFPR between men and women in some subregions is attributed to progress in education and female employment in the tradable sector.

Despite that narrowing, women in Asia are on average 70% less likely to be in work than men, with the country-to-country percentage varying anywhere from 3 to 80%, and wages that are one half to two thirds those of men in the same jobs (ADB, 2015). This gap persists despite economic growth, decreasing fertility rates and increasing education, in a disparity largely influenced by how women allocate their time between market and non-market activities.

Women can gain from international trade, especially through better wages and working conditions when export-oriented multinationals invest in labour-intensive sectors (Silvander, 2013). Evidence is compelling that participation in GVCs can generate more jobs for women when labour-intensive manufacturing sectors join international production networks. Electronics and garment sectors are good examples. More than 75% of Bangladesh's 4 million garment industry workers are women in the labour market for the first time and mostly from poor families (Bangladesh,

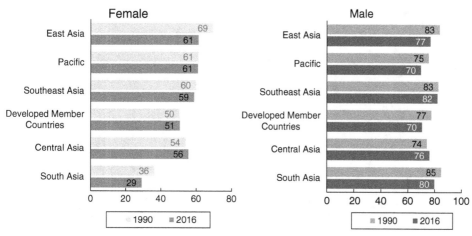

Figure 15.10   Female and male labour force participation rates, 1990 and 2016 (%).
Source: ADB calculations using data from International Labour Organization (n.d.a).
Note: Developed member countries refers to ADB members Australia, Japan and New Zealand.

Planning Commission, 2016). Export-oriented market jobs can generate incentives for training and educational opportunities, raising a country's human capital (Heath and Mobarak, 2015).

Value chains include services which create new types of employment. For example, software and business process outsourcing sectors hire educated women. In India, more than 1.3 million of 3.7 million people employed in information technology and business process management are women, who outnumber men as entry-level hires (PricewaterhouseCoopers and NASSCOM, 2016). In the Philippines, the business process outsourcing industry counts mostly women among its 1.3 million employees (Errighi *et al.*, 2016).

MSMEs For More Inclusive Growth and Sustainable Development

Micro, small and medium-sized enterprises (MSMEs) account for a significant share of firms in most economies – both developing and developed – as well as employment. Using the most recent figures between 2004 and 2014 for economies with available data, MSMEs in Asia and the Pacific totaled 77.4 million, employing 168.3 million people. On average, there are 22 MSMEs per 1000 people across the countries covered in the region, with almost 50% operating in the services sector. MSMEs employ a majority of employees in the private sector, but account for less than half of total value added in the economy (SME Finance Forum, n.d.).

However, despite their impressive growth and contribution to employment, the share of MSMEs in value added remains significantly lower, and the direct participation in international trade is even more negligible, especially compared to larger firms (Figure 15.11). Data show that only about a fifth of SMEs in Asia are engaged in export markets, compared to 34.5% of large enterprises (Figure 15.12). Interestingly, exporting is more prevalent in firms with a female top manager.

A primary reason MSMEs are largely unengaged in export markets is that they are more vulnerable to risks and face greater challenges, especially in exposure to trade

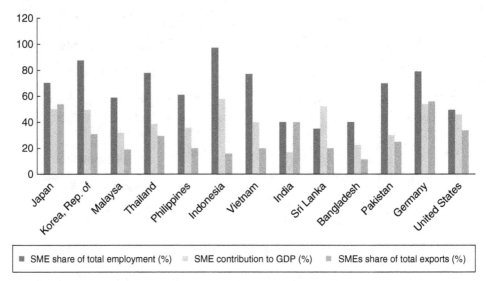

Figure 15.11   Contribution of SMEs to economic activity and trade.
Source: Yoshino and Wignaraja (2015).

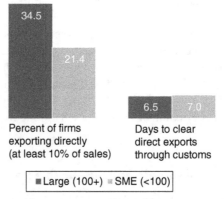

Figure 15.12   Exporting activity in Asia and the Pacific by firm size.
Source: ADB calculations using data from World Bank (n.d.d).
Note: Regional averages are computed by taking a simple average of country point estimates.
For each economy, only the latest available year of survey data are used in this computation.
Only surveys posted during 2010–2017 and adhering to the Enterprise Surveys Global
Methodology are used to compute these regional and subregional averages.

costs. For one, exporting implies fixed upfront costs that are disproportionately larger
for small firms: data show that the average days it takes to clear exports through customs is longer for SMEs than for large firms (Figure 15.12). Moreover, SMEs are
largely constrained in access to trade finance. Approximately 74% of the rejections of
trade finance proposals impact on MSMEs and midcap firms (Figure 15.13; DiCaprio
et al., 2017). In particular, female-owned firms face 2.5 times more rejections than
male-owned firms. Overall, these rejections lead to non-completion of trade transactions, estimated at around 60%. The WTO estimated the value of unmet demand for
trade finance of SMEs in developing Asia at US$700 billion.[6]

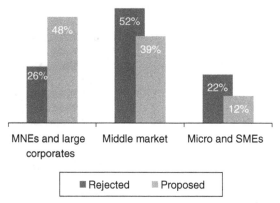

Figure 15.13   Proposals received and rejected transactions by firm size.
Source: DiCaprio et al., 2017.
Note: MNEs = multinational enterprises. SMEs = small and medium-sized enterprises.

It is imperative that efforts continue to lower trade costs and bridge trade finance gaps to boost the participation of MSMEs and marginalised groups in global and regional trade and value chains.

The Future of Inclusive, Trade-Driven Growth – Services Trade and Digitalisation?

Services contribute importantly to GDP, create jobs and provide inputs necessary for economies to thrive. The services sector employs 60% of the global workforce (and 70% of the female workforce). More importantly, "services are key inputs in the production of goods: information and communication technology (ICT) services, for example, help boost productivity and increase competitiveness in an economy. Financial services facilitate capital accumulation for productive investment and innovation, transport and logistics services are vital for moving goods and people and improving connectivity, and good health and education services improve human capital" (ADB, 2017c, p. 38). Given its heterogeneity, intersectoral linkages and wide coverage of economic activities, services can contribute to achieving inclusive growth. If harnessed properly, geographically challenged economies, MSMEs and marginalised communities stand to gain the most from a competitive and productive service economy.

The contribution of services towards Asia and the Pacific's total output and employment has been increasing over time (Figures 15.14a, b). Services now account for about 52.8% of regional gross domestic product and 41.8% of total employment, up from 46.2% and 28.9%, respectively, in 1996. While services already account for a substantial share of developing Asia's output and employment, room for further growth is ample. As Asia's middle classes rapidly expand, the demand for services, such as education, healthcare and financial, is expected to result in significant parallel growth (Park and Noland, 2013).

Similarly, the importance of services in the region's total trade is also increasing. Between 2005 and 2017, exports and imports of services in the region more than doubled to US$2.8 trillion from US$1.2 trillion. Services trade accounted for 5.4% of developing Asia's GDP during 2010–2017.[7] Pacific and Southeast Asian economies

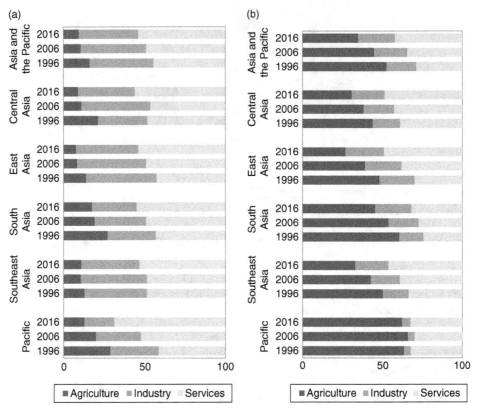

Figure 15.14 Sectoral distribution of output. (a) % of GDP; (b) % of total employment.
Source: ADB (2017d); International Labour Organization (n.d.a).
Note: Asia refers to developing Asia. Regional and subregional aggregates are calculated using data available for the respective year headings and no imputations are made for missing values. Moreover, aggregates are provided for subregions/regions where at least two thirds of the countries are represented.

were most open to trade in services, while Central Asian economies were least reliant. In fact, services trade is growing more rapidly than merchandise trade in 2012–2016, both regionally and globally, and was also less adversely affected by the post-GFC global trade growth slowdown (Figure 15.15).

Asian economies are also among the major services traders globally, accounting collectively for about one fifth of global services trade between 2000 and 2015.[8] By far the largest services traders have been the East Asian economies, accounting for 56.7% of Asia's total services trade with the world between 2000 and 2015, with the PRC alone contributing 20.3% (Figure 15.16). This reflects the size of East Asian economies and their wealth and integration into GVCs. East Asia's average services trade with the world nearly quadrupled to US$1.4 trillion in 2015 from US$383 billion in 2000. Southeast Asia is a second major contributor, capturing about a quarter of the region's services exports and imports during 2000–2015.

The sectoral distribution of total services trade within Asia over 2000–2015 shows the predominance of transportation, travel and other business services for all

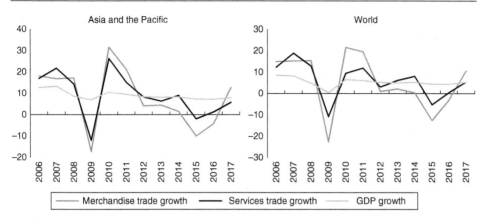

Figure 15.15 Merchandise and services trade growth and GDP growth – Asia and the Pacific and world (%, year over year).
Source: ADB calculations using data from World Trade Organization (n.d.a); International Trade Centre (n.d.a).
Note: Figures are based on the sixth edition of the IMF *Balance of Payments and International Investment Position Manual* (BPM6; IMF, 2009).

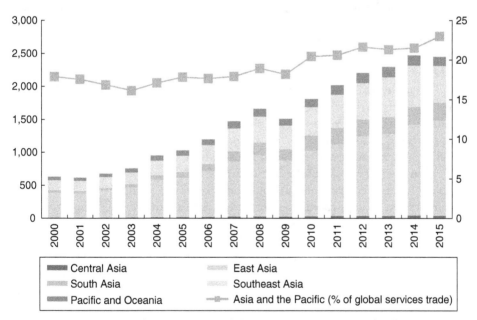

Figure 15.16 Services trade across Asia and the Pacific, 2000–2015 (US$ billion).
Source: ADB calculations using data from United Nations (n.d.a).
Note: Figures are based on Extended Balance of Payments Services (EBOPS) 2002 (United Nations, n.d.b).

subregions except Central Asia and South Asia (excluding India), where trade in these services is lower. Notably, computer and information services are more important in services trade in the PRC and India than they are in the rest of the region. Especially in India, computer and information services are the biggest contributor to the services trade, followed by other business services.

Despite the positive outlook for Asia's services trade, barriers to trade and investment in services are prevalent. A recent World Bank research project found that services barriers in both high-income and developing countries are higher than those for trade in goods, and that barriers in developing countries are generally much higher (Borchert *et al.*, 2014). Facilitating trade in services requires continual trade liberalisation. For this, adequate policy interventions and coherent approaches are necessary to shore up growth and maximise the benefits of the services economy and trade. At the very least, national regulations and administrative capacities have to be in sync so as not to undermine the intended purposes of regulations and policies and create unintended consequences. No one size fits all, but coordinated and harmonised approaches to regulation can reduce gaps and overlaps.

In this regard, services sectors and their reforms in trade negotiations need a prominent role. Yet, low-income countries' neglect of services in negotiations carries a significant opportunity cost, in that trade liberalisation can drive productivity and increase access to better services (Hoekman, 2017). To expand progress in this area and liberalise trade in services, first, governments could create mechanisms (services knowledge platforms) to bring together regulators, trade officials and stakeholders to discuss regulatory reform (Hoekman and Mattoo, 2011). Moreover, there is a need for a new approach to negotiations in the WTO, with countries that account for the bulk of services production agreeing to lock in applied levels of protection and pre-committing to reform policies that affect FDI and international movement for services providers.

Second, broad-ranging capacity constraints make it difficult for companies in developing economies to produce and trade services. Measures to help remove these hurdles should target availability and appropriateness of human capital (technical, export-related and entrepreneurial abilities) and financial capital (notably, access to credit to underpin productivity-enhancing investment). Also important are infrastructure improvements. Developing standards for services sectors and engaging companies in key services sectors to meet these is another area for attention (Hoekman and te Velde, 2017). Also needing to be addressed is the lack of accurate services sector data, a major stumbling block to effective reforms and trade liberalisation policy.

Third and most importantly, services trade can benefit greatly from digital technology and e-commerce platforms (Box 15.1), the rise of which has facilitated the upsurge in services trade. This has led to greater connectivity and participation in GVCs, especially for SMEs, and transformed the growth and tradability of services themselves. However, it is only a matter of time before this growth starts to slow, unless countries continue to find ways to shore up digital trade (Park *et al.*, 2017a).

Shoring up Digital Trade in Services

Digital trade in services capitalises on information and communication technologies (ICTs), which have facilitated the computerisation of work (e.g. via automated business processes, remote working mechanisms) and digitalisation of output (e.g. software and media products and services). This allows service providers to unbundle and relocate work to groups/areas with lower labour cost but high-quality and timely services. With developments in the adoption and usage of ICT, the entry of multinational enterprises was also facilitated into developing economies with low wages, thereby encouraging FDI.

Box 15.1   E-commerce for inclusive growth.

Asia and the Pacific is the world's largest retail e-commerce market with the bulk of sales (47%) coming from the PRC. Total sales are expected to almost triple from US$1 trillion in 2016 to US$2.7 trillion in 2020, driven by an expanding middle class, rapidly increasing mobile and internet penetration, growing competition among sellers and improving logistics and infrastructure.

However, e-commerce remains largely domestic and nascent in some parts of the region due to underdeveloped digital payments infrastructure and a weak logistics framework (ADB, 2017c). For instance, in the six major economies of Southeast Asia – Indonesia, Malaysia, Philippines, Singapore, Thailand and Vietnam – e-commerce comprises less than 1% of national output (Box Figure 15.1; Park *et al.*, 2017b).

Overall, for e-commerce to thrive in Asia and the Pacific, access to reliable and afford-able ICT services is paramount. Internet penetration remains varied, high in the region's relatively high-income economies but very low in many developing economies, with only about a third of people in the region having access. Moreover, given the low credit/debit card penetration in the region, the availability of secure electronic payment systems that operate in several countries remains another huge challenge for cross-border e-commerce

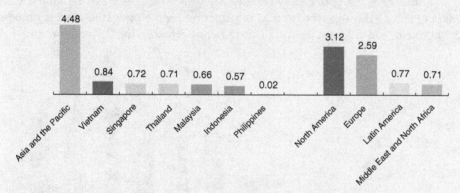

Box Figure 15.1   Share of e-commerce in GDP (%).
Source: eCommerce Foundation (2016); eMarketer (n.d.); and World Bank (n.d.b).
Note: E-commerce sales include products or services ordered online via any device and payment method, excluding travel and event tickets. Data for Asia and the Pacific, North America, Europe, Latin America and Middle East and North Africa refer to 2015; and for Southeast Asian economies, 2016.

development in Asia and the Pacific. Other challenges relate to high costs of shipment and poor logistics infrastructure – developing robust shipping networks, strengthening logistics and streamlining customs processes are critical for shoring up investments needed to seize the trade opportunities e-commerce can bring for Asia's economies.

Ultimately, it is imperative to develop the necessary legal and regulatory frameworks to facilitate online transactions. The legal and regulatory framework for e-commerce encompasses legislation on e-transactions, consumer protection, data protection/privacy and cybercrime. The increasingly cross-border nature of e-commerce calls for coordinated regional and global efforts to promote ICT and e-commerce and enforce related laws. Closing data gaps and limitations is also paramount given that e-commerce has already reached a critical mass in business transactions and increasingly impacts global trade.

More importantly, ICTs are the main enablers for increased access to information and inputs for business services such as telecommunications, finance and professional/technical services. Enhanced access to information and inputs is creating more efficient and cost-effective ways to deliver goods and services primarily through the reduction of transaction costs and improved logistics networks. Ultimately, the ICT revolution can set off the evolution of services trade from basic call centers, software coding and digital content to more complex business processes such as system design, research and development, human resources, sales and marketing and finance, i.e. ICT-enabled services.

Developing Asia's total trade in ICT and ICT-enabled services increased from US$284.7 billion in 2005 to US$772.3 billion in 2016, and accounted for more than one third of the region's total trade in services during the period 2005–2016. Trade in the telecommunications, computer, information and other business services – which accounted for the bulk (71.9%) of ICT-enabled services during the same period – rose to US$561.8 billion in 2016 from US$207.8 billion in 2005. Furthermore, exports of ICT-enabled services grew faster than all other services since 2011, on average, 16.8% compared to 3.7% (Figure 15.17).

India and the Philippines are setting good examples: the sector accounts for 67.3% and 74.6% of total service exports, respectively, with ICT-enabled outsourcing and offshoring services (e.g. information technology (IT) business process management and business process outsourcing) representing 3.7 million and 1.3

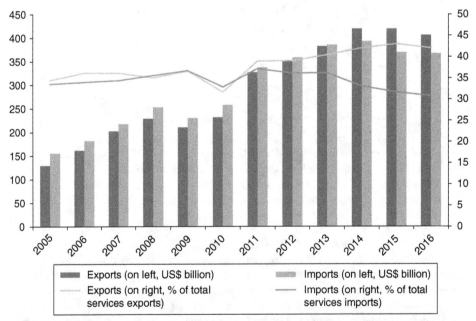

Exports (on left, US$ billion)
Imports (on left, US$ billion)
Exports (on right, % of total services exports)
Imports (on right, % of total services imports)

Figure 15.17 Exports and imports of ICT-enabled services, 2005–2016 (US$ billion, %).
Source: ADB calculations using data from International Trade Centre (n.d.a).
Note: ICT-enabled services include those in the following service categories based on the sixth edition of the *Balance of Payments and International Investment Position Manual* (BPM6; IMF, 2009): telecommunications, computer and information services; insurance and pension services; financial services; charges for the use of intellectual property; other business services; and personal, cultural and recreational services.

million workers, respectively, in these countries. For further growth in digital trade in services, expanding access to ICT infrastructure is crucial. Much progress has been made, particularly in terms of internet, mobile cellular and fixed broadband penetration (Figure 15.18). However, the progress has not been uniform across the region and within countries, with geographically challenged landlocked and sea-locked economies, the rural population and smaller businesses still significantly lagging behind.

Policy reforms and targeted interventions can help create and foster an enabling environment for competitive services markets to unleash the potential of trade in services. These include improving regulatory regimes, enhancing connectivity, promoting openness to FDI and modern trade facilitating solutions such as digital trade.

In particular, economies in Asia and the Pacific can consider the following policy actions to shore up digital trade in services. First, bridging information and infrastructure gaps by improving ICT infrastructure is a vital starting point. This primarily includes expanding access and reducing the cost of accessing ICT devices and services, as well as encouraging cross-border data flows. Closing the information and infrastructure gaps does not only promote greater connectivity in domestic and global markets but also enhances the transparency and accountability of (public and private) services delivery.

Second, establishing the supportive regulatory and legal environment is integral to facilitating digital trade in services. ICT-enabled trade is not exempt from traditional tariff and non-tariff barriers to goods and services trade. For digital trade in services to occur, lowering entry barriers and eliminating market access restrictions to services sectors are crucial. Further, a regulatory framework, particularly in the telecommunications sector, that fosters greater competition among services providers and an adequate legal framework that encompasses legislations

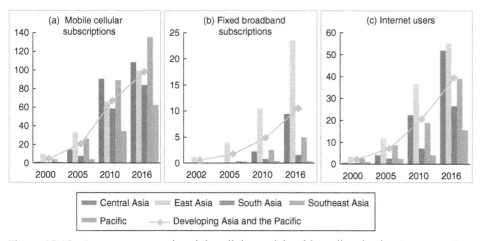

Figure 15.18   Internet users and mobile cellular and fixed broadband subscriptions in Asia and the Pacific, 2000–2016 (per 100 people).
Source: International Telecommunication Union (n.d.a); World Bank (n.d.b).
Note: For fixed broadband subscriptions, 2002 reported the required (earliest year) data for the largest number of constituent countries in each subregion.

on e-transactions, consumer protection, data protection/privacy and cybercrime are essential to promote innovation and expanded access to services, encourage transparency and reduce online transaction risks, and strengthen national e-commerce laws.

Third, there is a need to advance new services trade rules to address existing and emerging digital trade restrictions. For example, the General Agreement on Trade in Services (GATS) rules already cover some disciplines that support digital trade, including an Annex on Telecommunications Services. However, there are emerging challenges in digital trade that require new rules. For instance, government restrictions on the free flow of data – while some are for legitimate reasons such as for protecting data privacy and ensuring cybersecurity – can downgrade the potential of online platforms for international trade.

In this context, ongoing free trade agreement (FTA) negotiations provide opportunities for developing a more robust digital trade agenda. The member states of ASEAN provide an example on this front under the overarching framework of the e-ASEAN Initiative. The ASEAN-Australia-New Zealand Free Trade Area (AANZFTA) for instance covers provisions on transparency and online consumer protection. Under the Regional Comprehensive Economic Partnership (RCEP) negotiations, issues on intellectual property rights and other areas of e-commerce are also addressed. Strengthening regional efforts and individual commitments of governments and participating stakeholders in this regard is vital.

Ultimately, securing policy coherence and convergence of actions between and among Asia's economies in improving digital regulations and improving connectivity infrastructure is key to create an enabling environment for digital trade in services. To this end, the new Framework Agreement on the Facilitation of Cross-Border Paperless Trade in Asia and the Pacific can serve as a valuable tool to facilitate cross-border digital trade and better equip economies to implement the WTO Trade Facilitation Agreement. The agreement is expected to benefit the region by providing a multilateral intergovernmental platform, offering a strong capacity-building programme with emphasis on sharing knowledge, enabling pilot projects on cross-border data exchange, setting action plans based on countries' state of readiness and fostering recognition among stakeholders to achieve the agreement's goals (UNESCAP, 2016).

Policies to Unlock Trade Potential in Achieving SDGs

Much remains to be done to realise potential trade outcomes for inclusive growth. Trade costs are still generally significant. Restrictive policies and poor regulatory environments hinder trade connectivity and the development of competitive goods and services markets. The global trading architecture is uncertain due to the weakening of multilateral trade arrangements and proliferation of bilateral FTAs. Moreover, amidst the rise of anti-globalisation sentiments due to trade-related adjustment that creates both winners and losers, increasingly inward-oriented trade policies are taking hold.

In this context, there is a need to promote trade facilitation and revitalise the multilateral trading system. Aid and targeted interventions can help to build the infrastructure and productive capacity to expand trade, improve the business climate to attract more investment and foster regulatory reforms and stronger legal institutions in order to reduce complexity and cost.

Trade Facilitation for Inclusive Growth

Trade facilitation eases the cross-border movement of goods by cutting costs and simplifying trade procedures (OECD, 2009), in the process increasing trade flows and ultimately sustainable and inclusive growth. It lowers direct costs by raising efficiency among interacting businesses and administering agencies. Prices fall as they indirectly benefit from simpler, transparent border procedures. Even modest cost reductions show a *positive link* between trade facilitation and increased trade. All countries stand to gain, especially the developing ones, and those that improve border procedures will benefit most.

According to the UN Survey on Trade Facilitation and Paperless Trade Implementation (UNESCAP, 2017; United Nations, 2017), in Asia, the trade facilitation implementation rate reached 50.4% in 2017 from 44.8% in 2015 (Figure 15.19), but varied widely across subregions.[9] The Pacific Islands is lowest (28%) and East and Northeast Asia highest (around 74%), implying room for improvement. Across trade facilitation measures, transparency has the highest implementation rate, followed by transit facilitation measures. Meanwhile, women in trade facilitation is the least implemented. Although trade facilitation indicators and the trade facilitation implementation rate have been improving, cost to trade still remains high in Asia compared to the European Union (Table 15.5).

With the relatively low tariffs, removal of quotas and proliferation of FTAs, barriers to trade have shifted to non-tariff and technical impediments. Trade facilitation, which decreases trade costs, is perceived as crucial to unlocking "further gains from international trade" (ADB and UNESCAP, 2013). Indeed, ADB & UNESCAP (2017) estimates that fully implementing trade facilitation measures could reduce trade costs by up to 16%. And despite the upfront investment costs, the long-term benefits far outweigh the initial costs (Hoekman and Shepherd, 2015). Several studies also reveal the considerable potential gains from trade facilitation, such as increased trade flows (Martinez-Zarzoso and Marquez-Ramos, 2008) and higher income (Fox *et al.*, 2003), leading to sustainable and inclusive economic growth (Rippel, 2011).

Meanwhile, in the face of proliferating FTAs, the multilateral trading architecture received a boost when the WTO's Trade Facilitation Agreement came into force on 22 February 2017 upon ratification by two thirds of WTO members after over a decade of negotiations. The WTO estimates that full implementation of the agreement would lower trade costs by an average of 14.3% and increase global exports by between US$750 billion and US$1 trillion per year, depending on the speed and extent of implementation (WTO, 2015).

Least developed countries are expected to reap the greatest reduction in trade costs. Full implementation of the agreement is expected to reduce time to import by over a day and a half (a 47% reduction) and time to export by almost two days (a 91% reduction), with volume of exports increasing by 7–18%, benefitting these countries more. Ultimately, the Trade Facilitation Agreement would help raise global GDP by 5.4–8.7% by 2030, adding average economic growth to developing countries of around 0.9% per year.

Aid for Trade Helps Promote Inclusive Growth and Sustainable Development

Official development assistance to promote trade, or aid for trade (AfT), is an important modality for multilateral development banks and other donors to

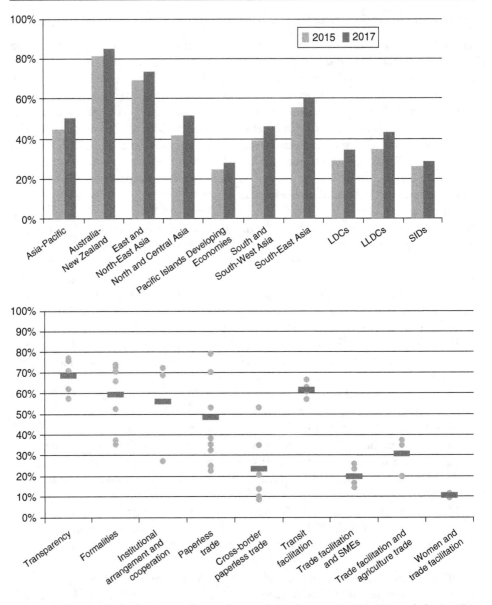

Figure 15.19   Trade facilitation and paperless trade implementation in Asia and the Pacific.
Source: UNESCAP (2017).
Note: Blue circles represent regional average implementation level of individual measures
within each group; red lines are average regional implementation level by groups of measures.
LDCs = least developed countries, LLDCs = landlocked developing countries, SIDs = small
island developing countries, SMEs = small and medium-sized enterprises.

help developing – and especially least developed – economies improve their
trade and productive capacities, their infrastructure and their institutions to
maximise the benefits of trade liberalisation. For instance, ADB (2017c) finds
that, overall, AfT is positively associated with job creation, employment and
lower unemployment.[10]

Table 15.5 Intra-regional and extra-regional comprehensive trade costs (excluding tariff costs), 2010–2015

Region	ASEAN-4	East Asia-3	Russian Federation and Central Asia-4	Pacific	SAARC-4	AUZ-NZL	EU-3
ASEAN-4	76% (6.7%)						
East Asia-3	76% (4.1%)	51% (-2.9%)					
Russian Federation and Central Asia-4	343% (-5.4%)	167% (-9.9%)	116% (-0.9%)				
Pacific	172% (-9.0%)	173% (-3.1%)	370% (21.6%)	130% (-8.8%)			
SAARC-4	130% (3.5%)	123% (-2.1%)	302% (7.7%)	300% (-4.6%)	119% (12.9%)		
AUZ-NZL	101% (2.9%)	87% (-5.4%)	341% (-4.9%)	82% (-8.9%)	136% (-6.7%)	51% (-4.9%)	
EU-3	105% (-3.4%)	84% (-3.4%)	150% (-7.1%)	204% (-7.1%)	113% (0.3%)	108% (-2.3%)	42% (-8.1%)
United States	86% (8.0%)	63% (0.4%)	174% (-3.5%)	161% (-5.4%)	112% (6.7%)	100% (2.9%)	67% (-0.4%)

Source: UNESCAP (2017).
Note: Trade costs may be interpreted as tariff equivalents. Percentage changes in trade costs 2004–2009 and 2010–2015 are in parentheses.
ASEAN-4 = Indonesia, Malaysia, Philippines, Thailand. East Asia-3 = People's Republic of China, Japan, the Republic of Korea. Central Asia = Georgia, Kazakhstan, Kyrgyz Republic. Pacific = Fiji, Papua New Guinea. SAARC = South Asian Association for Regional Cooperation; SAARC-4 = Bangladesh, India, Pakistan, Sri Lanka. AUS-NZL = Australia, New Zealand. EU-3 = Germany, France, United Kingdom.

Globally, AfT disbursements in annual official development assistance (ODA) grew from US$9.5 billion in 2002 to US$38.8 billion in 2016, at a faster rate than official development assistance (Figure 15.20). It comprised 20.9% (US$416.7 billion) of total ODA.

Asia and the Pacific is among the largest recipients of AfT. From a low base of US$4.0 billion in 2002, AfT disbursements to the region increased steadily to reach US$12.5 billion in 2016. Between 2002 and 2016, the region received US$142.1 billion in total AfT disbursements accounting for 31.1% of the total official development assistance.

Support for trade-related infrastructure equips developing countries with the preconditions to trade and promotes investments in quality infrastructure

Abundant evidence from empirical studies and case stories demonstrates that improving trade-related infrastructure helps reduce trade and transport costs, facilitates greater trade flows and market access, improves logistics performance and services delivery, enhances productivity and competitiveness and expands employment opportunities. For instance, Donaldson (2010) shows that India's railroads reduced trade costs and price differences across regions, increased inter-regional and international trade and raised real incomes and welfare. A more recent study by Lee (2017) also finds that AfT to infrastructure positively and significantly (though marginally) impacts bilateral exports of goods, particularly of mining and manufacturing products, as well as bilateral imports of mining products.

Case stories also point to related benefits. For instance, the Pacific Regional Connectivity Program – a programme financing an undersea fiber optic cable system linking Tonga to Fiji via the Southern Cross Cable – has facilitated high-speed internet connectivity and brought a wide range of benefits to Tongans, including

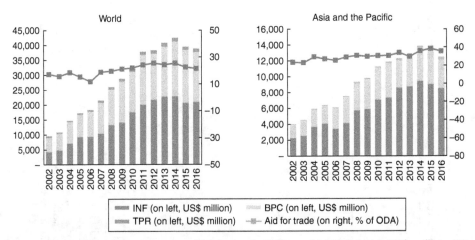

Figure 15.20   Official development assistance and aid for trade, 2002–2016 (US$ million, %).
Source: ADB calculations using data from OECD (n.d.a).
Note: Total aid for trade (AfT) is the sum of INF (aid for infrastructure), BPC (aid for building productive capacity), and TPR (trade policy and regulations and trade-related adjustment).

reducing connectivity costs by 60%; increasing international trade opportunities, specifically in tourism and business outsourcing; improving education and health services; and better facilitating other services such as bills payment, remittances and communication services at more affordable rates.

In Pakistan, the public and private sectors are increasingly getting involved in ICT infrastructure development and have made strides in providing a wide range of electronic services (including social welfare payments, citizen liaison services and automated border control), as well in driving e-commerce growth and developing innovative payment systems (Shah, 2017).

Meanwhile, under the Central Asia Regional Economic Cooperation Program (CAREC) Transport and Trade Facilitation Strategy, coordinated improvements of transport infrastructure and trade facilitation are recognised as key elements to improve the region's competitiveness and expand trade among member economies and with the rest of the world (ADB, 2009). These improvements were envisioned to result in significant and measurable reductions in transport costs and time for local, cross-border and transit traffic, and for trade along the corridors. The action plan for the Strategy focused on developing roads, railways, border crossing points along CAREC corridors, ports and a shipping route and airports. Significant progress was made in implementing the Strategy. As of end of 2012, 80% of the total 8640 km of the CAREC corridors had been built or improved (ADB, 2016b).

However, much remains to be done to improve connectivity and develop high-quality infrastructure networks in the region. ADB (2017e) estimates that the region's infrastructure investment needs amount to US$1.7 trillion per year, or US$26 trillion from 2016 to 2030, if the region is to keep up its growth momentum, eradicate poverty and respond to climate change.

Moreover, investments in upgrading ICT and energy infrastructure are needed more and more given fast-growing e-commerce and digital trade and the vast opportunities these offer to spur inclusive, trade-driven growth. Asia and the Pacific's e-commerce growth is contingent to the accessibility, affordability and reliability of ICT and energy infrastructure.

Support for building productive capacity helps promote employment and a more favorable business environment

Significant legal, regulatory and institutional constraints continue to hinder developing Asian economies from further enhancing their supply-side capacities and from tapping the contribution of other economic actors and stakeholders, especially the private sector. Building productive capacities can contribute by addressing market failures and advancing proactive industry-specific policies. In particular, aid to build productive capacities can make an impact by strengthening the capacity of domestic institutions; increasing efficiency in legal and regulatory reforms; raising firms' access to finance, markets and credit, especially for SMEs and female-owned enterprises; and capitalising on export-oriented services such as business services and tourism that have high potential to contribute to GDP and employment growth (ADB, 2017c; Hynes and Lammersen, 2017).

Aid targeted at tradable services sectors can be an important catalyst in promoting inclusive economic growth and structural transformation

A dynamic services economy can be a key driver of development, more so a functional and tradable services economy fosters universal access and helps ensure more efficient and equitable delivery. Digital technology in particular has been shown to offer a widening conduit for economies to increase trade and promote inclusive growth, and its great potential is recognised in its capacity to link businesses to markets that otherwise would be well beyond their reach.

However, the quality of policies, regulations and institutional frameworks remain significant hurdles to realising the full potential of the services and digital economies. Efforts to draw coherent domestic and international policies can improve the performance and competitiveness of services sectors, which provide vital support for all parts of an economy and play increasingly important roles in creating jobs and in opening up entrepreneurial opportunities for women. Regulations can facilitate modern trade in services and also deepen integration into regional markets, especially for those economies of Asia and the Pacific that face difficult trading conditions due to being remote.

AfT can boost trade in services and overcome regulatory barriers and other supply-side capacity constraints. Figure 15.21 shows that Asia and the Pacific is one of the major recipients of AfT in services, accounting for 37.6% of global AfT in services from 2002 to 2016. The largest beneficiaries have been Southeast, South and East Asian economies, while transport/storage and energy were the largest recipients by sector.

Finally, support for trade policy and regulatory reforms can broaden and strengthen the participation of developing countries in the institutions of global governance

Well-designed and economically sound trade policies play a significant role in improving domestic regulations and facilitating integration in international markets. Moreover, strong institutions cultivate the establishment of rule-based, transparent and accountable trading networks. However, without these institutional preconditions to trade, a dynamic and functional trading economy with the capacity to generate inclusive growth remains elusive.

Through aid for trade policy and regulations, AfT can help economies acquire the institutional preconditions to trade and be better equipped in adopting and implementing international cooperation and sustainable development strategies. In particular, AfT can contribute by providing trade education and training to national bodies involved in trade policies and regulations and reforms; equipping institutions in the analysis and implementation of trade agreements; and improving or fully implementing trade facilitation measures, such as simplification and harmonisation of international import and export procedures, among others. Further, AfT-related adjustment helps developing countries deal with the costs associated with trade liberalisation, as well as mitigate and compensate for the adverse impacts of trade changes and policy reforms, especially as they impact economically vulnerable groups (Hynes and Lammersen, 2017).

Given the volatility (and sometimes, even irony) of structural and regulatory reforms, AfT-related adjustment can make an impact by helping developing countries effectively adapt to changes in trade processes and cope with the negative socio-economic impacts and/or unintended consequences of trade liberalisation and regulatory reforms. In the case of employment and working conditions, AfT can contribute by supporting the

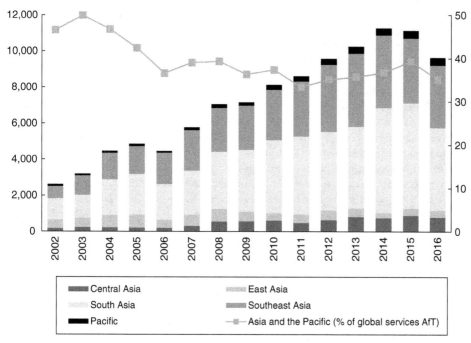

Figure 15.21   Distribution of aid for trade in services in Asia and the Pacific (US$ million).
Source: ADB calculations using data from OECD (n.d.a).
Note: In this study, aid for trade in services includes sectors that boost economic infrastructure – transport and storage, energy and communications – and those that increase productive capacity in an economy, which broadly are banking and finance, tourism, and business and other services.

Regardless of the level of development of the recipient economy, aid that enhances economic infrastructure and boosts productive capacity is positively correlated with services trade across Asia and the Pacific (ADB, 2017c). Empirical analysis shows a statistically and economically significant impact of AfT on services trade across all of Asia's subregions, most pronounced for South Asia and Southeast Asia. In particular, a 10% rise in AfT for services directly increases services trade by 0.4%.[11] Drawing from these results, well-targeted AfT interventions can generate inclusive growth, especially by boosting trade in services and e-commerce.

implementation of labour market policies that promote labour market efficiency and just employment practices; adjustment programmes that provide workers with social safety nets; and labour laws and programmes that help workers transition from one workplace to another (ADB, 2017c; Vandenberg, 2017). Ultimately, AfT can help countries achieve policy coherence by ensuring accountability and fostering a multi-stakeholder approach at the domestic and international levels.

Notes

1   The authors thank Kijin Kim for valuable comments, Eric van Zant for copy-editing the manuscript and Zemma Ardaniel and Ricardo Ang for research support. As indicated in the text, some sections of the chapter draw from the following Asian Development Bank publications listed in the references: ADB 2016a, 2017c; ADB and UNESCAP 2017.

2   Due to data limitations, earliest and latest years presented are those with most data available for Asian economies.

3   Because bilateral FDI flows before 2001 are not available, the intra-regional share cannot be calculated for years prior to 2001.

4   A firm-level data source that provides detailed information linking the global ultimate headquarters of multinationals and their affiliates (together with the international trade orientation of these affiliates) allows identifying the investments projects aimed at linking to international production networks/global value chains, i.e. GVC-FDI.

5   ADB broadly defines inclusive growth as growth with social equity and comprising (i) high, sustainable growth to create and expand economic opportunities; (ii) broader access to these opportunities to ensure that members of society can participate and benefit from growth; and (iii) social safety nets to prevent extreme deprivation (ADB, 2014).

6   To curb financing gaps, financial technology must address the due diligence challenges associated with performance and compliance risks. In particular, implementing firm identification solutions and harmonising digital standards in the financial and trade sectors are crucial (DiCaprio *et al.*, 2017).

7   Including the developed economies of Australia, Japan and New Zealand, services-trade-to-GDP ratio is equivalent 5.7% during the same period.

8   Including the developed economies of Australia, Japan and New Zealand.

9   In 2012, the UNESCAP Secretariat – in conjunction with the Asia-Pacific Trade Facilitation Forum organised by UNESCAP and ADB – conducted the first regional survey on the implementation of trade facilitation and paperless trade. A second regional survey was conducted in 2017. It covers 47 trade facilitation measures divided into seven groups: (i) general trade facilitation measures, (ii) paperless trade, (iii) cross-border paperless trade, (iv) transit facilitation, (v) trade facilitation for SMEs, (vi) agricultural trade facilitation and (vii) women in trade facilitation. (More details on methodology and the survey questionnaire are available at https://unnext.unescap.org/content/global-survey-trade-facilitation-and-paperless-trade-implementation-2017.) Asia includes Afghanistan, Armenia, Azerbaijan, Bangladesh, Bhutan, Brunei Darussalam, Cambodia, Federated States of Micronesia, Fiji, India, Indonesia, Japan, Kazakhstan, Kiribati, Kyrgyz Republic, Lao PDR, Malaysia, Maldives, Mongolia, Myanmar, Nauru, Nepal, Pakistan, Palau, Papua New Guinea, People's Republic of China, Philippines, Republic of Korea, Samoa, Singapore, Solomon Islands, Sri Lanka, Tajikistan, Thailand, Tonga, Tuvalu, Uzbekistan, Vanuatu and Vietnam.

10 More specifically, a 10% increase in AfT disbursement is associated with a 1.77% increase in the labour force participation rate for women and 1.22% for men; further segregating into AfT's primary components, a 10% increase in AfT disbursement for building productive capacity promotes 1.57% more labour force participation.

11 Besides services trade, ADB (2017c) finds that AfT has positive implications for FDI – that is, AfT increases greenfield FDI in all industries (primary, manufacturing and services industries) and boosts cross-border mergers and acquisitions in manufacturing and services industries. In general, this direct impact of AfT on services trade and foreign investment can contribute to economic growth and fuel the trading potential of recipient economies.

References

Acemoglu, D. (2003) Labor- and Capital-Augmenting Technical Change. *Journal of European Economic Association*, 1(1), 1–37.

Akamatsu, K. (1962) A Historical Pattern of Economic Growth in Developing Countries. *Developing Economies*, 1(1), 3–25.

Antras, P. & Yeaple, S. (2014) Multinational Firms and the Structure of International Trade. *Handbook of International Economics*, 4, 55–130.

Asian Development Bank (2009) CAREC Transport and Trade Facilitation: Partnership for Prosperity. Retrieved from: https://www.adb.org/sites/default/files/publication/27534/carec-transpo-trade-facilitation.pdf (accessed 12 July 2019).

Asian Development Bank (2014) Midterm Review of Strategy 2020: Meeting the Challenges of a Transforming Asia and Pacific. Retrieved from: https://www.adb.org/sites/default/files/institutional-document/34149/files/midterm-review-strategy-2020-r-paper.pdf (accessed 12 July 2019).

Asian Development Bank (2015) *Women in the Workforce: An Unmet Potential in Asia and the Pacific*. Manila: ADB.

Asian Development Bank (2016a) *Asian Economic Integration Report 2016: What Drives Foreign Direct Investment in Asia and the Pacific?* Manila: ADB.

Asian Development Bank (2016b) Central Asia Regional Economic Cooperation: Midterm Review of the Transport and Trade Facilitation Strategy and Implementation Action Plan. Retrieved from: https://www.adb.org/sites/default/files/project-document/184512/46263-001-tcr.pdf (accessed 12 July 2019).

Asian Development Bank (2017a) *Asian Development Outlook (ADO) 2017: Transcending the Middle-Income Challenge*. Manila: ADB.

Asian Development Bank (2017b) *Asian Economic Integration Report 2017: The Era of Financial Interconnectedness. How Can Asia Strengthen Financial Resilience?* Manila: ADB.

Asian Development Bank (2017c) *Aid for Trade in Asia and the Pacific: Promoting Connectivity for Inclusive Development*. Manila: ADB.

Asian Development Bank (2017d) *Banking on the Future of Asia and the Pacific: 50 Years of the Asian Development Bank*. Manila: ADB.

Asian Development Bank (2017e) *Meeting Asia's Infrastructure Needs*. Manila: ADB.

Asian Development Bank (2018) *Asian Economic Integration Report 2018: Toward Optimal Provision of Regional Public Goods in Asia and the Pacific*. Manila: ADB.

Asian Development Bank & UNESCAP (2013) *Designing and Implementing Trade Facilitation in Asia and the Pacific: 2013 Update*. Retrieved from: https://aric.adb.org/pdf/Trade_Facilitation_Reference_Book.pdf (accessed 12 July 2019).

Asian Development Bank & UNESCAP (2017) *Trade Facilitation and Better Connectivity for an Inclusive Asia and Pacific*. Manila: ADB.

Aswicahyono, H., Brooks, D. & Manning, C. (2014) Exports and Employment in Indonesia: The Decline in Labor-Intensive Manufacturing and the Rise of Services. In: Khor, N. & Mitra, D. (eds.) *Trade and Employment in Asia. Abingdon*: Asian Development Bank and Routledge, pp. 176–203.

Athukorala, P. (2014) Intra-Regional FDI and Economic Integration in South Asia: Trends, Patterns and Prospects. *South Asia Economic Journal*, 15(1), 1–35.

Athukorala, P. (2017) Global Productions Sharing and Local Entrepreneurship in Developing Countries: Evidence from Penang Export Hub, Malaysia. *Asia and the Pacific Policy Studies*, 4(2), 180–194.

Bangladesh, Planning Commission (2016) *Seventh Five-Year Plan FY2016–FY2020*. Retrieved from: http://plancomm.portal.gov.bd/sites/default/files/files/plancomm.portal.gov.bd/files/aee61c03_3c11_4e89_9f30_d79639595c67/7th_FYP_18_02_2016.pdf (accessed 12 July 2019).

Bentolila, S. & Saint-Paul, G. (2003) Explaining Movements in the Labor Share. *Contributions to Macroeconomics*, 3(1), 1–31.

Borchert, I., Gootiiz, B. & Mattoo, A. (2014) Policy Barriers to International Trade in Services: Evidence from a New Database. *World Bank Economic Review*, 28(1), 162–188.

Cai, F. & Du, Y. (2014) Exports and Employment in the People's Republic of China. In: Khor, N. & Mitra, D. (eds.) *Trade and Employment in Asia*. Abingdon: Asian Development Bank and Routledge, pp. 120–141.

Constantinescu, C., Mattoo, A. & Ruta, M. (2015) The Global Trade Slowdown: Cyclical or Structural? *IMF Working Paper* WP/15/16. Retrieved from: https://www.imf.org/external/pubs/ft/wp/2015/wp1506.pdf (accessed 12 July 2019).

Dao, M.C., Das, M., Koczan, Z. & Lian, W. (2017) Drivers of Declining Labor Share of Income. Weblog. Retrieved from: https://blogs.imf.org/2017/04/12/drivers-of-declining-labor-share-of-income/ (accessed 12 July 2019).

DiCaprio, A., Kim, K. & Beck, S. (2017) 2017 Trade Finance Gaps, Growth, and Jobs Survey. *ADB Briefs* No. 83. Retrieved from: https://www.adb.org/sites/default/files/publication/359631/adb-briefs-83.pdf (accessed 12 July 2019).

Donaldson, D. (2010) Railroads of the Raj: Estimating the Impact of Transportation Infrastructure. *NBER Working Paper* No. 16487. Retrieved from: http://eprints.lse.ac.uk/38368/1/ARCWP41-Donaldson.pdf (accessed 12 July 2019).

Dutt, P., Mitra, D. & Ranjan, P. (2009) International Trade and Unemployment: Theory and Cross-National Evidence. *Journal of International Economics*, 78, 32–44.

eCommerce Foundation (2016) Global B2C E-commerce Report 2016. Retrieved from: http://www.netcommsuisse.ch/dam/jcr:969b0986-e927-4a40-baf3-ad4aa123fecd/Ecommerce%2520Foundation_Global%2520B2C%2520Ecommerce%2520Report%25202016_SeC16.pdf (accessed 12 July 2019).

Edmonds, E. & Pavcnik, N. (2004) International Trade and Child Labor: Cross-Country Evidence. *NBER Working Paper* No. 10317. Retrieved from: https://www.nber.org/papers/w10317.pdf (accessed 12 July 2019).

eMarketer (n.d.) Retrieved from: https://www.emarketer.com/ (accessed 24 July 2019).

Errighi, L., Bodwell, C. & Khatiwada, S. (2016) Business Process Outsourcing in the Philippines: Challenges for Decent Work. Retrieved from: https://www.ilo.org/wcmsp5/groups/public/---asia/---ro-bangkok/---sro-bangkok/documents/publication/wcms_538193.pdf (accessed 12 July 2019).

Felbermayr, G., Prat, J. & Schmerer, H.J. (2011) Trade and Unemployment: What Do the Data Say? *European Economic Review*, 55(60), 741–758.

Fox, A., François, J. & Londono-Kent, P. (2003) Measuring Border Crossing Costs and their Impact on Trade Flows: The United-States-Mexico Trucking Car. Retrieved from: https://www.gtap.agecon.purdue.edu/resources/download/1492.pdf (accessed 12 July 2019).

Harrison, A. & Rodriguez-Clare, A. (2010) Trade, Foreign Investment, and Industrial Policy for Developing Countries. In: Rodrik, D. & Rosenzweig, M. (eds.) *Handbook of Development Economics*, Vol. 5. Amsterdam: North Holland, pp. 4039–4214.

Heath, R. & Mobarak, A.M. (2015) Manufacturing Growth and the Lives of Bangladeshi Women. *Journal of Development Economics*, 115, 1–15.

Hoekman, B. (2017) Supporting Services Trade Negotiations. In: Hoekman, B. and te Velde, D.W. (eds.) *Trade in Services and Economic Transformation: A New Development Policy Priority*. London: Overseas Development Institute. Retrieved from: http://cadmus.eui.eu/bitstream/handle/1814/45504/SET-essays_2017_02.pdf?sequence=1&isAllowed=y (accessed 12 July 2019).

Hoekman, B. & Mattoo, A. (2011) Services Trade Liberalization and Regulatory Reform: Re-invigorating International Cooperation. *World Bank Policy Research Working Paper* No. 5517. Retrieved from: http://documents.worldbank.org/curated/en/259531468153848623/pdf/WPS5517.pdf (accessed 12 July 2019).

Hoekman, B. & Shepherd, B. (2015) Who Profits from Trade Facilitation Initiatives? Implications for African countries. *Journal of African Trade*, 2(1–2), 51–70.

Hoekman, B. & te Velde, D.W. (eds.) (2017) *Trade in Services and Economic Transformation: A New Development Policy Priority*. London: Overseas Development Institute. Retrieved from: http://cadmus.eui.eu/bitstream/handle/1814/45504/SET-essays_2017_02.pdf?sequence=1&isAllowed=y (accessed 12 July 2019).

Hynes, W. & Lammersen, F. (2017) Facilitate Trade for Development: Aid for Trade. In: Helble, M. & Shepherd, B. *Win–Win How International Trade Can Help Meet the Sustainable Development Goals*. Tokyo: Asian Development Bank Institute, pp. 488–529. Retrieved from: https://www.adb.org/sites/default/files/publication/327451/adbi-win-win-how-international-trade-can-help-meet-sdgs.pdf (accessed 12 July 2019).

International Labour Organization (n.d.a) ILOSTAT. Retrieved from: http://www.ilo.org/ilostat/ (accessed 1 November 2017).

International Monetary Fund (n.d.a) Direction of Trade Statistics. Retrieved from: http://data. imf.org/ (accessed 1 October 2017a).

International Monetary Fund (2017b) World Economic Outlook: Gaining Momentum? Retrieved from: https://www.imf.org/~/media/Files/Publications/WEO/2017/April/pdf/text. ashx (accessed 12 July 2019).

International Monetary Fund (2009) *Balance of Payments and International Investment Position Manual – Sixth Edition* (BPM6). Retrieved from: https://www.imf.org/external/ pubs/ft/bop/2007/pdf/bpm6.pdf (accessed 19 July 2019).

International Telecommunication Union (n.d.a). Retrieved from: https://www.itu.int/en/ ITU-D/Statistics/Pages/stat/default.aspx (accessed 1 June 2018).

International Trade Centre (n.d.a) Trade Map. Retrieved from: http://www.trademap.org (accessed June 2018).

James, W.E., Naya, S. & Meier, G.M. (1989) *Asian Development: Economic Success and Policy Lessons*. Madison: University of Wisconsin Press.

Krueger, A.B. (1999) Measuring Labor's Share. *The American Economic Review*, 89(2), 45–51.

Lee, H.H. (2017) Effects of Aid for Trade (AfT) on Trade and Foreign Direct Investments: A Comprehensive Analysis. Background paper prepared for Aid for Trade in Asia and the Pacific Report 2017. Manuscript.

Lee J.-W. & Hong, K. (2012) Economic growth in Asia: Determinants and Prospects. *Japan and the World Economy*, 24, 101–113.

Martinez-Zarzoso, I. & Marquez-Ramos, L. (2008) The Effect of Trade Facilitation on Sectoral Trade. *The B.E. Journal of Economic Analysis & Policy*, 8(1), 1–46.

Milberg, W. & Winkler, D. (2013) *Global Value Chains in Capitalist Development*. Cambridge: Cambridge University Press.

Monetary Authority of Singapore (2016) The Evolving Pattern of Production and Trade Networks in Asia. *Macroeconomic Review*, XV(2), 80–90. Retrieved from: https:// www.mas.gov.sg/-/media/MAS/resource/publications/macro_review/2016/Oct-16/ SF-A--The-Evolving-Pattern-Of-Production-And-Trade-Networks-In-Asia.pdf (accessed 12 July 2019).

Moore, M. & Ranjan, P. (2005) Globalization and Skill-Biased Technological Change: Implications for Unemployment and Wage Inequality. *Economic Journal*, 115, 341–422.

OECD (n.d.a) Creditor Reporting System. Retrieved from: https://stats.oecd.org/Index. aspx?DataSetCode=CRS1 (accessed June 2018).

OECD (2009) Overcoming Border Bottlenecks: The Costs and Benefits of Trade Facilitation. OECD Trade Policy Studies. Paris: OECD Publishing.

Park, C-Y. (2011) Asian Financial System: Development and Challenges. *ADB Economics Working Paper* No. 285. Retrieved from: https://www.adb.org/sites/default/files/publication/30442/ economics-wp285.pdf (accessed 12 July 2019).

Park, D. & Noland, M. (eds.) (2013) *Developing the Service Sector as an Engine of Growth for Asia*. Manila: ADB.

Park, C., Khan, F. & Justo, C.J. (2017a) Unlocking Trade Potential in Services through Digitalization. Weblog. Retrieved from: https://blogs.adb.org/blog/unlocking-trade- potential-services-through-digitalization (accessed 12 July 2019).

Park, C., Khan, F. & Justo, C.J. (2017b) How Southeast Asia Can Maximize e-Commerce Opportunities. Weblog. Retrieved from: https://blogs.adb.org/blog/how-southeast-asia-can- maximize-e-commerce-opportunities (accessed 12 July 2019).

Penn World Tables Version 8.0 (n.d.a). Retrieved from: http://cid.econ.ucdavis.edu/pwt.html (accessed 1 November 2017).

PricewaterhouseCoopers & NASSCOM (2016) Making Diversity Work: Key Trends and Practices in the Indian ITBPM Industry. Retrieved from: https://www.pwc.in/assets/pdfs/ publications/2016/making-diversity-work-key-trends-and-practices-in-the-indian-it-bpm- industry.pdf (accessed 12 July 2019).

Redding, S.J. & Turner, M.A. (2015) Transportation Costs and the Spatial Organization of Economic Activity. In: Duranton, G., Henderson, J.V. & Strange W.C. (eds.) *Handbook of Regional and Urban Economics*, Vol. 5A. Amsterdam: Elsevier, pp. 1339–1398.

Rippel, B. (2011) Why Trade Facilitation is Important for Africa. *Africa Trade Policy Notes* No.27:Retrievedfrom:http://documents.worldbank.org/curated/en/676621468201835737/pdf/663200BRI0AFR00757B000PUBLIC00trade.pdf (accessed 12 July 2019).

Rodrik, D. (1998) *Capital Mobility and Labor*. Cambridge, MA: Harvard University Press.

Shah, T. (2017) Pakistan's Digital Economy: National Perspectives on Bridging the Digital Divide. Public Sector Case Story 87. OECD-WTO. Retrieved from: http://www.oecd.org/aidfortrade/casestories/casestories-2017/CS-87-Pakistan-Digital-Economy.pdf (accessed 12 July 2019).

Silvander, J. (2013) *Gender Equality in Global Value Chains and the Role of Aid for Trade in Promoting Gender Equality and Women's Employment in Developing Countries*. Helsinki, Ministry for Foreign Affairs of Finland.

SME Finance Forum (n.d.) MSME Country Indicators Database. Retrieved from: https://www.smefinanceforum.org (accessed 1 June 2017).

UNESCAP (2016) Framework Agreement on Facilitation of Cross-border Paperless Trade in Asia and the Pacific. Retrieved from: http://www.un.org/ga/search/view_doc.asp?symbol=E/ESCAP/RES/72/4&Lang=E (accessed 12 July 2019).

UNESCAP (2017) Trade Facilitation and Paperless Trade Implementation in Asia and the Pacific: Regional Report 2017. Retrieved from: https://www.unescap.org/sites/default/files/Regional_Report%20-%20v3%2B%2B.pdf (accessed 12 July 2019).

United Nations (n.d.a) Commodity Trade Database. Retrieved from: https://comtrade.un.org/data/ (accessed June 2017a).

United Nations (n.d.b) Extended Balance of Payments Services Classification 2002 (EBOPS 2002). https://unstats.un.org/unsd/tradekb/Knowledgebase/EBOPS-2002 (accessed 19 July 2019).

United Nations (2017b) UN Global Survey on Trade Facilitation and Paperless Trade Implementation 2017. Retrieved from: https://unnext.unescap.org/AP-TFSurvey2017/ (accessed 12 July 2019).

United Nations Conference on Trade and Development (n.d.a) UNCTADstat. Retrieved from: http://unctadstat.unctad.org (accessed 1 October 2017).

United Nations Conference on Trade and Development (2013) *World Investment Report 2013: Global Value Chains: Investment and Trade for Development*. Geneva: United Nations. Retrieved from: http://unctad.org/en/PublicationsLibrary/wir2013_en.pdf (accessed 12 July 2019).

Vandenberg, P. (2017) Can Trade Help Achieve the Employment Targets of the Sustainable Development Goals? In: Helble, M. & Shepherd, B. *Win–Win: How International Trade Can Help Meet the Sustainable Development Goals*. Tokyo: Asian Development Bank Institute, pp. 139–174. Retrieved from: https://www.adb.org/sites/default/files/publication/327451/adbi-win-win-how-international-trade-can-help-meet-sdgs.pdf (accessed 12 July 2019).

Vere, J. (2014) Trade and Employment in Hong Kong, China: Towards a Service Economy. In: Khor, N. & Mitra, D. (eds.) *Trade and Employment in Asia*. Abingdon: Development Bank and Routledge, pp. 142–175.

World Bank (n.d.a) Analytical Income Classification of Economies. Retrieved from: https://datahelpdesk.worldbank.org/knowledgebase/articles/906519-world-bank-country-and-lending-groups (accessed July 2019).

World Bank (n.d.b) World Development Indicators. Retrieved from: https://data.worldbank.org (accessed October 2017a).

World Bank (n.d.c) PovcalNet Database. Retrieved from: http://iresearch.worldbank.org/PovcalNet/home.aspx (accessed 1 June 2018).

World Bank (n.d.d) Enterprise Surveys. Retrieved from: http://www.enterprisesurveys.org/ (accessed 1 November 2017b).

World Bank (1993) *The East Asian Miracle: Economic Growth and Public Policy*. Oxford: Oxford University Press.

World Trade Organization (n.d.a) Statistics Database. Retrieved from: http://stat.wto.org (accessed 1 June 2018).

World Trade Organization (2015) *World Trade Report 2015 – Speeding up Trade: Benefits and Challenges of Implementing the WTO Trade Facilitation Agreement*. Geneva: World Trade Organization. Retrieved from: https://www.wto.org/english/res_e/booksp_e/world_trade_report15_e.pdf (accessed 12 July 2019).

Yoshino, N. & Wignaraja, G. (2015) SMEs Internationalization and Finance in Asia. Presentation at Frontier and Developing Asia: Supporting Rapid and Inclusive Growth, IMF-JICA Conference, Tokyo, 18 February. Retrieved from: https://www.imf.org/external/np/seminars/eng/2015/jica2015/pdf/1-B1.pdf (accessed 12 July 2019).

Chapter 16

Institutional Capacity, Trade and Investment in African Economies

Roseline Wanjiru and Karla Simone Prime

Introduction

In recent times, diverse African economies have made efforts to integrate their economies into international trade and investment networks as a result of intensified globalisation. The consequent reorganisation of their economic and political institutions to support and absorb foreign trade and investment flows has drawn academic and policy attention to the region, enhancing the scrutiny of regional trade and investment policies. Enduring debates over the domestic impacts of foreign investment persist, notwithstanding the reality of public interventions by governments to lift barriers as part of investment promotion and an international competition for capital flows (Phelps *et al.*, 2007). Following the last global recession, multiple African economies continue to demonstrate considerable resilience against a turbulent background characterised by steadily declining global investment inflows.

Official estimates underline the contraction of foreign direct investment (FDI) flows into Africa; in 2017, FDI contracted by 21% (totalling US$42 billion), in contrast to record flows of investment recorded over the preceding decade, exceeding US$72 billion in 2008 for example (UNCTAD, 2013; 2018). Alongside these declines, the distribution of flows across economies has been varied. The largest flows of investment to Africa in 2016 went to Angola (US$14.4 billion), Egypt (US$8.1 billion), Nigeria (US$4.4 billion), Ghana (US$3.5 billion) and Ethiopia (US$3.2 billion). Total flows going into African economies, however, pale in comparison to the flows into other developing regions for the same period. In Asia, for example, the largest flows in 2016 went to Singapore (US$61.6 billion), India (US$44.5 billion) and Vietnam (US$12.6 billion); while for the Latin America and Caribbean region, the largest flows went to Brazil (US$58.7 billion), Mexico (US$26.7 billion), Colombia (US$13.6 billion), Chile (US$11.3 billion) and Peru (US$6.9 billion) for

The Handbook of Global Trade Policy, First Edition. Edited by Andreas Klasen.

the same period (UNCTAD, 2017). It is therefore apparent that total FDI flows into Sub-Saharan Africa (SSA) make up only a small fraction of total global flows.

The distribution of investment flows into SSA remains primarily concentrated within narrow extractive sectors reliant on natural resources. Recent shifts into services and the manufacturing sectors have been noted in isolated economies of southern and eastern Africa where they comprise small but growing shares of inward FDI. The entry of new trade partners from China, India and Brazil and the rise of intra-regional trade with South Africa have generated new sources of investment, contributing to new patterns of investment for the region.

This chapter investigates the changing trade and economic performance of African economies and the influence which institutional capacities in different host economies have on the country's economic performance. Building upon insights from existing empirical studies, we focus on the role of institutions and their respective influence on trade and investment performance within African host countries. In this study, we specifically investigate institutions as key factors impacting the current performances on trade and inward FDI flows within African economies.

The rest of this chapter is set out as follows; an overview of the literature on foreign investment and trade is followed by a section on institutions for trade policy and investment in Africa. We next discuss the impact of institutional quality on inward FDI flows in the studied African economies and set out the framework and data used to empirically estimate the relationship between institutional quality and FDI. Subsequent sections outline the data and methods used to test this relationship, followed by a section setting out the results and the subsequent discussion of the findings. The concluding section addresses the implications of our results and discusses areas for further research.

Foreign Direct Investment, Trade and Economic Growth in Africa

The role of FDI in economic growth within Africa has received significant attention in academic and policy research. Policy concerns on the necessity to address investment gaps and limited access to technology are prevalent in official government statements and echoed in multiple World Bank and development partners' engagements within the African continent.

Established academic research on the contribution of FDI towards economic growth has focused on the impacts as well as determinants of FDI in the economic growth of developing economies. FDI is argued to contribute to capital for investment (Borensztein et al., 1998; Kohpaiboon, 2003) and to enhanced opportunities for employment of local workers, as well as access to improved managerial skills and expertise and access to enhanced technology (Asiedu, 2002; Bannaga et al., 2013; Bénassy-Quéré et al., 2007; de Mello, 1999; Ullah and Khan, 2017).

In evaluating the determinants of trade performance and FDI flows on economic growth, a range of studies further demonstrate the relevance of macroeconomic factors such as stability, market size, productivity, labour costs, infrastructure and tax regimes (Ang, 2008; Asiedu, 2006; Bevan and Estrin, 2004; Billington, 1999; Buckley et al., 2007; Faeth, 2009). The importance of political stability is further highlighted (Gani, 2007; Kolstad and Villanger, 2008; Mengistu and Adhikary, 2011; Morrissey and Udomkerdmongkol, 2012; Naude and Krugell, 2007; Obwona, 2001;

Ok, 2004). Both factors are demonstrably imperative in the ability of countries to attract investment inflows. These political and macroeconomic stability factors are particularly relevant when analysing the performance of African economies in attracting and absorbing FDI to support economic growth. Cross-country trends of FDI inflows vary significantly among African countries, with particular countries seen to perform better at attracting FDI compared to their counterparts.

Alongside conventional stability measures, an established body of research supported by empirical studies emphasizes the relationship between the quality of a country's institutions and the resulting investment inflows. These studies investigate the institution-growth relationship specifically within emerging markets (Bussiere and Fratzscher, 2008; Contractor *et al.*, 2014; Strange *et al.*, 2009) and additionally in developing countries (Buthe and Milner, 2008; Globerman and Shapiro, 2002; Jensen, 2008; Li, 2006; Li and Resnick, 2003; Neumayer and Spess, 2005). This study seeks to contribute to this debate by investigating these factors within the African context.

In this chapter, we build upon the insights of existing empirical studies with a specific focus on the role of different types of institutions in trade and investment performance within host countries in SSA. The study investigates institutions as key factors impacting the current performance of trade and inward FDI flows within African economies.

The Influence of Institutions on Trade Policy and Inward FDI in Developing Countries

Existing literature provides a broad framework suggesting that institutions play a significant role in the attraction of FDI and the support of trade. Institutions are defined by North (1991) as "humanly devised constraints that structure political, economic and social interaction", and these are a key channel by which FDI can be attracted and trade activities facilitated. Institutions are observable through individual purposive behaviour within societies and economies (Tauheed, 2013). This "effect" approach enables the analysis of institutions to focus on their operational classification, ranging from patterned behaviour and practices; social relations and interactions; cultural beliefs, norms and expectations; rules and procedures; ideology; social policies; legal systems and statuses; to constraints, hierarchies and power. North (1990) summarises institutions in terms of incentives in human exchange, whether political, social or economic. Institutions are not concerned with the aggregation of individual behaviour, but with the high-order factors that influence societal processes as well as outcomes tending to produce patterns or stasis.

Longstanding differences on which are the most appropriate policies that governments should adopt towards inward and outward investment persist. These differences form the backdrop against which countries offer tax breaks or preferential regulations in efforts to attract and maintain FDI. Within African economies, attention is paid to the role of trade policies and incentives provided by African host governments to encourage foreign investors. It is important to recognise that the investment decisions taken by multinational enterprises to locate within particular African countries are influenced to a large extent by endogenous institutional factors. As part of neoliberal opening up of domestic markets (Wanjiru, 2013; Phelps *et al.*,

2007), a variety of incentives have been widely adopted by multiple African governments in efforts to achieve competitiveness. As demonstrated by Petrović-Ranđelović *et al.* (2013), these decisions may be weighed up against other factors, particularly when taken together with the source of FDI, and whether the investment is from advanced economies like the United States, United Kingdom, France or Germany, where home firms are offered foreign tax credits. In such instances, certain types of fiscal incentives offered by host countries may have very little effect on the firms' eventual location decisions.

Host countries with market-based institutions that constrain opportunistic behaviour can encourage foreign competition and allow multinational enterprises (MNEs) to exploit overseas ownership advantages (Bailey, 2018). These types of governance infrastructure can have the effect of reducing costs and increasing host-country attractiveness for FDI (Grosse and Trevino, 1996). In this regard, market-legitimising institutions are beneficial as they permit efficiency-seeking investors to realise cost-saving benefits of internalising production and protect intellectual property from being appropriated (Bailey, 2018; Rodrik *et al.*, 2004). Trade policies designed to promote trade openness on average tend to have a robust positive effect on growth and investment rates (Wacziarg and Welch, 2008).

Second, the type of investment project influences the investment decision; where the project is short-term, "footloose" investment, such as banking, insurance, internet etc., tends to benefit the most from fiscal incentives such as tax holidays compared to their alternatives. Third, there is need to pay attention to the investors' motivation for the investment. If the investment is natural-resource or market seeking, fiscal incentives offered could only be a relatively minor determinant of inward FDI. Pike *et al.* (2015) suggest that the cost of domestic labour and the state of the governance infrastructure are more significant determinants of inward FDI. Lower labour costs and "good" governance infrastructure provide investors with assurances that their investment will remain "safe" and not likely to be vulnerable to expropriation.

When categorising institutions, emergent typologies consider which institutions may be "good" or "bad" for economic growth. "Good" institutions are expected to exert a positive influence on FDI inflows through a reduction in transaction costs (Bailey, 2018; Grosse and Trevino, 1996; Rodrik *et al.*, 2004); by reducing the liability of foreignness (Nelson and Sampat, 2001; Pike *et al.*, 2015); and by providing certainty and higher rates of returns (Bénassy-Quéré *et al.*, 2007; Buchanan *et al.*, 2012a; Daude and Stein, 2007; Globerman and Shapiro, 2003; Kurul, 2017; Kurul and Yalta, 2017). "Bad" institutions, on the other hand, act as a tax and increase the cost of FDI, with particular attention to the weak enforcement of property rights: the imperfect implementation of contracts, risk of expropriation of assets, high levels of corruption and political instability which all increase the uncertainty of future returns from investment (Buchanan *et al.*, 2012a; Daude and Stein, 2007; Globerman and Shapiro, 2002, 2003).

Sound institutional environments within Sub-Saharan African economies could therefore be expected to reduce perceived risks to investments. The majority of the cited studies investigating the role of institutions have tended to focus on larger, more developed and well-resourced economies as the cases for their conclusions. Conversely, a study by Wanjiru and Prime (2018) investigated the influence of institutions within smaller, more vulnerable and less well-resourced developing economies such as those in the Caribbean. This study, which focused on the impact of institutions on productivity and output, highlighted the influence of regulatory and legitimising institutions on the levels of economic productivity achieved by developing countries, and concluded that certain types of institutions appeared to matter more for growth than others.

The quality of institutions within empirical studies is often measured in terms of government efficiency, the incidence of minimal policy reversals, efficient and strong enforcement of property rights and the stability of legal systems. A key limitation when investigating the effects of these particular institutional measures as applied within policy and academic research is the problem of reverse causality. Higher levels of GDP per capita can increase the national capacity to improve institutions; at the same time, improved institutions increase the national capacity for productivity thereby increasing GDP per capita. Similarly, increased FDI flows can put pressure on governments to improve the quality of their existing institutions (Selowsky and Martin, 1997), alongside the reverse where improved institutions are argued to lead to increased FDI inflows. A positive correlation between institutions and FDI could be the result of the correlation between institutions and GDP per capita (Rodrik *et al.*, 2004). In addition, institutions and their quality are endogenous, shaped in part by income levels in respective countries. As a result, this may create issues of endogeneity and reverse causality in empirical studies of the interrelationship among the three factors.

Country-specific political and legal institutions can be defined as the governance infrastructure in a country (Globerman and Shapiro, 2003). The quality of the governance infrastructure affects the overall investment environment within a country for both domestic and foreign investors (Buchanan *et al.*, 2012b; Globerman and Shapiro, 2003). Daude and Stein (2007) contend that better governance infrastructure has a positive and economically significant effect on trade performance and FDI, with some institutional aspects being more important than others are for attracting investment. Governance infrastructure affects FDI through two main channels: (i) increasing transaction costs of FDI by acting as an additional tax (Bailey, 2018); or (ii) weak governance structures increasing uncertainty and perceived risk of investments (Buchanan *et al.*, 2012b; Daude and Stein, 2007; Globerman and Shapiro, 2002, 2003; Kurul, 2017).

Institutional frameworks comprise both formal and informal institutions in an economy. North describes these as a continuum, with unwritten taboos, customs and traditions at one end and constitutions and laws governing economics and politics at the other (1991). In the absence of formal rules, social networks in a particular economy begin to develop through customs, laws, trust and normative rules that create the informal institutional frameworks (Leftwich and Sen, 2011). The absence of formal rules or useful rules or even the existence of suboptimal rules or the poor enforcement of formal rules all contribute to weak governance structures, as is common in many developing and emerging economies in Africa, Asia and Latin America.

A measure of rights is required to protect economic exchanges through policing and enforcement of agreements. The more complex the economic exchange, the more costly it becomes to protect economic exchanges which occur through the institutional framework. If the costs of protecting those exchanges are prohibitive,

Aaron (2000) suggests it may not be worth devising rules, causing rights to remain undefined. Similarly, existing rules may not be enforced, where the enforcement and monitoring are too costly. A governance structure comprised of institutions that encourage long-term contracting may be therefore essential for investment and economic growth (Aaron, 2000).

Nelson and Sampat (2001) argue that institutions define a structure for behaviour within the market by securing private property, providing clarity and enforcing contracts. These "good" institutions make certain kinds of transactions and interactions within the market more attractive or easier, supporting the productivity of labour and capital (Nelson and Sampat, 2001). This view is supported by Hall *et al.* (2010), who find evidence that "good" institutions as characterised by social, political and legal rules (which provide secure property rights, unbiased contract enforcement) appeared to have a positive impact on productivity through improved levels of physical and human capital accumulation. Conversely "poor" institutions resulted in higher returns to investment in rent-seeking activities which plunder the wealth of others and hinder levels of productivity (Hall *et al.*, 2010). The differences in capital accumulation and productivity across countries can therefore be attributed to differences in institutions and government policies that determine the economic environment. As identified in an empirical study by Hall and Jones (1999), countries with long-standing policies favourable to productive activities produced much more output per worker, compared to those where there was diversion through expropriation, confiscatory taxation or corruption by the government. A favourable governance infrastructure promotes rules and institutions that support productive activities, skills acquisition, invention and technology transfer and protect output from predation and diversion (Hall and Jones, 1996; 1999).

Good institutions clearly define the boundaries within which MNEs can interact with the host-country economy, thereby enabling transactions at lower costs. The logical outcome of good institutions is, therefore, increased incentive to invest. Over the past two decades, there have been numerous papers that have examined the relationship between economic growth and inward FDI. Fewer researchers have examined the impact of governance infrastructure on incentives for inward FDI. Researchers have demonstrated that governance characteristics that define the rules of the game have an impact on inward FDI, as opposed to other factors such as geography and economic growth. In particular, studies have argued that the nature of property rights, legal institutions and labour market institutions is key for inward FDI. However, the results have been mixed and the debate about the nature of the relationship between governance structures and inward FDI is far from over.

To the extent that governance and institutional quality are complements, institutional quality may increase inward FDI. Aizenman and Spiegel (2006) argue that countries that have weak enforcement of property rights should experience lower inward FDI. The institutional distance between the investment home country and the host country should have a negative impact on bilateral FDI. What the academic literature refers to as the "psychic distance" contributes to the impact of institutional quality on the levels of inward FDI. Higher "psychic distance" could increase the perceived risks associated with investment. "Psychic proximity" reduces investors' perceived uncertainty or learning costs about target countries (Bénassy-Quéré *et al.*, 2007). Similar economic and social history, including colonisation, have an influence on the "psychic proximity" between investor and target countries, which may be observed in the persistence of historical factors on institutional quality – "persistence" here referring to the causal effect of the historical level of the quality of institutions on their contemporary levels.

Measuring Institutional Quality in African Developing Economies

Cross-country comparisons of institutions can be often difficult to measure as institutions are multifaceted and encompass a range of attributes. Indeed, different institutional attributes could matter at different stages of economic development within particular developing countries. De Crombrugghe and Farla (2012) view this "institutionally heterogeneous world" as comprised of complex relationships between institutional indicators, income levels, growth rates and growth volatility.

It remains unclear which type of institutions matter the most for trade performance and inward FDI in African economies. The classification of institutions under general socio-political or institutional categories can often cloud the different channels through which institutions impact economic performance and inward FDI (Das and Quirk, 2016). Additionally, there is a blurred distinction between policy and institutions, and often empirical research does not make the distinction (Voigt, 2013). The categorisation of institutional quality is therefore quite important for interpreting institutional effects, as they may indicate how effectively existing frameworks are implemented and enforced. This study investigates institutional quality based on the evaluation of their performance.

A basic characteristic of the institutional argument is that prior institutional choices limit available future options (Krasner, 1988). Possible options available at any given point in time are constrained by available institutional capabilities and these capabilities are themselves the product of choices made during some earlier period. Therefore, economic outcomes at a given point in time cannot be understood in terms of the preferences and capabilities of actors existing at the same point in time. Additionally, the nature of economic actors cannot be understood except as part of the larger institutional framework. The effect of institutions on inward FDI may arise either from their initial state or from changes in their quality over time. Where there are weak institutions and inefficient or no enforcement of property rights, firms may pursue only short-term horizons (Petrović-Ranđelović et al., 2013).

A range of studies indicate that contemporary institutional frameworks are the product of historical legacies. Aaron (2000), Acemoglu and Robinson (2008), Dixit (2007) and Marinescu (2014) propose that the development of institutions is path dependent, which suggests that there should be some persistence of the institutional framework as a result of previous outcomes and not based on current conditions (Puffert, 2016). History matters for path dependence and has an enduring influence. Choices made on the basis of transitory conditions may persist long after those conditions have changed. Therefore, explanations of the outcomes of path-dependent institutional evolution require an examination of the impact of history on the process of institutional evolution, rather than simply examining contemporary conditions of institutional structures and preferences existing in African economies. Such contemporary conditions are arguably the result of previous states of affairs (Boschma and Frenken, 2006) where institutions become "carriers of history" maintaining existing norms and cultural patterns through time (Vergne and Durand, 2010). Within African economies, the impact of historical conditions is therefore argued to be evidenced in the current state of institutional structures and preferences.

In an empirical study covering 60 countries, Law *et al.* (2013) investigated the causal relationship between institutions and economic growth using Granger causality tests based on Hurlin and Venet (2001) and vector autoregressive (VAR) lag-length selection criteria. In their study covering an 18-year period (1990–2008) and using institutional proxies from International Country Risk Guide (ICRG) and the World Governance Indicators (WGI), they concluded that a bi-directional causality existed between institutions and economic growth that was highly heterogeneous within the sample economies. Levine and Renelt (1992) had found evidence to suggest that growth-related policies (such as trade openness, macro stability, fiscal and monetary policy and legal quality) are highly correlated. Keho (2017) concluded that trade openness has positive effects on economic growth both in the short and long term, demonstrating a positive and strong complementary relationship between trade openness and capital formation in promoting economic growth. However, the issue of heterogeneity between economies with respect to trade policies, economic conditions and technological and institutional development complicates the assumptions of cross-sectional regressions.

Multiple empirical studies use reduced-form models that make it difficult to disentangle the direct and indirect effects of institutions, and potential issues of omitted variables and reverse causality may also arise. To mitigate issues of collinearity and endogeneity, studies use historical or geographical variables as instruments for contemporary institutional quality. The resulting regression coefficients need to be interpreted in terms of the time lag between the instrument and the contemporary measure. In this study we use a framework that includes various "historical" instruments that exert an impact on the outcome variable, which enables us to account for violations of the exclusion restriction.

To estimate the effect of institutional quality on inward FDI, we follow Acemoglu *et al.* (2001) and include mortality rates expected by European settlers as an instrument for the exogenous source of variation in institutions. Acemoglu *et al.* (2001) argued that potential settler mortality was a major determinant of European settlements which were major determinants of early institutions. In their study they used settler mortality as their instrument, income per capita as the output variable and institutional quality as the regressor. The results indicate a strong correlation between early institutions and contemporary institutions.

Testing for the Influence of Institutional Quality on Africa's FDI Stocks

Our contribution towards the understanding of the influence of institutional quality on FDI and economic growth in SSA is twofold. First, using principal component analysis, we investigate the quality of the multiple institutions which may be affecting FDI and economic growth in Africa by deriving an aggregate institutional index of institutional quality indicators. Second, we examine the effect of institutions on FDI stock levels in the given countries.

Data on institutional quality is derived from the Economic Freedom of the World (EFW) database computed by Gwartney *et al.* (2016). This database has been utilised in multiple empirical studies investigating the impact of economic freedom on investment, economic growth, income levels and poverty rates (Atukeren, 2005; Bennett and Nikolaev, 2016; Flachaire *et al.*, 2014; Góes, 2016; Le, 2009; Siddiqui and Ahmed, 2013; Sonora, 2014). In this study, we use available institutional quality indicators for the period 1985–2014. The EFW database ranks the degree to which different African countries' policies and institutions are supportive of economic freedom, based on the assumption that all members of the society have equal access to economic institutions. The institutional component ratings are constructed with 42 data points from data sourced from the International Monetary Fund (IMF), the World Bank (WB) and the World Economic Forum (WEF).

First, to investigate the quality of institutions, our aggregation of multiple institutional indicators into a single institution index allows us to isolate the underlying correlation of institutional quality indicators and explain variance with the fewest components, and avoid issues of collinearity that may arise from strong correlations among institutional indicators (Bartels *et al.*, 2014; Everitt and Skrondal, 2010; Siddiqui and Ahmed, 2013). Since institutions develop endogenously, this can increase the potential for contemporaneous correlation among any proxy which is used to examine institutional quality (Aaron, 2000; Boettke and Fink, 2011; Fabro and Aixalá, 2013). Additionally, endogeneity issues can lead to biased and inconsistent parameter estimates that make it impossible to arrive at a dependable inference of the relationship between different institutional dimensions and any other variable (Angeles, 2010; Slesman *et al.*, 2015; Wintoki *et al.*, 2012).

Second, to empirically examine the effect of institutions on FDI stock levels, we estimate the relationship between institutional quality and levels of income per capita on levels of FDI stock, using the Arellano and Bond (1991) difference general method of moments (GMM) estimator. This method uses the first-difference lagged instruments to get a consistent parameter and eliminate individual fixed effects, especially when the sample size is small (Arellano and Bond, 1991; Góes, 2016). Several empirical studies on the relationship between institutional quality and FDI rely upon fixed-effects instrumental variables estimation (2SLS). However, the results of first-stage statistics of the 2SLS regression may indicate that instruments are weak. With weak instruments, the fixed-effects instrumental variable (IV) estimators are likely to be biased. The use of exogenous instruments and lagged levels of the endogenous regressors in difference GMM makes the endogenous variable predetermined and not correlated with the error term (Arellano and Bond, 1991). The use of first differences also removes the country-specific effect that does not vary with time. The first-differenced lagged dependent variable is also instrumented with its past levels.

We analyse the long-run effect of the quality of institutions on contemporary levels of FDI. Acemoglu *et al.*'s (2001) earlier work demonstrated the links between colonisation and its influence on the quality of current institutions. In this study, we test for the persistence of institutional quality in Africa and the long-run effect on FDI. Following Acemoglu *et al.* (2001), our analysis uses historical instruments for contemporary endogenous regressors. First, we assume that the effect of historical instruments on the persistence of institutional quality is linear. The outcome variable is the natural log of FDI stock levels in 2016 and we use several instruments, including the log of absolute value of latitude (derived from *The World Factbook*; CIA, 2016) and the natural log of population size and length of independence, as controls for the potential correlation between settler mortality and geography, which may also affect our outcome variable.

Our analysis of the data revealed the existence of relationships between the length of independence in studied African countries and the quality of their institutions. Following Acemoglu's work on the link between colonisation and the current quality of institutions, our results indicate that the length of the time gap between the initial shock of settler mortality and the measurement of institutions has an impact on the quality of institutions in this sample (presented in the results section). Although the timing of each initial shock will vary and is difficult to exactly pinpoint, we are able to extract the persistence of institutional quality and its long-run effect on FDI. We estimate that for a one-unit increase in the quality of institutions, we expect to see on average a 2% increase in FDI stock levels (presented in the results section). Table 16.3 presents our results, which confirm a long-run relationship between institutional quality and inward FDI in the selected African countries.

Data and Model

Traditionally, examination of the main determinants of trade and FDI inflows has focused on economic factors such as market size, labour costs, exchange rates and infrastructure as critical factors determining a host country's ability to attract or deter FDI (Caves, 1974; Dunning, 1980). This study focuses on the influence of institutional quality on host country attractiveness for inward investment; it hypothesises the following:

1. The quality of contemporary governance infrastructure, defined as the political and legal institutional framework, affects the overall investment environment of the host country. Better governance structures will have a positive and statistically significant effect on levels of FDI stock.
2. Historical changes have a long-run effect on the quality of contemporary institutions.

The study explores these relationships within 19 Sub-Saharan African countries over the period 1980 to 2016 (Table 16.1). The sample countries are a mix of North African, West African, Central African, East African and Southern African low-,

Table 16.1   List of countries and income groupings

Low income	Lower-middle income	Upper-middle income
Burkina Faso	Cameroon	Angola
Gambia	Congo	South Africa
Democratic Republic of the Congo	Cote d'Ivoire	
Madagascar	Gabon	
Mali	Ghana	
Niger	Kenya	
Senegal	Nigeria	
Sierra Leone		
Togo		
Uganda		

lower-middle- and upper-middle-income countries. Countries were included or omitted in this study on the basis of the availability of data for all indicators.

This analysis involves two steps. The first step derives a component for the quality of institutions that can impact inward FDI flows into African economies. The second examines the impact of contemporary institutional quality on contemporary levels of FDI stock. Following Acemoglu *et al.* (2001), we use the log of potential settler mortality, and following Hall and Jones (1999), we use absolute latitude as instruments for institutions. Acemoglu *et al.* (2001) is the most prominent study that uses historical instruments for contemporary endogenous regressors. Both Acemoglu *et al.* (2001) and Hall and Jones (1999) argue that geography may be correlated with settler mortality and can therefore affect contemporary institutional quality.

We suggest that these instruments do not have a direct effect on inward FDI and are therefore valid instruments. The advantage of this approach is that settler mortality more than 100 years ago should have no effect on inward FDI today, other than through its effect on institutions (Acemoglu *et al.*, 2001). As evidenced in Figure 16.1, there is no linear relationship between log potential settler mortality 100 years ago and contemporary levels of FDI stock). Our tests also show that absolute latitude does not have an independent effect on inward FDI. This validates our use of these instruments in our model.

To avoid issues of collinearity arising from strong correlations among institutional indicators, this study uses factor analysis to isolate the underlying correlation structure. Endogeneity issues can lead to biased and inconsistent parameter estimates that make it impossible to arrive at a dependable inference of the relationship

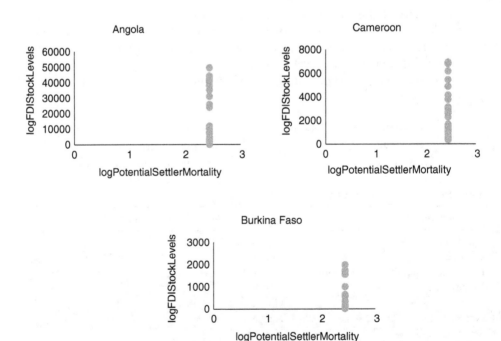

Figure 16.1 Scattergram of relationship between log FDI stock levels (1980–2016) and log potential settler mortality for three countries of the full sample (other country graphs omitted for space constraints).

between different institutional dimensions and levels of FDI stock (Angeles, 2010). Factor analysis reduces the institutional indicators to fewer factors that better explain the variance of correlation among all institutional indicators (Bartels *et al.*, 2014; Everitt and Skrondal, 2010; Siddiqui and Ahmed, 2013). Principal component analysis has been similarly used to extract new institutional indicators for a larger subset of correlated institutional indices in studies by Narayan *et al.* (2014, 2015) and Siddiqui and Ahmed (2013), who used institutional indices from the ICRG to study the effect of institutional quality on stock market returns. Siddiqui and Ahmed (2013) used indicators from ICRG, Business Environment Risk Intelligence (BERI) and the World Bank Worldwide Governance Indicators (WGI) to examine how institutional quality influences economic growth in the theoretical framework proposed by North (1990). Atukeren (2005), Bennett and Nikolaev (2015), Czegledi (2017), Flachaire *et al.* (2014) and Sonora (2014) used data from EFW to investigate the impact of economic freedom on investment, economic growth, income levels and poverty rates.

The list of institutional variables is presented in Table 16.2.

Following Siddiqui and Ahmed (2013), an expectation-maximisation (EM) algorithm using an iterative method was used to find the maximum likelihood estimates of missing values. This yielded a total of 323 observations per country. Utilising the Kaiser (1960) criterion, the first factor was retained as it significantly explained 46% of the variance of the data while the following factor only 12% and the remaining factors explain progressively smaller portions of the variance but are uncorrelated with

Table 16.2   Institutional variables used in model

Variable
Judicial independence
Impartial courts
Military interference in rule of law and politics
Integrity of the legal system
Legal enforcement of contracts
Regulatory restrictions on the sale of real property
Reliability of police
Tariffs
Non-tariff trade barriers
Foreign ownership/investment restrictions
Capital controls
Interest rate controls/negative real interest rates)
Hiring regulations and minimum wage
Hiring and firing regulations
Centralised collective bargaining
Hours regulations
Mandated cost of worker dismissal
Conscription
Administrative requirements
Extra payments/bribes/favouritism
Licensing restrictions
Tax compliance

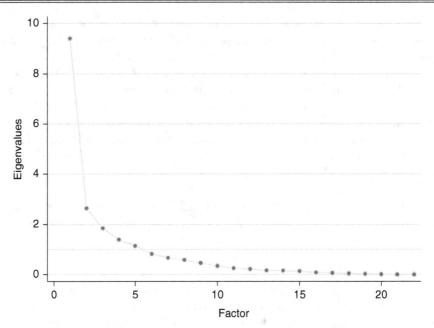

Figure 16.2   Scree plot of eigenvalues of institutional variables before factor rotation.

each other (Figure 16.2). This factor's loading indicates the relative importance of the remaining institutional indicators in explaining the correlation relationship among the larger sample of institutional indicators. A higher correlation coefficient means that the indicator is more relevant in defining the component.

Following Comrey and Lee (2013), coefficient loadings with an absolute value ≥ 0.40 were used as the cut-off for retaining heavily loaded indicators in the new institutional factor (Table 16.3). The new institutional factor captures a quarter of the variance in correlation among all the institutional variables. The retained factor has all positive values and is expected not to have an inverse impact.

An Arellano-Bond dynamic panel GMM model was used to examine the relationship between institutional quality and levels of FDI stock. FDI stock was used as FDI inflows are considered more volatile and may be distorted by one or two large takeovers. Bénassy-Quéré *et al.* (2007) argue that FDI stocks should be used for regression analysis relative to flows, as the former are based on accumulated flows – hence presumably less volatile – and are the relevant decision variables for firms in the long run. FDI stock accounts for FDI being financed through local capital markets could provide a better estimation of capital ownership (Devereux and Griffith, 2002). FDI stock levels for 2016 were taken from UNCTAD (2017).

The relationship between levels of FDI stock in 2016 and institutional quality are tested using the following model:

$$\text{FDI}i = \beta 0 + \beta 1 Y i_t - 1 + \beta 2 I i_t + \in i_t \tag{1}$$

The subscript "t" represents one of the 36-year period, "i" represents country, "Y" is log real per capita GDP, "I" is the institutional factor and "ϵ" represents the error term. GDP is correlated with FDI stock, and GDP growth is expected to have a direct

Table 16.3 Loadings of rotated institutional variables

Variable	Factor 1	Factor 2	Factor 3	Factor 4
Judicial independence	0.8841			
Impartial courts	0.8371			
Military interference in rule of law and politics	0.6684			
Integrity of the legal system			0.8829	
Legal enforcement of contracts		0.7457		
Regulatory restrictions on the sale of real property				
Reliability of police				
Tariffs	0.6762			
Non-tariff trade barriers	0.6028			
Foreign ownership/investment restrictions	0.7303			
Capital controls	0.5845			
Interest rate controls/negative real interest rates)				
Hiring regulations and minimum wage	0.4319	0.4917		
Hiring and firing regulations				
Centralised collective bargaining			−0.7975	
Hours regulations				
Mandated cost of worker dismissal				
Conscription		0.8508		
Administrative requirements				0.7668
Extra payments/bribes/favouritism	0.8089			
Licensing restrictions				0.7552
Tax compliance				

effect on inward FDI. All variables enter the equation in log form except I. Both GDP and institutions are endogenously determined. For this reason, GMM-based estimation is used for instrumental variable estimation in preference over ordinary least squares (OLS) and conventional IV estimators. A traditional IV estimator is ineffectual in the midst of heteroscedasticity.

GMM uses orthogonality conditions to allow for efficient estimation in the presence of heteroscedasticity (Arellano and Bond, 1991). Our model uses a one-step difference Arellano-Bond estimator with robust standard errors and takes the first difference form of Equation 1. When the regressor is transformed into first difference, potential biases caused by omitted variables and fixed country-specific effects, which could be correlated with the explanatory variables, are removed.

Results

Results of the GMM regression are presented in Table 16.4.

Our models examine the relationship between FDI stock levels in 2016, GDP per capita and institutional quality. All figures, except institutional quality, enter the equation as log and first difference. The parameter of interest is the "long-run effect" of historical changes in endogenous institutional quality on the contemporary dependent variable, FDI stock levels in 2016. Our estimations are based on instrumental variables from Acemoglu et al. (2001). We hypothesise that a change in institutional quality in 1800 from the lowest to the highest score in the EFW index leads

Table 16.4 GMM regression results

Dependent variable: FDI stock (2016) (log)	(1)	(2)	(3)	(4)	(5)	(6)	(7)	(8)	(9)
LogFDI stock (lag)								0.968***	0.964***
								(0.014)	(0.015)
GDP per capita (log)	5.317***	0.675	0.765	0.766	0.765	13.644***	0.765	0.135	0.765
	(0.112)	(0.471)	(0.471)	(0.468)	(0.471)	(0.876)	(0.470)	(0.128)	(0.471)
Lag GDP per capita (log)						-8.497***	-0.643		-0.643
						(0.904)	(0.456)		(0.456)
Institutional quality index	0.103***	0.028**	0.021*	0.021*	0.021*	0.125***	0.021*	0.021*	0.021*
	(0.011)	(0.010)	(0.010)	(0.010)	(0.010)	(0.021)	(0.010)	(0.010)	(0.010)
Latitude (log)	0	0.000	0.000	0.000	0.000	0.000		0.000	0.000
	(.)	(.)	(.)	(.)	(.)	(.)		(.)	(.)
N	669	649	649	649	650	649	651	649	649
LogSettlerMortality[a]	yes	no	no	no	yes	yes	yes	yes	yes
LogPopulation[b]	yes	yes	yes	yes	no	yes	yes	yes	no
Legal origin[c]	no	no	no	yes	no	no	no	no	no
Length of Independence[d]	no	no	yes	no	no	no	no	no	no
Serial correlation test (p-value)[e]									
AR(1)	0.04	0	0	0	0	0	0	0	0
AR(2)		0.14	0.14	0.14	0.76	0.14	0.026	0.143	0.15
Sargan test (p-value)[f]	1	1	0.95	0.97	1	1	1	1	1
dr_r	666	644	644	644	644	646	645	647	644

* p<0.05; ** p<0.01; *** p<0.001.
[a] Potential European Settler Mortality (Acemoglu et al., 2001).
[b] Total Population (La Porta et al., 1999).
[c] Legal origin of the latest European coloniser, indicating whether a country was a British, French, Portuguese or Belgian colony (La Porta et al., 1999).
[d] Date of independence is the first year that the country achieves independence from the latest European coloniser (Acemoglu et al., 2001).
[e] The null hypothesis is that the errors in the first-difference regression exhibit no serial correlation.
[f] The null hypothesis is that the instruments used are not correlated with the error terms.
Values in parentheses are standardised beta coefficients. All variables are in first differences, there is no intercept.

to on average a minimum 2.1 standard deviation change in FDI stock levels in 2016. This effect is both statistically and positively significant on FDI stock levels.

Our first model uses log of potential settler mortality capped at 250 per 1000 as the instrument in our GMM regression. The uncapped settler mortality variable is obtained from Acemoglu et al. (2001). Building upon Acemoglu et al. (2001), we appreciate that settler mortality may be correlated with region-specific factors, such as geography, which can also have an effect on contemporary FDI stock levels. Several studies have suggested that settler mortality is correlated with other contemporary variables, such as GDP per capita. For these results to be valid, we assume that settler mortality has affected GDP per capita through historical changes to institutional quality. To mitigate these issues, we include controls for the log of the absolute value of latitude of a country's approximate geodesic centroid obtained from *The World Factbook* (CIA, 2016).

We also include the log of population to help distinguish the effects of characteristics of physical location and characteristics of people living in that location. If African countries with good historical institutional quality attract population flows from other countries, this may affect the adjusted level of contemporary FDI stock levels, through the size of the potential market. Similarly, African countries with poor historical institutional quality may be vulnerable to smaller market sizes, which would also affect contemporary FDI stock levels. Arellano-Bond first-difference GMM estimation assumes that the variables are weakly exogenous, which means that they could be affected by dependent variables but not correlated with the error term. The Sargan test of over-identifying restrictions tests the overall validity of the instruments (Arellano and Bond, 1991). Our models have Sargan results of 1.00, therefore the null hypothesis can be rejected and the model is reliable and the error term is not correlated with the variables.

Conclusions

These results demonstrate institutions have a long-run effect on investment flows, in line with existing literature arguing that historical events have a long-run effect on contemporary inward FDI (Spolaore and Wacziarg, 2013; Wacziarg and Welch, 2008). Interpreting the magnitude and importance of regular findings is often problematic due to the complex interrelationships among the variables used in many empirical tests, which hinders the direct translation of empirical findings into policy advice relevant for policymakers in developing African economies. The framework suggested in this study addresses this by using instrumental variables that precede the endogenous regressor in time, to investigate the interpretation of the regression coefficients. We apply these instruments to estimate the long-run effect of changes in historical conditions on the quality of institutions and inward FDI.

A key implication of this chapter is in clarifying the effects of institutional quality on contemporary inward FDI flows. The method used here enables the consideration of the underlying data used to generate empirical results. The results are closely related to work by Acemoglu and Robinson (2010), who argue for the importance of using theory to make sense of empirical results. Our results indicate that to further increase economic benefits from rising trade participation and inward investment in African economies, there is need to pay attention to the role of effective institutions in regulating business, and implementation of supportive institutions more adapted to entrepreneurs and investors in high-risk environments. From the findings, we additionally note the role of supportive and sustained trade and investment facilitation measures. As outlined, the quality of institutions is measured in terms of government efficiency, minimal policy reversals, efficient and strong enforcement of property rights and the stability of legal systems. This chapter's findings therefore emphasise the role of institutions as key factors influencing trade and inward investment performance within selected host countries in SSA.

References

Aaron, J. (2000) Growth and Institutions: A Review of the Evidence. *The World Bank Research Observer*, 15(1), 99–135.

Acemoglu, D. & Robinson, J.A. (2008) Persistence of Power, Elites and Institutions. *American Economic Review*, 98(1), 267–293.

Acemoglu, D. & Robinson, J.A. (2010) The Role of Institutions in Growth and Development. *Review of Economics and Institutions*, 1(2), 1–33.

Acemoglu, D., Johnson, S. & Robinson, J.A. (2001) The Colonial Origins of Comparative Development: An Empirical Investigation. *American Economic Review*, 91(5), 1369–1401.

Aizenman, J. & Spiegel, M.M. (2006) Institutional Efficiency, Monitoring Costs and the Investment Share of FDI. *Review of International Economics*, 14(4), 683–697.

Ang, J.B. (2008) Determinants of Foreign Direct Investment in Malaysia. *Journal of Policy Modeling*, 30(1), 185–189.

Angeles, L. (2010) Institutions and Economic Development. New Tests and New Doubts. *SIRE Discussion Papers, 2010-75*. Retrieved from: http://repo.sire.ac.uk/bitstream/handle/10943/204/SIRE_DP_2010_75.pdf?sequence=1&isAllowed=y (accessed 12 July 2019).

Arellano, M. & Bond, S. (1991) Some Tests of Specification for Panel Data: Monte Carlo Evidence and an Application to Employment Equations. *The Review of Economic Studies*, 58(2), 277–297.

Asiedu, E. (2002) On the Determinants of Foreign Direct Investment to Developing Countries: Is Africa Different? *World Development*, 30(1), 107–119.

Asiedu, E. (2006) Foreign Direct Investment in Africa: The Role of Natural Resources, Market Size, Government Policy, Institutions and Political Instability. *World Economy*, 29(1), 63–77.

Atukeren, E. (2005) Interactions between Public and Private Investment: Evidence from Developing Countries. *Kyklos*, 58(3), 307–330.

Bailey, N. (2018) Exploring the Relationship between Institutional Factors and FDI Attractiveness: A Meta-analytic Review. *International Business Review*, 27(1), 139–148.

Bannaga, A., Gangi, Y., Abdrazak, R. & Al-Fakhry, B. (2013) The Effects of Good Governance on Foreign Direct Investment Inflows in Arab Countries. *Applied Financial Economics*, 23(15), 1239–1247.

Bartels, F.L., Napolitano, F. & Tissi, N.E. (2014) FDI in Sub-Saharan Africa: A Longitudinal Perspective on Location-Specific Factors. *International Business Review*, 23(3), 516–529.

Bénassy-Quéré, A., Coupet, M. & Mayer, T. (2007) Institutional Determinants of Foreign Direct Investment. *World Economy*, 30(5), 764–782.

Bennett, D.L. & Nikolaev, B. (2016) Factor Endowments, the Rule of Law and Structural Inequality. *Journal of Institutional Economics*, 12(4), 773–795.

Bevan, A.A. & Estrin, S. (2004) The Determinants of Foreign Direct Investment into European Transition Economies. *Journal of Comparative Economics*, 32(4), 775–787.

Billington, N. (1999) The Location of Foreign Direct Investment: An Empirical Analysis. *Applied Economics*, 31(1), 65–76.

Boettke, P. & Fink, A. (2011) Institutions First. *Journal of Institutional Economics*, 7(04), 499–504.

Borensztein, E., De Gregorio, J. & Lee, J.W. (1998) How Does Foreign Direct Investment Affect Economic Growth? *Journal of International Economics*, 45(1), 115–135.

Boschma, R.A. & Frenken, K. (2006) Why is Economic Geography Not an Evolutionary Science? Towards an Evolutionary Economic Geography. *Journal of Economic Geography*, 6(3), 273–302.

Buchanan, B.G., Le, Q.V. & Rishi, M. (2012a) Foreign Direct Investment and Institutional Quality: Some Empirical Evidence. *International Review of Financial Analysis*, 21(Supplement C), 81–89.

Buchanan, B.G., Le, Q.V. & Rishi, M. (2012b) Foreign Direct Investment and Institutional Quality: Some Empirical Evidence. *International Review of Financial Analysis*, 21, 81–89.

Buckley, P.J., Clegg, L.J., Cross, A.R. *et al.* (2007) The Determinants of Chinese Outward Foreign Direct Investment. *Journal of International Business Studies*, 38(4), 499–518.

Bussiere, M. & Fratzscher, M. (2008) Financial Openness and Growth: Short-Run Gain, Long-Run Pain? *Review of International Economics*, 16(1), 69–95.

Buthe, T. & Milner, H.V. (2008) The Politics of Foreign Direct Investment into Developing Countries: Increasing FDI through International Trade Agreements? *American Journal of Political Science*, 52(4), 741–762.

Caves, R.E. (1974) Causes of Direct Investment: Foreign Firms' Shares in Canadian and United Kingdom Manufacturing Industries. *The Review of Economics and Statistics*, 56(3), 279–293.

Central Intelligence Agency (2016) *The World Factbook 2016–17*. Washington, DC: CIA.

Comrey, A.L. & Lee, H.B. (2013) *A First Course in Factor Analysis*: Hove: Psychology Press.

Contractor, F.J., Lahiri, S., Elango, B. & Kundu, S.K. (2014) Institutional, Cultural and Industry Related Determinants of Ownership Choices in Emerging Market FDI Acquisitions. *International Business Review*, 23(5), 931–941.

Czegledi, P. (2017) Productivity, Institutions, and Market Beliefs: Three Entrepreneurial Interpretations. *Journal of Entrepreneurship and Public Policy*, 6(2), 164–180.

Das, K. & Quirk, T. (2016) Which Institutions Promote Growth? Revisiting the Evidence. *Economic Papers*, 35(1), 37–58.

Daude, C. & Stein, E. (2007) The Quality of Institutions and Foreign Direct Investment. *Economics & Politics*, 19(3), 317–344.

de Crombrugghe, D. & Farla, K. (2012) Preliminary Conclusions on Institutions and Economic Performance. *UNU-MERIT Working Paper Series, Institutions and Economic Growth* IPD: WP04. Retrieved from: https://www.merit.unu.edu/publications/wppdf/2012/wp2012-035.pdf (accessed 12 July 2019).

de Mello, J.L.R. (1999) Foreign Direct Investment-Led Growth: Evidence from Time Series and Panel Data. *Oxford Economic Papers*, 51(1), 133–151.

Devereux, M.P. & Griffith, R. (2002) The Impact of Corporate Taxation on the Location of Capital: A Review. *Swedish Economic Policy Review*, 9(1), 79–106.

Dixit, A. (2007) Evaluating Recipes for Development success. *World Bank Research Observer*, 22(2), 131–157.

Dunning, J.H. (1980) Toward an Eclectic Theory of International Production: Some Empirical Tests. *Journal of International Business Studies*, 11(1), 9–31.

Everitt, B.S. & Skrondal, A. (2010) *The Cambridge Dictionary of Statistics* (4th ed.). Cambridge: Cambridge University Press.

Fabro, G.E. & Aixalá, J.P. (2013) Do the Models of Institutional Quality Differ According to the Income Levels of the Countries? The Case of the Low-Income Countries. *Review of Public Economics*, 206(3), 11–26.

Faeth, I. (2009) Determinants of Foreign Direct Investment – A Tale of Nine Theoretical Models. *Journal of Economic Surveys*, 23(1), 165–196.

Flachaire, E., García-Peñalosa, C. & Konte, M. (2014) Political versus Economic Institutions in the Growth Process. *Journal of Comparative Economics*, 42(1), 212–229.

Gani, A. (2007) Governance and Foreign Direct Investment Links: Evidence from Panel Data Estimations. *Applied Economics Letters*, 14(10), 753–756.

Globerman, S. & Shapiro, D. (2002) Global Foreign Direct Investment Flows: The Role of Governance Infrastructure. *World Development*, 30(11), 1899–1919.

Globerman, S. & Shapiro, D. (2003) Governance Infrastructure and US Foreign Direct Investment. *Journal of International Business Studies*, 34(1), 19–39.

Góes, C. (2016). Institutions and Growth: A GMM/IV Panel VAR Approach. *Economics Letters*, 138, 85–91.

Grosse, R. & Trevino, L.J. (1996) Foreign Direct Investment in the United States: An Analysis by Country of Origin. *Journal of International Business Studies*, 27(1), 139–155.

Gwartney, J., Lawson, R.A. & Hall, J.C. (2016) *Economic Freedom of the World: 2016 Annual Report*. Vancouver: Fraser Institute.

Hall, J.C., Sobel, R.S. & Crowley, G.R. (2010) Institutions, Capital, and Growth. *Southern Economic Journal*, 77(2), 385–405.

Hall, R.E. & Jones, C.I. (1996) The Productivity of Nations. *NBER Working Paper* No. 5812. Retrieved from: https://www.nber.org/papers/w5812.pdf (accessed 12 July 2019).

Hall, R.E. & Jones, C.I. (1999) Why Do Some Countries Produce So Much More Output Per Worker than Others? *Quarterly Journal of Economics*, 114(1), 83–116.

Hurlin, C. & Venet, B. (2001) Granger Causality Tests in Panel Data Models with Fixed Coefficients. *Cahier de Recherche EURISCO, September, Université Paris IX Dauphine*.

Jensen, N. (2008) Political Risk, Democratic Institutions, and Foreign Direct Investment. *Journal of Politics*, 70(4), 1040–1052.

Kaiser, H.F. (1960) The Application of Electronic Computers to Factor Analysis. *Educational and Psychological Measurement*, 20, 141–151.

Keho, Y. (2017) The Impact of Trade Openness on Economic Growth: The Case of Cote d'Ivoire. *Cogent Economics & Finance*, 5(1), 1332820.

Kohpaiboon, A. (2003) Foreign Trade Regimes and the FDI-Growth Nexus: A Case Study of Thailand. *The Journal of Development Studies*, 40(2), 55–69.

Kolstad, I. & Villanger, E. (2008) Determinants of Foreign Direct Investment in Services. *European Journal of Political Economy*, 24(2), 518–533.

Krasner, S.D. (1988) Sovereignty: An Institutional Perspective. *Comparative Political Studies*, 21(1), 66–94.

Kurul, Z. (2017) Nonlinear Relationship between Institutional Factors and FDI Flows: Dynamic Panel Threshold Analysis. *International Review of Economics & Finance*, 48(C), 148–160.

Kurul, Z. & Yalta, A.Y. (2017) Relationship between Institutional Factors and FDI Flows in Developing Countries: New Evidence from Dynamic Panel Estimation. *Economies*, 5(2), 1–10.

La Porta, R., Lopez-De-Silanes, F., Shleifer, A. & Vishny, R. (1999) The Quality of Government. *Journal of Law Economics & Organization*, 15(1), 222–279.

Law, S.H., Lim, T.C. & Ismail, N.W. (2013) Institutions and Economic Development: A Granger Causality Analysis of Panel Data Evidence. *Economic Systems*, 37, 610–624.

Le, T. (2009) Trade, Remittances, Institutions, and Economic Growth. *International Economic Journal*, 23(3), 391–408.

Leftwich, A. & Sen, K. (2011) "Don't Mourn; Organize" Institutions and Organizations in the Politics and Economics of Growth and Poverty-Reduction. *Journal of International Development*, 23, 319–337.

Levine, R. & Renelt, D. (1992) A Sensitivity Analysis of Cross-Country Growth Regressions. *American Economic Review*, 82(4), 942–963.

Li, Q. (2006) Democracy, Autocracy, and Tax Incentives to Foreign Direct Investors: A Cross-National Analysis. *Journal of Politics*, 68(1), 62–74.

Li, Q. & Resnick, A. (2003) Reversal of Fortunes: Democratic Institutions and Foreign Direct Investment Inflows to Developing Countries. *International Organization*, 57(1), 175–211.

Marinescu, C. (2014) Why Institutions Matter: From Economic Development to Development Economics. *European Review*, 22(3), 469–490.

Mengistu, A.A. & Adhikary, B.K. (2011) Does Good Governance Matter for FDI Inflows? Evidence from Asian Economies. *Asia Pacific Business Review*, 17(3), 281–299.

Morrissey, O. & Udomkerdmongkol, M. (2012) Governance, Private Investment and Foreign Direct Investment in Developing Countries. *World Development*, 40(3), 437–445.

Narayan, P.K., Narayan, S. & Thuraisamy, K.S. (2014) Can Institutions and Macroeconomic Factors Predict Stock Returns in Emerging Markets? *Emerging Markets Review*, 19, 77–95.

Narayan, P.K., Sharma, S.S. & Thuraisamy, K.S. (2015) Can Governance Quality Predict Stock Market Returns? New Global Evidence. *Pacific-Basin Finance Journal*, 35(A), 367–380.

Naude, W.A. & Krugell, W.F. (2007) Investigating Geography and Institutions as Determinants of Foreign Direct Investment in Africa Using Panel Data. *Applied Economics*, 39(10–12), 1223–1233.

Nelson, R.R. & Sampat, B.N. (2001) Making Sense of Institutions as a Factor Shaping Economic Performance. *Journal of Economic Behavior & Organization*, 44(1), 31–54.

Neumayer, E. & Spess, L. (2005) Do Bilateral Investment Treaties Increase Foreign Direct Investment to Developing Countries? *World Development*, 33(10), 1567–1585.

North, D.C. (1990) *Institutions, Institutional Change and Economic Performance*. Cambridge: Cambridge University Press.

North, D.C. (1991) Institutions. *The Journal of Economic Perspectives*, 5(1), 97–112.

Obwona, M.B. (2001) Determinants of FDI and Their Impact on Economic Growth in Uganda. *African Development Review-Revue Africaine De Developpement*, 13(1), 46–81.

Ok, S.T. (2004) What Drives Foreign Direct Investment into Emerging Markets? Evidence from Turkey. *Emerging Markets Finance and Trade*, 40(4), 101–114.

Petrović-Ranđelović, M., Denčić-Mihajlov, K. & Milenković-Kerković, T. (2013) An Analysis of the Location Determinants of Foreign Direct Investment: The Case of Serbia. *Procedia – Social and Behavioral Sciences*, 81, 181–187.

Pike, R., Neale, B. & Linsley, P. (2015) *Corporate Finance and Investment: Decisions and Strategies* (8th ed.). Harlow: Pearson.

Phelps, N., Powers, M. & Wanjiru, R. (2007) Learning to Compete: The Investment Promotion Community and the Spread of Neoliberalism. In: England, K. &Ward, K. (eds.) *Neo-liberalization: States, Networks, Peoples*. Oxford: Blackwell, pp. 83–109.

Puffert, D. (2016) Path Dependence in Technical Standards. *New Palgrave Dictionary of Economics*. London: Palgrave Macmillan. Retrieved from: https://link.springer.com/content/pdf/10.1057%2F978-1-349-95121-5_2846-1.pdf (accessed 12 July 2019).

Rodrik, D., Subramanian, A. & Trebbi, F. (2004) Institutions Rule: The Primacy of Institutions over Geography and Integration in Economic Development. *Journal of Economic Growth*, 9(2), 131–165.

Selowsky, M. & Martin, R. (1997) Policy Performance and Output Growth in the Transition Economies. *The American Economic Review*, 87(2), 349–353.

Siddiqui, D.A. & Ahmed, Q.M. (2013) The Effect of Institutions on Economic Growth: A Global Analysis Based on GMM Dynamic Panel Estimation. *Structural Change and Economic Dynamics*, 24, 18–33.

Slesman, L., Baharumshah, A.Z. & Ra'ees, W. (2015) Institutional Infrastructure and Economic Growth in Member Countries of the Organization of Islamic Cooperation. *Economic Modelling*, 51, 214–226.

Sonora, R. (2014) Institutions and Economic Performance in Mexican States. *MPRA Paper* No. 58368. Retrieved from: https://mpra.ub.uni-muenchen.de/58368/1/MPRA_paper_58368.pdf (accessed 12 July 2019).

Spolaore, E. & Wacziarg, R. (2013) How Deep are the Roots of Economic Development? *Journal of Economic Literature*, 51(2), 325–369.

Strange, R., Filatotchev, I., Lien, Y.C. & Piesse, J. (2009) Insider Control and the FDI Location Decision Evidence from Firms Investing in an Emerging Market. *Management International Review*, 49(4), 433–454.

Tauheed, L.F. (2013) A Critical Institutionalist Reconciliation of "Contradictory" Institutionalist Institutions: What is an Institution? *Journal of Economic Issues*, 47(1), 1470–1167.

Ullah, I. & Khan, M.A. (2017) Institutional Quality and Foreign Direct Investment Inflows: Evidence from Asian Countries. *Journal of Economic Studies*, 44(6), 1030–1050.

UNCTAD (2013) *World Investment Report 2013: Global Value Chains: Investment and Trade for Development*. Retrieved from: https://unctad.org/en/PublicationsLibrary/wir2013_en.pdf (accessed 12 July 2019).

UNCTAD (2017) *World Investment Report 2017: Investment and the Digital Economy*. Geneva: United Nations. Retrieved from: https://unctad.org/en/PublicationsLibrary/wir2017_en.pdf (accessed 12 July 2019).

UNCTAD (2018) *World Investment Report 2018: Investment and New Industrial Policies*. Geneva: United Nations. Retrieved from: https://unctad.org/en/PublicationsLibrary/wir2018_en.pdf (accessed 12 July 2019).

Vergne, J.-P. & Durand, R. (2010) The Missing Link between the Theory and Empirics of Path Dependence: Conceptual Clarification, Testability Issue, and Methodological Implications. *Journal of Management Studies*, 47(47), 36–59.

Voigt, S. (2013) How (Not) to Measure Institutions. *Journal of Institutional Economics*, 9(1), 1–26.

Wacziarg, R. & Welch, K.H. (2008) Trade Liberalization and Growth: New Evidence. *World Bank Economic Review*, 22(2), 187–231.

Wanjiru, R. (2013) Free Trade Zones and the Attraction of FDI to New Locations in Peripheral Regions: Perspectives from Sub-Saharan Africa, "Enterprise Zones: In Search of Best Practice". *Regions*, 291(1), 13–15.

Wanjiru R. & Prime, K.S. (2018) Institutions, Economic Growth and International Competitiveness: A Regional Study. In: Castellani, D. Narula, R., Nguyen, Q.T. *et al.* (eds.) *Contemporary Issues in International Business*. AIB Book Series. New York: Springer International.

Wintoki, M.B., Linck, J.S. & Netter, J.M. (2012) Endogeneity and the Dynamics of Internal Corporate Governance. *Journal of Financial Economics*, 105(3), 581–606.

Part IV Financing Trade

Chapter 17

Financing Trade: The Role of the WTO and Recent Initiatives

Marc Auboin

Introduction

For decades, the expansion of trade finance supported that of international trade. The continued expansion of trade finance was largely taken for granted by analysts, until the regional and global financial crises of the 1990s and 2000s raised the policy profile of this topic. Interest in the subject matter had suffered from the lack of international statistics on trade finance and the poor understanding of spillover effects of financial crises onto the real economy until the 1990s. Even within the financial system, trade finance remained a relatively underrated activity.

Nonetheless, interest in the role of trade finance has grown in the context of the financial crisis of 2008–2009 and the subsequent economic downturn, just as policymakers' interest was once caught by the Asian Financial Crisis. The lessons learned by policymakers in the context of the Asian and Latin American financial crises led to a better understanding of the role of trade finance, and the functioning of markets in this area. Markets have actually grown to become very large with trade and investment globalisation (cross-border flows are counted in trillions of dollars).

This chapter summarises some of the economic and policy knowledge developed by analysts and policymakers in the past decade or so. The first section describes broadly what trade finance is. The second section examines the links between trade and trade finance. The third section analyses the markets, large, liquid but prone to temporary or permanent gaps – the problem being that these gaps affect the promising traders in the trade scene. The fourth section looks at challenges affecting developing countries, part structural, part linked to the retrenchment of the global financial industry from countries seen as "challenging" since the 2009 financial crisis. The fifth section discusses recent efforts to evaluate global trade finance gaps, and final section describes policy initiatives to address them.

The Handbook of Global Trade Policy, First Edition. Edited by Andreas Klasen.
© 2020 John Wiley & Sons Ltd. Published 2020 by John Wiley & Sons Ltd.

What is Trade Finance?

Only a small part of international trade is paid cash in advance, as importers generally wish to pay, at the earliest, upon receipt of the merchandise in order to verify its physical integrity on arrival. Exporters, however, wish to be paid upon shipment.

In order to bridge the gap between the time at which exporters wish to be paid and the time at which importers will pay, a credit or a guarantee of payment is required. Trade finance provides the credit, payment guarantees and insurance needed to facilitate the payment for the merchandise or service on terms that will satisfy both the exporter and the importer. Most trade credit, payment guarantees and insurance are short-term, with a standard maturity of 90 days, but trade credit is extended for longer periods of time, particularly for categories of goods subject to longer production and delivery cycles such as aircraft and capital equipment.

A key aspect of trade finance is that it helps mitigate the risk of cashless trade transactions. There are two main forms of trade finance: inter-company credit, and bank-intermediated trade finance. Inter-company credit is accorded by the buyer to the seller ("buyer's credit"), or inversely by the seller to the buyer ("seller's credit"). Such simple transactions nevertheless become complex given the shape of modern trade, characterised by large "eco-systems" of supply chain relationships. In such supply chains, the ability of firms (i.e. large suppliers) to extend credit to their trading counterparties (buyers) is enhanced by opportunities to discount their receivables (receiving cash immediately against documentation such as the export contract, a process called "factoring"), or to mitigate payment risk by purchasing trade credit insurance.

Banks are also important intermediaries in trade finance. They provide solutions to the needs of traders, such as letters of credit, which are widely used in commodity trading and other particular sectors. The letter of credit provides the seller with a guarantee that the purchase will be paid, and carries a number of obligations for the seller (delivery conditions, submission of documentation) and the buyer (notably the guarantee that if the buyer is unable to pay, the bank will cover the outstanding amount). Banks are also increasingly providing supply chain solutions for their clients, helping them manage the increasing flows of receivables and payables.

Estimating the Size of Trade Finance Markets

The Bank of International Settlements (BIS) has noted that there is no single, comprehensive source of statistics allowing for an evaluation of the exact composition and size of trade finance markets (BIS, 2014b). However, it found that the market for trade finance, considered in its widest definition, is very large – certainly well above US$12 trillion annually out of US$18 trillion of exports (or imports).[1] For bank-intermediated short-term trade finance, the BIS determined that "a flow of some US$6.5–8 trillion […] was provided during 2011, of which around US$2.8 trillion was L/Cs [letters of credit]". It added that "about a third of global trade is supported by one or more bank-intermediated trade finance products", and that "he remainder was financed by inter-firm trade credit" (non-bank-intermediated).

Trade Finance and Risk

While the commercial risks involved in an international trade transaction seem in principle to be larger than in a domestic trade transaction – non-payment, loss or alteration of the merchandise during shipment, fluctuating exchange rates – trade finance is considered to be a particularly safe form of finance since it is underwritten by strong collateral and documented credit operations.

The low-risk nature of short-term trade finance is supported by data collated in the International Chamber of Commerce's (ICC) Trade Finance Loss Register, established in 2011. According to the ICC's *Global Risks Trade Finance Report 2013*, the average transaction default rate on short-term international trade credit is no more than 0.021% (a rate that has remained stable according to post-2013 ICC trade finance register reports), of which 57% is recovered though the sale of the underlying asset, the merchandise.[2] Table 17.1 provides more detailed risk characteristics across specific categories of short-term trade finance instruments.

The conclusion to be made from these statistics is that: trade finance is one of the safest forms of finance, among the various segments of the financial industry; in the discussion that took place with Basel regulators in the period 2011–2013 (see the section on "Avoiding the unintended consequences of Basel III"), these statistics were instrumental in keeping a relatively light capital treatment for short-term trade finance.

The Links between Trade and Trade Finance

The "trade finance" hypothesis gained popularity as economists fell short of plausible explanation to explain the great trade collapse of late 2008 to late 2009, when global trade outpaced the drop in real GDP by a factor of 12, a figure much larger

Table 17.1   Risk characteristics of short-term trade finance products, 2008–2013

CATEGORY	Transaction default rate	Implied maturity (days)	Recovery rate[1]	Defaulted transaction loss rate[2]	Specific transaction-level loss rate
Import letters of credit	0.020%	80	71%	42%	0.008%
Export confirmed letters of credit	0.016%	70	40%	68%	0.011%
Loans for import	0.016%	110	45%	64%	0.010%
Loans for export: Bank risk	0.029%	140	32%	73%	0.021%
Loans for export: Corporate risk	0.021%	70	51%	57%	0.012%
Performance guarantees	0.034%	110	18%	85%	0.029%
Total	0.021%	90	52%	57%	0.012%**

Source: ICC (2013), pp. v, 23.

[1] Observed recoveries as a percentage of defaulted exposure across products.

[2] Estimated economic loss rate as a percentage of defaulting exposure after discounting and costs.

** The total average and the product-level annual transaction-level loss compare favourably with the average observed annual credit loss rate for Moody's customers over the same period of 1.49%.

than anticipated by standard demand models. Normally, the "reaction" (elasticity) of trade to changes in aggregate demand is much smaller, even during periods of economic depression.

The validity of this hypothesis has often been discussed by economists. While authors generally agree that the fall in demand has been largely responsible for the drop in trade flows, the debate focused on the extent to which other potential culprits, such as trade restrictions, a lack of trade finance, vertical specialisation and the composition of trade, may have played a role.

The "trade finance" hypothesis is based on the intuition that major disturbances in inter-bank markets were hit by contagion of the supply of short-term trade credit, which in turn is linked with trade. The dependence of trade on short-term financing is explained, notably in the above section, by the fact that a relatively small proportion of international trade is paid in cash. The existence of a time lag between the shipment of goods and the payment, justifying the need for credit and/or a guarantee, raises the suspicion that a squeeze in credit supply may end up seriously disrupting trade.

From Correlation to Causality

Empirical work on trade finance has been limited by the lack of a comprehensive dataset. However, progress was made by several academics in highlighting the link between financial conditions, trade credits and trade at the firm level. Amiti and Weinstein were able to establish a causality link between firms' exports, their ability to obtain credit and the health of their banks (Amiti and Weinstein 2011). They established in particular that the trade finance channel accounted for about 20% of the decline in Japanese exports during the financial crisis of 2008–2009. One reason is because exporters, more than any other producers, are reliant on trade credit and guarantees. Small and medium-sized exporters are more likely to be associated to ailing banks than large enterprises, hence increasing their sensitivity to financial downturns. Bricongne *et al.* (2012) found similarly, in France, that sectors which were highly dependent on external finance had been most severely hit by the financial crisis and experienced the largest drop in their export activity. Small and large firms, at the two ends of the spectrum of the 50,000 exporters' dataset, have been most affected by the shortage in trade credit.

At the macro level, the Organisation for Economic Co-operation and Development (OECD; Korinek *et al.* 2010) found a strong statistical relationship between insured short-term trade credit, as a proxy for total trade finance, and trade flows. When extending the same dataset over a full cycle, 2005–2012, a strong correlation was found by Auboin and Engemann (2014) between insured trade credit and trade flows (Figure 17.1).

The Auboin and Engemann paper identified the effect of insured trade credits on trade at the macro level, hence moving "from correlation to causality", using the Berne Union database, the largest available on trade credit. For the significance of macroeconomic analysis, it was important that the total amount of trade credit recorded annually the data (close to US$1.8 trillion for 100 countries) was somewhat proportionate to trade flows (US$16 trillion annually for global merchandise trade) and the overall credit in the countries tested. A two-stage approach was used to link up global economic and financial conditions (GDP and liquidity) and trade

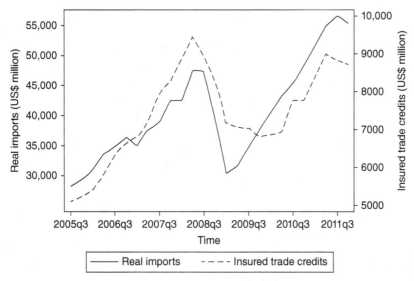

Figure 17.1   The relation between imports and insured trade credits in million US$ (averaged over all countries).
Source: Auboin and Engemann (2014).

credit availability, in the first stage; and trade credit availability and trade flows (imports since the breakdown of trade credit data is by destination country), in the second. This approach aimed at avoiding endogeneity problems linked to reverse causality between trade credit and trade, as the volume of trade demand impacts on the demand for trade credit, and trade credit availability impacts trade as well. Besides the data on insured trade credits, the Berne Union data also contained information on claims on unpaid trade credits, which measured the actual risk of trade credit insurance. Under the first stage, the study found that the volume of insured trade credit available was affected by overall economic and financial conditions over a full economic cycle – from the upswing of 2005 to the peak of the financial crisis in 2009, and the stabilisation of activity in 2010–2011. Trade credit was indeed determined by the level of liquidity in the economy and by GDP as a measure of national income.

The second stage of the study aimed at introducing trade credit as a determining factor in the standard import equation, which included, as described by the economic theory, GDP/national income and real effective exchange rates. Trade credit was found to be a significant and robust determinant of imports, with elasticities being stable and robust to tests around 0.4–0.5%. Real GDP and relative prices of foreign and domestic goods, the two traditional explanatory variables of standard import equations, also come out as the strongest determinants of imports.

Trade Finance Market Characteristics and Behaviour

If so Safe, Why is Trade Finance Prone to Disruptions?

The short answer to this question is that the systemic nature of financial crises experienced in the most recent periods, say, since the Asian Financial Crisis, no longer spares trade finance from being hit by the contagion of massive financial disruptions emanating from other segments of financial markets. The problems detected in the post-Asian crisis analysis, which could qualify as market failures (herd behaviour, increased gap between the level of risk and perception of risk, fragility of the market due to a relatively limited number of leading banks, confusion between country and counterparty risk, lack of visibility on the market situation due to the lack of statistics on short-term movements), have re-emerged in the cocktail of factors which characterised the global tensions in trade finance markets in 2008–2009 (Chauffour and Farole, 2009).

In the past, trade finance used to be relatively "protected" in the 1960s through the 1990s by a relatively well-established methodology and preferred treatment in handling officially guaranteed trade credit in the case of sovereign default. In these cases, commercial claims of private nature were in parallel "handled" by the London Club – generally in the form of restructuring, the interest of both governments and private sector banks being that the flow of trade should not be interrupted by efforts to restructure (or reschedule) old debt. This was regarded to be necessary to keep trade flowing and for the balance of payments to turn around. While officially guaranteed credit represented an important part of trade between developed and developing countries in the 1970s and 1980s, private markets have expanded more rapidly and took over the short-term trade finance segment as the expansion of local banking sectors allowed for the establishment of global inter-bank links helping to connect traders from the "North" and the "South".

These links have been temporarily disturbed, but in a massive way, during the Asian and Latin American financial crises of the late 1990s, when foreign "correspondent" banks reconsidered existing exposures to local banks, in the context of a solvency crisis affecting local financial institutions. In the most extreme cases, credit lines for available financing have been interrupted and outstanding debt left pending. In crisis-stricken countries, the stoppage of trade finance interrupted trade flows as well, delaying the recovery of the trade-reliant economies to redress their balance of payments. In the specific case of Indonesia, for example, the high import content of exports (over 40%) explained why the export growth was seriously affected by the difficulty of financing imported inputs for use in its export sectors. To alleviate the problem, the Indonesian government and Central Bank extended guarantees to foreign banks for letters of credit opened by Indonesian banks, and they encouraged a steering committee of private borrowers and lenders to find an arrangement to maintain trade finance facilities and settle arrears. Episodes of credit crunches in Asia and later in Latin America raised uncertainty in private markets in the absence of reliable information about risk, specifically country risk and individual risk.

Standard economic theory in such circumstances indicates that the demand for credit emanating from companies with good credit ratings should meet supply at a higher price. In periods of acute crisis, however, this supply did not exist in certain countries, raising suspicion of a market failure. In Indonesia, the total value of trade finance bank limits fell suddenly from US$6 billion from 400 international banks to US$1.6 billion from 50 banks (World Trade Organization, 1998). In order to avoid a prolonged interruption of regional and international trade flows, targeted intervention by public or semi-public entities took place in the middle of the crisis to restore a minimum of confidence in trade markets, even before exchange rates stabilised.

Market participants regarded the ad hoc solutions proposed by regional development banks as successful in terms of having suffered no defaults or losses while keeping minimum cross-border trade finance available. Both the Inter-American Development Bank and the Asian Development Bank (ADB) extended guarantee facilities to international banks confirming local banks' letters of credit. Some export credit agencies from developed countries provided short-term insurance for credit extended during the crisis period on bilateral trade. Urgency trade finance schemes, which were largely inspired by the trade finance facilitation programme of the European Bank for Reconstruction and Development (EBRD), have become more standardised since the Asian crisis.

The common element of all these ad hoc mechanisms was to offer risk mitigation to induce endorsing entities to accept commitments to pay. Although some local financial systems in East Asia had collapsed, in many cases the underlying trade links had not been broken – and contracts illustrated the existence of a solvable demand. Risk mitigation devices such as guarantees of payment in case of default proved to be an effective tool for the implementation of contracts.

The fact that a credit crunch could affect both exports and imports to the point of stoppage induced the international financial and trading communities to organise a "debriefing" exercise, involving the International Monetary Fund (IMF), World Bank, World Trade Organization (WTO), regional development banks and private sector actors. This exercise aimed in particular at identifying and analysing any market failure, best practice and cooperative policy action during a crisis period (IMF, 2003).

Excursus: Trade Finance Markets: Market Failure? How and When?

The IMF and WTO analysed the factors behind the fall in trade finance during the financial crisis of emerging economies in Asia and Latin America in the period 1997–2001. The IMF attributed such declines to "the response by banks as leveraged institutions, to the lack of insurance when it was needed, and to herd behaviour among banks, official export credit agencies (ECAs), and private insurers" (IMF, 2003). Moreover, the declines were often associated with weak domestic banking systems. The IMF also pointed to a relatively concentrated market for trade finance: "the consolidation of the international banking sector in recent years may also have had a bearing on the decline in trade finance during recent crises".

The IMF acknowledges an element of market failure as "the contraction in trade finance [has been] widely perceived to be more than would be justified by fundamentals and the risks involved [...]. The extent to which trade credit lines [have been] withdrawn was unprecedented, especially in countries (such as Brazil) with virtually no defaults on such credit lines and where policies were supported by a substantial international financial package" (IMF, 2003). The Fund explained it as owing to

- [...] the interaction between perceived risks and the leveraged positions of banks,
- the lack of sufficient differentiation between short-term, self-liquidating trade credits, and other categories of credit exposure by rating agencies,
- herd behaviour among trade finance providers such as banks and trade insurers, as decision-making by international providers of trade finance during crises is

often dominated by perceptions rather than fundamentals [an acknowledgement of failures in risk appraisal in periods of stress],
- and weak domestic banking systems.

These factors, already identified in 2003, do not differ fundamentally from the factors at play a few years later in the 2008–2009 financial crisis of developed economies. In its own analysis of the 1997–2001 financial crisis episode, the WTO points to the widening of the gap between the actual levels of risks and the perceived levels of risks during periods of financial crisis, as well as the confusion between the company risk and the country risk, which, altogether, led foreign banks to cut exposure for all customers rather than to adopt a differentiated approach. "Through a 'natural selection' process, one could have imagined that banks would have concentrated their portfolio on their best (and most solvable) customers, while taking advantage of the higher prices of credit. Instead, the contraction of trade finance seems to have been beyond what the 'fundamentals' would have suggested, thereby raising suspicions, as indicated above, about the existence of some market failure" (Auboin and Engemann, 2013).

The "herd behaviour" resulting in a general withdrawal by international banks from any type of activity regardless of the type of lending and of risk has been encouraged by the lack of transparency and adequate information regarding companies' balance sheets in the countries concerned, as well as worrying signals sent by credit rating agencies, which, after having failed to detect the onset of the crisis, had to rapidly downgrade the affected countries severely. While trade finance instruments help to mitigate commercial risks, there are still a number of risks to be borne, including the exchange rate risk. During the currency crises of 1997–1998, large swings in exchange rates increased the perception of risk in engaging in commercial transactions, which, in the region, were essentially invoiced in dollars. The WTO also discussed some of the weaknesses in supply chain finance arrangements. In periods of crisis, buyer–supplier open account arrangements were disrupted, with buyers no longer extending liquidity or favourable payment terms to their suppliers (IMF, 2003; WTO, 2004).

In its 2003 paper, the Fund had suggested a "framework for trade finance in crisis resolution" with recommendations that multilateral development banks (MDBs) extend risk-sharing agreements, and that export credit agencies and private insurers step into the market; it was said in the Fund paper that "multilateral development banks' trade finance facilities, properly designed and implemented, [could] be effective in mobilizing additional private sector funding during a period of heightened risk aversion". Central banks could also provide temporarily "liquidity to the export sector by purchasing export bills of exchange from export enterprises", "provide guarantees to enhance the acceptance of L/C issued by domestic banks", or "make foreign exchange available for appropriately documented pre- and post-shipment export trade finance transactions".

The WTO's 2004 paper also recognised the case for public intervention and indicated that ad-hoc solutions developed by regional development banks had been regarded as successful, in terms of having "suffered no default or losses while keeping minimum cross-border trade alive". It recommended that trade finance facilitation schemes become more standardised across multilateral development institutions. The

WTO paper also identified regulatory issues to be dealt with, as a way to "secure a greater availability of trade finance in the long-term". The paper pleaded for "a better interaction between the regulatory framework and market conditions, one aspect of the problem [being] the implementation of new 'Basel II' rules, [with] some significant increase in the risk weighting for short-term trade finance activities, from a level which has already been considered excessive for this relatively low-risk activity".

Both the IMF and the WTO had noted the poor state of international statistics on trade finance, a problem that remains unresolved, as of now. As indicated by the IMF (2003), "data on trade credit are not readily available, complicating efforts to carry out comprehensive empirical analysis. In the cases where data are available, they are often only partial. As a result, many participants of trade finance suggested a systematic effort involving country authorities, multilateral institutions as well as the private sector to be launched to collect data to facilitate future empirical research". Since then, the efforts by statistical compilers to redress the situation have been limited.

Many of the problems detected in the post-Asian crisis analysis have re-emerged in the cocktail of factors which characterised the global tensions in trade finance markets in 2008–2009. Many of the ad hoc solutions that have been devised during the Asian crisis and that have been analysed as being successful in the IMF and WTO documents, have therefore been used again in the crisis response to the 2008–2009 crisis, albeit in a more systematic and planned way. The "return from experience" offered by the IMF and WTO in 2003 greatly contributed to expanding some embryonic programmes put in place in Eastern Europe and Asia, such as trade finance facilitation programmes. During the recovery and expansion period of the global financial sector (2001–2008), the International Finance Corporation (IFC), the Asian Development Bank and the Inter-American Development Bank have inaugurated such facilities. The EBRD expanded its own substantially.

What Has Happened in 2009 and What Was the Policy Reaction?

It became clear that in the course of 2008 the overall liquidity squeeze on money markets was hitting trade credit supply, as the refinancing of such credit became more difficult with the liquidity squeeze, and as lending was also affected by the general reassessment of risk linked to the worsening of global economic activities. Beginning in the autumn of 2008 and continuing into 2009, indications of shortages in the trade credit market came from exchanges with key bankers and MDBs in the context of the WTO Expert Group on Trade Finance – a contact and consultative group which had started to meet regularly at the WTO after the end of the "debriefing" exercise which had followed the Asian Financial Crisis (above section). After the failure of Lehman failure, the secondary market for trade bills dried up and inter-bank liquidity became too tight for trade orders to be financed.

While the state of statistics had not improved much since 2003, one of the achievements of the Expert Group on Trade Finance had been to develop relatively comprehensive market surveys relying on bank information on the state of trade finance markets. So, contrary to the Asian crisis period, policymaking could rely on a "thermometer" of the market, as provided by both the International Chamber of Commerce's (ICC) Banking Commission and the Bankers Association for Finance and Trade. By the time of the London G20 (Group of Twenty) Summit, in April 2009, the surveys had confirmed the deterioration of trade finance markets. Calculated on a year-on-year basis, by the end of the third quarter of 2008, the flows of trade finance to some developing countries' regions had fallen more than the flows of trade for the same period. The fees on letters of credit in these regions had increased sharply under the combined effects of scarce liquidity and reassessment of customer and country risks. Spreads on 90-days letters of credit had increased from 20 to 30 basis points above London Inter-bank Offered Rate (LIBOR) prior to the crisis to levels of 250 to 500 basis points. The closure of the secondary market for letters of credit, directly linked to the freeze in inter-bank transactions on short-term refinancing instruments, had left a capacity gap estimated at US$20 billion per month. Market specialists had noted that, while demand for trade was falling as well, some of such demand remained unfinanced. Using the surveys as well as capacity reduction linked to the closure of some markets, it was estimated in the Expert Group that the "supply" gap at the period of the market crisis had reached between US$200 billion and US$300 billion – mainly felt in developing regions.

The process which led the G20 Summit in London, in response to these concerns, to step in and commit to the availability of extra capacity of US$250 billion for trade finance has been well explained and documented (Auboin, 2009; Chauffour and Malouche, 2011). The commitment to support the provision of short-term trade finance was one element in a wider set of fiscal, monetary and financial actions undertaken by the international community to support the continued functioning of international trade and financial markets during a period of acute stress. The G20 agreed to provide temporary and extraordinary crisis-related trade finance support that would be delivered on a basis that respected the need to avoid protectionism and would not result in the long-run displacement of private market activity. It relied on public guarantees and risk co-sharing agreements between banks and national and international public institutions. It consisted of three main "products":

- An increase in credit insurance and risk mitigation capacity by export credit agencies (ECAs). Some ECAs also provided working capital and credit guarantees aimed mainly at small and medium enterprises. Several large ECAs extended these facilities to imports as well.
- Regional development banks (RDBs) and the IFC of the World Bank Group increased guarantees for letters of credit under their trade facilitation programmes, before the G20 Meeting, and after. The increase was manifest in credit guarantee products and risk participation agreements.
- Some RDBs also provided liquidity windows as part of their trade finance facilitation programmes. In a period of liquidity squeeze, the demand by banks for such access had increased significantly, particularly for transactions involving the poorest markets. To this aim, the IFC reinforced its global trade finance facility through the introduction of the Global Trade Liquidity Pool (GTLP), allowing for a 40–60 % co-lending agreement between the IFC and commercial banks.

Above and beyond the G20 trade finance package, central banks have also provided support, notably by extending foreign exchange resources to traders which needed it, as the peak crisis period was marked by a US dollar shortage that reflected the tensions in the US money market. Central banks with large foreign exchange reserves also supplied foreign currency to local banks and importers, generally through repurchase agreements (Korea). Other central banks opened temporarily "discount windows" for local traders willing to discount foreign trade receivables and other bills (Japan). The US Federal Reserve Board helped central banks that did not have sufficient reserves in US dollars with the conclusion of 14 swap agreements, aimed at facilitating the payment of trade transactions. Most of these mechanisms were time-bound and waived when market conditions returned to normal. It considerably helped banks and importers in developing countries acquire scarce foreign exchange resources to conduct trade operations at one of the most difficult times of recent history.

The G20 established a "follow-up" working group aimed at monitoring the implementation of the London trade finance initiative. The package being demand-driven, the idea was to monitor commitments and utilisation rates, partly to make sure that it did not last longer than necessary. The working group indicated that most of the support initially promised for a period of two years had been front-loaded, and hence used during the first year of the initiative. Overall, some US$140–150 billion have been used out of the total commitment of US$250 billion (Auboin, 2015). Given these developments, G20 members began to scale back their support after the G20 Summit in Toronto in 2010. While perhaps the trade finance-related G20 programme was only a minor part of the overall effort to increase liquidity in financial markets at a time of illiquidity, the capacity put in place allowed exporters with existing orders to count on lending and trade credit insurance to be able to ship their goods. While the counterfactual may be difficult to establish, the non-delivery of orders could have had a chilling effect on trade for a longer period when the economic cycle rebounded.

An Uneven Recovery

According to ICC surveys in particular, trade finance markets improved continuously between the middle of 2009 and early 2011, with falling prices and increasing volumes of transactions. Recovery was uneven across countries though. The recovery was most evident in the main "routes" of trade, in line with the recovery of trade demand and improved financial market conditions within North America, Europe and Asia and between Asia and the rest of the world. In these areas, spreads had fallen, albeit not to pre-crisis levels, with a difference between traditional trade finance instruments (letters of credit), for which prices fell to low levels on the "best" Asian risks, and so-called funded trade finance products (on-balance sheet, open account transactions), for which higher prices reflected relatively large liquidity premia – the latter prices being still up to 40–50% higher than before the financial crisis.

By contrast, traders in low-income countries remained subject to the greatest difficulties in accessing trade finance at affordable cost, particularly import finance. The same applied to small and medium-sized enterprises (SMEs) in developed countries, which relied on small or medium-sized banks. This situation was explained by a banking environment in which capital had become scarcer and the selectivity of risks greater.

Indeed, while quantitative easing made liquidity relatively abundant at the "higher end" of the market, allowing large corporates to benefit from easy financing at low rates, ICC global surveys insisted that the "appetite" of international banks to operate in developing countries, in particular the poorest, had fallen. In 2014, nearly 46% of the 500 banks surveyed by the ICC had terminated correspondent relationships, mainly due to the cost or complexity of compliance, while 70% of respondents reported declining transactions due to other regulatory requirements such as "know-your-customer" and anti-money-laundering obligations. The need to adjust balance sheets downwards (process of "deleveraging"), in the light of new and more stringent capital adequacy requirements, also contributed to the retreat of global banks.

Surveys also pointed to the fact, as early as 2012–2013, that, as a result of lower presence of international banks and their refocusing on bigger clients, SMEs, notably in developing countries, were the prime victims of the impact of reduced correspondent banking networks.

Before policy actions could be warranted, more analysis and evaluation was needed on the issues of regulation, concentration of the trade finance markets (and the impact of de-risking) and the importance of the remaining trade finance market gap in developing countries. These issues have been examined in recent years and are dealt with in the following section.

New Challenges Affecting Mainly Developing Countries

Avoiding the Unintended Consequences of Basel III: A Dialogue with Prudential Regulators

In a joint letter sent to the G20 leaders in Seoul (2011), the Heads of the World Bank Group and the WTO raised the issue of the potential unintended consequences of the Basel II and III frameworks on the availability of trade finance in low-income countries. While trade finance received preferential regulatory treatment under the Basel I framework, in recognition of its safe, mostly short-term character, the implementation of some provision of Basel II proved difficult for trade. The application of risk weights and the confusion between country and counterparty risks have not been particularly advantageous for banks willing to finance trade transactions with developing-country partners. Basel III added to these requirements a 100% leverage ratio on off-balance-sheet letters of credit, which are primarily used by developing countries. At a time when more risk-averse suppliers of trade credit revised their general exposure, the application of more stringent regulatory requirements raised doubts about profitability and incentives to engage in trade finance relative to other categories of assets.

Besides, the feeling increased that the preferential prudential status granted under Basel I to trade finance in relation to other categories of assets was being significantly reduced; in other words, the comparative advantage of supplying trade finance, a relatively low-profitability business, was being diminished.

As a result, and in the overall framework of paragraph 41 of the Seoul Summit Declaration (G20, 2010), these issues have been discussed by the Basel Committee on Banking Supervision's Policy Development Group and the institutions concerned with trade finance, notably the WTO, the World Bank and the ICC.

In the context of the WTO Expert Group on Trade Finance, the Director-General of the WTO encouraged the ICC's banking commission to collect the necessary data, and for the dialogue with banking regulators on trade finance to be fact-based. Since 2010, the ICC has been able to collect data on loss default for trade finance operations, with the world's main banks contributing. This "trade finance loss register" indicates that the average default rate on international trade credit operations is no higher than 0.2% globally, including during the recent period of financial crisis. This is lower than most domestic lending activities. Aggregate data were passed on to the Basel Committee on Bank Supervision to feed the discussion with its partners. According to the ICC, World Bank and WTO, the data indicate that cross-border trade finance is a safe financial activity, including in low-income countries. While it was fully justified to re-regulate the financial sector in view of recent difficulties, trade finance ought not to become an unintended casualty.

The Basel Committee on Banking Supervision (BCBS) discussed which measures of the prudential regulation affecting trade finance were most detrimental to trade and trade finance availability, with a particular focus on the beneficial effects for low-income countries. Proposals were made by the WTO and the World Bank to the Committee with a view to waiving the obligation to capitalise short-term letters of credit for one full year, when their average maturity was according to the registry between 90 and 115 days (consistent with the maturity of the vast majority of international trade transactions). This measure was "blocking" hundreds of millions of US dollars of unnecessary capital that could be used to finance more trade transactions. During the G20 Meeting in London, at the initiative of the Director-General and of the President of the World Bank, the G20 had already asked for a temporary relief from this regulatory measure to support trade in developing countries. The temporary relief will now be made permanent. Hence, 90 to 115-days trade letters of credit will be capitalised for that appropriate maturity.

Traditionally, trade finance – mainly letters of credit and other self-liquidating instruments of payments for trade – received preferential treatment from national and international regulators on grounds that it was one of the safest, most collateralised and self-liquidating forms of finance. This was reflected in the low credit conversion factor (CCF) determined under the Basel I framework for the capitalisation of these instruments, which was set at 20%, i.e. five times lower than any on-balance-sheet loan. However, as the banking and regulatory communities moved towards internal ratings-based and risk-weighted assets systems under the successor Basel II framework, issues regarding maturity structure and country risk emerged.

After the 2008–2009 financial crisis, in the context of prudential re-regulation of the financial system under Basel III, some requested that trade finance, which had suffered casualties by contagion from other segments of the financial industry, not be penalised. The unintended consequences of increased prudential requirements were to be avoided, notably in respect of the ability of developing countries to access affordable trade finance. At the end of 2011, the G20 asked that the WTO and World Bank on the one hand, and the BCBS on the other, engage in discussions aimed at improving a common understanding of trade finance and identifying any unintended consequences of prudential regulation. This dialogue proved extremely useful. The data collected by the ICC under the pilot trade finance register allowed prudential regulators to improve their understanding of trade finance and verify the low-risk character and absence of leverage in the industry. The aggregate data delivered covered more than 20 major international banks, over 5 million transactions and revealed fewer than 1150 defaults. Since 2011, the WTO and the World Bank have continued to hold discussions with the Basel Committee.

Since then, the BCBS has made three revisions reflecting the low risk of trade finance and improving its regulatory treatment:

- On 25 October 2011, the BCBS agreed to reduce the excessive risk-weighting requirements on low-income countries, and to waive the one-year maturity floors for letters of credit and related instruments. Both measures are of great importance in removing obstacles to trade finance in developing countries (BIS, 2011).
- On 6 January 2013, the new Basel III guidelines on liquidity (concerning the liquidity coverage ratio) proved to be favourable to short-term self-liquidating trade finance instruments. In its decision, the Committee allowed national regulators to set very low outflow rates – between 0 and 5%, significantly below previous levels – for contingent funding obligations from trade finance instruments. Banks are allowed to hold fewer liquid assets against contingent trade liabilities, thereby increasing the availability of trade finance (BIS, 2013).
- On 12 January 2014, the BCBS reduced the leverage ratio on trade letters of credit and other self-liquidating trade-related instruments from a 100% CCF to a 20% CCF for capital purposes and 50% CCF for trade guarantees (BIS, 2014a). The 2014 modification was hailed by the WTO Director-General: "[this is] of particular significance for the availability of trade finance in the developing world, where letters of credit are a key instrument of payment. This is good news for developing countries, for the expansion of their trade and for the continued growth of South-South trade flows" (WTO, 2014a).

The situation on the prudential front looks better than it did a few years ago, thanks to the institutional dialogues opened by the WTO and the Basel Committee, and the data support provided by the ICC. There is no doubt that such initiatives have contributed to improving the policy coherence between the prudential and central bank community on the one hand, and the trading community on the other.

Other non-prudential regulatory issues described as KYC requirements have been subject to discussion within the WTO's trade finance community. The debate does not focus on regulatory requirements, which legitimately aim to increase transparency in financial relations (including various informational requirements to combat illegal financing and tax evasion), but rather on the various ways that they are being structured, defined and implemented by and in different countries and regions. It was argued, although it was not always proven, that the accumulation of these requirements (very detailed information varying across jurisdictions about a customer's identity and the end use of money lent) led banks to terminate banking relations, including trade finance, with developing countries. Therefore more clarity is still needed to determine whether a lack of harmonised regulatory requirements discourages trade, particularly in developing countries. Some have suggested that the trade finance industry needs more fact-based evidence of trade foregone, lost correspondent banking relationships and other criteria before it can assess the impact of lack of regulatory harmonisation in this area (WTO, 2014c). Dialogue on this issue should of course take place within the appropriate governance structures, such as the OECD's Financial Action Task Force (FATF).

Challenges Stemming from the Concentration of Global Trade Finance Markets

A study by the BIS (2014b) revealed that a large share of international trade is supplied by a relatively small group of globally active international banks. This group of about 40 banks accounts for some 30% of international trade finance, with local and regional banks supplying the remainder. The market for trade finance, considered in its widest definition, is very large – certainly well above US$10 trillion annually. For bank-intermediated short-term trade finance only, the BIS (2014b) considered that the flow was between US$6.5 trillion and US$8 trillion during 2011, of which around US$2.8 trillion was letters of credit.

The main trade finance banks are also dominant in other segments of financial services. Since the financial crisis of 2008–2009, global banks have been subject to more stringent capital and lending rules, and have had to recalibrate their balance sheets accordingly. As indicated above, global banks have also been subject to additional compliance requirements, generally linked to OECD standards and codes of good conduct (anti-money laundering, anti-terrorism financing, anti-tax evasion etc.). Some global banks have argued that there had been a causal relation between the reduction of their networks of correspondent banking relationships and the cost of compliance. While it may be difficult to attribute de-risking to only one cause such as the cost of compliance, for some banks the increased cost of doing business in very small or poor countries may have been balanced by the amount of fees generated in this business. A comprehensive survey was completed by the World Bank (2015) on the reduction in correspondent banking relationships – which is not affecting only trade finance but other cross-border flows as well (remittances etc.). The BIS also thought about the impact of increased due diligence costs on banking (2015).

Regardless of the causes, deleveraging has reduced the ability of global banks to provide trade finance globally and locally. While there is at least anecdotal evidence that part of the market share left is filled by local and regional banks, the withdrawal of a global bank from a country or a region leaves a temporary gap. In finance, size matters to make the heavy investment to establish a larger footprint. One important factor is the ability to offer traders global issuance and confirmation of letters of credit at an affordable rate. Another one is the ability to supply clients with US dollars, the most widespread currency in international trade. Finally, large banks are able to offer alternative services, such as factoring and other supply chain financing solutions that smaller banks are not necessarily able to provide locally.

Vulnerability of Small Businesses in Accessing Trade Finance

SMEs (i.e. companies defined as employing 250 or fewer workers) constitute the vast majority of companies registered in both developed and developing countries. Their role in economic activity, generating growth and innovation cannot be overstated. According to the World Bank, SMEs contribute to over 60% of total employment in developed countries and 80% in developing ones, including the estimated informal sector (World Bank, 2013). Also, according to OECD figures, SMEs account for 40% of exports of OECD countries,[3] and a somewhat smaller share in developing countries, where concentration of exports is highest among the largest firms (World Bank, 2013).

Recent research suggests that an absence of, or weak access to, finance can strongly inhibit formal SME development, regardless of the level of per capita income of countries. Market failures, notably in financial markets (be they financial crises or "information asymmetries"), fall disproportionally on SMEs, resulting in more credit rationing, higher costs of "screening" and higher interest rates from banks than for larger enterprises (Stiglitz and Weiss, 1981; Beck and Demirgüç-Kunt, 2006). SMEs tend to be associated with smaller banks, to the extent they are banked at all.

Credit constraints are particularly reflected in access to trade finance. A survey of 2350 SMEs and 850 large firms by the US International Trade Commission (USITC) showed that 32% of SMEs in the manufacturing sector and 46% of SMEs in the services sector considered the process of obtaining finance for conducting cross-border trade "burdensome". Only 10% of large firms in the US manufacturing sector and 17% in the services sector experienced the same difficulties. The USITC study also revealed that lack of access to credit is the main constraint for SME manufacturing firms and one of the top three constraints for SME services firms seeking to export or expand into new markets (see Figure 17.2). Even some sectors showing significant levels of creditworthiness and collateral (transport equipment, information technology and professional services) considered that securing finance was an "acute" problem (USITC, 2010).

Other surveys found similar results in Europe and Japan. In a study covering 50,000 French exporters during the financial crisis of 2008–2009, credit constraints on smaller exporters were found to be much higher than those placed on larger firms, to the point of reducing the range of destinations for business or leading the SMEs to stop exporting altogether (Bricongne et al., 2009). In Japan, SMEs were more likely to be associated with troubled banks, hence exporting SMEs were more vulnerable in periods of financial crisis (Amiti and Weinstein, 2011). In general, credit-constrained firms – mostly likely to be found among SMEs – were also less likely to export (Bellone et al., 2010; Manova, 2013).

In less capital-intensive or less-developed economies, or economies with lower savings rates, local banks are even more conservative about supporting developing countries' exporters and importers. In developing countries, local banks may lack the capacity, knowledge, regulatory environment, international network and/or foreign currency to supply import- and export-related finance. Equally, traders

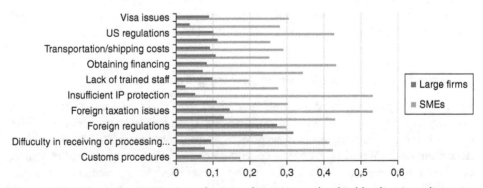

Figure 17.2 US services SMEs view obtaining financing as the third leading impediment to engaging in global trade.
Source: USITC (2010), pp. 6–11.

may not be aware of the available products, or of how to use them efficiently. Other obstacles in developing countries include banking or country risk, particularly in the context of regional and global financial crises. Exports from Asian countries, in particular during the Asian Financial Crisis, suffered from the contagion of regional financial crises, in certain cases causing interruptions of imports and exports due to the lack of trust of confirming banks in letters of credit issued in crisis-stricken countries (WTO, 2004). More recently, exports from sub-Saharan and other low-income countries have been particularly affected by the Global Financial Crisis because they are more dependent on bank-intermediated finance than other regions. The next section discusses recent MDB studies seeking to quantify the shortage of trade finance required for all trade transactions in developing countries, where the risk capacity or likeliness to support SMEs is even lower than in developed countries.

Estimating the Global Trade Finance Gap

The Global Trade Finance Gap Survey (Asian Development Bank)

The Asian Development Bank (ADB, 2017) estimated that the global trade finance gap was US$1.4 trillion in 2017, against an estimated gap of US$1.6 trillion in 2015 and US$1.4 trillion in 2014. The survey is the outcome of a major cooperative effort by several institutions, including the WTO, MDBs, private banks participating in the Banking Commission of the International Chamber of Commerce, factoring companies, export credit agencies and firms belonging to several networks (SME forum, UN International Trade Centre, the Netherland's Centre for the Promotion of Imports). Over 500 banks and 1300 firms in over 100 countries (mostly developing countries) have been surveyed for the 2017 ADB trade finance gap survey.

While the 2017 global trade finance gap looks stable relative to the 2015 and 2014 ones, one could have expected a fall, given that trade in US dollar value has fallen by 16% in the previous two years. Geographically, 40% of the gap comes from Asia, 23% from Latin America and 15% from Africa and the Middle East. Banks had reported in the survey that 74% of their total rejections of trade finance requests came from micro and small and medium-sized enterprises (MSMEs) and midcap firms.

One impact of such high rejection rates is foregone trade. Firms were asked what happened to the trade transaction after rejection of trade finance requested. About 60% of responding firms reported that they failed to execute the trade transaction. The remaining 40% of firms were able to complete the sale without bank-intermediated trade finance. Taking a different approach to the question of what happens after a transaction is rejected, more than half (53%) of surveyed firms did not look for alternative sources of financing when a transaction was rejected. Among those respondents that found an alternative (both formal and informal solutions), only half used it – the other half found it too expensive. Respondent banks in Africa and in Latin America resorted to informal financial providers more than firms from other regions.

Almost a third of transactions are rejected by the banks due to their reluctance to undertake due diligence (KYC) requirements for transactions which are regarded as

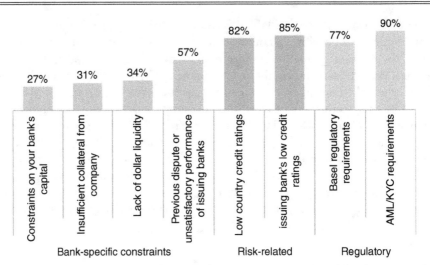

Figure 17.3 Constraints to supplying trade finance: percentage of banks' respondents. Source: ADB (2016).

either of insufficient profitability or too small in value (see Figure 17.3 regarding constraints to supplying trade finance). The lack of collateral against lending is also one of the main reasons for the rejection of requests for trade finance by banks. KYC, low profitability and lack of collateral explain three quarters of rejections. The ADB concludes that a lot of requests for trade finance could be accepted/financed if firm identity solutions were implemented to address challenges in KYC due diligence. The ADB pleads for the adoption of the Legal Entity Identifier (LEI), a harmonised global identification system which is also promoted by institutions such as the BIS and the IMF; more trade finance transactions could be accepted if MDBs were further supporting supply chain finance arrangements. Unlike traditional methods of financing that focus on financials and collateral, where SMEs tend to be weak, supply chain financing assesses risk performance based on payment history and the "stickiness" of the supply chain relation – the buyer having an interest in encouraging banks to support its supplier.

Banks are digitising their internal processes to reduce costs. Still, 70% of surveyed firms are unfamiliar with digital finance. This is not surprising. Financial technology (fintech) currently considered foresees the possibility for companies to do transactions through open ledgers using the internet. This requires, inter alia, company identification, registration systems, book-keeping, legal recourse etc., which do not always exist in low-income countries. Besides, the lack of compliant book-keeping and other related company infrastructures is already among the reasons for which traders are denied credit.

The African Development Gap Survey (Regional)

The African Development Bank (AfDB, 2014) released a survey similar in methodology to the ADB's, limited to Africa. The survey was updated in 2016. The results revealed that between 2011 and 2014, the trade finance gap in Africa fluctuated between US$90 billion and US$120 billion. Only one third of Africa's trade had been supported by bank-intermediated finance, suggesting that a significant share of Africa's trade relies on inter-firm trade credit through open account and cash-in-advance transactions – formally or informally. In terms of distribution by the type of clients/companies, almost 60% of bank-intermediated trade finance had been granted to the banks' top ten clients. Although SMEs accounted for more than 80% of businesses in the continent, they only accounted for 28% of banks' trade finance portfolio. This extreme concentration towards the larger firms was worrying as quality banking services were not reaching SMEs. The AfDB survey also suggested that unmet demand was much higher in fragile and low-income countries (LICs) in Africa than in middle-income countries (MICs).

The main reasons for rejecting financing requests (Figure 17.4) were a lack of creditworthiness or credit history, insufficient limits granted by endorsing banks to local African issuing banks, small balance sheets and limited capital of African banks, and insufficient US dollar liquidity. Some of these constraints are structural and can only be addressed in the medium-to-long run: the African banking sector is not very concentrated, hence limiting the financing capacity of individual banks; the lack of US dollar availability is chronic; and many African banks are risk-averse in view of the limited collateral guarantees presented by small traders. In the light of such constraints, the survey argued that the ADB's Trade Finance Facilitation Program as well as those of other development finance institutions are needed and are particularly well-suited to addressing some of these obstacles.

Prices for trade-related lending provide another useful proxy for the trade financing gap. Just as market prices reflect supply and demand, evidence of gaps in certain regions is logically translated into the price of trade finance instruments. Based on the spreads for emerging market trade credit instruments published by Omni Bridgeway – a leading firm in trade finance restructuring – a large number of African countries have encountered extremely high spreads on trade financing, consistently high over the years, as evidenced in Table 17.2.

For instance, in 2014, interest rates on trade loans peaked at 49% per annum in Kenya and 70% in Angola. Apart from a few countries for which political risk may be the main factor, such prohibitive terms on African countries reflect a disconnect between perceived and actual commercial risk.[4]

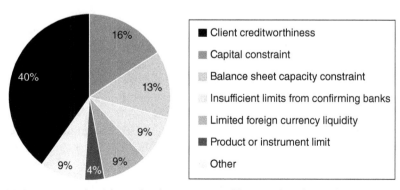

Figure 17.4   Reasons for African banks' rejection of letters of credit applications.
Source: AfDB (2014), p. 29.

Table 17.2   Africa trade credit pricing (annual interest rate, %)

Country	Price range as of May 2011		Price range as of April 2014	
	LOW	HIGH	LOW	HIGH
Angola*	60	65	65	70
Cameroon	14	20	18	24
Congo	22	26	22	26
Democratic Republic of the Congo	16	20	22	27
Ghana	78	82	74	78
Kenya*	39	49	39	49
Mozambique	20	26	20	26
Senegal	12	16	12	16
Sudan	15	19	9	14
Tanzania	10	13	25	35
Uganda	14	16	16	18
Zambia	13	20	13	20

* Spreads are corrected for inflation.
Source: Omni Bridgeway (2011, 2014).
Note: Trade credits and their documentation differ from case to case and price ranges should therefore be considered as benchmark only. Price ranges are based on a monthly compilation of sources and analytics. Liquidity on most instruments is very limited and trading may not have taken place for some time.

Other Surveys

Qualitative surveys can help position the lack of trade finance relative to other structural supply-side problems faced by exporters in poor countries. Unsurprisingly, lack of access to finance is one prime concern when operating in international markets. A variety of sources indicate that it is a major obstacle for traders in Africa. Other developing regions are also affected too. These results are apparent in the 2014 World Economic Forum (WEF) "Global Enabling Trade Report" and the ICC global survey (ICC, 2014). The WEF report ranked the lack of access to trade finance as one of the most problematic factors for exporting in Africa (see Figure 17.5).

The ICC global survey for 2014, based on data from 298 banks in 127 countries, confirmed such findings. Forty-one per cent of respondent banks acknowledged the existence of a shortfall in global trade finance supply, with an emphasis on SMEs and Africa. Among the main obstacles limiting SME access to trade finance are the increasing compliance and regulatory burdens as well as low country and local bank credit ratings (see Figure 17.6). Seventy per cent of respondent banks recognised a role for MDBs in providing access to trade finance.

Finally, with regard to the issue of financing trade in the context of global value chains: a survey conducted by the WTO and the OECD in 2013 as background for the Fourth Global Review of Aid for Trade concluded that lack of access to trade finance was a key obstacle to low-income countries participating in global value chains (see Figure 17.7).

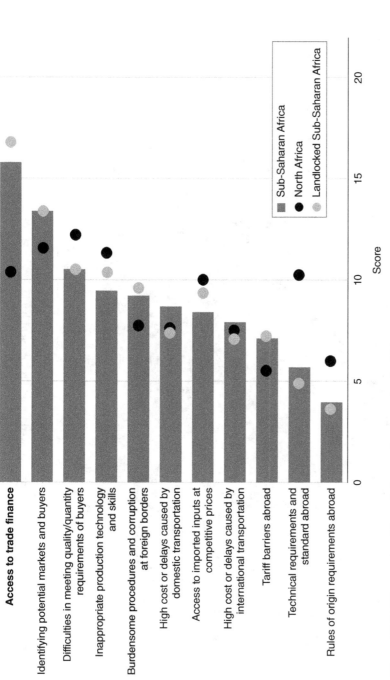

Figure 17.5 The most problematic factors for exporting in Africa.
Source: WEF (2014).
Note: From the list of factors above, respondents were asked to select the five most problematic ones for trading in their country and to rank them between 1 (most problematic) and 5. The bars in the figure show the responses weighted according to their rankings.

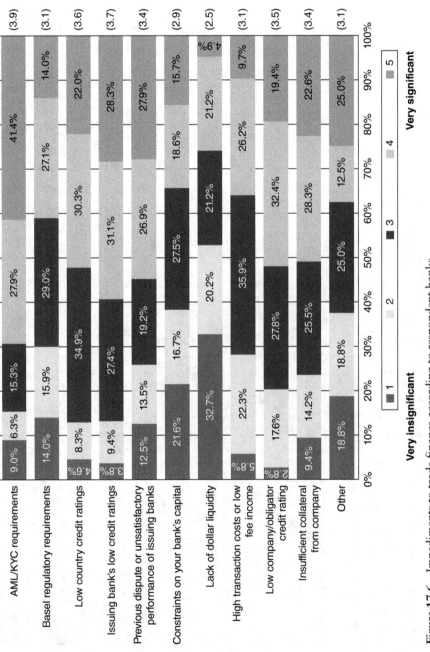

Figure 17.6 Impediments to trade finance according to respondent banks.
Source: ICC (2014), p. 97.
Note: Numbers in brackets are weighted averages of ratings. The closer the average rating is to 5, the higher the level of significance. An average rating close to 1 indicates a low level of importance.

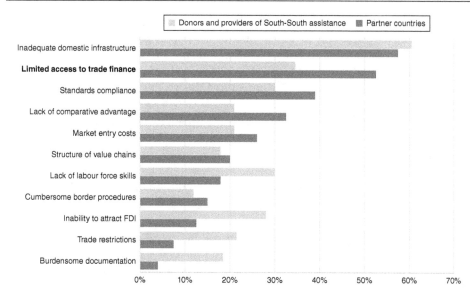

Figure 17.7   Public views of the main barriers in connecting firms to value chains (percentage of responses).
Source: WTO-OECD (2013), p. 24.

WTO Director-General Calls For New Action

Based on the above diagnosis, various stakeholders had policy discussions in the past year on how to address the challenges faced by developing countries, in particular their SMEs, in accessing trade finance after the financial crisis. On 26–27 March 2015, WTO members held a seminar to discuss this topic with government officials, bankers and multilateral development institutions. During the seminar, participants highlighted a number of key points, inter alia: trade financing gaps were due to a mix of structural and developmental factors (lack of know-how and capacity of the financial sectors in many developing countries) as well as the falling appetite of global banks to invest in developing countries after the financial crisis; developing local and regional trade finance industries took time, as it required knowledge dissemination, build-up of institutions and specific support by multilateral development agencies; the WTO and its Director-General should pay greater attention to these gaps – notably gaps in the poorest countries in which the need was the largest while the potential growth of trade was also the strongest.

In his introductory address to the seminar, the WTO Director-General Roberto Azevêdo promised to highlight the issue at the third United Nations Conference for Financing for Development in Addis Ababa in July 2015, which he did, and to come back to WTO members with concrete proposals.

In the first half of 2016, the Director-General issued a report, "Trade Finance and SMEs" (WTO, 2016), looking at these issues in detail and proposing a number of further steps that could be taken, including the following:

- Enhancing existing trade finance facilitation programmes to reduce the financing gaps. While trade finance facilitation programmes were not designed to eliminate all market gaps, they allowed SMEs and their banks locally to engage into international trade, thereby building capacity and experience.

- Reducing the knowledge gap in local banking sectors for handling trade finance instruments by training at least 5000 professionals over the next five years; professional organisations from the private sector would cooperate with MDBs in helping to pool the many training initiatives, where this is useful and when it generates economies of scale. The creation of the ICC Academy would be a useful tool in this regard.
- Maintaining an open dialogue with trade finance regulators to ensure that development considerations are reflected in the implementation, and eventually design, of regulations.
- Improving monitoring of trade finance in provision. The mapping of global trade finance gaps needs to be improved to better target policy action and respond to such gaps, particularly relating to any future crises.

In the past two years, progress has been recorded in several areas, thanks to the joint action of partner institutions such as MDBs and the ICC. Director-General Roberto Azevêdo continued to take the lead in favour of actions reducing trade finance gaps. He has worked in particular with the heads of MDBs. He met them collectively on the margins of the 6th Global Aid for Trade Review, and individually on specific occasions, including the 2017 WTO Public Forum and the 2017 Annual Meeting of the IMF and World Bank. Subsequently, MDBs have been stepping in, as demand for their financing or guarantees has increased.

In 2017, total financing and guarantees provided by MDBs under trade finance facilitation programs in developing countries reached close to US$30 billion, up from about US$22 billion in 2016. With the recovery of global trade flows forecast in 2018, demand for MDB credit and guarantees facilities are likely to be increased. However, representatives of MDBs indicated to the Director-General that there was "only so much more" they could do. The solution was hence to bring the private sector back into the most challenging markets, if the gap was to be narrowed down significantly.

One way was to develop co-financing and co-risk sharing operational among MDBs where geographical coverage overlapped, and between MDBs and commercial banks. For example, the International Financial Corporation (IFC, World Bank Group) and the Islamic Trade Finance Corporation (ITFC, Islamic Development Bank Group) recently signed a Memorandum of Understanding to conduct joint trade finance operations in Western Africa.

MDBs also agreed to boost capacity-building on trade finance in countries in which trade was growing rapidly. In 2017, the combined number of courses delivered by the IFC, ITFC, EBRD and the ICC Academy totalled over 2500, well above the aspirational target of 1000 recommended in the Director-General's publication.

MDBs also asked for a regulatory dialogue with the Financial Stability Board (FSB). MDBs, in their support to local banks in developing countries, were already doing much to get these banks to comply with international norms, notably to promote the pooling of information for compliance purposes, and hence facilitate flows of international trade finance to developing countries. In particular, more was needed to help clarify relevant regulatory requirements, notably by way of increased capacity-building. Philippe Le Houérou, Chief Executive Officer of the IFC, and Director-General Azevêdo wrote to the Chairman of the FSB to encourage an inter-institutional dialogue to this aim. After consultation of FSB members, the FSB agreed to seek IFC and WTO input, as far as trade finance was concerned, in their own clarification work. Director-General Azevêdo will continue his advocacy and technical work with the heads of multilateral agencies, the FSB and other stakeholders.

Notes

1 The trade transaction would not be financed twice. In the case of an inter-company credit, there is a seller's credit or a buyer's credit, not a credit on both the export and the import.
2 This would imply a transaction-level economic loss rate of approximately of 0.012% (i.e. 0.021% x 57%) for short-term trade finance transactions. By comparison, the average level of non-performing loans for main banks in the United States over the past 20 years has been 3% (World Bank data).
3 Data is available at http://www.oecd.org/std/its/trade-by-enterprise-characteristics.htm.
4 Unfortunately, the data in Table 17.2 is not available after 2014, as it is no longer published.

References

African Development Bank (2014) Trade Finance in Africa. Retrieved from: https://www. afdb.org/fileadmin/uploads/afdb/Documents/Publications/Trade_Finance_Report_AfDB_ EN_-_12_2014.pdf (accessed 12 July 2019).
Amiti, M. & Weinstein, D.E. (2011) Exports and Financial Shocks. *The Quarterly Journal of Economics*, 126(4), 1841–1877.
Asian Development Bank (2016) 2016 Trade Finance Gaps, Growth, and Jobs Survey. *ADB Briefs* No. 64. Retrieved from: https://www.adb.org/sites/default/files/publication/190631/ trade-finance-gaps.pdf (accessed 12 July 2019).
Asian Development Bank (2017) 2017 Trade Finance Gaps, Growth, and Jobs Survey. *ADB Briefs* No. 83. Retrieved from: https://www.adb.org/sites/default/files/publication/359631/ adb-briefs-83.pdf (accessed 12 July 2019).
Auboin, M. (2009) Boosting the Availability of Trade Finance in the Current Crisis: Background Analysis for a Substantial G-20 Package. *CEPR Policy Insight* No. 35, June 2009. Retrieved from: https://cepr.org/sites/default/files/policy_insights/PolicyInsight35.pdf (accessed 12 July 2019).
Auboin, M. (2015) Improving the Availability of Trade Finance in Low-Income Countries: An Assessment of Remaining Gaps. *Oxford Review of Economic Policy*, 31(3–4), 379–395.
Auboin, M. & Engemann, M. (2013) Trade Finance in Periods of Crisis: What Have We Learned in Recent Years? *WTO Staff Working Paper* ERSD-2013-01. Retrieved from: https:// www.econstor.eu/bitstream/10419/80075/1/736008144.pdf (accessed 12 July 2019).
Auboin, M. & Engemann, M. (2014) Testing the Trade Credit and Trade Link: Evidence from Data on Export Credit Insurance. *Review of World Economics*, 150(4), 715–743.
Bank for International Settlements (2011) Basel Committee on Banking Supervision, Treatment of Trade Finance under the Basel Capital Framework. Retrieved from: http://www.bis.org/ publ/bcbs205.pdf (accessed 12 July 2019).
Bank for International Settlements (2013) Group of Governors and Heads of Supervision Endorses Revised Liquidity Standard for Banks. Retrieved from: https://www.bis.org/press/ p130106.pdf (accessed 12 July 2019).
Bank for International Settlements (2014a) Amendments to Basel III's Leverage Ratio Issued by the Basel Committee. Retrieved from: http://www.bis.org/press/p140112a.htm (accessed 12 July 2019).
Bank for International Settlements (2014b) Trade Finance: Developments and Issues. *CGFS Papers* No. 50. Retrieved from: https://www.bis.org/publ/cgfs50.pdf (accessed 12 July 2019).

Bank for International Settlements (2015) Correspondent Banking: Consultative Report. Committee on Payments and Market Infrastructures. Retrieved from: https://www.bis.org/cpmi/publ/d136.pdf (accessed 12 July 2019).

Beck, T. & Demirgüç-Kunt, A. (2006) Small and Medium-Size Enterprises: Access to Finance as a Growth Constraint. *Journal of Banking and Finance*, 30(11), 2931–2943.

Bellone, F., Musso, P., Nesta, L. & Schiavo, S. (2010) Financial Constraints and Firm Export Behaviour. *The World Economy*, 33(3), 347–373.

Bricongne, J.-C., Fontagné, L., Gaulier, G. *et al.* (2012) Firms and the Global Crisis: French Exports in the Turmoil. *Journal of International Economics*, 87, 134–146.

Chauffour, J.-P. & Farole, T. (2009). Trade Finance in Crisis: Market Adjustment or Market Failure? *World Bank Policy Research Working Paper* WPS 5003. Retrieved from: http://documents.worldbank.org/curated/en/673931468336294560/pdf/WPS5003.pdf (accessed 12 July 2019).

Chauffour, J.-P. & Mallouche, M. (2011) *Trade Finance during the Great Trade Collapse.* Washington, DC: The World Bank Group.

Group of Twenty (2010) The Seoul Summit Document: Framework for Strong, Sustainable and Balanced Growth. Retrieved from: https://www.mofa.go.jp/policy/economy/g20_summit/2010-2/document.pdf (accessed 12 July 2019).

International Chamber of Commerce (2013) *Global Risks Trade Finance Report 2013.* ICC Banking Commission. Retrieved from: https://cdn.iccwbo.org/content/uploads/sites/3/2013/02/Global-Risks-Trade-Finance-Report-2013.pdf (accessed 12 July 2019).

International Chamber of Commerce (2014) *Rethinking Trade and Finance. ICC Global Trade and Finance Survey 2014. ICC Banking Commission.* Retrieved from: https://cdn.iccwbo.org/content/uploads/sites/3/2014/07/Global-Survey-2014-Rethinking-Trade-and-Finance.pdf (accessed 12 July 2019).

International Monetary Fund (2003) Trade Finance in Financial Crises: An Assessment of Key Issues. IMF Policy Development and Review Department. Retrieved from: https://www.imf.org/external/np/pdr/cr/2003/eng/120903.pdf (accessed 12 July 2019).

Korinek, J., Le Cocguic, J. & Sourdin, P. (2010) The Availability and Cost of Short-Term Trade Finance and its Impact on Trade. *OECD Trade Policy Papers,* 98. https://doi.org/10.1787/5kmdbg733c38-en.

Manova, K. (2013) Credit Constraints, Heterogeneous Firms, and International Trade. *Review of Economic Studies*, 80, 711–744.

Omni Bridgeway (2011) Debt Prices. Omni Bridgeway News, May 2011.

Omni Bridgeway (2014) Debt Prices. Omni Bridgeway News, April 2014.

Stiglitz, J. & Weiss, A. (1981) Credit Rationing in Markets with Imperfect Information. *The American Economic Review*, 71(3), 393–410.

United States International Trade Commission (2010) Small and Medium-Sized Enterprises: Characteristics and Performance. Investigation No. 332-510. USITC Publication No. 4189. Retrieved from: https://unstats.un.org/unsd/trade/s_geneva2011/refdocs/CDs/USA%20-%20ITC%20-%20Small%20and%20medium%20sized%20enterprises%20(Nov%202010).pdf (accessed 12 July 2019).

World Bank (2013) Evaluation of the World Bank Group's Targeted Support for Small and Medium Enterprises. Independent Evaluation Group (IEG) Approach Paper. Retrieved from: http://documents.worldbank.org/curated/en/520021468152101035/pdf/769830WP0Box370AP0evaluationof0SMEs.pdf (accessed 12 July 2019).

World Bank (2015) Withdrawal from Correspondent Banking: Where, Why and What to Do about It. *Working Paper* No. 101098. Retrieved from: http://documents.worldbank.org/curated/en/113021467990964789/pdf/101098-revised-PUBLIC-CBR-Report-November-2015.pdf (accessed 12 July 2019).

World Economic Forum (2014) *The Global Enabling Trade Report 2014.* Retrieved from: http://www3.weforum.org/docs/WEF_GlobalEnablingTrade_Report_2014.pdf (accessed 12 July 2019).

World Trade Organization (1998) Trade Policy Review: Indonesia. Geneva: WTO. Retrieved from: https://www.wto.org/english/tratop_e/tpr_e/tp94_e.htm (accessed 12 July 2019).

World Trade Organization (2004) Improving the Availability of Trade Finance during Financial Crises. WTO discussion paper by Auboin, M. & Meier-Ewert, M. Retrieved from: https://www.wto.org/english/res_e/booksp_e/discussion_papers2_e.pdf (accessed 12 July 2019).

World Trade Organization (2014a) Azevêdo Hails Basel Decision on Trade Finance as "Good News" for Developing Countries. Retrieved from: https://www.wto.org/english/news_e/news14_e/dgra_17jan14_e.htm (accessed 12 July 2019).

World Trade Organization (2014c) Report of the Working Group on Trade, Debt and Finance (2014) to the General Council. Working Group on Trade, Debt and Finance. Document WT/WGTDF/W/75. Draft, 14 November 2014. Retrieved from: https://docs.wto.org/dol2fe/Pages/FE_Search/DDFDocuments/128604/q/WT/WGTDF/W75.pdf (accessed 12 July 2019).

World Trade Organization (2016) Trade Finance and SMEs: Bridging the Gaps in Provision. Retrieved from: https://www.wto.org/english/res_e/booksp_e/tradefinsme_e.pdf (accessed 12 July 2019).

World Trade Organization & Organisation for Economic Co-operation and Development (2013) *Aid for Trade at a Glance 2013: Connecting to Value Chains*. Paris: OECD. Retrieved from: https://www.wto.org/english/res_e/booksp_e/aid4trade13_e.pdf (accessed 12 July 2019).

Chapter 18

How Trade Finance Works

Alexander Malaket

Introduction

International trade is, even under current geopolitical conditions that include protectionist and isolationist sentiment in various parts of the world, one of relatively few realms of commercial activity and economic value-creation that can be effectively influenced by policy, with the potential for global impact. It is also, as we were collectively reminded in the aftermath of the Global Financial Crisis, a decades-long driver of economic growth. Trade growth has lagged gross domestic product (GDP) growth over the past decade but is showing signs of recovering its position as an engine of growth, and with it, an effective channel for thoughtful, coordinated policy potentially advancing a wide range of global objectives. The conduct of trade is understood now to be dependent on adequate levels of timely and affordable financing, for one or more of the parties typically involved in international trade or, in a broader context, for groups of exporters, often small and medium-sized enterprises (SMEs), that sell into complex global supply chains. Simply put, trade does not take place without adequate levels of enabling liquidity, or financing.

The esoteric branch of finance that relates to the financing of cross-border trade and related activities has historically been referred to as "trade finance", covering techniques and instruments that have been in use for hundreds of years at least. Trade finance typically refers to financing of import and export transactions over the short and medium term, with financing time frames or tenors up to seven years or so. Transactions with longer time frames are covered under project finance. In addition to this traditional form of trade finance, evolving market practices and preferences have motivated the development of financing solutions that apply in the context of trade that flows through global supply chains. Supply chain finance (SCF) and its evolution is currently at the leading edge of the business of financing

The Handbook of Global Trade Policy, First Edition. Edited by Andreas Klasen.
© 2020 John Wiley & Sons Ltd. Published 2020 by John Wiley & Sons Ltd.

international commerce; however, traditional trade finance remains in use and supports about 10% of merchandise trade flows annually, worth in the range of US$1.5 trillion annually.

The majority of trade activity is currently conducted on so-called open account terms, where the buyer commits to payment at an agreed point in the transaction, such as the loading of cargo onto a vessel, or arrival at the port of destination. SCF has evolved explicitly with the objective of supporting open account trade flows. Estimates from various sources, including the World Trade Organization (WTO), suggest that 80% of global merchandise trade flows are dependent upon trade finance and SCF, which for practitioners includes financing as well as effective risk mitigation.

Trade drives the creation of economic value, and despite the acknowledged imperfections of the current system, trade is recognised as having helped to pull one billion people above the poverty line, as well as contributing materially to increased economic inclusion. In terms of the way trade finance works, the overarching point to note is the following. Trade financing is required to enable trade. Trade drives economic growth around the world, and facilitates economic inclusion. This linkage is a longstanding reality, but one where the role of the financing element has been in the background, and largely unappreciated outside a small community of practitioners. An understanding of this linkage, coupled with an awareness of the functioning of trade finance and SCF, has direct policy implications at national level and at the level of coordinated initiatives across jurisdictions. Trade finance and SCF become not only a critical enabler of trade, but an additional instrument of policy to impact trade, value-creation and economic inclusion. Accordingly, there are also policy opportunities that can support access to and delivery of trade financing, including areas like financial sector regulation, given the still significant role of banks as providers of trade finance around the world.

The Four Elements of Trade Financing

Commercial relationships involve a range of complexities, challenges and opportunities, some of which are magnified in the context of cross-border business, such as international trade. Examples include:

- commercial risk between the trading parties given distance, complexity of due diligence;
- intercultural negotiation and related complexities;
- political and country risk considerations;
- extended relationship, business development and sales cycles;
- extended sourcing and production timelines;
- extended payment time frames.

The foregoing factors, along with numerous others, combine to amplify familiar complexities of domestic commerce in the context of international trade. Businesses often require financing in order to enable and support their activities, whether on the seller side or the buyer side. This is particularly true of small businesses, where a shortage of financing and cash flow is a recurring issue in most markets around the world. With extended sales cycles and payment time frames, the situation can become even more acute for SMEs pursuing opportunities in international trade. Additionally, the risk factors to be assessed and mitigated are significantly more for companies operating in international markets. Trade financing, including traditional trade finance as well as SCF, encompasses a range of practices, products and solutions addressing financing as well as risk mitigation requirements, all of which, taken collectively, have enabled the successful conduct of trade under the most complex and difficult of conditions. Trade financing can involve complex techniques and financial structures. Irrespective of the complexity of a particular transaction, trade financing is about devising a solution that best combines the four elements to meet the needs of trading parties, including what can be very large commercial ecosystems driving trade through global supply chains. The four elements are:

1. The facilitation of appropriate, secure and timely payment across borders.
2. The provision of financing to one or more parties in a transaction or supply chain.
3. The effective mitigation or optimisation of a range of risks, as dictated by the characteristics of the transaction or trade flows, and the risk tolerances of trading parties.
4. The flow of information about the physical movement of the goods or services, and/or the related financial flows.

It is worth noting that the four elements provide a useful framework with which to appreciate trade financing, whether reference is made to traditional mechanisms like documentary letters of credit, documentary collections or guarantees, for example, or whether focus is on the "newer" techniques of SCF elaborated later in this chapter.

Secure and Timely Payment

Payments across borders today can be triggered by simple instruction, and can arrive at destination very quickly. In the context of a trade transaction, the triggering of a payment (or a payment promise at a future date) is ideally tied to the exporter having delivered goods as agreed, or having met other agreed conditions. Most such payments are effected through a bank-owned messaging network called SWIFT – (Society for World Interbank Financial Telecommunications), based in Belgium, that allows for secure, authenticated messaging and financial transactions between banks (and more recently member corporates). SWIFT is also the network through which formatted messages are used to send authenticated trade finance instruments like documentary credits, documentary collections and various forms of guarantees, together with amendments, settlement instructions, payments and related messages.

Financing

International trade involves transaction life cycles or timelines that are typically longer than domestic commercial transactions, in addition to involving a series of additional risks. In this context, it is common for one or more parties – including banks – to require financing over the course of a transaction. An SME exporter may require funds in advance of producing or shipping the agreed goods, in order to acquire inputs to production. An importer may need short-term financing in order to pay for the goods, with the loan repaid from the proceeds of sale. A bank (typically in an emerging market) may require financing from another bank in order to be able to discharge its own obligations, or in order to access funds at lower cost than could be done locally. Attractive financing packages can be a useful competitive advantage for exporters seeking to sell overseas, and such packages typically involve an exporter agreeing to payment at a future date to help enhance the buyer's cash position. The exporter can then request their bank to discount the obligation and effect immediate payment – a form of financing which is repaid once the buyer remits funds.

Risk Mitigation

As noted earlier, international transactions involve greater complexity – and a broader set of risks – than typical domestic transactions: political and country risk, the risk of loss or damage of the goods in transit (including the occasional shipping container lost at sea, for example), as well as risk related to currency volatility. Trade finance and international banking mechanisms have evolved to address, very effectively, a wide spectrum of risks. Risk insurance, guarantees, specific features of trade finance instruments, together with risk mitigation options offered through government or quasi-government entities, multilateral development banks and private sector insurers combined offer a comprehensive suite of risk management options. It should be noted that good will and the genuine desire to do business are fundamentally important in trade; fraud, or attempts to take advantage of certain aspects of a trade transaction, still require careful monitoring.

Information Flow

In trade as in many other endeavours, the role and importance of data and information are increasingly critical, and increasingly valuable as technology enables access to more granular data, and more complex analysis, more quickly than ever before. In trade finance, detailed information about the status of a shipment, for example, can (and increasingly does) inform financing decisions. The use of radio frequency identification (RFiD) technology helps track a container and ensures it remains in transit or flags the point at which ownership transfers from exporter to importer, again potentially informing the financing process. The four elements can be combined and optimised to best meet the particular needs of a buyer and seller, the maturity of their relationship and the risk character of the markets in which they each operate.

Payment and Financing

In traditional bilateral trade transactions typically involving one seller or supplier and one buyer, the seller or exporter wishes to have some level of assurance that payment will be made – and received – as agreed in exchange for the production and delivery of the goods or services contracted. The buyer or importer wishes to ensure delivery of the goods or services in the agreed time frame, and with the characteristics and quality contracted, and will want to ensure that payment is effected only once contract terms have been met.

Instruments and mechanisms have long existed to help protect the interests of importers and exporters engaging in cross-border trade activity. An important consideration in the choice of instrument relates to the nature of the trading relationship: new and unproven or mature and trusted. Equally important is the risk profile of the transaction, which, in trade, is only partially linked to the commercial relationship. Risk can be related to the conditions prevailing in-market, the stability of the local banking and financial sector or the commercial relationship, among other things.

This combination of factors – relationship and risk – should inform the choice of settlement and financing option (including related risk mitigation features) selected by trading partners. New relationships involving one or more high-risk markets pose a different set of challenges than established and trusted relationships operating in stable, secure markets. The former may emphasise risk mitigation and financing out of the four elements, whilst the latter may suggest greater focus on prompt delivery and payment (Figure 18.1).

Even highly trusted, proven relationships where the parties wish to ensure the completion of a transaction and are acting in good faith, may not provide sufficient assurance if one of the partners' home markets erupts in civil war, for example; the best intentions of two commercial enterprises will not likely mitigate the imposition of exchange controls, or the expropriation of enterprises by political authorities.

Similarly, the most stable of markets can still present significant risk if the trading counterparty is not well known, and could either engage in fraudulent activity or simply not be able to perform the tasks necessary to deliver (or effect payment) as contracted.

The four elements of trade finance are combined and emphasised to varying degrees, based on the nature of the transaction and the needs of the parties engaged in the transaction. More recent practice and thinking around international trade has evolved beyond the two-trader, bilateral view, to a perspective built on global supply chains. This is a view of cross-border commerce based on supply chain ecosystems, and commercial communities that can involve a global buyer with suppliers

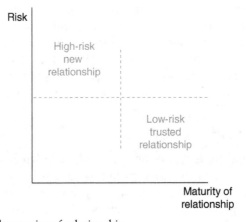

Figure 18.1   Risk and maturity of relationship.

numbering in the thousands or tens of thousands. Even in this complex environment, with evolving financing techniques, the "four elements" construct remains relevant, and a useful way to think about the financing of international trade.

The financing of international trade today can be thought of as encompassing two core tracks of activity – one referred to as "traditional" trade finance, and one labeled SCF. An understanding of the way trade-related financing functions today requires an appreciation of techniques and practices on both tracks. One challenge is that the two areas of activity overlap, and that some familiar and long-established techniques are core to the "new" SCF.

Traditional Trade Finance

Traditional trade finance has evolved over hundreds of years to meet the needs of a single buyer and a single seller (periodically with the inclusion of a broker to facilitate transactions). Techniques and products in use include:

- cash on delivery;
- documentary collections;
- documentary credit/confirmed documentary credit;
- payment in advance.

An importer or buyer will clearly prefer to make payment on delivery of the agreed goods or services, as this effectively lowers risk to negligible levels (Figure 18.2). This is the riskiest option for an exporter or seller, as it requires sourcing of inputs, production of the agreed goods and the shipment and delivery of those goods to the buyer. Risk exposure is with the exporter, with all costs incurred ahead of time. The exporter would prefer to be paid in advance, enabling the use of the funds to finance production and shipment, along with a profit margin.

The foregoing options can be utilised in the context of trading relationships where one or the other party has leverage or market power. A large buyer can use leverage on small suppliers or exporters, for example, and demand that initial sales be paid on delivery only. Similarly, exporters may produce something unique or difficult to access from alternate sources, possess unique intellectual property or have access to technology that enables the delivery of a differentiated product. In that instance, the supplier could apply pressure to require payment in advance, thus shifting risk to the importer or buyer.

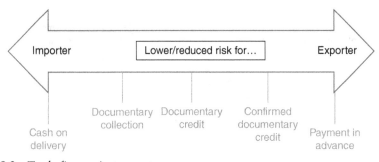

Figure 18.2 Trade finance instruments.

Documentary Collection

A documentary collection is a trade finance product where one or two banks will act to enable an exchange of shipping documents presented by the exporter, for payment by the importer. This will include documents of title that confer ownership of the cargo, as well as other documents that enable customs clearance in the country of destination – in summary, a set of documents that reflect what the exporter has done in terms of production and shipment to meet the terms agreed with the importer, and that, on receipt, will allow the importer to claim the goods on arrival. Documentary collections typically involve one or two banks (usually one bank acting in the importing country and one in the exporting country) to facilitate what amounts to an exchange of documents for the agreed payment. The presence of banks in the process provides some basic assurance to the two trading partners in that an exchange is being facilitated, but does little else to secure the interests of the two parties.

The process and practice around the use of documentary collections globally is guided by "The Uniform Rules for Documentary Collections", published by the International Chamber of Commerce (ICC) Banking Commission. These rules, like numerous other ICC publications that guide the use of commercial and trade financing instruments, are very widely adhered to, and enjoy the status of quasi-law, having been woven into the judicial interpretations and decisions of major legal traditions like the British Common Law and its various derivatives. Documentary collections are intended for use by trading partners that have concluded successful transactions and for whom the overall risk profile of the trading relationship or particular transaction is acceptable. In terms of the four elements view, documentary collections involve limited risk mitigation and relatively prompt payment, with financing options available to the buyer or seller or both.

Documentary Credits

Documentary credits are another core instrument of traditional trade finance, but one which more fully balances the protection afforded to both importer and exporter (Figure 18.3). Under a documentary credit, also referred to as a (commercial) letter

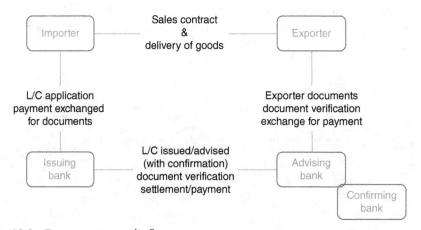

Figure 18.3 Documentary credit flow.

of credit or an L/C, the buyer and seller agree to settlement (payment) on the basis of an L/C. The importer completes an application for an L/C, the details of which align with the underlying sales contract between the two parties.

The application is completed with the importer's bank, referred to as the issuing bank, as this institution will issue the L/C. An L/C is a binding undertaking by the issuing bank that payment will be effected in favour of the exporter, provided all terms and conditions in the L/C have been met by the exporter. These instruments are referred to as "documentary" because the exporter, called the "beneficiary" of the L/C, must follow, strictly, all terms and conditions specified in the credit. L/C terms include an expiration date, a "latest shipment date" to indicate the date by which the contracted goods must be aboard a ship or other mode of transport. Additionally, a credit lists the documents that must be presented by the exporter in support of a request for payment, or a "drawing". Documents required under an L/C could include:

- draft or bill of exchange;
- commercial invoice;
- packing list;
- bill of lading or transport document;
- certificate of origin;
- certificate of inspection.

L/C terms and conditions can be simple and straightforward, or they can be comprehensive and complex. In any event, the terms of the credit reflect the underlying sales contact between buyer and seller, and are arrived at by mutual agreement, though the instrument is an obligation of the issuing bank. An exporter can request amendment to a credit, with agreement from the importer. Once the L/C is issued, it is routed, most commonly now through a global network run by SWIFT to a bank based in the home market of the exporter. This is the "advising bank", so-called because its task is to review the credit, authenticate its source and "advise" it, or send a copy of the L/C, to the exporter.

On receipt of the credit the exporter reviews it to ensure the specified terms and conditions can be met, and works with a freight forwarder and others, to collect the documents listed in the credit, ensuring that any documentary condition specified in the L/C is reflected in the documentation prepared for presentation. In the simplest variation of an L/C, documents are collected and presented by the exporter to the advising bank, typically the exporter's bank, with a drawing, or a request for payment under the L/C.

The advising bank verifies documents presented by the exporter against the L/C for compliance, and makes a determination whether the terms and conditions have been fully met, or whether there are any discrepancies, or instances of non-compliance. The documentary credit guided by the ICC's Uniform Customs and Practice for Documentary Credits (UCP) provides for a range of roles to be taken by banks providing trade finance services to clients on the basis of L/Cs. The variations and nuances are numerous. For purposes of this publication, an understanding of the more common transaction structures is sufficient.

Following this initial verification, the documents are sent by courier to the issuing bank, for an additional verification against L/C terms and conditions. If the documents are deemed to be in compliance, the issuing bank effects payment to the exporter, or undertakes to effect payment at an agreed future date. In the event that the exporter was unable to meet all terms and conditions specified in the L/C, the issuing bank informs the importer accordingly. If there is sufficient time, and the discrepancies can be corrected, this is an option. Alternatively, the buyer can waive the discrepancies and accept the documents as tendered, and thus the underlying shipment, or the importer can elect to refuse the documents, refuse to trigger payment and leave it to the exporter to incur the costs of returning the shipment, or of selling the goods at destination, typically at a deep discount.

While the L/C is an instrument – and an undertaking – of the issuing bank, and thus the ultimate decision on compliance or non-compliance rests with the issuing bank, the practical reality is that the importer is a bank client, and there is frequently dialogue and consultation between the applicant and the issuing bank. In some instances, an importer will use the threat of refusal of the shipment to force a discount from the exporter.

At its core, the L/C aims to ensure that the exporter is paid only in the event of full compliance, and that the goods are released to the importer only upon triggering of a payment or a future-dated payment undertaking. Documents flow from exporter to importer through the intermediating banks, while payment flows in the opposite direction, from importer to exporter through the banking system. With reference to the four elements perspective, there are two features worth highlighting:

- the option to arrange a "sight" or "term" L/C; and
- the option to add a confirmation to the L/C.

Financing, in its most basic form, is some variation of a loan, often to cover a shortfall of cash or working capital, certainly in the context of short-term trade flows, which still tend to involve longer time horizons for payment than most domestic transactions. An exporter may require financing to assist in the production and shipment of goods, or an importer may require financing in the form of delayed payment against the L/C, pending the sale of the goods purchased and the generation of revenue and profit, some portion of which may be used to cover the financial obligation represented by the L/C.

A "term" letter of credit is an L/C that contemplates payment against compliant documents at an agreed future date, for example, 90 days after shipment date, or 60 days (after) sight, meaning 60 days after a set of documents have been received and verified by the bank empowered to make a decision on their compliance against L/C terms (Figure 18.4).

A draft or bill of exchange is a document recognised in finance and at law as a representation of a financial obligation. Drafts indicate the amount and timeline of the obligation, and if it reflects maturity at a future date, the draft is "accepted" for payment at maturity, creating a banker's acceptance. This instrument can be traded in the market, or it can be discounted for immediate payment. A term L/C allows the importer to postpone debit to their account until maturity. Financing allows for immediate payment to the exporter through a discount of the draft, with the designated bank carrying the exposure until maturity. As with other aspects of this

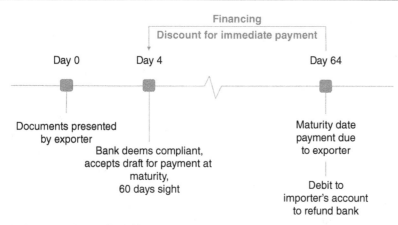

Figure 18.4   Financing under L/C terms.

presentation of trade financing, there are numerous variations and nuances as well as technically correct language and terminology which guides industry practice, but which is less critical to a conceptual treatment of the topic.

Confirmed Letter of Credit

There is the option, in the event of sufficient (actual or perceived) risk in a transaction, for the L/C to be "confirmed". In cases where the exporter is not sufficiently comfortable to rely on the payment undertaking of the issuing bank for any number of reasons, the exporter can request that the L/C be issued with the option to add a confirmation. Confirmation of an L/C involves the addition of a separate and independent payment undertaking by another bank – typically the exporter's bank located in the exporter's home market – in consideration of appropriate fees and charges. Once added, a confirmation allows the exporter to present documents to the confirming bank, and to request payment against those documents, provided they are in full compliance with the terms and conditions of the L/C. This has the practical – and very valuable – effect of protecting the exporter from risks related to the stability of the importing market, the financial viability of the issuing bank or even the technical competency of that bank in examining documents under an L/C.

The confirming bank must typically have risk appetite and credit lines to cover exposure to the importing country and the issuing bank; given that confirmations are usually requested in the context of high-risk markets or transactions, the confirming bank may wish to mitigate its exposure through some form of guarantee or insurance option. Private sector insurers offer such solutions, as do public sector (or hybrid) entities like export credit agencies (ECAs), mandated to support the export aspirations of local businesses. Documentary credit insurance might cover 85% of the exposure represented by the L/C, leaving the rest of the risk to be shared between the exporter and the confirming bank, for example.

The option to confirm an L/C is often the determining factor in enabling an exporter to pursue opportunities in high-risk markets that can prove lucrative, or to engage in trade with a new, untested counterparty. Confirmation of an L/C enables economic inclusion and engagement in trade, by markets and counterparties that might otherwise find it difficult or prohibitively expensive.

To bring the practicalities into focus, confirmation of an L/C allows an exporter to collect payment for goods produced and shipped in full compliance with L/C terms and conditions, even in the event of extreme circumstances such as the bankruptcy of the issuing bank, or sudden economic or political instability in the home country of the importer, that would otherwise impede successful conclusion of the trade deal. Perhaps equally importantly, the option of using a confirmed L/C can sometimes be a determining factor in the willingness of an exporter to explore a new trading relationship, and/or a new market. It is worth noting too that the ability of an exporter to combine a product or service with attractive payment terms – or a financing package – can become a compelling differentiator, and can assist the exporter in closing a deal or launching a new trading relationship.

Other Aspects

Traditional trade finance involves long-established instruments and mechanisms, together with commensurately mature market practice, supported by evolved legal treatment across most jurisdictions in the world. The policy environment around traditional trade finance is equally advanced. One major area of evolution in this form of trade financing involves the shift from documentation to digitisation, and it is in this area that policymakers have significant work to do. Digitisation of trade-related documentation is a significant undertaking requiring coordination across the globe, and across a range of areas of activity – transport and logistics, insurance, inspection and certification and a variety of others – that enable trade.

Effective trade financing, both the traditional mechanisms and the more recently evolving SCF techniques, is anchored in expert understanding of the commercial, economic and political context in which trade takes place. This requires macro-level understanding of country and political risk issues, just as much as it demands an appreciation for the impact of currency volatility, or the often very material differences in the cost of financing across markets. In the latter instance, trade finance and SCF techniques can be utilised to facilitate access to funding at more economical rates, by ensuring that the trading party with access to those lower funding costs arranges the financing. In the last decade in particular, there has been a notable and near-global shift from trade on the basis of traditional trade financing mechanisms like the documentary L/C and the documentary collection, to trade on open account terms. This has been driven largely by corporates who determined that traditional mechanisms are costly, time-consuming and transactionally complicated.

Supply Chain Finance

The shift to trade on open account terms created a dynamic in the market where the disintermediation of banks from trade financing and trade flows became a serious consideration: one that prompted banks, as providers of traditional trade finance, to work on devising solutions aimed at supporting open account trade.

SCF is the evolution of financing propositions in trade, designed to respond to the broader view of international commerce – a view that has shifted from a bilateral perspective, involving one buyer and one seller, to an ecosystem view built on the arteries of global commerce called supply chains. Supply chains involve a buyer and a community of suppliers and service providers that can number in the thousands, perhaps even tens of thousands, and can encircle the globe.

According to the standard definition by the ICC and its partners, SCF is defined as the use of financing and risk mitigation practices and techniques to optimise the management of the working capital and liquidity invested in supply chain processes and transactions. SCF is typically applied to open account trade and is triggered by supply chain events. Visibility of underlying trade flows by the finance provider(s) is a necessary component of such financing arrangements which can be enabled by a technology platform.

SCF is in relatively early stages of development; so much so that techniques and terminology are still under development and in market uptake mode. Some use the expression SCF to refer to a particular technique, though SCF is in fact broader, programmatic in nature, encompassing a range of techniques that can address financing requirements across the supply chain ecosystem. A two-year, multi-association initiative mandated to devise a baseline set of standard definitions around SCF has led to the development and promulgation of a series of definitions and detailed descriptions of SCF techniques. The importance of a common global understanding extends beyond importers, exporters and the global community of financiers, to regulatory authorities, professional service providers, investors and multiple stakeholders. The Definitions Drafting Group of the ICC and its partners defined a specific structure and scope to the treatment of the subject matter (ICC and Partners, 2016) (Figure 18.5).

Just as traditional trade finance has long underpinned and enabled trillions in global trade flows, SCF is taking its place as a fast-growing, high-impact form of financing that now supports the majority of trade activity worldwide. While traditional trade finance mechanisms support about 10% of global trade flows, worth somewhere between US$1.5 trillion and US$2 trillion annually, SCF and its growing suite of techniques addresses open account trade flows, easily now the majority of trade activity globally.

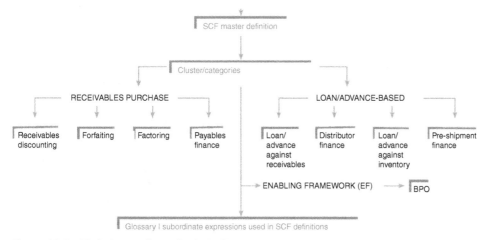

Figure 18.5 Techniques of supply chain finance.
Source: ICC and Partners (2016).

One of the most widely adopted techniques in SCF is the technique termed "payables finance", but also referred to by several other names, including "buyer-backed SCF".

This technique involves an approach where large global buyers work with their bankers to put into place a programme through which key suppliers are invited to avail themselves of financing through the buyer's bank, which is accessible on the basis of the bank's reliance on the credit standing and borrowing capacity of the buyer. In this context, qualified suppliers invited to access the programme, most commonly based in emerging markets, gain access to financing at costs that can be significantly lower than the cost of financing available locally. Payables finance techniques, well-structured, offer a win-win to buyers and their suppliers. The buyer assures the health, sustainability and financial viability of key suppliers in the ecosystem, assuring the functioning of the supply chain. Suppliers, as noted, access affordable financing on an as-needed basis. While payment terms can be extended, for example, from 30 days to 60 days, the SCF provider will include an option in the programme for the suppliers to be paid earlier at an agreed discount. Payment time frames are extended to the benefit of the importer, whilst invoice settlement can be accelerated to the benefit of the exporters participating in the programme (Figure 18.6).

Regardless of the nature of the technique or the specific circumstances in which that trade financing technique is applied, the overarching reality is that trade financing – be it traditional or SCF – is required in order for trade to take place. Trade cannot happen without trade financing. The post-crisis environment led directly to the broad realisation of the critical role of trade financing in the conduct of international commerce. While this relationship is known to trade financiers, the global crisis has highlighted the long under-appreciated role of trade financing for

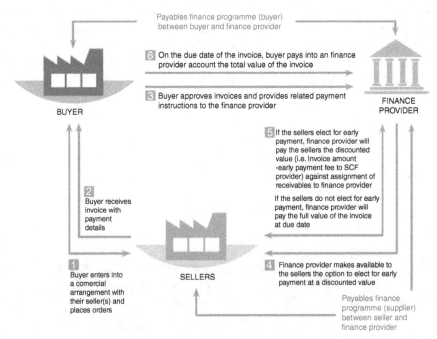

Figure 18.6 Supply chain finance overview.
Source: ICC and Partners (2016).

the international community, leading to unprecedented attention being given to the subject matter, generating robust and varied research around the topic and underpinning advocacy efforts previously unseen in support of this esoteric form of financing. Relatedly, investments in the form of new technology and new value propositions are being directed to trade financing, all while new providers of trade financing evolve in the market.

SCF is the area in which a number of these evolutions and innovations is most in evidence, and most likely to have the widest impact, given the widening adoption of a supply chain-based view of trade, and the imperative to develop and deploy financing solutions from pre- to post-shipment, and across the entire supply chain. While payables finance programmes are now mainstream for leading providers of trade financing, including numerous non-banks, other SCF techniques are still very much in development and market adoption phase, while still others (various forms of factoring, for example) are long-established and finding favourable positioning in the wider context of SCF. In addition to broadening the solution set across a trade transaction lifecycle, providers are also working to drive financing options deeper into global supply chains, to help address the needs of the suppliers representing the largest procurement spend, but also those of small sub-suppliers in the farthest-reaching end of the supply chain ecosystem – the so-called long tail of suppliers.

Risk Mitigation

Though we routinely speak of trade finance and SCF, placing emphasis on the lending or financing element, the reality is that effective mitigation – ideally, optimisation – of risk is as important, or even more important, an element of the value proposition brought to market by trade financing. As noted at the start of this chapter, international trade encompasses every challenge and complexity related to the pursuit of commercial opportunity in the domestic market, plus a range of others that take risk to an entirely different level.

Doing business with a buyer or supplier whose reputation, performance and financial health can be quickly assessed through local contacts, credit bureau reports and other elements of due diligence that are taken for granted in some parts of the world presents one set of risks. Pursuing a relationship with a counterparty halfway around the world, without the benefit of audited financial statements, trusted credit reports or access to a local network to check bona fides, presents a substantially higher risk. Couple that with instability or other risks related to the importing or exporting market, risks related to loss or damage of cargo in transit, or fundamental differences in legal tradition, and the picture quickly comes into focus: international trade demands a degree of risk tolerance. Success in international trade demands the expertise – or good advice – needed to be able to assess and effectively optimise a wide range of risks that do not arise in the context of domestic commerce.

Risk Examples

Consideration of even a few of the most common risks quickly brings into focus the challenges, complexities and nuances of international commerce. There are countless country risk and international risk analyses and tools available, some directly aimed at businesses and stakeholders involved in international trade, others taking a rather broader view. The World Economic Forum Global Risks Report for 2017 illustrates the wide variety of risks being tracked, and a quick review illustrates how many of those could or do impact the pursuit or the conduct of trade across borders. A few examples that require attention from trade financiers, or from entrepreneurs/senior executives in businesses engaged in trade, include:

- political and country risk
- bank risk
- currency risk
- non-performance or non-payment risk and the complexity of addressing cross-border regulatory and compliance risks including:
  o anti-money laundering
  o terrorism finance
  o supply chain security
  o cybersecurity

Some of the risks to consider have been a part of the trade landscape since the earliest days of cross-border exchange – political risk, currency volatility and others, whilst certain risks, such as supply chain security risks are, if not "newer", perhaps a matter of more recent and increasing concern. In the context of trade finance, it is illustrative to explore the ways in which traditional trade finance techniques and mechanisms address familiar risks in order to enable trade – and the creation of economic value – that might otherwise never take place. Well-structured commercial relationships tend to reflect a positive correlation between risk and reward – higher risk, more attractive return. This is true in international commerce, where margins can be significantly more attractive than in domestic activity, and where other benefits, such as access to new technology, skill sets or production inputs, or the ability to extend the lifecycle of a product line that has reached maturity at home, can prove as compelling as financial profitability.

Dealing with Risk in Trade

Risk cannot be completely eliminated (and if that were possible, the cost would tend to be prohibitive in any case), thus a degree of risk tolerance is necessary in the pursuit of opportunity in international markets, even those considered safe and stable. The discussion shifts then to the notion of risk optimisation: what is the right balance between acceptable risk/exposure and commensurate, cost-effective mitigation of risk? Risk can be managed and mitigated between counterparties in various trade finance transactions and structures: one core objective of the most basic documentary credit transaction is to transfer risk from a commercial entity (the importer) to a bank (the issuing bank). Instead of relying on the importer for payment, an exporter agrees to settlement via L/C, and thus shifts the payment obligation (and related risk) from the importer to the issuing bank. This transfer of risk is attractive in cases where the issuing bank is believed to be more robust and financially healthy than an importing corporate, and represents both a transfer of risk and an enhancement of the credit quality of the transaction.

Political and country risk can also be mitigated through documentary L/Cs, as illustrated earlier, by arranging for a confirmation (a separate and standalone payment undertaking) to be added to the L/C by a trusted confirming bank, most commonly allowing for payment in the home country of the exporter. This eliminates the impact of political unrest, imposition of exchange controls preventing payment in the currency of the L/C and any number of other risks related to the importing country, the issuing bank and ultimately the importer, provided documentation accompanying the request for payment is in full compliance with the terms and conditions specified in the L/C.

Continuing with fundamentals, a trade finance product or structure can help mitigate exposures to currency fluctuations, depending on which trading party has the stronger negotiating leverage and can thus determine the currency in which an L/C is denominated. A buyer in the United States settling on the basis of a US dollar-denominated L/C paying a supplier in Brazil effectively places the risk of currency volatility on the Brazilian supplier. The majority of trade flows today are denominated in US dollars; thus, currency exposure is a concern for most trading parties. A bank (or banks) intermediating or facilitating a trade transaction could offer to assist one or both parties to the transaction to remove the risk related to currency exposure and volatility. This can be achieved by offering to pay the exporter in their domestic currency, and offering to debit the account of the importer in their home currency when the time comes for the importer to return to a bank funds that were used to settle with the exporter. Such a service involves the payment of applicable fees and margins, and eliminates the need for trading parties to use forward contracts, options or other currency hedging strategies.

It is worth noting that in trade finance, there is the option to leverage correspondent banking networks to arrange for payment through a branch or financial institution that is located outside the importing and exporting countries, perhaps in the country of the currency of the L/C, for example (Figure 18.7). Thus, a US dollar-denominated L/C issued by a German bank in favour of a Kenyan supplier could be settled through a US bank in New York, if so desired.

The discipline of trade financing has evolved numerous proven and highly effective risk mitigation techniques that can be incorporated into financing instruments and structures through features of the instruments themselves, or through long-established

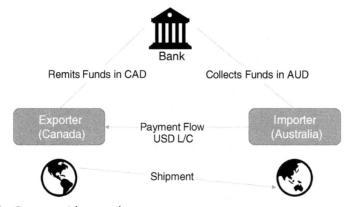

Figure 18.7 Currency risk example.

industry practice. The use of various forms of guarantees, standby L/Cs, bid and performance bonds and other such instruments is illustrative. This group of instruments, though often used in domestic transactions, is commonly managed out of the trade finance departments of banks due to the similarities the instruments share with documentary L/Cs. Guarantees and standbys might involve an issuing and an advising bank and are issued on behalf of an applicant to a beneficiary, typically to back-stop or provide a guarantee in support of a contractual obligation of the applicant to perform or to remit funds. If the applicant fails in the relative obligation, the beneficiary can claim payment under the guarantee or standby, often on the basis of a simple demand.

Such instruments are sometimes used in combination with trade financing instruments or structures, or SCF programmes, to support particular obligations and to provide additional comfort or assurance to one or more of the parties involved in a trade transaction.

Additional Risk Mitigation

Additional risk mitigation – and even financing – is available in support of international trade, through export credit and insurance agencies and through several multilateral development banks. These organisations, whose role and relevance were once the subject of debate, proved that they are indispensable during the Global Financial Crisis, and have remained strong contributors to trade, the creation of economic value and economic inclusion.

Multilateral development banks

All major multilaterals have developed trade finance and SCF programmes, with the first such programme launched by the European Bank for Reconstruction and Development in 1999, with operations in 27 countries and transactions approaching 20,000 valued at nearly US$15 billion. The more recent programmes have been established by other multilaterals, including the International Islamic Trade Finance Corporation (IITFC) and the African Development Bank.

The International Finance Corporation (IFC) is a multilateral with a global (as opposed to regional) mandate, and has a far-reaching trade financing programme with multiple value propositions for the market, ranging from guarantee programmes aimed at supporting the engagement of developing market banks in trade finance, to financing, risk mitigation and SCF solutions, and propositions aimed at specific sectors of trade activity. IFC's programme, launched in 2004, operates across 90 countries and has completed US$53 billion in transactions globally, with a network of 1300 correspondent banks.

These programmes have numerous distinctive features, including elements particularly suited to their target and constituent markets, for example, the IITFC explicitly seeks to support and promote trade between members of the Organization for Islamic Cooperation (OIC) or trade involving coffee exports from Indonesia, for example. The multilaterals offer a broad and growing range of products and solutions aimed at encouraging and enabling trade, including combinations of traditional techniques with emerging SCF techniques and a wide variety of guarantee schemes and risk mitigation mechanisms.

Several programmes work closely with banks in developing economies to encourage their involvement in trade finance activity, with a view to increasing the trading capacity of those countries where the financial sector is being supported. Specifically, considering traditional mechanisms like confirmed documentary credits, international banks will confirm L/Cs issued by local, developing market banks only in cases where country and bank credit capacity is in place. The standing and credit profile of developing market banks is often such that other banks are unlikely to confirm credits issued by these banks due to unacceptable risk characteristics or credit quality. In such instances, multilaterals can step in and add guarantees to the instruments issued by approved local banks, so that international banks will accept to engage as confirming banks.

These risk mitigation and guarantee programmes aim to increase engagement in trade, to increase capacity in the global system and, relatedly, to increase technical competencies in trade financing among local bankers, through training programmes, knowledge transfer and capacity-building programmes that run alongside the various guarantee programmes. In addition to the demonstrably important role of multilateral development banks in trade finance, SCF and risk mitigation, the contributions of ECAs and export insurers are equally key. ECAs are public sector or hybrid (quasi-public sector/private sector) organisations typically mandated to support the development of exports. The remits of ECAs vary significantly, as do the business and operating models of those organisations.

Export credit agencies

Certain ECAs or "export-import banks" focus on export development and remain relatively traditional and tightly focused. The Export-Import Bank of the United States (US Exim), for example, has a congressional mandate that requires it to exit business activities in cases where the private sector begins to undertake these activities that were previously considered a "market gap". US Exim has faced a difficult period in the United States as a result of ideological debates about the role of state institutions in supporting private enterprise, to the extent that the reauthorisation of its mandate was fundamentally in question. Operating models for ECAs in markets like Germany and France have a hybrid character, which includes a public sector component and a market-driven, purely commercial dimension. There are numerous nuances, and perhaps as many variations in approach as there are ECAs. At the top level, the combination of commercial considerations and public policy has important implications: hybrid ECAs can and will undertake financing and risk mitigation activity that is commercially unviable – that is, excessively risky or perhaps unprofitable – for the sake of supporting a policy objective, including variations of domestic national interest/benefit, and other targets like contributions to international development through trade. The scope of activity and breadth of remit of ECAs can vary significantly, with certain ECAs empowered to provide direct lending support or even to take equity positions in businesses that present clear trade-related potential and benefits. Some ECAs are viewed as taking a partially competitive posture relative to private sector banks and other providers of trade finance, whilst other ECAs take explicit care not to "crowd out" the private sector.

In the context of traditional trade finance, specifically in the use of confirmed documentary credits, banks that provide confirmations to L/Cs accept risk on the issuing bank, and may keep the exposure on their books, or may decide for various reasons to reduce that exposure, by securing insurance against a portion of that exposure – commonly, 85% of the face value of the L/C. Documentary credit insurance is one product available through ECAs which helps to reduce risk, but also creates additional trade financing capacity in the market, by reducing exposure and freeing up credit risk capacity to allow for the underwriting of additional business. ECAs and private sector insurers also offer other solutions such as foreign accounts receivable insurance, insurance against unfair claims for payment under bonds and guarantees and a wide spectrum of related products that can be indispensable in the pursuit of opportunities in international markets. While it may seem intuitively clear that such products would be attractive when a deal involves a higher-risk developing economy, or a market that is experiencing political instability, the reality is that even so-called advanced economies present risks that are wisely assessed and mitigated through such mechanisms.

ECAs and private sector entities can be a source of robust market intelligence, and often provide a range of support services to assist businesses – including SMEs – to engage in international trade. One notable evolution related to ECAs is that many, even those with a public sector focus, operate far beyond their home markets. Those that are in hybrid mode can extend their remit globally, so that an exporter unable to secure support from their domestic ECA now has many more options to explore.

The majority of ECAs, especially those with a public sector component to their structure and remit, belong to an industry association called the Berne Union, whose members collectively provide some form of support to enable about 11% of global trade flows worth nearly US$2 trillion annually. Berne Union members report having paid about US$40 billion in claims related to trade activity since 2008. The geographic distribution of exposure and related data points is notable for the fact that it reflects numerous advanced economies – a reflection of relative trade volumes as much as risk.

While banks remain core providers of trade finance, particularly traditional trade finance, and are increasingly active in the development of propositions linked to SCF, the role of multilateral development banks and ECAs is of fundamental importance, and adds significant net capacity to the global market, both through risk mitigation and through additional access to financing. Both types of organisations operate in the short- and medium-term end of the market, and ECAs are likewise engaged in project finance which involves long-term infrastructure projects such as dams, bridges, mining operations and a range of others, with timelines extending as far out as 20 years or more.

Although ECAs are mature parts of the trade financing ecosystem, the variety of ECA structures, mandates and approaches to the market opens up a range of policy considerations related to these entities, be they driven primarily by government objectives, by commercial imperatives or by some combination of the two. Policy priorities can be defined for ECAs that determine what posture they take with banks and other trade finance providers: whether they focus on enabling SME activity in trade or pursue big-dollar, large client transactions. Policy can also determine complementary elements to a mandate, such as supporting development finance activities, or the priority assigned to the environmental or social impact of the deals being financed.

The scope and size of projects financed or supported by ECAs has resulted over time in significant attention being paid to the environmental and social impact of those projects, with various non-governmental organisations such as ECA Watch tracking the practices, behaviour and impact of ECA activity. The notion of responsible financing has been particularly compelling in light of the reality that many ECAs are at least partially supported through public funds. The importance of this issue is highlighted by the creation of the Equator Principles in 2010 – a risk management framework initially focused on ensuring that social and environmental impact, particularly risk, is taken into account in trade and project finance activity.

Supply chain finance instruments

Even as SCF grows in uptake and impact, and non-bank providers like multilaterals, ECAs and others remain key to the ecosystem, other long-established market actors, such as factoring houses that provide financing against invoices, are growing their cross-border activities and becoming increasingly central to the overall global capacity for trade-related financing. Factors Chain International, a leading industry body, has been reporting double-digit growth in cross-border factoring for several years, and factoring featured prominently in the "Standard Definitions for Techniques of Supply Chain Finance" mentioned earlier (ICC and Partners, 2016). The fast-paced growth of SCF has given rise to a number of non-bank boutique firms, including those with a financial technology or "fintech" character, aiming to provide financing and/or risk mitigation services in the context of SCF and open account trade flows.

The risk mitigation element of trade financing and SCF points to several policy considerations that have the potential to support greater trade activity through access to trade finance and SCF solutions. The nature and mandate of numerous ECAs today is governed through an informal agreement among Organisation for Economic Co-operation and Development (OECD) economies in particular that sets out parameters within which ECAs can and should operate, in order to minimise distortions in the market and in order to ensure that these institutions do not become *de facto* channels for state subsidy of trade flows. Certain jurisdictions have openly questioned the value of ECAs, largely on the basis of ideological leaning, whilst others, notably high-growth emerging markets, are leveraging various ECA models in support of economic development and trade-driven growth. An increasing number of systemically important ECAs operate outside the OECD agreement. There are opportunities, at the level of international, regional and domestic policy, to sharpen and update the mandates of ECAs, particularly those that operate partly with a public sector mandate. Engagement with the Berne Union can further refine the efficacy of policy targeting trade financing and risk mitigation accessible through ECAs. Perhaps relatedly, to the extent that specific jurisdictions support trade-based development, it can prove effective to direct funds to multilateral development agencies in support of their trade finance and trade facilitation programmes.

The Role, Value and Impact of Information

As with many areas of business and human endeavour, the role, value and impact of information has been greatly amplified through technology, advanced analytics and the ability to manage and mine massive amounts of data to extract strategically

valuable insight. This is equally true in consumer spending, where loyalty programmes track patterns and provide a trove of buyer behaviour information, as it is
in the context of international commerce, where trade activity is rich in data across
a range of levels, sectors and types of activity. The notion of "event-based" or "event-
triggered" financing highlights the very practical link between data flows and access
to financing, including trade financing. The concept is that financing offers can be
associated with specific events in a transaction lifecycle, or in the trade cycle, such as
the issuance of a purchase order, the acceptance of an invoice for payment by a
buyer, the transfer of ownership of a cargo in transit from supplier to buyer, based
on the agreed Incoterm (International Commercial Term), or any number of other
such events or triggers.

Determinations about transaction status and trigger points are often made on the
basis of timely information flow about the status of transactions at the level of the
production, shipment and delivery of goods – the physical supply chain. These flows,
and the triggers that relate, have direct impact on the flow of financing and
payments – the financial supply chain. The use of radio frequency identification technology, when applied to track the movement of a container across the ocean, can
also be directly relevant to a financing option or trigger, and can assist a lender in
tracking the status of a shipment after funds have been disbursed, especially in cases
where the cargo has been taken as collateral against the related financing. This
element of trade finance will become even more critical as production and shipment
dynamics are disrupted by 3-D and 4-D printing, where trading parties effectively
exchange a blueprint via email and the component or product is printed at destination, and used in the context of additive manufacturing activities. Transaction time
frames will compress, and the need for financing may change accordingly. In any
event, the question can then be posed, is trade finance now about financing the flow
of product, or the flow of intellectual property, or some combination of both? In the
latter instances, the quality of information flow is critical, and the trust in information
channels will need to be extremely high.

Another key aspect linked to information flow relates to one of the major challenges in trade financing today: regulation and compliance. Trade financiers will
acknowledge that the regulatory expectations around cross-border financial activity,
from correspondent banking to trade finance, have never been more stringent. There
are very legitimate reasons for this, including the critical need to combat money
laundering linked to organised crime and terrorism, the imperative to ensure that
sanctioned countries and individuals are not able to circumvent sanction provisions
and, relatedly, the increasingly disciplined requirements in the area of due diligence
in providing financing to parties around the world.

Additionally, behaviour by global, top-tier financial institutions, from the triggering of the Global Financial Crisis of 2008 to interest rate fixing to financing narcotics
gangs to facilitating deals for sanctioned regimes – the list goes on – has effectively
guaranteed that compliance and regulatory standards would become more stringent.
Anti-money-laundering (AML) and combating-the-financing-of-terrorism (CFT) considerations are presented in the context of the information flow element of trade
finance, with a view to the need for trade financiers to collect, review and assess
information necessary to assure compliance with regulatory standards. Notably,
financial institutions are expected to do more than report to authorities, they are

required to proactively assist police and intelligence authorities with investigative and enforcement activity. The matter of regulation and compliance is also germane to the topic of risk, relative both to trade financiers and to counterparties in trade transactions and relationships. On one level, trade finance providers assist with due diligence and, in so doing, help reduce the risk of their clients engaging in business that facilitates the laundering of illegal funds, or that is linked to organised crime or terrorism. This is in addition to the relevance of this topic to the banks and trade finance providers themselves – given the significant reputational and financial risk arising from applicable fines. The stringent levels of due diligence demanded by regulatory authorities have had material impact on the commercial realities of the provision of trade finance, raising the cost – and reputational risk of non-compliance – materially.

There are, in this aspect of trade financing, significant opportunities for enhanced, effective policy, both on the compliance side, and in terms of capital adequacy requirements that guide the amount and composition of capital to be held in reserve against the amount of trade finance underwritten by bank providers. Reserve requirements are meant to be aligned with the risk profile of the business lines meant to retain the capital reserve. While there has been progress in achieving risk-aligned capital treatment of trade finance, more work is to be done in education, advocacy and policy development. The financing of international trade has long been a discipline that has enabled global commerce, but has done so in the background and with limited appreciation for its critical role, except among practitioners around the world. The post-crisis environment has brought sharply into focus the role of trade finance – and its four elements – in enabling trade, the creation of economic value and inclusion in markets around the globe.

At the macro level, there are ample opportunities to advance trade by helping assure adequate levels of trade financing. These include, for purposes of illustration:

- programmes aimed at ensuring ease of access to trade financing for SMEs;
- policies that include support of and contribution to international entities like the WTO, the ICC and others, that seek to advance trade and trade financing globally;
- initiatives that enhance professional competencies and technical skills in trade financing, both domestically and internationally;
- policies that support access to trade financing for emerging sectors of activity such as service sector trade, or emerging modes of trade such as online platforms or trade conducted in a digital context;
- policies that drive adoption of health and safety standards and practices, anti-corruption measures and anti-slavery programmes across global supply chains, with incentives built into financing programmes if needed.

Technology, Digital Trade and Digitised Trade Finance

Traditional trade finance has been in existence, largely unchanged in substance and in practice, for hundreds of years, if not longer. An early example of a documentary L/C preserved at the museum of the Banca Monte Dei Paschi in Italy dates back to the 15th century and illustrates the robust nature of these instruments that, still today, enable about 10% of trade flows globally. The robustness of these instruments is such that the processes and practices linked to them have remained largely unchanged, even as entire industries have reinvented themselves. The creation and promulgation of guiding rules, such as the UCP, has been one relatively modern development in the practice of trade financing, and their wide adoption has been critically important to the successful pursuit of commerce around the globe. There have been attempts, particularly notable since the late 1990s, to advance the business model and proposition of trade financing through the application of technology. Such early attempts began with the promise of transformation, and the threat of making banks irrelevant to the financing of international commerce.

In reality, progress has been limited, in part because of limitations in technical capability, and because of limited market interest in and uptake of these ground-breaking, technology-enabled models. Instead of fundamentally reshaping practices and processes linked to trade finance, these early initiatives focused on incremental improvements to existing models. The nature of trade, and the uneven access to information and communication technology (ICT) around the world, resulted in a certain resistance among trading parties, government authorities and trade financiers to move to processes that are less paper-, process- and people-intensive. The post-crisis environment and developments in the commercial, legal and policy context have, however, combined to encourage a shift to more efficient business models, including now those underpinned by electronic documentation and data and automated decisioning. The application of optical character recognition (OCR) and artificial intelligence (AI) to trade finance processes will soon be mainstream in industry practice.

Bank Payment Obligation

One illustration of the evolution of trade financing is the development of the bank payment obligation (BPO). The BPO is now referred to as a trade financing framework, applicable in the context of traditional trade transactions as well as in the context of trade conducted on open account terms, extending therefore to SCF. The BPO is a joint initiative of SWIFT and the ICC, combining a business model with a set of guiding rules and practices akin to the UCP to help drive market acceptance and adoption. At its core, the BPO replicates the logic and flow of a documentary credit, but does so on the basis of data extracted from the export side and the import side of a transaction which is then compared through a data matching engine (the TMA, or transaction matching application) to determine consistency between the datasets – put another way, compliance by the exporter as illustrated by data consistency between (for example) a purchase order on the import side and a commercial invoice on the export side. The two datasets to be compared are agreed upfront by the importer and exporter; in the event of a match, payment or financing can be triggered. If there is a mismatch, data may be corrected and resubmitted, or the buyer can waive the mismatch and accept the shipment.

The BPO is an inter-bank instrument to secure payments against the successful matching of trade data (Figure 18.8). As per the uniform rules for bank payment obligations, the BPO means "an irrevocable and independent undertaking of an

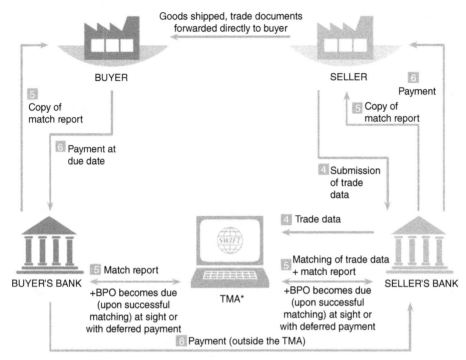

Figure 18.8 Bank payment obligation.
Source: ICC and Partners (2016).

obligor bank to pay or incur a deferred payment obligation and pay at maturity a specified amount to a recipient bank following submission of all datasets required by an established baseline and resulting in a data match or an acceptance of a data mismatch" (ICC, 2013).

While the first BPO transaction was announced in 2010, market uptake has been limited, in part because banks have prepared themselves to adopt the BPO, but have largely stayed on the sidelines waiting for others to lead, and because, arguably, corporate clients were not made aware of this alternative quickly enough or with sufficient energy. Efforts continue to encourage greater adoption of the BPO; however, key questions related to compliance, capital treatment and accounting and reporting expectations have remained open and thus impeded the rate of market acceptance and adoption. More recently, driven in part by the accelerating pace of growth of SCF and the entry of non-banks into the market for trade financing, the impetus to advance the practice of trade financing has picked up significantly, and the drive to apply technology to the financing of trade has likewise accelerated. Initiatives from the private sector and from public sector authorities to advance the digitisation of trade and of global supply chains have shown significant progress with a longstanding challenge – the digitisation of marine bills of lading and other transport documents (particularly those that are also documents of title) has been achieved and is showing significant levels of market adoption. Likewise, technology-enabled transformation in the physical supply chain is motivating greater receptiveness to transformational evolution in the financial supply chain.

Other Initiatives

A striking illustration of the fundamental shift in innovation energy around trade finance is perhaps the annual Singapore FinTech Festival, where the monetary authority of Singapore and partners in the festival devised 100 problem statements and asked members of the local fintech community to work on proposed solutions to each. Three of those related directly to the financing of international trade.

In the past several years, as distributed ledger technology (DLT) has gained momentum, visibility and market uptake, numerous proofs of concept (PoCs) have been presented to the market that, again, relate to the financing of international commerce. These include PoCs linked to the issuance of traditional instruments of trade financing, like guarantees and standbys, or PoCs that seek to leverage DLT and blockchain as one variant, or PoCs aimed at the reduction of fraudulent attempts to access funds through trade financing, for example, by attempting to finance an invoice multiple times through different financiers.

The application of OCR to data extraction or AI to document and data analysis as a means of effecting a payment or financing decision remain areas of significant potential, with the possibility of allowing a shift of specialised trade finance resources away from operational tasks like document verification in traditional trade, to activities that are more relationship focused. Technology has only recently become a material factor in the financing of international trade, at least as a transformational element, but its role is now entrenched and irreversible, particularly – but not exclusively – in SCF, where non-banks and fintechs are applying technology as a matter of course, and where platform-based, technology-enabled propositions are the norm. The pace of application of technology to trade finance and SCF will only accelerate as banks and fintechs collaborate and as technology and changing commercial practice continue to transform supply chains around the world.

The policy opportunities here are also significant – from aligning or including financing components to digital trade initiatives and single-window market access programmes, to creating enabling regulatory environments that allow for the mainstreaming of digital documentation, advancements in enabling technologies and the entry of non-banks, as well as the effective and balanced regulation of fintechs, so that they may also enter the global enabling architecture for trade.

Conclusion

Trade has been a part of the human experience for thousands of years, from the Phoenicians on the coast of modern-day Lebanon to the original Silk Road through today's ambitious and transformative Belt and Road initiative launched by China. Even today, the pursuit of trade and the global architecture of institutions, policies and practices that enable trade are fraught with imperfection, even injustice. Financing is a critical enabler of international commerce, facilitating 80% of merchandise trade flows alone worth US$15 trillion or more annually.

In this context, trade financing (whether traditional or SCF) shares both in the tremendous success created through cross-border commerce and in the responsibility to address its imperfections, by ensuring access to adequate, affordable trade financing in developing economies. This includes supporting police and intelligence agencies where needed, motivating the adoption of decent, human environmentally aware commercial practices across supply chains, and generally enhancing the positive impact of trade around the globe. It is no exaggeration to say that robust, mutually beneficial trade contributes to international security, as nations that trade together are less likely to shoot at each other.

Policy measures that help develop a healthy and robust trade finance market will by direct extension contribute to a dynamic capability to trade, and in the end, despite appearances, the core of trade financing is not difficult to grasp. The four elements of trade finance provide an adequate framework to do so, and even brief consideration of the value and impact of trade around the globe quickly brings into focus the opportunities that can derive from closing the US$1.5 trillion trade finance gap.

References

International Chamber of Commerce (2013) *Uniform Rules for Bank Payment Obligations*. Paris: ICC. Retrieved from: http://store.iccwbo.org/Content/uploaded/pdf/ICC-Uniform-Rules-for-Bank-Payment-Obligations.pdf (accessed July 20 2019).

International Chamber of Commerce & Partners (2016) Standard Definitions for Techniques of Supply Chain Finance. Retrieved from: https://cdn.iccwbo.org/content/uploads/sites/3/2017/01/ICC-Standard-Definitions-for-Techniques-of-Supply-Chain-Finance-Global-SCF-Forum-2016.pdf (accessed July 20 2019).

World Economic Forum (2017) *Global Risks Report 2017*. Geneva: World Economic Forum. Retrieved from: http://www3.weforum.org/docs/GRR17_Report_web.pdf (accessed 14 July 2019).

Chapter 19

Export Credit Arrangements in Capital-Scarce Developing Economies

Benedict Okey Oramah

Introduction

Public export credit agencies have been in existence since shortly after World War I as the preferred institutional form of export credit administration. Following the United Kingdom's establishment of its Export Credits Guarantee Department in 1919, almost all other advanced economies created national export credit agencies (ECAs) as instruments of trade, foreign policy and investment promotion and financing (although there are a few private credit insurers, the focus of this chapter is on officially supported ECAs). They served as instruments for boosting the competitiveness of national exports through government-backed loans (in the form of direct lending or interest rate subsidies), guarantee schemes and insurance to corporations seeking business opportunities in foreign countries. Against ECA cover, commercial banks in Organisation for Economic Co-operation and Development (OECD) countries were able to finance manufactured and investment goods exports to developing economies that were considered to be risky markets.

With respect to developing countries, Mexico, South Africa and India established ECAs as early as 1937, 1956 and 1957, respectively. However, it was not until the 1970s–1990s that ECAs became important in the developing world – first in Latin America and Asia (Krauss, 2011) and much later in a number of African countries. The emergence of ECAs in developing economies, particularly in developing Asia and parts of Latin America, coincided with these countries' industrial take-off in the late 1970s to early 1990s. Prior to that, almost all developing-economy exports were centred on primary commodities that did not require elaborate medium- or long-term export credit support.

By the 1980s, some developing economies, especially in Southeast Asia, as well as in India and China, began to shift from a strategy of import substitution to export-led

The Handbook of Global Trade Policy, First Edition. Edited by Andreas Klasen.
© 2020 John Wiley & Sons Ltd. Published 2020 by John Wiley & Sons Ltd.

industrialisation with initial emphasis on light manufactures. Whereas advanced economies created ECAs as instruments to support national exports to seemingly risky markets, developing economies created ECAs to serve three distinct but related needs: (i) to finance the import of equipment needed to retool factories and convert them from import substitution to export orientation; (ii) to finance non-traditional exports (that is, manufactures); and (iii) to open new markets, largely developing-economy markets, to non-traditional exports through market research and by putting exporters of these products on near-equal footing to those of traditional exports.

During the first half of the 20th century, almost all ECAs were created in economies with deep financial markets that could finance capital goods and other exports if risks were sufficiently mitigated. It is perhaps for this reason that most advanced-economy ECAs, with the exception of the United States and a few others, did not directly offer loans, but rather guarantees and credit insurance. Deep financial markets, coupled with the unwillingness of commercial banks in advanced economies to provide short-term credit for export of consumption goods to new and fragile markets with very limited credit histories, created unique opportunities for the growth of ECAs during that time. Interestingly, in the 1970s, ECAs began to emerge in developing economies with shallow financial depth and limited industrial bases. While most ECAs in developing Asia have survived and have supported industrial growth across the region, some ECAs in other developing economies, particularly Africa, have failed, with many ceasing to exist.

One important question that follows is what form developing market ECAs should assume to deliver meaningful impact. Stephens (1999) asserts that there is no typical ECA; neither is there any single perfect model for an ECA applicable at all times and in all countries. Ascari (2007) points to a number of factors that significantly altered the operating model of advanced-economy ECAs during the 1990s: the global debt crisis of the 1980s, which led to massive credit defaults and restructurings by ECAs; a new vision of the world stemming from the fall of the Berlin Wall, which favoured liberalism and a greater role of markets and private agents in the growth process of both industrialised and developing economies; and limitations imposed by individual countries on state aid. These developments resulted in changes to OECD regulations of ECAs, including stricter and more conservative underwriting policies, and brought issues of pricing, environment and bribery to the fore (Ascari, 2007).

Given that developing-economy ECAs have been in place for over 30 years and were established and have operated under conditions different from those faced by traditional (advanced-economy) ECAs, it is important to understand the factors that drive their operations and their effectiveness. This understanding has become increasingly relevant in light of the growing interest among several African economies (for example, Ghana, Côte d'Ivoire and Rwanda) to establish national ECAs and attempts by others to refocus (South Africa) or revamp (Nigeria, Zimbabwe, Egypt) their ECAs. To that end, this chapter addresses the following key questions:

- What is the rationale behind the use of ECAs in export promotion in capital-scarce economies, which would ordinarily not be in positions to export capital goods or offer export credits?
- What are the differences, if any, between traditional (advanced-economy) ECAs and developing-economy ECAs, and why? Are ECAs that are designated as

export-import (Exim) banks more prevalent in advanced or developing economies, and why?

- How have ECAs in developing economies evolved as economies have moved up the development ladder? Is there a tendency towards convergence with traditional arrangements as developing economies accumulate capital?
- What important lessons can be learned from the foregoing for developing economies contemplating setting up ECAs?

This chapter traces the historical evolution of export credit agencies (ECAs) across the world and highlights some lessons from experience and policy implications for capital-scarce developing economies attempting to establish or revamp national or regional ECAs. The following section traces the origin and history of ECAs. The third section describes various forms of ECAs, followed by a section presenting an analysis of the changing roles and functions of ECAs as the economic development process evolves. The fifth section provides two case studies, of the Nigerian Export-Import Bank (NEXIM) and the African Export-Import Bank (Afreximbank), and the final section concludes the chapter.

Origin and History of ECAs

Publicly supported ECAs are known to have first emerged in 1919 when the United Kingdom established its Export Credits Guarantee Department. The first private entity to offer export credit was Euler American Credit Indemnity, created in 1893 to provide insurance coverage for both export and domestic accounts receivables, covering sales to over 160 countries worldwide. Federal of Switzerland, another private entity, began offering export credit insurance in 1906. According to Krauss (2011), the rationale for the publicly supported British programme, which was copied by other countries, was to aid employment and to re-establish export trade disrupted by World War I. Gianturco (2001) and Krauss (2011) further state that, in addition to export credit insurance, the British government established a trade finance programme, offering up to six years of finance of exports at a preferential rate. The British arrangement was supported by the treasury, with the provision that income be sufficient to cover potential losses.

Following the success of the British arrangement and in response to the economic dislocations caused by World War I, many other countries launched their own ECAs, with export credit guarantee and insurance schemes emerging in Belgium (1921), The Netherlands (1923), Finland (1925), Germany (1926; as a transformation of Euler Hermes from a private to a public scheme), Austria and Italy (1927), France and Spain (1928) and Norway (1929). Gianturco (2001) argues that the major rationale for establishing these schemes was to revitalise industries devastated by World War I; to re-establish exports; and to expand trade with the Soviet Union, which posed special risk challenges to European exporting firms and also needed credit. The Great Depression of the 1930s and the onset of World War II in 1939 threatened trade flows and triggered a new impetus for officially supported export credit schemes. As a result, the 1930s saw a number of countries establish export credit programmes: Japan (1930); Czechoslovakia, Latvia and Poland (1931); Sweden (1933); the United States (1934); and Ireland (1935). Most of the export credit was focused on facilitating exports to the Soviet Union.

Gianturco (2001) points out that only the United States offered direct credit pro-grammes (as opposed to guarantees and insurance facilities), while other countries concentrated on guarantees and insurance, with backup discount lending to commercial banks to reduce interest rates. Another notable characteristic of most of these schemes is that they operated as governmental departments. This changed later, with autonomous government or quasi-government institutions taking over the functions in many countries. The focus on risk-bearing (guarantees and insurances), rather than on direct lending, may be explained by the depth of financial markets of those economies, as indicated by the large share (over 30%) of private sector credit in gross domestic product (GDP) (Figures 19.1 and 19.2). In addition, as shown in Figure 19.3, in countries that established ECAs in those early years, manufactured exports as a share of total merchandise exports were relatively high (over 35%).

Until the 1970s, most developing economies were not in positions to create ECAs because these countries were characteristically dependent on the production and export of primary commodities, which did not require sophisticated export financing, as they were mainly traded on a cash-against-document basis and, for the most part, paid for within a few days of shipment. International banks, traders and a few local banks provided financing for these types of exports. As a result, until 1970, only Mexico (1937), Morocco (1949), South Africa (1956), India (1957) and Ecuador

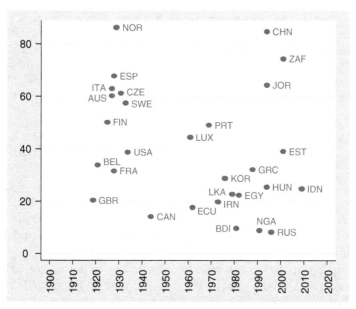

Figure 19.1 Private sector credit (% of GDP) and year of establishment of ECA, 1900–2016. Source: World Bank (n.d.); Jordà-Schularick-Taylor Macrohistory Database, International Trade Statistics, 1910–1960 (http://www.macrohistory.net/data/).
Note: AUS – Australia; BDI – Burundi; BEL – Belgium; CAN – Canada; CHN – China; CZE – Czech Republic; ECU – Ecuador; EGY – Egypt; ESP – Spain; EST – Estonia; FIN – Finland; FRA – France; GBR – Great Britain; GRC – Greece; HUN – Hungary; IDN – Indonesia; IRN – Iran; ITA – Italy; JOR – Jordan; KOR – Korea Republic; LKA – Sri Lanka; LUX – Luxemburg; NGA – Nigeria; NOR – Norway; PRT – Portugal; RUS – Russian Federation; SWE – Sweden; ZAF – South Africa.

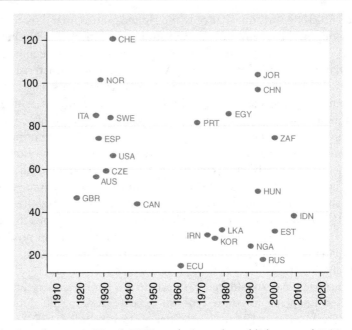

Figure 19.2 Broad money (% of GDP) and year of establishment of ECA, 1900–2016.
Source: Jordà-Schularick-Taylor Macrohistory Database (http://www.macrohistory.net/data/).
Note: AUS – Australia; BDI – Burundi; BEL – Belgium; CAN – Canada; CHN – China;
CZE – Czech Republic; ECU – Ecuador; EGY – Egypt; ESP – Spain; EST – Estonia;
FIN – Finland; FRA – France; GBR – Great Britain; GRC – Greece; HUN – Hungary;
IDN – Indonesia; IRN – Iran; ITA – Italy; JOR – Jordan; KOR – Korea Republic; LKA – Sri
Lanka; LUX – Luxemburg; NGA – Nigeria; NOR – Norway; PRT – Portugal; RUS – Russian
Federation; SWE – Sweden; ZAF – South Africa.

(1964) had established export credit insurance schemes. However, a number of
factors later combined to give impetus to the emergence of ECAs across the developing world, including the following:

- *The myriad of debt- and commodity price-induced global economic and financial crises of the 1970s to the 1990s, which led to drastic cuts in short-term
  trade finance lines to developing economies.* During the second half of the
  20th century, ECAs in industrialised economies not only supported exports to
  developing economies but were also labelled as exporters of debt to these
  countries. The activities of developing-economy ECAs led to a rapid
  accumulation of debt by governments of developing economies (Wiertsema,
  2008), such that by the end of 1982, the external debts of developing economies totalled US$700 billion (3% of the combined GDP of developing econ-
  omies), of which a significant portion consisted of direct public or publicly
  guaranteed loans (Wilkens, 1983). It is also estimated that a significant
  proportion of the debt was created by ECAs, accounting for 30–40% of total
  official public sector debt.
- *Development of the financial services sector in many developing economies,
  particularly those in Asia.* This created the necessary environment for effective
  implementation of guarantees and insurance programmes. Figures 19.1 and 19.2

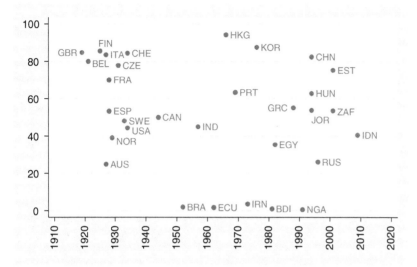

Figure 19.3 Manufactures (% of total exports) and year of establishment of ECA 1900–2016.
Source: World Bank (n.d.); Jordà-Schularick-Taylor Macrohistory Database, International Trade Statistics, 1910–1960 (http://www.macrohistory.net/data/).
Note: AUS – Australia; BDI – Burundi; BEL – Belgium; CAN – Canada; CHN – China; CZE – Czech Republic; ECU – Ecuador; EGY – Egypt; ESP – Spain; EST – Estonia; FIN – Finland; FRA – France; GBR – Great Britain; GRC – Greece; HUN – Hungary; IDN – Indonesia; IRN – Iran; ITA – Italy; JOR – Jordan; KOR – Korea Republic; LKA – Sri Lanka; LUX – Luxemburg; NGA – Nigeria; NOR – Norway; PRT – Portugal; RUS – Russian Federation; SWE – Sweden; ZAF – South Africa.

show that this was the case for China and South Korea, which, at the time of establishing their ECAs, recorded levels of credit to the private sector as a percentage of GDP well within those of advanced economies.

- *Improved manufacturing capacities of several developing economies, which led to a rapid growth in industrial activities and a rise in the export of capital goods and light manufactures in Asia and Latin America and a few African countries during the 1980s and 1990s.* As shown in Figure 19.3, manufactures as a share of total merchandise exports of some of the developing economies that created ECAs (mainly Asian economies – China, South Korea, Indonesia – and South Africa) approached the levels of those of developing economies during the dates of the establishment of the ECAs.
- *The potential for ECAs to promote the growth of exports and improve foreign currency earnings.* A number of developing economies combined their competitive advantages (lower labour costs) with access to export credit made possible by their national ECAs to expand industrial capacities. As a result, many Asian developing economies experienced a post-World War II boom in trade and economic growth, while other developing economies saw their exports plateau during the same period (see Figure 19.4).
- *Changes in national development priorities/strategies.* Increased export orientation rather than import substitution and/or protectionism led many countries to introduce more aggressive ECAs.

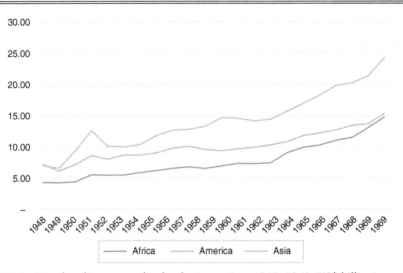

Figure 19.4 Merchandise exports by developing region, 1948–1969 (US$ billion).
Source: UNCTADstat (https://unctadstat.unctad.org/wds/TableViewer/tableView.
aspx?ReportId=101).

Accordingly, during the 1970s and 1980s, a new group of countries – India (1982; apart from Export Credit Guarantee Corporation of India (ECGC) created in 1957, the government of India established the Export-Import Bank of India in 1982), Iran (1973), South Korea (1976), Sri Lanka (1979) and Egypt (1982) – developed export credit schemes or reformed existing ones. By the 1980s, some developing economies, especially those in Southeast Asia, as well as India and China, began to shift from import substitution to export-led industrialisation with initial emphasis on light manufactures. The changes in economic strategies among developing economies, coupled with the break-up of the Soviet Union and deepening economic crises across the world, led to an unprecedented growth in the establishment of official ECAs during the 1990s. The 1990s saw the emergence of ECAs in China (1994), the Czech Republic (Czech Republic Export Guarantee and Insurance Corporation in 1992 and the Czech Export Bank in 1995), Hungary (1994), Poland (1991), Russia (1996), Slovakia (1997) and Slovenia (1992). In Latin America, several countries (Brazil, Colombia and Venezuela) reconfigured their export finance agency structures, and Chile opened its doors to a foreign-owned private sector export credit insurance company. In Africa, a number of countries emerging from the devastating consequence of the debt crises of the 1980s and early 1990s established national export credit schemes, including Nigeria (1991), Egypt (1992), Ghana (1994), Algeria (1996), Botswana (1996), Zimbabwe (1999), South Africa (2001), Tunisia (2003) and Tanzania (2005). In 1993, African governments, with the support of the African Development Bank (AfDB) created the Afreximbank to, among other things, spearhead the financing of African trade using various instruments, including guarantees, insurance, direct lending and advisory services.

Form and Function of ECAs

Since the establishment of the first ECA in the early 1900s, several variants of ECAs have emerged, each designed to meet host countries' particular needs in accordance with their prevailing financial and economic conditions (Klasen,

2014). This section explores (i) the structural and functional differences between ECAs in advanced (capital-rich) and developing (capital-scarce) economies, (ii) the extent to which the nomenclature of ECAs differs across countries, and (iii) whether ECAs that are classified as Exim banks are different from other ECAs. The analysis is based on a comprehensive list comprising 96 national ECAs, as identified in US Exim (2017) plus five regional/multilateral ECAs.

Categorisation and Definition of ECAs

Export credit schemes across the world have generally been designated as "Exim banks", "export credit guarantee and insurance agencies (ECGIs)", or simply "export banks". In a few cases, publicly supported ECAs are referred to as "departments", as was the case until recently with the United Kingdom's Export Credit and Guarantee Department. To help standardise ECA naming conventions, the Committee for Economic and Commercial Cooperation of the Organization of Islamic Cooperation divides ECAs into three categories: (i) full-service ECAs (providing lending, insurance and other products); (ii) insurance-only ECAs (providing only insurance and guarantees with no direct lending); and (iii) insurance and lending, in two separate entities (COMCEC, 2015).

A bank, as defined by the Business Dictionary Online (www.businessdictionary.com/), is an establishment authorised by a government to accept deposits, pay interest, clear checks, make loans, act as an intermediary in financial transactions and provide other financial services to its customers. It follows then that an Exim bank, apart from performing these standard banking functions, provides financing to facilitate exports from, and imports to, its host country.

An agency, as defined by the *Oxford Dictionary*, is a "business or organisation providing particular services on behalf of another business person or group" or a department or body providing a specific service for a government or other organisation. It follows then that the definition of an ECA is a department or body providing export credit services for a government. In line with this, Kraus (2011) defines an ECA broadly as: (i) a highly specialised bank, insurance company, finance corporation or dependency of the government; (ii) offering loans and/or guarantees, insurance, technical assistance and so forth to support exports; (iii) covering both commercial and political risks related to export sales; (iv) with the backing or the approval of the national government; and (v) dedicated to supporting a nation's exports.

These various definitions and designations raise the following questions.

1. *Are ECAs in developing economies structurally or functionally different from those in developed economies?*
   Table 19.1 compares ECAs (for which data are available) in advanced and developing economies in terms of product offering, ownership, corporate structure, mandate and operational aspects. A total of 83% of developing-economy ECAs are wholly public, 34% were set up as joint-stock companies or similar arrangements and 42% were created by specific statutes, compared to 92%, 51% and 32%, respectively, of advanced-economy ECAs. There appears to be no significant difference with regard to the role of the state in appointing senior

executives or members of the board of directors. In the area of mandate/mission, while advanced- and developing-economy ECAs are mandated to finance their countries' exports, only 3% of developing-economy ECAs had additional mandates of foreign policy and promoting the rule of law and human rights in other countries, compared to 11% for advanced economies. About one third of advanced-economy ECAs list foreign policy/international economic cooperation as one of their objectives, while 11% add rule of law promotion. In addition, ECAs in advanced economies are more likely to be profitable (88%) than those in developing economies (84%), even though very few of the ECAs in both cases have explicit profit motives. In terms of sectoral focus, manufacturing is the principal focus of both groups of ECAs; agriculture and construction/infrastructure are also very important for developing-economy ECAs, as are construction and transport/logistics for advanced economies. Developing-economy ECAs have a more evenly distributed regional focus than do developing-economy ECAs.

2. *Are ECAs in developing economies predominantly referred to as Exim banks?*
Table 19.1 shows that 11% of ECAs in advanced economies are designated as Exim banks, compared to 27% in developing economies. When developing economies are further classified into upper-middle-income and lower-middle-income categories, nine of the ECAs in lower-middle-income economies (representing 32%) are referred to as Exim banks, compared to approximately 23% of the agencies in upper-middle-income countries. Less-developed economies are more likely to refer to their ECAs as Exim banks, perhaps to emphasise that those agencies provide direct lending (Table 19.2 indicates that all Exim banks are most likely to engage in direct lending).

3. *Are ECAs that are designated as Exim banks functionally, organisationally or operationally different from others?*
To answer this question, product offerings of the various ECAs are reviewed, as presented in Table 19.2. The data show that Exim banks are more likely to provide: (i) direct credit on their own (100% of Exim banks); (ii) financing for export-generative imports into their countries (81%); (iii) guarantees covering a broad spectrum of activities, including export, investment and project finance guarantees (86%); and (iv) other long-term financing, exceeding seven years (81%). Only 29% of Exim banks provide concessional loans, perhaps reflecting the dominance of Exim banks as the preferred type of developing-economy ECA. Such economies, being capital-scarce, may be constrained in providing concessional loans.

Export banks provide services and show characteristics similar to those of Exim banks. In this regard, all export banks provide direct credit: 77% provide long-term credit and 41% provide guarantees. None of the export banks provide concessional credit. Furthermore, 66% of ECGIs provide direct export credit; a smaller proportion (38%) offers financing of imports. In addition, ECGIs provide concessional (tied) credit to a limited extent, but to a greater extent than other ECAs (48%), and support long-term investments of their countries in other markets (71%). These numbers point to an improvement, as, in recent years, some ECAs that previously had not provided direct credit (especially those in advanced economies) have expanded their

Table 19.1 Developed and developing countries export credit arrangements (ECAs), 2016

	Advanced economies		Developing economies		Total	
	Number of ECAs	% of total	Number of ECAs	% of total	Number of ECAs	% of total
Number of ECAs	37	36.63	64	63.37	101	
Type of ECA						
Export-import bank	4	10.81	17	26.56	21	20.79
Export bank	10	27.03	12	18.75	22	21.78
Export credit guarantee and insurance agency	23	62.16	35	54.69	58	57.43
Core mandate						
Economic growth and export expansion	37	100.00	64	100.00	101	100.00
Foreign policy/international or economic cooperation	12	32.43	4	6.25	16	15.84
Social development in low-income countries (alleviate poverty, promote rule of law and human rights in least-developed countries)	4	10.81	2	3.13	6	5.94
Profitability						
Profit motive	6	16.22	5		11	10.89
Profitability in 2016	31 (5 made losses)	83.78	28 (of the 32 that had information in Annual Report)	87.50	59	58.42
Sectoral focus	25		17		42	
Agriculture	8	32.0	11	64.7	19	45.24
Manufacturing	24	96.0	14	82.4	38	90.48
Construction/infrastructure	18	72.0	10	58.8	28	66.67
Transport, tourism, logistics (including warehousing)	17	68.0	7	41.2	24	57.14
Metals and mining	10	40.0	6	35.3	16	38.10
Oil and gas/energy	15	60.0	5	29.4	20	47.62
Telecommunications	7	28.0	1	5.9	8	19.05

(Continued)

Table 19.1 (Continued)

	Advanced economies		Developing economies		Total	
	Number of ECAs	% of total	Number of ECAs	% of total	Number of ECAs	% of total
Regional focus						
Africa	19	76.0	10	58.8	29	69.05
Asia	24	96.0	9	52.9	33	78.57
Americas	23	92.0	9	52.9	32	76.19
Europe	24	96.0	11	64.7	35	83.33
Middle East	16	64.0	4	23.5	20	47.62
Product offering						
Direct credit	20	54.1	35	53.0	55	53.4
Export credit	19	51.4	35	53.0	54	52.4
Import finance	8	21.6	20	30.3	28	27.2
Long-term finance	21	56.8	34	51.5	55	53.4
Credit insurance	25	67.6	49	74.2	74	71.8
Guarantees	26	70.3	37	56.1	63	61.2
Concessional credit	16	43.2	25	37.9	41	39.8
Corporate structure						
Appointment of CEOs and Board						
Government	27	75.00	52	81.25	79	78.22
Company	9	25.00	15	23.44	24	23.76
Legal form (for establishment)						
Set up by specific law/statute	12	32.43	27	42.19	39	38.61
Set up as government company or initially created as part of government agency/department	8	21.62	13	20.31	21	20.79
Company (through joint stock, public/private, joint venture or other arrangements)	19	51.35	22	34.38	41	40.59
Ownership						
Government	34	91.89	53	82.81	87	86.14
Public/private	4	10.81	13	20.31	17	16.83

Source: Author's computation.

Table 19.2 Activities of export-import banks compared with other export credit arrangements (ECAs)

Classification	Export-import banks		Export banks		Export credit guarantee and insurance agencies	
	Number of ECAs	% of total	Number of ECAs	% of total	Number of ECAs	% of total
Number of ECAs	21	20.39	22	21.36	58	79.61
Product offering						
Direct credit	21	100.00	22	100.00	38	65.52
Export credit	21	100.00	17	77.27	22	37.93
Import finance	17	80.95	11	50.00	17	29.31
Long-term finance	17	80.95	17	77.27	41	70.69
Credit insurance	12	57.14	4	18.18	58	100.00
Guarantee	18	85.71	9	40.91	49	84.48
Concessional credit	6	28.57	0	-	28	48.28
Profitability						
Profit motive	2	9.52	11	50.00	9	20.45
Profitability in 2016 (number of ECAs that made profit)	18	85.71	8 (out of 14 entities with available information)	57.14	36 (out of 44 entities with available information)	81.81
Corporate structure						
Appointment of CEOs and Board						
Government	20	95.24	17	77.27	45	77.59
Company	1	4.76	5	22.73	32	55.17
Legal form (for establishment)						
Set up by specific law/statute	14	66.67	6	27.27	19	32.76
Set up as government company or initially created as part of government agency/department	3	14.29	7	31.82	11	18.97

(Continued)

Table 19.2 (Continued)

Classification	Export-import banks		Export banks		Export credit guarantee and insurance agencies	
	Number of ECAs	% of total	Number of ECAs	% of total	Number of ECAs	% of total
Company (through joint stock, public/private, joint venture or other arrangements)	4	19.05	9	40.91	28	48.28
Ownership						
Government	20	95.24	18	81.82	42	72.41
Public/private	1	4.76	4	18.18	16	27.59
Regional focus					29	
Africa	11	55.0	8	36.36	24	82.8
Asia	14	70.0	12	54.55	25	86.2
Americas	14	70.0	11	50.00	24	82.8
Europe	18	90.0	15	68.18	27	93.1
Middle East	4	20.0	5	22.73	16	55.2
Total number of ECAs considered based on availability of information	13		12		33	
Sectoral focus						
Agriculture	6	46.2	5	41.7	18	54.55
Manufacturing	13	100.0	8	66.7	24	72.73
Construction/infrastructure	8	61.5	6	50.0	19	57.58
Transport, tourism, logistics (including warehousing)	11	84.6	6	50.0	21	63.64
Metals and mining	9	69.2	4	33.3	17	51.52
Oil and gas/energy	7	53.8	9	75.0	22	66.67
Telecommunications	4	30.8	6	50.0	16	48.48

Source: Afreximbank staff computations.

offerings to better support their countries' exports in an environment where international banks are increasingly de-risking and exiting certain markets perceived to present high compliance risk. The core mandate of ECGIs is to provide credit insurance (100%) and guarantees (84%), as well as long-term finance (71%).

Further, Table 19.2 shows the structural and functional differences among Exim banks, export banks and ECGIs in terms of product offering, profitability, corporate structure and regional and sectoral focus. The data shows that ECAs, for the most part – 95% of Exim banks, 82% of export banks and 72% of ECGIs – are public (government) entities, with a few constituted as public–private arrangements. Over 70% of Exim banks or export banks were established by specific law or as part of government departments or parastatals, compared to about 38% for other forms of ECAs. Fewer Exim banks and export banks (19% and 41%, respectively) were set up as joint-stock companies, compared to 48% of ECGIs. This distribution appears to reflect the move, during the 1990s, by many developing economies that led to the privatisation of some ECA activities – a tendency that appears to be under revision today. Regarding sectoral focus, most ECAs promote manufactured exports (over 67%), while Exim banks also place emphasis on tourism and logistics (85%) and export banks tend to focus on natural resource sectors (75%). Natural resources (metals and minerals), transport and logistics, and construction and infrastructure were the most important sectors for ECGIs. In line with global trade flows, most ECAs targeted Europe (over 66%) and the Americas (over 50%), with Africa becoming increasingly important. Only a few ECAs have a profit motive; nevertheless, the majority of ECAs across all groups made a profit (86% of Exim banks, 82% of ECGIs and 57% of export banks).

In sum:

- Most Exim banks are located in capital-scarce developing economies, with the majority focused on direct lending to exporters. This is due to the relative shallowness of the financial sector in many developing economies, where financial deepening – measured by commercial bank credit to the private sector as a share of GDP – ranges from 4% in Sierra Leone to 141% in China. For the most part, access to credit is low, and the cost of credit is very high, putting many developing-economy exporters at a disadvantage in the global market. In some cases, developing-economy governments borrow from multilateral development banks at relatively cheap rates and on-lend to their ECAs. Further, many commercial banks in developing economies (mostly in the least-developed economies) have weak capitalisation and lack knowledge of foreign markets, making it difficult for them to run viable export finance businesses, even if supported by ECA guarantees. As a consequence, in many capital-scarce economies, ECAs essentially act as export lenders of last resort.
- Unlike ECAs in advanced economies, a large proportion (30%) of ECAs in developing economies finance imports of capital goods that support export generation, especially in the area of manufacturing. In recent years, the globalisation of supply chains has made it necessary to finance the import of intermediate goods for further in-country processing for export within a supply chain.
- ECAs in developing economies are more likely to operate profitably and to provide financing for exports of manufactures and agricultural products. Among ECAs, Exim banks are most profitable.

- With regard to control, developing-economy ECAs tend to be government controlled by virtue of their establishment laws and ownership and appointments of senior executives.
- Finally, there are indeed some differences in the natures and characters of ECAs, depending on whether they are designated as Exim banks, export banks or ECGIs. Exim banks are more likely to be profitable, provide direct financing for exports and imports, provide long-term finance and be located in developing economies. Their sectors of interest vary, although all strongly support manufacturing.

Timewise Evolution of ECAs in Selected Economies

As mentioned above, during the early to mid-1900s, OECD countries created ECAs as tools to promote industrial growth, innovation and job creation by way of de-risking industrial value-added exports to new and developing markets considered risky. ECAs contributed to the rapid industrialisation of the early 1900s, which also helped support the recovery from the Great Depression.[1] However, questions arise as to what drove the rapid emergence of ECAs across the developing world, how they have evolved over the past few decades and to what extent the natures of ECAs are converging across advanced and developing economies.

To address these questions, this section reviews the timewise evolution of ECAs in five countries – China, India, South Korea, Nigeria and South Africa – and across Africa as a whole. China and South Korea are included in the sample, given their economies' dramatic transformation from the time publicly supported ECAs were first put in place. India features because many developing economies planning to set up export credit schemes have sought the country's advice in that regard. Africa is included based on its particular interest to this chapter's author and the existence of a continent-wide export-import bank (the Afreximbank) with unique features, including preferred creditor status in each of its African member states. Nigeria and South Africa are included because they represent the largest African economies and have had relatively long experiences with export credit schemes.

To obtain an effective understanding of the drivers of the creation of ECAs in selected developing economies, trends in the following key economic variables are analysed: credit to the private sector as a percent of GDP (a proxy for credit availability); broad money as a percent of GDP (a proxy for financial deepening); domestic interest rates as a measure of the state of demand and supply of credit; GDP per capita, supplemented by the World Bank's classification of the developmental status of each economy (that is, low-, middle-, or high-income); total merchandise exports; foreign exchange reserves; current account balance; and the external debt-to-GDP ratio. The period selected covers the dates of establishment of publicly supported ECAs in each of the countries.

Capital, Debt and Credit in Developing Economies

Table 19.3 shows that the level of development of the financial sector (measured by private sector credit and broad money as proportions of GDP) varies widely across the sample of countries – from as high as 85% and 97%, respectively, in China to as low as 9% and 24%, respectively, in Nigeria. This suggests some possible differences

Table 19.3 Macroeconomic indicators of selected economies at year of creation of national export credit arrangement

Macro-economic indicator	United Kingdom (1919, Export Credits Guarantee Department (ECGD)	United States (1934, US Export-Import Bank)	Japan (1950, Japan Export-Import Bank)	China (1994, China Eximbank)	India (1982, Export-Import Bank of India)	Korea Rep. (1976, Korea)	Nigeria (1991, Nigeria Export-Import Bank)	South Africa (2001, Export Credit Insurance Corporation)	Africa, (1993, African Export-Import Bank)
Real GDP growth rate (%)	5.45	16.78	16.95	13.08	3.48	13.46	-0.62	2.70	0.96
GDP per capita	4,870.41	5,113.61	1,920.72	471.76	279.66	874.64	279.28	2,705.78	534.00
Debt (% of GDP)	1.43	0.40	0.14	17.90			134.44	20.89	
Private credit (% of GDP)	20.43	38.78	23.70	84.69	22.30	28.82	8.95	74.43	31.84
M2 (broad money) (% of GDP)	46.71	66.14	32.58	96.82	35.48	27.71	24.02	57.31	34.04
Merchandise exports (US$ billions)	2.75	2.12	0.82	121.00	9.36	7.72	12.26	29.26	91.56
Manufactures exports (% of total merchandise exports)	84.70	44.26	84.76	82.31	49.19	87.41	0.69	53.51	24.17
Lending rate (%)	3.48	1.00	11.00	10.89	16.50	18.00	20.04	13.77	n.a.
Foreign exchange reserves (US$ billions)				52.91	4.32	1.97	4.44	6.04	453.12

Sources: World Bank (n.d.); Jordà-Schularick-Taylor Macrohistory database (http://www.macrohistory.net/data/).

in the motives for the establishment of ECAs in China as compared to other developing economies with weak financial systems. Based on the data in Table 19.3, a case for capital scarcity and rising external debt as possible drivers for the establishment of the ECAs can only be made for Africa, Nigeria and India, but not for South Korea, China or South Africa. In fact, the AfDB (1992) and Oramah *et al.* (1995) cite rising external debt as the reason for the establishment of the Afreximbank and NEXIM, respectively. The same holds true for the establishment of the Export-Import Bank of India (India Exim Bank).[2]

The data do not explain why all of the countries in the sample, except South Africa, started off with Exim banks, which (as discussed in the section "Form and Function of ECAs", above) provide direct loans. It does, however, support why South Africa started off with an export credit insurance agency and not an Exim bank. It also helps explains why China and South Korea established export credit guarantee and insurance arrangements as separate institutions shortly after creating their Exim banks. In fact, Nigeria provides a clear example of where financial market realities forced the choice of scheme to implement. In this regard, Oramah *et al.* (1995) state, "NEXIM was initially conceived as an export credit guarantee institution similar to Britain's Export Credit Guarantee Department (ECGD). The enabling decree for this named it Nigerian Export Credit Guarantee and Insurance Corporation. It was, however, discovered that conceived solely as an export risk management institution, the organisation would only have a limited impact on the country's non-oil export performance. Thus, a successor decree was promulgated in 1991 which broadened its mandate to include the provision of risk bearing, credit, and trade information services". Oramah *et al.* (1995) add that the relatively high cost of funds and limited export credit that were being extended to the export sector meant that there was an urgent need to increase the level of credit available to the sector. In addition, the AfDB (1992) notes that one of the compelling reasons for creating the Afreximbank was the scarcity of trade finance in Africa.

ECA Creation: A Response to Economic and External Sector Developments

Many developing economies created ECAs mostly in response to the deteriorating economic situation that ensued during the 1970s and 1990s from a myriad of economic and financial crises. It would appear that each of the developing economies witnessed significant economic deceleration by the time they first established their ECAs. For instance, China's economic growth rate weakened from 13.5% in 1985 to 3.9% in 1990 before recovering strongly to 13.9% in 1993, a year before the country established its Exim bank (China Exim Bank) (Figure 19.5). Similar growth decelerations occurred in India, South Africa and Nigeria, with the most severe in Nigeria during 1990–1995.

While macroeconomic conditions may have influenced ECA creation in developing economies, other variables – the state of industrial development, overdependence on commodities (which added to economic vulnerability) and national goals of boosting access to the global market and enhancing global competitiveness – were the primary drivers. Apart from China and South Korea, whose shares of manufactured exports relative to total exports were at comparable levels to those of developing economies at the time their ECAs were created, all other developing economies

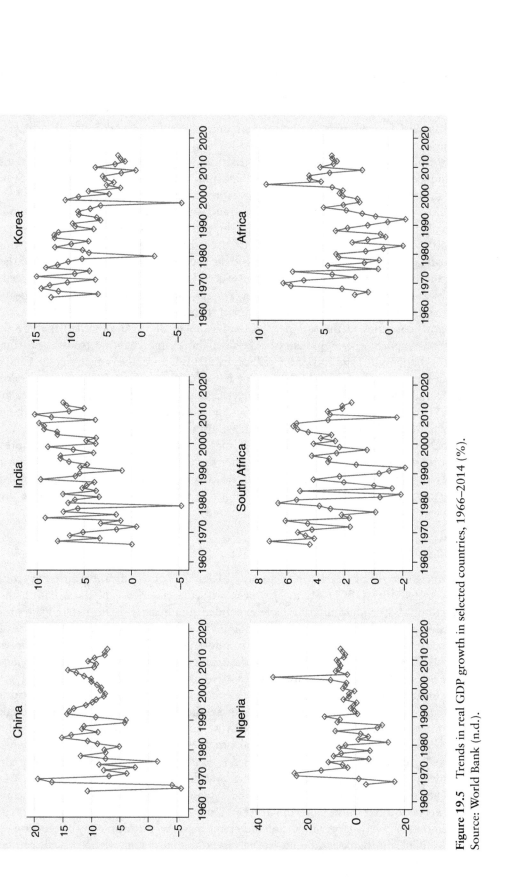

Figure 19.5 Trends in real GDP growth in selected countries, 1966–2014 (%).
Source: World Bank (n.d.).

had a relatively weak manufacturing base, with manufactures' export share of total national exports below 50%, and much lower for Nigeria and Africa as a whole. It is therefore plausible that the motives for the creation of ECAs in relatively advanced/ industrialised developing economies were much different from those of other developing economies.

In China, the primary aim of China Exim Bank and the China Export & Credit Insurance Corporation (also known as Sinosure) was to extend China's influence in the global market through trade and investment. Sinosure is a state-funded, policy-oriented insurance company established and supported by the state to promote China's foreign economic and trade development and cooperation. In the case of NEXIM and the Afreximbank, and as discussed in the section "Evolution and Performance of ECAs in Africa: Lessons from Two Case Studies", below, one of the key incentives that led to their creation was to boost value-added exports. Indeed, for most countries in the sample, except Nigeria, the share of manufactures exports surged in the years following the creation of their first ECAs (Figure 19.6).

In all countries in the sample, the establishment of ECAs preceded the rise of national exports and/or industrial take-off. China's merchandise trade rose from US$360 billion in 1994 to US$0.6 trillion by 2011. During the same time, the China Exim Bank and the China Development Bank had become the largest suppliers of trade and investment finance to other developing economies, disbursing as much as US$110 billion between 2009 and 2010 – an indication of China's policy of forging new patterns of China-led globalisation within the context of its broader push for global-export expansion. Additionally, merchandise exports and manufactures exports rose in India and South Korea after the creation of national ECAs. While a case can be made for the contribution of the ECAs to the growth of national exports, the exact impact is subject to further empirical investigation, which is outside the scope of this chapter.

Product Offering

Products offered by developing-economy ECAs are not significantly different from those offered by OECD ECAs. However, with the emergence of Exim banks, the functions and product offering have expanded significantly. Exim banks were predominantly created in developing economies in recognition of the need to provide capacity for capital imports essential for industrial development. Table 19.4 shows the broad product offerings by each of the arrangements in each of the sample countries. All countries, except South Africa, started off with Exim banks. Accordingly, at the time of their inception, each country's export credit scheme, except that of South Africa, provided loans in support of exports either directly to exporters or through the intermediary of banks, or both. NEXIM, in particular, operated at that time solely through the intermediary of banks to "veil off the government" and ensure some degree of independence. All schemes, except South Africa's, also provided trade finance (that is, L/Cs, forfaiting, factoring, and the like).

The commencement of lending can be explained by poor capital and financial-market conditions in the cases of Africa and in India, but not China or South Korea, given the relatively deeper financial and credit markets at the time of the creation of the China Exim Bank and South Korea's Export-Import Bank (KEXIM).[3] It can be

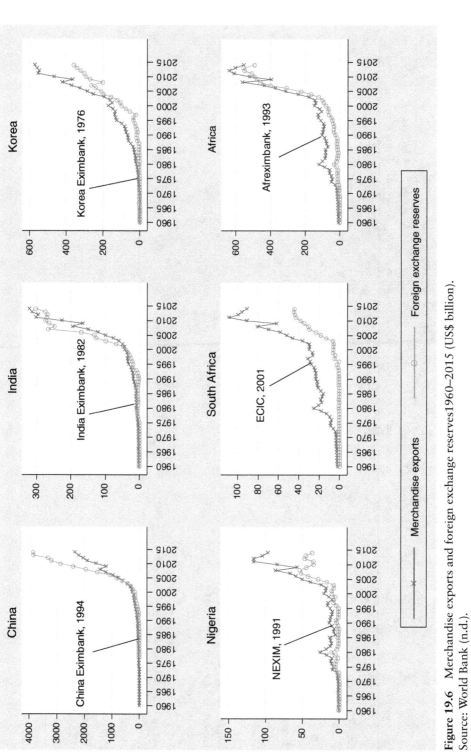

Figure 19.6 Merchandise exports and foreign exchange reserves1960–2015 (US$ billion).
Source: World Bank (n.d.).

Table 19.4 Characterization of selected export credit arrangements (ECAs)

Country/type of ECA	Year created	Export loans	Import loans	Overseas investment loans	Guarantees	Credit insurance	On-lending loans (national)	On-lending loans (foreign)	Concessional lending
Korea									
Korea Export-Import Bank	1976	1980	1980	1980	1980	Nil	1980	1980	1980
Korea Trade Insurance Corporation	1992	Nil	Nil	Nil	Nil	1992	Nil	Nil	Nil
India									
Export Import Bank of India	1982	1982	1982	1982	1982	Nil	1982	1982	1982
Export Credit and Guarantee Corporation of India	1957	Nil	Nil	Nil	1957	1957	Nil	Nil	Nil
China									
China Export-Import Bank	1994	1995	1995	1995	1995	Nil	1995	1995	1995
China Export and Credit Insurance Corporation	2001	Nil	Nil	Nil	Nil	2005	Nil	Nil	Nil
Nigeria									
Nigerian Export-Import Bank	1991	1991	1991	Nil	2005	Nil	2005	1995	Nil
Africa									
African Export-Import Bank	1993	1995	1995	1995	1995	Nil	1995	1995	Nil
South Africa									
Export Credit Insurance Corporation	2001	Nil	Nil	Nil	Nil	2005	Nil	Nil	Nil

argued that China Exim Bank's lending operations reflected its broad mandate as a policy bank, being one of the institutional banks (the others are the China Development Bank and Agricultural Development Bank) in China chartered to implement state policies in industry, foreign trade, diplomacy, economy and provide policy and financial support so as to promote the export of Chinese products and services.

At the time of their respective creations, all ECAs (except South Africa's) handled on-lending loans for foreign entities. For instance, NEXIM, at the time of its inception, managed an Export Stimulation Loan in the amount of about US$245 million, made available to the federal government of Nigeria by the AfDB; the China Exim Bank managed several on-lending facilities, including concessional loans from Japan; and the Afreximbank and India Exim Bank were beneficiaries of lines of credit from foreign commercial banks. Advisory services were the only other services offered by all agencies in the sample in the early periods of their respective operations.

All ECAs in the sample – except for the South Korea Trade Insurance Corporation (K-SURE), Sinosure and South Africa's Export Credit Insurance Corporation (ECIC) – offered import loans in their early years of operation to finance the import of export-generating imports and, in the case of China Exim Bank and the Afreximbank, "strategic" imports into their respective countries. Indeed, each country recognised the need for such import financing to support the acquisition of technologies to help make their manufactured exports competitive. The India Exim Bank, for instance, launched a programme for the financing of information technology (software and so forth) in 1985, which played a key role in subsequently making India an important information and communication technology hub. All Exim banks in the sample also offered trade finance and guarantee products at the times of their inceptions; none of the other institutions offered these products. However, only the non-Exim institutions (Sinosure, ECIC and K-SURE) offered export credit insurance from the times of their inceptions. Only KEXIM and the China Exim Bank started off by offering concessional loans to overseas clients. The India Exim Bank later followed. China Exim Bank, KEXIM and India Exim Bank acted as managers of grants and concessional loans granted by their respective governments to overseas governments.

By 2005, when almost all countries in the sample had operated ECAs for over a decade, there were no major changes in their export credit offerings. As shown in Table 19.4, China and South Korea had by then introduced separate institutions offering export credit insurance, a reflection of the need to extend comprehensive support to their exporting entities. This move also made it possible for respective Exim banks to expand lending. Throughout the sample period, all institutions remained publicly held and managed. Although comprehensive data are not available, all institutions, except NEXIM, appear to have maintained good profitability and strong capitalisation from the times of their inceptions to 2016.

By 2005, China Exim had begun to expand activities beyond traditional ECA services into activities consistent with its broad mandate. For instance, it started intervening in certain commercial transactions, including syndicated loans, not directly linked to China's trade but intended to strengthen China's financial sector. It also began promoting the growth of China's capital markets by supporting the issuance of "Panda" bonds by way of guarantees. CEXIM, KEXIM and, more recently, the Afreximbank have established, or have begun investing in, funds. The Afreximbank, for instance, by 2017, finalised arrangements to launch the Fund for Africa's Export Development. Programmes in support of supply chain financing have also been launched by India Exim Bank, China Exim Bank, KEXIM and the Afreximbank.

Converging Natures

US Exim (2017) discusses the changes that traditional (advanced-economy) ECAs are making to counter the support being provided by ECAs in Asia, especially China, India, Korea and other Asian countries. The paper argues that since the Global Financial Crisis of 2008, ECAs have become part of the "strategic big picture" and that this strategic connection has led to increased funding for, and expanded mandates of, ECAs around the world, as well as a shift from the role of lender of last resort to a more proactive role in meeting a variety of export financing needs. A natural consequence of this strategic importance is the rapid expansion of "trade-related" programmes that are outside of OECD arrangement rules (for example, investment and untied support). Noticeable changes seen in advanced-economy ECAs include the following:

- Renewed government involvement in export credits. For instance, the government of France, in 2016, transferred its guarantee programme from Compagnie Française d'Assurance pour le Commerce Extérieur (Coface) (a private agency) to Banque publique d'investissement (Bpi) France, which is a government bank. The goal is to make guarantees more accessible to French exporters and therefore more potent.
- A number of agencies that had previously relinquished short-term businesses are beginning to take them back. Many have started offering supply chain and working capital finance guarantees.
- Some advanced-economy ECAs are also considering having (or already have) buyer-direct lending, in recognition of the constraints that compliance risk is posing to their host countries' commercial banks. In this regard, the advantage that their deep financial markets offer, with respect to attracting commercial banks into export credit activities, appears to be increasingly disappearing, as banks accelerate de-risking due to high compliance costs.
- Some advanced-economy ECAs have also followed in the footsteps of South Korea to provide so-called untied and market-window support – programmes supporting major projects of significant national interest.[4]

As such, there has been a tendency towards convergence, with Asian ECAs leading the way. This is perhaps not surprising, given that as economies become more developed, their strategic trade interests begin to resemble those of advanced economies. At the same time, developed-economy ECAs are beginning to recognise the limits of commercial banks under current global conditions and are increasingly beginning to strengthen government support for their exporters in a highly competitive world market.

Evolution and Performance of ECAs in Africa: Lessons from Two Case Studies

Unlike other developing regions – developing Asia in particular – that have used ECAs to transform the structures of their economies, the experience in Africa has not been successful. Almost all ECAs created in Africa during the late 1960s to early 1980s have collapsed or become ineffective. This section reviews two case studies (NEXIM and the Afreximbank) – institutions similar in some ways but very different in their historical performances.

The Nigerian Export-Import Bank

Background

NEXIM was the Nigerian government's response to the country's deteriorating economic situation during the late 1970s and most of 1980s. Over-concentration of exports on a few commodities and an underdeveloped financial sector meant that the country's external sector was highly exposed to volatility in commodity prices and economic shocks emanating from other regions. The bulk was petroleum, with most of the total exports (89.6%) of the country destined for the United States and Europe. Moreover, over 75% of non-oil exports were paid for under L/C terms. Interest rates were in excess of 25% a year during most of the period after 1986, compared to average global inflation of less than 10%, thereby reducing the competitiveness of Nigeria's exports.

NEXIM was established in 1991 as a replacement for the Nigerian Export Credit Guarantee and Insurance Corporation established in 1988 to promote and foster diversification of Nigeria's exports through the use of insurance products. With an initial capitalisation of ₦500 million (US$50 million in 1991 US dollars), NEXIM was tasked to perform the following actions:

- Provide export credit guarantees and export credit insurance facilities to its clients;
- Provide credit in local currency to its clients in support of exports;
- Establish and manage funds connected with exports;
- Provide foreign exchange credit from a revolving fund to exporters who need to import foreign inputs to facilitate export production;
- Provide trade information and export advisory services in support of export business;
- Provide domestic credit insurance where such a facility is likely to assist exports;
- Provide credit insurance in respect of external trade and transit trade;
- Purchase and sell foreign currency and transmit funds to all countries; and
- Provide investment guarantees and investment insurance facilities.

Governance

NEXIM's governance structure is similar to that of other ECAs created in the early 1900s. The institution is wholly owned by the government of Nigeria and falls under the purview of the Ministry of Finance and the Central Bank. The President of Nigeria appoints the nine members of the board of directors and the managing director/chief executive officer (CEO) on the recommendation of the governor of the central bank. He also appoints two executive directors to assist the CEO. The CEO appoints other staff members. Due to the nature of the shareholding, annual general meetings are not held. Rather, the board, which is chaired by a deputy governor of the central bank, usually reports separately to the Central Bank and the Ministry of Finance. All policy documents are approved by the board. The CEO is usually appointed for a term of five years, renewable once.

While other ECAs have become either fully or partially independent and others privatised, NEXIM has remained essentially state-owned. In that vein, due to the political nature of the appointment, NEXIM has had six CEOs since the time of its inception (an average of one every four years). This might have negatively affected NEXIM's policy and strategy consistency and the ability to follow through on strategic initiatives.

Product offering and evolution

With a clear mandate, NEXIM launched a unique set of products aimed at creating domestic capacity for export production and diversification of the economy away from commodities. It launched the Export Credit Rediscounting and Refinancing Facility (RRF) to provide pre- and post-shipment finance in local currency through commercial banks, which enabled exporters to have access to expanded export portfolios of banks at preferential rates. Through the RRF, local banks provided pre-shipment credit for a maximum duration of 120 days and post-shipment credit for a maximum duration of 60 days. Recognising the need to create domestic capacity for value addition, NEXIM's Foreign Input Facility (FIF) provided foreign exchange to export manufacturers for imports of capital equipment, packaging materials and raw materials for the production of finished or semi-finished export products. The FIF, which at inception was provided through banks, was made to benefit export manufacturers. In addition to the FIF, NEXIM introduced the Repurchase Facility to ameliorate the burden of repayment on enterprises financed under the FIF but which encountered unanticipated difficulties that made it difficult for them to meet repayment obligations in a timely manner. With the Repurchase Facility, the participating bank repurchased not more than two instalments of a loan that had fallen due but could not be repaid. In addition, NEXIM's Stocking Facility, provided through banks in local currency, enabled manufacturers to procure an adequate stock of raw materials (which are seasonal in nature) to keep their production at optimal levels, particularly during periods in which raw materials were scarce. The facility had a maximum maturity of 18 months.

Some 12 years following the establishment of NEXIM, the product mix changed, essentially driven by limits on NEXIM's sources of funds rather than by a deliberate strategic realignment. For instance, due to the depletion of RRF resources as a result of inflation and the absence of an injection of additional funds, the RRF is no longer available (Table 19.5). Since 2010, facilities in operation include the Direct Lending Facility (DLF) and a very low level of export guarantees. Funding that has sustained the FRF/DLF consists of loans from the Afreximbank; naira lending is made possible by funding received from the Bank of Industry (a Nigerian government agency) and a loan from the federal government of Nigeria. The DLF is made available directly to exporters and not through commercial banks – a major shift from the original operational model.

Table 19.5 Loans and advances (outstanding) by type of facility offered by Nigeria Export-Import Bank, 1995–2015 (US$ million)

Type of facility	1991	1992	2007	2008	2009	2010	2013	2014	2015
Rediscounting/refinancing facility	123.67	70.84	9.21	0.92	6.97	-	3.04	2.82	2.48
Foreign exchange revolving fund	240.53	262.08	-	-	-	-	-	-	-
Direct lending	-	-	30.28	19.33	13.41	18.81	186.66	240.56	235.14
Medium-term direct lending	-	-	-	-	-	-	*154.34*	*205.56*	*175.94*
Short-term direct lending	-	-	-	-	-	-	*29.32*	*35.00*	*59.20*
Working capital/stocking facility	9.09	14.40	-	8.26	-	13.27	-	-	-
Repurchase facility	3.9	24.87	-	-	-	-	-	-	-
Export guarantee	0.66	0.38	28.38	-	0.01	27.47	1.36	0.19	0.19
Medium-term	-	-	28.10	-	-	-	-	-	-
Short-term	-	-	0.28	-	0.01	-	-	-	-
Others	-	-	-	-	-	6.23	-	-	-
Total	364.85	333.30	67.88	28.50	20.40	65.78	225.23	287.30	343.62

Sources: Nigerian Export-Import Bank annual reports (http://www.neximbank.com.ng/downloads-centre/); Oramah *et al.* (1995).

Operational and financial performance

Oramah *et al.* (1995) assessed the viability and performance of NEXIM during its first three years of operation. This section expands on that work by evaluating the operational and financial performance during the past 25 years. At the time of NEXIM's inception in 1988, exporters faced low country and buyer risk, but they were also met with limited and costly export credit. Credit to the export sector was unattractive to commercial banks and was therefore consistently in lower supply than that to importers and others engaged in domestic trade (Figure 19.7). These factors combined to favour the introduction, on the part of NEXIM, of credit facilities over risk-bearing facilities. Mindful of the need to keep administrative overheads low, NEXIM restricted operations to wholesale banking, taking advantage of the extensive branch network of commercial and merchant banks to avail subsidised export credits to exporters across the country. The arrangement was also reflective of NEXIM's role as a supplementary, rather than a competitive, source of export financing.

In 1991, banks' outstanding export credit liabilities to NEXIM stood at ₦942.5 million, representing 65% of total export credit outstanding in the banking system (Table 19.6). By 1993, these liabilities rose to ₦1,574 million, representing 91% of total export credit outstanding, indicating that NEXIM had, within three years of commencing operations, become the dominant source of export credit to the sector. This was most likely due to liquidity problems that banks in Nigeria faced in 1992–1993, along with prevailing macroeconomic policies that did not provide banks with incentives to finance exports (Oramah *et al.*, 1995). An analysis of NEXIM's export credit RRF by product group reveals that the number of commodities financed grew from 14 in 1990 to 16 in 1991, rising further to 28 in 1992, before peaking at 29 in 1993. In support of export projects, NEXIM also expanded activity under its FIF, Repurchase and Stocking Facilities.

A number of challenges – rising domestic inflation, inadequacy of working capital, delays in equipment installation, poor project appraisals and the relatively short

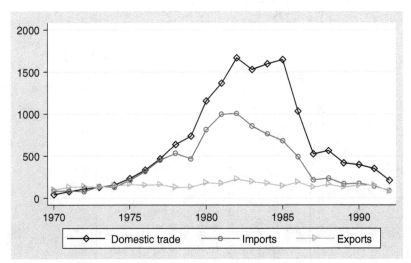

Figure 19.7 Banking system outstanding credit to import, exports and domestic trade, 1970–1992 (US$ million).
Source: Oramah et al. (1995).

Table 19.6 Nigeria Export-Import Bank short-term export credit

Year	(1) Nigeria Export-Import Bank's outstanding export credit (₦ million)	(2) Banking system's outstanding export credit (₦ million)	(1) As a percentage of (2)
1991	942.5	1,449.2	65.0
1992	1,457.0	1,682.6	86.6
1993	1,574.0*	1,727.1	91.1

Source: Nigeria Export-Import Bank; Central Bank of Nigeria.

maturity (five years) of the FIF – made it difficult for some beneficiaries to meet their obligations in a timely manner. In response, NEXIM introduced a Rescue Facility under which it repurchased repayment notes that had fallen due to provide sufficient time for projects to bring production to a capacity that would allow for obligations to be met. In 1991, the total volume of repurchases stood at US$3.9 million, involving six banks and eight projects. Repurchase facilities of US$24.87 million were granted to 76 projects through 65 banks in 1992. Over time, however, this rescheduling initiative could not achieve its objectives and was therefore discontinued. The Stocking Facility was designed as an input inventory-financing facility to assist manufacturers of value-added agricultural products to keep their production running at optimal levels, particularly during periods in which agricultural inputs were scarce (see Table 19.5 for loans granted under this facility). Like the FIF, the Stocking Facility ran into trouble in later years and was discontinued.

Since the late 1990s/early 2000s, NEXIM's operation has not been as impactful as it was during the early years, due to a lack of resources. By 2010, NEXIM's main facility was the DLF, at which time NEXIM's contribution to export credits outstanding in the Nigerian banking sector had become negligible. The current Nigerian government has decided to promote non-oil exports, and NEXIM is seen as key to that effort.

Sources of funding

At the time of its inception, NEXIM's major sources of funds were the Central Bank of Nigeria, which provided ₦1.2 billion in the form of an 8% perpetual debenture to support the RRF, and the AfDB, which provided about US$243.7 million under an Export Stimulation Loan to the government of Nigeria (Table 19.5). NEXIM also drew from guarantee funds put in reserve in anticipation of the introduction of risk-bearing facilities. Due to varying interest rates and fluctuating exchange rates, the average cost of NEXIM's funds depended on the relative share of the various sources in the volume of funds used in the period. Borrowings to fund the trade and project finance facilities accounted for the bulk of funds available to NEXIM, which rose from ₦3.8 billion in 1991 to ₦5.75 billion in 1992 – largely as a result of currency depreciation, which affected the nominal value of funds available under the FIF. Central Bank of Nigeria funding for the RRF accounted for 18.24% and 32.4% of total funds available in 1992 and 1991, respectively, while AfDB funding for the FIF accounted for 67.5% and 60.3%, respectively, of total funds available in 1992 and

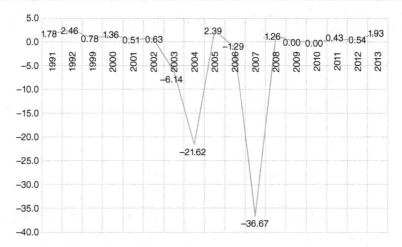

Figure 19.8 NEXIM profit/loss (US$ million).
Source: Nigerian Export-Import Bank annual reports (http://www.neximbank.com.ng/downloads-centre/).

1991. By 2013–2014, the sources of funds had shifted such that loans for exports stimulation made available by the government at an interest rate of 1% were dominant, with an amount outstanding of ₦6.5 billion. This was followed by an amount of US$50 million in loans made available by the Afreximbank. These two loans constituted about 80% of total NEXIM debt liabilities in 2013 and 2014.

With regard to financial performance, NEXIM's profit fell sharply, reflecting the wide disparity between interest rates on its loans and the inflation rate, as well as a large provision for doubtful debt with respect to its project finance operations (Figure 19.8). The almost complete reliance of banks on NEXIM for export financing meant that NEXIM devoted over 91% of its funds to credit operations, thereby constraining it from using other investment avenues to improve its operating profit. This, however, was justified in view of its export development focus. The cost of NEXIM operations was below the average interest charge it placed on its loans, which was about 12% in the early years. In 1992, the cost of administration was 1.8% of the total amount of loans – which, together with the average cost of funds of about 7.4%, put the cost of operation at 9.2%. However, high inflation and excessive currency depreciation, which contributed to large loan losses, exerted immense pressure on profitability, such that by 2003, NEXIM began to see losses or near-zero profits.

The Afreximbank: Brief History, Evolution and Performance

Background
The background to the creation of the Afreximbank (the Bank) is similar to that of the creation of national ECAs in most African and other developing regions. The debt crises that broke in Latin America (originating in Mexico, Brazil and Argentina) adversely affected African countries, as many international banks exited the continent due to perceived high credit and country risks. With limited availability of trade finance, banking sector credit to the private sector stagnated at about 15% of GDP

during the 1980s and early 1990s; Africa's merchandise exports declined by over 40% between 1980 and 1986; GDP, in both nominal and real terms, declined by over 20% over the same period; and inflation stood at hyper-levels (World Bank, n.d.).

At the 1987 annual meeting of the board of governors of the AfDB, held in Cairo, Egypt, African ministers of finance adopted a resolution requiring AfDB management to conduct a study on the desirability of establishing a regional institution to provide trade finance facilities to promote trade. Of great concern was the very low level of intra-African and Africa–South trade, the low level of value-added exports, a decline in financial flows to Africa, a worsening external debt situation of many African countries and a sharp reduction in trade financing to Africa by international commercial banks. The feasibility study initiated in 1987 by the AfDB's board of governors was completed in 1992 and formed the basis of the establishment of the Afreximbank in Cairo in 1993. The Afreximbank was established under the constitutive instruments of an agreement signed by member states, which confers on the Bank the status of an international organisation, and a charter signed by all shareholders, which provides the general framework for conducting the Bank's business. By signature of the Establishment Agreement, member countries agreed to confer on the Bank preferred creditor status in their countries.

Governance structure

The Afreximbank's shareholders are drawn from within and outside Africa and consist of both public and private investors. The majority of shareholders are from Africa. To encourage partnership on the basis of South–South and North–South cooperation, the Bank charter permits both African and non-African investors. At the time of the Bank's inception, shareholders were divided into three categories: (i) Class A, consisting of African states or their central banks, the AfDB and African regional and subregional financial institutions; (ii) Class B, consisting of African national financial institutions and African private investors; and (iii) Class C, consisting of international financial institutions and economic organisations, and non-African private investors. At the time of the Bank's inception, its charter allowed for maximum ownership of the Bank at full subscription of its shares as follows: Class A: 35%, Class B: 40% and Class C: 25%. As of the end of 2016, Class A shareholders held the majority of the shares (64%), and Classes B and C held 26% and 10%, respectively.

The Afreximbank's authorised share capital, at the time of the Bank's inception, amounted to US$750 million, of which US$364 million had been subscribed by the end of 1995. In 2012, an amendment to the charter of the Bank raised the authorised capital to US$5 billion and introduced Class D shares, which could be invested by anybody and which could be listed. As of December 2017, the Bank's shareholders' fund amounted to US$2.1 billion, with callable capital (subscribed, yet to be "called") amounting to US$655 million (Figure 19.9). Depository receipts linked to Class D shares were issued and listed on the stock exchange of Mauritius in October 2017.

At the top of the hierarchy is the general meeting of shareholders, the main purposes of which are as follows:

- To elect/remove directors and determine their remuneration;
- On the recommendation of the board of directors, to appoint/remove the president;

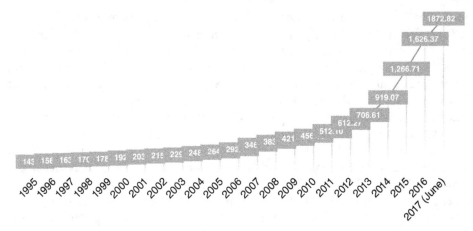

Figure 19.9   Afreximbank capital (US$ million).
Source: Afreximbank annual reports, 1995–2017 (https://www.afreximbank.com/research-and-knowledge/).

- To appoint the external auditors and determine their mandate and remuneration;
- To approve, after reviewing the report of the external auditors, the annual financial statements of the Bank and adopt the Annual Report; and
- To change the headquarters of the Bank.

The second level in the governance hierarchy is the board of directors. At the time of the Bank's inception, the board of directors was composed of ten members – four of these were elected by Class A shareholders, one of which was nominated by the AfDB; four were elected by Class B shareholders; and two were elected by Class C shareholders. Following an amendment to the charter in 2012, two independent directors (to be nominated by the board and approved by shareholders) were added. The amended charter provided for Class D shareholders to elect a board representation if Class D shares represent at least 10% of the total issued common stock of the Bank; in this case, the number of representations in Class B would be reduced by one.

The procedure for the appointment of the president is also well documented in the charter. On recommendation by the board of directors, the shareholders, during their general meeting, appoint the president by a simple majority of votes of holders of all issued shares of common stock and at least 40% of the holders of Class A shares. The charter prescribes specific attributes of the president of the Bank, including that the president be a national of an African state but not a national of the African state where the Bank's headquarters is situated. The president's term of office is five years, renewable once for a second term of equal length. Since its inception, the Bank has had three presidents, with the third currently in service. Each of the first two presidents served two full terms, which ensured stability of vision and operations.

Mandate
The Afreximbank's charter mandates the Bank to facilitate, promote and expand intra- and extra-African trade (particularly Africa–South trade) using three broad instruments – credit, advisory services and credit insurance. In 2012, the charter of the Bank was amended to expand its mandate to include the following: "To provide

capital to African corporates and importers through equity investments which shall include, but not be limited to, shares, share warrants, redeemable preference shares and loan and to do so whether or not in conjunction with the extension of credit".

Product offering

The Afreximbank began operations in September 1994. Given the broad mandate of the Bank, its management took a deliberate decision to focus on short-term trade financing, with emphasis on export financing. The rationale for this was as follows:

- Africa was not exporting a significant number of capital goods, and demand for export credit insurance, which usually would support such exports, was very low. It was also thought that combining credit insurance and direct lending under one balance sheet would not be prudent.
- Short-term trade finance was considered a priority, as international banks that usually provided short-term pre-export financing and letters of credit facilities had exited Africa as a result of the debt crisis of the 1980s. It was thought that the Bank's limited resources would better serve the short-term trade finance needs of the continent.
- Project finance was considered necessary but too risky for a young bank with limited resources.

Accordingly, the products offered by the Bank during its early years of operations included the Lines of Credit Programme, Direct Financing Programme, Syndications Programme and Special Risk Programme (including the Country Risk Guarantee Facility, Joint Bill Discounting and the Refinancing Facility). Over the years, the product offering expanded to include the following programmes: Note Purchase, Financial Future Flow Pre-Financing, Project-Related Financing, ECA Loans Facilitation and Export Development. Since 2012, a number of special products targeted at developing critical sectors have also been put in place, including the Construction and Tourism Linked Relay Facility in support of the development of the continent's tourism sector; the Africa Cocoa Initiative in support of value addition to cocoa; the Construction and Medical Tourism Relay Facility; the Countercyclical Trade Liquidity Facility, an emergency facility created in 2015 to enable orderly adjustments to commodity price shocks; the Food Emergency Contingent Trade Financing Facility; and the Central Bank Deposit Programme (CENDEP), for deposit mobilisation from African central banks.

Operations

Since the time of its inception, the Afreximbank's strategies have been targeted at attaining two broad objectives: trade developmental/macro-objectives and corporate objectives. While the macro-objectives are at the core of the Bank's mandate, the Bank cannot achieve them on its own – it can only facilitate their attainment through specific activities aimed at removing constraints to economic activity, mobilising other forces and so forth. The trade developmental objectives include promoting intra-African and Africa–South trade, promoting diversification of Africa's export products and markets and improving credit-risk perception of African entities and African counterparties, among others. The corporate objectives are those that are reasonably within the Bank's control and are geared towards specific issues that are likely to facilitate the attainment of the macro-objectives. They would normally include, among others, improving capitalisation, human capital, operational efficiency and financial performance. Highlights of the macro- and corporate achievements are discussed below.

At the macro-level, Africa's merchandise trade increased from US$234 billion in 1995 to over US$1 trillion in 2010 before retreating to under US$950 billion in 2015.[5] Intra-African trade rose from US$21 billion in 1995 to about US$146 billion in 2015, with the share of total trade rising from under 9% to 15% during the same period. All these were within range of the Afreximbank's strategic goals under the four strategic plans it has implemented since the time of its inception. Bank estimates indicate that it supported about 30% of the aggregate trade finance needs of its member countries in 2015–2016.

At the corporate level, the Bank deployed a menu of instruments to deliver trade and project finance solutions to the African continent. It provided direct financing to corporations that met certain criteria, while others were supported under lines of credit to banks. The Structured Trade Finance Instrument[6] (Oramah, 2015) was extensively used to mitigate credit risks. In 1995, soon after the Bank's creation, the Line of Credit, Direct Financing and Special Risk Programmes accounted for 6%, 74% and 10%, respectively, of total loan authorisations (Table 19.7). In terms of sectoral focus, commodities (agriculture, metals and minerals and energy) dominated, accounting for a combined share of 92% of the Bank's authorisations in 1995 (Table 19.8).

Over time, the Bank's operations have expanded both in size and in breadth in line with its strategic shift (in 2000) toward promoting and financing activities aimed at improving the continent's export competitiveness. In terms of sectors, the Bank has expanded its activities in the services sector (in support of services exports), manufacturing (agro-processing and light manufactures), telecommunications and transportation. In 2005, some 11 years after the Bank commenced operations, the share of commodities in loan authorisations declined to 26%, and it further declined to 12% at the end of 2016. Conversely, financing of manufacturing and trade-supporting infrastructure projects expanded significantly between 2000 and 2016.

Over the years, the Bank has expanded the use of commercial banks as intermediaries in the delivery of its services, such that their shares of authorisations reached 84% in 2016 (from 12% in 1995). This approach has enabled it to support more non-traditional export financing in a low-risk manner. Accordingly, the share of authorisations to all other sectors has been in decline (Tables 19.7 and 19.8). In terms of product offering, the three main products – Lines of Credit, Direct Financing and Special Risks – remain dominant instruments. However, new products have emerged, with the shifting emphasis from commodity financing to value added and services export financing. The Projects and Export Development Finance Facility became an important instrument starting in 2000, with facility approvals rising from US$10 million in 2000 to approximately US$880 million by 2016.

Funding sources

During its first two years of full operation (1995–1996), the Afreximbank's only source of funding was equity investments from shareholders. In 1997, the Bank, for the first time, accessed bilateral lines from international financial institutions in an amount of US$14 million (Table 19.9). Bilateral and money-market lines became the

Table 19.7 Historical trends in Afreximbank loan approvals by type of product offering

Type of product	Loan approvals (US$ million)					Percentage share				
	1995	2000	2005	2010	2016	1995	2005	2010	2015	2016
Line of credit	9.00	694.00	532.00	1,442.58	8,401.74	5.74	58.45	39.78	51.32	60.14
Note purchase	-	-	115.00	28.00	-	-	12.63	0.77	-	-
Receivables purchase/discounting	-	12.24	50.00	-	-	-	5.49	-	2.60	-
Direct financing programme	115.90	204.20	113.20	576.27	2,721.98	73.87	12.44	15.89	18.50	19.49
Project/export development finance	-	10.00	-	465.77	876.98	-	-	12.84	9.16	6.28
Special risk programme:	16.00	131.75	10.00	70.00	-	10.20	1.10	1.93	-	-
Future-flow pre-financing	-	-	-	73.90	-	-	-	2.04	-	-
Asset-backed lending	-	-	-	29.00	-	-	-	0.80	-	-
Syndications	92.70	181.00	90.00	940.68	1,968.70	59.08	9.89	25.94	18.43	14.09
Total	156.90	1,233.19	910.20	3,626.21	13,969.40	100.00	100.00	100.00	100.00	100.00

Source: Afreximbank annual reports, various issues (https://www.afreximbank.com/research-and-knowledge/).

Table 19.8 Historical trends in Afreximbank loan approvals by sector

Sector financed	Total approvals (US$ million)						Percentage share of total					
	1995	2000	2005	2010	2015	2016	1995	2000	2005	2010	2015	2016
Agriculture	71.90	29.00	80.00	199.60	280.90	249.80	52.91	2.91	8.82	7.43	5.57	2.08
Energy	24.00	212.50	130.00	302.04	698.90	1,052.00	17.66	21.31	14.33	11.25	13.87	8.74
Services	-	-	45.00	158.90	210.70	180.00	-	-	4.96	5.92	4.18	1.50
Metals and minerals	17.00	18.75	25.00	105.00	11.00	170.00	12.51	1.88	2.76	3.91	0.22	1.41
Transportation	-	34.24	15.00	88.55	150.00	33.50	-	3.43	1.65	3.30	2.98	0.28
Manufacturing	7.00	-	-	67.20	182.80	140.20	5.15	-	-	2.50	3.63	1.17
Telecommunications	-	100.00	20.00	352.54	65.80	119.50	-	10.03	2.21	13.13	1.31	0.99
Financial institutions	16.00	602.75	592.00	1,411.70	3,439.90	10,086.30	11.77	60.44	65.27	52.57	68.25	83.83
Total	135.90	997.24	907.00	2,685.53	5,040.00	12,031.30	100.00	100.00	100.00	100.00	100.00	100.00

Source: Afreximbank annual reports, various issues (https://www.afreximbank.com/research-and-knowledge/).

Table 19.9 Sources of non-equity funding

						(US$ million)					
Type of funds	1997	1998	1999	2000	2006	2009	2011	2014	2016
Money market and bilateral lines	14.0	102.6	123.0	157	75.4	150.0	229.3	250.0	952.1
Customer deposits	n/a	n/a	n/a	6.1	28.7	56.7	39.7	296.8	
Central bank deposit	n/a	n/a	n/a	n/a	n/a	n/a	n/a	n/a	3,234.4
Syndicated loans	n/a	n/a	60.0	100.0	150.0	610.8	821.3	763.3	1,180.3
Bonds	n/a	n/a	n/a	n/a	n/a	300.0	545.5	750.0	899.9
Export credit arrangement/development finance institution	n/a	n/a	n/a	n/a	n/a	n/a	293.7		254.3
Total	14.0	102.6	183.0	263.1	254.1	1,117.4	1,929.5	2,060.1	6,521.0

Source: Afreximbank annual reports, various issues (https://www.afreximbank.com/research-and-knowledge/).

principal instruments for raising treasury funding for the Bank's operations until 1999, when the Bank successfully tapped the euro syndicated loans market to raise US$60 million. The amounts raised through this instrument grew exponentially, surpassing bilateral and money-market lines after 2005. With its growing knowledge of the market, proven track record and strong relationships, the Bank began to introduce other sophisticated instruments following the attainment of investment grade rating in 2009. It launched a bond issuance in 2009, which was very successful and significantly oversubscribed. It also launched, in 2011, an ECA/Development Finance Institutions (DFI) Loans Facilitation Programme, through which it mobilised trade and project finance from ECAs and development finance institutions from regions outside of Africa, particularly Europe and Asia. In 2012, the Bank launched the CENDEP, an instrument designed to mobilise part of the growing foreign exchange reserves of African central banks. CENDEP has been very successful, with its share of total liabilities at over 49% in 2016. In addition, in 2016 and 2017, the Bank successfully raised funding through the issuance of Panda and Samurai bonds in the Asian markets.

Profitability

Due to its unique structure, being a public–private institution, the Bank ensured that it creates a balance between delivering economic value/development to its public sector shareholders (essentially African governments) and ensuring solid financial return on investment for its private sector shareholders. In this regard, since 1998, the Bank has consistently made profits and paid dividends to its shareholders. Table 19.10 shows that net income rose 28-fold – from US$5 million to over US$160 million – between 1995 and 2016. Return on equity has also remained well above 11% over the past two decades.

In terms of size, the Bank's total assets rose from US$144 million in 1995 to US$587 million in 2005 and further to US$1.9 billion by 2010. The Bank's activities quickened with the onset of the Global Financial Crisis in 2008, the Eurozone sovereign debt crisis of 2010 and the commodity price shock of 2014, which led to an explosion in demand for trade financing. As a result, the Bank's pipeline grew to US$50 billion from an annual average of about US$10–15 billion prior to that, and its total assets (largely loans) grew close to US$12 billion by the end of 2016 (Table 19.10).

Table 19.10   Afreximbank – summary financial performance indicators

	1995	2000	2005	2010	2016
Total assets (US$ million)	143.86	346.46	587.06	1,905.42	11,726.11
Equity (US$ million)	143.02	192.34	264.52	456.68	1,626.37
Net income (US$ million)	5.99	13.65	23.04	44.40	165.03
Key ratios (%)					
Return on average assets	4.2	4.2	4.1	2.7	1.750
Return on average equity	4.2	7.4	9.0	10.1	11.410
Cost-to-income ratio	41.2	21.8	21.1	28.0	18.27

Source: Afreximbank.

Survival of ECAs in Africa: Lessons from the Case Studies

It is clear from the analysis above that NEXIM and the Afreximbank have had varying operational success, even though they were established within the same environment and during the same period. Table 19.11 highlights the salient structural and functional differences that contributed to their divergent achievements.

Table 19.11   Key structural and operational differences between the Afreximbank and NEXIM

Factors	Afreximbank	Nigerian Export-Import Bank (NEXIM)
1. Governance structures	Established as an international public–private partnership. Its board of directors is elected by shareholders. The president and executive vice presidents are appointed through competitive processes. There is reasonable certainty of tenures and independence.	Established as a government institution. Appointments to the board and chief executive offices are made by the political leadership. This arrangement makes senior management and its board of directors susceptible to frequent changes, which negatively impact long-term planning and so forth.
2. Sources of funding	Funds itself through shareholders' equity and other market sources, including international bond markets, bilateral lines, export credit arrangement lines, syndicated loans markets and others. Was assigned investment-grade ratings by international rating agencies so as to be able to tap funding from international financial and capital markets.	Funded by the government or through government-guaranteed loans. Overreliance on government sources of funding limit operational independence. Further, funding of operations is a function of the state of health of the national economy. Poor funding and low capitalisation have been the greatest challenges of the institution.
3. Economic/operating environment	Given that economic shocks impact the Afreximbank's member countries differently, the Bank is able to diversify risks, limiting the impact of adverse economic developments on particular countries.	Operates in a single economic environment (Nigeria) and hence is very susceptible to country-specific economic shocks. Losses due to economic shocks are much higher. In addition, economic shocks hampered the Nigerian government's ability to capitalise/recapitalise NEXIM over time.
4. State of and capacity for export manufacturing	With operations in 50 countries, is able to support and finance value-added exports due to the existence of some manufacturing/processing capacities in a number of countries across the continent. Value-added exports, as a share of total exports, average about 20%.	Financing conditions were not favourable for value-added exports because the share of value-added exports at the organisation's inception was less than 1%.

Table 19.11 *(Continued)*

Factors	Afreximbank	Nigerian Export-Import Bank (NEXIM)
5. Market versus subsidy	Does not provide subsidised credit, which enables it to preserve capital over time.	Provides subsidised credit. This, combined with unfavourable macroeconomic environment (for example, a high inflationary regime), meant that its resources became depleted very quickly. These resources, when not replenished quickly by government, affect operational performance.
6. Shareholding	Broad and diversified shareholding, including public–private as well as non-African entities mean that the Bank operates with profitability in mind.	Lack of diversified shareholding, especially lack of private sector interests, denies the organisation of potential shareholder pressures for financial soundness.

Conclusions

In examining the nature and evolution of ECAs, this chapter attempted to answer the following key questions:

- What is the rationale behind the use of ECAs in export promotion in capital-scarce economies that are typically not in a position to export capital goods and offer export credits?
- What is the difference, if any, between traditional (advanced-economy) ECAs, and why? Why do developing economies prefer to operate Exim banks rather than other types of ECAs?
- How have developing-economy ECAs evolved as economies developed? Is there a tendency towards convergence with traditional ECAs?
- What important lessons are there to be learned from the evolution of ECAs?

The analysis shows that the general motivation for establishing ECAs has been the same across advanced and developing economies: countries have tended to establish ECAs to enable them to boost national exports – most notably, exports of manufactures.

Some differences have been observed among ECAs designated as Exim banks and those designated as export credit insurance and/or guarantee agencies, with Exim banks more likely to offer direct credit and guarantees, while others are more likely to offer credit insurance. Exim banks have also been more likely to operate profitably.

Developing economies have favoured Exim banks over other forms of ECAs and were more likely to offer direct credit. Developing-economy ECAs (most notably, Exim banks) have been more likely to finance imports into their countries than to have developing-economy ECAs.

The differences observed between advanced and developing-economy ECAs reflect the state of host countries' financial sectors. In developing economies, where access to credit is limited or expensive, ECAs have bridged the gap by providing direct lending to exporters.

Timewise evolution of export credit administration in selected economies indicates that, in the early stages, ECAs focused on direct credit, guarantees, import financing and long-term lending. Over time, countries introduced new arrangements, including export credit insurance and concessional financing.

The analysis also indicates that, as the development process progresses, the nature of developing-country ECAs has tended to converge with that of ECAs in advanced economies. The pace of convergence has been rapid in recent years, as China's dominance in the export credit space has driven developing-economy ECAs to expand their activities into other areas, including the so-called untied market-window support and direct lending.

Lessons arising from the foregoing analysis are as follows:

- ECAs in developing economies have a fair chance of operational and trade-promotion effectiveness if they operate as Exim banks. ECAs can be forces for promoting a country's exports, especially new exports in new markets, as demonstrated in China.
- For ECAs to succeed in developing economies, they must be insulated from political interference, manned by professionals and properly capitalised and funded. A stable macroeconomic environment, devoid of policy reversals and inconsistencies, is crucial, as is a well-articulated and documented external sector strategy that can help guide ECA managers.
- Using subsidised credit to promote exports in an unstable macroeconomic environment with high inflation and volatile exchange rates can compromise the effectiveness of an ECA over time. An ECA can only be sustained if the government is willing to continue to regularly recapitalise the ECA, which was the case in South Korea, but not in Nigeria. South Korea, for instance, recapitalised KEXIM in 1987, 1998 and 2011, raising its total equity from KRW150 billion to KRW1 trillion, KRW4 trillion and KRW60 trillion, respectively. In contrast, NEXIM did not experience any major recapitalisation, except for the relatively large capital infusion planned in 2017–2018.

The convergence of ECAs across advanced and developing economies is a strong indication that ECAs are dynamic and must change as dictated by market conditions. In this regard, ECAs should not shy away from unconventional activities and instruments if those activities can contribute to the overall attainment of their goals. For example, some ECAs have opened market windows to use the profits therefrom to support their riskier and unprofitable traditional operations.

Notes

1 See Schumpeter (1912); Greenwood and Jovanovic (1990); and Merton and Bodie (1995, 2004).
2 For more on the history of the Export-Import Bank of India, see https://accountlearning.com/export-import-bank-exim-bank-significance-functions/.

3 World Bank (n.d.).
4 See US Exim (2017) for more on the volume of untied and market windows offered by selected OECD and developing economies.
5 See Afreximbank annual reports, 1995–2017 (https://www.afreximbank.com/research-and-knowledge/).
6 Structured trade finance is the art of transferring risks in financing trade and trade-related transactions from parties less able to bear these risks to those more equipped to bear them in a manner that ensures automatic reimbursement of advances from the underlying transaction (see Oramah, 2015).

References

African Development Bank (1992) Feasibility Study Concerning the Establishment of an African Export-Import Bank (Afreximbank), presented to the Board of Governors of the AfDB, Abidjan. (Document available on demand from Afreximbank.)

Ascari, R. (2007) Is Export Credit Agency a Misnomer? The ECA Response to a Changing World. *ResearchGate Working Paper* No. 02. Retrieved from: https://www.researchgate.net/profile/Raoul_Ascari/publication/228800684_Is_export_credit_agency_a_misnomer_The_ECA_Response_to_a_Changing_World/links/568e29c908aead3f42ee26c8/Is-export-credit-agency-a-misnomer-The-ECA-Response-to-a-Changing-World.pdf (accessed 15 July 2019).

COMCEC (Committee for Economic and Commercial Cooperation of the Organization of Islamic Cooperation) (2015) Improving the Role of Eximbanks/ECAs in the OIC Member States. Retrieved from: http://www.comcec.org/wp-content/uploads/2015/08/5-Trade-Report.pdf (accessed 14 July 2019).

Gianturco, D. (2001) *Export Credit Agencies: The Unsung Giants of International Trade and Finance*. Westport: Quorum Books.

Greenwood, J. & Jovanovic, B. (1990) Financial Development, Growth, and the Distribution of Income. *The Journal of Political Economy*, 98(5), 1076–1107.

Klasen, A. (2014) Export Credit Guarantees and the Demand for Insurance. *CESifo Forum*, 15(3), 26–33.

Krauss, R.M. (2011) The Role and Importance of Export Credit Agencies. Washington, DC: George Washington University, Institute of Brazilian Business and Public Management Issues. Retrieved from: https://www2.gwu.edu/~ibi/minerva/Fall2011/Raquel.pdf (accessed 14 July 2019).

Merton, R.C. & Bodie, Z. (1995) A Conceptual Framework for Analysing the Financial Environment. In: Crane, D.B., Froot, K.A., Mason S.P. *et al.* (eds.) *The Global Financial System: A Functional Perspective*. Boston: Harvard Business School Press, pp. 3–32.

Merton, R.C. & Bodie, Z. (2004). The Design of Financial Systems: Towards a Synthesis of Function and Structure. *Harvard Business School Working Paper* No. 02-074. Retrieved from: http://www.afi.es/eo/Design%20paper%20final.pdf) (accessed 22 July 2019).

Oramah, B.O. (2015) *Foundations of Structured Trade Finance*. London: ARK Group and Trade and Forfaiting Review.

Oramah, B.O., Chukwurah, O. & Ojeifo, O. (1995) Non-Oil Export Financing under Nigeria's Structural Adjustment Programme: The Role and Performance of Nigerian Export-Import Bank. *African Review of Money Finance and Banking*, 1(2), 93–129.

Schumpeter, J.A. (1912) *Theory of Economic Development*. Leipzig: Dunker & Humblot.

Stephens, M. (1999) *The Changing Role of Export Credit Agencies*. Washington, DC: International Monetary Fund.

US Exim (2017) Report to the US Congress on Global Export Credit Competition for the Period January 1, 2016 through December 31, 2016. Retrieved from: https://www.exim.gov/sites/default/files/reports/508%20compliant%20version_EXIM%20Bank%20Competitiveness%20Report_June%202017.pdf (accessed 14 July 2019).

Wiertsema, W. (2008) Export Credit Debt How ECA Support to Corporations Indebts the World's Poor. *European ECA Reform Campaign Briefing Note 05*. Available at: Retrieved from: https://www.fern.org/fileadmin/uploads/fern/Documents/Export%20Credit%20Debt %20briefing.pdf (accessed 14 July 2019).

Wilkens, H. (1983) The Debt Burden of Developing Economies. *Intereconomics*, 18(2), 55–59.

World Bank (n.d.) World Development Indicators Database. Retrieved from: http://datatopics. worldbank.org/world-development-indicators/ (accessed 14 July 2019).

Chapter 20

Export Credit Insurance Markets and Demand

Simone Krummaker

Introduction

Engaging in international trade with partners in other countries offers manifold opportunities to sustain and grow a business, but companies are also facing several risks which might endanger the whole enterprise. Exporters and investors are facing heterogeneous political systems, economic conditions and cultural behaviour. Besides political risk and a different legal and regulatory environment, companies are exposed to different business and trade practices as well as several dimensions of financial risk, such as currency exchange risks, risk of default or delayed or incomplete payment

Questions of trade finance are becoming increasingly important in connection with export transactions. The ability to offer financing arrangements to buyers can have a positive impact on the likelihood of the purchase, in particular for capital goods or projects with long-term time horizons. Companies regularly provide and use trade or export credit when selling or buying goods and services without receiving an immediate payment. Credit terms usually define the type and time frame of payment, including e.g. early payment discounts. Trade credit can be used as an easily accessible source of short-term financing, is simple and quick to arrange and helps in managing the capital requirements of the company. Credit terms differ across companies but also across industries.

In this chapter, we will be focusing on aspects of managing the risk connected with the provision of trade credit in international trade. The seller agrees to ship and deliver goods and services before the payment is due. Selling on export credit increases the working capital requirements as the money is tied up in the credits until the buyer pays. When export credit has been provided and the services and goods have already been delivered, the seller bears a risk that the payment might default or be delayed. The different types of export credit insurance are the key tools available to mitigate export finance and credit risk.

Export Credit Insurance Markets and Products

The main ways for organisations to manage risk are risk avoidance, risk retention or risk transfer. Risk retention includes methods such as loss control (loss prevention or reduction) or risk financing (funded or unfunded), whereas risk transfer involves insurance and non-insurance transfers. Non-insurance risk transfers usually transfer risks to counterparties via contract, hedging or by incorporating a business. With insurance, the risk is transferred onto an insurance company via an insurance contract. The insurer accepts the risk against the payment of a risk-based, actuarially derived premium. Insurance is one of the key tools used in a firm's risk management to transfer risk.

An insurance contract can be used to transfer unsystematic risks. While for most companies, it leads to an efficient risk allocation when the insurer bears the risks, the use of insurance also frees up funds to finance uninsurable and undiversifiable risk. This means the entrepreneur can concentrate on bearing entrepreneurial risks (Gollier et al., 2005).

Companies make use of insurance to mitigate a variety of risks, such as fire, business interruption, product or directors and officers (D&O) liability and freight/transport insurance. Export credit insurance is a type of property and casualty insurance and is offered by private insurance companies as well as governmental export credit agencies (trade credit insurance for domestic trade is also available but this chapter focuses on international trade covered by export credit insurance). It covers the exporter against the loss of receivables due to non-payment by the importer (full or part default as well as protracted default) based on commercial risks (e.g. insolvency). Usually, a pre-shipment cover can also be obtained, that covers against risks of contract frustration during the manufacturing period. Therefore, export credit insurance protects the exporter's contract cash flows and consequently the firm's profits against unwanted volatility due to unsystematic risk.

As export credit insurance focuses on the commercial risk arising from contractual and financial rights and duties, it excludes a number of perils from coverage, in particular force majeure and political risks. Risk arising out of political aspects can be covered with a political risk insurance (sometimes also called investment insurance), which comes into play if legal or governmental measures prevent the exporter or the importer from fulfilling their contractual obligations. This includes, among others, if the buyer has to cancel the contract or refuses to accept the goods, if the foreign currency conversion or transfer of funds to the exporter's account is compromised, a moratorium, import or export licence withdrawals and acts of war, unrest or revolution.

The Export Credit Insurance Market

Export credit insurance is offered by private sector insurance companies as well as governmental organisations, so-called export credit agencies (ECAs). Additionally, some of the ECAs are underwriting marketable risks with their own private subsidiaries in competition with the other private sector insurers (e.g. Euler Hermes, Atradius or Compagnie Française d'Assurance pour le Commerce Extérieur [Coface]). Besides the exporters, who are on the demand side of the export credit insurance market, other important market participants are commercial insurance companies, public export credit agencies, intermediaries (mainly brokers and banks) and reinsurance companies.

Private export credit insurance providers

Private insurers are usually covering short-term export and trade credit risks for up to two years under normal market conditions. It is difficult for exporters to obtain coverage for medium- and long-term export credit risks via the private insurance market. Consequently, these risks are considered not to be marketable and are thus often covered by public ECAs (Auboin, 2009). The commercial insurance companies offer export credit insurance on negotiated terms and conditions against their capital and build technical provisions to take care of the liabilities inherent in this business. Some ECAs also have a private arm to offer export credit and political insurance to marketable risks. The public and private operations are in general strictly separated (Chinese wall), which includes a separation of administration and accounts as well as information exchange on the risk of foreign buyers.

The term "marketable risk" is used to describe risks for which in principle a market exists. With respect to export credit insurance, that means that insurance capacity is available in the private insurance sector. Basically, this also means that the insurance companies are able to obtain sufficient reinsurance capacities. The private sector for trade and export credit insurance consists of specialised monoliners as well as multiline insurance companies, which in general focus on offering short-term domestic and export credit insurance. In contrast to ECAs, private insurers do not care about the origin of the product, they also accept foreign content and they do not abide to the Organisation for Economic Co-operation and Development (OECD) agreement and can set premiums and terms and conditions freely.

The commercial market for export credit insurance is largely concentrated; the so-called big three private insurers, Euler Hermes, Atradius and Coface, traditionally dominate the markets. Recently, Sinosure, which covers 90% of all Chinese export credit insurance, has developed a similar market position. Together, these four companies account for roughly 78% of the global credit insurance market (Euler Hermes 26%, Atradius 15%, Coface 15%, Sinosure 22%; Swiss Re, 2014). This leads to the conclusion that the commercial domestic and export credit insurance market can be described as an oligopoly, however keen competition is between them (European Commission, 2005).

Export credit agencies

ECAs are official or quasi-official branches of their government. They are offering export credit insurance, guarantees and sometimes also financing for non-marketable risks, mainly with a medium- and long-term nature. ECAs are integral components of national governments' trade and foreign aid strategies. Their purpose is to foster international trade and to promote exports, and by doing so, to contribute to employment and economic growth. Governments use ECAs to increase the competitiveness and exports of their businesses by granting cover for both commercial and political risks or by providing direct lending. Most countries in the developed economies but also in many developing countries have created ECAs to address market failures and to insure and finance exports. Altogether, ECAs are the largest source of government funding for private businesses (Klasen, 2013; Morel, 2011).

As the use of ECAs might open the opportunity for hidden export subsidies and state aids, the provision of public export credit insurance and financing is highly restricted and regulated by international agreements, e.g. World Trade Organization (WTO) rules and the OECD agreement, and EU laws (European Union, 1998). Furthermore, ECAs cover risks in export transactions that have been mainly produced or sourced in the home country; most ECAs have to abstain from coverage if foreign content is above a defined level. However, more recently a move from national content to national interest requirements is observable among several ECAs. The national interest policy is more flexible in terms of assessing the socio-economic impact of ECA support (for example employment, economic growth etc.).

ECAs mainly cover transactions for high-risk regions where the private insurance market does not offer risk coverage, often in developing or emerging countries and those with export credit payment periods of longer than two years. ECAs are expected only to bear risk which the private market is unable or unwilling to cover to avoid crowding out of private offerings. However, the OECD has occasionally suspended some of the rules in times of economic crises, such as the Global Financial Crisis of 2008, to enable ECAs also to enter the short-term market after the shortfall of private market coverage (European Commission, 2009).

ECAs exist in many organisational forms and sizes and also their product portfolio varies greatly. In general, ECAs are considered to act as an insurer of last resort and are backed up or reinsured by their government. In contrast to private insurers, which have to put noticeable emphasis on maintaining their long-term solvency and to remain profitable, ECAs often only need to just break even and often they also do not have to hold provisions for the liabilities they take on with underwriting export credit insurance (Moser *et al.*, 2008; European Union, 2012, gives a good overview about the different organisational arrangements which can be found among the global ECAs). However, due to the diversity of organisational forms, financial requirements, product portfolios and government authorisations, the impact on the national economy might vary across the ECA landscape. Thus, despite strong efforts to create a level playing field for export promotion and trade support among the global ECAs, there is also competition among ECAs for the most favourable conditions within the global governance frameworks.

Exporters often experience that coverage available from private insurance companies is restricted in particular for transactions with more risky markets or capital goods with extended credit periods (Morel, 2011). Thus, to maintain an active trade relationship with those regions, exporters often have to rely on ECA support.

Market intermediaries and reinsurance

In commercial insurance it is common practice that companies negotiate and purchase their insurance contract using an insurance broker. This is also true for export credit insurance. The London market for more specialised or tailored insurance provision is also widely accessed via brokers. Lloyd's of London, the world's unique market for specialised and sophisticated insurance, does not accept direct access to their syndicates. Brokers are acting on behalf of their clients (in contrast to agents, which are acting on behalf of the insurer) and are usually paid by commissions from the insurer who gets the business. Brokers play an important role in reducing information asymmetries and are involved in the administration of policies as well as claims and recoveries (European Union, 2012).

Banks play a key role in facilitating trade finance and export credit insurance. They could also bridge the knowledge gap widely present in the small and medium-sized enterprise (SME) sector and intermediate these insurance services to their clients when being approached for loans to finance trade.

Reinsurance is a traditional tool for insurance companies to manage risks they take on their balance sheet as part of their business model (Swiss Re, 2014). It helps to reduce effects of information asymmetries and earnings volatility and is a means to increase underwriting capacity as well to replace solvency capital. ECAs have also started exploring the use of commercial reinsurance to complement government funding, but this is still rare (European Commission, 2005).

Export credit insurance associations

Two main industry associations play a role in the global export credit and political risk insurance market:

- The Berne Union (International Union of Credit & Investment Insurers) is the international association of the public and private export credit and investment insurance industry. It currently represents 84 members from 73 countries (Berne Union, 2018a).
- The International Credit Insurance & Surety Association (ICISA) currently numbers 55 members which cover about 95% of the global private credit insurance volume (ICISA, 2018).

The purpose of both associations is to support and facilitate international trade, to share expertise and information and to collaborate with members. They also liaise with international and multilateral governing bodies such as the WTO, OECD and European Union (EU).

Official support for medium- and long-term trade in 2017 was approximately US$211 billion, with Berne Union members providing coverage for 14% of global trade worldwide and total paid claims of over US$6 billion (Berne Union, 2018b, pp. 4–5; US Exim, 2018, p. 20). Figure 20.1 shows new export credit insurance business in relation to total exports worldwide since 2006.

Forms of Export Credit Insurance

In general export credit insurance can be categorised by four criteria (Häberle, 2002; Büter, 2007):

- *Risk*: coverage of elements of the export transaction process (pre- and/or post-shipment, delivery, debt claims after shipment etc.)
- *Insured organisation*: policies might cover exporters and/or export finance provider.

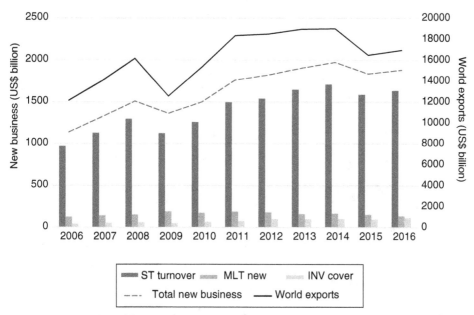

Figure 20.1 Total world exports and new export credit insurance business.
Source: Berne Union (2017).
Note: ST – short term, MLT – medium- and long-term, INV – investment insurance.

- *Scope of cover*: single transaction policy or whole turnover cover for many transactions.
- *Time horizon*: short-term insurance cover or medium- to long-term insurance cover.

First of all, export credit insurance is usually divided into short-term and mid- and long-term business. Short-term business includes exports with the repayment terms for the trade credit being less than one year, often 30, 60 or 90 days. Medium-term includes business of usually two to five years and long-term looks at tenures of over five years.

Some forms of export credit insurance mitigate the commercial risk of the exporter, while other forms cover the risk of lenders financing the export of goods or services. Most policies require the insured organisation to bear some proportion of the risk themselves, usually 5% for political risks and up to 15% for commercial risks. The policyholder has to retain the remaining risk of the uninsured part, which controls for moral hazard on the insured's side.

Typical forms of export credit insurance are described in the following paragraphs:

- *Whole turnover insurance*. This covers the value of an entire portfolio of export transactions with different buyers in different countries within an agreed period (of usually 12 months). In most cases it can be tailored to the needs of the exporter, e.g. which countries to cover. This is the most common form of export credit insurance which comprehensively protects the receivables of an exporter up to a pre-agreed limit (often 85–95%) against commercial risks but can be extended to political risk. The cover starts with the day of shipment. The premium is calculated as a percentage of the insured turnover.

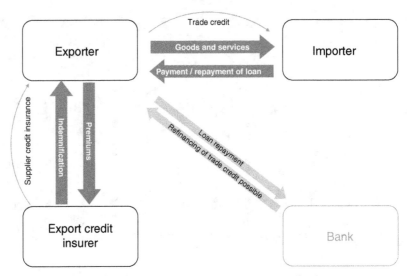

Figure 20.2   Supplier credit insurance.

- *Single transaction policies.* In contrast to whole turnover policies, single transaction policies cover only one particular transaction of the exporter's international trading activities. Mostly, single transaction policies are applied in medium- and long-term business, but the majority of export credit policies are whole turnover policies.
- *Supplier credit cover.* Supplier credits are the most common form of short- and mid-term trade finance, as the exporter gives the buyer time for payment after the delivery. Therefore, the supplier bears the risk of default, which can be covered with a supplier credit insurance. The supplier/exporter might refinance the trade credit granted to the buyer using e.g. banks. Then, the indemnification may be assigned to the refinancing organisation in the case of default of the buyer. Figure 20.2 illustrates this scheme.
- *Buyer credit cover.* In a buyer credit agreement, the buyer borrows funds from a bank or other lender to pay for the goods or services (see Figure 20.3). The buyer credit cover therefore insures the risk of the lender that the buyer might default on the repayment of the loan. For the exporter, a buyer credit arrangement has some advantages, as they do not have to get involved in negotiating terms of trade credit and can benefit from the proceeds of the trade immediately. This puts less stress on liquidity and cash flows.
- *Manufacturing risk cover.* This protects the exporter against the loss of direct and indirect production cost accrued up to the order value of the supplies or services under the export contract. This type of insurance is particularly beneficial if custom-made products are delivered, as these cost are difficult to recover should the order be withdrawn and cannot be remarketed.

The risks in the medium- and long-term business can be characterised as low-frequency/ high-severity risks. That means the probability of losses occurring are relatively low, but when they happen, the size of the loss can be rather large. The overwhelming majority (90%) of the claims here are due to commercial risk rather than political risk.

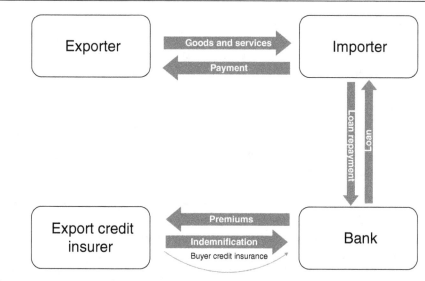

Figure 20.3   Buyer credit insurance.

Comparable to general insurance business lines, export credit insurance also experiences underwriting cycles. At the time of the writing of the chapter, the market was in a soft market phase with high competition in the private market, rather low pricing and higher claims. It is expected that soon loss ratios will become unsustainable leading the market slowly to another phase of the underwriting cycle (Berne Union, 2018a).

Benefits, Implications and Limitations of Export Credit Insurance

In general, any form of insurance as a means of risk transfer reduces the effects of asymmetric information and uncertainty on profits, lowers profit volatility and frees up capital for a more efficient use, and allows firms to focus on their core business and to focus on entrepreneurial risks. With respect to trade, export credit insurance fosters international trade by mitigating risk which otherwise would be unbearable for some companies, and it also provides liquidity by protecting trade receivables, covering credit risk of private lenders and thus increasing access to private trade finance. The benefits of export credit insurance can be summarised as follows:

- *Transfer of credit risk.* The transfer of the credit risk inherent in international trade transactions onto an insurance company leads to a more efficient allocation of risk. The insurer is an organisation that is actively assuming risk and is more professional and efficient in evaluating, pooling, diversifying and financing risk (Gollier *et al.* 2005). Furthermore, the exporter is relieved from allocating time, effort and money to manage export credit risk and thus can concentrate on bearing uninsurable and market risk.
- *Access to new markets and expanding relationships with existing customers.* International trade relationships are, among others, characterised by long distances and asymmetric information which can have a constraining effect on export activities (Moser *et al.*, 2008). As export credit insurance alleviates some

of these risks, it allows exporters to enter new markets or new relationships with foreign importers. Furthermore, it allows trade relationships to be sustained in times of financial distress and increased default risk. Another benefit is that export credit insurance allows for the adjustment of credit terms to buyers (e.g. to offer longer invoice payment periods) and for the expansion of existing trade relationships, which otherwise the exporter would not enter (Coleman, 2013).

- *Access to financing and increased liquidity.* With export credit insurance, the trade receivables are secured against the indemnification of the insurer or ECA. This often is a compelling argument for lenders to engage in the financing of an export transaction, on both the exporter's and the importer's side. Insurance also helps to lower the volatility of earnings as the impact of losses due to export credit risk is transferred away. Large uninsured losses reduce a firm's equity, so using insurance leads to a lower insolvency risk of the exporting firm too, thus they benefit from more favourable terms and cheaper access to debt financing. Insurance alleviates financial frictions as the exporter and the importer will have access to trade finance via banks which otherwise would not have been available. Furthermore, the indemnification payments of the insurer provide a "leverage-neutral" source of financing and do not affect the capital structure of the company (Doherty and Smith, 1993).

The insurer also provides valuable information about buyer and country risk which helps in evaluating whether the importer is creditworthy and in increasing the exporter's confidence and trust in international trade relationships (Coleman, 2013). With export credit insurance, the exporter can also maintain or enhance their liquidity, as trade receivables are covered against late or non-payment and therefore protect cash flows.

Research supports the positive effects of export credit insurance or guarantees on international trade, particularly the reduction of earnings uncertainty, the lowering of information asymmetries about country and counterparty risk and the enabling of exporters to gain experience in international trade including by lowering entry costs (Abraham and Dewit, 2000; Bernard and Jensen, 2004; Egger and Url, 2006; Moser *et al.*, 2008). There are some studies that find positive effects of ECA authorisations on national exports (such as Egger and Url, 2006; Moser *et al.*, 2008; Korinek *et al.*, 2010; Auboin and Engemann, 2014; van der Veer, 2015; Agarwal and Wang, 2018), which vary across industries. In the German example, these effects are largest in those sectors with capital goods and high time-to-build lags, such as shipbuilding or aviation, and smaller for those industries which are not subject to severe credit constrains (Felbermayr and Yalcin, 2013). According to Badinger and Url (2013), the effect is larger for companies/industries with higher credit risk.

On the other hand, adverse effects of ECA financing and guarantees are discussed. Unless market failure is addressed, economic efficiency might be lost, because government mandate and strategic trade policy asks ECAs to reallocate capital that could have been more efficiently used otherwise (Agarwal and Wang, 2018). Resources created by the taxpayer are redistributed from other areas of the economy. The criticism of ECAs also includes that they create market distortions themselves as they are mitigating risks and financing transactions for firms or sectors which in a free market would not have had access to this extent. Thus, ECA guarantees might be supporting inefficient transactions, firms or industries that are treated favourably because they represent a high priority on the government's agenda (Abraham and Dewit, 2000).

Export Credit Market Governance

The regulation of export credits is embedded on multiple levels, from supra-national to national to industry level. So, providers of export credit-related insurance, guarantees and finance have to comply with different rules of different regulators. Export credit guarantees and insurance are a policy tool for exporting nations and export credit insurers, and ECAs in different countries might be subject to different regulations and laws affecting the process and terms and conditions of providing export credit insurance.

The export credit markets and their participants are first of all regulated by national laws and regulations of their home jurisdiction. Furthermore, a distinction has to be made between the providers of private export credit insurance, which are private insurance companies, and the providers of export credit insurance, guarantees and finance on behalf of the government, the ECAs.

The private export credit insurers are subject to insurance and financial market regulation in their jurisdiction, which in the EU, for example, is driven by the Solvency II Directive (European Union, 2009), which was implemented in January 2016. The member states of the EU ratified the Directive into national law, which might be complemented by further national regulations. Beyond this, the private export credit insurance market in the EU is a fully private and competitive market.

Officially supported export credits by ECAs as discussed are a policy tool for the exporting nations and thus can be used to subsidise exporters to provide them with an advantage in international competition over financing or managing risk of export credits. Policy coherence by a coordination and harmonisation of international trade rules aims to create a fair and transparent environment which facilitates global trade.

The WTO has established a framework for trade policies, built in particular around the five principles of non-discrimination, reciprocity, binding and enforceable commitments, transparency and safety values. The key functions of the WTO are the implementation and administration of the WTO agreements and providing a forum for negotiations and settling disputes. For the 164 member states, the agreements of the WTO have binding character. Thus, the trade and export support policies of governments including the policies and operations on officially supported exports via the ECAs have to follow the WTO principles, specifically the Agreement on Subsidies and Countervailing Measures (SCM Agreement) (WTO, 2018).

More detailed regulations in the export credit context are formulated by the OECD. Since the 1970s, the OECD countries have started to coordinate their export credit policies as laid down in the "Arrangement on Officially Supported Export Credits" (OECD, 2018). This agreement is a gentlemen's agreement with no formal enforcement power and has currently nine participants: Australia, Canada, the EU (with 28 member states), Japan, Korea, New Zealand, Norway, Switzerland and the United States. Furthermore, Brazil participates in the Aircraft Sector Understanding and Turkey and Israel are observers. The main aim of the Arrangement is particularly to create a level playing field in the global export environment as well as coherence between national export credit policies. Furthermore, one key objective is to support the competition of exporters based on quality and price rather than favourable terms provided by their ECAs (Drysdale, 2014). This is supposed to minimise trade distortions and help competition by minimising subsidies related to ECA support.

The OECD arrangement sets out guidelines, which define the most favourable premiums, terms and conditions that may be granted by the ECAs for export credit insurance, guarantees, financing or interest rate support. It applies to all officially supported export credits provided by or on behalf of a government for exports with a tenure of two years or longer (OECD, 2018). The means to achieve the goals are particularly as follows:

- *A system of country risk classification.* Countries are classified according to their country credit risk into eight categories (country risk categories) from 0 to 7. Category 0 includes countries with a negligible country credit risk, and credit risk in transactions with buyers from this category is assumed to be mainly driven by the risk of the obligor/guarantor. Category 7 is deemed to be the most risky. The country credit risk consists of five elements: general moratorium, political events and/or economic difficulties, legal provisions regarding repayments, other governmental decisions or measures, cases of force majeure (a more detailed description can be found in OECD, 2018).
- *Sovereign risk and buyer risk classification.* Beyond the country risk classification, the OECD Arrangement also gives guidance to classify sovereign risk and buyer risk.
- *Minimum premium rates for credit risk.* The rules on insurance premium rates for supported export credits determine the minimum premium rate (MPR) which must be charged for any combination of risk and tenor. The aim is that the premium levels do not undercut premiums in the private market, and to avoid crowding out due to the availability of state support. The MPR is determined by several factors, such as the country risk classification, the time at risk, the buyer risk category and the percentage of risk retention (OECD, 2018).
- *Sector understandings.* The guidelines in the Arrangement are complemented by sector understandings which detail further specific guidelines with respect to particular sectors. This allows for the specific requirements of six sectors – (i) ships, (ii) nuclear power plants, (iii) civil aircraft, (iv) renewable energy, climate change mitigation and adaptation, and water projects, (v) rail infrastructure and (vi) coal-fired electricity generation projects – to be met (OECD, 2018).

The Arrangement and the sector understandings are regularly reviewed and adjusted in the light of market and policy developments.

Further regulation happens at EU level via the Directorate General for Trade in order to harmonise the policies and supported export credits among the member state's ECAs, and it also makes the application of the OECD Arrangement mandatory for EU ECAs. While the EU requires their ECAs not to provide cover for marketable risks and the private market provides plenty of cover for short-term exports, ECAs in the EU are very much focusing on medium- and long-term export credit coverage.

More trade in recent years has shifted into non-OECD countries; in particular, the BRIC countries (Brazil, Russia, India and China) account for large proportions of the growth in global trade. Thus, more trade and consequently more export credit financing and insurance transactions are provided outside the OECD Agreement. Countries that are not following the OECD arrangement are able to offer more flexible and competitive terms to exporters as they do not need to comply with the rules and limitations defined there. Additionally, in some non-OECD areas there are only few private export credit insurance providers, thus requiring ECAs to step in to provide coverage for short-term transactions (US Exim, 2018). Furthermore, a gap in private sector lending following the Global Financial Crisis has required that ECAs fill this gap to help their exporters carry on with their business (Ron and Terzulli, 2015).

Firm Factors Affecting the Demand for Export Credit Insurance

Insurance is one of the most important instruments for risk mitigation and risk transfer available to companies. Transferring insurable risks to an insurance company releases financial resources to cover other entrepreneurial or market risks which cannot easily be mitigated or transferred.

The general theory on insurance demand, which focuses on individuals and is based on risk aversion (often modelled using concave utility functions), demonstrates that individuals are willing to give up some wealth (pay a premium) to get rid of uncertainty. Mainstream theory considers companies (and mainly corporations) as a nexus of contracts and that for this reason they do not exhibit risk preferences (Jensen and Meckling, 1976). Therefore, the individual theory of insurance demand based on risk aversion is not applicable to explain firm's risk behaviour. However, companies account for about 50% of the world's premium income in property and casualty insurance, thus several researchers have developed theories that explain why companies buy insurance: asymmetric information and agency conflicts, transaction cost and cost of financial distress, insurance real services (e.g. Mayers and Smith, 1982, 1987; Main, 1982; Grillet, 1992). A number of empirical studies have been conducted to test the theories on firms' insurance demand (e.g. Core, 1997; Garven and Lamm-Tennant, 2003; Yamori, 1999; Hoyt and Khang, 2000; Zou et al., 2003; Thomann et al., 2012; Regan and Hur, 2007; Krummaker and Schulenburg, 2008; Aunon-Nerin and Ehling, 2008; Michel-Kerjan et al., 2015).

There also has been some research focusing particularly on export credit insurance, showing that it is an essential risk mitigation tool for exporters (e.g. Felbermayr et al., 2014, or Abraham and Dewit, 2000). Furthermore, it is important to understand which firm characteristics and context factors drive the demand for export credit insurance (Klasen, 2014). Research has identified several factors, which are described in the following subsections.

Ownership Structure and Risk Bearing

The ownership structure of a company is relevant for the implementation of risk management measures and thus also indicative of the demand for insurance. In individual enterprises, for example sole proprietorships, the owner bears unlimited liability and consequently is also tied in with his/her personal wealth. Here it can be assumed that insurance demand is explained by individual risk aversion (Mayers and Smith, 1982; Doherty and Smith, 1993).

In companies with separation of ownership and control and a more widespread ownership, individual risk aversion cannot explain a firm's risk management behaviour. But the presence of risk is costly and creates inefficiencies, and incentives for risk shifting exist. In particular in risky companies (e.g. with a considerable leverage that might lead to financial distress), there might be incentives for the management to engage in risk-taking activities which, in the event of success, will be fully to the benefit of the owners in the form of increased profits and dividends. But if unsuccessful, the debtholder will have to bear more risk as the likelihood of financial distress increases. Risk-shifting incentives differ according to the ownership structure of the company. The use of insurance alleviates the conflict as the probability of financial distress can be lowered by transferring insurable risk onto an insurance company.

In addition, owners of corporations are bearing enterprise risk only up to the value of their investment. In case of insolvency, they only lose this and their personal wealth is not affected, contrary to what happens to sole proprietors. Based on this, it is expected that companies with a closer ownership demand more insurance than companies with broader ownership structures.

Empirical studies have found evidence to support this assumption (e.g. Mayers and Smith, 1990; Regan and Hur, 2007), but there are also tests which did not find a relationship between ownership structure and insurance demand (e.g. Zou et al., 2003; Yamori, 1999). The only study on export credit insurance is supportive as well (Klasen, 2014).

Firm Size and Insurance Real Services

The size of a company influences the decision to buy insurance twofold. First, potential costs of insolvency can be alleviated with insurance as it lowers the probability of insolvency due to insurable losses. Smaller firms proportionally bear more of these costs, thus, they benefit more from insurance than larger companies (Mayers and Smith, 1982). This hypothesis is also supported empirically by e.g. Aunon-Nerin and Ehling (2008) or Core (1997), whereas Hoyt and Khang (2000) had mixed results.

Second, insurance companies have comparative advantages in evaluating, pooling and bearing risks (Gollier et al., 2005). When buying insurance, firms not only transfer their idiosyncratic risk to the insurance company, they also take advantage of further services of the insurer. These services, connected with risk assessment and pricing, loss prevention and processing claims, are an additional motivation to buy insurance. Companies are relieved from bearing cost and effort to evaluate and settle losses, which are a greater burden to smaller companies than for larger companies. They have fewer resources and less experience with risk management, and insurance often also increases the capacity to raise debt and equity. Furthermore, larger companies might benefit from better diversification opportunities, for example for different geographical reasons or different lines of business. Additionally, the services of ECAs help to find adequate financing, for the exporter but also for the importer (Bischoff and Klasen, 2012). Smaller companies can benefit more from these services as they experience difficulties in finding financing more often than large exporters do. In particular since the financial crisis, SMEs have had significant difficulties finding export finance in the commercial banking market. Additionally, SMEs, which often have less sophisticated risk management systems as well as less knowledge about export credit risk mitigation instruments than large corporations have, can benefit from this expertise offered by private or public credit insurers.

Therefore, it is expected that smaller companies demand more insurance (Mayers and Smith, 1982; Doherty and Smith, 1993).

Financing and Taxes

Risk management in general and insurance in particular help companies to reduce cash flow volatility and to smooth revenues as the adverse consequences of an insurable loss are mitigated (e.g. Zou *et al.*, 2003). This lowers the likelihood of insolvency but also is a signal to investors. Publicly listed corporations prefer low earnings volatility as this signals information about management quality and firm risk to capital markets. Additionally, it reduces the costs of external financing (Breeden and Viswanathan, 1998; Froot *et al.*, 1993). This is particularly important related to exports and financing export credits.

Business tax also plays a role in the demand for insurance. Several scholars demonstrate that particular tax regimes incentivise the purchase of insurance (Mayers and Smith, 1982; Main, 1982; MacMinn, 1987) and conjecture that companies with higher tax liabilities would buy more insurance.

Empirical results on financing- and tax-related incentives to demand insurance are mixed. Graham and Rogers (2002) find that companies do not hedge to respond to tax convexity but to increase debt capacity.

Export Quota and Buyer Risk

A few studies include export-related aspects in the research of insurance demand. Exporting companies can use export credit insurance or ECA coverage to manage the risk associated with the international trading partner and country (Ross and Pike, 1977; Klasen, 2014). The export quota of the selling company is hypothesised to have an impact on the demand of export-related insurance (Felbermayr *et al.*, 2014). Regan and Hur (2007) as well as Klasen (2014) give evidence for a positive relationship between the export quota and insurance demand. This means that exporters that export more will also buy more export credit insurance. Besides the risk of the buyer or the buyer's country, financing also plays a role in the demand for insurance. As export finance is often unavailable without appropriate export credit insurance coverage, but ECAs also give support in finding appropriate financing, this shows the interdependencies of finance and insurance in the international trade environment.

Exporters' Demand for Insurance

In summary, it can be stated that exporters are exposed to a wide range of risks associated with the process of exporting. Insurance helps to protect the balance sheet and working capital and to maintain liquidity. Furthermore, agency conflicts are alleviated, and internal funds are made available for more efficient use. As critical idiosyncratic risks are covered by insurance, companies can use their resources to manage entrepreneurial and market risks that are not insurable. The purchase of insurance and its positive effects also support or increase access to external funding, both debt and equity, which is increasingly important but also difficult to secure, particularly for small and mid-sized exporters. Export credit insurance from private and public providers thus has been proven beneficial to expand their business internationally and to safeguard the existing business from potential detrimental effects of global trading.

Current Issues and Conclusion

The Global Financial Crisis and the following decline in global trade, accompanied by higher claims volumes and an increasing risk environment, led to a market phase with increased premiums and reduced capacities in private export credit insurance. But as default risk rose, the demand for short-term export credit insurance increased as well (Morel, 2011). As a consequence of this increased demand, accompanied by some hesitation from the commercial markets, ECAs started to temporarily offer short-term coverage for risks which were deemed marketable until the financial crisis (European Commission, 2009). Since the financial crisis, ECAs have gradually assumed risk and addressed the lack of trade finance from the private sector by providing different forms of protection and financial support, e.g. direct lending (Berne Union, 2018).

The reduced risk appetite of European banks, despite improved market conditions, has led to a persistent lack of export funding, in particular for small and very large transactions, as well as for exports with long maturities. This is also due to tightened financial market regulation since the Global Financial Crisis, with the introduction of the rules under Basel 2.5 and Basel III which implemented tougher capital requirements and leverage ratios (Swiss Re, 2014; Berne Union, 2018). Consequently, together with higher requirements on KYC (know your customer) and anti-money laundering, small ticket transactions have become relatively more expensive, which incentivises banks to emphasise business with larger transactions or companies with substantial amounts of exports. Furthermore, the commercial banks mainly provide export finance for up to ten years in riskier markets, maybe longer in less risky regions (US Exim, 2018).

Despite lower risk portfolios as well as ample capital and capacity in the private insurance sector, which led to moderate premiums, a funding and insurance gap for SMEs still remains. The market supply for both has still not recovered to pre-crisis levels. The World Bank estimates an overall credit gap for SMEs of approximately US$1.2 trillion (World Bank, 2018). Besides stricter bank and insurance regulations, this is also due to transaction costs, which are larger in relative terms for coverage of smaller export volumes. Insurers claim that sometimes the premiums do not fully account for the cost associated with insuring SMEs. Thus, some insurers have set minimum premiums and turnover levels for SME export credit insurance. Therefore, export credit insurance for SMEs is more expensive than for large exporters (European Commission, 2005). One way to alleviate the issues related to export credit financing and insurance for SMEs could be for export credit insurers and ECAs to consider combined insurance and financing (Swiss Re, 2014).

Another challenge for SMEs with regards to their demand for export credit guarantees and insurance is the knowledge gap. In contrast to large exporters and multinational companies, SMEs have considerably fewer resources and less knowledge and experience in using these products. This gap in knowledge about available risk management, as well as the lack of funding sources, often means smaller or midsized companies abstain from engaging in international trade due to the risk being unbearable. This puts them in a significantly worse situation than their competitors. Various ECAs have started to address the needs of this clientele more specifically, as the transfer of products and processes mainly designed to suit large exporters with large transactions and export volumes is inappropriate. Additionally, efforts are being made to disseminate information about available export credit insurance offerings for SMEs. If SMEs start using ECA guarantees to mitigate export credit risks, it can be seen that they grow more confident to engage in international trade (Berne Union, 2018a).

Some other issues affecting trade and export credit insurance are consequences of globalisation and shifts in the geopolitical landscape. Furthermore, protectionist tendencies pose a threat to global trade. Another mega-trend is digitalisation and the emergence of big data, paving the way for technologies such as fintech, insurtech, blockchain, rapid prototyping and additive manufacturing, which might change the nature of trade for many industries. But this changing nature of how business and trade is conducted also introduces new risks, usually described as cyber risks.

With the changing nature of trade and export new risks and challenges arise. Export credit insurance, offered by private and public export credit insurance providers, will continue to be one of the most important tools for companies to mitigate risks associated with international trade.

References

Abraham, F. & Dewit, G. (2000) *Open Economies Review*, 11(1), 5–26.

Agarwal, N. & Wang, Z. (2018) Does the US EXIM Bank Really Promote US Exports? *The World Economy*, 41(4), 1378–1414.

Auboin, M. (2009) Restoring Trade Finance during a Period of Financial Crisis: Stock-Taking of Recent Initiatives. *WTO Staff Working Paper* ERSD-2009-16. Retrieved from: https://www.econstor.eu/bitstream/10419/57600/1/61763808X.pdf (accessed 16 July 2019).

Auboin, M. & Engemann, M. (2014) Testing the Trade Credit and Trade Link: Evidence from Data on Export Credit Insurance. *Review of World Economics*, 150(4), 715–743.

Aunon-Nerin, D. & Ehling, P. (2008) Why Firms Purchase Property Insurance. *Journal of Financial Economics*, 90(3), 298–312.

Badinger, H. & Url, T. (2013) Export Credit Guarantees and Export Performance: Evidence from Austrian Firm-Level Data. *World Economy*, 36, 1115–1130.

Bernard, A. & Jensen, B. (2004) Why Some Firms Export. *Review of Economics and Statistics*, 86, 561–569.

Berne Union (2017) Statistics 2012–2016. Retrieved from: http://cdn.berneunion.org/assets/Images/Berne-Union-2016-Year-End-Statistics.pdf (accessed 16 July 2019).

Berne Union (2018a) *Berne Union Yearbook 2017*. Retrieved from: http://cdn.berneunion.org/assets/Images/BU%20Yearbook%202017-lowRes.pdf (accessed 15 July 2019).

Berne Union (2018b) Berne Union Spring Meeting. *The Bulletin on International Trade, Finance and Investment from the Export Credit and Political Risk Insurance Industry*, 19.

Retrieved from: http://cdn.berneunion.org/assets/Images/6345be17-145a-4695-aaa1-44fa 4980b71c.pdf (accessed 16 July 2019).

Bischoff, B. & Klasen, A. (2012) Hermesgedeckte Exportfinanzierung [Export Finance Covered by the German ECA]. *Recht der Internationalen Wirtschaft*, 11, 769–777.

Breeden, D. & Viswanathan, S. (1998) *Why Do Firms Hedge? An Asymmetric Information Model*. Working paper, Duke University. Retrieved from: https://static.secure.website/ wscfus/8149792/uploads/Breeden_1991_Viswanathan_Why_Do_Firms_Hedge_ Unpublished.pdf (accessed 16 July 2019).

Büter, C. (2007) *Außenhandel: Grundlagen globaler und innergemeinschaftlicher Handelsbeziehungen* [Foreign Trade: Foundations of Global and Intra-Community Trade Relationships]. Heidelberg: Physica.

Coleman, J. (2013) Why Exporters Need Export Credit. *Global Policy*, 4(1), 110–111.

Core, J.E. (1997) On the Corporate Demand for Directors' and Officers' Insurance. *The Journal of Risk and Insurance*, 64(1): 63–87.

Doherty, N.A. & Smith, C.W. (1993) Corporate Insurance Strategy: The Case of British Petroleum. *Journal of Applied Corporate Finance*, 6(3), 4–15.

Drysdale, D. (2015) Why the OECD Arrangement Works (Even Though it Is Only Soft Law). In: Klasen, A. & Bannert, F. (eds.) *The Future of Foreign Trade Support*. Durham: Wiley, pp. 5–7.

Gollier, C., Eeckhoudt, L. & Schlesinger, H. (2005) *Economic and Financial Decisions under Risk*. Princeton: Princeton University Press.

Häberle, S.G. (2002) *Einführung in die Exportfinanzierung: Grundlagen der internationalen Zahlungs-, Finanzierungs- und Sicherungsinstrumente* [Introduction to Export Finance: Foundations of International Payment, Finance and Security Instruments]. Munich: Oldenbourg.

Egger, P. & Url, T. (2006) Public Export Credit Guarantees and Foreign Trade Structure: Evidence from Austria. *The World Economy*, 29(4), 399–418.

European Commission (2005) The Report on Market Trends of Private Reinsurance in the Field of Export Credit Insurance. Retrieved from: http://ec.europa.eu/competition/state_ aid/studies_reports/export_credit_insurance_report.pdf (accessed 16 July 2019).

European Commission (2009) State Aid N 384/2009 – Germany: Short-Term Export-Credit Insurance. C(2009)6225 final. Retrieved from: http://ec.europa.eu/competition/state_aid/ cases/232090/232090_983216_60_2.pdf (accessed 16 July 2019).

European Union (1998) Council Directive 98/29/EC of 7 May 1998 on Harmonisation of the Main Provisions Concerning Export Credit Insurance for Transactions with Medium and Long-Term Cover. Retrieved from: https://publications.europa.eu/en/publication-detail/-/ publication/0b824009-348a-413b-91f5-bba1e9e37f1b/language-en (accessed 16 July 2019).

European Union (2009) Directive 2009/138/EC of the European Parliament and of the Council of 25 November 2009 on the Taking-Up and Pursuit of the Business of Insurance and Reinsurance (Solvency II). Retrieved from: http://data.europa.eu/eli/dir/2009/138/ 2014-05-23 (accessed 16 July 2019).

European Union (2012) Study on Short-Term Trade Finance and Credit Insurance in the European Union. Retrieved from: https://publications.europa.eu/en/publication-detail/-/ publication/a1ae8477-930c-44df-8c41-b38fb9ad94a4/language-en (accessed 16 July 2019).

Felbermayr, G.J. & Yalcin, E. (2013) Export Credit Guarantees and Export Performance: An Empirical Analysis for Germany. *The World Economy*, 36(8), 967–999.

Felbermayr, G., Heiland, I. & Yalcin, E. (2014) The Role of State Export Credit Guarantees for German Firms. *CESifo Forum*, 15(3), 52–55.

Froot, K.A., Scharfstein, D.S. & Stein, J.C. (1993) Risk Management: Coordinating Corporate Investment and Financing Policies. *The Journal of Finance*, 48(5), 1629–1658.

Garven, J.R. & Lamm-Tennant, J. (2003) *The Demand for Reinsurance: Theory and Empirical Tests*. Working paper, Louisiana State University/GenRe. Retrieved from: http://www. revueassurances.ca/wp-content/uploads/2016/03/2003_71_no2_Garven.pdf (accessed 16 July 2019).

Graham, J.R. & Rogers, D.A. (2002) Do Firms Hedge in Response to Tax Incentives? *The Journal of Finance*, 57(2), 815–839.

Grillet, L. (1992) Corporate Insurance and Corporate Stakeholders: Transactions Costs Theory. *Journal of Insurance Regulation*, 11(3), 233–251.

Hoyt, R.E. & Khang, H. (2000) On the Demand for Corporate Property Insurance. *The Journal of Risk and Insurance*, 67(1), 91–107.

International Credit Insurance & Surety Association (2018) Yearbook 2017–18. Retrieved from: https://docplayer.net/81538515-Icisa-go-to-content-page-icisa-yearbook-st-edition-phone-31-0-registered-number.html (accessed 16 July 2019).

Jensen, M.C. & Meckling, W.H. (1976) Theory of the Firm: Managerial Behavior, Agency Costs and Ownership Structure. *Journal of Financial Economics*, 3(4), 305–360.

Klasen, A. (2013) Export Credit Availability and Global Trade. *Global Policy*, 4(1), 108–109.

Klasen, A. (2014) Export Credit Guarantees and Demand for Insurance. *CESifo Forum*, 3, 26–33.

Korinek, J., Cocguic, J.L. & Sourdin, P. (2010) The Availability and Cost of Short-Term Trade Finance and its Impact on Trade. *OECD Trade Policy Papers* No. 98. Retrieved from: https://www.oecd-ilibrary.org/docserver/5kmdbg733c38-en.pdf?expires=1563280700&id=id&accname=guest&checksum=2A9E49C5014838BE564EC35255647472 (accessed 16 July 2019).

Krummaker, S. & Schulenburg, J.M. Graf von der (2008) Die Versicherungsnachfrage von Unternehmen: Eine empirische Untersuchung der Sachversicherungsnachfrage deutscher Unternehmen [Corporate Insurance Demand: An Empirical Investigation of German Businesses' Demand for Non-Life Insurance]. *Zeitschrift für die gesamte Versicherungswissenschaft*, 97(1), 79–97.

MacMinn, R.D. (1987) Insurance and Corporate Risk Management. *Journal of Risk and Insurance*, 54, 658–677.

Main, B.G. (1982) The Firm's Insurance Decision. Some Questions Raised by the Capital Asset Pricing Model. *Managerial and Decision Economics*, 3(1), 7–15.

Mayers, D. & Smith, C.W. (1982) On the Corporate Demand for Insurance. *Journal of Business*, 55(2), 281–296.

Mayers, D. & Smith, C.W. (1987) Corporate Insurance and the Underinvestment Problem. *Journal of Risk and Insurance*, 54(1), 45–54.

Mayers, D. & Smith, C.W. (1990) On the Corporate Demand for Insurance: Evidence from the Reinsurance Market. *The Journal of Business*, 63(1), 19–40.

Michel-Kerjan, E., Raschky, P. & Kunreuther, H. (2015) Corporate Demand for Insurance: New Evidence from the US Terrorism and Property Markets. *The Journal of Risk and Insurance*, 82(3), 505–530.

Morel, F. (2011) Credit Insurance in Support of International Trade: Observations throughout the Crisis. In: Chaffour, J.-P. & Malouche, M. (eds.) *Trade Finance during the Great Trade Collapse*. Washington, DC: World Bank, pp. 337–356.

Moser, C., Nestmann, T. & Wedow, M. (2008) Political Risk and Export Promotion: Evidence from Germany. *The World Economy*, 31(6), 781–803.

OECD (2018) Arrangement on Officially Supported Export Credits. TAD/PG(2018)1. Retrieved from: http://www.oecd.org/officialdocuments/publicdisplaydocumentpdf/?doclanguage=en&cote=tad/pg(2018)1 (accessed 15 July 2019).

Regan, L. & Hur, Y. (2007) On the Corporate Demand for Insurance: The Case of Korean Nonfinancial Firms. *The Journal of Risk and Insurance*, 74(4), 829–850.

Ron, M. & Terzulli, A. (2015) Regulations, Subsidies and ECAs – Are We Sure the More the Merrier? In: Klasen, A. & Bannert, F. (eds.) *The Future of Foreign Trade Support*. Durham: Durham University and Wiley.

Ross, D.G. & Pike, R.H. (1997) Export Credit Risks and the Trade Credit Offer: Some Canadian Evidence. *Journal of Multinational Financial Management*, 7, 55–70.

Swiss Re (2014) Trade Credit Insurance & Surety: Taking Stock after the Financial Crisis. Retrieved from: https://www.swissre.com/dam/jcr:7eb9c972-cd6f-4065-8da7-151cf5c880d1/Trade_credit_insurance_surety_final.pdf (accessed 22 July 2019).

Thomann, C., Pascalau, R. & Schulenburg, J.-M. Graf von der (2012) Corporate Management of Highly Dynamic Risks: Evidence from the Demand for Terrorism Insurance in Germany. *The Geneva Risk and Insurance Review*, 37(1), 57–82.

US Exim (2018) Report to the US Congress on Global Export Credit Competition for the period January 1, 2017 through December 31, 2017. Retrieved from: https://www.exim.gov/sites/default/files/reports/competitiveness_reports/2018/EXIM-Competitiveness-Report_June2018.pdf (accessed 16 July 2019).

van der Veer, K.J.M. (2015) The Private Export Credit Insurance Effect on Trade. *Journal of Risk and Insurance*, 82(3), 601–624.

World Bank (2018) Small and Medium Enterprises (SMEs) Finance. Improving SMEs' Access to Finance and Finding Innovative Solutions to Unlock Sources of Capital. Retrieved from: http://www.worldbank.org/en/topic/smefinance (accessed 16 July 2019).

World Trade Organization (2018) Who We Are. Retrieved from: https://www.wto.org/english/thewto_e/whatis_e/who_we_are_e.htm (accessed 16 July 2019).

Yamori, N. (1999) An Empirical Investigation of the Japanese Corporate Demand for Insurance. *Journal of Risk and Insurance*, 66(2), 239–252.

Zou, H., Adams, M.B. & Buckle, M.J. (2003) Corporate Risks and Property Insurance: Evidence from the People's Republic of China. *The Journal of Risk and Insurance*, 70(2), 289–314.

Chapter 21

Climate Finance, Trade and Innovation Systems

Fiona Bannert[1]

Introduction

Global climate change has been recognised as among one of the biggest challenges in the 21st century. The comprehensive scientific evidence provided by successive reports of the Intergovernmental Panel on Climate Change (IPCC) has left little doubt that anthropogenic greenhouse gas emissions (GHG) are already changing the earth's climate system (IPCC, 2014). Climate change is no scientific phenomenon anymore, and countries in the developed and developing world have already started to feel the impacts of climate change, e.g. through intensified weather events such as heat waves and droughts, a change in weather patterns or water crises. Several studies are indicating that climate change will take the largest toll on poor and vulnerable people, as poverty and inequalities increase the risks from climate hazards (UN, 2016). It is also undeniable that shifting the global development path towards low-carbon green growth requires significant investment in renewable energies and energy efficiency, especially in emerging and developing countries. At last, with the Copenhagen Accord in 2009 and the Paris Agreement in 2015, fighting climate change has become a prominent theme of international political discussions between developed and developing countries, both as a measure for collaboration but also as potential for friction.

This chapter will look at climate finance from a variety of angles. It will start by outlining the current landscape of climate finance, its actors, instruments, final use and location. The chapter will then discuss the challenge of mobilising additional private investment and ways to leveraging public funds before making reference to the role of international trade in this setting. Finally, it will sketch out a theoretical framework, which – once refined – could be a helpful tool for placing the current discussions around climate finance in a holistic framework.

The Handbook of Global Trade Policy, First Edition. Edited by Andreas Klasen.

But let's start with the first question: what is climate finance? This rather simple question is surprisingly hard to answer. Up until now, no single definition for climate finance has been agreed upon within the international community, and different institutions and reports follow different approaches. One rather broad definition stems from the United Nations Framework Convention on Climate Change (UNFCCC) Standing Committee on Finance, according to which "climate finance aims at reducing emissions, and enhancing sinks of greenhouse gases and aims at reducing vulnerability of, and maintaining and increasing the resilience of, human and ecological systems to negative climate change impacts" (UNFCCC Standing Committee on Finance, 2014). This definition, arising out of convergence between nations, relates to the flow of funds to all activities, programmes or projects that support climate change-related projects, whether mitigation or adaptation, anywhere in the world. In a narrower sense, climate finance is also often used in the context of financial resources made available for assisting developing countries to help them reduce GHG emissions and adapt to a changing climate as set out in the Paris Agreement, which will be discussed shortly in more detail (Venugopal and Patel, 2013).

Given the lack of a common definition, the reported volume of climate finance can vary quite significantly depending on differences in objectives, reporting approaches and definitions of what kinds of projects meet the basic standards of climate finance. Last not but least, some finance flows, even if theoretically falling under this category, might be hard to capture due to the lack of available data. This is expected to be especially relevant for flows to developing countries from private actors. For consistency reasons, this chapter will follow – with few exceptions – the numbers provided by the Climate Policy Initiative (CPI), which publish a very comprehensive assessment of annual climate finance flows on a yearly basis. Their definition of climate finance refers to capital flows directed towards low-carbon and climate-resilient development interventions with direct or indirect greenhouse gas mitigation or adaptation benefits. Furthermore, it includes support for capacity-building measures as well as for the development and implementation of policies (Buchner *et al.*, 2017a).

Having narrowed down the definition, another important question would be: what are the determinants of climate finance? The current political economy of climate finance is made up of the triangle of climate science, financing needs and the political economy on a national and international level (Stewart *et al.*, 2009b, p. 4). Out of these three parameters, the first one is comparatively straight forward. Climate science is very clear that the increase in global temperature needs to be reduced to below 2° Celsius and – in best case – kept close to 1.5° Celsius, otherwise the world will face serious risks of far-reaching climate damage. And while critics may argue that the 2-degree mark is arbitrary, or even too low, there is little doubt that the global climate is changing (IPCC, 2014).

The picture becomes more complex when turning towards the second part of the triangle: the financing aspects. This is not only given the lack of a clear definition and coherent numbers reported by different institutions. In 2009 at the Copenhagen Consensus, three major commitments were made by the participating countries: First, to provide US$30 billion for mitigation and adaptation financing for the period 2010–2012. Second, to mobilise US$100 billion per year by 2020 to support developing countries in actions on climate change adaptation and mitigation. And last but not least, to make such funding new and additional, and sourced from public and private, bilateral and multilateral institutions (UNFCCC Standing Committee on Finance, 2016). This figure of US$100 billion has become the centre of political discussions around climate finance and was later reaffirmed at the Paris Conference in December 2015. The Paris Agreement, which was negotiated by representatives of 195 countries and was unanimously adopted, constituted a major breakthrough by the international community because it is the first climate change agreement that includes commitments by all signatories, in the form of Nationally Determined Contributions (NDC) (Streck *et al.*, 2016).

Even though international discussions now focus on the figure of US$100 billion, it is not clear if this sum will be sufficient as support for developing countries. According to a paper by Schalatek and Bird (2014), the real cost could run into hundreds of billions, if not trillions of US dollars annually by 2020. And this does not only refer to climate finance in developing countries. Whatever sum is needed, it will need to come from a variety of sources, public and private, bilateral and multilateral actors as well as alternative sources of finance. And given limited and often tight public budgets, an increasing share needs to come from private sources. But before looking into these issues in the following paragraphs, back to the last missing piece of the triangle of the political economy of climate finance: the national and international political economy.

Global climate policies are driven by policies and incentives on a national level. Major influencing factors in developed countries on the national level are, among others, the falling costs of technology, concerns about international competitiveness and the growing pressure from civil society for government and business to implement measures for green and sustainable growth. In developing countries, the impact of climate change has often already been felt more strongly, and governments are confronted with requests for emission limitations commitments by their own citizens but also by the international donor community (Reddy and Assenza, 2009).

As common in the political landscape, global policies are the outcome of many factors: domestic policies and strategies, bi- and multilateral discussions and negotiations, in which some countries prove to be more influential in defining global policies than others. When it comes to fighting climate change and discussing climate finance, states such the large European countries, the United States, Australia, Canada or Japan are not only driving interstate agreements but at the same time also setting limits to international discussions and progress given their own political agenda. An example is the announcement of the US government under President Trump in June 2017 to withdraw from the Paris Agreement. The United States has been the largest carbon emitter since records started and currently still ranks second after China in producing the largest amount of emissions per year. Nevertheless, the decision was made due to considerations driven by domestic politics despite the significant implications for the prospects for global compliance with the agreement (Stavins, 2017). The US withdrawal does not only undermine the universality of the agreement but can also impair states' confidence in international climate cooperation and sets a bad precedent for future collaboration. In addition, it is also likely to have wider implications reaching from the decline in overall climate finance and climate research funding available to a reduction of other countries' emission space and an increase in the emission costs, to name only a few (Zhang *et al.*, 2017).

However, in the fight against climate change it is not only the voice of developed countries that is important. The domestic policy preference and the economic power of the major emerging economies such as China, India and Brazil give them their own strong positions in international climate negotiations. Due to their economic rise, these countries have become important political players, but because of their growth, they have also become major GHG emitters and need to be on board, too. And even less politically powerful countries, both developed and developing, might have their special bargaining power in international negotiations, e.g. when they are essential for an international climate agreement actually to work. This could be relevant in cases where their unwillingness to vigorously follow domestic policies may distort and hinder the purpose of the agreements and unsettle the adherence of the more powerful states to them.

The exact analysis of the interplay of bargaining positions of different countries in international climate policy is a science of its own. A detailed discussion of the design, process and tactics of international climate negotiations can, for instance, be found in Van der Gaast (2016). What is worth mentioning in this context is that there is a "political cost curve" in national politics that deviates substantially from the economic cost curves that dominate in climate policy analysis (Stewart *et al.*, 2009a). In other words, some economically and environmentally attractive global options might not be pursued because the domestic political costs (or e.g. internal bargaining problems in a regional group like the European Union) would be too high. On the other hand, some measures that are neither economically efficient nor environmentally optimal may push through because they are preferred for domestic political reasons and are therefore adopted in order to achieve an overarching agreement.

A new tendency that has emerged during the negotiations for the Paris Agreement is that, for political and economic reasons, both developed and developing countries are now demanding greater flexibility in their international climate commitments and arrangements and want to manage climate mitigation on their own terms. As a result, the global climate regime, which started out with a top-down command approach used in the Kyoto Protocol, is moving towards a more flexible bottom-up setting. Whilst this tendency can be welcomed, and more flexibility clearly has its advantages, the challenge will be to avoid letting countries' individual freedom develop into too much plurality, decentralisation and fragmentation, which will make coordinated market arrangements and financing mechanisms even more difficult. This is an aspect the chapter will return to later. But first, it is time to map out the current climate finance landscape.

Assessing the Existing Climate Finance Landscape

Annual climate finance flows as recorded by the CPI have floated around US$360 billion per year since 2012 before reaching a peak in 2015 with US$437 billion (Figure 21.1).

The high was driven by a surge in private investments in renewable energy, particularly in China, and an increase of rooftop solar power projects in the United States and Japan. The following year, this volume could not be sustained, and total climate finance dropped to US$383 billion in 2016. This was due to several reasons, the most

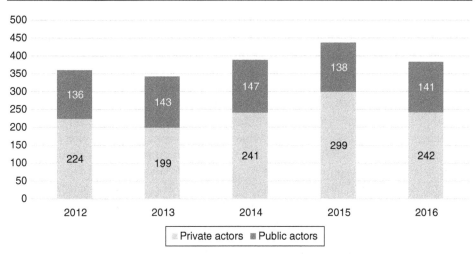

Figure 21.1 Breakdown of global climate finance by public and private actors, 2012–2016 (US$ billion).
Source: Buchner *et al.*, 2017a, p. 1.

important being falling technology costs but also lower capacity additions in some countries (Buchner *et al.*, 2017a). It is important to note that the figures stated here are not to be confused with amounts that may count towards the US$100 billion per year developed countries committed to mobilise in the Copenhagen Accord, and reaffirmed in Paris, to assist developing countries. The cited numbers rather refer to a broader definition of climate finance, i.e. all capital flows directed towards low-carbon and climate-resilient interventions with direct or indirect greenhouse gas mitigation or adaptation benefits, which could be recorded by the authors of the CPI reports (for details of the methodology used, see Buchner *et al.*, 2017b).

Establishing how much of the US$100 billion pledge is already being provided per year is difficult. UNFCCC reported climate finance flows from developed to developing countries in the range of US$40–175 billion per year in 2014 (UNFCC Standing Committee on Finance, 2014). The wide range is already an indication of the challenges of producing detailed and reliable numbers of current financial flows, with the lack of an internationally agreed definition being only one of them. Another challenge is the fact that the differentiation between a "normal" development project and a climate finance project can be blurred, even though the latter should be identified by "Rio markers". These are agreed markers within the OECD Development Assistance Committee (DAC) system to be applied to all bilateral official development assistance (ODA) flows (OECD, 2013). Donors are encouraged to indicate whether a project has a "principal" or "significant" objective of climate mitigation or adaptation or both. A further challenge is that it is often unclear how much of what is counted as climate finance meets the required additionality criteria. Finally, the calculation and inclusion of private sector co-financing as well as export credits are highly debated in this setting. Taking all these points together, some studies suggest that little of the climate finance flows reported under the US$100 billion goal in fact meets the required criteria (e.g. Government of India, 2015).

Where is the capital for climate finance coming from? Climate finance can generally come from public as well as private actors or institutions, with the majority coming from the private side (Buchner *et al.*, 2017a). Public sources include governments, bilateral aid agencies and climate funds as well as national, bilateral or multilateral development finance institutions (DFIs[2]). These actors often engage because of a specific political mandate, be it strengthening knowledge and technical capacity, reducing the costs and risks of climate investments for private actors or building the track record needed to enhance confidence in such investments. Most of the public institutions have also recognised the benefits of climate action for achieving their overarching policy goals, and that managing climate change effectively is in their national economic interest. Despite playing such an important part on various levels, overall public contribution in total climate finance dropped from 41% in 2013 to 36% in 2016 (Buchner *et al.*, 2017a, p. 1). The two main reasons were a disproportional increase of investments from private finance actors but also lower finance flowing from national DFIs.

Out of the overall flow provided by public resources, national, bilateral and multilateral DFIs accounted for the majority with funds of on average US$124 billion annually over the past five years (Buchner *et al.*, 2017a, p. 4). Of this number, almost half came from national DFIs, although their share experienced a gradual decrease over the years, from US$70 billion in 2013 to US$56 billion in 2016. This can be partly related to the fact that national DFIs in emerging markets have witnessed sharp downturns of up to 50% in climate finance lending due to economic volatility and its effect on budgets, including currency devaluations.

The contribution of national DFIs is closely followed by the involvement of multilateral DFIs. Among them, multilateral development banks (MDB) have come out with very strong commitments. Ahead of the Paris Agreement in 2015, the six largest MCBs had self-committed to wide-reaching targets to scale up climate finance, ranging between 25 and 40% of their total business by 2020. The Asian Development Bank (ADB), headquartered in Manila, committed to double its climate finance engagement from its own resources to US$6 billion annually by 2020 (ADB, 2015). Consequently, ADB's spending on tackling climate change is likely to rise to around 30% of its overall financing by the end of the decade. The African Development Bank (AfDB) even promised to nearly triple their climate financing commitment and to increase it to 40% of its total new investments by 2020, compared to an average of 26% from 2011 to 2014 (AfDB, 2015). And in 2015 the largest multilateral DFI, the World Bank Group, announced that it was steering to increase its own climate financing from US$10.3 billion to US$16 billion. Moreover, it planned to leverage an additional US$13 billion from other partners in support of these projects. A report in 2016 showed that, one year later, five of the six institutions were on track to meet their individual targets (MDBs, 2016). Likewise, new multilateral development financial institutions such as the Asian Infrastructure Investment Bank (AIIB) and the New Development Bank (NDB) announced their own commitments to a fixed share of renewable energy projects in their portfolio. NDB for example proposed to earmark as much 60% of its lending for renewable energy (NDB, 2016).

And finally, the smallest share of contributions from the three types of DFIs comes from the bilateral side, where annual contributions fluctuated between US$15 billion and US$20 billion over past years.

Compared to the contribution of the DFIs, the financing coming from the two remaining sources of public finance – governments and their agencies as well as climate funds – is much smaller. International finance from donor governments and their agencies to developing countries stayed constant throughout 2014–2016 at around US$14 billion. Multilateral climate funds, on the other hand, approved a record amount of climate finance grants and loans of US$2.45 billion in 2016, an increase of 40% compared to 2015. This can be explained by the coming into action of the Green Climate Fund (GCF), which was set up at the Durban Conference of the Parties (COP) back in 2010 and is expected to become a primary channel through which international public climate finance will flow over time. After far-reaching commitments had been made by 43 governments by the end of 2015, 2016 really was the first year of GCF's full operations, in which the Fund managed to develop a project portfolio of 35 projects, worth over US$1.5 billion (GCF, 2017). Given the recent setbacks of the Fund in July 2018, with the board failing to agree on any big-ticket decisions and the sudden resignation of the head of the secretariat, it remains to be seen if the Fund can live up to its full expectations. Other major climate funds include the Adaptation Fund (AF), the Climate Investment Fund (CIF) and the Global Environment Facility (GEF).

What many public actors have in common is that they do not only provide their own resources but also play a key role in creating the right incentives to encourage the participation of private players. As discussed later, reliable policy frameworks, positive market signals and predictable and stable revenues are key for private actors' financing decisions. But who are the players in climate finance on the private side?

The rather diverse list includes project developers, corporate actors, households and commercial financial institutions as well as institutional investors, private equity or venture capital funds. Among this large group, project developers are the party which is consistently providing the biggest volume of private finance, accounting for US$148 billion of finance in 2015 and slightly less, US$125 billion, in 2016 (Buchner et al., 2017a, p. 7). Such companies include dedicated energy project developers, engineering, procurement and construction (EPC) contractors, utilities and independent power producers. The second-largest group in 2016 was commercial financial institutions, which provided US$55 billion or 23% of total private climate finance in 2016. Their funding mainly went into renewable energy projects with established technology (solar photovoltaics [PV] and onshore wind) in East Asia, the Pacific and the Americas. Only little over 10% of their financing was used for other technologies. Commercial banks also take on an important intermediary role of originating investments and lending to corporates and households for small-scale projects. The latter two themselves account for around 10–15% of total private finance flows, of which a large percentage is spent on (home) solar PV systems. And finally, money from private equity, venture capital and infrastructure funds levelled at around US$2 billion per year, whereas money from institutional investors stood at around US$1 billion. It is important to note that this might only capture a fraction of institutional investors' actual contribution as the CPI report focuses on project-level primary financing data. It thereby excludes activities that are more typical for institutional investors, such as refinancing, or equity and debt investments into project developers, manufacturing companies and aggregation vehicles like funds.

There are two key take-aways from section. First, that one must carefully check the respective definitions of climate finance to understand the variance in numbers reported in different references. And second, that the landscape of climate finance is made up of multiple players with their own interests and agendas.

Instruments in the Existing Climate Finance Landscape

Looking at the current financial mix used to fund climate finance, the two biggest instruments are market-rate debt at project level (roughly 35%) provided in particular through development and commercial finance institutions on the one hand and balance sheet financing provided by project developers, corporate actors and households (around 40%) on the other hand. According to the data from Buchner *et al.* (2017a), the private side overall relies primarily on their own balance sheets to finance renewable energy projects, especially solar PV projects in high and upper-middle-income countries such as Japan, the United States and China. The authors, however, point out that this predominance of balance sheet financing might also reflect a bias in the data because many privately financed climate finance transactions may be subject to incomplete financial disclosures. In any case, the investors' tendency on balance sheets finance will also depend on the size of the project as it can make more sense and might be easier to finance small projects internally instead of incurring debt or high costs of external capital.

On the public side, finance mainly comes in the form of grants and concessional project debt as well as market-rate debt. Grants made up more than half of government entities' and climate funds' respective commitments, and most of those were spent on projects in low- and lower-middle-income countries. Public concessional or lower-than-market-rate finance, including loans with longer tenors and grace periods, plays a catalytic role through supporting the establishment of policy frameworks, strengthening technical capacity, lowering investment costs and reducing investment risks for the first movers in a market. Almost two thirds of national and bilateral DFIs' financing is coming in these forms. Multilateral DFIs tend to provide the majority of their commitments as market-rate loans – often blended with governments' and climate funds' concessional resources – primarily for sustainable transport and renewable energy generation projects. What is worth mentioning in this setting is the fact that DFIs also often manage quite a significant amount of external resources. When it comes to climate finance, those are mainly spent on greenfield renewable energy generation and mostly targeted at projects in Sub-Saharan Africa, East Asia and the Pacific, and Latin America and the Caribbean. In addition, DFIs also take on another important role by providing other financial instruments such as credit guarantees, political risk insurance and contingency recovery grants, which, in order to avoid double counting, are not included in the CPI reported figures. The enabling role of these public instruments for use in countries with political uncertainty or a challenging investment environment will be discussed further later in the chapter.

Final Use and Location

Having understood who is involved in climate finance and how the money is spent, the last important question is: what use and location does it go to? The answer to the first question is very straightforward: as of now, there is a heavy bias in the use of climate finance towards mitigation, i.e. measures to reduce the sources or enhance the sinks of greenhouse gases. Over 90% of current climate finance is going into these kinds of projects, mainly in the form of projects to promote renewable energy. Again, this substantial bias might also partly reflect the lack of data for private investments beyond the renewable energy sector. Most private investment went via balance sheet financing to small and large-scale solar PV and onshore wind projects, where risks and technology are relatively well defined. Public climate finance focuses on three main areas: renewables energy projects, energy efficiency and sustainable transport. Projects in these sectors benefited greatly from low-cost concessional loans.

Besides mitigation, the remaining climate finance flowed – a long distance – to spending on adaptation, i.e. adjustment in natural or human systems in response to actual or expected climatic stimuli or their effects. And finally, a small amount of funds also went to investments for dual use as well as for reducing emissions from deforestation and degradation (REDD).

When looking at the geographical distribution, there appears to be a strong domestic preference of investors, even though climate change is a phenomenon which does not stick to national borders. Buchner *et al.* (2017a) report that in 2016, 77% of finance was mobilised and deployed within the same country, mainly in high- or middle-income countries (Figure 21.2). This is consistent with observations of previous years and of different authors (e.g. UNFCC Standing Committee on Finance, 2016, p. 4). The tendency can be explained by investors feeling more comfortable in settings where country and institutional risks are well understood. It also highlights the importance of effective and reliable domestic policies to enable the unlocking of investment at scale.

Developing countries rely more on international capital in the sourcing of climate finance. According to Buchner *et al.* (2017a), almost US$50 billion per year went from OECD to non-OECD countries on average during 2015/2016. There also is a flow in the opposite direction, albeit very little with US$3 billion per year. The flow between developing countries during the same period amounted to roughly US$8 billion. In country terms, Western Europe and the Americas are the largest

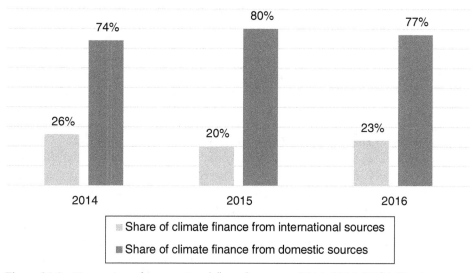

Figure 21.2 Domestic and international flows by source, 2014–2016 (US$ billion). Source: Buchner *et al.*, 2017a, p. 13.

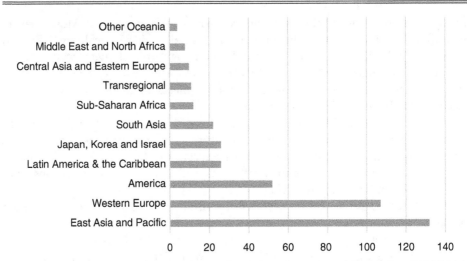

Figure 21.3   Average annual climate finance breakdown by region of destination, 2015/2016. Source: Buchner *et al.*, 2017a, p. 13.

destination within the OECD countries. In non-OECD regions, East Asia and the Pacific make the largest destination, which are also the two regions most prone to the impacts of climate change (Figure 21.3).

Challenge of Mobilising Additional Private Investment and Leveraging Public Funds

Given the challenge of attracting financing not only to deliver the US$100 billion promise but also to provide for continuing and growing finance flows globally to fight climate change, discussions have focused on two aspects: how to attract more private sector finance and how to best put the overall finance capacity into use through the leveraging role of public resources. At a narrow level, leverage generally refers to the ability of a public financial commitment to mobilise some larger multiple of private capital for investment in a specific project or undertaking. At a broader level, it also includes the potential for a more catalytical role of public investments or incentives to encourage much more widespread changes towards climate-friendly behavior by private firms and households across the whole economy rather than by only those involved in a specific climate-related project. A common way for this to be achieved is through addressing market failures or barriers to investment on a national level (OECD, 2011, p. 34).

The public hand can come in on a macro, i.e. policy level, as well as at the micro or project level. On the macro level, a primary requirement to attract private sector capital into low-carbon, climate-resilient investments is an appropriate policy framework. Almost all such investments can be categorised as policy-dependent in the sense that they normally have higher costs than carbon intensive options. Nearly as important as the national policy framework itself is that private investors perceive it as clear, stable and predictable. In addition to this assessment on the macro level, investors will of course be looking at the profitability of the potential investment at the individual project level, or more specifically the risk-reward ratios of the investment (either debt or equity) (Brown and Jacobs 2011, p. 2ff.). One of the most common examples of how government can provide all of the above is through a feed-in tariff (FiT) structure commonly applied in the renewable energy setting, e.g. for wind or solar plants. A FiT with a guaranteed fixed price – often at a higher than market rate – will make the revenue stream higher and predictable and thus increase the attractiveness for investors. This holds especially in settings where the energy market is not yet properly developed and tariff payments might otherwise not be secure. But even when the profitability of an investment seems to be given in a specific setting, the perceived and real risks might still be too high, and as a result, private capital might not be available at all or only at very high cost.

Project risk is very specific to the individual project and its setting, e.g. subsector, technology, participants and country, to name only a few. Risks in low-carbon projects can be categorised in different ways, and no generic list might be able to cover all the risks comprehensively. Brown and Jacobs (2011) suggest the following six categories, which are rather typical for renewable energy projects from an international investor's perspective:

- First, general political risk which takes into account the political stability and the security of property rights in the country as well as the risk (and generally higher cost) of working within unfamiliar legal systems.
- Second, legal and regulatory risks – as mentioned above – which reflect the stability and certainty of the regulatory and policy environment, including the longevity of incentives available for low-carbon investment and the reliability of FiTs and power purchase agreements (PPAs).
- Third, operation or performance risk where the (local) project developer/firm may lack the capacity and/or experience to execute the project efficiently; along with the general difficulty of operating in a foreign and unfamiliar country.
- Forth, foreign currency risk which can arise when project revenues and costs are denominated in different currencies. Foreign currency risk includes exchange rate risk (depreciation and devaluation of the local currency), convertibility risk (not being able to exchange local currency for foreign currency due to a policy action of the government) and transfer risks (not being able to transfer foreign exchange out of the country).
- Fifth, technology risk when implementing a new and relatively untried technology or system or using a known technology in a new environment.
- And last, a risk described by the authors as unfamiliarity risk. This is the case when one might require a considerable amount of time and effort to understand a project, and its setting, that has not been undertaken by the investor before.

In addition, common risks of course include financial risks, construction risks and potentially supply risks, all depending on the type of project.

There are a number of well-known financial tools that can be used to address the above-mentioned investment risks and potential barriers for private engagement. These instruments tend to be placed either on the equity or the debt side via direct public financing or through different forms of public guarantee structures. On the equity side, two common arrangements are pledge funds and subordinated equity funds (Brown and Jacobs 2011, p. 3). Pledge funds might be useful for projects that are either too small for equity investors to be considered or that simply cannot access sufficient equity despite having a strong internal rate of return. In this case, an equity capital "pledge" fund may be installed, where public sponsors – which could be developed-country governments or international financial institutions – provide a small amount of equity to anchor and encourage larger pledges from private investors, such as sovereign wealth funds, large private equity firms and pension funds.

Another alternative of public support on the equity side is through a so-called subordinated equity fund. This means that the public hand would put in public capital through the provision of subordinated equity, for which the repayment is of a lower hierarchy than the repayment of other equity investors in the cash flow waterfall. More specifically, this means that the fund would have access to profits only after rewards to other equity contributors were distributed. Through this mechanism, the subordinated equity gives some comfort to the private investor by ensuring that he has the first claim on the dividends of the project, thereby increasing its risk-adjusted returns.

On the debt side, public support tends to come in the form of loan guarantees, political insurance and foreign exchange rate liquidity facilities (Caperton, 2010, p. 3). Loan guarantees are used in countries with high political risks, in which the low-carbon market is often still in its infancy and where contracts have low legal certainty. In such a setting, loan guarantees by governments or international public finance institutions will ensure that the loan will be repaid if the borrower cannot make the payments. It transfers part or all of the risk from the lender, e.g. the commercial bank, onto the loan guarantor. Besides reducing the repayment risk, an additional impact is that the lender is in a position to be able to charge a lower interest rate on the loan due to the lower risk, thereby reducing the cost of capital and increasing its profitability.

To address risks which arise through the political environment and the regulatory setting, political risk insurance is another common tool. As with any insurance, the precise scope of coverage is governed by the terms of the insurance policy but it typically includes cover against the risk of governmental expropriation or confiscation of assets, governmental frustration or repudiation of contracts, political violence or business interruption. In a renewable energy setting, political risk insurance is bought by the lender specially to cover the risk of changes in the FiT structure or the revocation of licences or permits necessary to operate a project. Given that these risks can be quite substantial, private insurance companies might only be able to offer such policies to a certain extent, so public political risk insurance institutions, such as the Multilateral Investment Guarantee Agency (MIGA), step in, allowing for a more comprehensive cover.

And finally, the public side might also be important to offer solutions for foreign currency risks, e.g. in the form of foreign exchange liquidity facilities, as currency depreciation or devaluation is a common and significant risk to the loan repayment of international investors in projects where revenues are generated in a local currency. Such a facility, best set up early together with the loan facility, can help reduce the risks associated with borrowing money in a different currency by creating a line of credit that can be drawn on when the project company faces challenges to managing it debt repayments due to a devaluation of the local currency and can then be repaid when the project creates a financial surplus again.

The instruments provided by the public hand listed above are not all-encompassing, nor have the different mechanisms been described in all their detail (see Caperton, 2010; Brown and Jacobs, 2011). Nevertheless, the overview gives a suitable insight in how public institutions can address some of the concerns and risks holding back the engagement of private actors, and, in the best case, leverage additional finance from private sources. It also highlights that not all of these mechanisms will be equally applicable to every private actor or to every type of project. For instance, while sovereign wealth funds are suited to participation in a pledge fund or a subordinated equity fund, debt-specific instruments, such as loan guarantees and foreign exchange liquidity facilities, are more applicable to banks. Most of the debt-based mechanisms described above are also common tools used to mitigate risks in international trade transactions and, in this matter, are provided by DFIs or export credit agencies (ECAs). It is important to emphasise that, especially for larger projects, a mix of instruments might be required to address all the project-specific risks. And of course, there will be case where even a sum of public sector instruments will not be sufficient to take away all the concerns and reservations of the private players. The next section will look at some connections between climate finance and international trade and what contribution the latter can make in fostering the availability of capital for climate finance.

Interaction of Climate Finance, International Trade and Export Credits

The discussions around combating climate change concluding in the Paris Agreement in 2015 as the last major milestone were held across various disciplines. These included not only discussions at the scientific level but also politics and diplomacy, and development as well as international trade. Climate change and international trade are intermingled in various, sometimes more indirect, ways than other disciplines: the higher frequency of extreme weather events can and most probably will lead to climate-induced trade disruptions such as changes in natural resource trading or the inability to rely on previous trade routes due to a rise in sea level (Reiter, 2015). New legal aspects will need to be incorporated in the rules of the global trading system, such as the compatibility of WTO rules and domestic actions taken under the UNFCCC or other similar multilateral environmental agreements, including questions arising from climate regulatory law, such as renewable energy certificates or carbon trading (see e.g. Derwent, 2009; Marceau, 2009; Gallagher, 2016). And probably most importantly, behind every trade transaction stands a production and transport process and its associated GHG emissions. A recent study by Andrew *et al.* (2013) found that trade-related emissions account for roughly 26% of global emissions. Consequently, actions taken for climate protection addressing the production or transport process can have wider impacts, especially on developing countries which are focused on increasing their own productive capacities to strengthen their integration into the global economy and trading system. When it comes to the financing aspect of climate change, a global push for higher climate finance spending is also likely to increase the volume of trade in this specific area, as goods and new technologies will be needed in countries where such a production capacity might not yet exist or where the products can be sourced cheaper from elsewhere. For how these changes might look like, one just needs to look at China, which has emerged as a major hub for solar PV production over the past decade. As a result, Chinese companies are busy exporting their products and technology to projects around the world.

Matching global trade with related climate finance flows is not an easy exercise and has been done only in very narrow settings (e.g. OECD, 2017b; Global Economic Governance Initiative, 2016). This chapter will therefore rely on trade of low-carbon, climate-resilient investment supported by official ECAs as proxy. Export credit guarantees are financial instruments that foster exports and trade by mitigating the financial risk of transactions and projects. They are often provided by ECAs, normally official or quasi-official government institutions. The support can take the form either of official financing support, such as direct loans to foreign buyers, refinancing or interest-rate support, or of pure cover support, such as export credits insurance or guarantee cover for loans provided by private financial institutions. ECAs not only jointly account for the world's largest source of government financing for private sector industries, they also covered more than US$1.9 trillion of global trade in 2016 together with investment and private credit insurers, a record amount of more than 11% of international trade (Berne Union, 2017, p. 11). In addition, ECAs also are among the largest public institutions that support investment in energy projects worldwide and, as such, can play an important role in providing and encouraging climate finance.

In 2016, the total volume of projects reported by ECAs in support of low-carbon trade transactions amounted to almost US$3.3 billion, or 6.1% of their total commitment (OECD, 2017b). All projects fell under the category of renewable energy. The yearly percentage of total business in renewable energy supported by ECAs has been growing steadily over the past ten years, averaging around 3.7% per year. It is also significant that over two thirds of all projects were related to wind energy, a fact that relates well to the result of the CPI report discussed earlier.

ECAs are well aware of their official government mandate, as well as of the environmental responsibility that comes with it, and have started discussions on climate finance via different channels. One significant one is the export credit community within the OECD, which is an important forum for exchanging information on export credits systems and business activities as well as discussing and coordinating national export credits policies relating to good governance issues, e.g. environmental and social due diligence or sustainable lending. It also serves as a platform for monitoring, maintaining and developing the financial disciplines for export credits, which are contained within the Arrangement on Officially Supported Export Credits (the Arrangement). The Arrangement defines the most generous financial terms and conditions that member states may offer when providing officially supported export credits, in order to ensure a level playing field (OECD, 2017a). Major milestones in the discussions with regard to low-carbon financing have been the modification of the Sector Understanding on Export Credits for Climate Change Mitigation, Renewable Energies and Water Projects (CCSU) in 2012, which allows preferential terms for low-carbon transactions, e.g. favorable financial terms. The CCSU was later revised in 2014 to additionally incorporate climate change adaptation (OECD, 2014).

Another platform for discussion has been a workshop hosted by the Danish export credit agency EKF (Eksport Kredit Fonden) in 2013, which originated out of a work stream under the ministerial process initiated by the United States in

Washington earlier that year at the Ministerial Meeting on Mobilizing Climate Finance. The aim of the meeting in Copenhagen was to get ECA representatives as well as experts from international organisations and the private sector together to discuss the current and future role of ECAs in mobilising private climate finance. During the workshop, the participants developed and shared new ideas for scaling up climate finance approaches and instruments. On the basis of these discussions, EKF published a catalogue of seven ideas, and different working groups were created to develop some of these ideas further (EKF, 2014, p. 24). The ideas ranged from encouraging dialogue on new technical approaches that can be developed within individual ECAs or in cooperation between different ECAs, to ideas that require coordination in the appropriate political committees, such as the OECD, to political ideas that would need ministerial backing in order for ECAs to contribute further to mobilising private climate finance. Concepts included a risk-sharing pool of ECA capacities, an international climate fund insured by ECAs and a fund to cover project development costs.

A further idea referred to expanding the scope of ECAs from being the "back office" of a transaction to becoming more an arranger in a project as a link between developers, exporters, lenders and borrowers. Another suggestion encouraged the building of better bridges between ECAs, DFIs and national development authorities. There is much room for synergies: ECAs have expertise in financing commercial viable projects in specific sectors or regions defined by their exporters' focus. DFIs, on the other hand, often have a longer experience in developing countries and a deeper understanding of the regulatory and legal environments. In this capacity, they can enhance private actors' awareness of and ability to understand, appraise and manage climate change opportunities and thereby engage investors currently still at the sidelines of climate finance.

One example that has often been used as a case study to showcase how such synergies might look is the Lake Turkana Windfarm in Kenya. With a total investment of around US$680 million and a capacity of 310 MW, the project will be the largest wind farm in Africa and furthermore the single largest investment in Kenya to date. It includes the installation of 365 wind turbines, 436 km of transmission lines and the rehabilitation of more than 200 km of existing roads. Once completed, the wind project will increase the country's national electricity supply by around 15%, having been in the making since 2005. In early 2017, all turbines were up and ready for electricity generation; however, there was a delay in the completion of the transmission line, which was caused by financial difficulties experienced by the main Spanish contractor. Despite this and other difficulties arising during the project preparation and construction phase (among others, multiple delays occurred around land acquisitions), the Lake Turkana Windfarm has been seen as an example of innovative financing for low-carbon energy projects for a number of reasons (Swedfund, 2017). The project features a unique public–private mix (AfDB, 2018). The private project company is responsible for the construction of the wind farm, whilst the ancillary 428 km transmission line was procured and needed to be delivered by the public sector. Equity financing was provided by a number of private companies as well as funds, including the Norwegian Investment Fund for Developing Countries (Norfund), the Finnish Fund for Industrial Cooperation Ltd (FinnFund) and the Danish Investment Fund for Developing Countries (IFU). On the debt side, the

European Investment Bank (EIB) could leverage around €200 million into the project with guarantee structures from the Danish ECA EKF (as the wind turbines were sourced from the Danish company Vestas Wind Systems A/S) and from two South African banks. In addition, AfDB used its B-loan structure, allowing participant banks to benefit from its preferred creditor status. And finally, the project also profited from the support of the EU-Africa Infrastructure Trust Fund (EU-AITF), which provided capital participation to the project in order to close the equity gap.

This project was a good example to show how public and private players can work together successfully and use the synergies of each other's mandate and knowledge to set up a complex financing structure for a very large clean energy project. The experts involved in doing the financial structuring used some out-of-the-box thinking and tried to address the challenges of each of the players with a sophisticated risk-sharing exercise, combining different instruments and structures. The project also highlights the respective contribution of DFIs and ECAs in such a setting, by not only reducing the general risk for private investors but also backing the project with their political influence. Nonetheless, the Lake Turkana Windfarm also showed that even such a high-profile project with participation of financial heavyweights like AfDB and EIB is not exempt from encountering a substantial number of challenges. Nevertheless, after long delays, the project was finally inaugurated in July 2019 (*The EastAfrican*, 2019).

What can be taken away from this example for the general interaction of climate finance and international trade? Climate finance will in many circumstances come hand in hand with cross-border transactions of technical equipment. ECAs offer risk mitigation tools which address challenges inherent to a large part of low-carbon investment and as such, if put in place, can be an effective way to crowd in private capital. More and more systematic exchange is required between ECAs and DFIs in order not only to work together on projects case by case but to lift the cooperation to become a rule. Nevertheless, one should not forget in the discussions around the climate finance quest of ECAs that a major limiting factor for ECAs lies in the fact that climate finance as of now is only a secondary or derivate activity for ECAs. Their primary purpose remains to support their national exports and facilitate international trade. For this reason, they rely on the focus of their national exporting companies and their ability to compete in international bidding procedures for low-carbon projects. One additional challenge in this setting comes from the fact that, whilst equipment for low-carbon projects in theory can be sourced globally, in practice local content requirements often limit international sourcing possibilities (UNCTAD, 2014). Given the local content specifications set out in the OECD Arrangement, this can limit the ability of ECAs to participate and shape such projects.

An Innovation System Approach to Climate Finance

When looking at the current discussions about climate finance it becomes apparent that much of it is focused either around the more academic discourse of exact definitions and a detailed account of existing climate finance flows on the one side or on a more hands-on debate about ways to mobilise and leverage additional finance led by practitioners on the other side (McCollum *et al.*, 2013; UNFCCC Standing Committee on Finance, 2016; Blanc-Gonnet and Calland, 2013; Lütken, 2014).

Areas which are equally important but where less attention has been paid so far include the spending side. A range of issues can present challenges in accessing available climate finance funds, such as low levels of technical capacity to design and develop projects or programmes on a national or local level, difficulties in following the procedures to access the funds or a limited ability to monitor and evaluate progress. Other areas where more research is needed include the development of a deeper understanding of economic change and the barriers to innovation in the specific setting of climate finance and the design of the best institutional incentives and arrangements (Steckel *et al.*, 2017). Examples of research which investigates these aspects can be found in Van Kerkhoff *et al.* (2011), where existing funds for project-based financing are discussed, or in Cui *et al.* (2014), which looks at the distribution of climate finance funds at the country level. These case studies, while representing notable exceptions, were undertaken under a very specific financing modality that is the GCF.

While this research on a country- or even an investment type-specific level is highly needed, the author of this chapter believes that going forward a more holistic approach is required to understand climate finance in its whole complexity on a country but also on a global level. Only then will it be possible to deliver what is required to counter climate change, not only in terms of quantity but also in terms of quality. One theoretical approach which might be used to place climate finance in such a holistic framework is the innovation systems approach first featured by Christopher Freeman (Freeman, 1987). He was among the first to emphasise that countries differ not only in terms of economic performance but also with respect to patterns of creating and diffusing innovation and the national institutional frameworks supporting it. He tested this in his analysis of technology and economic performance in Japan, in which he highlighted the flows of technology and information among people, companies and institutions and their relationship as key to the innovation process. Over the years, Freeman's approach has been proven to be a useful tool in identifying the driving forces of innovation and in explaining the difference between economic performances in different countries (Casadella and Uzunidis, 2017; Fagerberg and Srholec, 2008).

Today, innovation is considered to be an important policy element to economic development and reaching the Sustainable Development Goals (SDGs) (Casadella *et al.*, 2015). In this context, the term "innovation" has moved on from being primarily associated with advances in science and technology, highly qualified personnel or a sophisticated working environment. It is rather understood as finding new ways of combining knowledge for solutions in response to current challenges or opportunities that arise in the social and/or economic environment (Fagerberg *et al.*, 2004). As such, innovation policy is not limited to science, technology and industrial areas but covers much broader issues such as the provision of infrastructure, human and financial resources and appropriate institutions in the form of legal frameworks, regulation and incentives (Martin, 2013). It also looks at emerging types of innovation, e.g. public sector innovation, social innovation and innovation for inclusive development. Given the nature of this theoretical framework, an advanced version of it might be a useful tool to understand the climate finance setting on a more systematic basis by mapping out key actors, institutions and networks and their engagement on an international and, in particular, on a national level, i.e. across the different government ministries and across society, including civil society and the private sector (Vidican, 2015, p. 229). Important aspects which need to be addressed within this analysis are the issue of ownership of climate finance, the alignment with national climate change priorities and overall public policies and strategies (UNFCCC Standing Committee on Finance, 2016, p. 83).

One paper that has already taken this approach is by Hogarth (2012), who looked at the function of and institutional arrangements for climate finance on a country level from an innovation systems perspective. In his analysis, he examined the barriers that prevent developing countries from transitioning to low-carbon and climate-resilient economies. He also explored public policy interventions which are necessary to overcome those barriers. Hogarth finds that the barriers to innovation and economic change are much more pervasive than a lack of incentives. These barriers include issues such as insufficient knowledge flows and technical capacity, inadequate network formation around value chains, capital constraints due to undeveloped capital markets and unstable and inappropriate policy regimes. In examining these barriers, his research provides multiple findings and potential actions for policymakers.

Conclusion and Policy Recommendations

This chapter has looked at the topic of climate finance from a variety of angles, proceeding in probably a rather unusual order. It started out by looking at the triangle that drives the political economy of climate finance: climate science, financing needs to counter climate change and the national and international political economy that defines the political discussions and climate agreement negotiations. It then assessed the current climate finance landscape in more detail: total volumes, the prevailing financing actors and their instruments, as well as final use and geographical location of the financial flows. The chapter subsequently proceeded by highlighting the challenge of mobilising additional private investment and ways of leveraging public funds by discussing different financial instruments. It underlined the importance of public institutions in providing risk mitigation tools as well as establishing the right frameworks and incentives for private investors. The following paragraph looked at the interaction of climate finance and international trade using projects supported by ECAs as a proxy for low-carbon, climate-resilient trade and investment. It referred to discussions around climate finance held on different platforms within the ECA community and listed some ideas on how ECAs as public institutions can play a bigger role in climate finance. This section finished by showcasing the Lake Turkana Wind Farm in Kenya, a cited example of the successful interplay of public and private investors and innovative risk structuring in a large energy project, even though the project itself has not been without its challenges. From this practical example, the chapter then took a step back and suggested that a more holistic approach is required to understand climate finance in its whole complexity on a country but also on a global level. This will be even more important going forward, given the current trend in the global climate regime to move from the initial top-down command approach used in the Kyoto Protocol towards a more flexible bottom-up approach as set out in the Paris Agreement. The innovation systems approach first mentioned by Freeman was sketched out as theoretical concept, which could potentially provide such a framework once a broader definition of innovation as well as current relevant trends in innovation have been identified and integrated into the approach. However, more research will need to go into matching an advanced theoretical framework of innovation systems with climate finance. This was beyond the scope of this chapter in terms of content but also because of the practical, more policy-orientated nature of the Handbook.

What should have become clear is that in order to fulfill the "US$100 billion by 2020" pledge but also to increase climate finance globally, a variety of new arrangements to generate public and private climate finance and engage developing countries in mitigation and adaptation activities are needed. The current climate finance regime already involves a large number of actors, independent funds and initiatives. And it is likely that this regime will become even more complex and diffuse in the coming years. A single uniform design for climate finance will be neither feasible nor desirable. Furthermore, finding more innovative, equitable and efficient use of available finance flows will be a major challenge, paired with continued efforts to mobilise new sources of finance. But despite, or rather because of, this new diversity of initiatives and mechanisms, new and sophisticated institutional arrangements or frameworks are needed to recognise, facilitate and coordinate the diversity of decentralised climate initiatives among both developing and developed countries, on a country as well as a global level.

Finally, I would like to end this contribution with three policy recommendations.

First, there is no way around an agreed definition of what constitutes climate finance on an international level, and this is not only important regarding the commitments made under the Paris Agreement. It is hard – if not impossible – to reach quantitative aims without knowing what exactly contributes to it. A clear understanding of what investments will be counted, where they will take place and what the underlying drivers are will help to identify and overcome the existing barriers to low-carbon private investment. In addition, improved tracking at the national level can help strengthen climate change policymaking processes and ensure effective management of public resources to deliver on national climate change policy goals.

Second, more attention should be spent on an appropriate national investment policy and the establishment of the right climate finance incentive framework on a country level. Sending unclear or uncertain policy signals and setting deficient frameworks can distort or inhibit low-carbon investment.

Third, it remains important to foster the dialogue and enhance the integration of climate change considerations into the financial system. Public actors of different types have the opportunity to drive investment from the wider financial system by providing other investors and financiers with the needed confidence to participate in climate projects. Institutions such as DFIs and ECAs have an important role to play in enhancing private actors' awareness of and ability to understand, appraise and manage climate change risks and opportunities, and thereby engage investors currently still at the sidelines of climate finance.

Notes

1   The views expressed here are solely those of the author in her private capacity and do not in any way represent the views of ADB.

2   The CPI report follows the following differentiation: multilateral DFIs are public finance institutions
    with multiple countries as shareholders and from which finance flows internationally. Bilateral DFIs
    are public finance institutions where finance also flows internationally but with a single-country own-
    ership, whilst national DFIs have a single-country ownership and finance flows are only directed
    domestically.

References

African Development Bank (2015) AfDB's Commitment: Supporting Climate Resilient and
    Low-Carbon Development. Retrieved from: https://www.afdb.org/en/topics-and-sectors/
    sectors/climate-change/our-strategy (accessed January–March 2018).

African Development Bank (2018) Lake Turkana Wind Power Project: The Largest Wind
    Farm Project in Africa. Retrieved from: https://www.afdb.org/en/projects-and-operations/
    selected-projects/lake-turkana-wind-power-project-the-largest-wind-farm-project-in-
    africa-143 (accessed January–March 2018).

Andrew, R., Davis, S. & Peters, G. (2013) Climate Policy and Dependence on Traded Carbon.
    Environmental Research Letters, 8, 2–8.

Asian Development Bank (2015) ADB to Double Annual Climate Financing to $6 Billion for
    Asia-Pacific by 2020. Retrieved from: https://www.adb.org/news/adb-double-annual-
    climate-financing-6-billion-asia-pacific-2020 (accessed January–March 2018).

Berne Union (2017) *Berne Union Yearbook 2017*. Retrieved from: http://cdn.berneunion.org/
    assets/Images/BU%20Yearbook%202017-lowRes.pdf (accessed January–March 2018).

Blanc-Gonnet Jonason, P. & Calland, R. (2013) Global Climate Finance, Accountable Public
    Policy: Addressing the Multi-Dimensional Transparency. *The Georgetown Public Policy
    Review*, 18(2), 1–16. Retrieved from: http://www.gppreview.com/wp-content/uploads/
    2013/04/jonason-and-calland.pdf (accessed January–March 2018).

Brown, J. & Jacobs, M. (2011) Leveraging Private Investment: The Role of Public Sector
    Climate Finance. Retrieved from: https://www.odi.org/sites/odi.org.uk/files/odi-assets/
    publications-opinion-files/7082.pdf (accessed January–March 2018).

Buchner, B., Oliver, P., Wanget, X. *et al.* (2017a) Global Landscape of Climate Finance 2017.
    Retrieved from: https://climatepolicyinitiative.org/wp-content/uploads/2017/10/2017-
    Global-Landscape-of-Climate-Finance.pdf (accessed January–March 2018).

Buchner, B., Oliver, P., Wanget, X. *et al.* (2017b) Global Landscape of Climate Finance 2017:
    Methodology. Retrieved from: https://climatepolicyinitiative.org/wp-content/uploads/
    2017/10/GLCF-2017-Methodology-Document.pdf (accessed January–March 2018).

Caperton, W. (2010) Leveraging Private Finance for Clean Energy. Retrieved from: https://
    cdn.americanprogress.org/wp-content/uploads/issues/2010/11/pdf/gcn_memo.pdf (accessed
    January–March 2018).

Casadella, V. & Uzunidis, D. (2017) National Innovation Systems of the South, Innovation
    and Economic Development Policies: A Multidimensional Approach. *Journal of Innovation
    Economics & Management*, 23(2), 137–157.

Casadella, V., Liu, Z. & Uzunidis, D. (2015) *Innovation Capabilities and Economic
    Development in Open Economies*. New York: Wiley.

Cui, L., Zhu, L., Springmann M. & Fan Y. (2014) Design and Analysis of the Green Climate
    Fund. *Journal of Systems Science and Systems Engineering*, 23(3), 266–299.

Derwent, H. (2009) Carbon Market Design: Beyond the EU Emissions Trading Scheme. In:
    Stewart, R., Kingsbury, B. & Rudyk, B. (eds.) *Climate Finance Regulatory and Funding
    Strategies for Climate Change and Global Development*. New York: New York University
    Press, pp. 125–134.

Eksport Kredit Fonden (EKF) (2014). *Export Credit and Climate Finance*. Retrieved from:
    https://www.ekf.dk/Docs/Handbook%20EKF%20climate%20financing.pdf (accessed
    January–March 2018).

Fagerberg, F. & Srholec, M. (2008). National Innovation Systems, Capabilities and Economic Development. *Research Policy*, 37(9), 1417–1435.

Fagerberg, J., Mowery, D. & Nelson, R. (eds.) (2004) *The Oxford Handbook of Innovation.* Oxford: Oxford University Press.

Freeman, C. (1987) *Technology and Economic Performance: Lessons from Japan.* London: Pinter.

Gallagher, K.P. (2016) Trade, Investment, and Climate Policy: The Need for Coherence. In: Gallagher, K.P. (ed.) *Trade in the Balance: Reconciling Trade and Climate Policy.* Boston: Boston University, pp. 5–13. Retrieved from: http://www.bu.edu/pardee/files/2016/11/Pardee_TradeClimate_110316final.pdf (accessed January–March 2018).

Global Economic Governance Initiative (2016) *Trade in the Balance: Reconciling Trade and Climate Policy*, edited by Gallagher, K.P. Boston: Boston University. Retrieved from: http://www.bu.edu/pardeeschool/files/2016/11/Pardee_TradeClimate_110316final.pdf (accessed January–March 2018).

Government of India (2015) Climate Change Finance, Analysis of a Recent OECD Report: Some Credible Facts Needed. Delhi: Government of India. Retrieved from: https://dea.gov.in/sites/default/files/ClimateChangeOEFDReport_0.pdf (accessed January–March 2018).

Green Climate Fund (2017) About the Fund. Retrieved from: http://www.greenclimate.fund/who-we-are/about-the-fund (accessed January–March 2018).

Hogarth, R. (2012) The Role of Climate Finance in Innovation Systems. *Journal of Sustainable Finance & Investment*, 2(3–4), 257–274.

Intergovernmental Panel on Climate Change (2014) *Climate Change 2014: Synthesis Report. Contribution of Working Groups I, II and III to the Fifth Assessment Report of the Intergovernmental Panel on Climate Change.* Geneva: IPCC. Retrieved from: https://www.ipcc.ch/site/assets/uploads/2018/05/SYR_AR5_FINAL_full_wcover.pdf (accessed January–March 2018).

Lütken, S. (2014) *Financial Engineering of Climate Investment in Developing Countries: Nationally Appropriate Mitigation Action and How to Finance It.* Cambridge: Anthem Press.

Marceau, G. (2009) The WTO and Climate Finance: Overview of the Key Issues. In: Stewart R.B., Kingsbury, B. & Rudyk, B. (eds.) *Climate Finance: Regulatory and Funding Strategies for Climate Change and Global Development.* New York: New York University Press. pp. 247–253.

Martin, B. (2013) Twenty Challenges for Innovation Studies. In: Fagerberg, J., Martin, B.R. & Sloth Anderson, E. (eds) *The Future of Innovation Studies.* Oxford: Oxford University Press.

McCollum, D.L., Nagai, Y. Riahi, K. *et al.* (2013). Energy Investments under Climate Policy: A Comparison of Global Models. *Climate Change Economics*, 4(4), 3–32.

MDBs (2016) 2015 Joint Report on Multilateral Development Banks' Climate Finance. Retrieved from: http://www.ebrd.com/2015-joint-report-on-mdbs-climate-finance.pdf (accessed January–March 2018).

New Development Bank (2016) NDB President: 60% of Funding Will Be for Renewables. Retrieved from: https://www.ndb.int/president_desk/ndb-president-60-funding-will-renewables/ (accessed January–March 2018).

OECD (2011) Mobilizing Climate Finance – Paper Prepared at the Request of G20 Finance Ministers. Retrieved from: http://www.oecd.org/env/cc/49032964.pdf (accessed January–March 2018).

OECD (2013) OECD DAC Rio Markers for Climate Handbook. Retrieved from: https://www.oecd.org/dac/environment-development/Revised%20climate%20marker%20handbook_FINAL.pdf (accessed January–March 2018).

OECD (2014) Climate Change. Retrieved from: http://www.oecd.org/tad/xcred/climatechange.htm (accessed January–March 2018).

OECD (2017a) Export Credits Work at the OECD. Retrieved from: http://www.oecd.org/tad/xcred/about.htm (accessed January–March 2018).

OECD (2017b) Trends in Arrangement Official Export Credits (2007–2016). Retrieved from: http://www.oecd.org/trade/xcred/business-activities.htm (accessed January–March 2018).

Reddy, S. & Assenza, G. (2009) Climate Change – A Developing Country Perspective. *Current Science*, 97(1), 50–62.

Reiter, J. (2015) What Does Climate Change Mean for the Future of Global Trade? What Can Policy-Makers Do about It? Retrieved from: https://www.ictsd.org/opinion/what-does-climate-change-mean-for-the-future-of-global-trade-what-can-policy (accessed January–March 2018).

Schalatek, L. & Bird, N. (2014) The Principles and Criteria of Public Climate Finance – A Normative Framework. Retrieved from: https://www.odi.org/sites/odi.org.uk/files/odi-assets/publications-opinion-files/9296.pdf (accessed January–March 2018).

Stavins, R. (2017) *Why Trump Pulled the US Out of the Paris Accord: And What the Consequences Will Be*. Retrieved from: https://www.foreignaffairs.com/articles/2017-06-05/why-trump-pulled-us-out-paris-accord (accessed January–March 2018).

Steckel, J.-C., Jakob, M., Flachsland, C. *et al.* (2017) From Climate Finance toward Sustainable Development Finance. *Climate Change*, 8(1).

Stewart, R., Kingsbury, B. & Rudyk, B. (eds.) (2009a) *Climate Finance Regulatory and Funding Strategies for Climate Change and Global Development*. New York: New York University Press.

Stewart, R., Kingsbury, B. & Rudyk, B. (2009b). Climate Finance for Limiting Emissions and Promoting Green Development Mechanisms, Regulation, and Governance. In: Stewart, R., Kingsbury, B. & Rudyk, B. (eds.) *Climate Finance Regulatory and Funding Strategies for Climate Change and Global Development*. New York: New York University Press, pp. 3–34.

Streck, C., Keenlyside, P. & Unger, M. (2016) The Paris Agreement: A New Beginning. *Journal for European Environmental & Planning Law*, 13, 3–29.

Swedfund (2017) Lake Turkana – Africa's Largest Wind Power Project. Retrieved from: https://www.swedfund.se/en/investments# (accessed January–March 2018).

The EastAfrican (2019) Kenya launches Africa's biggest wind farm. (19 July). Retrieved from: https://www.theeastafrican.co.ke/business/Kenya-to-launch-africa-biggest-wind-farm/2560-5202472-m7582y/index.html (accessed 21 July 2019)

UNCTAD (2014) Local Content Requirements and the Green Economy. Retrieved from: https://unctad.org/en/PublicationsLibrary/ditcted2013d7_en.pdf (accessed January–March 2018).

UNFCCC Standing Committee on Finance (2014) Biennial Assessment and Overview of Climate Finance Flows Report. Retrieved from: https://unfccc.int/files/cooperation_and_support/financial_mechanism/standing_committee/application/pdf/2014_biennial_assessment_and_overview_of_climate_finance_flows_report_web.pdf (accessed January–March 2018).

UNFCCC Standing Committee on Finance (2016) *Biennial Assessment and Overview of Climate Finance Flows Report*. Retrieved from: http://unfccc.int/files/cooperation_and_support/financial_mechanism/standing_committee/application/pdf/2016_ba_technical_report.pdf (accessed January–March 2018).

United Nations (2016) Report: Inequalities Exacerbate Climate Impacts on Poor. Retrieved from: http://www.un.org/sustainabledevelopment/blog/2016/10/report-inequalities-exacerbate-climate-impacts-on-poor/ (accessed January–March 2018).

Van der Gaast, W. (2016) *International Climate Negotiation Factors: Design, Process, Tactics*. Cham: Springer International.

Van Kerkhoff, L. Ahmad, I.H., Pittock, J. & Steffen, W. (2011) Designing the Green Climate Fund: How to Spend $100 Billion Sensibly. *Environment*, 53, 18–31.

Venugopal S. & Patel S. (2013) Why Is Climate Finance So Hard to Define? Retrieved from: http://www.wri.org/blog/2013/04/why-climate-finance-so-hard-define (accessed January–March 2018).

Vidican G. (2015) The Emergence of a Solar Energy Innovation System in Morocco: A Governance Perspective. *Innovation and Development*, 5(2), 225–240.

Zhang, H.-B., Dai, H.-C., Lai, H.-X. & Wang, W.-T. (2017) US Withdrawal from the Paris Agreement: Reasons, Impacts, and China's Response. *Advances in Climate Change Research*, 8(4), 220–225.

Index

Page references to Figures or Tables are followed by the letters 'f' or 't' respectively, while Notes are indicated by the letter 'n' and note number following the page number

The Handbook of Global Trade Policy, First Edition. Edited by Andreas Klasen.
© 2020 John Wiley & Sons Ltd. Published 2020 by John Wiley & Sons Ltd.